Choose Your Medicine

Choose Your Medicine

Freedom of Therapeutic Choice in America

LEWIS A. GROSSMAN

OXFORD

UNIVERSITY PRESS

OXFORD
UNIVERSITY PRESS

Oxford University Press is a department of the University of Oxford. It furthers
the University's objective of excellence in research, scholarship, and education
by publishing worldwide. Oxford is a registered trade mark of Oxford University
Press in the UK and certain other countries.

Published in the United States of America by Oxford University Press
198 Madison Avenue, New York, NY 10016, United States of America.

Library of Congress Control Number: 2021913108
ISBN 978–0–19–061275–7

DOI: 10.1093/oso/9780190612757.001.0001

1 3 5 7 9 8 6 4 2

Printed by Sheridan Books, Inc., United States of America

For Mom (the lawyer) and Dad (the doctor).

Contents

Acknowledgments

The completion of this book has been a long journey, and I have received valuable assistance at innumerable stops along the way. I would like to thank the participants in the many different forums in which I presented parts of this work, in some instances on multiple occasions: the American Society for the History of Medicine, the American Society for Law, Medicine & Ethics Annual Health Law Professors Conference, the American Society for Legal History, the American University Washington College of Law Faculty Speakers' Series, the Cornell Law School Faculty Workshop, the DC Legal History Workshop, the Georgia State University College of Law Faculty Workshop Series, the Harvard Law School Health Law Workshop, the Princeton Program in Law and Public Affairs (LAPA) Fellows Seminar Series and LEGS Seminar Series, the Seton Hall Law School Faculty Colloquium, and the Stanford Law School Bio LawLaPalooza.

I am grateful to the many academic colleagues who gave me advice, comments, and support. They include Aziza Ahmed, Jonathan Baker, Edward Balleisen, Peter Brooks, Susan Carle, Janie Chuang, Glenn Cohen, Angela Creager, Michael Dorf, Daniel Ernst, Amanda Frost, Paul Frymer, Leslie Gerwin, Hank Greely, Jeremy Greene, Stanley Katz, James May, Daniel Rogers, Ezra Rosser, Rachel Sachs, William Sage, James Salzman, Brenda Smith, David Snyder, Sidney Tarrow, Robert Tsai, Keith Wailoo, and Lindsay Wiley. (I apologize to those I may have omitted from this list.) You all helped me greatly, whether or not you realize it.

I had the privilege of meeting (personally or virtually) and receiving insights from some of the characters who appear in the pages of this book, including Frank Burroughs, Gregg Gonsalves, Mark Harrington, David Barr, Peter Staley, Jim Eigo, and Alan St. Pierre.

Deans Claudio Grossman and Camille Nelson of the American University Washington College of Law provided generous financial support. I am also thankful for the financial support, intellectual stimulation, and precious time to write I enjoyed as a Princeton University LAPA fellow.

American University Pence Law Library Directors Billie Jo Kaufman and Adeen Postar provided indispensable research assistance and advice, as did Associate Law Librarian Shannon Roddy. Thanks to Billie Jo, the Pence Law Library was for a short time perhaps the only academic law library in the country with a subscription to *High Times* magazine!

I am indebted to my student research assistants Brianna Gardner, Katherine Freitas, Steven Valentino, Amanda Bokshan, and Xochitl Halaby. Katherine and Steve deserve special thanks for reviewing every single citation in the final manuscript. I am also deeply grateful to an entire generation of students at the American University Washington College of Law who have listened to me hold forth and ruminate about the issues addressed in this book and have shared their own views with me.

I will never forget the great historians who taught me, inspired me, and instilled in me a love of the study of American history, especially Edmund Morgan, David Brion Davis, William Cronon, and Morton Horwitz.

Without Peter Barton Hutt's enduring mentorship, friendship, and infectious joy in his work, I would never have pursued Food and Drug Law as a practice area or as a beloved field of study. I treasure my long association and camaraderie with the lawyers in the Food, Drug, and Device Practice Group at Covington & Burling LLP, where I currently serve as a part-time Of Counsel. Nothing in this book represents the views of the firm or its clients.

Thanks to David McBride, my Acquisitions Editor at Oxford University Press, who gave me this opportunity, shepherded me through the process, suggested useful revisions, and demonstrated extraordinary patience.

I am grateful most of all to my family. My parents (Edward and Madeleine), my sister (Jill), my brother (Peter), my brother-in-law (David), and my sister-in-law (Lisa) unfailingly supported me, urged me forward, and expressed interest in my work. My mother heroically read and (lightly) edited the entire manuscript and expressed much-needed enthusiasm while doing so. My children, Elizabeth, Samuel, and Hannah, are the joys of my life. When I started this book, they were all delightful kids living at home; by the time it is published, they will all be magnificent young adults making their way in the world. I want to thank them for letting me spend so much time on this project with few complaints. I hope that I have been a compassionate, loving, and attentive father despite my devotion to my work.

It is difficult to put into words my gratitude and love for my wife, Lisa—my rock, my biggest fan, my intellectual partner, my TV-watching buddy, and my best friend.

Introduction

Traveling Abby's Road

At the dawn of the new millennium on January 1, 2000, Abigail Burroughs had many reasons to celebrate. The nineteen-year-old Falls Church, Virginia, resident had just completed a successful first semester of her second year at the University of Virginia. She attended UVA as an Echols Scholar, a prestigious honor the school bestows upon a small number of applicants based on their extraordinary academic achievement and intellectual leadership. Abigail ("Abby" to her friends) loved college. She was earning excellent grades, had a group of devoted friends, and was dating a third-year Economics major. The main annoyance Abigail confronted that fall was an irksome mouth sore that would not heal. But now even that nuisance was gone; her doctor had removed the sore in December.[1]

Then, just a few days into the new year, Abigail's world began to crumble. Her physician informed her that the sore was malignant. It was a squamous cell carcinoma of the head and neck (SCCHN), a cancer found primarily in much older patients with a history of tobacco or alcohol consumption. Abigail, terrified, underwent an additional procedure to remove the margins of the lesion. Afterward, buoyed by her doctor's assurances that there was a 90 percent chance the cancer would not recur, Abigail returned to UVA and forged on with her college career. She declared herself a Political and Social Thought major and joined the venerable Jefferson Literary and Debating Society.

That summer, Abigail discovered a lump in her neck. The cancer had returned and invaded her lymph nodes. Abigail underwent surgery to remove the mass and then, throughout the fall semester of her third year, received chemotherapy and excruciating radiation treatments at a hospital near the UVA campus in Charlottesville. Although this regimen seemed to arrest the cancer's growth for a while, in January 2001, scans showed new tumors in Abigail's neck and lungs. The Charlottesville doctors, out of ideas, referred her to the renowned cancer center at Johns Hopkins University in Baltimore.

Following another unsuccessful round of chemotherapy, Abigail's oncologist at Hopkins informed her that the only remaining recourse was to try an experimental treatment not yet approved by the Food and Drug Administration (FDA). Based on the characteristics of Abigail's tumors, the two most promising

Choose Your Medicine. Lewis A. Grossman, Oxford University Press. © Lewis A. Grossman 2021.
DOI: 10.1093/oso/9780190612757.003.0001

investigational drugs were gefitnib (Iressa®), manufactured by AstraZeneca, and cetuximab (C225), made by ImClone. By 2001, both had completed successful small, uncontrolled "Phase 1" clinical studies—the first stage of a three-phase research protocol ordinarily required by the FDA for drug approval. During Phase 1, a new drug is tested in twenty to eighty subjects to determine "the side effects associated with increasing doses and, if possible, to gain early evidence on effectiveness."[2] Iressa had not been studied at all in patients with head and neck cancer. C225 had been, however, and early results suggested it may have shrunk their tumors. Nonetheless, a drug's effectiveness can only be meaningfully established by the larger, controlled studies conducted at Phases 2 and 3.[3]

Abigail did not qualify for any of the ongoing clinical trials of Iressa or C225. She thus attempted to obtain them through an FDA procedure known as "compassionate use," which permitted companies to provide unapproved drugs to desperately ill individuals who had exhausted all other measures. Drug sponsors were not required to participate in this procedure, however, and they were generally hesitant to do so when asked. They did not want to divert eligible patients—or scarce supplies of the investigational drug—away from the controlled trials designed to obtain FDA approval. They feared that adverse events suffered by compassionate use patients might derail the approval process and expose them to tort liability. And importantly, the FDA did not permit manufacturers to charge patients for compassionate use drugs without prior agency authorization, and these charges, even when allowed, were capped at the amount necessary for cost recovery.

Unsurprisingly, therefore, Abigail and her family found only frustration when they reached out to AstraZeneca and ImClone in early 2001 seeking compassionate access to Iressa and C225. In denying Abigail's request, AstraZeneca accurately pointed out that Iressa had never even been tried in people with head and neck cancer. ImClone could not offer the same justification, because C225 had been administered to head and neck cancer patients with promising (though very preliminary) results. Instead, ImClone told Abigail that it simply could not choose among the hundreds of people requesting the drug. The company also explained that it did not want to sap resources away from the controlled clinical trials it was conducting to gain FDA approval. Harlan Waksal, ImClone's chief operating officer, declared, "We think truly the most compassionate thing to do for the oncology community is to get this drug approved."[4]

Frank Burroughs, Abigail's father, organized a public relations campaign to pressure the companies. About 2,000 friends, family, and supporters—including both US senators from Virginia—contacted the firms, urging them to provide their drugs to Abigail. More than 6,600 members of the UVA community signed a petition. These efforts were to no avail, however. On June 9, 2001, Abigail Burroughs died peacefully in her sleep at her home in Falls Church, without ever having had the opportunity to try an experimental treatment. (See Fig. I.1 for a portrait of Abigail.) Five years later, the FDA approved C225 (under the brand name Erbitux®) for treatment of squamous cell carcinoma of the head and neck.[5]

Soon after Abigail's death, a despondent but determined Frank Burroughs founded a new nonprofit organization called Abigail Alliance for Better Access to Developmental Drugs. In 2003, the Alliance joined with the Washington Legal Foundation (WLF), a conservative public interest group, to file a suit against the FDA in federal court in Washington, DC. The plaintiffs sought an injunction prohibiting the agency from barring sales of post–Phase 1 drugs to patients in desperate situations like Abigail's. They based their claim on the due process clause of the Fifth Amendment to the US Constitution.

In 2006, Abigail Alliance achieved a stunning victory in the US Court of Appeals for the District of Columbia (often called "the nation's second most important court"). In a 2–1 decision, liberal judge Judith Rogers (a Clinton appointee) and conservative judge Douglas Ginsburg (appointed by Reagan) ruled that mentally competent, terminally ill adult patients with no alternatives have a

Figure I.1 Abigail Burroughs. *Courtesy Frank Burroughs.*

fundamental right to obtain potentially life-saving medications after successful Phase 1 testing.[6]

The court used a test for substantive due process articulated by the Supreme Court in *Washington v. Glucksberg*, a 1997 case denying the existence of a fundamental right to physician-assisted suicide. The *Glucksberg* test requires judges to ask whether an asserted right is "objectively, deeply rooted in this Nation's history and tradition and implicit in the concept of ordered liberty." Judge Rogers observed, "A right of control over one's body has deep roots in the common law." She declared that for more than a century after the country's founding, "there was essentially no drug regulation in the United States." She then emphasized that although the FDA acquired authority to regulate drug safety early in the twentieth century, it did not obtain power to require proof of efficacy until 1962. Rogers concluded: "It cannot be said that government control of access to potentially lifesaving medication is now firmly ingrained in our understanding of the appropriate role of government, so as to overturn the long-standing tradition of the right of self-preservation."[7]

Unfortunately for the Alliance, the thirteen judges of the DC Circuit voted to vacate this three-judge panel decision and rehear the case *en banc* (that is, as a full court). In 2007, the court issued an 11–2 decision in favor of the FDA, with only Rogers and Ginsburg dissenting. Judge Thomas Griffith (the dissenter from the panel decision) wrote for the *en banc* majority. He read the historical record very differently from Judge Rogers. He pointed to a history of state and federal regulation of drug safety extending back to the country's earliest years, with federal regulation of efficacy added during the latter half of the twentieth century as the rise of modern clinical science made it practicable. "We conclude that our Nation has long expressed interest in drug regulation, calibrating its response in terms of the capabilities to determine the risks associated with both drug safety and efficacy." Therefore, he concluded, "the Alliance's claimed right is not fundamental." When the US Supreme Court declined to hear the case, Frank Burroughs's journey through the federal court system was over. Ever since, Abigail Alliance has focused its advocacy on the political and regulatory realms.[8]

I have taught *Abigail Alliance* in my Food and Drug Law course every year since the case was decided. The class discussion about the case is always a highlight for me and (I think) my students. Each year, I poll the students on which side they favor, and they invariably support letting patients like Abigail Burroughs purchase unapproved drugs—often by overwhelming margins. I then point out that if drug companies could sell unapproved drugs for a profit after Phase 1, they might never perform the Phase 2 and Phase 3 trials necessary to determine whether drugs are safe and effective. Even after my introduction of this problem, a majority of the class usually continues to support Abigail Alliance's position. The conversation is always lively, because it concerns a foundational question that students are eager to explore—namely, when is the government justified in restricting people's personal choices regarding their health?

When I first read *Abigail Alliance*, I was drawn to it not only as a teacher of Food and Drug Law, but also as a historian. After all, historical narrative and analysis comprised large segments of the panel and *en banc* decisions. Judges Rogers and Griffith painted very different portraits of the evolution of American views on drug regulation, and I wondered whose was more accurate. I thus started researching this history myself. I did not focus exclusively—or even primarily— on formal legal materials. I also examined petitions, speeches, popular magazine articles, legislative testimony, and slogans chanted at street demonstrations, to name just a few sources.

It soon became apparent to me that throughout most of American history, a broad swath of the population has believed that people have a right to choose their preferred medical treatments without government interference. This fact became especially obvious when I started considering the history of disputes over the regulation of medical *practice*. I learned that until the early twentieth century, medical freedom activists viewed state medical licensing laws, not drug regulation, as the primary threat to therapeutic choice. These "medical practice acts" threatened the very existence of the unorthodox medical sects that millions of Americans adhered to before the rise of modern scientific medicine. Some of these sects abjured the use of drugs altogether. Others were so firmly identified with the particular types of drugs they administered that state licensing laws were effectively a form of drug regulation.

Relatedly, I realized that demands for access to unapproved *orthodox* treatments were only part of story. For most of American history, freedom of choice activism was focused primarily, and sometimes exclusively, on *alternative* therapies rejected by the orthodox medical establishment. This activism, which persists today, has always evinced a very different style of argument from that used by groups like Abigail Alliance. Most people demanding access to pharmaceuticals earlier in the drug development process do not wholly reject the legitimacy of conventional science, FDA regulation, and drug companies, but rather seek to reform and democratize these institutions. By contrast, the medical freedom rhetoric of alternative medicine movements has always included a strain of thoroughgoing hostility to scientists, experts, bureaucrats, elites, and big business—a hostility sometimes fading over into paranoid conspiracy mongering. It is in this realm of distrust that activism in favor of giving patients access to their desired therapies has overlapped, ideologically and organizationally, with resistance to compelled measures such as mandatory vaccination and face masks.

My research, thus expanded, revealed that the framing of therapeutic choice primarily as a question of *bodily* liberty, as in *Abigail Alliance*, is a modern phenomenon. For most of American history, bodily liberty was only one of multiple strands of freedom rhetoric that featured prominently in therapeutic choice advocacy. Medical freedom activists also frequently invoked notions of economic freedom, freedom of conscience and religion, and freedom of inquiry.

I was struck by another feature of the historical record: the constitutional nature of many of the arguments for freedom of therapeutic choice, even when presented outside of court. As we will see, American courts (with some important exceptions) have only rarely ruled in favor of medical choice. But American medical freedom advocacy epitomizes "popular constitutionalism"—the creation of constitutional law by the people rather than by judges. Larry D. Kramer, in his book *The People Themselves*, describes how Americans historically shaped constitutional meaning in extrajudicial forums, such as mobs, boycotts, rallies, petition drives, elections, and jury service. Kramer contends that popular constitutionalism thoroughly dominated American constitutional understanding in the country's early years and remained an important force until the 1980s.[9] My research suggests that he stopped the clock too early.

Of course, advocacy in the public square does not typically include detailed exegeses of constitutional text. From the perspective of scholars of popular constitutionalism, however, the "constitution" is not limited to the US Constitution's detailed provisions as interpreted by the Supreme Court. It also includes the broad foundational principles of equality, liberty, and self-governance set forth in that document's Preamble and in the Declaration of Independence. Professor Mark Tushnet influentially dubbed this core of basic values the "thin Constitution." When medical freedom advocates invoke the Declaration's "inalienable rights" of "life, liberty, and the pursuit of happiness"—as they do constantly throughout this book—they are engaged in a form of "thin" constitutional argument.[10]

Still another theme that emerged from my research was the unusual politics around freedom of therapeutic choice. Rogers and Ginsburg's liberal-conservative collaboration in *Abigail Alliance* is representative of a broader phenomenon. American medical freedom advocacy has long defied and bridged conventional political categories. This book is populated by strange bedfellows battling alleged infringements of the right to therapeutic choice: right-wing Republicans and left-wing Democrats; fundamentalist Christians and counter-cultural hippies; conservative libertarians and progressive AIDS activists.

Some commentators instinctively reject the notion that popular campaigns for freedom of therapeutic choice are ever really impelled by the desires of patients rather than by the economic self-interest of practitioners and medical product manufacturers. When I have presented my research at conferences, some audience members have dismissed crusading patients and consumers as either the hapless dupes or paid shills of industry. I am not naïve. I know that medical product manufacturers and physicians' organizations have always wielded significant influence over American health regulation and have often cloaked their economic self-interest in a purported "public interest." I am also aware that some medical freedom activists receive financial support from industry. But in this book, I credit many proponents of freedom of therapeutic choice with independent agency and the sincerity of their own convictions, and I believe that I am justified in doing so. After all, consider Frank Burroughs. The pharmaceutical industry did *not* back his crusade. To the contrary, when Abigail Alliance filed its case, the Pharmaceutical Research and Manufacturers of America (PhRMA) publicly and vehemently opposed the idea of making drugs available after Phase 1 trials.[11] The Abigail Alliance litigation was motivated by Frank Burroughs's earnest belief that people like his daughter have a right to make their own health care decisions.

This book should not be read as an attempt to challenge the *Abigail Alliance* decision. My narrative does not necessarily demonstrate that a right to try potentially life-saving treatments—let alone treatments for less severe conditions—is so "rooted" in American history and tradition that it is entitled to special constitutional protection in court. Indeed, my account of two-and-a-half centuries of passionate debate and legal and political contestation might even support the opposite conclusion. I approached this project as a historian, not as an advocate. And as a historian, I am delighted to present a story far more complex and intriguing than the spare judicial accounts in *Abigail Alliance* might suggest.

Though this book is not itself making a constitutional argument, it demonstrates that a significant portion of Americans have embraced freedom of therapeutic choice as a constitutional value for most of the country's history. The *only* period in which medical liberty advocacy was a fringe cause with little impact on law and policy was the middle of the twentieth century, a time distinguished by unusually prevalent trust in the medical and scientific establishments, the government, the media, and even big business. As a product of the end of the Baby Boom (one of my earliest memories is watching the 1969 moon landing), I grew up assuming that such confidence in our society's major institutions was an entrenched feature of the American character. I considered the distrustful, antiauthoritarian mood of the 1970s to be a temporary departure. Today, however—having lived through decades of popular resistance to scientific expertise, orthodox knowledge, and establishment institutions—I view the mid-twentieth century as an anomalous moment in our history. From this perspective, the COVID skepticism of the past year, with its rejection of face masks, its embrace of unproven remedies, and its demonization of Dr. Anthony Fauci, has not been exceptional but rather a reversion to the norm.

In Chapter One, I will unearth the deep roots of therapeutic choice rhetoric in American history by examining the resistance to the country's first medical licensing schemes (in the late 1700s) and the medical liberty advocacy of

Benjamin Rush, the most prominent American physician of the early national period. Chapter Two explores the wholesale abandonment of state medical licensing in the antebellum years due to demands for freedom of therapeutic choice by followers of a wildly popular school of botanical medicine called Thomsonianism.

Chapter Three shows how therapeutic choice remained an influential theme in American policy and thought in the Gilded Age. It explains how despite the almost universal restoration of medical licensing after the Civil War, the new licensing regimes were drafted and enforced in ways that protected the rights of unorthodox practitioners and their patients. Chapter Four describes how in the Progressive Era, even as comprehensive public health statutes and apparatuses appeared, medical freedom proponents restrained the power of this "state medicine," often by portraying it as a tyrannical conspiracy between government officials and the orthodox medical establishment to deny citizens their treatments of choice.

Chapter Five discusses the 1930s through the 1960s—the atypical period discussed earlier during which Americans' confidence in government health regulators, the medical establishment, and pharmaceutical companies was at its peak. During this era, therapeutic freedom of choice advocacy occurred mainly on society's margins, among right-wing cranks and peddlers of fraudulent products. Chapter Six then explores how during the 1970s, broad swaths of society once again embraced the cause of therapeutic choice, as evidenced by health food activism, the women's health movement, and the astonishingly powerful social movement in favor of the alternative cancer drug Laetrile.

The remainder of the book proceeds thematically rather than chronologically. Chapter Seven examines the rise during the past half century of demands by patients for freedom of choice within orthodox scientific medicine. This chapter's main focus is the epic and influential struggle by AIDS activist groups in the late 1980s and early 1990s to persuade the FDA and Congress to permit early access to unapproved HIV/AIDS drugs and speed their approval. Chapter Eight considers the resurgence of alternative and complementary medicine since the 1970s and reviews the various ways that American law has accommodated rather than quashed this trend. It also discusses a feature of modern resistance to medical orthodoxy that became extremely prominent during the COVID-19 pandemic: broad-based opposition to health regulations and conventional pharmaceutical treatments as insidious instruments of a shadowy conspiracy among despotic government actors and rapacious private interests.

Chapter Nine tells the story of the largely successful modern movement to legalize the medical use of cannabis, with emphasis on the distinctive aspects of this campaign stemming from marijuana's primary use as a recreational drug. Chapter Ten discusses the recent, paradoxical assertion of a right to therapeutic choice in the context of reimbursed health care, where every hint of a limitation on insurance coverage provokes cries like "rationing!" and "death panel!" and even "keep the government's hands off my Medicare!" Finally, Chapter Eleven explores physician-assisted suicide, the issue addressed by *Washington v. Glucksberg*, the aforementioned 1997 Supreme Court decision. This chapter considers why Americans remain more ambivalent about physician-assisted suicide than the other treatments and products discussed in the book.

Throughout this volume, I will emphasize not only the sheer persistence of demands for freedom of therapeutic choice in the United States, but also other themes that I alluded to earlier in this Introduction: the "constitutional" nature of much extrajudicial medical freedom advocacy, the fluctuating combination of distinct strands of liberty that have contributed to this rhetoric, and the tendency of disputes over therapeutic freedom to forge alliances that defy conventional political categories. Moreover, I will highlight the important relationships between American therapeutic choice movements and other contemporaneous political and social movements. While relating the fascinating story of American struggles for freedom of therapeutic choice, I hope to also provide readers with broader insight into this country's character as it has developed—and remained the same—during the past 250 years.

1

Storming the Bastille of Orthodoxy

The Origins of American Health Libertarianism

The recently arrived first-year medical students at the University of Pennsylvania must have been filled with anticipation, and even awe, as they settled into their seats in Surgeons Hall in Philadelphia. It was November 3, 1801, and these young men were enrolled in the nation's oldest and most prestigious medical school. Philadelphia was the medical capital—indeed, the intellectual capital—of their young nation. And they were about to hear their faculty's leading light, Professor Benjamin Rush, deliver his annual introductory lecture on a topic of importance to the medical community.[1]

Rush, who lived from 1746 to 1813, is less celebrated than some of his fellow Founding Fathers, but he was an extremely prominent figure during the country's early years and an extraordinary Renaissance man almost on the level of Franklin and Jefferson. He was a member of the Continental Congress, a signer of the Declaration of Independence, a member of the Pennsylvania ratifying convention, an antislavery pamphleteer, a longtime Treasurer of the US Mint, and the founder of Dickinson College.[2] And of particular importance to his students, Rush was the most celebrated and influential physician in the United States, commonly referred to as the "American Hippocrates."[3] In 1787, he had helped found the College of Physicians (the country's first medical society) in Philadelphia. He was the nation's leading exponent of the then-dominant "heroic" approach to medicine, which relied primarily on enervating treatments such as bloodletting, blistering, and purging from both ends of the gastrointestinal tract.

But if the students expected this lion of American medicine to deliver a paean to the glories of the profession and its institutions, they would soon be surprised. Rush had a surprisingly fraught relationship with the medical establishment. Many physicians resisted his hyper-aggressive brand of heroic medicine. Moreover, many in Philadelphia's generally conservative medical community disdained Rush's radical Jeffersonian politics. He was barely on speaking terms with many of the city's doctors. The anodyne title of Rush's lecture—"The Causes Which Have Retarded the Progress of Medicine"—barely hinted at the belligerent polemic to come.[4]

Rush, his white hair tied back with a black ribbon, looked over the audience with penetrating grey eyes (Fig. 1.1). The doctor was a gifted orator who

Choose Your Medicine. Lewis A. Grossman, Oxford University Press. © Lewis A. Grossman 2021.
DOI: 10.1093/oso/9780190612757.003.0002

Figure 1.1 Benjamin Rush, M.D. (1745–1813) as a professor of medicine at the University of Pennsylvania. *Library of Congress.*

frequently spoke to paying crowds. He prepared assiduously for his lectures so he could appear spontaneous when he delivered them. Though he spoke from a seated position, he used voice modulations and hand gestures to imbue his talks with dramatic intensity. An ex-student who visited Rush's class around this time reported that the professor's performance "filled me with tumultuary and superstitious emotion. I was on enchanted ground and my friend was the grand Magician who animated and governed and directed the sorcery of the scene."[5]

When Rush began talking, he thus immediately captured the students' attention. He began: "The imperfection of medicine is a common subject of complaint, by the enemies of our profession. It has been admitted by physicians." He then enumerated the "causes which have retarded the progress of our science." He catalogued orthodox doctors' numerous clinical lapses: "The neglect to ascertain the nature, and strength of diseases by the pulse." "An undue reliance upon the powers of nature in curing diseases." "The exhibition of medicines, without a due regard to the different stages of disease." Rush also assailed physicians' arrogance—their use of Latin, their "undue attachment to unsuccessful, but fashionable modes of practice."

The primary theme of Rush's lecture was the unpardonable close-mindedness of "regular bred physicians." He denounced doctors' "undue attachment to great names . . . which has imposed a restraint upon free inquiry" and their "indolence and credulity in admitting things to be true, without sufficient examination." He blasted universities for their "refusal . . . to tolerate any opinions . . . which are not taught nor believed by their professors." Rush even condemned the medical profession's "neglect to inquire after, and record cures which have been . . . performed . . . by quacks or by the friends of sick people." Finally, Rush identified some legal obstacles to medical progress, including government bans on particular remedies and the exclusionary system of medical licensing supported by most of his orthodox colleagues.

By the end of Professor Rush's lecture, every first-year medical student at the University of Pennsylvania was aware that the most famous physician in America was a fierce advocate for medical freedom.

Early American Orthodox Medicine and Its Alternatives

Early American orthodox (or "regular") medicine was based almost completely on speculative deduction from the principle that good health was a balance of systemic forces in the body. From this perspective, illness was an imbalance characterized by excessive excitement or enfeeblement. "The fundamental objective was to restore the natural balance, which was accomplished by depleting or lowering the overexcited patient and by stimulating or elevating the patient enfeebled by disease."[6] Conventional medicine was later termed "allopathic" medicine by its homeopathic opponents, because it used drugs and remedies intended to produce effects opposite the symptoms being treated.[7] (In Greek, *allo* means opposite, and *pathos* means suffering.)

During the first decades of the nineteenth century, regular doctors widely believed that most diseases were overstimulating rather than enfeebling. The typical treatments used to restore the natural balance were thus depletive ones.[8] Mainstream doctors routinely enervated their patients through the use of therapies such as bleeding, the application of blistering plasters to the skin, and the administration of massive doses of mineral-based purgatives, emetics, and diaphoretics (which induced bowel evacuation, vomiting, and sweating, respectively). The two main symbols of this approach to medicine—among both its proponents and critics—were the lancet (an instrument used for bleeding) and calomel (a mercury-based purgative).

Later observers labeled this approach to healing "heroic" medicine because of the regular practitioners' commitment to aggressive, interventionist treatment. As stated by a leading medical historian, "During the first two-thirds of the nineteenth century . . . the physician's 'redemptive role,' his active therapeutic intervention in an effort to redeem patients from disease, was at the core of what it meant to be a physician in America."[9] The most famous—or, in the eyes of critics, infamous—episode of heroic medicine's reign occurred at the 1799 deathbed of George Washington, who was suffering from a severe throat infection. Physicians treating the stoic national hero—including one of Rush's students— dosed him with calomel and tartar emetic, applied blisters to his throat and legs, and drained about half of the blood from his body.[10]

Despite the frequent use of a single term, "heroic medicine," to describe early American orthodox practice, disagreements sometimes arose among orthodox doctors with regard to both principles and remedies. As noted earlier, in the 1790s, Rush's depletive system of heroic medicine was challenged by other regular doctors, who asserted that stimulative as well as depletive remedies had a useful role in treatment. Their view would reemerge in the middle of the nineteenth century, as orthodox practitioners increasingly prescribed stimulative therapies such as quinine (from cinchona bark), iron compounds, and alcohol. At mid-century, a growing number of regular doctors would also begin to articulate an attitude of therapeutic skepticism, suggesting that physicians should merely provide palliative care while letting nature take its course. Such trends, however, should not be overstated. Although bleeding largely disappeared during the 1800s, other depletive therapies were used—though often in smaller doses—throughout the century. And even those orthodox practitioners who embraced the rhetoric of skepticism remained committed to pharmaceutical intervention in practice.[11]

Who were these "regular" doctors? The borders defining the orthodox medical profession were quite indistinct in early American history. Regular physicians were likely to be members of local and state medical societies, and they increasingly also tended to be graduates of foreign or domestic medical schools. Yet neither of these credentials was a prerequisite for practice before the Civil War. As we will see, orthodox medical practitioners sought to secure the boundaries of their profession by encouraging the passage of state medical licensing requirements. The details of these laws varied greatly, but even the strictest of them posed relatively low barriers to entry. As Paul Starr observes in *The Social*

Transformation of American Medicine, "The preferred statuses—medical school graduate, society member, licensed practitioner—were continually invaded by the lower ranks of the profession as schools multiplied, societies became less exclusive, and licenses became easier to acquire."[12]

The boundaries defining the orthodox armamentarium were somewhat permeable, as well. A few important remedies used by regular physicians, such as inoculation for smallpox and powdered cinchona bark (the source of quinine) for malaria, originated in folk medicine. Alternative practitioners often condemned the regulars for using "mineral" remedies such as calomel rather than "natural" medicines derived from the plant kingdom. In fact, however, the orthodox pharmacopoeia was replete with botanical products. Consider, for example, the career of New York City's David Hosack. Best known today for serving as Alexander Hamilton's attending doctor during his fatal duel with Aaron Burr, Hosack was one of the most prominent and influential physicians in early America. In addition to holding the chair in *materia medica* at Columbia, he was also a professor of botany there. In 1801, he created the Elgin Botanical Garden near the current site of Rockefeller Center. This institution was dedicated to the cultivation of plants of medicinal and agricultural significance. Perhaps inspired by Hosack's example, Benjamin Rush himself attempted, but failed, to acquire funding to establish a medicinal garden in Philadelphia.[13]

The blurriness of the line dividing orthodox and unorthodox medicine does not, however, negate the fact that many practitioners were clearly outside the fraternity of regular physicians. Early America's medical landscape was populated by large numbers of indisputably lay practitioners, including botanical healers, midwives, bonesetters, unschooled inoculators, and abortionists. Native Americans, African Americans, and women were virtually excluded from the orthodox medical profession, but they were extremely well represented among the ranks of lay and folk healers. Indeed, women members of households were the nation's most important primary health care providers. Informed by oral tradition, by personal experience, and, increasingly, by published manuals on domestic medicine, many housewives were experts at the use of botanical and other household remedies. But there were always also white men who operated outside the formal system—by choice, due to geographical isolation or social ostracization, or, as the nineteenth century progressed, because they were unable to satisfy new state licensing requirements.[14]

The history of efforts to establish medical licensing in America commences well before independence. Prior to the Revolutionary War, orthodox physicians in America sporadically attempted to persuade colonial governments to pass laws mandating the examination and licensure of doctors. Their primary stated aim was to protect the vulnerable and ignorant public from "quacks" and "mountebanks." They also bemoaned the disrepute that untrained and unorthodox practitioners brought down on the entire profession. "It is very injurious to regular-bred physicians," one licensing advocate remarked, "that such impostors are suffered to deceive mankind and bring into contempt the honorable profession of physic."[15]

The early efforts to create licensing regimes were generally unsuccessful. Proposals to institute medical licensing prompted a reaction between indifference and outright opposition among the majority of citizens, suggesting the deep-rootedness of the American preference for freedom of therapeutic choice. The few licensing laws that passed were primarily (though not exclusively) honorific measures that did not penalize practice by unlicensed physicians. In the words of medical historian Richard Harrison Shryock, "Most men seem to have believed that a people who entrusted their souls to all sorts of preachers, could likewise entrust their bodies to all sorts of 'doctors.'"[16]

The strongest colonial licensing laws, at least on paper, were those enacted by New York in 1760 and by New Jersey in 1772. These statutes required that doctors be examined and licensed by lay officials, and they imposed fines on violators. The fate of these two laws, however, illustrates why it is often necessary to look beyond formal legal sources to determine citizens' attitudes toward medical liberty. The New York and New Jersey laws were extremely unpopular because they threatened the people's traditional freedom to choose from among a variety of types of healers. The colonial authorities thus rarely—perhaps never—enforced them.[17]

Therefore, on the eve of the Revolution, no effective constraint on practice by unorthodox and untrained doctors existed in the American colonies. One commentator facetiously remarked in 1774: "There is no law for *hanging* mountebanks, that I know of, in this land of liberty; and therefore they that are fond of them may . . . run after them as long as they please."[18] The same year, a committee of Connecticut doctors complained:

> The power of the magistrate is very seldom or ever exerted, or any Notice taken
> in this country for the preservation of health, or distinguishing the eminent,
> the learned, from the illiterate and the ignorant. . . . The importance of a proper
> medical police is either not understood or very little attended to or regarded.[19]

After the signing of the Declaration of Independence, states gradually began to enact medical licensing laws in response to pressure from the growing body of regularly educated physicians. By 1800, six states had medical practice acts of some kind on the books. State licensing regimes multiplied and strengthened starting around 1810, a development culminating with a flurry of legislative activity in the late 1810s and early 1820s. The medical practice statutes of the early national period generally required examination and licensing by state medical societies, which were often incorporated by the same laws. By the end of 1825, eighteen of the twenty-four extant states, plus the District of Columbia, had adopted medical licensing.[20]

The nature and severity of the sanctions set forth in these licensing statutes varied significantly from state to state and changed within states as the laws were amended. Some states' medical practice laws established no penalty whatsoever for violators, and others imposed fines too small to influence behavior.[21] For example, in some jurisdictions, the sole sanction was a prohibition against unlicensed practitioners suing for unpaid fees—a measure practitioners could circumvent simply by demanding payment before providing treatment. On the other side of the scale, about half of the states that enacted medical licensing laws during this era authorized the imposition of fines, and a few went so far as to allow the imprisonment of violators. The general trend during this period was toward stricter penalties.[22]

In New York—which, for a time, provided for imprisonment of unlicensed practitioners—the medical practice statute was "remarkably effective." By contrast, some other states' licensing statutes had little impact. In some jurisdictions, especially frontier states with sparse populations and small numbers of orthodox physicians, the licensing regimes failed due to halfhearted implementation and a lack of enforcement by government officials. Moreover, juries everywhere routinely refused to convict unlicensed practitioners. In 1811, the Maryland licensing examination committee grumbled that it was simply unable to bring violators of that state's medical practice act to justice.[23]

The steady proliferation of state licensing statutes during the United States' early decades may have been due mainly to organizational factors. During this era, regular physicians established many stable local and state medical societies. Irregular doctors, by contrast, could point only to a network of small "Friendly Botanic Societies" that Samuel Thomson, an ambitious herbalist healer from New Hampshire, started establishing around 1811. Orthodox medicine was thus logistically and financially much better positioned to sway lawmakers in legislative battles over licensing.[24]

Early Arguments against Medical Licensing

Due to alternative medicine's lack of organizational structure, and the relatively low literacy of its adherents, there is no noteworthy body of American medical freedom literature prior to the 1820s. This scarcity of written material makes it difficult to assess the precise basis for anti-licensing sentiment during the early national period (other than the economic self-interest of irregular practitioners). There are scattered clues, however.

The meager record indicates that those who opposed medical licensing in the late eighteenth century did so for various reasons that would persist throughout the antebellum period and beyond. One theme that emerges from early anti-licensing statements is the threat to economic freedom posed by government-granted monopolies. For example, in 1769, an opponent of medical licensing in Connecticut raised the specter of a doctors' monopoly exacting excessive fees from the people. He contended, "A combination of Doctors perhaps gives them a greater advantage to impose on mankind, by extravagant demands, than if no such combination had been formed."[25] When the Connecticut legislature in 1787 debated, and rejected, a bill that would have established a state medical society with licensing power, one representative protested that he "did not like this plan: . . . it was a combination of the doctors: . . . they cost more than they do good: this society . . . was directly against liberty: they might shut out every body else: it was a very dangerous thing."[26]

Anti-monopolism was widespread in Revolutionary America. Indeed, the American colonists' antagonism toward English grants of trade monopolies, such as the East India Company's monopoly over tea importation to the colonies, was a significant impetus for their bid for independence. Many Americans of this period, drawing on a long tradition of anti-monopolism in English jurisprudence and political thought, viewed exclusive charters as not only detrimental to society's economic interests, but also violative of individuals' economic *rights*. Indeed, Thomas Jefferson and six state ratifying conventions sought to include an anti-monopoly provision in the Bill of Rights of the US Constitution.[27]

A related reason for the early opposition to medical licensing was suspicion of the motives of the exclusive medical societies that would administer these schemes. Historian Gordon Wood has observed that late eighteenth-century Americans exhibited widespread "concern with the deceit and dissembling of sophisticated elites." They saw "designs within designs, cabals within cabals."[28] Any group or gathering perceived to have aristocratic pretensions was viewed not only as unrepublican, but also as a conspiratorial threat to liberty.[29] Thus another Connecticut legislator opposed to the creation of a state medical society with licensing power opined "[t]hat he was against all societies, whose constitutions & designs we did not know; such as [the Society of the Cincinnati], free-masons, and this medical society; that they were composed of cunning men, and we know not what mischief they may be upon."[30]

An additional premise in the sparse early record that would become an enduring theme in American medical freedom literature was the importance of freedom of inquiry. For example, in 1788, a Philadelphia newspaper observed that although the state legislature could address the problem of incompetent and ignorant practitioners through legislation, "it has never yet interfered, not only from an unwillingness to multiply restraint in a free country, but perhaps from a doubt, whether some equivalent advantage might not arise from the liberty of attempting medical experiments." This statement suggests that foes of medical licensing statutes thought that such laws not only constituted excessive state interference into citizens' private affairs, but also threatened the progress of medical science. The writer of this column further explained: "Unfortunate individuals suffer in the course of [the uneducated practitioner's] inquiries, but the community at large is sometimes benefitted by an accession to experimental knowledge."[31]

These two themes—first, the aversion to monopolies and elite fraternities that undermined economic freedom and republican values, and second, the need for free inquiry to advance medical knowledge—also dominated the medical freedom rhetoric of Benjamin Rush.

Benjamin Rush: Orthodox Advocate for Medical Liberty

One might assume that Rush, the nation's leading orthodox doctor, would have sided with the forces of exclusion and privilege. As a young man, he might have. During the Revolutionary years, Rush was a staunch Federalist, apprehensive about extreme democracy and hostile to Pennsylvania's radicals. By 1789, however, he had undergone a dramatic conversion, and for the remainder of his life he was a confirmed Jeffersonian Republican who railed against aristocratic conspiracies.[32]

Rush's transformation was not as surprising as it might seem. As Rush himself was acutely aware, he was in many ways an outsider to the elite medical community of Philadelphia and its well-off clientele. He came from a family of modest means and no connections. He was a Presbyterian in a city dominated by Quakers and Anglicans. Moreover, his role as a leading patriot in the American Revolution alienated him from the large portion of the city's upper class with loyalist sympathies.[33]

In his professional life, Rush enraged his orthodox colleagues by cooperating with unlicensed and unorthodox practitioners. As he described the situation in his autobiography, "I frequently exposed myself to reproach from the regular bred [sic] of physicians by attending patients with quacks, and with practitioners of physic [medicine] of slender education." Rush tried to mollify his colleagues by appealing to their elitist sensibilities. He recalled, "I justified this conduct by saying that I rescued the sick from the hands of ignorant men, and gave them a better chance of being cured, and at the same time instructed [the irregular doctors] in a regular mode of practice." At other times, however, Rush was more generous to unschooled and alternative practitioners, even maintaining that regular doctors could learn valuable lessons from them. He declared medicine to be "a science so simple" that it required little study and was "obvious to the meanest capacities." Such statements—not to mention Rush's accusation that physicians' use of Latin wrapped medicine in "mystery or imposture"—could not have failed to outrage Rush's snobbish orthodox brethren.[34]

In addition, many elite regular physicians in Philadelphia disdained Rush's medical theories. First, he infuriated the city's established doctors by embracing the nervous-system-centric theories of his Scottish mentor, William Cullen, while they stubbornly clung to the older views of Holland's Herman Boerhaave, who emphasized the role of bodily fluids. Then, in the late 1780s, after most of his colleagues had finally also accepted Cullen's teachings, Rush invited their wrath again by developing his own methods of treatment based on extreme bleeding and purging. (In severe cases, he recommended the removal of up to four-fifths of the blood from the body.) Although this approach would become widespread by the early nineteenth century, Philadelphia's fraternity of regulars did not immediately embrace it, and some never did. For these reasons, Philadelphia's medical elite refused to engage in consultations with Rush and even urged medical students to avoid his lectures.[35]

The acrimony between Rush and his local colleagues peaked in 1793, when a severe yellow fever epidemic ravaged the city. The medical establishment vehemently disagreed not only with Rush's hyper-aggressive approach to treating the epidemic's victims, but also with his views regarding the scourge's origins. As Rush later explained in his autobiography, he attributed the outbreak to "domestic origins" (a "noxious miasma"), whereas "nearly the whole College of Physicians . . . derived it from a foreign country," namely, the thousands of Frenchmen who arrived in Philadelphia after fleeing the Haitian Revolution. The rancor of this dispute was heightened by the curious fact that attitudes about the epidemic's source corresponded to political divisions, with the (pro-French) Republicans supporting Rush and the (anti-French) Federalists backing his opponents. By the time the yellow fever outbreak subsided, the rupture between Rush and the medical establishment was so severe that he resigned from the College of Physicians, the society he had helped to found.[36]

This background helps us understand how the most famous regular physician in America could deliver the lecture he did to the University of Pennsylvania's medical students in 1801. His political conversion from Federalist to Republican explains why the speech was deeply infused with Jeffersonian social egalitarianism and devotion to limited government. His ostracization by the Philadelphia medical establishment underlies his barely veiled attacks on the profession's snobbish conceit. And Rush's status as a medical dissident in his home city (even while serving as an orthodox exemplar elsewhere) illuminates why Rush became an outspoken advocate for tolerance of different medical views even while having what one biographer calls a "somewhat immutable conviction in the correctness . . . of his [own] ideas."[37]

Rush's lecture contained the seeds of three persistent medical liberty notions—freedom of conscience, economic freedom, and freedom of inquiry, respectively—that would reverberate down through American history. Consider three of Rush's enumerated "causes which have retarded the progress" of medicine:

21st. The interference of governments in prohibiting the use of certain remedies, and enforcing the use of others by law. The effects of this mistaken policy has [sic] been as hurtful to medicine, as a similar practice with respect to opinions, has been to the Christian religion.

22d. Conferring exclusive privileges upon bodies of physicians, and forbidding men of equal talents and knowledge, under severe penalties, from practising medicine within certain districts of cities and countries. Such institutions, however sanctioned by ancient charters and names, are the bastiles [sic] of our science.

23d. The refusal in universities to tolerate any opinions, in the private or public exercises of candidates for degrees in medicine, which are not taught nor believed by their professors, thus restraining a spirit of inquiry in that period of life which is most distinguished for ardour and invention in our science.[38]

In the first quoted paragraph, Rush seems to have been alluding primarily to actions by governments in Europe, rather than the United States; at the time Rush delivered the lecture, few if any American laws had ever actually prohibited or mandated the use of particular remedies. This paragraph anticipated an enduring theme in American medical freedom rhetoric by alluding to a parallel between medical freedom and religious freedom. Like many Jeffersonians, Rush was a committed religious pluralist and outspoken advocate of religious liberty.[39] He equated the state imposition of orthodox medical doctrine with the despotism of an established church and the truth-stifling effect of religious intolerance. Jefferson himself reached the same analogy from the other direction in a discussion about religious liberty in his *Notes on the State of Virginia*. Bemoaning various symptoms of "religious slavery," Jefferson remarked:

Reason and free enquiry are the only effectual agents against error. . . . Had not free enquiry been indulged, at the æra [sic] of reformation, the corruptions of Christianity could not have been purged away. If it be restrained now, the present corruptions will be protected, and new ones encouraged. Was the government to prescribe to us our medicine . . ., our bodies would be in such keeping as our souls are now. Thus in France the emetic was once forbidden as medicine.[40]

Religious liberty and freedom of inquiry were thus intertwined for both Jefferson and Rush.

The subsequent paragraph, by contrast, addressed what Rush perceived to be an extant and growing problem in his own country. As early as 1769, Rush's mentor and sometime nemesis John Morgan (the founder of Penn's medical school) had unsuccessfully petitioned the provincial legislature for authority to found a medical society with the power to examine and license practitioners. By the time of Rush's address in 1801, about six of the sixteen states had enacted medical licensing laws. Although Rush's own state, Pennsylvania, would not enact its first medical practice act until after the Civil War, many of his elite Philadelphia colleagues surely supported such a measure.[41]

By condemning the artificial privilege and monopoly perpetuated by medical licensing, Rush presaged the important role that the theme of economic freedom would play in American medical freedom rhetoric. Just how wide Rush himself would have flung open the door to the medical profession is not clear; he complained in the address only about the exclusion of "men of equal talents and knowledge." Nonetheless, Rush indisputably had a much less restrictive vision of the profession than many regulars. This opposition to special castes and exclusive privileges was a typical Republican position. Jeffersonians believed the granting of monopolies, particularly to favored elites, was "destructive of the principle of equal liberty" and inconsistent with a republican form of government.[42]

Rush's reference in the third quoted paragraph to the relationship between freedom of inquiry and scientific advancement illustrates yet another theme that would prove to be enduring. Rush's admonition earlier in the speech that orthodox physicians not neglect the "cures performed by quacks" reflected his conviction that medical progress depended on the inquiries of irregular practitioners as well as those of erudite medical students and physicians.[43] In a 1789 graduation speech at the University of Pennsylvania, he declared:

> Improvement in medicine is not to be derived only from colleges and universi-
> ties. . . . Those facts which constitute real knowledge, are to be met with in every
> walk of life. Remember how many of our most useful remedies have been dis-
> covered by quacks. Do not be afraid, therefore, of conversing with them, and of
> profiting by their ignorance and temerity in the practice of physic. . . . But fur-
> ther.—In the pursuit of medical knowledge, let me advise you to converse with
> nurses and old women. . . . Even negroes and Indians have sometimes stumbled
> upon discoveries in medicine. Be not ashamed to inquire into them.[44]

Rush's views regarding the value of experimentation by the common man were also typical of early nineteenth-century republicanism. Despite Jefferson's own belief in a "natural aristocracy," his followers increasingly asserted that popular knowledge was as accurate and beneficial as the knowledge of experts.[45]

Rush's Legacy

In March 1813, an unschooled itinerant herbal healer from rural New Hampshire walked into the Medical Department of the University of Pennsylvania. His name was Samuel Thomson, and he would eventually become the leader of the largest organized alternative medicine movement in America prior to the Civil War. At this point, however, he was a small-time practitioner who wandered around northern New England treating townsfolk with a botanical system of medicine he had invented. As Thomson reported in his widely circulated autobiography, he had traveled in February from New Hampshire to Washington, DC, where he had obtained a patent for his remedies after wearing down the resistance of a contemptuous clerk at the patent office. He had then journeyed by stagecoach to Philadelphia with the intention of seeing Benjamin Rush and his faculty colleague, Benjamin Smith Barton, "to confer with them upon the subject of introducing my system of practice to the world."[46]

Thomson recalled that Rush "was so much engaged, that I was unable to have but little conversation," but that he "treated me with much politeness; and said that whatever Dr. Barton agreed to he would give his consent." Thomson then had an extended chat with Barton, during which he "stated to [Barton] pretty fully my opinion of the absurdity of bleeding to cure disease." At the end of their conversation, Barton graciously agreed to accept some of Thomson's medicine and "make a trial of it." Unfortunately, Rush and Barton both died soon afterwards, thus depriving Thomson "of the influence of these two men, which I was confident would otherwise have been exerted in my favour."[47]

If Thomson's account is accurate, his visit to Penn was extraordinarily audacious. To put it in modern perspective, imagine an unknown, unlicensed naturopath from New Hampshire strolling uninvited into the National Institutes of Health and seeking a meeting with Anthony Fauci to recruit him for an antivaccination campaign.

As Thomsonian medicine grew in popularity, more and more Americans read his autobiography, which was bound in the same volume as his guide to his healing system.[48] Presumably, many (or even most) of Thomson's followers learned everything they knew about Rush from this memoir. In the autobiography, Thomson condemned Rush's methods even while praising his courteousness. He proclaimed that the widespread embrace of Rush's "absurd" approach of aggressively bleeding yellow fever victims had "destroyed more lives than powder and ball in this country."[49]

Nonetheless, the Thomsonian literature of the late 1820s and early 1830s, which we will examine in detail in the next chapter, regularly refers to Rush with adulatory phrases such as the "great Dr. Rush."[50] Thomsonian authors highlighted the fact that the "much-distinguished" Rush, like their own mentor, believed in the "unity of disease and of cure."[51] They depicted Rush (somewhat accurately) as open-minded and (inaccurately) as ambivalent about his own variety of heroic treatments.[52] One Thomsonian lecturer, with some justification, characterized Rush as believing that "some lonely weed, trampled in the earth, might furnish a cure which had baffled all the wisdom of the schools."[53] But another speaker confused Rush's willingness to consider the benefits of herbal medicine with a wholesale rejection of orthodox principles. This lecturer asserted that Rush "opened the cry" in the United States against the orthodox "practice of poisoning the human system."[54]

It is unclear if any Thomsonian author had access to a full copy of Rush's 1801 lecture. But in 1839, an American journal dedicated to the growing alternative school of homeopathy reproduced much of the address verbatim, including the passages quoted in this chapter.[55] Thereafter, medical licensing opponents quoted Rush's language opposing "exclusive privileges" with increasing frequency for the remainder of the nineteenth century.

Sometime after the turn of the twentieth century, opponents of restrictive licensing creatively expanded Rush's words into a *constitutional* argument for medical freedom. For instance, in 1907, the *Journal of the American Osteopathic Association* conjured up the following imaginary declaration by Rush:

> The constitution of this republic should make specific provision for medical freedom as well as for religious freedom. To restrict the practice of the art of healing to one class of physicians and deny to others equal privileges constitutes the bastiles [*sic*] of our science. All such laws are un-American and despotic. They are vestiges of monarchy and have no place in a republic.[56]

For more than century, this fictitious rendering of Rush's words has taken on a life of its own. A Google search today reveals thousands of web pages, many of them on the sites of health freedom organizations, ascribing this language (or some variant of it) to Rush. His imagined advocacy of a medical freedom amendment to the Constitution has become fact in cyberspace. The truth that he never actually called for such an amendment should not, however, obscure his actual emphatic opposition to state interference in medical affairs.[57]

2

"The Blood-Bought Freedom of Our Venerable Sires"

The Antebellum Battle for Medical Freedom

An editorial in the August 25, 1838, issue of the *Botanico-Medical Recorder* stressed the importance of the upcoming Ohio state election for those who treasured medical freedom.[1] Five years earlier, the Thomsonians had achieved a great triumph by conducting a successful campaign to erase a medical licensing requirement from the Ohio statute books. But their fortunes took a turn for the worse in December 1837, when a bill to charter the Botanico-Medical College of Ohio, a Thomsonian medical school in Columbus, failed to become law. The bill passed the Ohio House of Representatives but died after the chairman of the relevant senate committee (an orthodox doctor) reported against it. In hopes of reversing this result in the next legislative session, the editorial's author urged his readers to support candidates who were "honest, independent, substantial citizens . . . incapable of the rascality of creating monopolies in favor of parties and sects, and denying constitutional rights."[2]

The author of this editorial was almost certainly Alva Curtis, the publisher of the *Recorder* and the leader of a group of botanical practitioners known as the "Independent Thomsonians."[3] He was also the Botanico-Medical College's founder and sole instructor. Curtis ascribed the previous year's defeat to a nefarious plot between regular physicians and their lackeys in the state legislature to suppress the liberty of unconventional practitioners and their patients. He declared:

> There is something more involved in this question whether we shall have a charter for our School, than the prosperity of a single institution. It is the question whether any minority . . . who think proper to depart from fashion . . . shall be entitled to the common privileges of citizens. The trifling duty demanded on a cargo of tea in '76, was of small importance, but the consideration of the principle it involved very properly turned the whole harbor of Boston into one grand teapot. It will be well for the demagogues of Ohio, to remember that the blood of that tea party still lives and runs in their own Botanic constituents.[4]

Choose Your Medicine. Lewis A. Grossman, Oxford University Press. © Lewis A. Grossman 2021.
DOI: 10.1093/oso/9780190612757.003.0003

Curtis closed the editorial by seeking the support of "every man . . . who does not wish to be trampled in the dust and deprived of his constitutional liberty." In 1839, he got his charter.[5]

Curtis's editorial exemplifies the rhetoric of an extraordinarily successful Thomsonian-led movement for medical freedom in antebellum America. Although the war against orthodox domination of medical regulation had various fronts, its primary aim was the repeal of state licensing laws. The movement's overwhelming victory is reflected in the fact that between 1830 and the Civil War, the United States was transformed from a country that almost universally embraced some form of medical licensing to one in which this type of regulation was virtually nonexistent. The editorial illustrates how during this period, extrajudicial campaigns for freedom of therapeutic choice were waged on explicitly constitutional grounds, even when they invoked the nation's broad foundational principles of equality and liberty rather than particular constitutional provisions.

The Decline and Fall of Antebellum Medical Licensing

The 1820s were the fulcrum of a shift in state legislative activity with respect to medical licensing. Up until 1820, every pertinent measure passed in the United States was designed to either create or strengthen a licensing regime. In stark contrast, between 1830 and 1860, most relevant state legislation either weakened or entirely revoked medical licensing. Some states initially lowered the penalty for practicing without a license, exempted certain classes of irregular practitioners from the licensing requirement, or both. By the end of the 1850s, most states had repealed their medical licensing regimes altogether, and half of the medical practice acts that remained imposed no penalty on violators.[6]

An examination of the statutes alone actually understates the disintegration of medical licensing in the antebellum period. As noted previously, even at the apex of medical licensing in the late 1810s and early 1820s, the laws' effectiveness was uneven, at best. But as the century advanced, the shrinking number of licensing laws still on the books became increasingly irrelevant. Executive authorities, apparently aware of the public's growing distaste for restricting the practice of medicine, often simply failed to enforce the statutes. Some of the remaining licensing boards settled into a state of permanent hibernation.[7]

By the 1840s, contemporary commentators were observing that medical licensing was, for all practical purposes, finished. In an 1844 article, a New York observer of the national scene remarked:

The conclusion which may be drawn is, that when restrictive laws are really efficient and enforced, they protect the community against inexperience and its consequences, but that popular sentiment is opposed to them; consequently the law is either so drawn as to be inefficient, or is, in nine out of ten cases, openly violated with impunity, whilst its existence is such as to get up a feeling of hostility to the regular profession.[8]

In his renowned 1850 report on public health in Massachusetts, Lemuel Shattuck wryly observed: "Any one, male or female, learned or ignorant, an honest man or a knave, can assume the name of a physician, and 'practice' upon any one, to cure or to kill, as either may happen, without accountability. 'It's a free country!' " According to one scholar, "By the time of the Civil War, no effective medical licensing existed in any of the states."[9]

What happened? The antebellum medical licensing regimes succumbed to the country's first broad popular movement promoting medical freedom, led by the Thomsonians. In petitions, journals, and speeches, the Thomsonians framed a successful, multidimensional libertarian argument against medical licensing. And although they advanced their case entirely outside of court, their contentions were unmistakably constitutional.

The Thomsonians

Samuel Thomson, whom we met last chapter on his 1813 visit to the University of Pennsylvania, was born in 1769 and raised on a remote New Hampshire farm in humble circumstances. He lacked any formal education. As a boy, Thomson became fascinated by herbal remedies under the tutelage of a local widow. At age nineteen, he sustained a severe ankle wound and credited botanical cures for his recovery. In his early twenties, he watched in horror as regular doctors' aggressive interventions apparently hastened his mother's death from tuberculosis. The following year, he dismissed the team of physicians attending his young wife during severe complications following childbirth ("they were doing more harm than good") and sent for "root doctors" instead. Thereafter, Thomson completely renounced orthodox medicine.[10]

Thomson began developing his own healing system while treating his family and neighbors. In 1805, he started roaming around northern New England, offering his services to townsfolk and establishing a few medical offices. The commercially savvy Thomson soon conceived an innovative business plan; he sold the right to use his system and proprietary remedies to families in advance of any illness. He fiercely guarded his intellectual property in both his medicines and his publications. Eventually, Thomson (depicted in Fig. 2.1) built a nationwide business empire, which included an army of agents, thirteen editions of his bestselling *New Guide to Health*, a network of Friendly Botanic Societies, and

Figure 2.1 Samuel Thomson (1769–1843), the founder of Thomsonian botanical medicine. *National Library of Medicine.*

annual US Thomsonian Botanic Conventions.[11] Thomsonianism became wildly popular in the 1830s, especially in the South and Midwest. In 1839, Thomson himself boasted that three million Americans—approximately 20 percent of the population—were adherents of his method. One modern scholar surmises that Thomson's estimate, though likely exaggerated, did not vastly exceed the true number.[12]

While the Thomsonians stridently disparaged regular doctors' use of dangerous mineral remedies, their system shared certain central characteristics with orthodox medicine, including a reductionist understanding of disease as a fundamental bodily imbalance and a uniform therapeutic method based on the evacuation of bodily fluids. Thomson posited that all illness derived from the body's loss of natural heat, and his treatment regime was designed to restore the patient's "vital warmth" by clearing bodily obstructions through perspiration, purging, and vomiting. The emblematic components of the Thomsonian healing system were lobelia (an emetic herb), cayenne pepper, and steam baths. Despite its resemblance to regular medicine, Thomson's course of treatment was probably less enfeebling than the use of calomel and bleeding. Many were attracted to the Thomsonians' use of "natural" vegetable-based remedies instead of mineral compounds such as calomel.[13]

Although Thomson derived his system largely a priori from unproven premises about the nature of the human body and disease, Thomsonians took pride in being more "empirical" than the regulars. Compared to orthodox physicians, they ascribed more value to actual experience and less to abstruse theory. Whereas orthodox doctors often used the term "empiric" as an insulting moniker for undereducated alternative practitioners, the Thomsonians embraced the label. They condemned orthodox medicine for its abstract speculation, as well as for its ineffective and dangerous treatments.[14]

The 1830s were a tumultuous decade for Thomsonians. Samuel Thomson himself became progressively more self-important, fanatical, and vengeful. He tolerated no variation from his therapeutic methods and denied that conventional scientific and medical education had any value whatsoever. But the patriarch's unquestioning disciples were increasingly outnumbered by flexible advocates of a more general botanic cause. Alva Curtis was the most prominent of these open-minded Thomsonians. In 1836, he defied Thomson on the education issue by founding the initially unchartered Botanico-Medical College of Ohio, whose curriculum incorporated lectures and texts on basic science. In 1838, Curtis led a secession of "Independent Thomsonians" away from the purists—a schism impelled by the Independents' desire for freedom to explore improvements to Thomson's system, including expansion of its *materia medica*. Despite this development, Curtis remained committed to the core aspects of Thomsonian medicine.[15]

The Thomsonians and Jacksonian Liberty

Issues of social status swirled around the Thomsonian movement. Though it attracted some middle-class and wealthy followers by the 1830s, it remained at its core "a rural and lower-class phenomenon." Thomsonians were driven by populist passion—a rejection of elite practitioners, institutions, and knowledge. In this respect, they were representative of a broad, egalitarian political culture with affinity to President Andrew Jackson's Democratic Party—a political culture that frequently exhibited a fierce libertarian opposition to government intrusion into private affairs.[16]

Most Jacksonian Democrats were not laissez-faire absolutists; they embraced some economic regulation not deemed to advance the interests of self-aggrandizing moneyed aristocrats. Nonetheless, they, along with their Jeffersonian Republican forebears, probably had the most comprehensive libertarian philosophy of any major political culture in American history. As described by Marvin Meyers, Jacksonians believed that a "laissez-faire society . . . would re-establish continuity with that golden age in which liberty and progress were joined inseparably with simple yeoman virtues." Whereas the Jacksonians' Whig opponents supported an active role for the government in funding and facilitating economic development, the Jacksonians tended to reject such measures as "special legislation" favoring privileged patricians. They had an almost paranoid view of the grasping "money power's" ability to control the organs of government. Jacksonian laissez-faireism was thus populist in spirit, reflecting a view that economic regulations were the instruments of corrupt, scheming elites—whether industrialists or orthodox physicians—striving to increase their wealth and power at the expense of the common man. The Jacksonian journalist William Leggett believed (in Marvin Meyers's words): "Freedom is . . . freedom *from* chartered exploitation, from 'aristocratic innovation.' "[17]

The Whigs and Jacksonians also disagreed about government's appropriate posture with respect to religion and the regulation of private behavior. The Whigs believed the state should enforce moral standards and promote cultural homogeneity; accordingly, they supported temperance laws, obligatory Sabbath observance, and a broad partnership between church and state to advance a "national religion." Jacksonians, on the other hand—with the support of the vast majority of the nation's Catholics—opposed temperance laws, embraced the strict separation of church and state, and generally "made room for widely divergent private behavior."[18]

In short, in the words of historian Daniel Walker Howe, "Whigs had a positive conception of liberty; they treasured it as a means to the formation of individual character and a good society. Democrats, by contrast, held a negative conception of liberty; they saw it as freeing the common (white) man from the oppressive burdens of an aristocracy." The popular Jacksonian magazine *Democratic Review* maintained that the "principle of [America's] organization" was a collection of four freedoms: "freedom of conscience, freedom of person, freedom of trade and business pursuits, [and] universality of freedom and equality." The Thomsonians would embrace all of these in their fight against medical licensing statutes.[19]

The Thomsonians' Constitutional Struggle

The Thomsonians' battle for medical freedom was an explicitly constitutional one, even though they apparently never attempted to challenge a state medical practice act in court. The Thomsonians and their supporters instead waged their successful struggle against the orthodox medical establishment by using the press, petitions, and party politics to sway legislators and governors. Citizens also used their power as jurors to undermine medical licensing statutes, and executive officials often responded to popular opposition to such laws by declining to enforce them.

Why did the Thomsonians not use lawsuits to advance their cause? Perhaps they believed that such actions would be futile. Jacksonians generally viewed the courts as bastions of antidemocratic aristocracy, especially in states that had not yet embraced judicial elections. The Thomsonians may thus have viewed judges as prejudiced in favor of the privileged class of regular physicians. Furthermore, opponents of medical licensing were likely aware that antebellum courts did not typically strike down legislation based on the application of broad constitutional principles. Legal historian Mark Graber has observed: "Remarkably, hardly any constitutional question arose in the antebellum United States that was resolved into a judicial question."[20]

Finally—and importantly—Americans during the Jacksonian era simply did not view courts as the exclusive, or even primary, arena for contesting constitutional principles. All the nonjudicial methods that had been used to shape constitutional meaning during the Revolutionary period—except perhaps mobbing—were still considered valid vehicles for popular constitutionalism. The important change was that party politics had become the chief means by which the people expressed their constitutional understandings. The legislative and executive departments were deemed to have at least as much of a role in constitutional interpretation as the courts, and the people sought, through a wide variety of party-based activities, to ensure that these elected branches acted in accordance with their constitutional vision. In Larry Kramer's words, "Democratic-dominated governments at both the state and national levels successfully marginalized the judiciary . . . and reasserted popular control over constitutional development."[21] Therefore, the fact that the Thomsonians advanced their arguments outside of court should not obscure the fact they were *constitutional* arguments and that, for them, medical liberty was a *constitutional* imperative.

The earliest suggestion I have found of a widespread challenge to the constitutionality of medical licensing is contained in an 1824 message by Pennsylvania governor Andrew Shulze accompanying his veto of a medical practice statute. In this document, Schulze questioned "the expediency of enacting a law, which a large and respectible [sic] portion of the community believe to be contrary to the best established principles of the constitution."[22] Shulze's message offers an intriguing hint that citizens were already (perhaps in an organized manner) voicing constitutional arguments for freedom of therapeutic choice to elected officials.

Another early assertion of the unconstitutionality of medical licensing came from the pen of a prominent member of the academic medical elite—Professor

Benjamin Waterhouse of Harvard. Waterhouse was a personal friend of Samuel Thomson's and one of the few members of the regular medical profession to (somewhat) respect his work. In an 1825 letter from Waterhouse to a New York physician, delivered by Thomson himself, the Harvard professor asked, "How came your Legislature to pass so unconstitutional an act as that called the *anti-quack* law?"[23]

In the early 1830s, the growing Thomsonian movement took the lead in advancing constitutional arguments against licensing. Consider, for example, a lengthy 1832 piece in the *Thomsonian Recorder* titled "An Essay in Relation to the Unconstitutionality, Injustice, and Injurious Effects, Resulting from Our Present Aristocratical Medical Law in the State of Ohio." This article, authored in Revolutionary-era fashion by "Honestus," reads like a legal brief or bill of particulars. Honestus condemns Ohio's 1824 licensing statute as "contrary to the letter and spirit of the constitution and a direct and undeniable violation of the oath of legislators, whereby they are sworn to maintain that sacred charter of our liberties." He asserts that the law violates various "natural and unalienable rights" protected by the Ohio Constitution, including "enjoying and defending life and liberty, acquiring, possessing and protecting property, pursuing and obtaining happiness and safety." Honestus also contends that the licensing statue violates the state constitution's prohibition against laws impairing the validity of contracts.[24] Shortly before this article appeared, Ohio citizens presented a petition to their legislature similarly declaring that the medical practice act violated their "unalienable and constitutional rights."[25]

In addition to relying on state constitutions, Thomsonians also appealed frequently to the US Constitution. For example, in 1834, the Friendly Botanic Society of New York City adopted resolutions against New York State's medical practice law. The resolutions' preamble stated, "We . . . feel ourselves aggrieved by the passage of such an act, because we are restricted from and denied the privilege of exercising those dear rights guaranteed to us by our forefathers in the invaluable Constitution of our beloved nation."[26]

The Thomsonians' "constitutional" arguments frequently appealed not only to the state and federal constitutions, but also to fundamental rights embodied in the Declaration of Independence and vindicated on the battlefields of the Revolutionary War. Take, for instance, a lengthy 1837 editorial in the *Thomsonian Recorder* titled "The Declaration of Independence." The author of this unsigned piece (possibly Alva Curtis) starts: "On July 4th, 1776, it was declared by the Representatives of these United States, in Congress assembled, to be 'self-evident, that all men were created equal and endowed by their Creator, with certain inalienable rights, among which are life, liberty, and the pursuit of happiness.'"[27] He then asserts that the state and federal constitutions were formed "[i]n accordance with these principles" and therefore that "all enactments of men . . . which are opposed to these principles, are null, void and of no effect." The author continues:

These propositions [from the Declaration of Independence], having been admitted for sixty-one years to be self evident, . . . *all the laws* in the United States which make it a misdemeanor for any but a member of "the Regular Medical Faculty" to administer remedies to cure the sick, or for any person to employ and pay whom he pleases as his physician; or that prevent any man from recovering, by process of common law, a just reward for medical services that had been voluntarily solicited and faithfully performed, are unconstitutional, oppressive, and wicked.

The editorial's final call to action is addressed to the "sons of the patriotic sires who nobly resisted laws made without their consent; who, half clothed and half starved, poured out for seven years their treasures and their blood, to secure to you, their posterity, equal enjoyment of your inalienable rights."[28]

The Multiple Strands of Medical Freedom

The Thomsonians' more specific arguments against medical licensing demonstrate that they had a multidimensional vision of the constitutional right to freedom of therapeutic choice. In their view, medical freedom implicated various categories of inalienable liberties protected by the country's founding documents and by higher law.

Bodily Freedom

To modern ears, the Thomsonian arguments that sound most familiar are those concerning the right of control over one's body. Whereas many of the strands of medical liberty advanced by the Thomsonians echoed themes articulated by Benjamin Rush decades earlier, the bodily freedom theme was a more original contribution.

One version of this argument was the assertion that people have a right to decide what and what not to put into their bodies. In particular, the Thomsonians insisted that citizens should be free to avoid the dangerous remedies employed by regular physicians. Honestus asked, "If I be conscientiously opposed to bleeding, blistering, mercurialising, or poisoning with emetic tartar, opium, arsenic, or prussic acid, shall I be compelled to employ a law-made doctor, who deals almost exclusively in these potent remedies?" The author of the "Declaration of Independence" maintained, "To give poisons, is to deprive men of sound health, if not the whole of vitality or life; and, therefore unconstitutional and wicked." A legislative committee considering repeal of the New York medical practice law painted an especially vivid picture, stating that the legislature should not "thrust calomel and mercury down a man's throat while he wills to take only cayenne or lobelia."[29]

A related Thomsonian argument with parallels in modern rhetoric was the contention that individuals have a right to choose what steps to take to protect their physical well-being. For instance, in resolutions adopted in 1834 by the Friendly Botanic Society of New York City against New York State's licensing requirement, the Society maintained a "freedom to choose the means which we believe are best calculated to secure to us health and life." This document further stated, "A large majority of us are private citizens [i.e., not practitioners], and are deprived of the privilege . . . of calling on such physicians as we prefer, that we may have health restored to us when suffering from the inroads of disease." An 1831 or 1832 petition against the New Jersey medical practice act declared: "In matters which concern our LIVES, we conceive it to be *our* interest, and that it should be *our privilege*, to choose such Physicians for our relief, as we have most confidence in."[30]

Economic Freedom

References to economic freedom were even more common in the Thomsonian literature than those to bodily freedom. Before we review these arguments, it is important to stress that the Jacksonians' support of economic liberty was tied to their broader vision of political and human liberty. It was not based merely on a wish to maximize economic efficiency and growth.

Moreover, it bears repeating that unlike many later proponents of the laissez-faire principle, the Jacksonians were not impelled by a desire to protect wealthy individuals and large businesses from the government. To the contrary, their opposition to economic regulation was directed primarily against "special legislation," such as the bestowal of monopolies, which promoted the interests of the affluent and influential rather than advancing the common good. Consequently, when the New York Thomsonians contemplated forming a third party to push for repeal of the New York medical licensing statute, they called it the "Anti-Monopoly Party." Their bête noire was not simply economic regulation in the medical field, but regulation used to prop up an aristocratic monopoly. As Honestus proclaimed, "The coalision [*sic*] of the medical faculty in this state [Ohio], and the protection of that coalision by legislative patronage, we confidently affirm to be contrary to the letter and spirit of the constitution."[31]

Because they believed that licensing was a monopolistic plot by the medical establishment, the Thomsonians were certain that the medical practice acts' purported goal of protecting health was mere camouflage for mercenary motives.

This conviction was bolstered by the fact that many states, rather than prohibiting the unlicensed practice of medicine altogether, merely forbade the collection of fees or banned suits for unpaid compensation. New York's legalization of free botanical medical services led the *Thomsonian Recorder* to quip: "Quacks may kill whom they please . . . if they do not take any money for the commission of the act."[32]

The battle over medical licensing was thus a quintessential Jacksonian-era conflict, pitting "equality against privilege, liberty against domination; . . . natural dignity against factitious superiority; . . . progress against dead precedent."[33] The Thomsonians saw themselves as commonsensical, empirical, and democratic, in contrast to the pretentious, doctrinaire, and cliquish regular physicians they struggled against. Whereas the regulars were attempting to fortify their economic and social position through the establishment of an artificial monopoly, the Thomsonians were fighting for an open medical services market in which the price and availability of different therapeutic approaches would reflect their actual value to patients. According to a Maine senator advocating the repeal of that state's medical practice law, the public demanded:

> that it will be the judge of its own wants—it will select its own servants. . . . —
> that there shall be no bar to competition between two classes of physicians; but
> that each individual shall stand or fall on his own merits—that he who pretends
> to superior attainments or endowments, shall support his claims, not by ap-
> pealing to his lineage or associations, but by what he accomplishes.[34]

The Thomsonians viewed their fight for medical freedom as part of a larger war being fought by the country's honest, productive citizens against aristocratic privilege and power. Calling for revocation of the New York practice law, the *Poughkeepsie Thomsonian* contended:

> Nothing short of such a measure can wrest the reins of government from the
> polluted hands of aristocracy, and place its inhabitants on an equal footing.
> This step must eventually be taken, in order to break down that disgusting
> monopoly which has long been sapping the very foundations of American
> freedom. . . . Thomsonians are by no means the only class that suffer from cor-
> rupt legislation. Farmers, mechanics, and laborers in general experience . . . the
> demoralizing influence of unfair and unjust speculation, set on foot by the anti-
> republican nabobs that infest our country. These drones of community feast
> and fatten at the expense of the honest and industrious parts of society.[35]

Despite the Thomsonians' emphasis on aristocratic conspiracies and class con-flict, they also viewed medical licensing statutes as direct infringements of their *individual* economic rights. Undergirding their Jacksonian attack against special legislation were two fundamental constitutional norms of economic liberty: the law should not take the property of one citizen and give it to another and the law should not impair the obligation of contracts. The Jacksonians reaffirmed a traditional constitutional view (articulated in 1798 by Supreme Court Justice Samuel Chase) that even when such laws were not directly forbidden by particular constitutional language, they were violative of "certain *vital* principles in our *free republican governments*" and "contrary to the *great first principles* of the *social compact*."[36]

The Thomsonians sometimes referred to specific constitutional provisions helpful to their arguments. For example, Honestus contended that the Ohio medical practice act's prohibition against suits for fees by unlicensed practitioners violated the state constitution's bar against laws impairing the validity of contracts. Overall, however, the Thomsonians tended to base the economic liberty strand of their medical freedom arguments not on the letter of the state and federal constitutions, but on basic principles. For example, the editorial titled "Declaration of Independence" invoked general free labor and free contract notions. "Our tradesmen and mechanics are permitted and encouraged to hire themselves for what they can earn, and to bring forward the fruits of their labor and sell them for what they are worth, without being questioned where, with whom, or how long they served as apprentices. . . . So should it be with the doctor." A proposed petition to the New York legislature, presented in the voice of patients, contended: "It is one of the privileges of an independent people to pay their money to whom they please, and for what they please, without the direct or indirect interference of any one."[37]

In this "thin constitutional" mode, the Thomsonians sometimes combined their arguments regarding economic freedom with appeals to bodily freedom. For instance, an editorial in a New York botanical newspaper, attacking the state's prohibition against compensation for unlicensed practitioners, explicitly linked the law's tyrannical economic coercion against unlicensed practitioners with an equally oppressive bodily coercion against patients:

Here we are gravely told by law that we shall not command our own property. If A. employs B. because he is a skilful [*sic*] practitioner, C. steps in and says if A. pays B. any thing [*sic*] for his services he will have B. fined and imprisoned for taking it. C. therefore commands the will and purse of A. and prevents B. from doing the service that A. must have done in order to save his life. But B. in consequence of being jeopardized both in his "*life, liberty and property*," and having a family to support, must go into other business, thereby throwing the sick man, or A. and his property into the power of a set of men in whom he has no confidence, or he must go without a doctor until he will come to the terms that are dictated to him, and be poisoned "*Secundum Artem*" [according to the accepted practice of the profession], and according to law.[38]

This paragraph illustrates how the different aspects of medical freedom in the Thomsonian literature were sometimes almost inextricably intertwined. The next strand of medical freedom we will consider—freedom of inquiry—similarly cannot be viewed in isolation from the other strands.

Freedom of Inquiry

The Thomsonians directed their anti-monopoly arguments not only at regular physicians' efforts to control the market for medical services, but also at their efforts to control the marketplace of medical ideas.

Like Benjamin Rush, the Thomsonians railed against the orthodox medical establishment's squelching of competing systems of medical knowledge. They and their allies defended the right of free inquiry as a necessary feature of a free and democratic society. For example, in a report advocating repeal of that state's medical licensing statute, New York State Senator George Scott declared, "A people accustomed to govern themselves, and boasting of their intelligence, are impatient of restraint. They want no protection but freedom of inquiry and freedom of action."[39] The Thomsonian essayist Honestus maintained:

Learning and property are the elements of political power. These elements combined and put in operation, are the most efficient means for the elevation of the few and the subjugation of the many. . . . This monopolizing spirit constitutes . . . a literary aristocracy, a privileged order, whose ends and aims have been, are now, and ever will be hostile to the equal and unalienable [*sic*] rights and privileges of society at large.[40]

The Thomsonians not only considered free inquiry to be essential for equality and political liberty; they also deemed it necessary for intellectual progress. Honestus lamented that the elite "renounce the demonstrations of reason, received from honest inquiry, devoutly idolize antiquated traditions, and in philosophy, medicine, and their kindred sciences adhere . . . pertinaciously . . . to the impress of superstition." In emphasizing the need for open inquiry, Honestus stressed a theme that would reverberate throughout the history of American medical liberty advocacy—the incompleteness and imperfection of present scientific knowledge. Because of "the defective limitedness and imperfection of human intellect," he maintained, many supposedly established "facts and demonstrations . . . lie open for free enquiry and the most ample discussion."

Honestus explained that freedom of inquiry was necessary "not because there are no fixed immutable principles . . . existing inherently in the nature and fitness of things," but because these principles "have never been perfectly understood, and therefore never fully developed by the boldest researches of science and time."[41]

Consistent with their egalitarian Jacksonian worldview, the Thomsonians and their allies frequently proclaimed that if people of all classes were liberated to exercise their natural genius, common folk would be at least as likely as book-trained physicians to advance medical knowledge. In a Georgia Senate debate on a bill that would revise the state medical practice act so as to permit botanical physicians to charge for their services, Senator Norborn B. Powell declared: "I feel unwilling to fetter the human mind, to bind men by law to any particular system of physic. Such a course must curtail the range of human intellect. Have not some of the most important discoveries in science been made by those in the humblest walks of life?" In response to his own rhetorical question, Powell pointed to the contributions that the "illiterate dairy-women of England," the "unlettered Indians of Peru," and the "cannibals of Brazil" had made to medicine by discovering the therapeutic qualities of cowpox matter, cinchona bark, and ipecac, respectively.[42]

Such celebrations of common people's medical achievements usually presumed not that the unschooled masses possessed great intellectual sophistication, but rather that medicine was a relatively uncomplicated discipline. A Maryland legislative committee observed, "Of all sciences, the knowledge of disease and the means of cure, must be supposed . . . as most simple and easy of attainment. It is, essentially, a science of experience."[43] When medicine was viewed in this way, the "free inquiry" required for its progress was not complex scientific analysis, but simple practical experimentation, uncorrupted by abstract theory. In his autobiography's preface (written in the third person), Samuel Thomson himself remarked:

> Dr. Thomson . . . had nothing to guide him but his own experience. He not having had an education, has received no advantages from reading books, which left his mind unshackled by the visionary theories and opinions of others; his whole studies have been in the great book of nature, and his conclusions have all been drawn from that unerring guide; by this he was enabled to form correct opinions of the fitness of things.[44]

Samuel Thomson was not himself a paragon of free inquiry, at least later in his life. Committed to protecting the purity of his system, he increasingly condemned explorations into improved or supplemental therapies as "mongrelism." But the increasingly dominant Curtis and his Independents were deeply devoted to free inquiry; indeed, their schism from the purists was based in large part on their commitment to this ideal. The Independent Thomsonians opened the pages of their journals and the curricula of their classrooms to both conventional science and other alternative medical systems of the era, including Grahamism, Mesmerism, phrenology, and hydropathy. In 1837, Curtis defended his Botanico-Medical College of Ohio from the Thomsonian purists' attacks by boasting, "We have given the utmost freedom and latitude to inquiry, cheerfully confessed our ignorance where we felt it, and advised submission to nothing but demonstration by the best evidences that the nature of the cases would admit."[45]

Freedom of Conscience and Religion

Finally, the Thomsonians' medical liberty arguments also invoked the principle of freedom of conscience. For example, in his essay, Honestus proclaimed himself "conscientiously opposed" to orthodox medicine and then rhetorically queried:

> Might I not with equal propriety, and with equal justice, be compelled to attend at, or to erect and support certain places of worship, or maintain a patented clergy, either Papal or Protestant without my consent and against my con- science, as to be compelled to employ a physician of a certain class, contrary to my best judgment, and utterly against my will?[46]

It is difficult to determine exactly what the Thomsonians meant when they asserted that "freedom of conscience" required freedom of therapeutic choice. On the one hand, they may have believed that this term was synonymous with freedom of religion—and thus that a person's choice of a health practitioner was in some way an exercise of religion. On the other hand, they may have believed that "freedom of conscience" was a broader concept that embraced both freedom of religion and medical freedom as distinct but analogous notions. Dictionaries of the time did not limit the word *conscience* to religious belief. But as legal scholar Michael McConnell has observed, in the country's early years, "outside of dictio- naries, the vast preponderance of references to 'liberty of conscience' . . . were either expressly or impliedly limited to religious conscience."[47]

At times, the Thomsonians demanded freedom of thought in the broadest sense. A letter to the *Thomsonian Recorder* proclaimed: "Legislatures may enact laws against Thomsonianism, but, thank heaven, they cannot bind the mind of man. . . . For freedom of thought and speech are the unalienable rights of man." Honestus implored, "In this land of freedom . . . shall we not as a free, magnani- mous and independent people, dare to think and act for ourselves, to assume our proper rank and dignity in the scale of being . . . ?"[48]

But echoing Rush before them, the Thomsonians routinely linked their pleas for freedom of "conscience" or "thought" to religious liberty. For example, immediately following this statement, Honestus urged the people to "shake off the reckless aspirations of a clerical, legal, and medical denomination, that invades our rights and holds them in contempt." Thomsonians frequently compared orthodox medicine to an established church and equated the right to choose a physician with the right to choose a minister. For instance, an unsigned editorial in the *Thomsonian Recorder* declared: "We could never see what right any man, or any body of men, can have in the nature and fitness of things to control us in our choice of a lawyer, preacher or physician." Samuel Thomson himself opened the introduction to his *Guide to Health* by equating the orthodox physicians of his own day to the priests of ages past, who "held the things of religion in their own hands, and brought the people to their terms."[49]

One scholar has observed that although "little in [Thomsonianism] could be called overtly or distinctively religious," it nonetheless "had deep roots in the Second Great Awakening, which accentuated the role of humans in effecting the Kingdom of God on earth." The Thomsonians sometimes strengthened the link between medicine and religion by suggesting that the "natural" botanical remedies of their system were divinely sanctioned. The very first page of the first issue of the *Thomsonian Recorder* claimed a divine foundation for the Thomsonian system, bemoaning the persecution of any practitioner "who dares to remove disease with healing medicine, which the God of Nature has so profusely scattered for the benefit of all."[50] The previously mentioned New Jersey petition against medical licensing similarly declared:

> We believe, the God of Nature has bountifully caused to grow in our own country, and placed within our reach, medicines for the alleviation and cure of the various maladies with which we are from time to time afflicted; and we conceive it an infraction of our rights to debar us from the use of such remedies, or from employing such physicians as administer them.[51]

The US Constitution's free exercise of religion clause was not deemed to limit state law until the twentieth century, and I have found no instance in which a Thomsonian-era commentator directly contended that a medical licensing statute violated a state constitutional religion clause. Nonetheless, the perceived link between medical and religious choice was so close that when the Arkansas territorial governor vetoed a medical practice law in 1831, he asserted in his veto message that government should not control a citizen's "will and faith" on the subject of the choice of medical practitioners.[52]

As we will see, after the Civil War, groups with more explicitly spiritual agendas would become leading advocates for medical freedom, and the association between medical and religious liberty would become ever stronger.

The Battle in New York

The Thomsonians' popular constitutionalist demand for therapeutic freedom, with its four contributing strands, achieved its greatest triumph in 1844, with the revocation of the medical practice law of the nation's most populous state.

New York had had a medical licensing statute on the books since colonial times, and the legislature had ratcheted up the penalties until, by 1827, unlicensed practitioners were subject to fines and imprisonment, at least in theory. The Thomsonians' struggle for medical liberty in New York began in the late 1820s, when they conducted a statewide petition campaign that persuaded the legislature, in 1830, to exempt from the licensing requirement any person "using or applying, for the benefit of any sick person, any roots, barks, or herbs, the growth or produce of the United States." Four years later, however, the regulars persuaded the legislature to repeal this provision. The 1834 amended statute allowed botanical doctors to perform their services, but only "without fee or reward."[53] Thus commenced a decade-long crusade, led by the Thomsonians, to revoke the state's medical practice statute altogether.

In September 1834, the New York Botanic State Convention, comprising delegates from local botanic societies throughout the state, launched a campaign against the revised medical practice law. As described by the editor of the *Botanic Watchman*:

> A spirit of unanimity pervaded the convention in all its deliberations, and as they felt the weight of their oppression, they were unanimously resolved to apply at the source of evil [the legislature] for a redress of their grievances, and a mitigation of the abuses, that have been unwarrantably heaped upon them, until the right of a free selection of their favorite physician, is left unfettered by legal restraint. If every state in the Union would pursue a similar course, we might ere long, throw off the shackles of despotism, which the lordly faculty are endavoring [sic] to make fast, until the people are entirely lost to a sense of their freedom, and the right to exercise their constitutional privileges.[54]

The convention appointed two committees, one to write resolutions expressing the views of the convention and another to draft a petition for repeal of the medical practice law. Samuel Thomson's son, John, was appointed to both.[55] The resulting documents, to be discussed in detail, are notable both for their explicit invocation of the Constitution and for their reference to all the strands of medical freedom discussed earlier.

The convention ordered the printing of one thousand copies of the resolutions and five hundred copies of the petition. In February 1835, the *Thomsonian Recorder* reported that "petitions are pouring in to the Capitol from every portion of the Empire State," and three months later the same publication claimed that the number of petitioners had "swelled to 40,000." A revocation bill passed the House but lost in the Senate. The Thomsonians nevertheless energetically continued their petition campaign; on one occasion John Thomson paraded into Albany pushing a wheelbarrow containing a petition bearing so many signatures that it stretched thirty-one yards. Three additional times, the petitioners obtained the same disappointing result (passage in the House, defeat in the Senate). Finally, in 1844, they triumphed. The legislature repealed the New York medical practice statute and enacted a law explicitly stating: "No person shall be liable to any criminal prosecution or to indictment, for practising physic and surgery without license, excepting in cases of mal-practice, or gross ignorance, or immoral conduct in such practice."[56]

An examination of the petition and resolutions demonstrates that the New York Thomsonians viewed themselves as vindicating fundamental constitutional principles. The petition declared, "We believe said law is a direct infringement of our constitutional privileges." The resolutions attacked an unholy alliance of orthodox physicians and legislators that was usurping New York citizens' constitutional rights. The introduction to the resolutions characterized legislators who supported medical licensing as "traitors to their constituents, and assassins to the principles of a liberal and just government." It continued, "Upon such men should not the mark of disapprobation be branded, so plainly as to warn all others from encroaching in like manner upon our constitutional rights?"[57]

In detailing the rights the despised statute invaded, the convention members used every libertarian argument in the Jacksonian arsenal. Because the 1834 New York law did not prohibit botanical practitioners from administering their remedies to patients, but only from receiving compensation, the petition and resolutions gave special emphasis to the idea of economic freedom. Indeed, the petition (a much shorter document focusing on the ban against compensation) rested almost exclusively on principles of free contract and free labor. First, the petition declared from the perspective of patients:

> We have a right, beyond doubt, to employ any person whom we may think proper, as our physician, without jeopardizing his life, liberty or property. If we employ a person to administer to us as our physician, common law and justice should give him a reasonable compensation for his services.

Assuming the voice of practitioners, the petition then asserted: "In all matters of business, we have a right to manage our own affairs, and that right we wish to exercise unmolested by those who may make it their interest to thwart and perplex us in our just and legal avocations."[58]

The resolutions echoed these themes, asserting, for example, that law should "leav[e] all professions to stand or fall by their own merits, regulated by a fair competition, and an accountability to their employers." But the committee on resolutions also offered a broader, typically Jacksonian attack on corrupt special legislation favoring the economic aristocracy. Although the resolutions vigorously attacked legislators who supported the medical practice law, the primary villains were the "medical men," who had captured the legislative process to "invade in an unjust manner [our] rights and privileges." One resolution declared that the law "was obtained through the influence of a designing faculty, and expressly calculated to force a monopoly of practice into their own hands by the exclusion of all others." Another pledged, "We will use all laudable endeavors to counteract the influence of all medical monopolies in the halls of Legislation, and to produce an equalized system of practice, resting on its respective merits."[59]

The New York Thomsonians' arguments were not solely economic, however. The resolutions asserted a right to control one's body and the treatment of it:

> We are all sensitive beings, both in mind and body, and it is to protect these functions from insult and injury, that we object to the [law]. If we are distressed in body, what greater privilege can we enjoy than the free and independent right in the selection of our Physicians to relieve our maladies?

The Thomsonians proclaimed that the right to employ one's choice of physician was part of the "blood-bought freedom of our venerable sires, which was purchased by them on the field of battle for their posterity." The resolutions bolstered their argument for bodily freedom by reference to the dangers of heroic orthodox medicine. "It were better to have no laws regulating the practice of medicine, than to place all power in the hands of a privileged few, and those using the most dangerous poisons for medicine."[60]

The resolutions also invoked the parallel between medical freedom and religious freedom. "If our minds are diseased, who would have the audacity to dictate to us our spiritual Physician: would we not all of us consider ourselves fully competent to select the Physician for our souls as well as bodies?" This argument proved to be persuasive to the legislative committee considering repeal measures. In supporting the petitioners, the committee remarked, "Men cannot be legislated out of one religion and into another."[61]

Finally, although the resolutions did not greatly emphasize freedom of inquiry, they did allude to the merits of "unshackled" science. The committee that drafted the resolutions, like Thomsonian commentators generally, embraced a populist empirical vision of medical science, in which therapeutic systems are "tested by experience" and any law restricting free access to different types of practitioners unfairly "charges the people with ignorance, and infringes on their rights."[62]

In short, the documents emerging from the 1834 New York Botanic Convention epitomize the Thomsonians' multidimensional view of medical rights as constitutional rights. Moreover, the tactics used by the Thomsonians in New York exemplify how medical freedom advocates, like others in Jacksonian America, did not treat courts as the only forum, or even the preferred forum, for asserting constitutional rights. Finally, the result of these struggles demonstrates that such extrajudicial constitutional campaigns could be astonishingly successful.

Conclusion

The Independent Thomsonians continued to exist, under a series of different names (Botanic-Medicals, Physio-Medicals) until the early 1900s. However, following the completion of their largely successful campaign against medical licensing by the mid-nineteenth century, there was a discernible change of character in the group. They lost their grass-roots, popular fervor (and much of their following) and assumed all the trappings of orthodox medicine, including state medical societies and a small network of diploma-granting medical schools. Meanwhile, the purist Thomsonian faction shriveled away and disappeared following the dissolution of the US Thomsonian Society in 1840 and the founder's death in 1843. During the second half of the nineteenth century, botanical medicine proponents who traced their roots back to Samuel Thomson transformed from a "remarkable socio-medical movement" to "a small, ineffectual, and pseudo-scientific cult."[63]

Nevertheless, other botanical systems continued to prosper through the 1800s. Before the Civil War, a botanical practitioner named Wooster Beach founded a distinct branch of botanical medicine that came to be known as the "eclectics." Eventually, many Independent Thomsonian schools and practitioners converted to eclecticism, and the eclectics became (along with the regulars and the homeopaths) one of the three major organized medical sects during the latter part of the nineteenth century.[64] Moreover, as we will see, botanical medicine was just the first in a long list of popular unorthodox medical approaches that would emerge over the course of the century. While these different systems produced a kaleidoscope of theories and philosophies, they tended to embrace the same cluster of attitudes: skepticism toward orthodox medical science, an embrace of more "natural" and lower-risk alternatives to regular drugs, a populist suspicion of nefarious conspiracies involving the medical elite, and a firm conviction that freedom of therapeutic choice was every American's constitutional right.

3

Orthodoxy and "The Other Man's Doxy"

Medical Licensing and Medical Freedom in the Gilded Age

On March 24, 1894, the *Boston Evening Transcript* contained a letter to the editor titled "The Medical Registration Act." The author—William James, M.D., of Cambridge—began, "I have just signed a petition . . . begging our legislature not to pass a bill now pending, of which the purpose is to 'regulate' the practice of medicine and surgery."[1]

William James, the brother of novelist Henry James, is remembered today as the father of American academic psychology and as a cofounder of the American philosophical school known as "pragmatism." Although he had produced only a small portion of his influential body of work by 1894, he was already a familiar figure to the *Transcript*'s Brahmin readership. The fifty-two-year-old Harvard professor's orations on a variety of topics attracted large and enthusiastic audiences. Though he increasingly identified as a philosopher, James's scientific credentials were also impressive. He had earned a medical degree from Harvard, had started his academic career teaching anatomy and physiology, and had established the country's first experimental psychology laboratory. James was thus a persuasive commentator on matters of medical policy.[2]

The bill that James resisted would have prohibited any person from practicing medicine in Massachusetts unless he either possessed a degree from a "reputable" medical school or passed an examination administered by a state board of examiners. In his letter, James offered various objections to the creation of such a medical licensing regime. First, he asserted that the bill "is too grandmotherly, and goes against the best political habits and traditions of our state." He declared that it would be a "grotesque and puerile anomaly" for the commonwealth to stand between a citizen and the therapeutic advisor of his choice. "If the word 'sacred' can be applied to any personal right, surely the right to treat one's own body as one chooses may claim the title."

Second, James maintained that the proposed scheme offered little actual protection to citizens, for the "*serious* therapeutic inadequacy which the population of Massachusetts . . . is exposed to is the inadequacy of the regular educated profession." He observed that despite undoubted advances in anatomy and diagnosis, treatment remained a matter of guesswork for doctors—a task "still

Choose Your Medicine. Lewis A. Grossman, Oxford University Press. © Lewis A. Grossman 2021.
DOI: 10.1093/oso/9780190612757.003.0004

beyond their powers." James remarked, "There is no more epigramatic instance of that combined greatness and littleness of man's mind . . . than this capacity to give interminable clinical lectures over patients to whom we are radically unable to afford real help." Although he did not explicitly claim that drugless approaches, such as Mind Cure and Christian Science, produced results superior to those of regular medicine, he came close. The truth of the alternative practitioners' *theories* might be uncertain, James remarked, but "their *facts* are patent and startling."

Finally, James (depicted in Fig. 3.1) reached perhaps his most important point: "The suppression of certain practitioners will hinder the progress of therapeutic knowledge as a whole." The drugless healers' "brilliant" results demonstrated that "the agency of the patient's mind" was a critical aspect of the

THE PSYCHOLOGICAL PILLAR OF THE HARVARD TEMPLE
Professor William James, "the centre of a cultured and admiring circle," is accused by some critics of being no true scientist.

Figure 3.1 William James, M.D. (1842–1910), Harvard professor of psychology and philosophy. *National Library of Medicine.*

treatment of disease. If the proposed Medical Registration Act suppressed these practitioners' treatments, scientists would lose the opportunity to observe and study them, and a "public calamity" would result.

James and his allies ultimately prevailed. Although the legislature passed a revised version of the bill, the enacted statute expressly exempted "clairvoyants [and] persons practising hypnotism, magnetic healing, mind cure, massage methods, christian science, cosmopathic, or any other method of healing." And on March 2, 1898, at a thronged hearing before the Massachusetts Committee on Public Health, James and other prominent medical freedom activists persuaded legislators to kill a bill that would have revoked this exemption four years after its passage.[3]

These developments in Massachusetts were typical of the American experience generally following the Civil War. Although almost every state embraced medical licensing during the Gilded Age, the legislation was written and implemented in ways that largely preserved citizens' ability to choose their preferred therapeutic approach.[4] And the struggle to shape this second wave of medical licensing laws generated its own rich body of medical liberty literature.

Medical Practice in the Gilded Age

Gilded Age arguments about the regulation of medical practice were not merely a reprise of the antebellum debates. The scientific and professional contexts had changed in ways that significantly shaped the dispute.

Over the course of the nineteenth century, regular physicians increasingly questioned the efficacy of the profuse bleeding and liberal administration of purgatives, emetics, and blistering agents that characterized early American "heroic" medicine. Even before the Civil War, doctors in the United States— under the influence of the "Paris clinical school"—began embracing a more empirical, scientific approach that led them to doubt the usefulness of these depleting treatments.[5] After the war, some elite physicians developed an extreme therapeutic skepticism and urged doctors to rely primarily on nature's healing power.

In practice, even these skeptics never fully rejected conventional therapeutics. Nonetheless, the regular profession as a whole undeniably embraced a humbler and more flexible attitude as the century progressed. Doctors virtually abandoned bloodletting, administered depleting drugs less frequently and in smaller doses, and added stimulating therapies to their armamentarium. These changes made it increasingly difficult for rivals to paint the regulars as doctrinaire bleeders and poisoners. They also, however, complicated orthodox physicians' efforts to portray themselves as indispensable, uniquely qualified healers.[6]

The regulars hoped that scientific progress would bolster their standing. European researchers had been making significant discoveries since mid-century. The most important such development was the proof and elaboration of the germ theory of disease by Louis Pasteur and Robert Koch. Although American physicians embraced the germ theory more slowly than their European counterparts, many did so by the 1890s. By this time, research science was arguably the most important source of regular medicine's professional authority.[7]

Clinical research was a relatively weak basis to support orthodox medicine's reputation, however, unless it generated useful new therapies. A few important treatment breakthroughs occurred during this period—most notably, antiseptic surgery, aspirin, and diphtheria antitoxin. But overall, therapeutics did not advance at the nearly same rate as medical knowledge during the late 1800s. According to one modern commentator, only about six "reliable and effective pharmaceutical preparations" existed at the start of the twentieth century.[8] This dearth of effective orthodox remedies was an important rhetorical weapon for alternative sects in the wars over medical licensing.

Meanwhile, alternative practice itself evolved in ways that made it harder for mainstream physicians to cast all unorthodox practitioners as uneducated quacks. The dominant irregular sects after the Civil War were the homeopaths and the eclectics. In stark contrast to the early Thomsonians, these movements embraced the need for medical education and rigorous training, evinced a growing willingness to borrow remedies from other schools, and—particularly in the case of the homeopaths—attracted many well-off followers.[9]

Homeopathic medicine, the brainchild of German practitioner Samuel Hahnemann, was based on two main principles: (1) the "law of *similia*," which stated that diseases could be cured by drugs that produced symptoms in healthy individuals resembling those that appeared in people suffering from the disease in question, and (2) the "law of infinitesimals," according to which a drug's efficacy rose as the dose was reduced through extreme dilution to the point where the active ingredient was undetectable. Homeopathy reached America's shores in the 1820s and steadily attracted adherents. By the time of the Civil War, it was orthodox medicine's ("allopathy's") largest rival. Homeopaths, who viewed themselves as members of a scientific profession, established numerous schools, associations, and journals. Eventually, the movement fragmented between Hahnemannian purists and "eclectic" homeopaths who abandoned the law of infinitesimals and used some non-homeopathic remedies. The latter dominated the field by the 1880s.[10]

The other leading postwar sect, eclectic medicine, focused on botanical cures. It derived from a botanical healing movement founded in the 1820s by New York physician Wooster Beach, as well as from Alva Curtis's Independent

Thomsonianism. Although never as popular as homeopathy—or as respectable among elites—eclectic medicine also had many followers during the Gilded Age. As the sect's name indicates, it was generally nondogmatic and willing to borrow therapies from other schools. Like the homeopaths, the eclectics embraced professionalization and founded numerous medical colleges.[11]

In the late nineteenth century, orthodox medicine, homeopathy, and eclectic medicine thus resembled each other in various ways. They had parallel institutional structures. They evinced a similar professional ethos. They borrowed methods from each other and referred patients back and forth.[12] And they mutually disdained the growing popularity of drugless healing approaches.

The founders of drugless sects shared an interest in the theories and practices of Franz Anton Mesmer, a German physician who effected cures by supposedly transferring a universal spiritual force to his patients—an invisible "fluid" he dubbed "animal magnetism." Whereas Mesmer sought to provoke violent convulsions in his patients, his followers refined his technique to induce a peaceful, trance-like state. This "hypnotic" form of mesmerism, commonly known as magnetic healing, became extremely widespread in the United States by the 1840s and remained on the scene until the early twentieth century.[13]

In the Gilded Age, the combination of mesmerism with mystically infused belief systems such as Swedenborgianism, Transcendentalism, and Spiritualism spawned a variety of additional healing schools emphasizing immaterial, and sometimes divine, forces. Many of these drugless healers, under the influence of American mesmerist Phineas Parkhurst Quimby, emphasized the mind's power over the body and the importance of healthy mindedness and "right belief." Two of Quimby's followers launched important Boston-based mental healing movements. In 1879, Mary Baker Eddy founded the Church of Christ (Scientist), whose practitioners rejected the use of drugs and surgery and purported to cure disease by persuading their patients of God's goodness and the unreality of sin, sickness, and death. Around the same time, Quimby disciple Warren Felt Evans helped forge a spiritual (though less explicitly scriptural) school of thought known as the Mind Cure or New Thought movement, which stressed the healing power of positive thinking.[14]

Like adherents to homeopathy, many followers of Christian Science and Mind Cure were highly educated, urbane, and economically privileged, and thus difficult for the regulars to dismiss as gullible rubes. In 1898, a sympathetic observer remarked that "no theory of cure in the history of the healing art has grown in favor so rapidly among intelligent people as mental therapeutics." Another remarked, "The mental scientists and the healers are among the most reputable people in [Massachusetts]."[15]

As the late nineteenth-century battle over licensing raged, American medicine was thus divided into three main clusters of practitioners: (1) the regulars, (2) the homeopaths and eclectics, and (3) practitioners of various types of mental, spiritual, and religious healing approaches. The regulars were the driving force behind the return of medical licensing. The latter two camps and their followers fought, with great success, to ensure that the new licensing regimes would not discriminate against them.

The Resurgence of Medical Licensing

As we saw in the previous chapter, by 1861 most states had revoked their medical practice laws, and the few remaining statutes were dead letters. The nationwide re-embrace of medical licensing after the Civil War thus represents a remarkable U-turn. States began enacting new medical licensing schemes in the late 1860s. About seventeen states had such laws on the books by 1880, a number that rose to about forty by 1890. By 1901, every single state and the District of Columbia had a medical licensing regime of some sort in effect.[16]

The Gilded Age saw not only the proliferation of medical licensing systems, but also their inexorable strengthening. The only prerequisite for obtaining a license under the earliest postbellum laws was a diploma from a medical school—any medical school, including one of the inferior or wholly fraudulent institutions that arose to exploit this lack of standards. In the early 1880s, states began to require that the diploma be from a "reputable" institution, as determined by a state board of examiners. Many states also permitted candidates without a medical school diploma to earn a license by passing a uniform examination administered by the board. During the final decades of the century, all but a few states began to mandate that *every* aspiring physician pass such an examination, regardless of his education. Consequently, by 1900, the majority of states required both a diploma from a reputable medical school and passage of an examination.[17]

Some medical freedom activists of the time ascribed the wide adoption of medical licensing during this period to the evil designs of the American Medical Association (AMA), the national organization for regular physicians founded in 1847. This explanation is unconvincing; although the AMA certainly encouraged licensing, it was neither large nor powerful enough yet to play a significant direct role in the state legislative arena. Some modern scholars have attributed this second wave of licensing to revolutionary developments in medical science— particularly the rise of the germ theory—and the accompanying recognition that physicians must be well educated. As others have pointed out, however, the germ theory did not achieve widespread acceptance among American doctors until most states had already adopted licensure.[18]

A combination of other factors probably impelled the rise of licensing during the Gilded Age. One was the growing political influence of state medical societies, which were dominated by orthodox physicians. These organizations supported licensing as a means of limiting competition and boosting the regulars' self-identification as an exclusive and learned profession. In addition, the resurgence of medical licensing was a manifestation of a growing fondness among America's professional and business classes generally for appointed boards of scientific experts.[19]

One might assume that the broad embrace of medical licensing after the Civil War showed that the American ethos in favor of freedom of therapeutic choice was fading away. In fact, however, late nineteenth-century Americans still broadly favored allowing patients a free choice among different schools of practitioners. As we will see, licensing legislation favoring orthodox medicine regularly elicited potent resistance not only from alternative practitioners, but also from common citizens.

The Legal Impact of Popular Opposition

Nondiscriminatory Licensing Legislation

Most late nineteenth-century medical practice laws were drafted in ways that protected the interests of unorthodox practitioners and their patients. This preservation of freedom of therapeutic choice reflected the views of the citizenry as voiced in petition campaigns, mobbed legislative hearings, and medical liberty literature. The participants in this social movement for medical choice represented a broad swath of Americans. Harvard Medical School Professor Reginald Fitz, a supporter of strong medical licensing regimes, complained: "[The] opposition is diverse. . . . On the one hand is to be found the entire class of those likely to be shown to be ignorant, unskillful, dishonest, or corrupt. . . . On the other hand we see intelligent theorists and educators, at time leaders in thought and morals, who object to the infringement of personal rights."[20]

In some states, the widespread commitment to medical freedom successfully thwarted the passage of any licensing legislation at all—at least for a while. For example, mass opposition defeated an 1880 medical licensing bill in Massachusetts, even though the measure accommodated the interests of homeopaths and eclectics. A proponent of the law snidely described its adversaries as "deceitful clairvoyants, long-haired spiritualists, necromancers, wizards, witches, seers, magnetic healers, [and] pain charmers." But a modern scholar's research demonstrates that the petitions against the bill were signed by a wide variety of people, ranging from laborers to professionals and businessmen.[21]

Under pressure from medical freedom forces, legislatures in other states included explicit nondiscrimination clauses in the licensing bills they enacted. For example, Virginia's 1884 law instructed that no applicant for a medical license be rejected for his "adherence to any particular school of medicine or system of practice, nor on account of his views as to the method of treatment and cure of diseases." Rhode Island's 1895 measure stated, "Nothing in this chapter shall be so construed as to discriminate against any particular school or system of medicine." Texas elevated medical nondiscrimination to a constitutional principle: its 1876 state constitution provided, "The Legislature may pass laws prescribing the qualifications of practitioners of medicine in this State, and to punish persons for malpractice, but no preference shall ever be given by law to any schools of medicine."[22]

Legislatures that did not include broad nondiscrimination clauses protected the rights of alternative practitioners and their patients in other ways. For example, almost all late nineteenth-century medical practice acts gave homeopaths a role in administering medical examinations and issuing licenses, and most gave eclectics a place at the table as well. Indeed, these sects often had their *own* tables; almost a quarter of states created either two boards (regular and homeopathic) or three (regular, homeopathic, and eclectic). And more than two-thirds of states with a single board guaranteed sectarian representation on that body.[23]

These developments did not arise primarily from the gradual decline of dogmatism among regular physicians. A more important factor was probably the medical establishment's recognition that because of homeopaths' and eclectics' popular appeal, any viable medical licensing regime had to include them. Regulars also had a monetary motivation for entering this alliance; they increasingly received referrals from doctors in the other sects. The impulse to preserve orthodox purity was once so strong that the original AMA Code of Ethics, written in 1847, effectively banned consultation with irregular doctors. The authors of the 1903 amended Code omitted this provision, deeming it to be unreasonable, anachronistic, and impractical.[24]

Some states accommodated unorthodox practitioners by omitting topics of fundamental controversy between the different schools from licensing examinations. The most commonly excluded subjects were therapeutics and *materia medica*. In most other states, applicants from the alternative sects were examined on these subjects (or sometimes all subjects) by representatives from their own school. The authors of a 1907 AMA survey of state licensing laws noted a widespread conviction "that an examination for a license should be purely a test of technical knowledge and of facts which are established beyond dispute . . . and that, having demonstrated a sufficient knowledge of the composition and functions of the human body, the applicant should be allowed perfect freedom in the choice of remedial agents or choice of treatment."[25]

Developments in New York State exemplify the dynamics of legislative battles over medical licensing during the Gilded Age. The state legislature, which revoked medical licensing in 1844, revived it in 1874. The new statute was non-discriminatory; it mandated merely that applicants have either a diploma from *any* chartered medical school or a certification of qualification from *any* of the state's "several medical societies" (including the homeopathic and eclectic societies).[26]

In 1885, the orthodox-dominated Medical Society of the State of New York began pressuring the legislature to establish an examining and licensing board that would administer a single general examination to all candidates. The *New York Times*, while praising this proposal as a "discreet and well-considered attempt" to suppress quackery, expressed concern that it would founder because of quarreling between the "zealots" of different schools. The bill indeed failed, apparently because the regulars insisted that their society have the power to appoint six of the board's nine members and that the mandatory examination cover therapeutics. According to one observer, "Every attempt to secure legislation made by regular practitioners [was] strenuously opposed by homeopaths and eclectics, as well as by an army of Christian scientists, clairvoyants, magnetists, mind curers, faith curers, truss-makers, and all those wishing to engage in the business of healing the sick without training or study."[27]

The regulars promoted a similar bill in 1889, but the alternative sects successfully pressured the Senate committee considering the bill to shelve it. In 1890, the alternative practitioners countered with a measure that would create separate allopathic (regular), homeopathic, and eclectic boards of examiners. The regulars dismissed this approach as "ridiculous on its face." The *Times* disagreed, opining: "The homeopaths and the eclectics claim the same right to license their own graduates that the different churches possess, and there does not seem to be any good reason why it should not be conceded to them."[28]

In response to the "Three Board Bill," the orthodox Medical Society presented yet another bill creating a single board of examiners. This effort failed, too. "Throughout the length and breadth of the State, circulars and petitions had been scattered, pledges had been exacted; and when we appeared before the legislative body with our bill, we found the greatest stumbling-block in the fact that almost every member had been solicited . . . to vote against any bill which did not include three separate Boards of Examiners." Later in 1890, the governor finally signed an amended version of the bill pushed by the alternative sects. The statute established three distinct boards. Although it mandated a largely uniform examination for all license applicants, it provided that "in the department of therapeutics, practice and *materia medica* the questions shall be in harmony, with the tenets of the school selected by the candidate."[29]

The homeopaths and eclectics enjoyed similar triumphs in state after state. Ironically, however, victory in the licensing wars marked the beginning of the end for these sects. Except for purist Hahnemannians, homeopathic and eclectic practitioners essentially melted (both methodologically and organizationally) into the great mass of regular physicians. A leading scholar observes: "When homeopathic and Eclectic doctors were shunned and denounced by the regular profession, they thrived. But the more they gained access to the privileges of regular physicians, the more their numbers declined. The turn of the century was both the point of acceptance and the moment of incipient disintegration."[30]

Statutory Exemptions for Drugless Practitioners

Unlike the homeopaths and eclectics, Mind Curers, Christian Scientists, and other drugless healers sought total exemption from the licensing regimes rather than a role in administering them. In their eyes, any requirement that mental and religious healers be educated and examined in subjects like anatomy and physiology was self-evidently pointless and thus a barely disguised ploy to suppress their practices altogether. Judge Clifford Smith remarked: "Of course no one expects that Christian Scientists will betake themselves to medical colleges to study a system which they do not intend to practise, and go before a board of medical doctors to ask their official permission to practise Christian Science. That is not the purpose of such a law."[31]

The legislatures of many states were receptive to such arguments and carved out exceptions for drugless practitioners in their medical licensing laws. Four New England states—Connecticut, Massachusetts, Maine, and New Hampshire—provided the broadest range of exemptions. Connecticut's story is illustrative.

On March 8, 1893, the Connecticut House of Representatives held a public hearing on a licensing bill that (like New York's statute) established a mandatory examination administered by separate allopathic, homeopathic, and eclectic boards. Prior to the event, a Boston-based medical freedom organization called the National Constitutional Liberty League disseminated a circular throughout Connecticut urging "those who would maintain their constitutional liberty of choice of physician or healer [to] personally appear to signify their determination to defend this inherent and inalienable right." Opponents of the bill flooded the hearing. A reporter observed that "Christian scientists were there, and those of the faith cure school, and the auditors of the gentler sex were very audible in their applause."[32]

Most witnesses at the hearing testified in support of the bill, emphasizing the need to protect patients. The exasperated secretary of the Connecticut Board of

Health asked, "How could there be objections to such a bill?" A homeopathic doctor, speaking in favor of the law, forcefully rejected the charge that his school "was persecuting others after having been persecuted itself." He insisted, "Any physician should know how to detect diseases, to make a diagnosis and discriminate." But the hearing was dominated by the lawyer, politician, and orator Joseph L. Barbour, who blasted the bill as a monopolistic plot by regular physicians and an infringement of personal liberty. He waved petitions against the bill signed by "hundreds of remonstrants." The *Hartford Courant* observed that "Mr. Barbour . . . made the 'regulars' wince." According to the National Constitutional Liberty League, his presentation "rightfully elicited round after round of irrepressible applause."[33]

After the hearing, thousands more Connecticut citizens signed petitions opposing the licensing bill. One such petition declared it "unnecessary and unwise to legally forbid further improvement in the healing art, and deny to posterity the constitutional liberty of choice and the possible benefit of such improvement." Additional hearings were similarly mobbed by adversaries of the bill. After the final hearing, the *New York Times* reported, "The Medical Practice bill . . . has excited greater interest and opposition than the whole lot of public acts that have been considered since the session began."[34]

In the face of such antagonism, supporters of the measure accepted major amendments to enable its passage. As finally enacted in May 1893, the Connecticut medical licensing law explicitly stated that it did not apply "to any chiropodist or clairvoyant who does not use in his practice any drugs, medicines or poison, nor to any person practicing the massage method, or Swedish movement cure, sun cure, mind cure, magnetic healing, or Christian science, nor to any other person who does not use or prescribe in his treatment of mankind, drugs, poisons, medicine, chemicals, or nostrums."[35]

Similar events transpired elsewhere in New England. In 1894, as described at the start of this chapter, protests and petitions impelled the Massachusetts legislature to table a measure requiring the licensing of all healers and to pass an alternative exempting "clairvoyants [and] persons practising hypnotism, magnetic healing, mind cure, massage methods, christian science, cosmopathic, or any other method of healing." Soon thereafter, Maine and New Hampshire enacted medical practice laws that echoed Massachusetts' exemption language almost exactly, although they clarified "any other method of healing" by restricting it to practitioners who did not use drugs or perform surgery.[36]

Although no medical licensing statutes outside New England contained similarly broad exceptions for drugless practitioners, a growing number of jurisdictions exempted treatment by prayer generally, or Christian Science in particular. By 1907, Christian Scientists were exempted from medical licensing in eleven states—a number that would grow to twenty-eight by 1917. During this same period, however, six state legislatures passed bills designed to *suppress* Christian Science and other drugless therapeutic systems, most commonly by broadening the range of practitioners subject to examination and licensing requirements. Moreover, states sometimes prosecuted Christian Science practitioners and parents for manslaughter when treatment of a child tragically failed. Nonetheless, the clear trend around the turn of the century was toward noninterference with Christian Scientists and other religious, spiritual, and mental healers. Indeed, governors vetoed three of the six laws directed against such practitioners that legislatures passed. Their veto messages—one of which we will examine later in this chapter—contained ringing defenses of the right to choose one's healer.[37]

Jury Nullification

Despite alternative medicine activists' widespread success in shaping legislation during the Gilded Age, in various states at various times the licensing laws effectively outlawed much irregular healing. In these jurisdictions, practitioners faced criminal liability if they could not qualify for a license but continued to treat patients anyway. But any analysis of popular views about medical licensing must consider enforcement and conviction patterns as well as the law in the books. Because of jurors' tolerance for medical diversity and sympathy for therapeutic choice, prosecutors had great difficulty convicting, or even indicting, unlicensed alternative practitioners. An 1899 treatise on law and medicine observed: "Sometimes, especially in rural districts and small towns . . . both grand and petit jurors, swayed by personal predilections, decide the issues in violation of their oaths, not upon the testimony, but upon their sentiments or information extraneous to the case."[38]

One modern researcher has identified only about thirty criminal cases of any type brought against Christian Scientist practitioners between 1887 and 1915, compared with "scores of others" in which coroners and grand juries failed to indict. Of the seventeen juries that issued verdicts in cases charging Christian Scientists with the unlicensed practice of medicine, only ten found the defendant guilty—even though the state usually had little trouble establishing the facts in these matters.[39] And these figures do not reflect the uncountable number of prosecutors who—because of their own sympathy for unlicensed practitioners or a sense of futility—did not pursue indictments in the first place.

Legislatures responded in various ways to the lax enforcement of medical licensing statutes. In 1876, the Texas legislature—clearly exasperated by jury nullification—amended its medical practice act to provide that "it shall be the duty of the Judge . . . to charge the grand jury with the necessity of preserving this act inviolate, and to admonish them of their duty to find presentments against any and all persons guilty of its infraction." Other legislatures appear simply to have given up; the enactment of many statutory provisions accommodating or exempting alternative practitioners likely reflected, at least in part, lawmakers' recognition that the medical practice acts were not being enforced against them, anyway.[40]

The Role of the Courts

Sometimes, practitioners accused of practicing without a license turned to judges for help, asking them to hold that state medical practice laws unconstitutionally violated their liberties and those of their patients. Judges almost always rebuffed such claims, however. During this era, the legal profession was engaged in its own campaign to control access to the bar through examination and licensing, and judges were thus likely inclined to support the parallel efforts of their medical brethren. In any event, the US Supreme Court virtually extinguished the possibility that medical licensing statutes were unconstitutional with its momentous 1889 decision in *Dent v. West Virginia*.[41]

Under an 1881 West Virginia statute, three categories of individuals were entitled to receive a certificate to practice medicine from the state Board of Health: (1) doctors who had practiced medicine in the state for at least ten years prior to enactment; (2) graduates of any "reputable medical college"; and (3) individuals who passed a state examination. When the law took effect, Dr. Frank Dent and his father were partners in a thriving Newburg, West Virginia, medical practice founded by Frank's great-grandfather. Because Frank had been practicing for only six years and had never attended medical school, he faced the unpleasant prospect of taking an examination.[42]

Rather than subject himself to such an ordeal, Dent migrated to Kansas and ministered to patients there. Although he considered himself a regular physician, he briefly attended and earned a degree from the American Medical Eclectic College of Cincinnati (AMEC) in Ohio. Diploma in hand, he returned home to West Virginia and resumed his Newburg practice. When he presented his medical degree to the Board of Health and demanded a certificate, the board, populated by regulars, refused because it did not consider AMEC to be a "reputable medical college." Dent continued to treat patients nonetheless and was tried and convicted for the unlawful practice of medicine. He challenged his conviction on constitutional grounds, contending that the statute deprived him of his property—his "vested rights and estate in his profession"—in violation of the due process clause of the Fourteenth Amendment.[43] The trial court and the West Virginia Supreme Court both rejected this argument, so the beleaguered doctor appealed the matter to the US Supreme Court.

Dent had reason to be optimistic. Three years earlier, the Court had declared in *Yick Wo v. Hopkins*: "The very idea that one man may be compelled to hold his . . . means of living . . . at the mere will of another, seems to be intolerable in any country where freedom prevails, as being the essence of slavery itself." Justice Stephen Field seemed particularly likely to embrace Dent's argument, for he had repeatedly emphasized citizens' constitutional right to practice their professions. For example, in his influential dissent in the 1873 *Slaughterhouse Cases*, Field had emphatically asserted a fundamental right of every citizen "to pursue his happiness by following any of the known established trades and occupations of the country."[44]

Nevertheless, the Court affirmed Dent's conviction unanimously and without hesitation in an opinion written by Justice Field himself. Field's decision is not as surprising as it might seem. Despite his celebrated paeans to economic liberty, he gave significant latitude to state legislatures when he concluded they were genuinely trying to protect the safety, health, or morals of the community pursuant to their valid "police power." Field's true aversion was to "special legislation" or "class legislation"—statutes that, though disguised as neutral exercises of the police power, were in fact intended to economically advantage particular people or groups.[45] He simply did not perceive the West Virginia medical practice act to be such a law.

In *Dent*, Field reaffirmed "the right of every citizen of the United States to follow any lawful calling, business, or profession he may choose." He acknowledged, however, that states could limit this right if the restrictions were "general in [their] operation," "appropriate to the . . . profession," "attainable by reasonable study or application," and imposed "for the protection of society."[46] In Field's view, the West Virginia licensing statute met these tests and was thus legitimate. He explained:

> Few professions require more careful preparation by one who seeks to enter it than that of medicine. It has to deal with all those subtle and mysterious influences upon which health and life depend, and requires not only a knowledge of the properties of vegetable and mineral substances, but of the human body in all its complicated parts, and their relation to each other, as well as their influence upon the mind. The physician must be able to detect readily the presence of disease, and prescribe appropriate remedies for its removal. Every one may have occasion to consult him, but comparatively few can judge of the qualifications of learning and skill which he possesses. Reliance must be placed upon the assurance given by his license, issued by an authority competent to judge in that respect, that he possesses the requisite qualifications.[47]

Dent virtually destroyed the theory that medical licensing unconstitutionally violated a physician's property rights in his trade. Afterward, few litigants even bothered to raise the point.[48] But *Dent* did not address the distinct question of whether a medical licensing statute might be unconstitutional if, as written or applied, it *discriminated* in favor of the regulars and against alternative medical approaches.

At first glance, one might assume that *Dent* extinguished this theory, as well. After all, orthodox physicians in West Virginia had championed licensing precisely to drive unorthodox practitioners from the field. But a closer look shows that neither the parties nor the justices viewed the case as having anything to do with discrimination among different medical theories. The statute at issue was explicitly nondiscriminatory; under pressure from concerned citizens, the legislature in 1882 had amended it to require that a qualifying diploma be issued by a "reputable medical college *in the school of medicine to which the person desiring to practice belongs.*" Furthermore, Dent never claimed that the Board of Health, in violation of this provision, had rejected his diploma because it was from an eclectic institution.[49] Consequently, the question of unconstitutional discrimination between sects was not before the Court.

It is unclear why Dent did not advance such a claim. Perhaps Marmaduke Dent, Frank's cousin and attorney, concluded that any focus on AMEC's "reputability" would harm rather than help his client. The real problem was that AMEC was at best a fly-by-night, second-rate institution and perhaps a completely fraudulent diploma mill. Marmaduke might have framed the case differently—indeed, the board might not have denied Frank's application in the first place—if Frank had earned his degree from the Eclectic Medical Institute, Cincinnati's largest medical school of any type and the most respected eclectic institution in the country.[50]

It is interesting to imagine how Justice Field, the nemesis of special legislation, would have ruled if Dent had presented a well-supported medical discrimination claim. A careful reading of the passage from *Dent* quoted earlier suggests that Field would not have endorsed a licensing scheme that privileged orthodox medicine. The opinion refers to medicine not as a settled or certain science, but rather as one concerning "subtle and mysterious influences." Field's reference to "vegetable and mineral substances" implies that he deemed the former, favored by the eclectics, to be as useful as the latter, preferred by the regulars. Furthermore, his obscure, perhaps inverted, reference to the body's "influence upon the mind" indicates that he recognized the potential validity of non-materialistic approaches to disease like Mind Cure and Christian Science.

Notably, Stephen Field's own medical history made him skeptical about, and perhaps downright contemptuous of, the regular medical profession. As a young man, he had bashed his knee against the wheel of a cart and developed a serious infection. His physician—apparently a regular doctor with a "heroic" bent—dosed him with the mercury-based purgative calomel and nearly killed him. The damaged knee bothered and hobbled Field for the rest of his life, and, according to his family, he always believed that the injury's severity resulted "principally . . . from the medicine taken." Field consulted "eminent surgeons," but they offered him "very little relief." He thus resorted to hydropathy, visiting "different watering-places whose waters were supposed to possess healing virtues."[51]

In short, there is good reason to suspect that Justice Field—personally distrustful of orthodox medicine, disdainful of discriminatory special legislation, and suspicious of anticompetitive schemes disguised as public health measures—would have been sympathetic to allegations that particular medical licensing systems were designed specifically to exclude irregular practitioners. He never considered such a claim, however.

Following *Dent*, American courts invariably denied claims that uniform educational and testing mandates applicable to all medical license applicants constituted unconstitutional discrimination. For example, even though the Ohio Supreme Court recognized medical discrimination as a cognizable constitutional interest, it rejected a Christian Science practitioner's contention that the state's licensing law unconstitutionally "discriminate[d] against Christian Science, or in favor of certain schools of medicine" by requiring a Christian Scientist to "take the same examination as the regular practitioner, in other words, [to] understand the use of drugs and medicines, none of which . . . does he ever use." Parallel claims brought by magnetic healers in other states similarly failed.[52]

When Gilded Age courts evinced sympathy for freedom of therapeutic choice, they usually did so not through constitutional interpretation, but through statutory interpretation. Their primary vehicle for exercising such leniency was cases in which unlicensed alternative practitioners were prosecuted for the unauthorized "practice of medicine." State licensing laws contained a variety of definitions of this phrase, and in many instances no definition at all.[53] When faced with either ambiguity or silence, courts tended to interpret this language to acquit drugless healers, especially Christian Scientists.

Judges initially did not demonstrate such tolerance for drugless healers. In an 1894 case, *State v. Buswell*, the Nebraska Supreme Court held that Christian Science practitioners were covered by the state's medical practice act, which imposed licensing on anybody "who shall operate on, profess to heal, or prescribe for or otherwise treat any physical or mental ailment of another." Rejecting the defendant's argument that the law regulated only practitioners of "medicine, surgery, or obstetrics, as generally or usually understood," the court concluded that the statute's "provisions are not limited to those who attempt to follow beaten paths and established usages."[54]

Four years later, however, a Christian Science practitioner prevailed in a similar case in Rhode Island. In *State v. Mylod*, the Rhode Island Supreme Court limited the meaning of "practice of medicine" in the state's licensing statute to its "popular understanding." The court explained that in common parlance, the "practice of medicine" requires "a knowledge of disease, its origin, its anatomical and physiological features, and its causative relations; and, further, it requires a knowledge of drugs, their preparation and action." Healing by prayer, therefore, "does not constitute the practice of medicine in the popular sense." The court further opined that a nondiscrimination clause in the statute ("nothing in this chapter shall be so construed as to discriminate against any particular school or system of medicine") compelled an exemption for Christian Scientists. In light of this provision, the court concluded that it would be "absurd" to subject practitioners of a healing system to requirements with which they could not comply, because such a construction "would operate not as a discrimination only, but as a prohibition." Fortunately for Christian Scientists and other mental and religious healers, *Mylod* proved to be far more influential than *Buswell*.[55]

On occasion, a judge construing the meaning of a medical practice act would transcend technical statutory interpretation and proclaim the importance of medical liberty. For example, in *Bennett v. Ware*, a court considering the case of a "magic healer" declared that limiting application of Georgia's act to those who prescribed drugs was "the better rule and one more in consonance with reason and in harmony with the republican character of our institutions." The North Carolina Supreme Court, in *State v. Biggs*, interpreted that state's licensing requirement not to apply to a drugless practitioner who treated patients with physical manipulation and dietary advice. It explained: "In the cure of bodies, as in the cure of souls, 'orthodoxy is my doxy, heterodoxy is the other man's doxy.' . . . This is a free country, and any man has a right to be treated by any system he chooses."[56]

The *Biggs* court asserted that its interpretation of the North Carolina medical practice act was dictated by the principles of the US and state constitutions. *Biggs* may thus have been the only judicial decision of the era to conclude that mandatory licensing of drugless practitioners was in and of itself unconstitutional. Nevertheless, the nationwide battle against the suppression of alternative sects was a "constitutional" movement. Medical liberty advocates routinely advanced constitutional arguments outside of court, and there they often found receptive audiences.

Constitutional Rhetoric Outside of Court

It is telling that one of the leading organizations in the Gilded Age anti-licensing movement was named the National *Constitutional* Liberty League. In legislative chambers and the public sphere, campaigners for medical liberty frequently framed their arguments in constitutional terms. For example, opponents of the 1893 medical licensing bill in Connecticut asserted that the law "would trespass upon the rights of the individual; that its purport is hostile to the spirit of our institutions, and that its enactment would be illegal and its enforcement unconstitutional." In his magazine *The Arena*, medical freedom activist Benjamin Orange Flower characterized medical licensing statutes as "unjust and un-American legislation which makes unfair distinctions and unconstitutional discriminations."[57]

In these extrajudicial arenas, anti-licensing activists invoked the nation's fundamental values more frequently than specific constitutional language. But like their antebellum forebears, they considered themselves to be making "constitutional" arguments when doing so. Their Constitution was not simply the collection of provisions contained in the document itself, but also the broad principles of freedom and equality that the Founding Fathers proclaimed in the Declaration of Independence, fought a war to vindicate, and reiterated in the Constitution's Preamble. In other words, they invoked the bundle of foundational national values that Professor Mark Tushnet has termed the "thin Constitution."[58]

Gilded Age medical freedom literature contained ubiquitous references to the Declaration of Independence's "inalienable rights" of "life, liberty, and the pursuit of happiness." In his 1893 article "Medical Slavery through Legislation," Henry Wood characterized these rights as "constitutional guarantees" that included "the right of individual judgment in regard to . . . interior, sacred, personal experiences and choices." He continued, "Society robs one of all these when . . . it makes one's irregular healer . . . a criminal." Alzine A. Chevaillier declared that "the right of a man to save his body from disease and death . . . certainly is 'a pursuit of happiness.'" She mistakenly assigned this phrase to the Constitution itself.[59]

Like their antebellum counterparts, Gilded Age medical licensing foes often portrayed their cause as a continuation of the American Revolution. After the 1898 victory in Massachusetts, the *Boston Transcript* cheered: "The regulars are as signally whipped as they were at Bunker Hill." J. W. Lockhart invoked an even longer history of Anglo-American freedom. He wrote that the notion that "people are not capable of choosing their own medical advisers" was "refuted at Runnymede when the Magna Charta [*sic*] was forced from King James, . . . at Independence Hall when the Liberty Bell pealed forth the joyous proclamation of political, religious and social freedom; when the Declaration of Independence proclaimed the 'inalienable rights of man' and when the Fourteenth Amendment was incorporated into the organic law of this country."[60]

Some anti-licensing advocates proceeded more legalistically. Robert Chapin Bayly, for example, cited a grab bag of specific constitutional provisions. He invoked the due process and equal protection clauses of the Fourteenth Amendment and Article I's prohibition against ex post facto laws. He contended that Article IV's "full faith and credit" and "privileges and immunities" clauses prohibited one state from denying the right to practice to a physician authorized to do so in another. He even unconvincingly contended that medical licensing violated the Article IV provision that obligates the United States to "guarantee to every state . . . a republican form of government." Ultimately, however, even Bayly favored broad incantations of American's fundamental rights—the "great principles of organic law transmitted to us by the Fathers of the Republic." He argued that state medical practice acts were illegitimate under guarantees "emphatically declared in the Declaration of Independence before the Constitution was made."[61]

The Four Strands of Medical Freedom

When elaborating on such arguments, Gilded Age medical licensing opponents referred to the same four strands of liberty as their antebellum predecessors: bodily freedom, economic freedom, freedom of conscience, and freedom of inquiry. The rhetoric of the two periods differed, however, particularly with respect to the relative emphasis given to these different themes.

Bodily Freedom

Before the Civil War, an important trope in anti-licensing literature was the appalling image of a patient who, denied access to botanical cures, had no choice but to subject his or her body to the brutal, debilitating, and "unnatural" remedies administered by regular doctors. As orthodox medicine became less "heroic" during the nineteenth century, this scenario became increasingly implausible, and licensing foes evoked it much less often. It did not vanish from anti-licensing arguments altogether, however. An opponent of the 1893 Connecticut measure fretted, "I am anxious for the defeat of this bill that I may have the liberty . . . of employing a doctor who, I feel sure, will give me no arsenic, strychnine, corrosive sublimate, rattlesnake virus, nor any other deadly thing." Alexander Wilder, a physician, journalist, and prominent medical libertarian, warned: "If it is imagined that the blood-letting practise has disappeared, not to return, we have only to remember that there are recurrences of epidemic 'fads' among medical men."[62]

Increasingly, though, those opposed to mandatory licensing for alternative practitioners focused less on the right to *avoid* unwanted remedies and more on the right to *access* one's preferred treatments and advisors. Wilder remarked, "It would be an act of tyranny to force a person to take medicine if he did not believe in its efficacy, and it is equally such to compel him to do without advice and service where he does so believe." Christian Scientist Herbert W. Packard contended: "When we come to the right to seek and preserve health, we come to a right than which there is none more sacred, for it is an axiom that self-preservation is the first law of nature." In his 1894 letter to the *Boston Evening Transcript*, William James condemned "paternalism so solicitous . . . as to stand between [the citizen] and the therapeutic adviser whom he would naturally select."[63]

Sometimes, activists linked medical freedom to a broader vision of bodily freedom. Herbert Packard insisted that the state had no more right to interfere with one's choice of medical advisors than "to prescribe the kind of food a man shall eat, the clothes he shall wear, or the work he shall engage in." Reverend Benjamin Fay Mills, testifying at the 1898 Massachusetts Committee on Public Health hearing mentioned at the start of this chapter, proclaimed: "You might as well say that a man should not walk on the slippery part of the sidewalk, or that he should eat boiled meat and not fried." More than a century before adversaries of the 2010 Affordable Care Act compared that law's health insurance mandate to requiring people to eat broccoli, these men were voicing similar arguments.[64]

The Gilded Age literature foreshadowed modern bodily freedom rhetoric in other ways, as well. For example, in his letter to the *Transcript*, James declared: "If the word 'sacred' can be applied to any personal right, surely the right to treat one's own body as one chooses may claim the title." Similar language would reappear some seventy years later in the arguments of the abortion rights movement. For example, in 1973, an *amicus* brief filed by pro-choice groups in *Roe v. Wade* asserted, "Surely none of the rights can be seen as more basic, fundamental or worthy of protection than a woman's right to control her body."[65]

It is thus important to take special note of this strain of advocacy in the Gilded Age anti-licensing literature, for such arguments retain a currency today that some of the others advanced then do not.

Economic Freedom

Many Gilded Age political reformers were inveterately suspicious that statutes, regardless of their ostensible goals, were "special legislation" or "class legislation" intended mainly to benefit the legislators' wealthy patrons. These reformers routinely opposed state interventions in the free market that they perceived to be promoting the interests of particular individuals or groups. Examples of such legislation included laws restricting free trade, distributing bounties to industry, or creating artificial monopolies. Like the Jacksonians before them, Gilded Age reformers condemned special legislation not only as unwise policy, but also as a violation of Americans' fundamental liberties.[66]

This is the lens through which late nineteenth-century medical freedom activists viewed licensing. They considered the postbellum proliferation of medical practice acts to be a corrupt plot by regular physicians to exclude competitors from the market. Alexander Wilder asserted that "legislators who vote for such enactments are little else than dupes of those who seek them." The licensing laws, he said, reflected nothing more than "lust of power and lust of gain."[67] R. C. Bayly described these statutes as "a sample of the worst and most damnable class legislation on record in any free country." He asserted that "legalized cormorants . . . have entered into a conspiracy, widespread as the United States, to maintain a kind of medical trust."[68]

The allegation of a "medical trust" was a common and significant feature of Gilded Age medical freedom literature. Resistance to government-supported monopolies in private trades had deep roots in American libertarian thought. Hence, William Lloyd Garrison II (the son of the great abolitionist), testifying against expanding licensing requirements at the 1898 Massachusetts hearing, drew from a deep well of indignation when he contended: "Ostensibly an act to protect the community from malpractice, in reality its motive is to restrict competition and secure the monopoly of treating disease to those who bear the credentials of an established and recognized school." In an article titled "Socialistic Medical Legislation," J. W. Lockhart proclaimed: "The medical monopoly, like all other monopolies, is socialistic . . . in the matter of preventing competition and maintaining large fee bills, and despotic in regard to all other matters pertaining to the public health."[69]

As illustrated by Justice Field's opinion in Dent, even those fiercely opposed to special legislation acknowledged there was a sphere of legitimate state police power. But laissez-faire constitutionalists frequently dismissed the purported public health goals of disputed legislation and ascribed its passage to selfish ulterior motives. For instance, in the famous 1905 case Lochner v. New York, the Supreme Court struck down a maximum hours law for bakers, observing: "Many of the laws of this character, while passed under what is claimed to be the police power for the purpose of protecting the public health and welfare, are, in reality, passed from other motives."[70]

Medical freedom activists expressed similar misgivings about licensing statutes. Indeed, Herbert Packard attacked them by quoting this very passage from
Lochner. Wilder observed: "When protection [of the people] is talked about it is
time to be on the lookout for jobbery and trickery." Bayly maintained: "I have not
known of one instance where [medical licensing] laws were enforced for the protection of the people. Such laws are always championed through the legislature
by political scoundrels in the interest of some nefarious combination or trust
directly opposed to the welfare . . . of people and to all free government." Such
cocksure rejections of the possibility of a genuine health motivation for medical
licensing may seem paranoid to us today, but it is important to remember that
at the time, orthodox medicine was not clearly more efficacious than its rivals.
Moreover, most states did not prohibit unlicensed practitioners from providing
services *for free*, and this curious exception heightened suspicions that the medical practice acts' true purpose was to protect the regulars' market share, rather
than the public health.[71]

Medical freedom proponents also contended that licensing laws violated the
individual economic rights of practitioners and patients. Like other proponents
of laissez-faire in the late nineteenth century, medical licensing foes believed that
invalid assertions of the police power constituted unconstitutional invasions
of personal freedom, including the "freedom to practice a trade" and "liberty
of contract." Bayly thus contended: "The State Board of Health has no more
authority to regulate the practice of medicine than [any other] common business. . . . The State, in the exercise of its police power, has no authority whatever to
deprive a citizen of the United States of the right to freely engage in the business
of his choice, provided, that the rights of others are not infringed." And Wilder
asserted: "Of the right of an individual to make his own contracts there can be no
rational question. He may engage whomsoever he pleases to cure him; and the
person, having rendered a meritorious service, has a moral right to a reasonable
compensation."[72]

Although the economic freedom arguments of Gilded Age medical licensing
foes resembled those of their antebellum counterparts, they lacked the same
populist tone. Thomsonianism was primarily a rural and working-class phenomenon, and its followers portrayed regular doctors as an intellectually and socially
pretentious cabal plundering the common folk. By contrast, leading post–Civil
War campaigners against medical licensing, drawn largely from the middle
and upper classes, were much less likely to vilify orthodox physicians for their
wealth or elitism. Nevertheless, like other reformers of their era, these medical
freedom advocates utterly despised special legislation as a matter of principle.
And to them, medical practice acts were a prime example of such legislation, the
product of a corrupt alliance between a powerful interest group and unscrupulous party politicians.[73]

Freedom of Conscience and Religion

Freedom of conscience and freedom of religion played an even larger role in medical liberty arguments after the Civil War than before. This development was due largely to the increasing importance of spirituality in alternative medical systems in the later nineteenth century. Thomsonianism was a secular movement that generally did not invoke the healing power of spiritual or divine forces. By contrast, such forces were integral components of many later healing systems. Hahnemannian homeopaths ascribed "spiritual power" to their drastically diluted medicines.[74] And for drugless sects such as Mind Cure and Christian Science, cure of the body was virtually inseparable from cure of the soul.

The post–Civil War struggle against medical licensing was thus led by people who vigorously rejected the purely materialistic approach of regular medicine. Judge Thomas E. Grover, testifying on behalf of the Boston Metaphysical Club at the 1898 Massachusetts Committee on Public Health hearing, declared that "there is a close, . . . unknown and unexplained connection between the unseen mind and the visible body."[75] At the same hearing, Reverend T. E. Allen testified:

> It is notorious that many physicians are confirmed materialists, convinced . . . that . . . man is wholly material and death ends all. Over against this, we find that the heretical healing schools believe that man is an immortal spirit. . . . Believing this, then, as a part of their religious systems, their theories of healing are dominated by the same idea, and they necessarily attach more importance to the operation of spiritual and mental forces than do many others in the community.[76]

To those for whom physical and spiritual health were inextricably linked, medical freedom was essentially indistinguishable from freedom of belief. In their view, it was precisely medicine's basis in faith rather than science that made government regulation of it inappropriate. As Herbert Packard argued: "In matters about which there is a right to exercise judgment and discretion, and about which men are not agreed, and have not come to definite and fixed conclusions, the majority of the people, through the legislature, cannot substitute their judgment and opinion for that of their fellowmen and make them conform thereto, without depriving men of natural and unalienable rights protected under the Constitution."[77]

Explicitly religious themes were prominent in the medical freedom literature. Bayly proclaimed, "The establishment of a State system of medicine . . . is just as tyrannical in its methods, as subversive of the liberty and rights of the citizens, as any system of religion backed by the civil power, ever dared to be." Flower declared: "The right of every man to employ whomsoever he desires in matters pertaining to his physical health is as sacred as his right to employ whosoever he desires to minister to his spiritual welfare." Joseph Barbour ended his testimony at the 1893 Connecticut legislative hearing by remarking that under the proposed licensing law, St. Peter would have been prosecuted for healing the lame man at the Temple.[78]

Nevertheless, Gilded Age medical licensing opponents were much more likely to assert violations of freedom of belief in general than infringements of *religious* liberty in particular. The worldviews with which many drugless healing systems overlapped, such as Transcendentalism, Swedenborgianism, and Theosophy, were not religious creeds so much as amalgams of philosophical, mystical, and religious ideas.[79] Many advocates thus analogized medical and religious liberty rather than equated them.

Even Christian Scientists only gradually began to condemn government interference as a direct violation of their religious liberty. The early Scientists— including, initially, Mary Baker Eddy herself—tended to view their movement as a healing system more than as a religion. As one historian observes, "Although there appeared to be a symbiotic relationship between sin and sickness in Christian Science . . . the practical reality was that most people initially came to Science for a cure from sickness."[80]

The Scientists remained conflicted about how to classify their rights into the twentieth century. Consider, for example, two nearly contiguous articles in the 1905 volume of the *Christian Science Journal* addressing the constitutionality of licensing Christian Science practitioners. In his contribution, Herbert Packard discussed Christian Science as a "system of healing" and contended that there is a "right to seek and preserve health" in our "fundamental principles of government." A few pages later, by contrast, Clifford Smith depicted Christian Science first and foremost as a "system of religious teaching" and based his argument against licensing chiefly on "the constitutional guaranty of religious freedom."[81]

Invocations of religious liberty were clearly ascendant, however. When Nebraska governor John Mickey vetoed a licensing bill the same year, he asserted: "In the Christian Science religion the ideas of worship and of divine healing are so intermingled that it is impossible to draw the line of demarcation, and hence interference with the one is an interference with 'the rights of conscience' and thus becomes an infringement of the constitutional guaranty of religious freedom." After the New Hampshire Supreme Court definitively characterized Christian Science as a religion in a 1912 dispute concerning Eddy's will, Scientists relied principally on religious freedom arguments.[82]

Freedom of Inquiry

Freedom of inquiry was the main theme of Williams James's 1898 testimony to the Massachusetts Committee on Public Health opposing the previously mentioned bill that would have revoked the licensing exemption for drugless practitioners.[83] He opened by reminding the committee of his Harvard medical degree and his long record of teaching scientific subjects at the university. He quipped: "The presumption is that I am . . . interested in Science. I am indeed; and it is, in fact, because I see in this bill . . . a movement in favor of ignorance, that I am here to oppose it. It will inevitably trammel the growth of medical experience and knowledge."

James proceeded to articulate themes that he would develop at length four years later in his masterpiece *The Varieties of Religious Experience*, particularly in the chapter titled "The Religion of Healthy-Mindedness."[84] One such theme was the contingency of truth. Although James did not, in his testimony, directly deny the possibility of objective medical truth, he flirted with this conclusion by suggesting that medical knowledge was in a state of permanent flux. "Both as to principle and as to practice our knowledge is deplorably imperfect. The whole face of medicine changes unexpectedly from one generation to another." James characterized medicine as a collection of "vital mysteries," "personal relations of doctor and patient," and "infinitely subtle operations of nature." Whereas licensing might be appropriate if medicine were a "finished science," it had not nearly achieved this status.

The other main theme of James's testimony—one that he also elaborated on in *Varieties*—was the idea that practical experience is the only valid measure of medical truth. "Whatever you do," he urged the committee, "you are bound not to obstruct the growth of truth by the freest gathering of the most various experiences." He mocked regular and homeopathic medicine for their mutual refusal to consider experiential evidence of each other's efficacy, noting that their conflict was more akin to a disagreement between philosophers or "theologists" than one between scientists. He then rebuked the regulars for taking the same dismissive stance toward Mind Cure:

> One would suppose that any [set] of sane persons interested in the growth of medical truth would rejoice if other persons were found willing to push out their experiences in the mental-healing direction, and provide a mass of material out of which the conditions and limits of such therapeutic methods at last become clear. . . . But instead of rejoicing, [regular doctors] adopt the fiercely partisan attitude of a powerful trades union, demanding legislation against the competition of the "scabs."

James attacked the licensing bill on the grounds that "the Commonwealth of Massachusetts is not a medical body, has no right to a medical opinion, and should not dare to take sides in a medical controversy." He urged the legislature to stay its hand in view of "the confusion, the deplorable imperfection of the most expert knowledge, . . . the conscientious divergences of opinion, the infinite complication of the phenomena, and the varying and mutually exclusive fields of experience." The measure under consideration, he contended, would "convert the laws of this Commonwealth into obstacles to the acquisition of truth" by destroying "a whole department of medical investigation . . . together with the special conditions of freedom under which it flourishes."

James did not scorn regular medicine. Indeed, he conceded that if forced to choose only one type of practitioner, "I should unhesitatingly vote to license the Harvard Medical School type." Such a choice was unnecessary, however. Massachusetts should continue allowing the Mind Curers to do their work, because "our state needs the assistance of every type of mind, academic and nonacademic." And if mental healers proved incapable of adequately interpreting their own results, "why then let the orthodox M.D.s follow up their facts, and study and interpret them. But to force the mind curers to a State examination is to kill the experiments outright."

Unlike his 1894 letter to the *Transcript*, James's 1898 testimony focused almost exclusively on freedom of inquiry, and he promoted this concept chiefly on utilitarian grounds rather than out of concern for individual rights. He stated that his duty was to "the larger society, the commonwealth" and to the "real interests of medicine." James's testimony was nonetheless a strong libertarian statement. "Above all things," James concluded," let us not be infected with the Gallic spirit of regulation and reglementation for their own abstract sakes."

The Committee on Public Health apparently found James's testimony (and that of his allies) persuasive. It unanimously voted against revoking the exemption for drugless practitioners, and the bill's supporters backed down.[85]

Following James's address, freedom of inquiry became perhaps the most common theme in American anti-licensing literature. Just three months later, Benjamin Flower wrote an article opposing medical licensing in which he extensively quoted the testimony and concluded, "Medical freedom . . . fosters science and aids progress; and the safety of the people is conserved under freedom." A few years later, Alexander Wilder opined: "The concept that medical or other progress may be promoted by restrictive laws is absolutely contrary to the experience of mankind. It is not possible to devise any kind of government handcuff . . . that can help progress."[86]

Such reasoning appealed to the early twentieth century's rising progressive impulse, which, at least in some of its manifestations, was concerned with societal improvement more than with individual rights. Medical freedom activists continued passionately to advance arguments based on personal liberty as well. But as we will see in the next chapter, the contention that unrestricted medical inquiry generated community-wide health benefits would be an extremely important addition to their rhetorical arsenal in the Progressive Era.

Governor Thomas's Veto Message

In 1899, Colorado governor Charles Spaulding Thomas vetoed a bill that would have subjected drugless practitioners to a state medical licensing system administered by a board comprising regular physicians, homeopaths, and eclectics. His veto message wove together all the Gilded Age's main strands of medical freedom rhetoric in a way that makes it emblematic of the period.[87]

Thomas began by emphasizing the uncertainty of medical knowledge. He contended that in its current state, "Medicine is not a science. . . . It is a series of experiments more or less successful, and will become a science only when the laws of health and disease are fully ascertained and understood." Building on this theme, Thomas stressed the importance of freedom of inquiry. He asserted that medical knowledge would be advanced "not by arresting the progress of experiment, and binding men down to hard and fast rules of treatment, but by giving free rein to the man who departs from the beaten highway and discovers hidden methods and remedies in the wayside." The governor warned: "Innovation and experiment will always languish when held in thralldom by the censorship of a powerful commission founded upon a rigid and exacting statute."

Next, Thomas emphasized economic liberty. He denied the state's authority to "deprive practitioners . . . of the right to continue their business." The governor declared that "if [medical practitioners'] livelihood can be made to depend upon such oppressive conditions, the independences of the individual must disappear, and servitude in its worst form will inevitably follow." Thomas claimed that he would have vetoed the bill even if it advanced the public health, "for disease is . . . preferable to the unrestricted power of punishment and confiscation." But the legislature's references to health were in fact a "subterfuge." He observed, "all measures designed to promote a specific interest or protect an existing evil are ostensibly labeled 'for the benefit of the people.'" The true goal of the licensing bill was to establish a "medical trust . . . which shall regulate demand and supply by absolute control of the product which forms its basis."

Finally, Thomas turned to freedom of belief and bodily freedom, which—in a move typical of his era—he blended into a single line of argument. "The fundamental vice of the bill," he maintained, "is that it denies absolutely to the individual the right to select his own physician. This is a right of conscience, and is that which enables the citizen to worship God as he may desire. It is indeed the same right manifesting itself in a parallel direction." Thomas emphasized that the preservation of this right of conscience would benefit citizens' bodily health, for "confidence of the patient in the healer does more to restore him than all the drugs that ever medicined [*sic*] man." The governor pointed out that followers of drugless healing recognize "a power to overcome disease by the operation of mind and personal influence," and he insisted that "the cures they narrate are not imaginary." He asked, "Shall the government enact by statutes that these people shall not longer enjoy their beliefs or put them into daily practice?"

Gilded Age Medical Libertarianism

Notably, Governor Thomas did not confine his argument to these distinct strands of medical freedom. Near the end of his veto message, he broadly declared that the medical licensing bill, "like all kindred forms of paternalism, assumes that the citizen cannot take care of himself. The States must lead him as a little child, lest he fall into trouble unawares. . . . Such a system . . . crumbles into ashes in the crucible of experience." Thomas thus nodded toward a comprehensive libertarian philosophy of a type never quite voiced by the antebellum Thomsonians. Other Gilded Age medical licensing opponents routinely made similar statements. William James, for example, insisted that the "Massachusetts principle has always been to allow freedom of choice in personal matters and to let the citizen bear the consequences."[88]

Medical licensing foes drew from various intellectual and cultural sources in forging this all-embracing libertarian worldview. One was the English political theorist Herbert Spencer. American medical freedom advocates enthusiastically adopted the "first principle" that Spencer articulated in his 1851 book *Social Statics*: "Every man has freedom to do all that he wills, provided he infringes not the equal freedom of any other man." Spencer himself elaborated this principle into a condemnation of slavery, economic regulation, censorship, state religion, women's inequality—and medical licensing. Americans frequently borrowed from Spencer in their own jeremiads against licensing. Reverend T. E. Allen, for example, stated: "The essence of liberty is to allow each person to follow his own choice wherever he may do so without infringing the equal liberty of others. The instance you say 'I will give you liberty to do the thing that appears right or wise in my eyes,' you enter upon a policy of coercion, and become at heart a tyrant."[89]

Spencer's own attack on medical licensing had a ruthless, survival-of-the-fittest justification: "Unpitifying [*sic*] as it looks, it is best to let the foolish man suffer the appointed penalty of his foolishness." American licensing opponents assiduously avoided quoting this merciless language. Instead, they asserted, like Alexander Wilder, "Our American fellow-citizens are intelligent and able to take care of themselves, and need no such babying and swaddling by government." In addition, the Americans portrayed medical choice as just one aspect of a more general freedom of choice implicit in the United States' democratic system. Henry Wood explained: "Democracy takes it for granted that citizens are not imbeciles but free, intelligent moral agents. Within proper limits, they are to exercise the power of choice . . . even where the choosing may not always be the best."[90]

American medical freedom activists also drew ideas and inspiration from a homegrown tradition of "radical libertarianism," which emphasized the protection of individual autonomy against invasion by the state. In the antebellum years, this ideology was evident among not only Thomsonians, but also abolitionists, labor reformers, women's rights advocates, and freethinkers. In the decades following the Civil War, the somewhat diminished but still-robust cohort of radical libertarians embraced medical freedom as one of a cluster of causes that also included women's rights, anti-imperialism, freedom of speech, and sexual freedom (including access to contraceptives).[91] They carried these views into the twentieth century.

Consider, for example, the leading medical freedom activist Benjamin Flower, who lived from 1858 to 1918. According to one scholar, as a young man, Flower "came under the spell of Herbert Spencer and abandoned himself to the perils of free thought." He embraced the Mind Cure movement, explored spiritualism, and helped found the American Psychic Society.[92] His libertarianism extended well beyond medical issues. Near the end of his life, he echoed abolitionist Wendell Phillips's call for "entire unshackled freedom for every man's life, no matter what his doctrine—the safety of free discussion, no matter how wide its range."[93] Throughout his career as an editor and commentator, Flower was an exponent of freedom of speech, academic freedom, religious toleration, and women's rights.[94] His dedication to the last of these extended not only to suffrage and property rights, but also to access to contraceptives, because women should be "given absolute control of their bodies."[95]

Or consider William Lloyd Garrison II, who testified alongside William James at the 1898 Massachusetts hearing. Born in 1838, he grew up immersed in his father's abolitionist philosophy and fought for African Americans' rights until his death in 1909. He also became an ardent proponent of women's rights and a passionate anti-imperialist. Underlying all these positions were Garrison's commitment to the freedom of every individual and his fierce opposition to "the enthronement of privilege in fundamental law."[96]

Interestingly, at least some Gilded Age medical licensing foes eventually strayed from libertarian orthodoxy in one very important respect—namely, their attitude toward economic regulation. In the 1890s, as they confronted the social problems accompanying industrialization, urbanization, and growing wealth disparity, they began to support extensive government intervention in the economic realm. Flower, for example, abandoned laissez-faire economics over the course of this decade and embraced a series of redistributionist measures, including large-scale public works programs, Henry George's single tax, and government ownership of some industries. He became an admirer of populists like Tom Watson and William Jennings Bryan, progressives like Robert La Follette, and even the socialist Edward Bellamy. Garrison's views seem to have undergone a similar evolution. And Colorado governor Charles Thomas was elected in 1898 on a fusion Democratic-Populist ticket; twice enthusiastically supported Bryan for president of the United States; publicly endorsed and signed a bill establishing a maximum eight-hour workday in the state's smelting and mining industries; and proposed the establishment of a state inheritance tax.[97]

Licensing is, at its essence, a form of economic regulation. So why did such men continue battling medical licensing even after they began to endorse other government interventions in the economy? The answer lies in part in the fact that they never lost their antipathy for *special* legislation. Their opposition to a state-supported medical monopoly directly paralleled their denunciations of government grants of special privileges within other industries and trades.

But more important factors were also in play. Because of its connection to health and mortality, medicine is never simply another trade. The regulation of doctors raises profound issues of sovereignty over one's body that are not similarly raised by the regulation of railroads, for example. Moreover, in the Gilded Age, many Americans remained unconvinced that regular physicians' purely materialist understanding of disease was superior to that of schools that emphasized the role of the mind and spirit. Consequently, medical freedom activists believed that state suppression of alternative approaches would interfere not only with people's bodily autonomy, but also with their personal beliefs and with scientific progress. In other words, to the era's medical freedom proponents, medical licensing not only granted an *economic* monopoly to the regulars, but also gave them an *intellectual* monopoly and established their system of belief as a sort of state *creed*.

As we will see, the twentieth century brought new challenges to medical libertarians. One was the wide embrace of a Progressive political philosophy that prioritized societal welfare over individual rights in the health arena. The other was the emergence of increasingly effective orthodox treatments and the consequent growth of the view that modern scientific medicine was a uniquely valid approach to battling illness.

4

Reining In Progressive "State Medicine"

On May 3, 1900, the American School of Magnetic Healing got no mail.[1]

The postman's failure to appear was notable because the ASMH—housed in a sprawling mansion in the town of Nevada, Missouri—ordinarily received about 3,000 letters per day. Indeed, its voluminous correspondence so overwhelmed the local post office that the federal government would soon erect a new, larger facility. Despite its name, the institution was not merely a "school." It administered as well as taught magnetic healing, and it offered both its educational and therapeutic services by mail as well as onsite. The ASMH's daily mountain of correspondence consisted largely of requests and payments for "absent treatment," a method devised by the School's founder, Sidney A. Weltmer. The ASMH advertised this therapy in newspapers around the country. In exchange for a $5 monthly fee, a patient seeking a cure for her ailments would receive a letter from Weltmer instructing her to lie down at two specified times per day—wherever she happened to be—and make herself "passive to me." If she followed his directions scrupulously, Weltmer promised, "my positive healing thought force will enter your body and reconstruct it."[2]

Somebody from the ASMH—probably Joseph H. Kelly, the business manager—walked over to the post office to see what the problem was. There he learned that the local postmaster, J. M. McAnnulty, had that day received a telegram from the postmaster general of the United States instructing him to withhold all the School's mail "pending consideration for the issuance of a fraud order."[3]

Within days, Weltmer and Kelly were in Washington, DC, attempting to ward off disaster. While there, Weltmer put on an exhibition for Post Office Department officials to demonstrate the validity of his methods. He rubbed the forehead of a volunteer from the audience who complained of a pain over his right eye. Unfortunately, Weltmer succeeded only in shifting the pain to the left.[4]

On May 15, the postmaster general issued a formal order instructing McAnnulty to stamp the word "fraudulent" on all letters addressed to the ASMH, or to Weltmer or Kelly as individuals, and return these letters to their senders. McAnnulty was further instructed to categorize all such correspondence lacking a return address as "dead matter" and dispose of it. The postmaster general issued this order pursuant to a federal postal statute (known as a "lottery statute") targeting schemes for obtaining money through the mail "by means

Choose Your Medicine. Lewis A. Grossman, Oxford University Press. © Lewis A. Grossman 2021.
DOI: 10.1093/oso/9780190612757.003.0005

of false and fraudulent pretenses, representations, and promises."[5] Two weeks later, the School filed a federal lawsuit seeking to force the postmaster general to withdraw the order. Thus commenced litigation that would culminate, two years later, in the most influential medical freedom opinion ever issued by the US Supreme Court.

Sidney Weltmer was born in 1858 to highly educated parents, in either Pennsylvania or Ohio. By the time he was a teenager, his family had moved to Missouri, where he resided until his death in 1930. When Weltmer was thirteen years old, his oratorical skill at a town celebration earned him the nickname "Professor"—an honorific he would continue to use as an adult to compensate for (or disguise) his lack of formal education. At age fourteen, he started studying orthodox medicine under the tutelage of a local physician, but he abandoned his hopes of becoming a doctor five years later because he believed he was afflicted with consumption (tuberculosis), a debilitating and then incurable disease. The teenage Weltmer also voraciously consumed books about religion and mesmerism. These volumes ultimately proved more relevant to his career than the standard medical texts.

For the first two decades of his adult life, Weltmer bounced around among a variety of vocations: Southern Baptist preacher, schoolteacher, farmer, librarian, business college instructor. He founded a children's school, an education journal, and a local library. Then, in the mid-1890s, he began devoting himself exclusively to mesmerism and related phenomena. As a traveling healer in 1895 and 1896, Weltmer combined therapeutic services with "hypnotical entertainment." In 1897, however, he abandoned such frivolity. It was inconsistent with the professional and scholarly image he sought to project that year when he settled in Nevada, Missouri, and founded the Institute of Suggestive Therapeutics—soon to be renamed the American School of Magnetic Healing.[6]

Joseph Kelly was his partner in this venture. Kelly, who worked as a hardware store clerk before joining forces with Weltmer, was probably a huckster seeking a quick path to wealth on the backs of gullible customers. Weltmer, by contrast, was a well-read, cerebral, and earnest striver who almost certainly believed in the efficacy of his own healing system. He was in the long line of nineteenth-century American mental healers described in the last chapter, comprising practitioners of Mind Cure and Christian Science. Even Weltmer's provision of "absent treatment" was not novel; the influential Mind Curer Phineas P. Quimby and others had previously engaged in similar practices.[7]

What, then, made "Weltmerism" original enough to merit its own name? As Weltmer himself explained in a treatise, his method, unlike his predecessors', did not depend on either the personality of the healer or on any mindful effort on the part of the recipient. Instead, its curative power was based entirely on an omnipresent, imperceptible, unconscious force ("universal substance" or "universal intelligence") that pervaded all forms of matter. A healer could channel this force, in the form of a thought, into the mind of a passive patient, triggering unconscious "thought-vibrations" of the brain cells that would cure the body. Although Weltmer explicitly equated this force with the God of the New Testament, he more rigorously analogized it to scientific phenomena such as heat, light, sound, and, especially, electricity. "[My healing theory] may sound strange," he acknowledged, "but it is not more strange than wireless telegraphy, and operates on the same principle."[8]

Around the turn of the century, the ASMH was one of Missouri's largest treatment providers (Fig. 4.1). While a small army of female "typewriters" handled the daily deluge of correspondence, Weltmer and his staff of twenty healers (including one orthodox physician who performed diagnoses) ministered to as many as 400 patients per day in-house. Within the facility, the transmission of mental vibrations was sometimes accompanied by the "laying on of hands" or, occasionally, more vigorous manual manipulation—in one instance so vigorous that a young woman received a $7,500 malpractice verdict for back injuries

Weltmer School of Healing. Nevada, Mo.

Figure 4.1 A photograph of the American School of Magnetic Healing in Nevada, Missouri, from an undated postcard.

inflicted by an overenthusiastic staff member. President William McKinley, bandmaster John Philip Sousa, and other luminaries visited the ASMH. The thriving institution's overall annual revenues—which also included fees for teaching Weltmer's methods—totaled about $40 million in today's dollars.[9]

In 1899, "Professor" Weltmer brought a defamation suit against a Methodist minister who branded him a "miserable charlatan." A parade of satisfied customers testified on Weltmer's behalf at trial, and a jury awarded him damages of $750. (The Missouri Supreme Court would later overturn the verdict.) Magnetic healing was so popular that by 1900, at least fourteen competing establishments had set up shop among Nevada's 7,500 residents. The rise of magnetic healing vexed the orthodox medical establishment. Dr. E. L. Priest devoted an 1899 speech before the Missouri State Medical Association to attacking magnetic healers. He used this address as a springboard for a successful effort to persuade the state legislature to pass a more stringent medical licensing statute in 1901.[10]

Orthodox doctors were thus no doubt extremely pleased when, in October 1900, a federal circuit court judge ruled in favor of the government and upheld the postmaster general's order in *American School of Magnetic Healing v. McAnnulty*. (For technical reasons, McAnnulty, the local postmaster, was the named defendant.) Two years later, however, their satisfaction turned to dismay when the US Supreme Court issued an astonishing 7–2 opinion reversing the lower court. In an irate editorial, the *Journal of the America Medical Association* blasted the Court's "queer" decision in favor of the "fraudulent pretender" as "a judicial blunder."[11]

The briefs filed in the Supreme Court focused primarily on the complex constitutional question of whether the postal fraud statutes deprived persons of property without due process of law. But Justice Rufus Peckham, writing for the Court, explicitly avoided this issue and instead based his decision on a point of statutory interpretation that the victorious ASMH had barely hinted at in its filings. In doing so, he struck a blow at the very notion of medical "science."

Peckham held that the phrase "false or fraudulent" in the federal postal statute did not—could not—apply to the School's business. Why? In language strikingly reminiscent of William James, the justice asserted:

> Just exactly to what extent the mental condition affects the body, no one can accurately and definitely say. . . . Because the [ASMH] might or did claim to be able to effect cures by reason of working upon and affecting the mental powers of the individual . . . who can say that it is a fraud, or a false pretense or promise within the meaning of these statutes? . . . Those who might deny the existence

or virtue of the remedy would only differ in opinion from those who assert it. *There is no exact standard of absolute truth by which to prove the assertion false and a fraud.*[12]

Peckham observed that even if a majority of people embraced regular medicine, "the effectiveness of almost any particular method of treatment of disease is . . . a fruitful source of difference of opinion." Therefore, he argued, magnetic healing and virtually all other alternative medical approaches fell outside the meaning of "false or fraudulent" in the statute. Peckham cited electrical therapy and homeopathy as other healing methods beyond the postmaster general's power because their efficacy was not reducible to a question of fact. He then twisted the knife by noting that the same was true of orthodox medicine. Comparing regular medicine to homeopathy, he remarked, "Both of these . . . schools of medicine have their followers, and many who believe in the one will pronounce the other wholly devoid of merit." Because there was "no precise standard by which to measure the claims of either," the law should hinder neither.[13]

A few years later, Peckham would author the famous decision in *Lochner v. New York*, striking down a New York maximum hours law for bakers on the basis of liberty of contract. It is therefore notable that his opinion in *American School of Magnetic Healing* hardly nodded at healers' and patients' economic freedom. The difference in tone between the two opinions is also striking. Whereas Peckham wrote *Lochner* in a manner that invited the dissenters to (perhaps unfairly) accuse him of blindly embracing the truth of laissez-faire economic theory, his *Magnetic Healing* opinion is soaked with epistemological uncertainty with respect to medical theory.[14]

It is interesting to surmise why Justice Peckham decided and wrote *Magnetic Healing* the way he did in November 1902. The opinion's clear echoes of William James's *Varieties of Religious Experience* suggest that Peckham may have recently read that book, a bestseller published five months earlier. The justice's skepticism about medical science might also reflect tragic circumstances in his family life. Three years earlier, Peckham's younger son, Rufus Jr., had suffered an agonizing death due to an unknown ailment beyond the help of doctors. And when the Court issued the opinion, Henry, the justice's only remaining child, was residing in the tuberculosis colony at Saranac Lake, New York, incapacitated and fading toward his inevitable demise in 1907. These events throw a melancholy light on Rufus Sr.'s defense of magnetic healers: "If they fail, the answer might be that all human means of treatment are also liable to fail, and will necessarily fail when the appointed time arrives." At a time when orthodox medicine itself could claim few therapeutic triumphs, Peckham's attitude was hardly unusual.[15]

Medicine in the Progressive Era

One might assume that the Progressive Era, the ill-defined period running from approximately 1890 to 1920, was an unpropitious time for advocacy in favor of freedom of therapeutic choice. Progressive reform is generally identified with a growing embrace of government regulation guided by scientific expertise and a corresponding decline in individualism. Indeed, such attitudes greatly influenced the medical field during the Progressive Era. The states, while administering their now-entrenched medical licensing regimes, also exerted authority in areas such as public sanitation, school health inspections, and mandatory vaccination. In a ringing defense of this phenomenon— dubbed "state medicine" by both its proponents and detractors—the Pennsylvania commissioner of health proclaimed at the 1907 annual meeting of the American Medical Association (AMA): "Submission to reasonable personal restrictions intended for the welfare of all is the very foundation stone of civilized liberty." The US Supreme Court famously embraced this principle in 1905, when it upheld the authority of states to enforce compulsory vaccination laws in *Jacobsen v. Massachusetts*.[16]

Medical freedom activists perceived, behind these developments, the machinations of an increasingly powerful orthodox medical establishment, embodied by the AMA. The professionalization and organization of educated occupations was another prominent aspect of progressivism, and medicine was an obvious example of this trend. In 1901, the AMA revised its constitution in a way that both rationalized the organization's structure and incentivized membership, which exploded from just eight thousand members in 1900 to seventy thousand (about half of American physicians) a decade later.[17]

Although the AMA was a private entity, it exercised so much power that medical sectarians deemed it a government-supported trust. One significant AMA initiative was the 1905 creation of a Council of Pharmacy and Chemistry, whose determinations of drug safety and efficacy influenced both physicians' prescription practices and the acceptance of advertisements by medical journals. The AMA also created a Council on Medical Education, which in 1906 inspected and graded the nation's 160 medical schools on the basis of curriculum, admissions standards, finances, and other criteria. The Council approved only eighty-two. The AMA then asked the Carnegie Foundation to conduct its own review of medical schools. The resulting 1910 report by Abraham Flexner, a prominent education reformer, sought to ensure that "the professional training of the physician is . . . securely established on a scientific basis." Its recommended approach was the closure of inferior schools and the improvement of the remaining ones. The Flexner Report argued that medical schools should be strengthened through, among other steps, the adoption of rigorous standards for admission, the implementation of a uniform and scientifically rigorous curriculum, and the encouragement of faculty research.[18]

The winnowing of medical schools had already commenced due to state licensing boards' imposition of heightened educational requirements. The states' widespread embrace of the Flexner Report accelerated this process. Between 1910 and 1922, the number of schools nationwide plummeted from 131 to 81. While university-based medical schools endured, this era saw the rapid disappearance of for-profit schools, rural schools, African American schools—and sectarian schools. The Flexner Report dripped with contempt for the homeopathic, eclectic, osteopathic, and physio-medical institutions he visited. He disparaged their admissions standards, instructional quality, and infrastructure. Most important, he condemned the very notion of a sectarian medical school as unscientific, because medical sects (unlike modern orthodox medicine) were built on preconceived dogma rather than on observable facts. Flexner visited thirty-two irregular medical schools; by 1920, only five of them (four homeopathic and one eclectic) remained.[19]

Flexner could not claim sole, or even primary, credit for the disappearance of sectarian medical schools. It reflected a broader decline of homeopathy and eclectic medicine as they effectively merged into regular medicine. Although some homeopathic purists clung to Hahnemannian principles in the early twentieth century, most displayed a growing willingness to use orthodox remedies. Eclectics—who were always less rigid than homeopaths—also borrowed extensively from the regular armamentarium. Throughout the Progressive Era, some representatives of both sects continued loudly to proclaim the superiority of their therapeutic theories and the importance of medical freedom, but this chorus grew quieter as their followers became less doctrinaire.[20]

The AMA, after decades of hostile conflict with homeopaths and eclectics, adopted a strategy of conciliation and absorption. In 1903, the organization revised its code of ethics to abandon the prior version's prohibitions against association with sectarians. Despite faltering efforts to preserve their separate professional organizations, more and more homeopaths and eclectics joined the regular state medical societies. Meanwhile, states with separate licensing boards (regular, homeopathic, and eclectic) tended to replace them with unified boards. The *New York Times*, advocating such a step in New York in 1907, observed: "The sacrifice is not a heavy one, for the present divisions among the real doctors are along vague and wavering lines, which most or many them already ignore occasionally in everything except theory." Later that year, New York revised its medical practice law to create a single examining board of nine members, with no sectarian allocation of seats.[21]

None of this is to say that Progressive Era Americans participated in a wholesale abandonment of alternative medical systems. In a 1923 survey by the orthodox Chicago Medical Society, 93 percent of respondents acknowledged at least sometimes turning to "cults" and "pseudo-science" when they were sick. The following year, a Philadelphia physician reported that 34 percent of his recent patients had sought such care within the three months prior to visiting him. Even as late as the end of the 1920s, the proportion of sectarian practitioners to orthodox doctors (approximately 1:4) was seemingly a bit *larger* than it had been a half-century before.[22]

What changed was the *types* of sects that thrived; the (slow) decline of homeopathy and eclectic medicine was accompanied by the growth of other approaches. While Mind Cure and magnetic healing persisted, Christian Science membership exploded. Meanwhile, a new sect called naturopathy blossomed. Founded around the turn of the century by Benedict Lust, a German immigrant, naturopathy was a hodgepodge of daily practices, outdoor activities, and "natural" botanical remedies. Within twenty years of its inception, multiple naturopathy schools had sprouted up around the country and ten states had enacted naturopathic licensing laws.[23]

Perhaps most important, the Progressive Era witnessed the growth of osteopathy and chiropractic, comprehensive systems of treatment that relied on manual manipulation of the body. Although these two sects would eventually become almost entirely mechanistic, they originated in the same late nineteenth-century metaphysical impulse that gave rise to Christian Science and Mind Cure. Both Andrew Taylor Still, who founded osteopathy in the early 1890s, and Daniel David Palmer, who developed chiropractic about five years later, had backgrounds in mesmerism and magnetic healing, and they both believed that physical manipulation could ensure the free flow of nonmaterial vital forces through the body. Osteopathy's popularity and institutional structures grew more quickly, and the legal status of its practitioners was already an active topic in state legislatures and courts by 1900. Disputes regarding chiropractors arose somewhat later.[24]

Although state medical licensing regimes were now firmly entrenched, they did not markedly inhibit the growth of the drugless sects and other irregular medical approaches. Organized medicine continued to try to strengthen licensing after 1900, but (with a few exceptions) these efforts failed in the state legislatures in the face of popular resistance. Conversely, a growing number of states—totaling twenty-eight by 1917—expressly exempted Christian Science from their medical practice acts, either specifically or along with all treatment by prayer. One scholar has designated the years from 1900 to 1915 as the era of "legal recognition" for Christian Scientists. Prosecutions against Christian Science practitioners, whether for unlicensed practice of medicine or manslaughter, ground to a virtual halt.[25]

Osteopathy was also deemed to fall outside the "practice of medicine" in most states, and thus outside the medical licensing statutes. In 1897, just two months after the Illinois Court of Appeals upheld the conviction of osteopath Eugene Eastman for practicing medicine without a license, an appeals court in Ohio overturned Eastman's conviction for the same violation in that state. The Ohio statute defined the "practice of medicine" to include "prescrib[ing], direct[ing], or recommend[ing] for the use of any person, any drug or medicine, or other agency for the treatment, cure or relief of any wound, fracture or bodily injury, infirmity or disease." The court explained: "If it was the intention of the general assembly to prohibit the practice in this state of osteopathy, clairvoyance, mind healing, faith cure, hypnotism, massage, and Christian science, it should have been specifically mentioned, and not left to mere inference from the general words *other agency*." Most courts subsequently opining on the applicability of their own states' medical practice acts to osteopathy reached the same conclusion as *Eastman*.[26]

Unlike the Christian Scientists, the osteopaths ultimately sought official legitimacy through the creation of their own licensing regimes. In 1896, the governor of Missouri (where osteopathy was born alongside Weltmerism) vetoed an osteopathic licensure bill because of inadequate educational standards. Andrew Taylor Still responded by expanding the curriculum of the American School of Osteopathy (located in Kirksville, Missouri) to include all the subjects taught at orthodox medical schools except for *materia medica*. Persuaded by these educational reforms and a fierce lobbying campaign, the governor of Missouri signed an amended osteopathic bill in 1897. By 1913, thirty-eight additional states had enacted osteopathic practice laws.[27]

The licensing of chiropractic—scorned by the osteopaths themselves as a physically brutal, sham imitation of osteopathy—came later, primarily in the late 1910s and 1920s. In the absence of chiropractic licensing laws, chiropractors were prosecuted for practicing medicine without a license far more frequently than their osteopathic counterparts had been. Although juries acquitted the majority, thousands (including Palmer himself) were convicted. The contrasting legal fortunes of unlicensed osteopaths and chiropractors were due to various factors. The former had greater success in gaining explicit exemptions from state medical practice acts. Moreover, belligerent osteopaths joined forces with the regulars in attempting to suppress chiropractic, often by invoking the crime of practicing *osteopathy* without a license. But perhaps the most important factor was chiropractors' willingness to serve jail time, both to make a stand for medical freedom and to promote business.[28]

Why did millions of Americans continue to seek unorthodox cures during the Progressive Era, a period in which orthodox doctors were increasingly identified with a burgeoning scientific research establishment accumulating significant medical discoveries? The answer lies largely in the fact that the dramatic advances in understanding and diagnosing diseases in the late nineteenth and early twentieth centuries were not accompanied by similarly impressive progress in therapeutics. This is not to say that orthodox medicine achieved nothing in its fight against illness during this period. Most notably, advancements in bacteriology, combined with American physicians' belated embrace of the germ theory, yielded important life-saving practices, including the adoption of aseptic surgery and the implementation of new public health measures.[29]

Pharmaceutical innovation was less dramatic, however. At the start of the Civil War, the very short list of drugs that were effective by today's clinical standards included quinine (for malaria), digitalis (for heart failure), and smallpox vaccine. When the United States entered World War I in 1917, the number of effective medicines was not all that much larger. Some significant new products were introduced between the 1880s and early 1910s, including antipyretics for the reduction of fever and pain (most famously aspirin); vaccinations for diphtheria, tetanus, and typhoid; and a pioneering chemotherapy for syphilis called salvarsan. But when the doughboys sailed for France, there were still no effective drugs for most of the country's deadliest diseases, including pneumonia, influenza, tuberculosis, kidney disease, and cancer. Countless minor ailments also lacked effective pharmaceutical remedies. It is thus not surprising that Americans continued to try unorthodox treatments.[30]

The Federal Government Steps In

Through the end of the nineteenth century, the federal government was only minimally involved in medical and health matters. In 1798, Congress created a marine hospital fund for the "relief of sick and disabled seamen." From 1813 to 1822, a federal agent preserved and distributed smallpox vaccine pursuant to the Vaccine Act of 1813. The federal government's administration of the District of Columbia, the territories, Indian reservations, and the military inevitably entangled it in medical issues. Moreover, starting in the mid-nineteenth century, various federal departments collected statistics, issued publications, and performed research related to public health. Nevertheless, the federal government's overall involvement in health issues remained modest, and it imposed no nationwide *restrictions* on medical commerce.[31]

The postmaster general's efforts at the dawn of the twentieth century to enforce the lottery statutes against the ASMH and some patent medicine companies was thus a groundbreaking development, and a harbinger of the striking growth in the federal government's public health role during the Progressive Era. Additional exercises of federal power in the medical arena quickly followed. In 1902, after contaminated diphtheria antitoxin and smallpox vaccine killed children in St. Louis and Camden, respectively, Congress passed a new Biologics Control Act. This law gave the Hygienic Laboratory of the Public Health and Marine Hospital Service (the ancestor of the National Institutes of Health) the power, through inspection and licensing, to ensure that biological products were "safe, pure, and potent." Four years later, Congress—with AMA support—passed the Pure Food and Drug Act of 1906, a landmark piece of federal progressive legislation.[32]

The 1906 law was directed against unsafe and deceptively labeled medicines sold in interstate commerce, as well as adulterated and misbranded food. The Act's drug provisions were motivated largely by "The Great American Fraud," a multipart exposé of the patent medicine industry by the muckraking journalist Samuel Hopkins Adams published in Collier's Weekly. "Patent medicines" were remedies that, in contrast to the "ethical" drugs marketed to physicians, relied primarily on direct-to-consumer advertising, made explicit therapeutic claims, and failed to disclose their ingredients. In an age in which many of the remedies prescribed by doctors provided little or no relief, patent medicines were a popular recourse. But as Adams revealed, some of these products contained potentially dangerous ingredients (such as alcohol, morphine, opium, cocaine, and chloroform), and many made baseless—often preposterous—claims.[33]

The 1906 Act declared that a drug (or food) was misbranded if its package or label bore "any statement, design, or device regarding such article, or the ingredients or substances contained therein which shall be false or misleading in any particular." Soon after the passage of the Act, the Department of Agriculture's Bureau of Chemistry (the agency that administered the law before the FDA) began vigorously to use this provision against purveyors of patent medicines making groundless therapeutic claims. Through the end of 1909, the Bureau invoked this provision, with uniform success, in at least twenty-eight enforcement actions (civil seizures and criminal prosecutions) targeting such claims.[34] The very first defendant facing a misbranding charge based on false or misleading therapeutic claims (the manufacturer of the ingeniously named Harper's Cuforhedake Brane-Fude) was convicted after pleading not guilty. For the next few years, manufacturers facing similar charges did not even bother to fight them in court.

Then the Bureau of Chemistry went after O. A. Johnson of Kansas City, Missouri, the owner of the Doctor Johnson Remedy Company.

The Supreme Court Intervenes: *U.S. v. Johnson*

In November 1909, a grand jury indicted Johnson for selling a collection of misbranded drugs—tablets, a tonic, and four topical products applied to the skin—marketed together as "Doctor Johnson's Mild Combination Treatment for Cancer." Johnson promptly moved to quash the indictment by advancing a novel theory. He contended that the "false or misleading in any particular" language of the 1906 Act simply was not intended to address claims of efficacy. The provision, he argued, was applicable only to representations concerning the *identity* of the drug and its chemical ingredients. In January 1910, probably to the government's astonishment, a US district court agreed and dismissed the charges against Johnson. The judge declared that "by no possible construction can [the Act] be extended to an inquiry as to whether or not the prescription be efficacious or worthless to the effect the remedy claimed for it."[35] The government appealed the case to the US Supreme Court, which heard arguments in spring 1911.

Although the question for the Supreme Court was, on the surface, a technical dispute over statutory interpretation, Johnson framed the case in a way that touched on profound issues of medical freedom and the meaning of scientific truth. Johnson's basic argument, echoing *American School of Magnetic Healing v. McAnnulty*, was that Congress could not have intended to regulate therapeutic claims, because such a claim was "not a statement of an existing fact, but is . . . in the nature of things an expression of opinion." He maintained, "Congress cannot . . . be deemed to have intended by this legislation to invade a field so speculative and conjectural."[36]

For various reasons, Johnson was in a stronger position to advance this argument than most peddlers of nostrums. First of all, Ora Alexander Johnson, MD, was not a medical ignoramus. He was an 1897 graduate of the Bennett College of Eclectic Medicine and Surgery in Chicago. The Flexner Report criticized the "frankly commercial" ethos of this for-profit institution, its "nominal" compliance with Illinois entrance requirements, and the "wretched" condition of its building. Nevertheless, the school was credible enough to earn a B rating ("probation") rather than a C ("unapproved") from the AMA's Council on Medical Education in 1906, to affiliate with Loyola University in 1910, and eventually to become the Loyola University School of Medicine. Dr. Johnson ran a thriving practice in Kansas City, specializing in cancer and chronic diseases, and was a member of the local, state, and national eclectic medical societies. In 1907, when the allopath-dominated Missouri Board of Health petitioned to revoke Johnson's license to practice on the grounds that he falsely claimed to cure cancer, a state court rejected the petition following two weeks of testimony from supportive sectarian doctors and satisfied patients.[37]

A second strength of Johnson's case was that his topical treatments were not inert substances, but rather caustic ones that really could destroy external cancerous tissue. Reputable eclectic and homeopathic medical experts, and even some regulars, rejected the orthodox remedy of surgical excision in favor of an "escharotic" (caustic) approach to treating some cancer, particularly skin cancer.[38] While the government assiduously tried to link the "Mild Combination Treatment for Cancer" with the infamous fraudulent "patent medicines," Johnson's lawyers avoided that term entirely and instead presented the remedy—particularly its caustic elements—as a product embraced by professionals.

By framing the dispute as one in which government officials, under the sway of regular physicians, were seeking to suppress unorthodox approaches, Johnson's lawyers cleverly removed the case from the realm of fraud and made it about monopolistic abuse of power in violation of medical freedom. Johnson accused the government of "manifesting a dogmatic frame of mind emanating from the surgical Keen Cutters of that profession known as the allopaths." He contended that "the biggest trust in the United States today is the medical trust dominated by the so-called regular physicians," a combination that would "hail the day when . . . all rival schools of medicine should be put completely out of business." Johnson further maintained that the government's interpretation of the Pure Food and Drug Act inappropriately "extends its provisions . . . into the field of theories, ideas and beliefs—a field in which freedom has always been the policy of our government." The government lawyers were forced to insist, defensively, that the Act "invades no right of conscience. . . . It simply condemns fraud."[39]

Johnson relied heavily on the *Magnetic Healing* decision—particularly its assertion that "there is no exact standard of absolute truth by which to prove [a therapeutic claim] false and a fraud." In other words, Johnson's argument was largely an epistemological one about the contingency of medical fact. He pointed to the "great number of schools of medicine" in the country and challenged the notion that any one of these sects was in a superior position to determine whether another's "opinion of curative properties of drugs and medicines is or is not well founded."[40] Johnson elaborated:

The theory of the American Medical Association and the allopaths . . . is that no remedy advocated by any other school or profession . . . is a remedy for anything, . . . and that every physician in the country who does not adopt their theory, should be subject to indictment. . . . By the same token every allopath physician could be indicted and convicted if on the other hand the Eclectic or Homeopath should go upon the stand and condemn their remedies. Thus it is seen that the subject is not and cannot be one of determination of fact as the determination of fact is recognized in the law. It does now, and must forever remain a subject incapable of proof, and must forever remain so unless a quietus is to be put upon medical discoveries.[41]

In making his argument, Johnson exploited the still-rudimentary state of clinical research. To establish the effectiveness of his cancer remedy, Johnson presented the Supreme Court with quotations from medical texts and journals, along with excerpts of testimony by sympathetic doctors and patients in the 1907 Missouri trial in which he successfully defended his license. With the possible exception of patient testimonials, this was exactly the type of evidence that orthodox doctors themselves routinely relied on in assessing the efficacy of drugs in 1911. Although some academic reformers were advancing a program of "rational therapeutics" based on laboratory work, animal experimentation, and carefully designed clinical experimentation, they had little impact on the views of practicing doctors. Indeed, even most scientists—such as the professors staffing the AMA's Council on Pharmacy and Chemistry—often lacked data from experimentation and relied instead on "the opinions and recommendations of trusted colleagues." Surveying the scene in 1914, a British physician bemoaned the fact that "not one single drug has been carefully studied so as to understand its full effect on the human system."[42]

Johnson's legal strategy was successful. In May 1911, the Supreme Court ruled 6–3 in the doctor's favor. The majority opinion, by Justice Oliver Wendell Holmes Jr., concluded that the phrase "false or misleading in any particular" in the Pure Food and Drug Act was aimed only at statements regarding "the identity of the article." Holmes reasoned that Congress would be unlikely to punish merely "mistaken" therapeutic claims. Holmes also questioned whether Congress would have referred questions of "medical effect" to the Bureau of Chemistry, a body not obviously equipped to assess drug efficacy.

Although Holmes (once a close friend and intellectual playmate of William James) disclaimed the need to "go into considerations of a wider scope," he nonetheless offered "a word as to what Congress was likely to attempt." Citing *Magnetic Healing*, he concluded: "[Congress] was much more likely to regulate commerce in food and drugs with reference to plain matter of fact, so that food and drugs should be what they professed to be, when the kind was stated, than to distort the uses of its constitutional power to establishing criteria in regions where opinions are far apart."[43]

The Path Forward: Focus on Fraud

U.S. v. Johnson reflected a widespread view that the law should not choose sides in therapeutic disputes between people of good faith. But what about patent medicines foisted on an unwitting public with claims their manufacturers *knew* were false? Although the purveyors of such nostrums fought to preserve their right to sell them—often by waving the flag of medical freedom—courts and legislatures had much less sympathy for these grifters than for earnest followers of alternative medical philosophies.

Following *Johnson*, there thus appeared to be a general consensus that honest differences of medical opinion were beyond the reach of the law, but downright fraud was not. The task of implementing this consensus was taken up by Congressman Swagar Sherley of Kentucky. Shortly after the Court decided *Johnson*, Sherley introduced a bill to amend the Pure Food and Drug Act by adding a provision stating that a drug was misbranded "[i]f its package or label shall bear or contain any statement . . . regarding the curative or therapeutic effect of such article or any of the ingredients or substances contained therein, which is false and fraudulent." The very next day, President William Howard Taft issued a special message to Congress urging it to amend the Act to allow the federal government to combat patent medicine manufacturers who knowingly sold worthless nostrums.[44]

During hearings on Sherley's proposed legislation, his colleagues expressed concern about potential interference with the sale of products rejected by orthodox doctors but earnestly embraced by their vendors. One representative, for example, asked Sherley "if a conviction could be had under this amendment where there was a diversity of opinion between the various schools of medicine in regard to the merits of the medicine?" Sherley emphatically dismissed this concern. He insisted that in any case in which "the man who offers the drug as a cure subscribes himself to that school that believes in [its] curative properties," a conviction would be impossible "where there was any diversity of opinion" as to the drug's efficacy.[45]

Sherley emphasized that his amendment protected unorthodox medical creeds by, unlike the other misbranding violations in the Pure Food and Drug Act, requiring a showing that the statement in question was "false *and fraudulent*." Therefore, a claim that a drug was a "cancer cure" would not constitute misbranding unless "that cure was absolutely no cure and known to be such by the manufacturer of it."[46] This explanation, however, raised the question of whether the Sherley Amendment left the government with sufficient power to fight the useless remedies peddled by the patent medicine industry. Representative Harry J. Covington, a supporter of the amendment, assured his colleagues that it did. He explained: "There is . . . a wide field in medicine within which the curative or therapeutic effect of drugs is as well known and as definitely determined as is the law of gravitation. Within that field, apart from any question of opinion, the fact that a so-called remedy is absolutely worthless and its label false and fraudulent is easily susceptible of proof."[47]

Congress passed the Sherley Amendment in August 1912, and the Bureau of Chemistry promptly resumed bringing criminal and civil enforcement actions against patent medicines making baseless therapeutic claims. Despite the new requirement that the government show fraud, the Bureau met with great success. The United States prevailed in case after case, almost always by a default judgment or guilty plea.[48] However, one litigious patent drug manufacturer—the Philadelphia-based Eckman Company—fought back and ultimately forced the government to defend the constitutionality of the Sherley Amendment in the Supreme Court.

The dispute commenced in December 1912 when the government seized thirty-four bottles of Eckman's Alterative on the premises of an Omaha, Nebraska, drug distributor. ("Alterative" was a generic synonym for "remedy" favored by many nostrum manufacturers.) The product was a quintessential patent medicine—a liquid of indeterminate composition with labeling making broad and bold therapeutic claims. The label on the bottle declared that the drug worked for "all throat and lung diseases including Bronchitis, Bronchial Catarrh, Asthma, Hay Fever, Coughs and Colds, and Catarrh of the Stomach and Bowles [sic], and Tuberculosis (Consumption)." A circular inserted into the package proclaimed: "We know it has cured and that it will cure Tuberculosis." The only information Eckman's provided about ingredients was the presence of alcohol (14 percent by volume)—a disclosure specifically mandated by the 1906 Act.

The government focused its allegations on Eckman's claims regarding tuberculosis—one of the great, unconquerable scourges of mankind prior to the development of an antibiotic treatment (streptomycin) in the 1940s. The United States contended that the statement "will cure tuberculosis" was false and fraudulent because "in truth and in fact said article of drugs would not cure tuberculosis . . . there being no medicinal substance . . . known at present which can be relied upon for effective treatment or cure of tuberculosis."[49] In other words, rather than relying on a chemical examination of the drug and a refutation of each ingredient's remedial power, the government simply accused Eckman's Alterative of claiming to be a cure for an incurable illness. A federal district court ultimately agreed and declared the seized product to be misbranded.

In challenging this determination in the Supreme Court, the Eckman Manufacturing Company contended that the Sherley Amendment was unconstitutional.[50] The company relied largely on Justice Peckham's assertion in *Magnetic Healing* that "the effectiveness of almost any particular method of treatment of disease is, to a more or less extent, a fruitful source of difference of opinion." Eckman asserted that the Amendment's restriction on its ability to advance its "opinions" regarding the drug's curative properties violated its property rights under the Fifth Amendment. The company further argued that the Amendment violated the Sixth Amendment's requirement that "the accused . . . be informed of the nature and cause of the accusation." According to Eckman, behind any criminal prosecution or condemnation of property "must be an act measurable by fixed standards that in law can be determined, and not merely by the speculative theories and contrary tenets of experimental science."[51]

In its January 1916 opinion, the Court rejected these arguments. Writing for a unanimous Court, Justice Charles Evans Hughes seemed to acknowledge that there might be a constitutional problem if the Sherley Amendment "enter[ed] the domain of speculation" in the manner condemned by *Magnetic Healing*. But, Hughes explained, it did not do so. In drafting the amendment, "Congress deliberately excluded the field where there are honest differences of opinion between schools and practitioners. It was plainly to leave no doubt upon this point that the words 'false *and fraudulent*' were used." At the same time, however, "Congress recognized that there was a wide field in which assertions as to curative effect are in no sense honest expressions of opinion but constitute absolute falsehoods and in the nature of the case can be deemed to have been made only with fraudulent purpose."[52] *Eckman's* was such a case.

With *Eckman's*, the Supreme Court thus protected sincere proponents of unorthodox drugs while allowing the government to pursue mendacious manufacturers of useless nostrums. Even if the Bureau of Chemistry had been inclined to bring enforcement actions against authentic homeopathic and eclectic remedies, it now knew that such actions would be fruitless. The post-*Eckman's* jury instructions delivered by trial judges virtually guaranteed this result. For example, in *Kar-Ru Chemical Co. v. U.S.*, the judge instructed the jury: "It is not proper in such a case as this to try rival well-established schools of medicine, and, if you find that the defendant has only used in its several preparations homeopathic remedies for the alleviation of ailments, then your verdict should be not guilty."[53]

Accordingly, even though authentic homeopathic drugs frequently contained no detectible amount of any potentially active ingredient, the Bureau of Chemistry appears never to have challenged the efficacy of such products (most of which did not make labeling claims, in any event). Notably, the product at issue in *Kar-Ru* was not a recognized homeopathic drug administered by trained homeopathic practitioners for specific ailments, but an over-the-counter patent medicine with a broad range of indications and a total absence of any conceivably therapeutic ingredient. The Kar-Ru company seems to have embraced homeopathy only after being indicted. The jury saw through this ploy.[54]

The botanical active ingredients in most eclectic medicines were well-recognized pharmaceutical substances. Unlike homeopathic products, eclectic drugs contained these ingredients in easily detectible amounts. Indeed, the most prominent line of eclectic products—the "Specific Medicines" manufactured by the Lloyd Brothers company of Cincinnati—were much *more* concentrated than the standard "tinctures" sold by conventional pharmaceutical houses. Lloyd Brothers, which marketed its drugs largely to physicians and professional compounding pharmacists, scrupulously complied with the labeling requirements of the Pure Food and Drug Act.[55] Unsurprisingly, the FDA left Lloyd Brothers alone.

The requirement of a showing of fraud protected not only sellers of drugs used by established unorthodox sects, but also dissenters and innovators within the orthodox medical community. For example, the maker of a drug called Tuberclecide claimed that it was a remedy (though not a cure) for tuberculosis and got away with it, even though most orthodox physicians had long ago rejected the notion that the drug's primary active ingredient (creosote carbonate) was effective for that ailment. Pointing to evidence offered by the defense that at least some physicians still endorsed use of the drug, the judge—overturning a jury's guilty verdict—declared: "We all know . . . that doctors disagree. . . . Can it fairly be said that a man is practicing a fraud when he acts upon the advice of a physician, although other physicians disagree with him?"[56]

In light of these cases, the Bureau of Chemistry, from the late 1910s onward, focused its enforcement actions on drugs making claims that any well-informed person would know were false. These included nonhomeopathic drugs containing only inert substances, drugs claiming to treat an unrealistically broad range of illnesses, and drugs labeled as curing then-incurable ailments such as tuberculosis and internal cancers.

Because the Pure Food and Drug Act gave the Bureau of Chemistry jurisdiction over *products* (drugs) rather than *procedures*, the statute did not even potentially interfere with the drugless therapies—osteopathy, chiropractic, Christian Science—that increasingly dominated alternative medicine during this period. Nonetheless, the courts' reasoning about the appropriate reach of the law in the face of medical uncertainty was equally applicable to these other healing schools, which were subject to the postal fraud statutes.

As a formal matter, these Pure Food and Drug Act cases concerned the rights of drug manufacturers, not patients or doctors. There was, however, at least one major Progressive Era dispute in which the entire universe of alternative medicine proponents joined together to assert their constitutional right to freedom of therapeutic choice. To find it, we must look outside the judicial realm and visit the arena of pure politics.

The NLMF's Campaign against a National Health Department

June 30, 1906, the day that President Theodore Roosevelt signed the Pure Food and Drug Act and the Meat Inspection Act into law, arguably represented the high-water mark of federal progressive health legislation. After this date, progressives at the national level continued striving to implement their ideas of professionalization, bureaucratic efficiency, and regulation through national health regulation. These efforts, however, resulted in few successes and one spectacular failure. This failure was the defeat of a plan—seemingly uncontroversial at first—to establish a National Department of Health.

In the early twentieth century, the federal government's modest health-related responsibilities were dispersed widely throughout the sprawling federal bureaucracy. Congress had allotted them to the Public Health and Marine-Hospital Service (a component of the Department of Treasury) and to various bureaus within other departments, including Agriculture, Interior, and the short-lived Department of Commerce and Labor. In 1906, the AMA's National Legislative Council advocated gathering these functions within a single national department. The same year, two prominent Yale professors of political economy, Irving Fisher and J. Pease Norton, also promoted this idea. In 1907, the American Association for the Advancement of Science formed a "Committee of One Hundred on National Health" to examine the subject. This body—with Fisher as its president—commenced a long and ultimately fruitless campaign for the creation of a national health department.

The initiative had widespread and bipartisan support. The 1908 Democratic platform endorsed the establishment of a "national bureau of public health." The outgoing and incoming Republican presidents—Roosevelt and William Howard Taft—supported the concept, too, although they favored consolidating the scattered health-related agencies within an existing department rather than creating a new one. In February 1910, Taft officially embraced a plan by the Committee of One Hundred to create a new bureau of health within the Department of Commerce and Labor. But the momentum quickly swung to a bolder approach when Democratic senator Robert L. Owen of Oklahoma introduced a bill establishing a separate Department of Public Health led by a cabinet-level secretary of public health.[57]

The entity proposed by Owen would encompass all existing agencies (except those within the Department of War and the Department of the Navy) "affecting the medical, surgical, biological, or sanitary service, or any questions relative thereto." In addition to assuming the component agencies' existing duties, the department would gather data, enforce quarantine regulations, and establish "chemical, biological, and other standards."[58]

In April 1910, a Senate committee held hearings on Owen's bill. The measure received unanimous support from, among other witnesses, Professor Fisher and Dr. William Welch, the president of the AMA. A progressive-minded representative of the Metropolitan Life Insurance Company hailed the proposed federal department's capacity to bring about "coordination, cooperation, prevention of duplication, [and] prevention of waste," and to "educat[e] . . . the public generally along modern lines for the prevention of disease and the prolongation of life." The witnesses anticipated only one significant objection to the plan, namely, that it inappropriately interfered with the states' primary jurisdiction over health matters. The bills' supporters sought to quell this concern with assurances that the new department's power was primarily advisory, investigative, and cooperative. When the president of the Conference of State Boards of Health testified in favor of the bill, it seemed on the way to becoming law.[59]

Then, in mid-May, an advertisement assaulting the Owen bill appeared in many of the nation's leading newspapers. Its bold headline asked, "Do You Want the 'Doctors' Trust' to be able to Force Its Opinions on You?"[60] The advertisement was sponsored by a previously unknown organization called the National League for Medical Freedom (NLMF).[61] The ad identified the AMA (the "political doctors") as the motivating force behind the measure. It warned that the legislation's "concealed purpose" was "to commit the United States Government to the establishment of a system of medicine, denying to the people the right to determine for themselves the kind of medical treatment they shall employ." Newspaper readers were urged to join the NLMF and contact their representatives in Washington. Two additional, similarly alarmist NLMF ads appeared soon afterward.

The NLMF was the brainchild of Benjamin Orange Flower (1858–1918), who served as its president and guiding spirit. Flower was a reformist magazine editor who, with his round glasses and generous dark mustache, looked like a country schoolteacher.[62] Born in rural Illinois, Flower abandoned his plans for a career in the ministry when he became enamored of the philosophy of Herbert Spencer, the English libertarian philosopher. By his own account, Flower's lifelong interest in the issue of medical freedom was triggered by Spencer's condemnation of medical licensing in *Social Statics*. In that work, Spencer blasted English physicians' efforts "to establish an organized, tax-supported class, charged with the health of men's bodies as the clergy are charged with the health of their souls."[63]

Flower moved to Philadelphia in the early 1880s to work as a secretary in the unorthodox medical practice of his brother, Richard, an unscrupulous man eventually arrested at least twice for financial swindling. Richard soon relocated to Boston and started a successful patent medicine business, the Flower Medical Company. Benjamin followed his brother to Massachusetts and, from 1885 to 1889, served as the company's president. This decision to briefly work for a corporation selling quack remedies would later come back to haunt him.

Flower's true interests were journalism and literature. After moving to Boston, he started a modestly successful literary journal, *The American Spectator*. In 1889, Flower merged this magazine into a new publication, the *Arena*, a political and literary review that he edited from 1889 to 1896 and again from 1900 to 1909. Though never reaching an audience as large as the first-tier progressive magazines, *McClure's* and *Collier's*, the *Arena* achieved a circulation of about 100,000 by the early twentieth century and was an important forum for articles about social reform.[64]

Flower's own contributions to the *Arena* illustrate his rapid political and intellectual transformation. When he founded the journal, he was a libertarian moral reformer who scorned most legislation as schemes by moneyed interests to gain special privileges. He evolved into an enthusiastic proponent of government interventions in the economy, such as large-scale public works programs and the socialization of certain industries. Flower supported most of the leading populist and progressive causes of the age, including urban renewal, abandonment of the gold standard, child labor reform, direct democracy through the initiative and referendum, and women's rights. Flower's role as a progressive magazine editor led one scholar to dub him "Father of the Muckrakers."[65]

Flower also immersed himself in the movements swirling around Boston that examined the relationships between body, mind, and spirit. He helped found the American Psychical Society and its journal, the *Psychical Review*, both dedicated to the "investigation of the phenomena of Modern Spiritualism in accordance with the scientific method." He was an active member of the national New Thought (Mind Cure) organization, called the International Metaphysical League. Although not an adherent of Christian Science, he published a book-length defense of it in December 1909, just months before starting the NLMF.[66]

Likely because of his involvement in these movements, Flower started participating in medical liberty activism years before the appearance of the Owen bill. As early as 1898, he contributed an article to the *Arena* blasting state medical licensing laws as "despotic" obstacles to "science, progress, justice, and the liberty of the citizen."[67] Therefore, he was well prepared, in 1910, to organize the opposition to what he perceived to be a conspiracy to rob Americans of their freedom of therapeutic choice.

Within three weeks of its formation, the NLMF already had 69,800 members. Although there was no charge for membership, the organization quickly received enough generous contributions to fund the aggressive advertising campaign discussed earlier. According to John L. Bates, an ex-governor of Massachusetts and the NLMF general counsel, these donations came primarily from ordinary people who "believed themselves to have been healed of diseases where the regular physicians had given them up."[68]

The NLMF's emergence had an immediate impact on the debate over the national health department. In early June, at House of Representatives hearings on the companion bill to Owen's, committee members reported that telegrams opposing the legislation were pouring into their offices. The tone of these proceedings was dramatically different from that of the earlier Senate hearings. The witnesses in favor of the bill were followed by a passionate parade of people speaking against it, almost all of them NLMF officers or board members (though not Flower himself).[69]

The sudden rise of the movement against the Owen bill sapped the legislation's momentum. The House tabled the companion measure in January 1911. Senator Owen tried again, introducing an amended version that April. The Oklahoman made various changes to mollify the opposition. The new bill was vague as to whether the director of the proposed department would be a cabinet-level officer. Moreover, to reassure practitioners and followers of unorthodox sects, Owen added a guarantee that the department "shall recognize no so-called school or system of medicine."[70]

Meanwhile, the bill's supporters sought to delegitimize the NLMF. Shortly after Owen introduced the amended legislation, Collier's attacked the organization as a "bad bunch" that was "doing a tremendous amount of damage by its opposition to needed medical legislation." The article suggested that the NLMF was financially backed by the patent medicine industry, supporting this allegation in part by citing Flower's stint in his brother's drug company a quarter-century earlier. Owen himself repeated this attack in an impassioned speech on the Senate floor.[71]

The NLMF's response was fierce—and effective. In early July 2011, Senator John D. Works of California, a Christian Scientist, took to the floor to flat-out deny any connection whatsoever between the NLMF and the patent medicine industry. He defended the members of the rapidly growing organization (which already numbered more than 200,000) as "people who are simply standing for the principle that every sort of healing medium, whether it be the doctors of this profession or that profession, this school or that school . . . shall have the right and freedom to exercise their rights as American citizens." After reading extensively from the Supreme Court's Magnetic Healing decision, Works declared, "It would be a violation of the very spirit of the Constitution to forbid me the right to resort to that sort of help that I believe to be most efficient in my own case."[72]

In September 1911, NLMF released the first issue of Medical Freedom magazine, a monthly edited by Flower. A month later, the publication's (self-reported) circulation was already 100,000. That autumn was punctuated by NLMF-organized mass meetings around the country in favor of medical freedom. A "large and enthusiastic" rally in New York's Carnegie Hall was followed by gatherings of thousands in Chicago and San Francisco. Owen's amended bill died.[73]

Owen offered a third version of his bill in April 1912. This iteration explicitly stated that the new national health agency would have no power "to regulate the practice of medicine" or "to interfere with the right of a citizen to employ the practitioner of his choice." Senator Works assaulted this measure, as well, reading William James's entire 1898 Massachusetts testimony into the record. In August, as the NLMF's membership climbed past 300,000, Owen's cowed colleagues rejected his bill in favor of a law that merely shortened the name of the health agency within the Treasury Department to the "Public Health Service" and modestly increased its employees' salaries and research responsibilities. The dogged Owen made a couple of other fruitless attempts at establishing a national health department, but these efforts were doomed to failure after the 1914 outbreak of World War I diverted lawmakers' attention to more pressing matters. No significant reorganization of the federal government's health bureaucracy would occur until the creation of the Federal Security Agency (a forerunner of today's Department of Health and Human Services) in 1939.[74]

The Paranoid Style in American Medical Politics

In his famous 1964 article "The Paranoid Style in American Politics," historian Richard Hofstadter identified a persistent strain of "heated exaggeration, suspiciousness, and conspiratorial fantasy" in the country's political rhetoric. The medical freedom activists who squelched Owen's attempt to create a national department of health were exemplars of this phenomenon. Their campaign's central thesis was that a cabal of "political doctors" was secretly scheming to capture the federal governmental apparatus and undermine Americans' fundamental rights.[75]

Consider, for instance, the following statement by Fred A. Bangs, the NLMF's Associate Counsel, at the 1910 House hearings:

> The object behind these various bills is to establish a state medicine, and to make the American Medical Association a thoroughgoing, active medical trust, and to place the people of the United States of America completely under the dominion and domination of this association in all things related to the sanitary and health service.[76]

And what would the AMA do with the power it sought? The NLMF warned that this "very un-American organization" would suppress all unorthodox medical approaches and eliminate Americans' freedom of therapeutic choice. The self-described mission of the NLMF was "to protect the people in the enjoyment of one of the most sacred rights for which man has had to contend against privilege-seeking classes—the right to select the practitioner of his choice in the hour of sickness." At the Carnegie Hall mass meeting, one opponent of the Owen bill trumpeted: "At a time . . . when the common people are asserting their inalienable right to life, liberty, and the pursuit of happiness, this effort of the American Medical Association to secure restrictive, exclusive and prohibitive legislation is harking back to the ignorance and superstitions of feudalism."[77]

Two claims thus lay behind the NLMF's campaign: first, that the AMA was directing the drive for a national health department, and second, that the AMA intended to use the new department to eliminate unorthodox medical practice from the country.

NLMF representatives advanced the first claim relentlessly, asserting, for example, that the Owen bill was "the result of long years of political intrigue on the part of . . . the [AMA]." In fact, Senator Owen developed his plan independently of the AMA, which was utterly surprised by the introduction of his first bill. Nonetheless, there was some truth behind the NLMF's efforts to link the AMA to the legislation. The AMA was an early and consistent supporter of the creation of a national health agency. In the words of one historian, the organization "gave greater attention to [the establishment of a federal health department] than to any other national issue in the last half of the Progressive era." The AMA drafted a statement in favor of Owen's legislation, and AMA representatives testified in favor of it at congressional hearings.[78]

Much more outlandish was the NLMF's allegation that the AMA was not only behind the Owen bill, but also intended to use the new department to squelch nonorthodox practitioners and thus deprive Americans of medical choice. This is not to say that the AMA could not reasonably be accused of pursuing a monopolization strategy, at least at certain times in its history.[79] But the creation of a national health department was not a component of this strategy. After all, as the legislation's proponents pointed out again and again, it said nothing about medical licensing.

Indeed, at least one medical maverick testified *in favor* of the bill because he did not perceive any threat to unorthodox medical approaches. This witness was Dr. John Harvey Kellogg, the co-inventor of Corn Flakes. Kellogg was hardly a conventional physician. Among other quirks, he fixated on inhibiting masturbation. (He advocated anesthesia-free surgical intervention to address the problem when his recommended dietary regimen—including breakfast cereal—did not do the trick.) Despite his own unorthodox healing methods, Kellogg supported the Owen bill, declaring: "So far as any restriction of freedom in medical practice is concerned, I could have nothing to do with that at all; I can not imagine how any intelligent person who reads the bill could see anything of that sort in it."[80]

As the Owen bill's supporters repeatedly emphasized, a national health department could not constitutionally regulate medical practice, in any event. Under then-controlling Supreme Court jurisprudence, any attempt to control medical licensing at the federal level would have been beyond Congress's power under the Constitution's commerce clause and thus an invalid intrusion into the states' sphere of responsibility. An editorial in the *Journal of the American Medical Association* accurately remarked, "The proposed department of health would have just as much authority to determine what 'kind of medical treatment' the people should employ as the Department of Agriculture has to dictate to the farmer regarding the . . . company he shall buy his plows of."[81]

Foes of the national health department pointed to a provision of the Owen bill that that they claimed might be broad enough to encompass medical licensing—namely, language giving the new department the authority "to supervise all matters within the control of the Federal Government relating to the public health." Of course, this clause presented no such danger if medical licensing was beyond the federal government's constitutional power in the first place. Nevertheless, Owen twice amended the measure to assuage his adversaries' concern—ultimately by explicitly forbidding the new department from regulating the practice of medicine or interfering with citizens' choice of doctors. Yet the opposition remained as passionate as ever. Indeed, Senator Works denied that *any* statutory language could adequately address his fear that the allopathic establishment would use the department to suppress unorthodox medicine.[82]

This is where the medical freedom advocates' "paranoid" style became most evident. They essentially argued that the tyrannical AMA would wield the national health department as a weapon against medical choice *regardless* of what the statute and Constitution said. One NLMF representative described the AMA's clandestine plot as follows:

> To have and secure at the hands of the Government a law which would give them the absolute control of all things medical in the United States. Whether the legislation which they have proposed and which they are fathering at the present time would, if passed, give them such power as they are seeking, I do not undertake to say, but . . . I am satisfied that should you grant to them any legislation . . . looking toward paternalism in medicine, they would take advantage of any such law and either with or without additional laws obtained later seek to regulate and control the administering of medicine throughout the entire United States.[83]

As evidence of this grand conspiracy, NLMF members ripped stray comments by AMA officials and Committee of One Hundred members out of context. For example, they repeatedly pointed to AMA president Welch's remark, in Senate testimony, that "it may be that the Federal Government can exercise larger powers in this matter than is generally supposed to be the case."[84] In fact, Welch was referring to government sanitation measures, not to the regulation of medical practice. Nevertheless, the NLMF's dissemination of such quotations helped convince hundreds of thousands of Americans that if the Owen bill passed, they would no longer be able to seek care from homeopathic, eclectic, osteopathic, chiropractic, mental, or religious healers. The organization's campaign to defeat the legislation thus succeeded. As the twentieth century progressed, this feverish anti-AMA rhetoric would persist in medical freedom movements, but victories would become much rarer.

The NLMF's Medical Freedom Philosophy

The successful campaign against the Owen bill was a "constitutional" movement even though it occurred entirely outside the courts and only rarely invoked the US Constitution itself. The pages of *Medical Freedom* regularly invoked the country's foundational values and the key historical moments that vindicated those values. The magazine's cover bore images of, for example, the minuteman statue in Concord and the signing of the Declaration of Independence in Philadelphia. A typical editorial, under the headline "Spirit of '76," declared that the NLMF's "nearest prototype is the Patriot movement . . . resulting in the separation of the American Colonies from England." Articles proclaimed the Declaration's inalienable right to "the pursuit of happiness" and particularized it to "the pursuit of happiness by way of health." And when the actual language of the founders was insufficient, *Medical Freedom* liberally repeated Benjamin Rush's mythical statement that the "Constitution of this Republic should make special provision for medical freedom."[85]

Although the NLMF's assessment of the threat posed by the Owen bill bordered on irrational, the medical libertarian philosophy it framed in opposition to the legislation was coherent and sophisticated. The campaign against a national health department featured all four strands medical libertarianism prominent in American medical freedom literature since the country's earliest years.

Economic Freedom

The NLMF condemnation of the Owen bill as a scheme to empower and enrich the AMA drew from the long-standing American tradition of resistance to "special legislation" discussed in previous chapters. Flower, for instance, described the drive for a national health department as an "organized attempt by a privilege-seeking class to secure special legislation" and thus gain "increased emoluments . . . that would be impossible if the people enjoyed their rightful freedom."[86]

"Special legislation" could take various forms, from land grants to tariffs to rate regulation. But in the psyche of many Progressive Era Americans, the most odious type of all was the government-supported monopoly. A deep-rooted strain of American libertarianism considered the exclusive grant of commerce to a particular entity to be unethical government favoritism and a violation of excluded

AS THE PEOPLE WANT IT

Uncle Sam: "It's up to you—You're free to choose!"

Figure 4.2 The National League for Medical Freedom's ardent commitment to freedom of therapeutic choice fueled its opposition to "state medicine." This cartoon is from the December 1914 issue of *Medical Freedom* magazine.

competitors' economic freedom. One defining feature of progressivism was its antagonism to monopolies of all sorts (whether or not explicitly state-supported), from the great corporate trusts to municipal streetcar and utility franchises.[87]

Unsurprisingly, therefore, antimonopolism was one of the NLMF's primary refrains. It was the main theme of the organization's national advertisements against the Owen bill. For example, one ad entreated, "Have You Protested Against the Medical Trust?" before warning that the legislation "would create a monopoly more odious than was ever before conceived." At the House committee hearings, the NLMF's Fred Bangs remarked: "Talk about monopoly—the Standard Oil Company would be a mere unsophisticated tyro in comparison with such a trust." As evidence of the orthodox doctors' monopolistic designs, the NLMF pointed not only to the Owen bill, but also to state medical societies' publication of suggested fee schedules—an alleged price-fixing scheme—and the AMA's purported intention to control the medical publishing and drug trades.[88]

The NLMF's economic liberty argument was a powerful one. But the Owen bill's opponents emphasized that the corrupting effect of a close link between the federal government and medicine would threaten other types of freedom, as well.

Freedom of Conscience and Religion

American promoters of freedom of therapeutic choice had long linked medical liberty and religious liberty. During the Progressive Era, the connection between the two was particularly obvious because of Christian Scientists' prominence in medical freedom campaigns. As a member of the NLMF advisory board observed: "There is to-day a large and constantly growing class with whom the two terms are practically synonymous; so that, in the enactment of any legislation which effects [sic] in any way the medical freedom of any citizen, you are approaching very closely an encroachment upon his religious freedom."[89]

But when the Owen bill's opponents declared that the law threatened "sacred rights," their warning was not limited to followers of medico-religious sects. Rather, they were contending that medical beliefs, like religious beliefs, were exercises of the "conscience" immune from government intervention. Hence the president of the Arkansas State Eclectic Board of Examiners told the House committee considering the companion bill: "Anything that thus tends to interfere with liberty of conscience is undemocratic and constitutionally repugnant."[90] In a magazine article, Benjamin Flower opined:

> There are two rights that free men throughout Western civilization have . . . striven to secure and maintain even at the risk of their lives. One is the right of the individual to select the priest or clergyman of his choice to minister to his spiritual welfare or the health of his soul. . . . Another analogous demand quite as intimate and, to many, quite as sacred, was the right of the individual to choose the physician of his choice for his bodily ills.[91]

The analogy to religious freedom was particularly useful in the context of opposition to a national health department, because religious liberty in the US Constitution's First Amendment has two distinct, though related, components: a prohibition against an established church and a guarantee of the free exercise of religion. The NLMF and its allies drew on the anti-establishment notion by asserting that "state medicine is akin to state religion."[92] They thus coopted the term "state medicine"—a phrase originally coined in a positive light by AMA members—to launch a quasi-constitutional assault against the proposed health department. This line of attack was premised on the idea that the establishment of a "state medicine" would imperil dissenting medical sects in the same way that the establishment of a state church would imperil dissenting religious sects.

The NLMF forces had no doubt that the national health department would be "an allopathic department straight through" and that America's "state medicine" would thus be regular medicine. After all, they observed, the existing Medical Corps of the Public Health and Marine-Hospital Service included only regular physicians, due to discriminatory entrance requirements and civil service exam questions. In the House hearings, one activist opined that due to the overwhelming orthodox bias of the examinations, irregular practitioners were excluded from the Medical Corps "as effectually as though the plain letter of the law provided such exclusion." Another witness asserted, based on a survey of all federal departments: "There is no record of a man in the government service who is not of the regular school." Why would the proposed national department be any different?[93]

In the view of the Owen bill's foes, the very existence of an allopathic national health department would constitute a threat to liberty through "establishment" distinct from the "free exercise" problem posed by discriminatory medical licensing. Indeed, the department would undermine medical freedom even if its functions were limited to collecting and disseminating information. Senator Works declared: "When the Government becomes the publisher and distributor of information obtained by and relating to [the orthodox] school of medicine, it establishes a State medicine and makes it strictly sectarian. . . . The Government has no more right to sanction or support sectarianism in medicine than in religion. One is just as much a violation of the freedom of the citizen as the other." Hugh Spenser Williams, a Presbyterian minister, similarly asserted that the Owen bill "would confer a distinction and recognition of one particular school of medicine as superior to all others; that would be detrimental to all other schools and practitioners. It would stamp the allopathic school as the orthodox one and all others as heretics."[94]

Freedom of Inquiry

Since the country's earliest days, American medical freedom activists had contended that laws hindering nonorthodox medical practice squelched medical progress by inhibiting experimentation. This line of argument continued into the twentieth century. One broadside against the Owen bill, probably written by Flower himself, stated: "The history of civilization teaches few lessons more clearly than that in all fields of experimental research freedom, and not restriction, is the condition essential to scientific advancement and to human happiness and well-being."[95]

In the Progressive Era, this reasoning gained additional traction by its overlap with antimonopolism. Another column likely written by Flower explained:

> Special legislation which enables a privilege-seeking class to enjoy monopoly in commercial fields is an evil, placing as it does the people at the mercy of the favored few. The injustice and iniquity of such legislation, however, is small compared with the injury wrought by monopolistic legislation in fields of experimental knowledge, affecting matters so vital as a man's physical health and life; for here the laws enable the privileged few to close the door of hope and life against the invalid while retarding scientific advancement.[96]

As with the freedom of conscience arguments discussed earlier, arguments against the national health department based on freedom of inquiry maintained that government participation in medicine was potentially as problematic as government restriction of it. Senator Bates, for example, asserted that "medical research would be retarded and discouraged if there was one great central department that was supposed to being doing all that kind of work." American civilization's unmatched inventiveness required "personal, free, and independent" research, which would not occur if people "depended on the Government to do these things." Moreover, "when you have men working along lines where those lines are all determined by one central authority you get men working in grooves." Another foe of the national health department declared: "Were there a hundred laboratories established by Congress at Washington . . . it would remain, for the most part, for the doctor working quietly and diligently at the bedside of his truly needy patient and with microscope and paraphernalia in his private office to discover and give to the world the clearest conception of the malady in question and the most direct method of eradicating it." As the twentieth century progressed, and the age of the controlled clinical trial and government-directed biomedical research emerged, such assertions would sound increasingly quaint.[97]

Bodily Freedom

To modern ears, perhaps the most surprising aspect of Progressive Era freedom of therapeutic choice rhetoric was the continuing subsidiary role of arguments based on bodily freedom. Of course, bodily autonomy was implicit in every paean to the "precious" right of people to choose their treatment of choice, but activists alluded to the body itself surprisingly rarely. When the topic arose, it was almost always in the context of protecting people from government-*compelled* treatment rather than of resisting government hindrance of patient choice.

Some NLMF members, particularly those from the anti-vaccination community, emphasized the risk of state compulsion. They warned that the national health department would force unwanted treatments and medical examinations on American citizens. For these activists, bodily violation was a central image. For instance, Diana Belais, president of the Anti Vaccination and Vivisection Society of New York City, testified that the Owen bill might "subject the public to methods of treatment which may be obnoxiously contrary to their own best judgment and convictions; the American spirit can not endure this idea very well upon any subject, but when it comes to encroaching upon our personal liberty, into the sacred rights that we are supposed to have over our own bodies . . . then it becomes not only an unbearable thing, but an appalling thing."[98]

Such statements were rare, however, when Progressive Era activists demanded freedom to choose desired remedies rather than freedom from medical compulsion. Not until the rise of the feminist health movement in the early 1970s would bodily autonomy become the central trope in all medical choice advocacy.

Conclusion

Was the movement against the national health department a "progressive" one? The challenge in answering this question is that early twentieth-century "progressivism" was an indistinct and multidimensional concept to both the progressives themselves and to scholars today. Historian Michael Willrich, in his marvelous study of Progressive Era opponents of compulsory vaccination, poses the question of whether these activists were progressive or anti-progressive and understandably declines to offer a definitive answer. The particular problem with applying such labels to the medical freedom controversies of the early twentieth century is that these disputes pitted two core impulses of progressivism against each other: antimonopolism, on the one hand, and a celebration of bureaucratic rationalization, professionalization, and scientific expertise, on the other.[99]

Proponents of freedom of therapeutic choice were extremely progressive with respect to the former impulse. Christian Science writer Clifford Smith could thus credibly contend that his resistance to medical practice regulation was part of the same progressive antipathy to privilege and monopoly that lifted Woodrow Wilson to the presidency in 1912. And Benjamin Flower, in his 1914 book *Progressive Men, Women and Movements of the Past Twenty-Five Years*, could without irony celebrate the medical freedom activists alongside populist and progressive figures such as William Jennings Bryan and Robert M. La Follette.[100]

At the same time, the medical freedom advocates' apparent rejection of centralized organization and scientific expertise can seem anti-progressive. But even here, the story is complex, because the NLMF and its supporters did not spurn science per se. To the contrary, by resisting bureaucratization and professional-ization, they viewed themselves as embracing a *pro*-scientific position. In their opinion, the path to scientific progress was not the elevation of the university and government researchers favored by the AMA, but free medical experimentation by a broad range of citizens. One witness against the Owen bill warned that the law would marginalize "independent thinkers carrying on independent research and making a great part of the progress that to-day is being made in the treat-ment of disease."[101]

Still, there is no doubt that the NLMF's vision of scientific inquiry rowed against the modernist current in a manner atypical of most people who consid-ered themselves to be progressives. It is therefore unsurprising that the defeat of the Owen bill would be the last victory at the national level by an American med-ical freedom movement for more than a half century. The NLMF (and *Medical Freedom* magazine) remained in existence until September 1916, when the or-ganization closed because of insufficient funds. The League ultimately could not survive the end of the threat (the proposed creation of a national health de-partment) around which it had coalesced in the first place. The final volumes of *Medical Freedom* continued to rail against the AMA's sinister schemes to con-trol American medicine, but they addressed state and local developments much more than federal issues. And although denunciations of discriminatory med-ical licensing continued to appear occasionally, the magazine focused primarily on other aspects of alleged medical despotism, such as compulsory vaccination, mandatory medical examinations, and eugenics laws of various kinds.

World War I would impel the creation of a massive US military medical appa-ratus that would make numerous important innovations in disease control. The years after the war would see increasingly robust cooperation between academic researchers and pharmaceutical companies, a relationship that would provide the groundwork for revolutionary therapeutic advancements by the orthodox medical establishment for decades to come. This flow of "wonder drugs" would start as a trickle in the 1920s, accelerate in the 1930s, and run strongly into the 1960s. During this same period, doctors would achieve the pinnacle of their so-cial standing and prestige. Americans would become less and less concerned about resisting the authority of regular medicine. The mid-century "Golden Age of Medicine" would not be a golden age for medical freedom activism.[102]

5

Conspiracy Theorists and Con Men

Freedom of Therapeutic Choice in the "Golden Age" of Medicine

In June 1956, FDA Commissioner George Larrick received a scathing letter from Gerald B. Winrod, a demagogic Baptist minister from Kansas whom a journalist nicknamed the "Jayhawk Nazi." Winrod rose to prominence in the 1930s as a fervent anti-Semitic and anti-Catholic opponent of Franklin Roosevelt, whom he claimed had a clandestine Jewish background. Winrod fawningly toured Hitler's Germany, promoted the fraudulent tract *The Protocols of the Elders of Zion*, and railed against a global Jewish-Communist conspiracy. He ran for the US Senate in 1938, finishing a strong third in the Kansas Republican primary. During World War II, he was charged with sedition for promoting disloyalty in the armed forces, but he evaded conviction when the federal judge presiding at his trial died during the proceedings. After the war, Winrod continued to disseminate his right-wing views on the radio and in his magazine, *The Defender*. One of his pet causes was the FDA's "dictatorial" battle against the Hoxsey treatment, a controversial cancer drug.[1]

Two months before receiving Winrod's letter, Larrick had issued an unprecedented "Public Warning" cautioning cancer patients and doctors not to resort to a popular though "worthless" herbal cancer remedy marketed by Harry Hoxsey, a former coal miner. Winrod called Larrick's action "disgraceful"—the latest step in the FDA's "master plan to dominate the lives of the American people by means of a health dictatorship." The minister linked the FDA's totalitarian proclivities to "concepts of government since the advent of the New Deal" and contended that it was "more infested with leftists" than any other federal agency. On behalf of Hoxsey and his supporters, Winrod proclaimed:

> We symbolize the rights of man, the liberties that make life worth living. . . . We symbolize in the minds of millions of people a *Right*. It is the right of choice—the individual's right to choose his faith, his doctor, the food he eats, and the place where he shall lay his head at night. You have no right, Mr. Larrick, to usurp or subvert, through health control, the sovereign rights of our people.

Choose Your Medicine. Lewis A. Grossman, Oxford University Press. © Lewis A. Grossman 2021.
DOI: 10.1093/oso/9780190612757.003.0006

Winrod concluded his letter by emphasizing that "our interest in the control and cure of so-called incurable diseases, including cancer, is religious rather than medical. We are guided by the principle that whatever relieves pain and suffering is, in a broad sense, part of the Christian program. . . . The Hoxsey cancer cure . . . is a blessing from God to our day and generation. Don't try to stop it!"[2]

According to a legend likely spun by Harry Hoxsey himself, his grandfather invented the family's eponymous cancer remedies in 1840, after witnessing a prize stallion cure himself of hoof cancer by standing in a particular clump of flowering plants and shrubs.[3] Harry's father, a veterinarian, purportedly inherited the secret formulas and administered the drugs to livestock and people in the early 1900s. Then, in the 1920s, Harry emerged from the Illinois coal mines and commenced his own career as a cancer healer. He seems initially to have treated only malignancies on or near the body's surface, using an arsenic-containing paste and other corrosive concoctions. Harry then added an herbal tonic to his armamentarium and began treating internal cancers as well. This brownish-black liquid contained potassium iodide and various permutations of herbal extracts, including cascara sagrada, red clover, prickly ash, and buckthorn. A pink version also included pepsin to relieve medicine-induced nausea.

The Hoxsey remedies carried a patina of plausibility. Doctors had long used arsenic to eat away cancerous tissue. And the oral preparations contained some ingredients with recognized (though generally outmoded) medical uses. But the notion that any of these ingredients cured cancer was apparently a Hoxsey invention.

Hoxsey administered his remedies in ephemeral facilities in various states before establishing what would become his permanent clinic in Dallas, Texas, in 1936. He was perpetually entangled in legal disputes. Multiple jurisdictions charged him with practicing medicine without a license, and he pled guilty to this crime several times. He tussled frequently with the AMA. In 1949, Hoxsey won a libel lawsuit against Morris Fishbein, the longtime editor of the *Journal of the American Medical Association* and author of an editorial titled "Hoxsey—Cancer Charlatan." Although Hoxsey demanded a million dollars in damages, the judge awarded him only one dollar, reasoning that he *benefited* from portraying himself as a victim of AMA persecution.[4]

In the late 1940s, Hoxsey sought—with the support of several congressmen— to persuade the National Cancer Institute, a recently created federal government entity, to independently investigate his cure. The NCI rejected Hoxsey's request because he failed to produce data satisfying its basic criteria for initial assessment of a cancer treatment. Hoxsey accused the NCI of bending to the will of the AMA.[5]

By the early 1950s, the Hoxsey facility in Dallas was the largest private cancer clinic in the United States.[6] Thousands of patients from around the country traveled there for treatment. Some sought to avoid the standard treatments of radiation and surgery; others had already tried these methods unsuccessfully. Hoxsey now evaded unauthorized practice of medicine charges by delegating cancer diagnosis and treatment to licensed eclectic, homeopathic, and osteopathic doctors on his clinic staff. At some point he obtained a Texas license to practice as a naturopath, but it is unclear how much direct patient care he provided even then.

The FDA set its sights on Hoxsey when he began to ship his medicines, misbranded as cancer cures, to doctors in other states. In 1950, the US government filed a civil injunction action against him, seeking an order prohibiting this activity. The trial pitted the government's highly regarded orthodox medical experts against the osteopaths and satisfied patients testifying for Hoxsey. The district court judge (whom FDA staffers suspected had himself sought treatment at the Dallas clinic) ruled in Hoxsey's favor, holding that the government had failed adequately to demonstrate that his cancer claims were false or misleading. In 1952, however, the US Court of Appeals for the Fifth Circuit reversed and instructed the district court to issue the injunction.[7]

The Fifth Circuit's decision differed dramatically from the Supreme Court's 1905 *American School of Magnetic Healing v. McAnnulty* ruling, with its "medicine is opinion" ethos. The court of appeals explained that it was guided by facts "so universally . . . accepted by the practically unanimous aggregate of medical science . . . that contradiction thereof does not raise a substantial issue of fact." It observed that a controlled laboratory experiment on mice conducted by physicians and scientists with "superior qualifications and extensive experience in such matters" concluded that the Hoxsey medication had no therapeutic effect on cancer. The Fifth Circuit also emphasized that "the aggregate of medical experience and qualified experts" recognized only surgery, X-ray, and radium as appropriate treatments for internal cancer, "even though the ghastly truth is that these methods frequently fail." The decision concluded that only "persons activated by self-interest or ignorance may be found to express a contrary opinion."[8]

In 1954, following two failed attempts by Hoxsey to obtain Supreme Court review, the district court injunction took effect, prohibiting him from shipping his drugs in interstate commerce. The Dallas clinic continued to thrive, however, and in 1955, another successful Hoxsey clinic opened in Portage, Pennsylvania. Commissioner Larrick searched for a method within the FDA's authority to reduce patient traffic to the clinics. He arrived at the idea of issuing a warning pursuant to a previously unused provision of the 1938 Food, Drug, and Cosmetic Act (FD&C Act) that allows the agency to disseminate information "in situations involving . . . imminent danger to health, or gross deception of the consumer." In April 1956, Larrick published the aforementioned "Public Warning against Hoxsey Cancer Treatment" that provoked the Reverend Winrod's wrath.[9]

The warning, discussed by all the major newspapers, advised cancer sufferers, their families, and their physicians not to resort to Hoxsey's "worthless" medicines. Larrick cautioned patients "not to be misled by the false promise that the Hoxsey cancer treatment will cure or alleviate their condition. Cancer can be cured only through surgery or radiation. Death from cancer is inevitable when cancer patients fail to obtain proper medical treatment." The FDA hung "Public Beware" posters containing similar information in 46,000 post offices around the country (Fig. 5.1).[10]

Figure 5.1 FDA poster warning the public against use of the Hoxsey cancer treatment, 1957.

Hoxsey responded by filing filed an ultimately unsuccessful lawsuit challenging the warning's legality. He invited the US government and the AMA to investigate his clinic, and he pledged to close it forever (and donate $100,000 to charity) if such an investigation failed to demonstrate his cure's efficacy. Hoxsey repeated versions of this offer at three mass meetings in California hosted by a new medical libertarian organization, the National Health Federation (NHF).[11]

In 1956 and 1957, at least tens of thousands of citizens, and perhaps hundreds of thousands, mailed letters and petitions in support of Hoxsey to the FDA and Congress. Many of these were sent by Winrod's listeners and readers at the minister's urging. (Hoxsey paid him $82,750 in "advertising and public relations" fees.) Unsurprisingly, therefore, the letters expressed not only the fundamental American values of "freedom" and "choice," but also Winrod's conspiratorial right-wing ideology. Winrod's forces were not the first to allege a monopolistic plot between the medical establishment and the federal government, but they went further than their Progressive Era counterparts by decrying Jewish, Catholic, and communist influence in the AMA and FDA and accusing them of undermining the nation's Christian foundation.[12]

The FDA did not back down. Under pressure from federal enforcement actions, the Pennsylvania Hoxsey clinic shut its doors in 1958, and the Dallas facility folded two years later. With these closures, Hoxsey cancer remedies essentially disappeared from the United States, although a Tijuana clinic founded by one of Hoxsey's nurses operated from 1963 until 1999. Winrod died in 1957, before the FDA's ultimate triumph. Harry Hoxsey himself expired in 1974—from cancer.[13]

As we will see, the battle over the Hoxsey treatment exemplified mid-century American struggles over medical freedom of choice. The fight was over a therapy for cancer, a deadly disease for which orthodox medicine still had few answers. It concerned a particular remedy, rather than a *type* of remedy or *philosophy* of medicine. Freedom advocates extolled the individual who invented and endorsed the medicine at issue. And, like many other medical liberty activists during the Cold War Era, Hoxsey's followers embraced a right-wing conspiratorial worldview—an outlook that also led some to condemn the fluoridation of drinking water as a communist plot to destroy America. Not since the radical Jacksonians championed Thomsonianism had a medical freedom campaign mapped so clearly onto a particular political philosophy.[14]

Finally, the crusade for the Hoxsey cure was emblematic of mid-century medical freedom activism in its total defeat. During this period, the FDA had great success in driving ineffective drugs and devices off the market. Despite the continued popularity of many quack remedies, the bulk of the public wholeheartedly supported the FDA's efforts to suppress them.[15] The courts consistently upheld the agency's regulatory initiatives. And proponents of unorthodox cures never came close to passing choice-expanding legislation at either the state or the federal level. To the contrary, California enacted an anti-cancer-quackery law in 1959, which in turn served as a model for similar legislation in several other states. Then, in 1962, Congress passed revolutionary amendments to the FD&C Act requiring manufacturers of new drugs to demonstrate that their products were effective as well as safe before introducing them to the market.

These legal developments reflected Americans' overwhelming trust in large establishment institutions in the years after World War II. The country had extraordinary faith in organized medicine, science, and the government. Though several unorthodox therapies developed large and noisy groups of supporters, these product-specific networks did not crystallize into full-scale social movements capable of shaping legislation or even surviving the deaths or departures of their charismatic leaders.[16]

In short, the mid-twentieth century was the one, idiosyncratic period of American history in which advocacy for freedom of therapeutic choice was a marginalized phenomenon with little impact on law or policy.

World War I through the 1920s

The robust medical freedom advocacy characteristic of the nineteenth and early twentieth centuries diminished but did not disappear during World War I. The activism that persisted focused more on resisting compulsory medical measures than on ensuring freedom of access. As the German army collapsed in the summer of 1918, the American Medical Liberty League (AMLL), a new organization dominated by anti-vaccinationists, was established in Chicago. Its publication, the *Truth-Teller*, contained broadsides against the AMA ("the medical octopus"), allopathic hegemony, and state medicine similar to those in Benjamin Flower's *Medical Freedom*. During the 1920s, the AMLL—with the vocal support of celebrated lawyer Clarence Darrow—strove with some success to build public resistance to mandatory vaccination and to erode confidence in the AMA.[17]

Another notable group of this era was the Citizens Medical Reference Bureau (CMRB), founded in New York City in 1919. Its leader, Harry B. Anderson, the author of a 1920 screed titled *State Medicine: A Menace to Democracy*, was a nationally prominent warrior against compulsory medical measures. In a harbinger of the future, the CMRB attracted the financial support of Harold and Raymond Pitcairn, backers of a right-wing political organization called the Sentinels of the Republic.[18]

The 1920s also saw widespread popular resistance to the prosecution of chiropractors for practicing medicine without a license. Juries—sympathetic to defense lawyers' invocation of medical freedom—rarely issued guilty verdicts in such cases. The few chiropractors sentenced to prison embraced their imprisonment as a badge of honor, and their patients organized demonstrations and parades to protest state medical tyranny. In 1923, the California governor pardoned all imprisoned chiropractors in the "interest of justice." Many states enacted chiropractic-specific licensing laws during this decade. By the early 1930s, the vast majority of states legally recognized the profession through such statutes.[19]

By this time, however, the medical freedom movement was shriveling—so much so that one author has asserted that when the AMLL's secretary, Lora Little, died in 1931, "basically medical liberty passed on with her."[20] The collapse of interest in the issue was almost certainly related to the 1929 start of the Great Depression, a cataclysm that turned Americans' attention primarily to economic matters. After President Franklin Delano Roosevelt took office in 1933, advocates of limited government viewed his New Deal interventions into the economy as a more imminent and dire threat to liberty than the AMA and "state medicine."

Another important reason that medical freedom activism waned during this era was the accelerating therapeutic progress of orthodox medicine. Medical liberty movements' popularity had always rested largely on their followers' perception that alternative practitioners had at least as much healing success as regular physicians. But it became increasingly difficult to maintain disdain for scientific medicine as its breakthroughs accumulated during the 1920s. This decade saw the introduction of insulin for diabetes, vitamin D for rickets, and plasmoquine for malaria. And even these advancements paled in comparison to the drugs to come.

The 1930s through the 1960s: "The Golden Age of Medicine"

Although some scholars have identified the entire first two-thirds of the twentieth century as American medicine's "Golden Age," there is little dispute that the middle few decades of the century were the most resplendent period of all. During these years, doctors enjoyed extraordinarily high public esteem and wielded unprecedented political power. The medical establishment's status was bolstered tremendously by the invention of numerous new drugs for previously incurable illnesses. Although medical historian Charles Rosenberg has cautioned against casually using the term "therapeutic revolution" to describe this period, that is exactly what most Americans perceived to be occurring. The country's industrial-government-academic biomedical complex, which coalesced during World War II, pushed out "wonder drugs" at an astonishing pace for several decades, including antihypertensives, hyperthyroidism treatments, antipsychotics, oral contraceptives, and early chemotherapy for cancer.[21]

The most significant development of all was the discovery of effective antibiotic treatments for bacterial infections—"the most spectacular therapeutic advance of medical history," in the words of one scholar. By the end of the 1930s, doctors were routinely prescribing sulfanilamides to successfully treat pneumonia and other infectious ailments. In the early 1940s, penicillin entered the market as the first of the modern class of antibiotics derived from naturally occurring microorganisms. The introduction of these drugs played an enormous role in elevating Americans' faith in physicians, medical researchers, and pharmaceutical companies. Within a rather brief historical moment, it became possible to vanquish bacterial infections that had plagued mankind for millennia—from tuberculosis to strep throat to gastroenteritis to gonorrhea to pink eye. Modern antibiotics saved innumerable lives; consider the fact that in 1930, tuberculosis was the sixth leading cause of American deaths, whereas by 1965, it was twentieth.[22]

The twentieth century also witnessed a revolution in medical research methodology. At the start of the century, physician case reports and expert testimonials remained the most common basis for assessing a treatment's efficacy. Around this time, however, researchers began testing remedies by allocating every other patient alternately to either a treatment group or non-treatment group and comparing the results. In the early 1910s, a German scientist studying diphtheria antitoxin administered inert horse serum to his unknowing untreated subjects, thus introducing the use of a placebo control group. In the 1940s, researchers began assigning patients to the experimental or control group randomly rather than alternately to prevent selection bias. Then, to avoid investigator bias, they began to blind researchers as well as patients to each patient's assignment. A 1948 British Medical Research Council investigation of the antibiotic streptomycin for treatment of tuberculosis is often identified as the first randomized, double-blind, placebo-controlled clinical trial. This form of randomized controlled trial (RCT) soon became the "gold standard" for assessing a treatment's efficacy in the eyes of researchers, practitioners, and regulators.[23]

The public slowly became aware of modern clinical research methods, although the use of untreated controls was difficult for many to embrace. This ambivalence is reflected in Sinclair Lewis's 1925 novel *Arrowsmith*, a semi-satirical portrait of Martin Arrowsmith, a physician and medical researcher. The protagonist is an employee of the fictional McGurk Institute in New York (a stand-in for the prestigious Rockefeller Institute). He develops a bacteriophage that may immunize people against the bubonic plague. When the plague breaks out on the fictional Caribbean island of St. Hubert, Ross McGurk, the Institute's benefactor, sends Arrowsmith down to test the vaccine:

"If I could trust you, Martin, to use the phage with only half your patients and keep the others as controls, under normal hygienic conditions but without the phage, then you could make an absolute determination of its value. . . ."

Martin swore . . . that he would observe test conditions; he would determine forever the value of phage by the contrast between patients treated and untreated and so, perhaps, end all plague forever; he would harden his heart and keep clear his eyes.[24]

Arrowsmith, with a fierce commitment to advancing scientific truth at all costs, proceeds to conduct the controlled experiment on the island's population. Local officials, citizen committees, and even his closest American colleague urge him not to take this "heartless" approach and instead to provide the phage to everyone. Arrowsmith resists their entreaties. The population snarls at him in the street, and boys throw stones at him for "willfully withholding their salvation." Only when Arrowsmith's beloved wife, Leora, dies of plague (literally killed by experimental science, as she is infected by a spilled sample in her husband's lab) does he prioritize benevolence over scientific progress. "He raged, 'Oh, damn experimentation!' and . . . gave the phage to everyone who asked."[25]

Researchers of the time really did sometimes hesitate to assign patients to untreated control groups and thus deny them promising therapies. The public itself also blanched, and sometimes rebelled, at this approach. For example, a 1935 polio serum trial on children was undermined when the investigators acceded to the demands of anxious parents and allocated small doses of the limited supply of serum to all the children rather than larger doses to only half of them. "Means for a careful appraisal were easy to devise; impossible to carry out," bemoaned the *New England Journal of Medicine*. "Our sentiment overruled our reason."[26] Eventually, however, the scientific community almost universally embraced the randomized controlled methodology, and the broader population became more cognizant and accepting of it. Not until the AIDS crisis of the 1980s would widespread resistance to controlled medical research reemerge—an episode we will explore in Chapter 7.

The event that best demonstrated Americans' faith in orthodox research methods was the successful 1954 trial of Jonas Salk's polio vaccine in schoolchildren. Although parents were informed that the investigation was randomized and (in most places) placebo-controlled, more than 60 percent of them consented to have their children participate. Ultimately, 1.8 million children joined the study, while hundreds of thousands of lay volunteers helped implement it. The announcement of the trial's positive results enormously boosted the public's already-robust enthusiasm for the country's scientific and medical institutions. In the midst of the Cold War, Americans viewed Salk's achievement as evidence of their country's scientific prowess and benevolent spirit. Dr. Salk himself, a bespectacled intellectual, became a national celebrity on the level of baseball star Mickey Mantle and movie idol James Dean.[27]

Throughout the postwar period, physicians were among the most admired people in American society. As late as 1966, over 70 percent of Americans expressed "great confidence in" the people running medicine—a figure higher than that for any other major institution. A rare skeptical observer sneered: "Most patients are as completely under the yoke of modern medicine as any primitive savage is under the superstitious serfdom of the tribal witch doctor."[28]

Orthodox Medicine's Embodiment in American Law

This widespread faith in the medical establishment found its way into American law, which in turn endorsed and supported orthodox scientific medicine. This phenomenon involved not only legislatures and courts, but also administrative agencies. Notably, the relevant federal agencies were now housed within the same department. During his second term, Franklin Roosevelt moved the Public Health Service and the FDA into the newly created Federal Security Agency— a precursor to what is now the Department of Health and Human Services. Although a few farm groups meekly objected to removing the FDA from the Department of Agriculture and "placing it under the control of a lot of doctors," these protests were ineffectual whispers compared with the roar of opposition that had derailed the proposed national health department in the early 1910s.[29]

In considering the relationship between law and medicine during the mid-twentieth century, it is important to recognize that Americans' trust in large establishment institutions extended to the institutions of government, as well. According to one late 1950s poll, 90 percent of Americans agreed that they "usually have confidence that the government will do what is right." In a 1964 survey, 77 percent of respondents stated that they could "trust the *federal* government to do what is right" just about always or most of the time. These results—astounding from the perspective of the present day—were typical of the time. The public's simultaneous trust in government and medicine enabled a situation in which an increasingly powerful regulatory state bolstered the goals and values of the medical establishment.[30]

State Developments

At the state level, the dominance of orthodox medicine was visible in the widespread introduction of "basic science examinations." States with composite boards responsible for licensing both regulars and sectarians had long required all applicants to demonstrate basic scientific knowledge in subjects such as anatomy, physiology, pathology, and bacteriology. By contrast, states with independent homeopathic, eclectic, osteopathic, and chiropractic boards often licensed these alternative practitioners without testing their knowledge of such topics. In the 1920s, under pressure from the AMA, states with multiple licensing boards began to require all applicants to pass a basic science examination administered by a Board of the Basic Sciences. By 1941, seventeen states had established basic science boards; this number climbed to twenty-four by the end of the 1950s.[31]

Some states outlawed medical *products* that failed to meet modern scientific standards for efficacy. The most notable example of this development was a 1959 California statute commonly known as the "cancer quackery law." It established a fifteen-member, governor-appointed "Cancer Advisory Council" comprising, among others, faculty from each of the state's approved medical schools and representatives of the nation's leading nonprofit cancer research institutes. The statute required this council to investigate the efficacy (as well as the composition and safety) of drugs and devices represented as diagnosing or treating cancer. If the council deemed a product ineffective, it was empowered to prohibit anyone from "prescribing, recommending, or using" it. Reflecting the consensus of the time—even in a state unusually hospitable to alternative medicine—the California Assembly approved this measure by a vote of 60–11. In the five years following the law's passage, the council ruled six products (including Hoxsey's Cure) unlawful. Several other states enacted cancer quackery statutes modeled on California's.[32]

Changes in Federal Law

Meanwhile, Congress, federal agencies, and the courts steadily abandoned the principle—articulated most famously in *American School of Magnetic Healing v. McAnnulty*—that therapeutic efficacy was a matter of opinion and thus outside the scope of appropriate government regulation in the absence of fraud. The first major step in this direction was the 1938 enactment of the Food, Drug, and Cosmetic Act (FD&C Act) to replace the 1906 Pure Food and Drug Act. The 1938 law (still in effect today, though much amended and expanded) created a comprehensive new regime for regulating drugs and also gave the FDA authority over medical devices.

The 1938 FD&C Act required each manufacturer to submit a new drug application (NDA) to the FDA demonstrating that its product was safe prior to putting it into commerce. Although this premarket application was not required to establish efficacy, another section of the statute established a new standard for assessing the legality of therapeutic claims for drugs once they were on the market. As we saw in Chapter 4, the 1906 Act (as amended by the Sherley Amendment) prohibited such claims only if they were made with fraudulent intent. FDA Chief Walter Campbell was barely exaggerating when he asserted in 1933 Senate hearings that the 1906 law permitted a person to sell an utterly worthless drug as a "cure for every disease" so long as he honestly believed that claim based on the advice of his "witch doctor."[33]

By contrast, section 502(a) of the 1938 FD&C Act, in language still in effect today, simply prohibits drug and medical device labeling that is "false or misleading in any particular." There is no fraud element, and the provision applies to therapeutic claims as well as other labeling statements. In other words, Congress in 1938 banned false efficacy claims even if they were made in good faith. Although the FD&C Act's misbranding provisions originally regulated only labeling, not advertising, in 1938 Congress also revised the Federal Trade Commission Act to ban "unfair or deceptive acts or practices in commerce" as well as the "false advertisement" of any of the categories of products regulated by the FDA—again, without a fraud requirement.[34]

These statutory changes opened a doorway through which modern clinical science could enter American law and render the *McAnnulty* line of cases (which usually required a directed verdict against the government when an honest difference of medical opinion existed) essentially irrelevant. It rode through this doorway on the backs of sick chickens.

United States v. 7 Jugs, Etc., of Dr. Salsbury's Rakos, a rarely discussed 1944 US district court opinion, marked the first clear embrace of modern clinical methodology by an American court. The FDA seized three veterinary drugs for violating section 502(a), alleging that their labeling contained "false or misleading representations" regarding their efficacy in treating poultry diseases. Apparently, some veterinarians believed these drugs worked. Citing *McAnnulty* and other cases we considered last chapter, the company requested the following jury instruction: "In the treatment of diseases of animals honest differences of opinion may arise between school [*sic*] and practitioners as to the therapeutic or curative value of drugs. Statements with reference to the curative value of drugs . . . are not to be deemed false and misleading merely because differences of opinion exists [*sic*] between groups of Veterinarys [*sic*]." The court denied this request, and the jury held in favor of the government.

In denying a motion for a new trial, the court explained its refusal to give the requested instruction. The court stated that *McAnnulty* remained good law; juries could not deem a therapeutic claim "false or misleading" in the face of competing medical opinions, but only "where the question of effectiveness is demonstrable as fact." But then the court took a quietly dramatic step; it held that when proper evidence is submitted, "the question of whether a remedy is effective is *always* a question of fact." In this case, the government had provided the necessary evidence—namely, controlled scientific investigations:

> In the experimentation [conducted by the government's experts], all factors were controlled and a complete identity of circumstances and environment for the experimental poultry was provided. The report of such tests showed conclusively that the remedies were absolutely worthless and without any benefit whatsoever. The infected, untreated experimental group showed the same rate of mortality and recovery as the infected, treated group. These tests were duplicated and corroborated away from the laboratory under so-called field conditions. These tests were recognized by outstanding men of science as constituting conclusive evidence by recognized scientific standards that the remedies were wholly ineffective.

The court went on to suggest that *McAnnulty* had no relevance in any case in which controlled studies had been performed. "Tremendous advancements in scientific knowledge and certainty have been made since the rule in the McAnnulty case was first announced. Questions which previously were subjects only of opinion have now been answered with certainty. . . . In the consideration of the McAnnulty rule, courts should give recognition to this advancement."

After the *Dr. Salsbury's Rakos* decision, the *McAnnulty* doctrine was barely breathing. In 1948, the US Court of Appeals for the Ninth Circuit virtually finished it off. The product at issue in *Research Laboratories v. U.S.* was a human drug, "Nue-Ovo," which the manufacturer represented as a treatment for arthritis and rheumatism. The active ingredients included a variety of traditional herbal remedies included in most eclectic *materia medica*.[35] The FDA seized the product as misbranded under section 502(a). At trial in US district court, the government offered the testimony of eight medical experts, two of whom (at the government's request) had performed controlled studies of Nue-Ovo at major universities. After the jury "condemned" the drug as misbranded, the judge denied the manufacturer's request for a judgment notwithstanding the verdict. In doing so, he thoroughly embraced the notion that modern experimental techniques rendered efficacy a question of fact rather than opinion.

> It is not an expression of opinion when the Government experts say they conducted clinical tests in which unknown to the patients, they gave some of them . . . the remedy Nue-Ovo and others they gave a placebo, each of them thinking they were taking a remedy that was an effective treatment for arthritis, and each of these patients unquestionably afflicted with arthritis in its advanced

stages. And in all instances the results of pain were almost identical. . . . Now that's a matter of fact.[36]

In upholding the district court, the Ninth Circuit obliterated *McAnnulty*'s precedential force. The court set forth three "limitations to the *McAnnulty* rule." First, the "jury may consider testimony as to actual experiments"—particularly "'controlled clinical studies' conducted by eminently qualified physicians and surgeons." Second, the jury may consider "testimony of experts as to consensus of scientific opinion." Finally, the court stated, "Even opinion [expert] testimony as to therapeutic value is admissible." The court justified its decision by quoting the *Dr. Salsbury* language regarding the "tremendous advancements in scientific knowledge and certainty." It also emphasized that, in contrast to *McAnnulty*, which concerned an action by the Postmaster General, this case involved "a well-equipped Federal agency [i.e., the FDA] capable of arriving at a professional conclusion."[37]

Thus, in 1948—the same year as the completion of the seminal British Medical Research Council streptomycin study—therapeutic value became a question of fact rather than opinion in federal law. Since then, no defendant has ever successfully deployed the *McAnnulty* rule against an FDA or FTC enforcement action.

The War against Quackery

Between the late 1940s and the early 1960s, American society's interest in the problem of medical quackery soared.[38] Even though millions of consumers continued to purchase ineffective nostrums and useless devices, most people apparently supported the government's efforts to suppress such products.[39]

The FDA commenced a concerted "anti-quackery" campaign in the early 1950s. It focused first on "nutritional quackery" and then turned its attention to "medical quacks" as well. By 1960, the *Wall Street Journal* was reporting that the FDA, FTC, and Postmaster General were conducting a "crusade on quacks." In Washington, DC, the following year, the FDA and AMA cosponsored a National Congress on Medical Quackery, where the federal government and organized medicine agreed to wage all-out war on worthless remedies. When the second Congress on Medical Quackery convened in 1963, the National Health Federation held a competing conference across town called the National Congress on Health Monopoly. Although this alternate meeting, intended to promote "freedom of choice in matters of health," garnered significant media attention, barely more than one hundred people attended—compared to approximately seven hundred participants at the FDA-AMA conference.[40]

The 1962 Drug Amendments

Meanwhile, in 1962 Congress amended the FD&C Act in a way that unambigu-ously and emphatically embraced the scientific standards of modern orthodox medicine. The trigger for the change was the thalidomide crisis. Thalidomide was a sedative available in other countries, but not sold in the United States due to tenacious resistance by a now-legendary FDA medical officer named Frances Kelsey. In 1962, the American populace learned about a public health disaster overseas: thousands of infants born to mothers taking thalidomide (primarily to treat morning sickness) experienced severe birth defects—most distinctively malformed and stunted limbs. Americans, grateful to have largely avoided this catastrophe, drew the following lesson from it (in the words of one scholar): "If given the discretion and the resources, FDA medical officers will make the right decision, most of the time." A few months after the thalidomide story broke, over three-quarters of respondents to a nationwide poll expressed their support for "more strict" control over drugs.[41]

Congress responded to this sentiment by converting a milquetoast set of FDA reforms already under consideration into the game-changing 1962 Drug Amendments. This law introduced the requirement that investigators no-tify the FDA prior to commencing any study of an unapproved drug in human beings and authorized the agency to disallow or halt any investigation that did not satisfy requirements (including human subject protections) set forth in agency regulations. The FDA's "Investigational New Drug" (IND) regulations, issued in 1963, established the enduring three-phase structure for human drug experiments familiar to researchers today: first, studies in a small number of healthy volunteers to assess safety (Phase 1), followed by controlled studies in a larger but limited number of subjects suffering from the target disease to assess efficacy as well as safety (Phase 2), and finally large controlled trials intended to gather all the information the FDA needs to perform an overall risk-benefit as-sessment of the drug and to review the proposed labeling (Phase 3).[42]

The 1962 Amendments also made important changes to the FDA drug ap-proval process. Whereas the 1938 system was formally a premarket notification system, in which the NDA would automatically go into effect unless the FDA stepped in, the 1962 law converted the procedure into a true premarket approval scheme, under which a manufacturer cannot legally market a new drug until the FDA has positively approved it. More important, the 1962 Amendments revised the FD&C Act to require the agency to reject an NDA, not only if the applicant fails to demonstrate that the drug is safe, but also if "there is a lack of substantial evidence that the drug will have the effect it purports . . . to have . . . in the pro-posed labeling."[43]

Another critical feature of the 1962 law was its definition of "substantial evidence" of effectiveness: "evidence consisting of adequate and well-controlled investigations, including clinical investigations, by experts qualified by scientific training and experience to evaluate the effectiveness of the drug involved." In construing the term "adequate and well-controlled investigations," the agency's regulations embraced the methodology broadly adopted by drug researchers in the 1950s: the randomized, double-blind, controlled study. The FDA's regulations, guidance documents, and practices soon established this type of trial as the "gold standard" for demonstrating drug efficacy.[44]

Although FDA employees were quietly assessing clinical evidence of efficacy when reviewing NDAs even before the passage of the 1962 Drug Amendments,[45] the enactment of this statute represented the moment when American law officially endorsed and embraced modern scientific standards of medical efficacy. The notion that efficacy was a matter of opinion—the pillar long supporting legal arguments for freedom of therapeutic choice—was now dust.

Alternative Medicine in the "Golden Age"

Decline and Persistence

As faith in scientific medicine rose, fewer Americans turned to unorthodox alternatives. A decline in the use of alternative medicine was evident even before the antibiotics revolution. A survey conducted around 1930 showed that only 5.1 percent of cases attended by medical practitioners were attended by non-MDs. Statistics for the subsequent decades are sparse, but scholars generally agree that far fewer people used unorthodox medicine in the middle of twentieth century than before. A 2002 US government report observed with respect to this period: "Although most of the [non-conventional] health care systems and their therapies did not disappear, they were considered by most of the public and the mainstream medical community to be unscientific relics of the past. As a result, many were practiced in relative obscurity."[46]

Nonetheless, Americans never completely abandoned unorthodox cures. Despite their soaring esteem for scientific medicine, they recognized it was not yet a panacea. In 1970, three decades after modern antibiotics began to conquer bacterial infections, numerous syndromes remained for which regular medicine often failed to provide satisfactory answers: the common cold, arthritis, depression, heart disease, and cancer, to name just a few. The number of deaths ascribed to the last two of these almost tripled between 1930 and 1970, as infectious disease mortality dropped. Americans also began to realize that modern drugs could have serious—sometimes horrific—side effects. The extensive news coverage of the thalidomide tragedy in 1962 spread this realization to much of the population.

Some Americans thus turned to unorthodox treatments even during medicine's "Golden Age." In the words of historian James Harvey Young, purveyors of such remedies "moved into the gray areas where medical science had not yet won major victories . . . or where scientific opinion had not yet fully crystallized as to the certain path a person should follow to retain or regain his health."[47]

The Waning of Organized Medical Sects

The established unorthodox sects did not fare well during this period. They all either shrank precipitously or, in a bid to survive, transformed themselves in ways that would have appalled their founders.

The sects' decline was due not only to the public's growing faith in conventional medicine, but also to concrete actions taken by the medical establishment that made it more difficult for sectarians to practice. In 1938, the AMA excluded all institutions of "sectarian medicine" from its list of approved medical schools. In states that required applicants for licenses to have a diploma from a medical school "of good standing," this de-listing presented an insurmountable obstacle to graduates of sectarian schools. The widespread introduction of basic science tests also had a devastating effect on these graduates, because compared with regular medical schools, sectarian schools matriculated students with less prior education and offered less rigorous scientific curricula. Consider the fact that during the late 1920s and early 1930s, these examinations, where required, blocked the licensure of almost *three-quarters* of chiropractic graduates who dared to take them, compared to barely more than 10 percent of MDs.[48]

Another obstacle confronted by sectarian doctors was their inability to gain admitting privileges to hospitals. Regular physicians controlled these privileges and rejected most non-MDs. This exclusion became an increasing problem for the sects with Congress's passage of the Hill-Burton Act of 1946, which led to a hospital construction boom and a corresponding shift of much health care into the hospital setting. Still another challenge for the sects was orthodox doctors' widespread refusal to refer patients to sectarian practitioners. In 1957, the AMA revised its Principles of Medical Ethics to reaffirm that "a physician should practice a method of healing founded on a scientific basis; and he should not voluntarily associate professionally with anyone who violates this principle."[49]

The major unorthodox sects followed various descending paths. Eclectic and homeopathic practitioners, already aging and dwindling in number at the beginning of the period, continued to join orthodox societies, abandon dogmatism, and melt into the general population of physicians. The last eclectic medical school closed in 1939. Two homeopathic medical colleges lingered until the 1950s, but the practice of "pure" homeopathy went nearly extinct. States with independent eclectic and homeopathic licensing boards dissolved them; by the late 1950s, only Maryland's homeopathic licensing board survived. By the 1960s, both of these sects had effectively disappeared as distinct entities. In 1972, the FDA was able to identify only five homeopathic pharmacies in the entire country.[50]

All but five of the twenty-five states that had established naturopathic licensing abandoned it, and most of the nation's naturopathic schools closed. By 1968, there were only 553 naturopathic practitioners in the country. Christian Science, which had seen robust growth during the first quarter of the century, began to shrink during the 1940s and suffered a steady drop in membership thereafter. Although various factors contributed to this decline (including the expansion of professional opportunities for women, who had always constituted a disproportionate number of Christian Science practitioners), the rise of modern medicine was perhaps the most important.[51]

The two main manipulative sects, osteopathy and chiropractic, survived the Golden Age only by straying significantly from their founders' visions. Osteopathy endured by both raising its standards and diminishing its distinctiveness. From the 1930s to the 1950s, osteopathic schools dramatically increased their graduates' pass rates on licensure examinations by becoming more selective and scientifically rigorous. Meanwhile, doctors of osteopathic medicine (DOs) reduced their dependence on manipulative therapy while increasing their use of orthodox modalities. Eventually, a visit to a DO became barely distinguishable from a visit to an MD. In 1961, the AMA's judicial counsel clarified that consulting with osteopaths was fine, so long as they practiced "osteopathic medicine" rather than the "cult" of traditional osteopathy.[52]

In 1962, California legally merged osteopathy into regular medicine and converted already-granted DO degrees into MDs. Although no other state went so far as amalgamation (largely because osteopaths elsewhere wanted to maintain some level of distinctiveness), by the early 1970s, DOs were eligible for unlimited licensure to practice throughout the nation. Eventually, most people did not view osteopathic medicine as "unorthodox" at all.[53]

Chiropractic, by contrast, maintained a distinct identity, but it did so by shrinking its scope of practice. Although the vast majority of states were licensing chiropractors under separate chiropractic practice acts by 1930, the spreading use of basic science examinations threatened the sect's very existence. Many chiropractic schools closed during the Great Depression, and the sect appeared to be in its death throes. Chiropractic responded to this challenge by upgrading its schools' admissions standards and scientific rigor (although never as success-fully as the osteopaths). It also resisted the further spread of the basic science examination. Chiropractors won a major victory on this front in 1942. In a cam-paign suffused with medical freedom rhetoric, they led the successful opposition to a California initiative sponsored by the state medical society that would have mandated the examination. Other states' adoption of basic science requirements subsequently slowed and then ceased altogether by the end of the 1950s, due to chiropractic activism and regular physicians' own concerns about interstate reciprocity.[54]

Chiropractic paradoxically thrived in the late 1940s and 1950s, despite Americans' widespread devotion to orthodox medicine. The sect, however, bore diminishing resemblance to the chiropractic system conceived by Daniel David Palmer in the late 1890s—that is, an all-encompassing healing method based exclusively on manual correction of "vertebral subluxations." In the postwar era, a withering remnant of Palmerite "straight" chiropractors was dwarfed by a growing community of "mixers," who combined spinal manipulation with other drugless treatments, such as physical therapy, electrical muscle stimula-tion, and nutritional supplements. Moreover, fewer and fewer chiropractors asserted that spinal adjustment could cure organic diseases as well as musculo-skeletal disorders. Their patients increasingly visited them primarily, or exclu-sively, for treatment of back and neck problems. Only within this subspecialty did chiropractors gain widespread public acceptance.[55]

The FDA Confronts New Sects

The FDA played only a marginal role in the regulation of most of the long-standing alternative sects. The agency's jurisdiction extended to products, not to practice, and therefore drugless and device-less healing approaches were beyond its reach. The FDA occasionally brought misbranding actions against devices marketed to chiropractic "mixers," but when the agency based these actions on the assertion that licensed chiropractors were not "practitioners" under the FD&C Act, courts struck them down as invalid intrusions into state regulation of medical practice.[56]

But even during the age of faith in orthodox medical science, a few new alter-native medical philosophies emerged over which the FDA found ways to exercise power. Probably the most important of these was the "health foods movement," which gathered adherents at a slow but steady pace from the late 1940s through the late 1960s, after which it surged in popularity. Its advocates embraced all things "natural," were ambivalent about the triumphs of modern medicine, and were downright hostile to many broader technological developments. They ascribed the prevalence of chronic diseases (cancer, heart disease, arthritis) and Americans' general poor health to improper eating. Health foodists favored the consumption of natural dietary supplements and food grown through "organic farming" techniques that used natural rather than commercial fertilizers and pesticides. Conversely, they opposed processed foods, chemical food additives, synthetic vitamins, and the fluoridation of water. The health foods movement— antimodernist, anti-urban, anti-corporatist—was difficult to categorize on the conventional left-right spectrum, but during its first two decades (in contrast to the 1970s) it drew more support from extreme conservatives than from progressives.[57]

Most early followers of the health foods movement were sincere proponents of its philosophy. But some of its loudest advocates, while perhaps earnest, also had a financial stake in its success. These included supplement manufacturers and health food store owners. In the 1950s and 1960s, the FDA targeted this commercial distribution chain, seizing many products and even bringing some criminal charges, with almost uniform success in court. The agency made "Nutrition Nonsense" one of the main planks of its "anti-quackery" campaign of this period.[58]

An illustrative enforcement action against a typical marketing scheme was the successful late-1950s misbranding prosecution of Victor Earl Irons, the founder of one the country's largest supplement manufacturers. The V. E. Irons company sold products such as Vit-Ra-Tox 21A (raw veal bone, defatted wheat germ, and concentrate of green cereal juices) and Vit-Ra-Tox 21B (garlic derivative, wheat germ, and lecithin). The company disseminated leaflets and newsletters claiming that these products treated or prevented specific diseases, while also laying out the health foods movement's broader doctrines regarding soil depletion, the nutritional deficiency epidemic, and the dangers of processed foods. The government successfully argued that the disease claims in this literature rendered the products illegal misbranded drugs, and Irons himself went to prison.[59]

Another new movement that the FDA confronted during this period was the Church of Scientology.[60] It originated with Dianetics, a secular mental health method devised by science fiction writer L. Ron Hubbard in the early 1950s. Several years later, Hubbard founded the Church, which placed Dianetics' doctrines within a more comprehensive religious belief system. Like its secular predecessor, Scientology used (and still uses) a process called "auditing" to clear the mind of painful memories, known as "engrams," and thus improve emotional, mental, and physical health.

The jurisdictional hook for the FDA was the auditing process's use of a machine called the E-Meter—a skin galvanometer—to identify the presence of engrams in the auditee. The Church sold E-Meters to its trained auditors. The FDA installed an undercover agent within the "Founding Church of Scientology" (formerly Hubbard's house) on Dupont Circle in Washington, DC. Based on the information the agent collected, the agency determined that the E-Meter was a medical device. In 1963, the government raided the building and seized a hundred of the machines along with literature it considered to be "labeling."

By this time, the notion of a right to freedom of therapeutic choice was so deflated that Scientology did not even advance it in court. Instead, Scientology disclaimed any intent to diagnose or treat disease and asserted that its goal was to treat the "spirit." It characterized the seizure as an act of religious persecution that violated the First Amendment. Although the district court initially ruled in favor of the government and issued a decree of condemnation and destruction of the E-Meters, the US Court of Appeals for the District of Columbia handed Scientology a temporary victory by ruling that "literature setting forth religious doctrines . . . cannot be subjected to courtroom evaluation and therefore cannot be considered 'labeling' of [the E-Meter] for purposes of the 'false or misleading' provisions of the Act."[61]

On retrial, US District Court Judge Gerhard Gesell determined that the bulk of the literature was "replete with false medical and scientific claims devoid of any religious overlay or reference." He thus condemned the E-Meters, in an opinion dripping with contempt for Scientology (a "religious cult" founded by a "facile, prolific author" trafficking in "quackery"). Gesell ordered the church to either destroy the devices or bring them into compliance with the FD&C Act by prominently warning that their use was permitted only as part of religious activity and that they were "not medically or scientifically capable of improving the health or bodily functions of anyone." The DC Circuit tweaked, but basically upheld, Gesell's order, and to this day both E-Meters and their accompanying literature include a warning that the device "is not medically or scientifically useful for the diagnosis, treatment, or prevention of any disease."[62]

The FDA Battles Quack Drugs and Devices

Much of the FDA's mid-century crusade against "medical quackery" was directed at drugs and devices not authentically connected to any particular medical sect or philosophy. The purveyors of such products—for example, Harry Hoxsey—sometimes managed to create quasi-movements that bore some resemblance to traditional medical sects. They had organized bands of supporters. They employed the same language of medical freedom that American sectarians had cultivated over two centuries. They often sold their wares to osteopaths, chiropractors, and naturopaths, and some even boasted of degrees from these sects' schools. Nevertheless, in contrast to medical sectarians, the sponsors of these quack drugs and devices generally exuded an odor of crass commercialism, promoted specific products rather than broader medical philosophies, and used scientific jargon and endorsements from conventionally credentialed experts to exploit the public's faith in orthodox medicine.

Consider, for instance, the quack medical device market. American medical device quackery is as old as the country, and sellers of fraudulent contraptions have never missed an opportunity to take advantage of the population's faith in emerging technologies—from electricity and radio waves to radar and television. During the first half of the twentieth century, electromagnetic gadgets sold directly to practitioners came to dominate this market. Albert Abrams, a German immigrant physician, became magnificently wealthy during the 1910s and 1920s peddling diagnostic and therapeutic devices based on a concept called the "Electronic Reactions of Abrams" (ERA). Though the AMA and *Scientific American* debunked Abrams and his "radionics" techniques, he spawned multiple postwar descendants. The most prominent of these was Fred J. Hart (1888–1975), a farmer and radio station owner with no scientific background. In 1946, he became president of the Electronic Medical Foundation, an organization founded by Abrams. Practitioners—primarily "mixer" chiropractors—would send a blood sample to the foundation for diagnosis by a worthless "Radioscope" and then treat the patient with one of thirteen equally worthless devices purchased from the foundation.[63]

During the 1950s and 1960s, the FDA devoted significant time and resources to combating such products, using the authority it had obtained over medical devices in the 1938 FD&C Act. The FDA won virtually every misbranding enforcement action it brought against quack devices during this period. It had little trouble persuading judges and juries that the contraptions at issue were useless products sold by profit-mongering charlatans. Fred Hart did not even put up a fight when the government sought an injunction against his devices in 1954; he entered into a consent decree declaring them illegal and then dissolved the Electronic Medical Foundation. Perhaps Hart was simply ready to start the next phase of his career; in 1955, he founded the National Health Federation, which would be the country's most influential medical freedom advocacy group for the next three decades.[64]

Another major category of unorthodox medical products targeted by the FDA during medicine's Golden Age was alternative cancer drugs. We have already examined the rise and fall of the Hoxsey cure. Another blockbuster quack cancer cure to emerge during this period was Glyoxylide, a quasi-homeopathic drug "discovered" by physician William F. Koch and distributed widely during the late 1930s and early 1940s. The US government's battle against the Koch drug was a dress rehearsal for the Hoxsey conflict a decade later, with far-right politicians and religious figures (including Gerald Winrod) defending Glyoxylide users against "treacherous" government officials and the "Jewish-controlled" AMA.[65]

Krebiozen, which we will consider in detail at the end of this chapter, was yet another hugely popular alternative cancer cure, with a heyday in the 1950s and early 1960s.

The popularity of alternative cancer cures during this era can be ascribed not only to the special dread that cancer caused, but also to regular medicine's agonizingly slow progress in taming the disease. This was not for lack of effort. Following World War II, cancer researchers and practicing oncologists made advancements in early diagnosis, surgical intervention, and radiation therapy. The 1960s saw the dramatic introduction of effective chemotherapy against Hodgkin's disease and childhood leukemia. Nonetheless, orthodox medicine remained largely perplexed about cancer's causes and mechanisms, let alone its treatment. When surgery, radiation, and chemotherapy failed, many cancer victims were willing to try almost anything, Moreover, some cancer patients— like the early nineteenth-century opponents of "heroic medicine"—weighed the pain, disfigurement, and debility caused by conventional treatments against their uncertain benefit and decided to eschew them entirely and opt instead for less enervating unorthodox approaches.[66]

Although the purveyors of these cancer remedies enthusiastically accepted the support of alternative medical practitioners, they did not usually claim to represent an alternative medical sect. Instead, they tended to embrace the discourse and authority of orthodox medicine. Koch, for example, emphasized his own background as a PhD chemist, MD, and medical school professor. As we will see, Krebiozen's most prominent champion was Dr. Andrew C. Ivy, a highly respected physiologist.

Right-Wing Medical Freedom Advocacy

In the late 1940s and 1950s, American politics and culture were consumed by the country's rivalry with the Soviet Union overseas and a Red Scare at home. Demagogic Wisconsin senator Joseph McCarthy and the House Un-American Activities Committee conducted fanatical hunts for communist conspiracies throughout American government and society. As historian Richard Hofstadter observed in "The Paranoid Style in American Politics," the right wing believed that treasonous communist operatives (including some at the highest level of government) controlled the entire American establishment and that leftist "cosmopolitans" and intellectuals were undermining American ideals.[67]

During this period, medical liberty activism was closely associated with this most reactionary segment of American society. Although conspiracy mongering was already a well-established aspect of American health freedom rhetoric, mid-century militants added allegations of communist and Jewish plots to the more traditional rants against the orthodox medical monopoly. We have already met Harry Hoxsey's reactionary champion, Gerald Winrod. Another prominent figure in these circles was Lawrence P. Reilly, one of the Koch cancer treatment's leading boosters. Reilly was an anti-Semitic, racist, isolationist Lutheran minister and the publisher of an anti-communist monthly, *The Eleventh Hour*. The American Rally for Peace, Abundance, and the Constitution, a far-right organization founded in 1952, fulminated against fluoridation and the polio vaccine. In 1956, it nominated William Langer, a right-wing senator from North Dakota, for US president and Harry Hoxsey (!) for vice president.[68]

Then there was the California radionics device magnate Fred Hart. In January 1955, soon after the FDA put him out of business, he incorporated the National Health Federation (NHF) and established its headquarters in San Francisco. In April, the organization released the first issue of the *National Health Federation Bulletin*, which would quickly become the nation's leading platform for medical freedom advocacy. (It is still published today, under the name *Health Freedom News*.) Hart's own political views before he founded the NHF were somewhat muddled. He seemed to combine cooperative rural progressivism with limited-government, anti-tax conservatism. He ran as a Republican in an unsuccessful race for the US House of Representatives in 1944. He was himself an evangelical Baptist pastor, although at that time this description did not necessarily equate with "conservative."[69]

In any event, as editor of the *NHF Bulletin*, Hart did not hesitate to use hysterical right-wing rhetoric. During its first four years of publication, through 1958, the *Bulletin* raised the specter of communism frequently, warning its readers of the "Red Octopus deeply rooted and well established . . . in the Government Health Agencies." One issue reproduced Winrod's vituperative letter to FDA Commissioner Larrick, along with an editorial by Hart describing the letter as "a masterpiece" and vilifying the FDA as "a ruthless enemy, as tiranical [sic] in its actions as any Russian bureaucrat." The *Bulletin* also republished an article from the reactionary *Capsule News* titled "America Wake Up," which described the imprisonment of two health food company executives as "the U.S. government's blackest day of infamy since Franklin Roosevelt engineered the slaughter of 3,000 Americans at Pearl Harbor." This piece contended that the "House of Rockefeller owns the drug, food, milk, serum, money, news and other trusts . . . [and] the Eisenhower Administration." It also gratuitously condemned the US Supreme Court for overturning the conviction of a "Negro rapist" on "technicalities" and "turning him loose on society."[70]

The NHF was motivated by commercial interests as well as ideological ones.[71] The initial Board of Governors included, in addition to Hart (the president), health foods magnates V. E. Irons and Royal Lee. But the distinction between profits and politics was blurry in this realm. For example, the board also included

John Minder of the Christian Medical Research League, a nonprofit corporation established by conservative pastors in the late 1940s to manufacture and sell Koch's medicines. The league worked intimately with both Winrod and Reilly.[72]

The NHF's Medical Freedom Philosophy and Agenda

Along with right-wing tirades emblematic of the height of the Cold War, however, the early volumes of the *NHF Bulletin* also included much rhetoric consistent with the two centuries of American medical freedom literature that preceded it. The NHF's "Program," published in the first volume of the *Bulletin*, included:

> 5. Do whatever is necessary to guarantee freedom for every individual to select the doctor or religious practitioner of his choice . . . and to oppose all laws, rules, and regulations which would deny individuals of this freedom.

> 6. Oppose all existing and proposed laws, rules and regulations which deny responsible individuals the right to accept or reject any form of medication, treatment, or procedure which affects his body. . . .

> 9. Have introduced into the Senate . . . a resolution calling upon the Senate Judiciary Committee to make an investigation . . . to determine if organized medicine and other groups have created a monopoly . . . and to determine if agencies of the Federal Government have contributed to such a monopoly if it exists.[73]

This mission statement combined the traditional religious, bodily integrity, and anti-monopoly strains of freedom of therapeutic choice rhetoric that we have traced throughout this book. Elsewhere, contributors to the *Bulletin* advanced the freedom of inquiry strain. One article, for instance, opposed laws that would "mean the end of the future Pasteurs and the slow decay of medical progress."[74]

Like prior health freedom publications, the *Bulletin* stressed how government regulation of medicine violated fundamental American principles. Every cover of the publication included the slogan "Americans Crusading for Health Liberty," accompanied by patriotic graphics of the Statute of Liberty and the Liberty Bell. Fred Hart (with an unfortunate enthusiasm for italics) expressly granted medical freedom quasi-constitutional status:

> The Constitution of the United States guarantees *Freedom of Speech*, *Freedom of the Press*, and *Freedom of Religion*. It implies *Freedom of Health*! But *we are*

losing this latter freedom. Bureaucratic regulations and medical monopolies are rapidly depriving Americans of their *Freedom* in all matters relating to *Health*.[75]

The *Bulletin* also revived the fabricated Benjamin Rush quote calling for a "health freedom" amendment to the US Constitution.[76]

Along with general paeans to liberty, the NHF strongly emphasized the anti-monopoly theme. One author argued: "Both Communism and monopoly are essentially opposed to capitalism. Both eventually deprive free men of their freedom. They are both un-American."

As in the Progressive Era, the AMA was the chief target of these arguments, but the increasingly powerful pharmaceutical industry now served as a co-villain. Hart denounced "the medical monopoly-drug trust combination which seeks to destroy your and my freedoms in all matters even remotely related to health. They would completely subjugate the American people to their dictates and crush all competitive systems and thoughts." Contributors to the *Bulletin* frequently alleged collusion between these private interests and the government—especially the FDA, which was both a "promoter" and "tool" of the Medical Monopoly.[77]

In the latter part of the 1950s, the *Bulletin* addressed a smorgasbord of issues of concern to medical freedom activists: the federal government's suppression of the Hoxsey treatment, Krebiozen, and natural supplements; the rights of chiropractors and naturopaths; the evils of fluoridation and of the Salk polio vaccine. Although the publication did not favor one alternative medical system over another, it was particularly loyal to the health foods movement.

During this period, the NHF conducted its first two major lobbying campaigns. The first was an attempt to secure a congressional investigation of the FDA and "its relationship with the A.M.A. and the Drug Trust." The organization unconvincingly claimed victory on this front in 1957, when the House Committee on Interstate and Foreign Commerce launched a broad review of "the execution of the laws" by all the agencies within its jurisdiction, which happened to include the FDA.[78]

The NHF's second major legislative initiative was its fight against the previously mentioned California cancer quackery law. The legislation, first introduced in 1957 and backed by the American Cancer Society and the California Medical Association, created a state board with the power to investigate anti-cancer drugs and devices and to issue cease-and-desist orders against useless products. The 1957 bill was sponsored by Caspar W. Weinberger, an assemblyman from San Francisco (and later a cabinet secretary under Presidents Nixon, Ford, and Reagan). The NHF led the opposition to the measure. It organized a letter-writing campaign, and Weinberger received stacks of mail containing sentiments such as "I hope you too get cancer" and "Your bill is un-American, dictatorial, and socialistic." Hart testified against the bill at a hearing in the California Assembly.

The assembly passed the bill nonetheless, but Hart's forces managed to derail it in a senate committee.[79]

This victory was only temporary. In 1959, despite the NHF's equally energetic lobbying efforts, the California Legislature easily passed a similar bill. The Cancer Law created a Cancer Advisory Council to investigate purported remedies. The NHF claimed partial success because it persuaded legislators to deny any enforcement powers to the Council itself; instead, the body was required to make recommendations to the State Board of Health, which could then outlaw the products in question and issue cease-and-desist orders. Nevertheless, the law's passage was a devastating defeat for the NHF. Pursuant to its procedures, the Board of Health outlawed six products in its first five years of existence, including Koch's and Hoxsey's cures.[80]

The California Cancer Law's enactment demonstrates the limits of the NHF's power during the peak of orthodox medicine's reign at the end of the 1950s. Despite having 10,000 members, thirty-eight local chapters, a Washington, DC, office, and regular invitations to testify at congressional hearings, it was unable to prevent a statute utterly antithetical to its stated mission from passing in its home state.[81]

The 1960s: Krebiozen Activism in a Time of Transition

On March 28, 1966, about fifty demonstrators occupied the foyer outside FDA Commissioner James L. Goddard's office. They refused to leave until they were given an opportunity to meet with the commissioner to demand access to the cancer drug Krebiozen. The group was led by Mrs. Laine Friedman of New York City, the founder of Cancer Survivors for Krebiozen. In 1963, despite this group's tireless activism, the FDA had banned Krebiozen as an unapproved new drug pursuant to the 1962 Drug Amendments. Months later, Laine had lost her beloved husband, George, to abdominal cancer. She was convinced that Krebiozen had extended his life by two precious years.[82]

An FDA representative informed the protestors that Goddard was not available. They stubbornly held their ground. When some of them refused to leave at the end of the workday, police arrived to clear the area. To the accompaniment of furious shouts, the police wrestled Max Rosenthal and Irving Lieberman out of the foyer (Fig. 5.2). They then carried away an unidentified matronly woman while she remained seated stolidly in her chair. Following the episode, an FDA official defended the agency's stance, saying that he would have told the demonstrators that "Krebiozen was not doing them any good."[83]

Krebiozen was introduced to the United States in 1949 by a mysterious Yugoslavian refugee doctor, Stevan Durovic. It was a whitish powder that

Figure 5.2 Laine Friedman demands access to Krebiozen outside FDA Commissioner James L. Goddard's office while police remove fellow demonstrator Max Rosenthal, March 28, 1966. © *Charles Tasnadi/AP Images*

Durovic said he derived from the blood serum of horses inoculated with the bacterium that causes "lumpy jaw" in cattle. He claimed that he had successfully treated cancer in cats and dogs with this "substance X." In the early 1950s, Durovic brought it to Andrew C. Ivy, an internationally renowned physiologist, a vice president at the University of Illinois, and the executive director of the National Advisory Council of the National Cancer Institute. Astonishingly, Durovic persuaded Ivy to perform a clinical trial on the drug without even confirming its contents. At a dramatic March 1951 press conference at Chicago's Drake Hotel, Ivy announced that his study, performed on twenty-two patients with advanced cancer, had been remarkably successful.[84]

Thus began the strange tale of Krebiozen, "the most publicized unorthodox cancer treatment in the whole span of American history" up to that time.[85] Seven months after the press conference, the AMA announced that a nationwide study of the drug in one hundred cancer patients had determined that Krebiozen had no beneficial effect.[86] Ivy was temporarily suspended from the Chicago Medical Society and forced to take a two-year leave from the university. In 1953, reactionary Senator William Langer introduced into the *Congressional Record* a report by a senate investigator declaring that Krebiozen was "one of the most promising materials yet isolated for the management of cancer." This report concluded that there appeared to be a "conspiracy of alarming proportions" involving the AMA to suppress research on the drug.[87]

As the 1950s progressed, Krebiozen was discussed favorably in multiple *NHF Bulletin* articles and in a book published by the same small house that had published L. Ron Hubbard's *Dianetics*. In 1956, the Henry Regnery Company, a conservative publisher, distributed a report by Ivy contending that further research demonstrated that Krebiozen had a palliative (though not necessarily curative) effect on cancer. Around 1958, the Krebiozen Research Foundation (founded by Durovic and his brother, with Ivy as president) commenced a years-long campaign to persuade the American Cancer Society or the National Cancer Institute to perform a double-blind test on Krebiozen. This effort failed because the foundation and Ivy demanded unacceptable terms for the study and failed to provide requested data. By 1962, over four thousand patients had been treated with the unproven drug.[88]

For years, despite Krebiozen's lack of an effective NDA, its backers had gotten away with distributing the drug by designating it an experimental product. The 1962 Drug Amendments dramatically changed the rules of the game. The exemption to the NDA requirement for experimental drugs was now heavily regulated; sponsors were required to submit an investigational new drug application (IND) setting forth detailed information regarding the drug and the proposed clinical testing, and the FDA could disallow any proposed study on scientific, human safety, or ethical grounds.[89]

In January 1963, the FDA declared that Krebiozen's makers had until June 7 to submit an IND. This announcement triggered the first round of protests by Laine Friedman and her comrades; they staged a "march on Congress" and held a Capitol Hill meeting hosted by Senator Paul Douglas of Illinois, a longtime ally. In early June, as the deadline loomed, Friedman and a dozen others picketed the White House with signs such as "Don't Let FDA Ban Our Life." The *Washington Post* published a photograph of Friedman being arrested for "incommoding the sidewalk" and a large advertisement by the "Massachusetts Emergency Anti-Cancer Committee" demanding that the president and Congress "uphold the Constitution which guarantees to each of the cancer victims the right to their lives."[90]

Durovic submitted an IND for Krebiozen at the last possible minute, but he quickly withdrew it after the FDA pointed to manufacturing irregularities and accused him of selling diluted doses. On July 14, 1963, the FDA announced that interstate distribution of Krebiozen was henceforth illegal. Senator Douglas's efforts to delay enforcement of this order pending additional testing by the National Cancer Institute foundered in the face of two events that fall. First, Alma Levan Hayden, a pioneering African American chemist at the FDA, determined that Krebiozen was merely creatine, a common amino acid naturally present in the human body, available from everyday foods, and sold by commercial laboratories for pennies per ounce. Soon afterward, an expert committee retained by the government determined (based on its examination of patient records provided by Durovic and Ivy themselves) that Krebiozen was entirely useless. In October 1963, the NCI declared that Krebiozen did not merit further testing: "From a scientific standpoint, we regard the case as closed."[91]

Still, the drug's supporters persisted. In February 1964, about 1,500 of them attended a rally at the Unitarian-Universalist Community Church in New York City. Drs. Ivy and Durovic addressed the crowd. Laine Friedman, recently widowed, was applauded repeatedly as she declared her commitment to continue the struggle. The following week, Krebiozen advocates picketed the American Cancer Society, carrying signs asserting that the organization "restricts freedom of medical choice." Demonstrations at the White House and the Department of Health Education and Welfare followed.[92]

Krebiozen supporters briefly tasted triumph in January 1966, when a Chicago jury acquitted Durovic and Ivy following a nine-month criminal trial alleging fraud and FD&C Act violations. Advocates of the drug swarmed the defendants in celebration at the courthouse following their acquittals.[93] Nonetheless, Krebiozen's reign as the nation's leading quack cancer cure was nearing an end. The March 1966 protest at the FDA described earlier was the last Krebiozen demonstration covered by the major media.

The Krebiozen crusade of the 1960s was not simply a continuation of 1950s right-wing medical freedom activism. Compared to the earlier campaigns in favor of Koch's Glyoxylide, Hoxsey's cure, and even Krebiozen itself, it was larger, more bipartisan, and more mainstream. Laine Friedman would *not* have broken bread with Gerald Winrod, the reactionary anti-Semitic minister. She was a Jewish immigrant from England, a supporter of the anti-fascist Abraham Lincoln Brigade in the Spanish Civil War, a civil rights activist, and advocate for national health insurance. Woody Guthrie and Pete Seeger, troubadours of the left, sang at her wedding to George. And Senator Paul Douglas was a liberal civil rights advocate who shared little in common with the reactionary populist William Langer, who died in 1959. In contrast to Senator Langer's lone-wolf legislative efforts on behalf of quack cancer medicines, Douglas's exertions in favor of Krebiozen attracted substantial support from colleagues of both parties.[94]

Medical historian Keith Wailoo has observed, "The Krebiozen controversy resonated with the antiestablishment sentiments of the time. . . . Medical paternalism, deference to scientific expertise, and unquestioning trust in government authority . . . were being undermined in the sixties." That said, Americans' trust in establishment institutions remained extraordinarily high in 1966, just before it plunged precipitously. Krebiozen activism was thus more a harbinger than an example of 1960s and 1970s antiauthoritarianism. Though suspicious of the medical establishment's motives, Krebiozen supporters remained wedded to the promise and ideals of modern medical science, as demonstrated by their reverential embrace of Andrew Ivy and their demand for government-run controlled trials. And they were hardly hippies. As Wailoo himself observes, "The Krebiozen movement had a middle-class appeal. . . . Housewives, U.S. Senators, and other elected officials of many stripes counted themselves among the legion of supporters who were frustrated with medical orthodoxy's refusal to endorse the drug."[95]

Despite its initial embrace of far-right ideology, the National Health Federation also became politically ambiguous by the 1960s. Alongside its health libertarianism, the organization started voicing positions that aligned it with Ralph Nader. In congressional testimony, it endorsed the 1958 law that gave the FDA premarket approval authority over food additives and banned carcinogenic additives. In hearings on the 1962 Drug Amendments, the NHF introduced and lobbied for the requirement that patients in any FDA-authorized drug investigation be provided with informed consent. In the pages of the *Bulletin*, the NHF supported mandatory health warnings on cigarettes, backed the "fight against smog," and lauded environmentalist Rachel Carson's "great book" *Silent Spring*.[96]

Then, in the early 1970s, the NHF latched on to two issues that transcended political categories and brought the organization to its peak of influence: vitamin pills and a purported cancer remedy derived from apricot pits called Laetrile.

6

The Spirit of the '70s

Vitamins, Yogurt, and Apricot Pits

During November 1973, the front-page headlines of the daily *San Francisco Examiner* were dominated by the Watergate scandal ("The President: I'm not a Crook"), the aftermath of the Yom Kippur War ("Egypt, Israel OK peace plan"), and the oil embargo that Arab nations imposed in the wake of that conflict ("The wild rush to buy gas cans"). The newspaper also contained numerous stories about the era's civil rights struggles: women's liberation, gay liberation, school desegregation, and Cesar Chavez's fight for the rights of Mexican American farmworkers. And on November 21, the *Examiner* reported that the English rock band The Who opened their national tour at the Cow Palace in Daly City, just south of San Francisco, and finished their "unglued, unmusical, and unimpressive" set with a drummer recruited from the audience to replace Keith Moon, who passed out after consuming a handful of horse tranquilizers with a brandy chaser.[1]

A couple of weeks earlier, the *Examiner* had covered a very different sort of event held at the Cow Palace: a "Health Freedom Rally." This gathering protested a series of August 1973 FDA final rules that toughened the regulation of vitamin and mineral supplements. One rule severely restricted the combinations and amounts of nutrients available in these products. Two others classified all high-dose vitamin and mineral supplements as drugs and all high-dose vitamin A and vitamin D products as *prescription* drugs. An ad hoc committee called Consumers for Health Freedom, made up primarily of health food store owners, organized the rally. They were trying to drum up support for federal legislation (the "Hosmer Bill") that would effectively overturn these regulations.[2]

The FDA rules were bound to be controversial in a country in which more than half of people regularly took vitamins or other dietary supplements. For millions of Americans, vitamin supplements were *the* symbol of the flourishing health food movement. Many people consumed them to replace the nutrients they believed had been stripped from the conventional food supply by chemical-loving agribusiness and food processors. Others embraced megavitamin therapy for the prevention and treatment of disease—a theory championed, most famously, by Linus Pauling, the Nobel Prize winner for chemistry in 1954.

Choose Your Medicine. Lewis A. Grossman, Oxford University Press. © Lewis A. Grossman 2021.
DOI: 10.1093/oso/9780190612757.003.0007

Three-quarters of Americans in 1972 believed that taking vitamins would help them achieve "super health," both physical and mental.[3]

A November 8 advertisement for the rally published in the *Examiner* trumpeted: "FDA restrictions can hurt every American concerned about his Health and Nutrition. . . . You Can Fight Back!" Three days later, about 3,000 health food enthusiasts from all over Northern California poured into the Cow Palace. Although the crowd likely comprised the entire political spectrum, left-leaning activists apparently predominated. The health food movement, despite its predominantly right-wing roots in the 1950s, had taken a strikingly progressive turn in the late 1960s and early 1970s, drawing support from the New Left, the counterculture, and the burgeoning environmental movement.[4]

The identity of most of the "top entertainers, political leaders, health authorities and athletes" who participated in the Health Freedom Rally is lost to history. One was a progressive US Representative from California, Leo Ryan, who five years later would be tragically gunned down on an airstrip in Guyana by members of Jim Jones's People's Temple cult. Ryan snarled into the microphone, "Where does the FDA come off telling people what they can eat?" The cavalcade of stars also included "Gypsy Boots," a sixty-ish health food enthusiast and entrepreneur who used to appear regularly on NBC's "Steve Allen Show" whipping up fruit "smoothies"—a term he coined. The long-haired, bearded proto-hippie had been pursuing and advocating a back-to-nature lifestyle since the 1940s. At the Cow Palace, Boots flung a football over 50 yards, ascribed his athletic prowess to vitamin supplements, and then led the crowd in chants of "Watergate and the FDA operate in the very same way."[5]

Meanwhile, in Washington, DC, health freedom forces were taking their fight directly to the federal government. The National Health Federation (NHF), which we encountered last chapter, was at the heart of this activity. The California-based organization's credo was "the absolute right of the people to enjoy the civil liberty of freedom of choice in matters of personal health care." The NHF now claimed 20,000 members. Although its membership included representatives of the pharmaceutical, dietary supplement, and health foods industries, it asserted that the vast majority were "average citizens having no ties with any health related industry or profession." Even the AMA, which condemned the NHF as a "rallying point for purveyors of food-faddist products . . . and promoters of questionable and fraudulent medical products and treatments," acknowledged that most of the federation's members were "undoubtedly sincere in espousing the dubious or mistaken health notions they have been taught."[6]

After California Republican Congressman Craig Hosmer introduced his vitamin deregulation bill in January 1973, the NHF's Washington, DC, office immediately began championing it. The *NHF Bulletin* urged its readers to write to their representatives in support of the legislation. The letter-writing campaign soon took on a life of its own. By the beginning of 1974, Congress had received over one million letters from vitamin enthusiasts. Vitamin deregulation was one of the four issues that generated the most mail to Congress in 1973—along with Watergate, the energy crisis, and the foundering economy.[7]

Due in part to NHF's efforts, a bipartisan parade of almost 220 representatives lined up to cosponsor Hosmer's bill. They included everyone from archconservative Republican Steve Symms of Idaho to liberal feminist Democrat Bella Abzug of New York. James K. Kilpatrick and Nicholas von Hoffman—the representatives of the right and left, respectively, in the popular "Point-Counterpoint" segment on CBS's *60 Minutes*—*both* wrote columns excoriating the FDA vitamin regulations.[8]

The week before the October 1973 House subcommittee hearing on the Hosmer bill, a group picketed the FDA offices in Washington, chanting "A and D for you and me. Let me be free with Vitamin C." At the hearing itself, supporters of the bill packed the room, wearing buttons protesting "Nutritional Tyranny." Republican William Broomfield of Michigan opined: "It seems to me that privacy and free choice is already at a minimum in this era of big government without the Food and Drug Administration getting into the act, too." Democrat B. F. Sisk of California stated: "It has become clear to me through countless letters from my constituents that the public disagrees with the FDA and wants to keep its right to free choice in matters such as this. And I concur."[9]

Senator William Proxmire, a Wisconsin Democrat, introduced a similar bill in the Senate in December 1973. His diverse collection of ten cosponsors ranged from Republicans Barry Goldwater and Strom Thurmond to Democrats Hubert Humphrey and George McGovern. In August 1974, a Senate subcommittee held a hearing on Proxmire's bill. The most ideologically robust (though economically motivated) testimony was offered by David King, a former congressman and the legislative counsel for a health food industry trade group. King voiced numerous themes that have characterized medical freedom rhetoric throughout American history. Freedom of choice. ("The American concept is that consumers must not only be free to choose, but free to have that choice uninfluenced by government interference.") Economic freedom. ("I willingly concede that in a free market some consumers will be disappointed, but how can we have it otherwise and still keep our market free?") Freedom of inquiry. ("It is always possible that even the FDA might learn something from the millions of sufferers who are willing to try out various nutritional remedies on themselves. . . . Would it not be better to adopt a policy designed to encourage rather than to discourage the inflow of more knowledge?") The indeterminacy of medical science. ("Health and nutrition are so subjective. Knowledge is so fragmentary.")[10]

Coincidentally, the week before this hearing, the US Court of Appeals for the Second Circuit—in a case brought by NHF, industry groups, and manufacturers—had struck down some of the FDA's vitamin regulations and stayed the enforcement of some others. This decision made the need for congressional intervention somewhat less urgent. Two years later, Congress invalidated what remained of the FDA's rules by enacting Proxmire's bill, now known as the Vitamin-Mineral Amendments of 1976. These amendments added section 411 of the FD&C Act, which to this day virtually eliminates the agency's power to regulate the potency and composition of vitamin-mineral supplement products. The legislation passed the House of Representatives without a dissenting vote and passed the Senate by voice vote.[11]

The 1970s vitamin wars showed that the American movement for freedom of therapeutic choice had changed dramatically since the 1950s. Once largely the domain of right-wing extremists, it was now both bipartisan and mainstream. As we will see, this transformation reflected changes that the 1970s brought to American society as a whole.

The Loss of Trust

In the late 1960s and 1970s, the United States experienced wide-ranging cultural shifts, including a loss of trust in establishment institutions and a heightened demand for rights against these institutions. Though these developments seemed revolutionary to many Americans at the time, they actually represented the restoration of an antiauthoritarian mindset that was extremely prominent in the United States from its founding through the first decades of the twentieth century.

It is hardly surprising that during this time there was a dramatic disintegration of public trust in America's dominant institutions and the politicians, professionals, and experts who ran them. After all, the era was marked by the Vietnam War debacle, racial strife, the Watergate scandal, an energy crisis, and a stagnated economy. Whereas in 1964, 76 percent of poll respondents said "you can trust the government in Washington to do what is right" either "most of the time" or "just about always," by 1980 only 25 percent answered this way. Americans' trust in the people running large corporations, the military, and education plummeted similarly during this period. Although confidence in these institutions has waxed and waned a bit over the past four decades, it has never come anywhere near its mid-1960s peak.[12]

Medicine and science were not immune to this phenomenon. The number of respondents expressing a "great deal of confidence" in the leaders of medicine plunged from 73 percent in 1966 to 30 percent by 1979. The proportion of Americans voicing "a great deal of confidence" in the leaders of the scientific community plunged from 56 percent to 32 percent just between 1966 and

1971. In 1972, only three years after the triumphal landing of Apollo 11, NASA shuttered its lunar program in the face of public apathy and budgetary cutbacks.[13]

Various highly publicized episodes helped depress Americans' faith in science and medicine. Following the closing of the Apollo program, the space agency stayed in the news by promoting the arrival of Comet Kohoutek in late 1973, a spectacle it promised to be "50 times brighter than the Halley comet." Instead, Kohoutek turned out to be a dim "celestial box office dud," leading one stargazer to grumble: "Watergate, then the energy crisis, and now the comet." In 1979, the terrifying partial meltdown of the Three Mile Island nuclear reactor outside of Harrisburg, Pennsylvania, vaporized hope that nuclear technology would provide a clean, safe, and limitless alternative source of energy.[14]

In the world of medicine, the decade's most confidence-crushing event was an immunization episode starkly different from the triumphant rollout of the Salk polio vaccine in the 1950s. In March 1976, President Gerald Ford, fearing the emergence of a devastating swine flu pandemic, committed the national government to vaccinating most of the American population. Top immunological experts (including Salk), the head of the AMA, and the entire federal health bureaucracy endorsed this effort. That fall, more than 40 million citizens dutifully rolled up their sleeves and received their shots. No swine flu epidemic materialized, however, and twenty-three people died from Guillain-Barré syndrome, a neurological disorder apparently triggered by the vaccination. The humiliated Ford administration abandoned the immunization campaign in December. Liberal columnist Nicholas von Hoffman assigned blame for the fiasco "to that portion of the medical profession who have lost whatever claims they ever had to be called scientists, and to the structure of American medicine in which rank, prestige, institutional sphere of influence, intellectual lockjaw and pride in poor performance . . . saw to it that . . . the inoculation program would go forward."[15]

The swine flu debacle reinforced an already-evident deterioration of the country's trust in medical experts.[16] In his unlikely 1974 bestseller *Medical Nemesis*, Croatian-Austrian philosopher Ivan Illich declared, "A crisis of confidence in modern medicine is upon us." This book was just one of the era's numerous nonfiction publications challenging the arrogance, avarice, and biological reductionism of the medical establishment and questioning the safety, effectiveness, and humaneness of conventional medical practice. They included *The Therapeutic Nightmare* (1965), *The End of Medicine* (1975), and *Doing Better and Feeling Worse* (1977). In *Coma*, the top-selling thriller of 1977, an elite Boston hospital intentionally induced brain death in surgical patients, stored their comatose bodies in a creepy high-tech facility, and harvested and sold their organs. These publications both reflected and accelerated the crumbling of Americans' mid-century faith in the medical profession, scientific medicine, and "wonder drugs."[17]

The Turn to Alternatives

The 1970s crisis of confidence in orthodox medicine was accompanied, un-surprisingly, by a turn to unorthodox medical philosophies, practitioners, and remedies. The signature new medical credo of the 1970s was "holism." Its proponents, heavily influenced by Asian medical approaches, reacted against the deficiencies of Western mainstream medicine. They emphasized the inextricable link between physical, mental, and spiritual health; strove for the "wellness" of the whole person rather than specific body parts; viewed patients as active participants in their own care; embraced the healing power of nature; and pro-moted daily "right living" through, for example, diet and meditation.

Vitamin therapy was far from the only type of alternative medicine that surged in popularity in the 1970s. A wide variety of additional healing methods took their place under the "holistic medicine" umbrella and gained count-less adherents. These included both long-standing modalities like herbal med-icine, homeopathy, and naturopathy, and methods previously unfamiliar to Americans, such as acupuncture, shiatsu, Rolfing, and visualization. In a 1979 poll, a majority of respondents opined that "for most illnesses and conditions there are alternative treatments available, varying in risk and cost, which often are equally effective" as those recommended by doctors. Around this time, many Americans (even some physicians) started using the term "alternative medicine" to describe practices they once would have scorned as "quackery."[18]

In particular, the 1970s saw a remarkable resurgence of medical approaches based on the healing power of spiritual or divine forces. Holistic medicine's em-phasis on the link between psychological states and health often blurred into more metaphysical worldviews regarding the inseparability of spirit and matter. We saw how a variety of late nineteenth-century sects (osteopathy, chiropractic, New Thought, Christian Science) were premised on the existence of unseen, im-material forces. Due in part to the influence of Eastern religions, this approach to medical treatment returned in the 1970s. Millions of Americans embraced metaphysically oriented and even paranormal healing systems, including ther-apeutic touch, Tai Chi, Yoga, acupuncture, psychic healing, and crystal therapy. By the late 1970s, a new term had emerged to encompass this wide variety of spirituality-infused approaches: New Age medicine.[19]

There have always been links between organized religious creeds and alter-native healing systems in America. Beyond the obvious example of Christian Science, consider the Mormons' attraction to Thomsonianism in the nine-teenth century and evangelical Christians' ardent embrace of Hoxsey's cure in the 1950s. New Age medicine was not connected to an organized church, but it was a religious phenomenon.[20] Consequently, New Agers' demands for the right to use their preferred modes of treatment inevitably overlapped somewhat with the broad notion of religious freedom, even if most left-leaning spiritual searchers were too wary of the word "religion" to ever directly invoke the First Amendment. Other strains of medical freedom rhetoric were more important in the 1970s, however—including the assertion of new rights that were products of this era.

Patients' Rights

The 1970s has frequently been described as the time of a "rights revolution." Concepts such as women's rights, gay rights, elder rights, environmental rights, disability rights, and consumer rights dominated the national conversation.[21]

"Rights talk" also extended forcefully into the world of health and medicine. An important aspect of the 1970s rights revolution was "patients' rights." The genesis of the patients' rights movement appears to have been the drafting in 1970 of twenty-six such rights by the National Welfare Rights Organization. This action precipitated a widespread discussion that culminated in the adoption of a "Patient's Bill of Rights" by the American Hospital Association in 1973. A central theme of this document was the protection of informed consent.[22]

The phrase "informed consent," as well as the very notion of a patient's *right* to full disclosure and to ultimate decision making, did not exist until the late 1950s. Before this time, to the extent that doctors provided information to and received consent from patients, they did so out of a sense of beneficence, not because they viewed their patients as having a right to autonomy. Even after informed consent first appeared as an issue, it did not immediately assume its current importance in medical ethics. A study in the late 1960s, for example, showed that 50 percent of physicians thought it medically appropriate for a doctor to perform a mastectomy based solely on a blanket consent form signed at the time of hospital admission, and 53 percent thought that it was ethically appropriate for a doctor not to tell a cancer patient that she was participating in a placebo-controlled study of an unapproved drug. The 1973 Patient's Bill of Rights thus represented a sea change. It unambiguously declared that a patient has the right not only to refuse treatment, but also "to obtain from his physician complete current information concerning his diagnosis, treatment, and prognosis, in terms the patient can be reasonably expected to understand," and the right "to receive from his physician information necessary to give informed consent prior to the start of any procedure and/or treatment."[23]

Although forged in the context of conventional medicine, the patients' rights movement increasingly made Americans view themselves as capable, rights-bearing medical decision makers outside the orthodox arena as well. In addition, the notion of patients' rights soon expanded beyond the right to *refuse* unwanted treatments to also include the right to *obtain* desired treatments, including un-conventional remedies. By the end of the 1970s, battles over access to alternative medicine were increasingly seen through this lens. A 1977 *Washington Post* ar-ticle about the fight over access to the alternative cancer cure Laetrile (an episode we will examine in detail at the end of this chapter) was titled "Laetrile Dispute Focuses Attention on Rights of Patients." The piece observed, "Thirty years ago few patients put claims of other patients ahead of belief in their physicians and organizations such as the AMA. Laetrile's popularity has blossomed in an era of ever-increasing awareness of patients' rights and the necessity of informed consent. It has come on the medical scene at a time when many patients think of themselves as consumers and are sometimes willing to listen to patient testimonials."[24]

The Women's Health Movement

Special attention should be paid to the relationship in the 1970s between medical rights and women's rights, as embodied in the women's health movement. This movement's greatest legal triumph was the Supreme Court's recognition, in *Roe v. Wade* (1973), of a woman's constitutional right to obtain an abortion. Written by Justice Harry Blackmun, the former in-house counsel for the Mayo Clinic, *Roe* was very much a medical rights opinion, though one focused at least as much on the doctor as the patient. The majority decision declared that during the first tri-mester, "the attending physician, in consultation with his patient, is free to deter-mine, without regulation by the State, that in his medical judgment, the patient's pregnancy should be terminated." In the years immediately following the issu-ance of *Roe*, both supporters and opponents of the holding tended to embrace a medical interpretation of the case, rather than one focused on women's rights, bodily integrity, or reproductive freedom.[25]

Roe v. Wade briefly promised to serve as a precedent for a general constitu-tional right to freedom of choice in medical matters. As we will see, courts ulti-mately did not embrace this reading of the case. Outside of court, however, the abortion rights movement's "freedom to choose" theme (often divorced from *Roe* itself) contributed greatly to the rhetoric of popular campaigns for access to alternative medicine (Fig. 6.1).[26]

The concerns of the women's health movement extended well beyond abor-tion. Feminists expressed general dissatisfaction with the patriarchal, tech-nocratic medical system and sought greater agency for women in decisions affecting their health. One aspect of this campaign was an effort to empower women to reject orthodox treatments recommended by their doctors. Indeed, the women's health movement originally coalesced around the demand that

Figure 6.1 A woman at a reproductive rights march in Pittsburgh, 1974. © *Barbara Freeman/Getty Images.*

women receive full and accurate information about the risks associated with oral contraceptives. A 1969 book by health journalist Barbara Seaman, *The Doctors' Case against the Pill*, inspired a January 1970 Senate hearing on contraceptive pill safety. Women in the audience repeatedly interrupted the all-male proceedings with shouted questions. A few months later, the FDA proposed a regulation requiring direct-to-patient warnings for oral contraceptive pills—the first-ever mandatory patient labeling for a prescription drug. In June 1970, the agency finalized this rule over the protests of the AMA and other mainstream medical groups, which contended that such labeling would "interfere with the physician-patient relationship."[27]

Seaman went on to cofound the National Women's Health Network (NWHN) in 1975. In December of that year, the organization conducted its first formal action, a protest at FDA headquarters. While an advisory committee held hearings inside the building on the safety of estrogenic drugs used by menopausal patients, NWHN staged a "memorial service" outside to honor all the women who had died from taking hormonal products. When the head of the FDA's drug division crossed paths with the demonstrators, he promised to require patient warnings on all hormone products. Two years later, the FDA mandated "patient package inserts" for estrogenic drugs. When establishment medical groups and the pharmaceutical industry challenged the rule in federal court as an unconstitutional interference with the practice of medicine, they audaciously cited Roe's companion case, Doe v. Bolton, in support of their position. The court responded: "To the extent that [the abortion and other privacy cases] have any bearing on the present issue . . . their rationale would appear to *support* the challenged regulation. The objective of that regulation is to provide the patient with the facts relevant to a choice about the use . . . of estrogen drugs."[28]

The women's health movement also demanded freedom to choose alternative practitioners. One major component of this campaign was the establishment of women's health centers. The idea germinated in 1971, when attorney Carol Downer publicly demonstrated cervical self-examination at a Los Angeles feminist bookstore. Following a national self-examination tour, Downer and Lorraine Rothman (the inventor of a menstrual extraction kit for self-administered abortion) resolved to spur the creation of a national network of feminist women's health centers (FWHCs). They founded the Los Angeles Feminist Women's Health Center in 1972, and within four years, about fifty FWHCs and other feminist clinics were operating in major cities and college towns throughout the country. These establishments provided comprehensive gynecological care, much of it delivered by female lay health workers.

The medical establishment fought back with the weapon it has always used against irregular practitioners—state medical licensing statutes. In September 1972, California law enforcement officers raided the Los Angeles FWHC, arrested Downer and another worker, and seized yogurt from the facility's refrigerator. The state charged Downer with practicing medicine without a license because she had spooned yogurt into a patient's vagina to treat a yeast infection. The "Great Yogurt Conspiracy Trial" received widespread media attention, inspired a rally in support of Downer, and galvanized the burgeoning women's health movement nationwide. A jury found Downer not guilty in December 1972. Nevertheless, other states would subsequently also charge feminist health center workers with the unauthorized practice of medicine, generating additional legal struggles.[29]

The other major front in the war between feminist health activists and orthodox medicine was the alternative birth movement, or lay midwifery. Through the end of the 1800s, most American births occurred at home, and the midwives who attended them were indispensable providers of obstetric care. The vocation of midwifery nearly vanished with the inexorable rise of hospital deliveries during the first decades of the twentieth century. In the 1970s, however, women's rising dissatisfaction with the "over-medicalization of birth" led to a minor resurgence in home birth and a corresponding demand for lay midwives. An alternative birth movement arose, and one of its main themes was choice—namely, the right to choose to give birth at home instead of in a hospital.

Orthodox medicine sought to co-opt this trend by establishing "alternative birth centers" in hospitals, staffed by certified nurse midwives. Meanwhile, complaints filed by obstetricians generated a wave of prosecutions of lay midwives for practicing medicine without a license. (Few of these prosecutions resulted in convictions by juries, suggesting broad public sympathy for the home birth cause.) The alternative birth movement fought back in state legislatures, campaigning for laws establishing licensure of non-nurse midwives. Eight states did so by 1985, and that number has climbed to about thirty-five today.[30]

Initially, the women's health movement did not focus nearly as much on other alternative medical services and products. Consider, for example, the evolution of *Our Bodies, Ourselves* by the Boston Women's Health Book Collective, one of the movement's foundational texts. The first edition, a stapled booklet the Collective began distributing in 1969, promoted an integrative and holistic approach to health care generally, but it did not discuss particular alternative treatments—except to reject the efficacy of folk abortifacients. The three subsequent editions, published in the 1970s as the book achieved bestseller status, slowly expanded coverage of non-mainstream medicine, but none contained a full chapter devoted to the topic. This permanently changed in 1984 with the release of the fifth edition, which contained a chapter titled "Health and Healing: Alternatives to Medical Care." The chapter not only discussed alternative medicine in detail, but also portrayed it as particularly well suited to women.[31]

Our Bodies, Ourselves was thus slow to appreciate the special relationship that has always existed between American women and alternative medicine. Since at least the early nineteenth century, women have been disproportionately represented in the ranks of alternative medicine practitioners, patients, and promoters. This phenomenon persists in the modern era. One scholar recently declared: "Women dominate alternative medicine, both as consumers and as service providers."[32]

Women also continue to be leading political advocates for alternative medicine (now widely known as complementary and alternative medicine, or CAM). An entire book, *Women Confront Cancer*, is devoted to interviews of female participants in the movement devoted to ensuring legal access to (and publicly funded research of) alternative cancer therapies. In the introduction to this volume, the authors state: "We interpret the interviews ... as political documents in the struggle for women's increased control over their bodies and the availability of diagnostic and therapeutic options." One interviewee is Pat Prince, a supporter of Laetrile. When Prince developed breast cancer in the late 1970s, she declined all conventional treatment and went to a Mexican Laetrile clinic instead. In 1980, she was arrested for carrying a personal supply of the drug back into the United States and ultimately pled guilty to a federal crime. Prince is certain that Laetrile saved her life—and indignant that American law forbade her to exercise her medical choice.[33]

Prince's story demonstrates how the women's health movement overlapped with the 1970s' emblematic campaign for freedom of therapeutic choice outside orthodox medicine: the battle for access to Laetrile.

The Laetrile Story

Laetrile's Early Years

Both the origins and the precise chemical identity of Laetrile have long been matters of dispute. Even its name is uncertain; the drug has variously been called Laetrile, laetrile (with a small "l"), amygdalin, and vitamin B-17. In 1977, the FDA Commissioner remarked, "There is, quite simply, no one answer to the question 'What is Laetrile?' "[34]

The drug's complex and murky early history has been described in detail elsewhere.[35] According to Laetrile's promoters, it originated in the 1920s, from the efforts of Ernst Krebs Sr., an American pharmacist and physician. Krebs purportedly extracted amygdalin (an already-recognized chemical) from apricot kernels for reasons unrelated to treating cancer. According to this narrative, Krebs's less-well-credentialed son, Ernst Krebs Jr., tweaked his father's process in 1949 and called the resulting amygdalin-like substance "Laetrile." This account attracts skepticism, however. Because the 1962 Drug Amendments exempted certain older products from the new regulatory regime, Laetrile's proponents had a powerful incentive to invent a remote origin for the drug. The more likely true story (originally told by Krebs Sr. himself) is that he first extracted Laetrile from apricot kernels in 1951, and his son coined the name soon afterward.

In any event, by 1952 the Krebses were investigating Laetrile's use as a cancer therapy. To explain its ostensible mode of action, they embraced the "trophoblastic" theory of cancer propounded by Scotsman John Beard early in the century. Building on this theory, the Krebses hypothesized that an enzyme that was present only in cancerous cells converted Laetrile into a targeted, cyanide-releasing killer of these cells, while a different enzyme present in healthy cells rendered the drug otherwise nontoxic. The Krebses started commercially producing and marketing an injectable form of Laetrile in Pasadena, California, sometime in the early 1950s. For the remainder of the decade, the Krebses sold Laetrile as an "investigational" cancer drug to a gradually expanding cadre of physicians in California and elsewhere. They successfully eluded federal and state regulators, in part by relying on word-of-mouth promotion instead of explicit anticancer labeling claims.

The FDA finally began taking legal steps against the Laetrile trade in 1960, when it seized an interstate shipment of the drug. In 1962, the agency rejected Krebs Jr.'s NDA (new drug application) for Laetrile as a cancer palliative. That year, he was convicted of federal crimes for selling a different unapproved drug, and he agreed as part of his probation deal to stop manufacturing and distributing Laetrile, as well. Papa Krebs took over the Laetrile operation until the mid-1960s, when the FDA compelled him to stop, too.

At that point, the only remaining significant Laetrile manufacturer in North America was Andrew McNaughton, a shadowy Canadian arms dealer and unorthodox medicine enthusiast, who happened to be the son of General Andrew McNaughton, the commander of the First Canadian Army in World War II. McNaughton produced the drug in Montreal until the Canadian government enjoined him from doing so in 1964. He then launched an underground Laetrile manufacturing operation in the San Francisco Bay Area. The California government—which in 1963 had banned the drug pursuant to its cancer quackery law—finally chased McNaughton out of the state in 1970. He next established a Laetrile factory in Tijuana, Mexico. This facility provided the drug to a cluster of nearby Laetrile clinics that catered largely to American cancer patients crossing the border from San Diego. When they returned to the United States, many of these patients illegally carried personal supplies of Laetrile with them. Meanwhile, smugglers transported much larger amounts of Mexican-produced Laetrile into the United States for national and international distribution. In a final bid for legitimacy, McNaughton submitted an investigational new drug application (IND) for the experimental use of Laetrile in 1970. Following a *pro forma* initial summary approval, the FDA denied the application.[36]

Laetrile's history up to this point resembled that of Krebiozen: an unorthodox remedy seeking the aura of orthodoxy. Both drugs were invented by physicians. Both were injectable products usually administered by doctors. Both had a highly esteemed, though idiosyncratic, champion from the medical establishment. (Andrew Ivy's equivalent for Laetrile was Dean Burk, the chief of the Cytochemistry Section of the National Cancer Institute.) Both were the subject of unsuccessful INDs submitted to the FDA.[37]

Moreover, both Krebiozen and Laetrile had patient advocacy groups led by reassuringly mainstream, middle-aged women. Laine Friedman's counterpart in the Laetrile campaign was Cecile Pollack Hoffman, a pastor's daughter, schoolteacher, and breast cancer survivor from San Diego. In 1963, Hoffman founded the International Association of Cancer Victims and Friends (IACVF), primarily to promote Laetrile access. In the late 1960s, this organization oversaw a "cancer underground to Mexico," where patients acquired Krebiozen as well as Laetrile.[38]

This quasi-orthodox first phase of the Laetrile story ended in 1970, when the FDA rejected McNaughton's IND application. Laetrile advocates responded to the denial with outrage, accusing the FDA and the cancer research establishment with conducting an insidious conspiracy to suppress unorthodox treatments. Around this time, Ernst Krebs Jr. laid the groundwork for the transformation of Laetrile into a 1970s-style alternative remedy. In a 1970 article in the *Journal of Applied Nutrition*, he asserted that Laetrile was a previously unrecognized type of vitamin, which he dubbed "vitamin B-17." Krebs also reframed cancer itself, describing it as a "chronic metabolic disease that arises from a specific vitamin deficiency." He wrote: "One might ask . . . whether we suggest that . . . Laetrile is an effective cancer drug. Our reply must be: it is not a drug; it is a vitamin." Journalists soon started using "vitamin B-17" as a synonym for Laetrile; by the middle of the decade, this usage was routine.[39]

Krebs's *Applied Nutrition* article focused largely on oral intake of Laetrile. He declared that about seven teaspoons of defatted apricot kernel would provide consumers with all the vitamin B-17 they needed to prevent cancer. Americans were soon munching on unprocessed apricot seeds they purchased at health food stores. Krebs certainly knew, however, that many would prefer to consume Laetrile in a more convenient dosage form. Indeed, in the early 1970s, Laetrile tablets and capsules (obtained on the black market or in Mexico) surged in popularity. Americans used them as a co-therapy with Laetrile injections or as a stand-alone cancer preventative.[40]

Krebs probably repositioned Laetrile as a vitamin pill in a futile effort to evade the more stringent federal requirements applicable to drugs. The FDA shrugged off this scheme and continued to aggressively attack Laetrile as an illegal unapproved cancer drug. Krebs's strategy nonetheless boosted Laetrile's popularity by enabling it to ride the surging wave of holistic medicine. As a "vitamin" derived from apricot kernels, Laetrile appealed to the growing population of Americans who embraced "natural" therapies, stressed the importance of diet and nutrition, and sought whole-person wellness. Though the Tijuana clinics continued administering Laetrile by injection, they did so as part of a comprehensive program that patients were expected to continue after they returned home with a concealed supply of Laetrile pills. Their prescribed regimen included consumption of other dietary supplements, an organic diet, a positive attitude, visualization, biofeedback, and sometimes prayer. Krebs had transformed Laetrile into a drug that both libertarian conservatives and New Agers could love.[41]

Laetrile advocacy exploded into a full-fledged social movement following the 1972 arrest of John Richardson, a California physician. Dr. Richardson had recently reinvented himself as a Laetrile-dispensing cancer specialist. In June, California law enforcement officers raided Richardson's clinic near Berkeley and arrested him for violating the state's Cancer Quackery Law. Richardson was an active member of the reactionary, fiercely antigovernment John Birch Society. His fellow Birchers responded to the "persecution" of Richardson by supporting his legal defense and raging against an anti-Laetrile conspiracy involving the FDA, the AMA, the American Cancer Society, and the National Cancer Institute. Although California authorities ultimately revoked Richardson's medical license, he avoided criminal liability thanks to two hung juries.[42]

Birchers allied with Richardson founded a new organization, the Committee for Freedom of Choice in Cancer Therapy, which quickly became a leading voice for Laetrile legalization. For a time in the early 1970s, the pro-Laetrile crusade took on the shape of a right-wing social movement akin to the one that promoted the Hoxsey cure in the 1950s. Religious conservatives, antigovernment extremists, and opponents of the fluoridation of public water supplies (a John Birch bugaboo) flocked to the Laetrile cause. But as sociologist David J. Hess has observed, "The Bircher spur was soon subsumed by increasing movement diversification, as people from across the political spectrum united under the libertarian banner of medical freedom." According to one observer, at Richardson's trial "there were McGovern-for-president left-wing hippies in the audience who were in favor of this John Birch doctor. . . . Here was an issue that was far beyond left and right."[43]

A politically diverse coalition fought alongside the Committee for Freedom of Choice in the struggle for Laetrile access. The National Health Federation joined the cause, while also railing against nuclear power, chemical pesticides, and air and water pollution. Another allied organization was the Cancer Control Society (CCS). Betty Lee Morales and Lorraine Rosenthal founded the CCS in 1973 after they were pushed out of Cecile Hoffman's IACVF by less activist board members. Morales was a quasi-celebrity nutritionist and Rosenthal was a Berkeley-educated laboratory technician; both owned LA health food stores. The CCS became (in Hess's words) "the more alternative, populist wing of the [Laetrile] social movement." Then, in 1976, members of Science for the People, a radical left-wing association, organized a pro-Laetrile group called Second Opinion among employees at New York City's Sloan-Kettering Cancer Center. Laetrile activists joked about "left-handed" and "right-handed" Laetrile—a double entendre referring to both the movement's political diversity and to the drug's molecular structure.[44]

The Laetrile movement's ambiguous politics made it an emblematic 1970s phenomenon. The worldviews of the left and the right began to overlap during this decade. Their shared terrain was a deep-seated distrust of government, other establishment institutions, expertise, and technology. Liberal and conservative proponents of alternative medicine have battled the orthodox medical system together ever since.[45]

1977: The Year of Laetrile

In March 1977, two months after taking office, President Jimmy Carter participated in an unprecedented live call-in radio show moderated by CBS TV anchorman Walter Cronkite. Mrs. Opal Dehart of Trinity, North Carolina, dialed in on behalf of her terminally ill father to plead for access to "Vitamin B-17, Laetrile." Politely but boldly, she told the president: "We need your help in checking this vitamin out so that it's made available to the American people." Carter was noncommittal during the program. Several days later, the FDA's acting commissioner called Mrs. Dehart and informed her that extensive studies had failed to demonstrate that Laetrile was useful against cancer.[46]

Laetrile was one of the top news stories of 1977. *Newsweek*'s June 27 cover asked, "Laetrile and Cancer: Should the Drug Be Banned?" All the country's major newspapers ran multiple articles about the drug, sometimes on their front pages. The editors of the *New York Times* and the *Los Angeles Times* urged government forbearance. ("The law has no business denying a citizen's dying wish to grasp at harmless straws," opined the latter.) In his nationally syndicated column, conservative James J. Kilpatrick condemned the FDA's "pompous, dictatorial, and hoity-toity" prohibition of Laetrile, insisting that the "gut issue here is freedom." His liberal counterpart, Nicholas von Hoffman, chastised organized medicine for "kicking up such an undignified fuss because some people want to swallow a few laetrile capsules."[47]

A July 1977 poll showed that 58 percent of Americans supported legalization of Laetrile, versus only 28 percent who opposed it. In a May 1977 editorial, the *Washington Post* observed that "cancer dread, anti-establishment sentiment and perhaps the 'forbidden fruit' aura have kindled a popular fire." The *Post* endorsed congressional intervention, because the "popular force behind Laetrile is a political fact [that] dictates a political solution." More strikingly, Franz J. Ingelfinger, the editor of the hallowed *New England Journal of Medicine*, declared that the best way to quell "Laetrilomania" would be to legalize the drug and then have a group "broadly representative of society" analyze the real-world results. Dr. Ingelfinger himself was certain that Laetrile was "another one of those quack cures that sweep relentlessly through our volatile society," but he concluded that "there are some situations in which rational medical science should yield and make some concessions."[48]

The FDA remained a stalwart foe of Laetrile. It publicized the drug's worthlessness, raided domestic manufacturers, and cooperated with other federal agencies in a vain attempt to suppress Mexico-based smuggling operations. Meanwhile, state legislatures passed Laetrile legalization laws. Alaska moved first, in 1976. Thirteen additional states with diverse political leanings followed in 1977. Eventually, twenty-seven states would enact such statutes. The genesis of these laws followed a predictable pattern. The introduction of a bill in the legislature would be followed by rowdy hearings packed with zealous Laetrile supporters. Scientific witnesses would challenge Laetrile's efficacy, while cancer survivors and Laetrile activists would plead for freedom of choice. Finally, a flood of mail to state lawmakers would culminate in the enactment of a legalization statute.[49]

These state laws would have little if any practical effect, however, so long as the FDA deemed Laetrile to be an illegal unapproved new drug under federal law. Only Congress could change this situation, and there was significant action on this front, as well. In 1976, Republican Representative Steven Symms of Idaho (a John Birch fellow traveler) had introduced a "Medical Freedom of Choice Bill." Inspired by the Laetrile dispute, this legislation would have wholly repealed the FDA's power to review the efficacy of new drugs. The bill attracted numerous cosponsors from both parties but did not advance. In the new Congress that convened in January 1977, Symms reintroduced the bill with a bipartisan grab bag of nineteen cosponsors ranging from the conservative Mississippi Republican Trent Lott (later the Senate Majority Leader) to the progressive New York Democrat Shirley Chisolm (earlier the first woman and first African American to seek a major political party's nomination for president). "Freedom is the issue," explained Symms. "The American people should be able to make their own decisions." The bill ultimately attracted 106 co-sponsors from both parties.[50]

In July 1977, a Senate subcommittee chaired by Ted Kennedy held a hearing on the FDA's ban on Laetrile (Fig. 6.2). On the first panel, FDA Commissioner Donald Kennedy testified in favor of the prohibition, alongside a collection of other federal health officials and cancer experts. The second panel consisted of law enforcement officials, who justified their actions against leaders of the Laetrile movement. Finally, the witness table was occupied by a group of these leaders, including Ernst Krebs Jr., John Richardson, and Robert Bradford, the president of the Committee for Freedom of Choice in Cancer Therapy. The senators tried (with limited success) to make the witnesses clarify their positions on various issues. What was the precise chemical identity of Laetrile? Would they accept the results of any conventional study demonstrating a lack of efficacy? Senator Kennedy took on the air of a prosecutor, virtually mocking the witnesses—to

Figure 6.2 FDA Commissioner Donald Kennedy and Senator Edward Kennedy (D-MA) chat prior to a subcommittee hearing on the agency's ban on Laetrile, July 13, 1977. © *AP Images*.

laughter from the audience. He prodded Richardson to voice his theory that a vast conspiracy involving the pharmaceutical industry, the FDA, the American Cancer Society, and the AMA was suppressing Laetrile. "Conspiracy is not unusual in any time in history," Richardson declared, "and particularly at this time." The witnesses' performance effectively ended any possibility there would be federal legislation legalizing Laetrile. Symms's bill never advanced out of committee in the House.[51]

Laetrile advocates now pinned their hopes on the third branch of government—the courts. They had reason for optimism. Two years earlier, Glen Rutherford, a Kansas seed salesman, had sought a federal court order directing the FDA to desist from interfering with his use of Laetrile after federal officials seized one of his shipments from Mexico. In October 1975, Judge Luther Bohanon of the US District Court for the Western District of Oklahoma ruled in his favor. Accepting the plaintiff's constitutional argument, the judge held that denying patients "freedom of choice for treatment by laetrile to alleviate or cure their cancer" violated their due process rights as guaranteed by *Roe v. Wade*. Bohanon issued a preliminary injunction ordering the government not to interfere with Rutherford's acquisition of Laetrile for personal use.[52]

In 1976, the US Court of Appeals for the Tenth Circuit upheld the injunction. It also, however, remanded the matter to Bohanon for a trial on the technical statutory question of whether Laetrile was a "new drug" subject to premarket approval under the FD&C Act. The Act's definition of this term excludes any drug that is "generally recognized as safe and effective" (GRASE) for its labeled uses among qualified experts. Moreover, older drugs eligible for either of two "grandfather" clauses (one dating from 1938 and the other from 1962) are also excluded from the "new drug" definition. Judge Bohanon in turn remanded the matter to the FDA and ordered the agency to conduct a hearing on these statutory issues and provide the court with a detailed administrative record.[53]

The FDA hosted this hearing in a Radisson Hotel ballroom in Kansas City in early May 1977. The unusual two-day proceedings, jammed with boisterous Laetrile supporters, took on an almost riotous atmosphere. Pro-Laetrile witnesses generally ignored the technical requirements of the GRASE and grandfather clauses and instead railed against the arrogance and iniquity of the medical establishment. Glen Rutherford snarled at the FDA, AMA, and American Cancer Society representatives, "You set yourself up as God and Jesus Christ all rolled up into one. And we don't have any rights." A recurring theme was an alleged "conspiracy" by the "cancer industry" to protect its profits by covering up Laetrile's efficacy. When a medical school professor challenged the audience, "Do you really think a quarter of a million physicians across this country . . . let people die because they want to make a profit off of them?" the crowd erupted with shouts of "Yes!"[54]

The allegation of a monopolistic plot by the medical establishment was, of course, a time-honored theme in American medical freedom discourse. Indeed, in this and other ways, the pro-Laetrile forces' rhetoric at the 1977 hearing uncannily echoed that of the Thomsonians 150 years earlier. Just as the Thomsonians had condemned the brutality and futility of "heroic" medicine, Laetrile supporters now attacked orthodox doctors' "militaristic" approach to cancer. They disparaged modern cancer therapy as "slash, poison, and burn" (referring to surgery, chemotherapy, and radiation). One Laetrile proponent challenged the FDA representatives: "Have you listened to [oncology patients] discuss the side effects of the 'orthodox methods' of treating cancer? Have you seen the burns and pain from cobalt therapy, the vomiting, loss of hair and bleeding from chemotherapy?" In addition, the Laetrile advocates' defense of a "natural" remedy derived from apricot pits echoed the Thomsonians' earlier embrace of "natural" botanical cures. Betty Lee Morales, testifying on behalf of the NHF, called Laetrile "a natural food component" and described cancer as a "disease of civilization" that could be addressed only by "returning to nature."[55]

All the strands of liberty invoked by American medical freedom activists since the early nineteenth century appeared in the Laetrile advocates' testimony at the

THE SPIRIT OF THE '70S 157

Kansas City hearing. One witness invoked economic liberty: "Over-regulation may destroy the market place [*sic*] as the ultimate laboratory by which to prove what is effective or not effective." Others invoked religious liberty. "FDA is in . . . violation of the First Amendment. . . . Our religious freedom entitles us to partake of God's bounty without hindrance from FDA or any other Agency." Freedom of inquiry was also a recurrent theme. Glen Rutherford excoriated the FDA for "consistently refus[ing] to allow the use or the testing of laetrile by anyone, even on an experimental basis, in the United States." Finally, a demand for bodily autonomy was implicit in most of the pro-Laetrile testimony. Norma Manke, a cancer patient, proclaimed: "In a free society, Americans should not be prevented by anyone or any institution in [*sic*] receiving any treatment which they feel will be effective for themselves."[56]

The pro-Laetrile witnesses also made appeal after appeal to a quasi-constitutional right of "freedom of choice." Manke characterized freedom of choice as "a basic principle that this nation was founded upon." Glen Rutherford's lawyer, Kenneth Coe, quoted Benjamin Rush's apocryphal statement that all laws restricting medical freedom are "un-American and despotic." He insisted that the right to freely seek out a cure "is not new thinking. It is not avant-garde. It has been with us as long we have had the American Republic. Freedom of treatment . . . is certainly a part of the Constitution, as well as the right of every American."[57]

Despite these many recapitulations of traditional themes, the pro-Laetrile testimony at the May 1977 hearing was in other ways very much a product of its time. No fewer than four witnesses brought up Watergate. One, for instance, asserted: "What we are confronted with is a scandal of Watergate proportions in which the truth about cancer is being systematically suppressed." The Laetrile advocates also piggybacked on the era's enthusiasm for "holistic medicine." Robert Bradford defined holism as the "concept of treating the whole man as a single entity, the sum of his parts," contended that holistic medicine was the "wave of the future in cancer management," and portrayed Laetrile-based metabolic therapy as the foundation of that approach.[58]

Unlike their nineteenth-century forebears, the Laetrile proponents had to reckon with the rise of modern scientific methodologies. By 1977, the FD&C Act and virtually the entire scientific establishment considered "adequate and well-controlled clinical trials" to be the sole legitimate basis for demonstrating a drug's efficacy. By this standard, not a single valid investigation of Laetrile's effectiveness had ever been performed. The pro-Laetrile witnesses adopted various tactics to counter this problem. One was to point out (accurately) the lack of controlled clinical research supporting many practices and products of *orthodox* medicine. Another was to contend that the very nature of holistic medicine defied conventional research protocols focusing on a single variable. Still another tactic was to charge the orthodox establishment with suppressing positive data about Laetrile and preventing further research. Finally, at least one witness bluntly defended the use of testimonial and anecdotal evidence.[59]

These arguments ignored the specific statutory questions at issue and thus were doomed to fail. A few months after the hearing, FDA Commissioner Donald Kennedy issued a decision in which he concluded that Laetrile was neither GRASE nor eligible for one of the grandfather provisions. Consequently, the drug was a "new drug" subject to the premarket approval requirement, and it was illegal to sell it in interstate commerce without an approved NDA. The commissioner's findings were entirely consistent with the regulation of other drugs; the FDA and the courts have always construed the GRASE and grandfather exceptions so stringently that few if any products qualify for them.[60]

Kennedy's more daring move was to include a lengthy and eloquent section (not requested by the court) attacking the premises of the Laetrile advocates' "freedom of choice" argument:

> The choice to use Laetrile is seldom . . . a free one. . . . A cancer patient is a person beset by immense stresses, physical, psychological, emotional and societal; and the persuasion that the patient and his family are subjected to by Laetrile proponents is seldom limited to a rational laying out of competing arguments. . . . The idea that a reasoned free choice is involved in the selection of Laetrile rather than legitimate therapy is thus ultimately an illusion.[61]

In December 1977, Judge Bohanon issued his second *Rutherford* opinion. Astonishingly, he again ordered the FDA to stop interfering with the importation, sale, and use of Laetrile. The judge disposed of Kennedy's decision like an unwanted piece of junk mail. He declared the FDA commissioner's findings and conclusions "unlawful" and "held for naught." Withholding the strong deference that courts almost always granted such FDA determinations, Bohanon held that Laetrile qualified for the 1962 grandfather provision and thus was not a "new drug."

Turning to the constitutional issues, Bohanon delivered one of the most emphatic endorsements of freedom of therapeutic choice ever articulated by an American judge. He ruled that Rutherford's access to Laetrile fell within the "right to privacy" established four years earlier by *Roe v. Wade*. Bohanon quoted Justice William O. Douglas's concurring opinion in *Doe v. Bolton* (*Roe*'s companion case), which explicitly embraced "the freedom to care for one's health and person." Like medical freedom activists of old, Bohanon then emphasized the uncertain state of medical science, observing that many "knowledgable and concerned individuals are questioning the effectiveness and wisdom of our orthodox approaches to combatting cancer." He continued:

Doubtless FDA desires to protect the public. Such good intention, however, is not the overriding issue. . . . Our political ideals emphasize that the right to freely decide is of much greater significance than the quality of those choices actually made. . . . As a nation . . . we are irrevocably committed to the principle that the individual must be given maximum latitude in determining his own personal destiny. To be insensitive to the very fundamental nature of the civil liberties at issue in this case, and the fact that making the choice, regardless of its correctness, is the sole prerogative of the person whose body is being ravaged, is to display slight understanding of the essence of our free society and its constitutional underpinnings.

Bohanon concluded: "By denying the right to use a nontoxic substance in connection with one's own personal health-care, FDA has offended the constitutional right of privacy."[62]

Bohanon's holding contained important limitations. First, he seemed to confine it to "nontoxic" substances. Second, he took pains to stress that although individuals had a constitutional right to *use* "innocuous" unproven remedies, vendors did not have a corresponding right to falsely or fraudulently *promote* them. Nevertheless, Bohanon's reasoning would have extraordinary implications for the FDA's authority over alternative medical products if other jurists embraced it. By his logic, the government could not constitutionally ban any "safe" treatment. Indeed, a few other courts soon applied *Roe* to different alternative remedies. A Florida appeals court suggested that the state had unconstitutionally violated the privacy rights of a physician and his patients by stripping his medical license as a penalty for administering chelation therapy for arteriosclerosis. A federal district court held that the Texas Medical Practice Act violated patients' constitutional privacy rights by limiting the practice of acupuncture to licensed physicians and thus virtually eliminating it from the state.[63]

Although Judge Bohanon's *Rutherford* decision made him a hero in the eyes of the John Birch Society, he was no Bircher. To the contrary, he was a liberal Democrat appointed by John F. Kennedy and an admirer of the late Chief Justice Earl Warren—against whom the John Birch Society had conducted a vicious impeachment campaign. In an earlier case, Bohanon had compelled the Oklahoma City Public School District to comply with the desegregation mandate of *Brown v. Board of Education* by adopting a busing plan. Despite his progressive ideals, however, Bohanon arrived at the same freedom of choice position with respect to Laetrile as the right-wingers. The "right to privacy" thus offered a potential bipartisan path forward for medical freedom activists.[64]

Judge Bohanon's December 1977 district court ruling was a triumphant and auspicious ending to an eventful year for Laetrile proponents. Their buoyancy would not last long.

The Decline and Fall of Court-Created Medical Freedom

Rutherford's good luck persisted for a while. In 1978, the US Court of Appeals for the Tenth Circuit upheld the district court, though on different grounds. It disregarded Bohanon's application of the grandfather clause to Laetrile, as well as his constitutional analysis. Instead, the court of appeals concluded, as a matter of statutory interpretation, that the terms "safe" and "effective" in the FD&C Act had no sensible application to drugs taken by dying cancer patients. It instructed the FDA to promulgate regulations that redefined "safe" and "effective" in this context. The appeals court left Bohanon's injunction in place, though only with respect to terminally ill patients seeking to procure intravenous injections of Laetrile. The court apparently excluded oral dosage forms because FDA Commissioner Kennedy and others had expressed concern that the drug could cause hydrogen cyanide poisoning when taken by mouth.[65]

The federal government appealed to the US Supreme Court, which heard arguments in April 1979. In June, the Court issued a decision in *United States v. Rutherford* that devastated the Laetrile community. It ruled unanimously that "no implicit exemption for drugs used by the terminally ill is necessary . . . to avert an unreasonable reading of the terms 'safe' and 'effective.' " Justice Thurgood Marshall's opinion explained, "If an individual suffering from a potentially fatal disease rejects conventional therapy in favor of a drug with no demonstrable curative properties, the consequences can be irreversible."[66]

Laetrile advocates' last hope for judicial rescue was the constitutional right to privacy, which neither the Supreme Court nor the Tenth Circuit had addressed. The wind was blowing in the wrong direction, however. In *People v. Privitera*, the California Supreme Court had recently rejected a constitutional privacy challenge to the state's Laetrile ban by a vote of 5 to 2, over a ringing dissent by the liberal chief justice, Rose Bird. Bird would have stricken the ban based on the "right to control one's body" elaborated in *Roe* and other cases. She also raised the long-standing theme of freedom of inquiry. She believed the prescribing doctor himself had a constitutional right to use an unorthodox modality on a consenting patient because state interference would "suppress innovation by the person [i.e., the physician] best qualified to make medical progress." The chief justice observed, "It is by alternatives to orthodoxy that medical progress has been made." She thus concluded, "A free, progressive society has an enormous stake in recognizing and protecting this right of the physician."[67]

Bird's *Privitera* dissent was the last gasp among American judges of a vision of *Roe v. Wade* that elaborated the holding into a generalized right to freedom of therapeutic choice. In February 1980, the Tenth Circuit (citing the majority decision in *Privitera*) rejected Rutherford's constitutional privacy claim. It declared, "The decision by the patient whether to have a treatment or not is a protected right, but his selection of a particular treatment, or at least a medication, is within the area of governmental interest in protecting the public health." In other words, although Americans had a constitutional right to refuse medical treatment altogether, the choice among specific therapies was not constitutionally protected. Two months later, the Ninth Circuit ruled similarly in another Laetrile case.[68] When the Supreme Court declined to re-view *Rutherford*, it ensured that American courts would never be a fruitful forum for vindicating the right of therapeutic choice.

In retrospect, *Roe v. Wade* was a flimsy foundation on which to attempt to establish such a right. Legal academics of diverse political leanings questioned the decision's reasoning from the moment it was issued in 1973. After 1980 and the rise of President Ronald Reagan, the conservative movement increas-ingly condemned *Roe* as the epitome of illegitimate, antidemocratic judicial activism. The very notion of a judicially declared constitutional right to pri-vacy became an abomination among conservative legal scholars, conserva-tive politicians, and the growing ranks of conservative judges.[69] And liberal occupants of the bench who embraced *Roe* tended to support rigorous health and safety regulation and thus hesitated to use a right forged in the specific context of abortion to eviscerate government oversight of medicine more generally.

And what happened to Laetrile itself? Americans' interest in the drug plummeted in the early 1980s. The 1980 death from cancer of movie star Steve McQueen, the world's most prominent Laetrile user, helped cool "Laetrilomania." Enthusiasm waned further with the 1981 announcement that trials performed by the National Cancer Institute had failed to demon-strate Laetrile's efficacy and had also produced evidence of potential cya-nide toxicity. Even Laetrile supporters soon began to moderate their claims. Congressional bills to eliminate the FDA's power to review drug efficacy stalled. State legislatures stopped passing Laetrile legalization statutes and repealed some existing ones. By 1983, major media stories about Laetrile had largely disappeared.[70]

None of this is to say, however, that the demand for access to alternative medi-cine died with the Laetrile movement. To the contrary, as we will see in Chapter 8, CAM advocates energetically continued the struggle with respect to other types of treatments, though mainly outside of court.

7

AIDS Activists, FDA Regulation, and the Amendment of America's Drug Constitution

The Parklawn Building, a massive, bland edifice erected in the late 1960s, looms over a neighborhood of nondescript office buildings and auto repair shops in Rockville, Maryland, about four miles outside the Washington, DC, Beltway. Until recently, the building contained the headquarters of the US Food and Drug Administration (FDA), as well as other Department of Health and Human Services (HHS) offices. It is an unlikely setting for a mass protest. For a thousand boisterous AIDS activists who stormed it on October 11, 1988, however, the Parklawn Building was the Bastille. Their demonstration sparked a profound transformation in the government's approach to regulating treatments for serious illnesses.[1]

The "Seize Control of FDA" protesters—many of them bused in by the year-old AIDS Coalition to Unleash Power (ACT UP)—demanded that the agency speed the availability of drugs for Acquired Immune Deficiency Syndrome (AIDS). Since it had emerged in the United States in 1981, AIDS had spread with particular virulence among gay and bisexual men. They dominated the crowd surrounding the Parklawn Building, although many women also joined the protest. For an entire workday, the demonstrators loudly condemned the federal government's inaction in the face of AIDS. They denounced the apathy of President Ronald Reagan and Vice President George H. W. Bush (the 1988 Republican presidential nominee). Their primary target, however, was the FDA itself.[2]

In truth, the FDA had not been completely inert in response to the horrific rise of the epidemic. In 1986, the agency had made azidothymidine (AZT)—an investigational antiretroviral drug that targeted the human immunodeficiency virus (HIV)—available to patients outside of formal clinical trials on a "compassionate use" basis. The following year, it had approved AZT's New Drug Application (NDA) with extraordinary speed. In addition, the FDA had issued a "treatment IND" rule in 1987, formalizing its long-standing ad hoc practice of allowing therapeutic use of investigational new drugs in desperate situations.[3]

Choose Your Medicine. Lewis A. Grossman, Oxford University Press. © Lewis A. Grossman 2021.
DOI: 10.1093/oso/9780190612757.003.0008

AIDS activists were nonetheless enraged in the fall of 1988. AZT remained the only FDA-approved therapy for HIV/AIDS. At best, this drug delayed the disease's inevitably fatal outcome, and many people with AIDS (PWAs) could not tolerate its severe side effects. In October 1987, an FDA advisory committee had recommended against the approval of ganciclovir, a promising drug for a blindness-inducing eye infection common among PWAs. Meanwhile, the treatment IND process was not significantly increasing access to AIDS drugs still under investigation. At the time of the Parklawn protest, the FDA had made only one AIDS-related experimental therapy available pursuant to the new procedure.[4]

American scientists were studying scores of other compounds, and many in the HIV-positive population were eager to try each one as soon as it showed the slightest evidence of efficacy, rather than wait the seven to ten years the FDA ordinarily took to approve a drug. Accompanied by whistles and noisemakers, the crowd around the Parklawn Building chanted its demands for pharmaceutical access. "AZT is not enough, give us all the other stuff!" "Release the drugs now!" Most provocatively, the demonstrators, referring to the FDA commissioner, yelled "Frank Young, you can't hide, we charge you with genocide!" Their placards and banners were no gentler. "AIDS Doesn't Discriminate—Our Government Does." "Federal Death Administration." Many signs displayed a pink triangle, evoking the patch sewn onto the uniforms of gay inmates in Nazi concentration camps.

The action's theatrical elements captured the attention of cameramen from the television networks and major newspapers. Protestors lay down on the street holding cardboard tombstones bearing epitaphs such as "RIP, Killed by FDA" and "I Died for the Sins of FDA" (Fig. 7.1). Others paraded around in "blood"-stained white doctors' coats. ACT UP's Peter Staley, a J. P. Morgan bond trader turned full-time activist, hoisted himself onto the portico over the building's main entrance, wearing a bandana that made him look, in the eyes of a fellow protestor, like the Karate Kid. Once there, he attached a giant "Silence=Death" sign on the façade and set off smoke bombs, to the cheers of the throng.

The event was peaceful overall. A glass door and a couple of windows were shattered. Six activists sneaked inside the building and briefly occupied some non-FDA offices. One protester was arrested after knocking a police officer off his motorcycle. Other demonstrators, some in T-shirts declaring "Gay and Positive," occupied the driveway in front of the building and refused to move. Eventually, police—some wearing latex gloves—escorted or dragged 175 handcuffed activists to buses, which carted them off to be booked for loitering. Despite the gravity of the cause, the event was characterized by inspired camp and an almost festive camaraderie. One activist recalled, "It was really fun. I mean, it was really fun."[5]

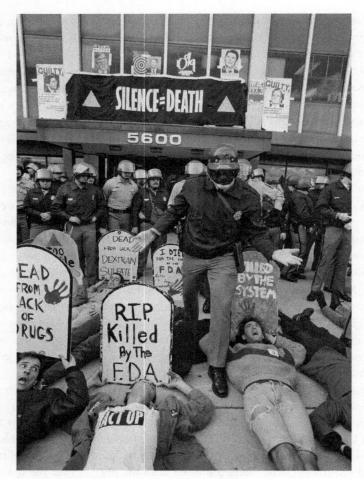

Figure 7.1 ACT UP demonstrators outside FDA headquarters in Rockville, Maryland, October 11, 1988. © *J. Scott Applewhite/AP Images.*

The day of the protest was not a productive one inside the Parklawn Building. Many employees stayed home or failed to breach the blockade. Those who managed to reach their desks spent hours peering through windows at the commotion outside.

When the workforce arrived en masse the next morning, things seemed back to normal. But in fact, the FDA never really resumed business as usual after ACT UP seized the agency in October 1988. The AIDS social movement spurred changes in the agency's implementation of the Food, Drug, and Cosmetic Act (FD&C Act) and, eventually, in the language of the statute itself. The resulting reforms have made access to potentially life-saving drugs a fundamental goal of the Act, alongside the protection of consumers from unsafe and ineffective products.

A recent scholarly trend, articulated most prominently by William N. Eskridge and John Ferejohn, focuses on how this country's foundational legal principles are contained not only in the US Constitution, but also in quasi-constitutional "superstatutes" and their implementation by administrative agencies. The 1938 FD&C Act is one such statute. Congress passed it largely in response to a crisis precipitated by insufficient government protection of drug consumers—namely, the death of more than a hundred people who consumed a medicine called Elixir Sulfanilamide. The statute was premised on the principle that the national government should shield consumers from unsafe products. The most significant subsequent increases in the FDA's power over medical products were also triggered by public health disasters. Congress enacted the 1962 Drug Amendments in reaction to the thalidomide crisis, and the 1976 Medical Device Amendments were inspired largely by a spate of severe injuries caused by the Dalkon Shield contraceptive device. In addition to granting the agency enhanced powers to protect consumers' safety, the 1962 and 1976 statutes also gave it premarket review authority over the *effectiveness* of drugs and devices. For most of the twentieth century, the American public broadly endorsed the FDA's gatekeeper role.[6]

The quasi-constitutional nature of the FD&C Act is reflected not only in the critical, deeply entrenched government structures and functions it has created, but also in its corresponding effect of restricting American consumers' choices within several fundamental product categories. As a formal matter, the Act curbs the conduct of manufacturers and distributors, not their customers. Nevertheless, when the FDA bans the sale of a product, it limits the rights of consumers who want that product. Americans usually quietly accept this constraint on their freedom of choice because they value the FDA's role in safeguarding their health. On occasion, however—and with increasing frequency since the 1970s— citizens have resisted FDA restrictions on the sale of certain products as unwarranted infringements on their autonomy. As we will see, these protests have been especially fervent with respect to potentially life-saving drugs, as patients have condemned government curbs on the distribution of such products as violations of the most fundamental right of all—the right to attempt to preserve one's own life.

The AIDS activists' struggle to change the FDA's approach to drug regulation can thus be viewed as a form of constitutional struggle, even though they rarely invoked the language of the US Constitution itself. By forcing a change in the FDA's regulatory practices, the campaign effectively amended what I call the country's "drug constitution." Before the AIDS movement took to the streets, the FDA viewed the sole core purpose of the FD&C Act as guarding the public health by protecting consumers from hazardous and ineffective products. By the time AIDS activism waned in the mid-1990s, the Act—as interpreted and applied by the agency—also embodied the (sometimes contrary) fundamental purpose of promoting the expeditious release of potentially effective treatments. Before the turn of the century, Congress would embody this transformation in the language of the FD&C Act itself.

A Movement for Freedom of Choice within Orthodox Medicine

Unlike their forerunners in the vitamin and Laetrile movements, the leading AIDS activists did not reject the scientific premises of modern drug development. To the contrary, they focused their demands on cutting-edge pharmaceutical treatments produced by the government-industrial-academic biomedical complex. AIDS activism was the first mass movement for freedom of therapeutic choice *within* orthodox scientific medicine.

The AIDS movement thus invited a fundamental tension into its ideology. American opponents of government restrictions on *alternative* therapies have long stressed the value of unfettered experimentation by practitioners and patients. By contrast, in modern scientific medicine, a treatment's efficacy is determined not by decentralized trial-and-error experimentation, but by meticulously designed, FDA-regulated, controlled clinical studies. Indeed, orthodox medical researchers believe that the unrestricted use of experimental drugs can *undermine* the quest for scientific truth by diverting patients away from such controlled studies. The AIDS activists thus pinned their hopes on a system in which the advancement of knowledge requires not *free* inquiry, but rather highly *regulated* inquiry. This tension between access and knowledge bedeviled the AIDS movement's campaign to reform FDA drug regulation.

The fact that AIDS activism was a movement for freedom of therapeutic choice *within* conventional medicine also impelled the AIDS community to embrace new tactics. Alternative medicine advocates have generally pursued their activism as outsiders, resisting establishment institutions and orthodox systems of knowledge. AIDS activists sometimes adopted an "outsider" approach, particularly when they engaged in disruptive direct actions, not only at the FDA, but also at the National Institutes of Health (NIH), St. Patrick's Cathedral, the New York Stock Exchange, AMA headquarters, and North Carolina senator Jesse Helms's house (which they sheathed in a giant condom).[7] But leading AIDS activists recognized that street protests alone could not achieve their more instrumental goal of reforming the FDA's approach to drug regulation. That mission, they concluded, required members of their movement to enter the halls of power and, using the technical language of modern scientific medicine, interact directly with the government, the pharmaceutical industry, and the clinical research community.

Consequently, an organized group of "treatment activists" emerged within ACT UP to lead the FDA reform effort. This determined coterie of eloquent laymen mastered the science of AIDS and the complexities of pharmaceutical research. Due to their emergence, the AIDS movement did not, like most social movements focused on science or medicine, simply attack the trustworthiness of "experts" or embrace an anti-scientific epistemology. Instead, as contemporaneously described by sociologist Steven Epstein:

> These activists wrangle with scientists on issues of truth and method. They seek not only to reform science by exerting pressure from the outside but also to perform science by locating themselves on the inside. . . . Most fundamentally, they claim to speak credibly as experts in their own right—as people who know about things scientific and who can partake of this special and powerful discourse of truth.[8]

This cluster of autodidacts engaged in highly technical discussions with the FDA and other stakeholders about how best to tackle the AIDS crisis. This "inside" complement to outside action was perhaps the defining characteristic of AIDS activism and subsequent movements for freedom within orthodox medicine. As we will see, however, it also represented a widening schism that ultimately tore ACT UP apart.

The Legal Framework of FDA Drug Regulation

Although the FDA arguably lacked sensitivity, creativity, and a sufficient sense of urgency in its early response to AIDS, nobody could charge it with violating the law by severely restricting access to drugs not yet definitively shown to be safe and effective. To the contrary, the agency was following the provisions of the FD&C Act to the letter. Unfortunately for PWAs clamoring for an opportunity to try new medications, that statute's primary goal was to keep unsafe and ineffective drugs off the market.

During the AIDS crisis, the FDA was operating within the regulatory framework established by the 1962 Drug Amendments. This still-intact framework, which we examined in Chapter 5, requires investigators to notify the FDA prior to commencing any study of an unapproved drug in human beings and authorizes the agency to disallow or halt any investigation that does not satisfy requirements set forth in FDA regulations, including human subject protections.

The "Investigational New Drug" (IND) regulations that the FDA issued to implement these provisions detailed the requirements for drug research and established the well-known three-phase structure for drug trials.[9]

Importantly, the 1962 Amendments further revised the FD&C Act to require the agency to reject a New Drug Application (NDA), not only if the applicant fails to demonstrate that the drug is safe, but also if it fails to provide "substantial evidence" of effectiveness.[10] Although the Amendments listed proof of safety and proof of effectiveness as separate requirements, the FDA immediately recognized the inextricable relationship between them and embraced a drug approval calculus that weighs benefit against risk.[11] This interpretation of the statute was sensible and probably inevitable. Many useful pharmaceutical products (including most AIDS and cancer drugs) pose significant risks. If the FDA considered the safety of such products in isolation from their benefits, it would reject many indispensable treatments. But this risk-benefit approach also exposed the FDA to a new type of challenge to its NDA decisions—attacks on the agency's policy judgments rather than (or in addition to) its scientific findings. After all, a decision by the FDA to reject an effective drug because of excessive risks is not merely a scientific conclusion. Rather, it is a determination that the product's risks so clearly outweigh its benefits that the government should deny patients and their physicians the opportunity to perform their own risk-benefit assessment and make their own treatment decision. The AIDS activists were among the first to attack FDA rulings on this basis.

The 1962 Amendments defined "substantial evidence" of effectiveness as "evidence consisting of adequate and well-controlled investigations, including clinical investigations, by experts qualified by scientific training and experience to evaluate the effectiveness of the drug involved." Congress left the precise meaning of "substantial evidence" to FDA regulation, however. The agency ordinarily interpreted it to require at least two successful Phase 3 trials demonstrating efficacy.[12] But as activists would realize, the agency's interpretation of this statutory standard was also a policy judgment subject to challenge, particularly in the context of an inevitably fatal disease whose victims might not demand the same level of certainty as people suffering from less serious ailments—or be able to wait as long.

Because of the rigorous, multistep drug development and approval process that Congress and the FDA imposed on manufacturers starting in 1962, many drugs took significantly longer to reach the market in the United States than in other advanced nations. The average interval that elapsed between the commencement of clinical research and final FDA approval grew from a little over four years in 1963 to more than ten years by 1990. While scholars and policymakers debated the significance and causes of this "drug lag," PWAs feared that without a change in approach, the AIDS treatments they needed would not reach the market until years after they had perished.[13] AIDS patients derived some solace from the FDA's March 1987 approval of AZT based on the results of just one successful Phase 2 study. Only twenty-two months passed between the start of clinical trials and approval of the NDA—a process so fast that one agency official likened AZT to a "greased pig."

AZT was not a cure, however, and it was intolerably toxic for many people at the prescribed dose.[14] PWAs desperately sought access to additional drugs. And they did not have time to wait for the FDA to complete even the most expedited approval process for these new medications. They wanted access to them *before* approval.

When the AIDS crisis arose, neither the FD&C Act nor FDA regulations explicitly allowed any use of unapproved drugs for the *treatment* of patients (as opposed to their administration for research purposes). Nonetheless, the agency had for decades sometimes permitted seriously ill patients with no satisfactory alternatives to obtain experimental drugs for treatment. It had done so on a largely ad hoc basis, under various rubrics, including "single patient exceptions" and "compassionate use INDs." The FDA had also overseen a number of programs in which larger numbers of patients used unapproved medications for treatment purposes. But in the words of legal scholar and former FDA chief counsel Richard Merrill, the FDA long believed that its primary job was "to prevent harm to consumers rather than facilitate the introduction of useful new medical products."[15] Consequently, preapproval access to drugs was a relatively rare phenomenon, as was rapid drug approval.

Conservative libertarians were the first to try to change the FDA's attitude.

The Reagan Administration and the Treatment IND

Ronald Reagan rolled into the presidency on a wave of anti-government fervor. The day after taking office in January 1981, he announced the establishment of a Presidential Task Force for Regulatory Relief chaired by Vice President (later President) George H. W. Bush. Later that year, the task force identified the drug approval process as one of twenty government regulatory programs in greatest need of reform. Although the administration's primary goal with respect to the FDA was shrinking the "drug lag," it also resolved to formalize the system by which severely ill patients with no alternatives could gain access to unapproved therapies. In June 1983, as part of a proposed broad reform of the IND requirements, the agency announced its intention to codify the agency's various pre-approval access practices under the name "Treatment IND."[16]

This initial proposal was rather restrained. It authorized the FDA to deny a request for a treatment IND whenever there was "not sufficient evidence of the drug's safety and effectiveness to justify its intended treatment use." Moreover, the proposal provided that investigational drugs would ordinarily become available for treatment use only after the end of Phase 2 studies. Finally, the FDA proposed that companies be permitted to charge for drugs released pursuant to a treatment IND only with the express written approval of the agency, based upon a showing that such sale was "required." This restriction was a major disincentive to participation by industry.

The treatment IND proposal was not a response to the AIDS crisis. At the time of its issuance in 1983, the disease had only recently emerged as a matter of public concern outside the gay community. Over the next few years, however, the treatment IND became closely linked to AIDS. As the disease spread virulently, PWAs learned to their distress that they could rarely obtain experimental therapies through the FDA's existing compassionate use programs. Between 1983 and 1987, the agency permitted the compassionate use of only two unapproved AIDS-related drugs. AIDS advocates thus began urging the administration to finalize the treatment IND rulemaking. Conservative libertarians joined PWAs in demanding that the FDA lower the regulatory barriers to AIDS drugs. For example, in a January 1987 New York Times op-ed column drawn from a Cato Institute report, Dale Gieringer declared: "Reform is needed to allow [AIDS] patients freedom of access to experimental drugs. . . . A country that honors free choice in religion, speech, and politics should also honor free choice in medicine."[17]

In March 1987, the FDA published a radical reproposal of the treatment IND rule shaped by deregulators within Reagan's Office of Management and Budget (OMB). It shifted the evidentiary burden onto the FDA, requiring the agency to approve a treatment IND request unless "the drug clearly does not provide a therapeutic benefit" or would expose patients "to an unreasonable and significant additional risk of illness or injury." It explicitly authorized the FDA to permit treatment use of experimental drugs prior to the completion of Phase 2 trials. Finally, the reproposal recognized that unless manufacturers could charge, "there might be no incentive . . . to supply investigational drugs for treatment use, thus denying the drug to patients who . . . choose to avail themselves of this treatment." It thus permitted drug sponsors to charge for treatment IND drugs after merely notifying the FDA, although it forbade them to commercially promote or market such products and allowed the agency to prohibit prices that were "manifestly unfair."[18]

The reproposal triggered a ferocious negative reaction. Unsurprisingly, the foes of the reproposal included the influential consumer protection organizations and their Democratic allies in Congress, the biomedical research establishment, and the FDA bureaucracy. Less expected, perhaps, was the opposition of the pharmaceutical industry. Although drug companies unambiguously favored a faster and less burdensome drug *approval* process, they were ambivalent at best about a rule that would facilitate *pre-approval* release. The distribution of investigational drugs for treatment use presented product supply challenges, posed tort liability risks, and threatened the completion of the clinical investigations required to obtain FDA approval. The Pharmaceutical Manufacturers Association (PMA), the trade association for large drug companies, did not take a public position on the reproposal, but FDA Commissioner Young later reported that PMA "would not live with" it. The *Wall Street Journal* editorial page, a champion of the treatment IND, angrily charged the PMA with obstructing the program.[19]

The combined forces arrayed against radical deregulation succeeded; the final rule, issued in May 1987, pulled back significantly from the reproposal. It authorized the FDA to deny a treatment IND for a drug "if the available scientific evidence, taken as a whole, fails to provide a reasonable basis for concluding that the drug may be effective for its intended use." Because the regulation did not define "reasonable basis," this provision gave the FDA latitude to block a treatment IND for any drug that had not completed Phase 2 trials. Moreover, the final rule capped the amount companies could charge for treatment IND drugs at the price "necessary to recover costs of manufacture, research, development, and handling" of the product.[20]

AIDS Activists Join the Fray

While this battle over the treatment IND rule raged, gay rights and AIDS organizations mostly sat on the sidelines. The gay community remained surprisingly uninvolved in FDA drug policy during the first five years of the epidemic. It focused more on other problems, such as widespread virulent homophobia and the potential imposition of coercive disease control measures. Influential people both inside and outside of the government publicly contemplated mandatory AIDS testing and quarantine. Conservative commentator William F. Buckley Jr. even appeared to recommend the compulsory tattooing of those found to be HIV-positive. As panic about the spread of AIDS grew, gay men increasingly found themselves fired from their jobs, evicted from their apartments, physically assaulted, and socially shunned.[21]

In this ominous environment, AIDS advocates initially embraced a primarily defensive agenda. Activist Gregg Bordowitz remembers: "Our first charge was to awaken the community to the possibilities of some very serious repressive actions against us, and to defend ourselves." The FDA demonstration in October 1988 thus represented an important pivot point for the AIDS movement. As Bordowitz later explained:

What [the] FDA [action] did was shift the group away from a defensive posture to an offensive posture ... and enabled us to come up with a vision for the
way that healthcare should be done in this country, the way that drugs should
be researched, and sold, and made available. Most importantly [sic] ... was the
idea that people with AIDS should be at the center of the public discussion on
AIDS.[22]

By the late 1980s, an important attitudinal shift was taking place within the
gay community. First of all, the widening availability of HIV tests meant that
a growing cadre of young gay men were learning they were infected while still
healthy and thus able to participate in treatment-oriented activism. Moreover,
the struggle with the FDA was bolstered by an intensifying sense of gay pride
and a fierce commitment to fighting societal apathy and hostility. The Parklawn
protest was not only an effort to mobilize the government against a horrific disease, but also a forum for the declaration of gay rights and for the assertion of
gay identity.[23]

The FDA demonstration also reflected the emergence of a new perspective
regarding the proper role of government in the AIDS crisis. Before 1988, representatives of the major gay rights and AIDS groups tended to cling to their pro-
regulation progressive roots and defend the FDA's authority. For example, Jeff
Levi, the executive director of the National Gay and Lesbian Task Force, opposed
the 1987 treatment IND reproposal. He sneered: "This is a scheme by the drug
companies to get rid of government regulation. ... This is Ronald Reagan trying
to deregulate the pharmaceutical industry."[24] But by the late 1980s, a new type of
AIDS advocate was moving to the forefront. These activists rejected the notion
that as "liberals" they should always favor more regulation. Their foremost goal
of "getting drugs into bodies" trumped all other concerns.

One such figure was San Francisco–based Martin Delaney, the founder of
Project Inform. Delaney, gay and HIV-negative, had been a Roman Catholic
seminarian, elementary school teacher, and management consultant before becoming a full-time AIDS treatment activist in the early 1980s. In April 1987, he
declared in his newsletter, *PI Perspective*, that the radically deregulatory treatment IND reproposal *did not go far enough*. After the more restrictive final rule
came out in October, Delaney called it a "sham" and "a lemon."[25]

For several years, Delaney had been helping to create an alternative method
for PWAs to obtain unapproved medications—importation from foreign countries. The FDA had long exercised enforcement discretion and permitted individuals to transport "personal use" amounts of such products into the country
in their luggage or by mail. After the start of the AIDS epidemic, Project Inform
coordinated efforts to import ever-increasing volumes of unapproved drugs
from Mexico and other countries, distribute them by underground networks,

and sell them in "buyers' clubs" and "guerrilla clinics." When in early 1988, the Customs Service seized packages of an unapproved AIDS drug mailed from Japan, Delaney personally lobbied FDA officials to clarify the personal importation policy. On July 23, 1988, in a widely publicized speech at a gay and lesbian health conference in Boston, FDA commissioner Frank Young announced a new "Pilot Guidance for Release of Mail Importations." Although an unnamed federal official speculated to *Science* magazine that Young had gone "temporarily insane," the guidance was in fact merely an affirmation of existing FDA policy. Nevertheless, it had immense symbolic import.[26]

Meanwhile, activists on the East Coast also began to demand that the FDA expedite access to AIDS drugs. One of the first was Marty Robinson, who in 1986 co-founded a group of aggressive AIDS protesters in New York called the Lavender Hill Mob. Like Delaney, he thought even the OMB-shaped reproposal of the treatment IND rule was too restrictive. At April 1987 congressional hearings, Robinson dismissed the reproposal as "tokenism and public relations, nothing more" and demanded "greater availability of drugs undergoing Phase II testing."[27]

By this time, Robinson's place at the vanguard of the East Coast AIDS movement was being assumed by Larry Kramer. Kramer was a confrontational and abrasive New York author and playwright who co-founded Gay Men's Health Crisis in 1982 but left the organization the next year following conflicts with less militant members. On March 10, 1987, Kramer—not yet aware that he was HIV-positive—delivered a speech at the Lesbian and Gay Community Services Center in Greenwich Village calling for the creation of a new AIDS organization committed to direct action. Two days later, Kramer and other activists (including Robinson) gathered at the Center and founded the group that would soon be named the Aids Coalition to Unleash Power—ACT UP. The organization's initial demands included the appointment of an FDA "undercommissioner" from within the AIDS community, the "*immediate* testing and expeditious release of experimental drugs," the elimination of placebo trials, and the removal of FDA's authority over trials of AIDS drugs.[28]

On March 23, Kramer wrote a scathing opinion essay in the *New York Times* titled "The F.D.A.'s Callous Response to AIDS." He scornfully dismissed the FDA's approval of AZT three days earlier as a "sop to the gay community." He also furiously attacked the agency's reluctance to allow pre-approval access to other medications. "Doctors everywhere are waiting to put into immediate use a battery of drugs that have passed Phase One safety trials," he insisted. "AIDS sufferers, who have nothing to lose, are more than willing to be guinea pigs. . . . We cannot understand for the life of us, or for what life in us many of us still cling to hungrily, why the F.D.A. withholds [these drugs] especially when the victims are so eager to be part of the experimental process."[29]

The next day, ACT UP conducted its first public demonstration—a march on Wall Street in which protesters demanded the immediate release of seven drugs and burned FDA Commissioner Young in effigy.[30] A year and a half later, ACT UP demonstrators descended on the Parklawn Building.

Getting Inside the Agency

The FDA was a tricky target for this burgeoning social movement. The FDA's decisions occurred behind a veil of scientific complexity, technical expertise, and administrative bureaucracy. The Administrative Procedure Act (APA) grants citizens a right to submit comments on rules proposed by the FDA and other agencies. Nevertheless, agencies maintain extremely broad discretion to reject commenters' objections and suggestions. The APA also compels agencies to provide interested persons the right to petition for new rules, but agencies have no obligation whatsoever to grant such petitions. In any event, specific drug approval decisions are not "rules" subject to the APA's public participation provisions. Finally, the country's widespread homophobia inevitably bled into the agency itself. Soon after the Parklawn action, an unnamed top FDA official corroborated the protesters' claim that the agency was lagging on AIDS drugs because the majority of PWAs were gay.[31]

The AIDS activists thus decided that their campaign for bodily freedom must commence with their mass bodily presence at the FDA itself. When they concocted the idea of a protest at FDA headquarters, ACT UP's David Barr and Mickey Wheatley explained:

> We have this idea for a strategy that would be very different than things that have been tried before in activism. . . . Many groups have gone to Washington and protested in front of the White House. Many groups have protested in front of Congress. For our movement, we need to go to the Food and Drug Administration. . . . This is an institution that is very specific to the issues that we're facing.

Years later, Barr—apparently unaware of the smaller FDA protests conducted by Krebiozen, vitamin, and women's health activists in the 1960s and 1970s—continued to insist that "there had never been a demonstration at the Food and Drug Administration before, ever."[32]

Importantly, the Parklawn action's organizers always viewed the event as merely a first step. Their ultimate objective was to be invited *inside* the building, to participate in the meetings where FDA employees forged drug policy with scientists and industry representatives. "The idea was to cut through the bureaucratic red tape of the Food and Drug Administration," Gregg Bordowitz later recalled. "But more than that, that people with AIDS should be involved in every level of decision-making concerning research for a treatment and a cure for our disease." It is telling that ACT UP titled the action "Seize Control of FDA" rather than, for example, "Burn Down FDA." Unlike the Laetrile protesters before them, most AIDS activists thought the FDA had an important role to play. Rather than seeking to eliminate FDA regulation of AIDS drugs, they strove to participate in the agency's processes and thus reform its scientific and regulatory vision.[33]

The outside component of ACT UP's outside-inside strategy was nonetheless vital to the movement's success. The mass action at the FDA helped not only to thrust the treatment activists inside the halls of government, but also to ensure that the federal bureaucracy and the public at large would perceive the development and release of AIDS drugs as a momentous matter of social justice. To this day, members of the "insider" treatment group credit their achievements to both aspects of the outside-inside approach.[34] As we will see, however, once ACT UP's treatment specialists gained access to the government policymakers, a growing divide developed between them and the broader AIDS activist community.

"With Friends Like These . . ."

Just hours after the Parklawn demonstration, ACT UP's Peter Staley (the aforementioned "Karate Kid") appeared on the CNN political debate show *Crossfire*. Patrick Buchanan, the often-intolerant interlocutor "on the right," told him: "Mr. Staley, this is going to astonish you, but I agree with you a hundred percent. I think if someone's got AIDS and someone wants to take a drug, it's their life and if it gives him hope he oughta be able to take it." Earlier that year, Buchanan had published a memoir in which he had scorned Gay Pride Week as a "celebration of sodomy" and condemned homosexuals as "the perpetrators of this epidemic that will kill more Americans than Korea and Vietnam."[35]

As the AIDS movement forged ahead with its FDA reform agenda, it confronted a major conundrum: how to manage its alliance with conservative deregulators. Leading AIDS advocates suggested publicly that they cautiously welcomed this partnership. Kramer, for example, acknowledged that conservative Republicans were "strange bedfellows" for his largely gay, overwhelmingly left-leaning movement, but he concluded, "What liberal support is there?"[36]

The two sides of this unlikely coalition agreed on breathtakingly little outside the narrow question of early access to AIDS drugs. Indeed, they even held starkly divergent views regarding the value of FDA regulation in general. The *Wall Street Journal*'s editors invoked the AIDS crisis in calling for the complete repeal of the

FD&C Act's requirement that manufacturers demonstrate efficacy prior to approval. The conservative Heritage Foundation went further, proposing that the FDA be stripped of its gatekeeping power over drugs altogether. By contrast, the *ACT UP FDA Action Handbook*, distributed to participants in the Parklawn demonstration, warned: "AIDS advocates must be careful to keep their agenda, supporting earlier access to promising life-saving drugs . . ., from becoming confused with the Bush deregulation/Wall St. Journal/Heritage Foundation agenda of sweeping drug industry deregulation. It would be a disaster for all American consumers, including people with HIV infection, if the Kefauver [1962] Amendments were repealed and drug companies were no longer required to prove safety and efficacy for most drugs."[37]

ACT UP campaigned for national health insurance and Kramer urged the establishment of a federal "Manhattan Project" to find a cure for AIDS. Conversely, President Reagan famously intoned "government is not the solution to our problem; government is the problem" and consistently underfunded AIDS research. In his 1986 budget, he proposed *cutting* the appropriation for this purpose by 22 percent.[38]

By necessity, treatment activists overcame their aversion to sitting in the same room as Republicans. Nevertheless, AIDS movement leaders recognized that this was, at best, an alliance of convenience and that they would have to manage the relationship carefully.

Articulating an Ideology of Liberty

If few members of the AIDS community embraced a thoroughgoing libertarianism like that of conservative deregulators, exactly what type of liberty were they advocating for?

Bodily freedom was always a central feature of the AIDS movement's rhetoric. As early as 1983, the quasi-constitutional "Denver Principles," drawn up at the National Gay and Lesbian Health Conference, listed among the "Rights of People with AIDS" a right "to full explanations of all medical procedures and risks, to choose or refuse their treatment modalities, to refuse to participate in research without jeopardizing their treatment and to make informed decisions about their lives." Such statements illustrate the AIDS movement's indebtedness to the patients' rights movement of the early 1970s and its emphasis on informed consent. The AIDS activists sought a level of bodily autonomy that transcended these earlier calls for patients' rights, however. First, their ideology of bodily freedom extended beyond health issues to sexual conduct and expression. Second, they demanded access to treatments that they could not legally obtain.[39] In both of these respects, the true progenitor of ACT UP's bodily freedom philosophy was the women's health movement of the 1970s.

From the time of its inception, ACT UP included a large cohort of women, many with experience in feminist, women's health, and reproductive rights advocacy. These women—many of them lesbians—shared their ideology and tactical experience with their gay male counterparts. ACT UP member Robert Vazquez-Pacheco opined: "ACT UP, historically, directly came from . . . the women's health movement." ACT UP's Women's Caucus in New York City compiled an enormous handbook on the women's health movement and presented it in a "teach-in" to hundreds of men. Risa Denenberg, a leader of the caucus, explained that feminism contributed directly to the AIDS activists' ideology, in particular the "empowerment that takes place . . . when concepts change about things that are as basic as who has control over your body. So if it came up to something like drugs into bodies, it was just nice to kind of have that perspective."[40]

The abortion rights aspect of the women's health movement was a particularly compelling model for ACT UP members. Brian Zabcik "always saw a very strong relationship" between abortion rights and AIDS advocacy. He explained, "In both instances, we were trying to work for a solution that would help people avoid being punished for their sexual mistakes." ACT UP members participated enthusiastically in pro-choice mobilization events because, in one member's words: "They're the same issue. It's about control over our bodies." Not coincidentally, "choice" became the most important word in ACT UP's verbal arsenal. Jim Serafini of ACT UP San Francisco declared of the group's agenda: "Sounds all-American, doesn't it? It is because it is about freedom and choice."[41]

As we saw, nineteenth-century movements for freedom of therapeutic choice were bolstered by a robust strand of economic freedom. During the AIDS crisis, some conservative deregulators similarly contended that FDA drug regulation improperly violated contractual liberty. For example, Sam Kazman of the Competitive Enterprise Institute opined:

> Restoring the right of contract might do more for [PWAs] than any other change in the world of law. . . . In cases of untreatable diseases . . . unapproved drugs would no longer be categorically barred. Instead, they could now be available by prescription, with a clear warning of their unapproved status. . . . Those who wished to rely on FDA's judgment could continue to do so. The rest of us could knowingly, and contractually, assume the risks of unconventional therapies. . . . Such an exercise of the right of contract is nothing more than what the Framers intended 200 years ago.

Mark Milano of ACT UP likewise suggested that the FDA require drug manufacturers to "put the data on the label" and let the "marketplace" decide. Such arguments were relatively rare among AIDS activists, however.[42]

Meanwhile, the freedom of conscience strain of medical liberty—so essential when the therapies defended were Christian Science and Mind Cure—were largely absent from the AIDS activists' campaign for FDA reform. Faith simply was not a central element of their modern scientific approach to finding a cure. The closest they came to acknowledging a nonmaterialist aspect of medicine were their occasional paeans to the value of "hope."

Finally, the most prominent AIDS treatment activists emphatically *rejected* the value to society of the fourth traditional medical liberty strand, "freedom of inquiry," at least to the extent this notion applied to unrestricted experimentation by individual patients and doctors. Unfettered trial-and-error was once thought to be the best method for advancing therapeutic knowledge. Since the middle of the twentieth century, however, scientific medicine (a system embraced by the AIDS movement's treatment experts) has deemed such individualized experimentation to be irrelevant to determining a treatment's true value. Instead, the FDA-regulated controlled clinical trial has become the "gold standard" for establishing effectiveness. Because such trials are randomized and controlled (ideally, placebo-controlled), this model of investigation is, at root, premised on *denying* participants a free choice of therapy. Indeed, because such studies are double-blind, patients and physicians are not even aware of what therapy (if any) each patient is taking. Moreover, from the perspective of modern medicine, the widespread use of experimental AIDS drugs outside of clinical studies was not merely irrelevant to the search for a cure, but threatened to undermine it. Why would a PWA enroll in a controlled clinical study of a promising new medicine and risk receiving the control when he could obtain the experimental drug for certain elsewhere? If too many patients were diverted away from clinical trials, these studies might never be completed, and nobody would know for sure whether new AIDS treatments provided any clinical benefit.

In the face of this tension, AIDS activists followed one of two paths. Some flatly insisted that PWAs' personal right to choose was more important than the advancement of medical knowledge. Others, by contrast, prioritized the acquisition of scientific understanding but tried to reconceptualize medical research so that the use of experimental drugs outside of traditional controlled studies would not interfere with research, and perhaps even contribute to it. Eventually, as we will see, these different approaches proved to be irreconcilable, and bitter conflict divided the movement. But first came some collective triumphs.

Modest Victory: Subpart E

The Parklawn action quickly bore fruit. Barely more than a week after the demonstration, the FDA issued a rule that, at least on its face, promised speedier approval of AIDS drugs.[43]

A chief demand of the AIDS activists was that the FDA should, when considering the NDA for a drug for an incurable fatal disease, require less conclusive proof of efficacy than usual and instead err on the side of approving the product and letting patients make their own risk-benefit assessments. Two months before the Parklawn protest, Vice President Bush, acting as chairman of the Task Force on Regulatory Relief, had charged the FDA with developing procedures for the expedited approval of therapies for AIDS and other life-threatening diseases. On October 19, 1988, the FDA suddenly announced an immediately effective new rule establishing procedures to speed the approval of drugs for "life-threatening and severely debilitating illnesses." The *Washington Post* reported that the FDA issued the rule "primarily to assuage AIDS activists."[44]

These "Subpart E" procedures (still in effect today and partially codified in the FD&C Act under the rubric "Fast Track") invite drug sponsors to request early meetings with the FDA regarding the design of animal and human studies. The most important such consultation is an "end-of-Phase 1 meeting" intended to discuss how the sponsor might design data-rich Phase 2 trials that will obviate the need to proceed to Phase 3 before approval. The Subpart E regulations also bind the FDA, when considering NDAs for drugs for life-threatening and severely debilitating illnesses, to perform a risk-benefit analysis that "tak[es] into consideration the severity of the disease and the absence of satisfactory alternative therapy." The preamble to the 1988 rule declared: "The agency recognizes that safety and effectiveness are not absolute . . . but must be assessed in light of what condition the drug treats." The FDA thus embraced the AIDS activists' essential argument regarding drug approval—namely, that victims of grave illnesses are willing to accept greater uncertainty and risk than are people suffering from less serious ailments.[45]

Although major newspapers gave the FDA's announcement of the Subpart E regulations front-page coverage, the AIDS community was unenthusiastic. Martin Delaney acknowledged that the rule represented "a touch of common sense," but he added, "We got a nickel when we needed a dollar." Some AIDS activists dismissed the FDA's action as a cynical campaign ploy by Bush, then in the final weeks of his ultimately successful presidential race. The rule's detractors asserted that it was merely a statement of flexibility that the FDA already possessed, as demonstrated by the rapid approval of AZT the previous year. Activists also bemoaned the agency's lack of resources to implement the new procedures.[46]

Triumph: Parallel Track

Genesis of an Idea

Despite their dissatisfaction with the Subpart E regulations, the activists quickly turned their attention to other matters. Because no anti-HIV drugs were nearing FDA approval in autumn 1988—even under the most expedited procedures— the activists focused instead on gaining access to unapproved drugs earlier in their development, before they had even entered Phase 2 trials.

As discussed earlier, the final version of the 1987 Treatment IND rule essentially required that there be a "reasonable basis" for concluding that the unapproved drug was effective. The FDA was thus unlikely ever to grant a treatment IND before positive results emerged from at least one Phase 2 trial. In practice, the agency tended to permit treatment use only after the completion of Phase 3. This regime frustrated AIDS groups, who began demanding access to experimental drugs based solely on Phase 1 results, even though these early uncontrolled studies are designed to assess safety and provide, at most, preliminary indications of effectiveness.

In an October 1988 speech before the Infectious Diseases Society of America, Martin Delaney presented one of the first detailed arguments in favor of allowing PWAs to try drugs for which there was only minimal evidence of effectiveness.[47] He opened by declaring: "If public and individual good are not clearly harmed, then the government should not stand in the way. That is the American way." He contended that therefore "the burden of proof should not be on those seeking access to experimental therapy but upon those who seek to deny such access." Delaney rejected the argument, frequently advanced by regulators, that PWAs must be protected from their own desperation. This view, he opined, "smack[ed] of 'big brother.'" He also dismissed the common assertion that PWAs should be denied experimental drugs because they "may do more harm than good." He declared, "It is often equally possible that the treatment may do more good than harm. . . . The question should be, 'who gets to decide what risks are acceptable: the bureaucracy in Washington or the patient whose life is on the line?'"

Finally, in a groundbreaking portion of his speech, Delaney addressed the concern that wide access to experimental drugs would make clinical research difficult or impossible to conduct. He observed that regardless of any impact on research, "many patients and their advocates find it morally repugnant to deny potentially life-saving treatment to the masses to force the few into clinical studies." Fortunately, a choice between individual liberties and the advancement of science was not necessary, because—contrary to widely held assumptions— early treatment use of unapproved drugs served both. Delaney urged his listeners to consider how clinical research actually proceeds "in the laboratory of the real world." He explained that because people join clinical trials for a variety of reasons (including "simple and admirable altruism"), researchers would find sufficient numbers of subjects for their controlled studies even if the experimental drugs were also available through other avenues.

Delaney then presented a daring and counterintuitive argument. He contended that providing wide access to unapproved drugs for treatment would actually *enhance* the clinical research enterprise. He explained:

> The real-world AIDS experience . . . shows us that the policy of restriction is itself destroying our ability to conduct clinical research. AIDS study centers throughout the nation tell of widescale concurrent use of other treatments; frequent cheating, even bribing, to gain entry to studies; mixing of drugs by patients to share and dilute the risk of being on placebo; and rapid dropping out of patients who learn that they are on placebo. . . .

> If patients had other means of obtaining treatment, force-fitting them into clinical studies would be unnecessary. Volunteers that remained would be more likely to act as pure research subjects, entering studies not solely out of a desperate effort to save their lives.

Delaney further argued that the simultaneous provision of experimental therapies for treatment use outside clinical studies "in a structured and monitored fashion" would itself provide "useful evidence of long-term benefits and drawbacks."

Delaney emphasized that the fight against AIDS, "the medical equivalent of war," demanded a new approach. "Inflexibly applied to the AIDS epidemic, regulatory practices contribute to the failure of science, demean the public good, and tread heavily on our civil liberties." He concluded: "Science and patient alike would be better served by a system that permits life-threatened patients some form of access to the most promising experimental therapies, peacefully coexisting alongside a program of unencumbered clinical research."[48] Although he did not use the precise words, Delaney had eloquently advocated the creation of what would soon come to be known as the "parallel track."

The term "parallel track" entered public discourse at the June 1989 International Conference on AIDS in Montreal. At this meeting, members of ACT UP's Treatment and Data (T&D) Committee presented a document titled "A National AIDS Treatment Research Agenda." This agenda proposed a "parallel track" procedure permitting the treatment use of experimental drugs while controlled efficacy trials were ongoing. A revised version of the agenda published three months later elaborated: "Parallel Track should encompass post-Phase I open-label [i.e., unblinded] treatment protocols for people unable

to participate in controlled clinical trials for AIDS and HIV-related treatments."
According to this document, various categories of HIV-infected patients should
be deemed "unable to participate" in clinical trials and thus eligible for parallel
track. They included, among others, people who could not tolerate the standard
treatment being used as the active control, people for whom that standard treatment had already failed, and people who were too sick to enroll in a clinical trial
or too distant from a study site. The agenda emphasized that safety and (if possible) efficacy data should be collected on parallel track subjects, thus providing
important early information on "real-world" usage of the experimental drug.
Finally, the document proposed that the parallel track program be implemented
by a newly created Parallel Track Advisory Committee composed of government
and industry representatives, AIDS primary care physicians, representatives of
community-based research groups, and—critically—"people with AIDS, HIV,
and their advocates."[49]

In the months following the Montreal conference, ACT UP began participating in policy discussions inside the federal bureaucracy. Simultaneously, and
perhaps inevitably, T&D activists who had achieved some mastery of the complex subjects of drug development and FDA regulation began to dominate the
organization's pharmaceutical-related efforts. Other than Iris Long, a straight female chemist, ACT UP's T&D Committee was composed of self-taught young
gay men. Jim Eigo, for example, was an HIV-negative avant-garde writer with
a graduate degree in theater but no post-secondary science education. Another
prominent ACT UP treatment specialist was Mark Harrington, an HIV-positive
aspiring screenwriter. Harrington, who had majored in visual and environmental studies at Harvard, had no background in medicine other than some
menial temporary jobs in a hospital. The tactics and attitudes of this cluster of
brilliant autodidacts increasingly differentiated them from the broad mass of
ACT UP members.

Enter Fauci

The person most responsible for ushering the treatment activists into the
decision-making processes of the federal government was Dr. Anthony
Fauci, the director of the National Institute of Allergy and Infectious Diseases
(NIAID) within NIH. Fauci initially opposed extensive pre-approval use of
AIDS drugs for treatment, fearing it would deter participation in clinical trials.
He changed his mind, however, both because of his growing distress over the
plight of dying PWAs and because AIDS activists persuaded him that clinical
research would survive, and perhaps even improve, if accompanied by treat-
ment access. Following the Montreal conference, Fauci invited some ACT UP

T&D Committee members to NIH to discuss their plan. Days later, on June 23, 1989, Fauci delivered a speech in San Francisco in which he outlined a new program, titled Parallel Track, that would make unapproved AIDS drugs available for treatment use as soon as they were proved safe, even as clinical trials were ongoing. In his pronounced Brooklyn accent, which would become so familiar to Americans three decades later during the COVID-19 pandemic, the NIAID chief acknowledged that this proposal resulted from "constructive pressure" from AIDS advocacy groups.[50]

Fauci did not confer with the FDA before delivering this speech—a striking lapse, in view of the fact that the FDA, not NIAID, would be responsible for designing and implementing any parallel track mechanism. FDA Commissioner Young quickly insisted, "I've been pushing [parallel track] as much as Tony has"—and then commenced the difficult work of putting flesh on Fauci's skeletal proposal. As one scholar remarked: "Overnight, Fauci became the hero of the activist community and . . . made the [FDA] regulators into the stumbling block to reform."[51]

Less than a month later, Young was sitting beside Fauci on a panel of government representatives promoting their parallel track plan before a House subcommittee. The subcommittee was chaired by Representative Henry Waxman, a traditional consumer protection advocate who opened the proceedings by emphasizing the FD&C Act's critical role of "protect[ing] consumers from dangerous products and from snake oil remedies." Waxman also defended the morality of imposing "a policy of limited distribution today, so that we will have adequate information for tomorrow." In response to Waxman's suggestion that the proposal was "an opening for laetrile," James Mason, the HHS assistant secretary in charge of the National AIDS program, assured the congressman that the program would be limited to drugs that showed "some promise" of efficacy—either in animal experimentation or in Phase 1. The panel expressed confidence that the existence of a parallel track would not discourage sufficient voluntary participation in clinical trials. Fauci emphasized that because only PWAs ineligible or unable to participate in a clinical trial were eligible for the parallel track, nobody could choose the parallel track *instead* of a controlled study, in any event.[52]

In his testimony, Martin Delaney took issue with Fauci's proposal to make the parallel track off-limits to anyone eligible and able to participate in a clinical trial. He opined that policymakers were still too concerned with preserving the integrity of the clinical trial process and too little concerned with protecting PWAs' medical autonomy. "Research outcomes are not the only objective of what we're trying to accomplish here, and there's a broad enough pool of patients here that we can give a degree of choice to those who are at the most near-term risk of losing their own lives. We think choice has to be given to those people."[53]

Advisory Committee Meeting

Later that summer, Young convened an FDA advisory committee (a body of outside experts) to help resolve the complex issues surrounding parallel track. The August 17, 1989, meeting of FDA's Anti-Infective Drugs Advisory Committee in Bethesda, Maryland, was an extraordinary event. Traditionally, advisory committee meetings had been the exclusive domain of government bureaucrats, scientists, industry representatives, and, sometimes, members of established consumer protection groups. In this meeting, AIDS activists played a prominent—even dominant—role. The FDA, sensing the shifting political dynamics, invited Delaney, Eigo, and several other AIDS activists to testify. About ten additional activists and patients took the microphone during the open public hearing. ACT UP bused in members to fill the spectators' seats. The result was a departure from the normally staid atmosphere of such events; the highly engaged audience punctuated the proceedings with applause and laughter dozens of times. The activists thus established an important precedent for extensive patient involvement in FDA advisory committee meetings.[54]

At the start of the meeting, Fauci and Young spoke favorably but guardedly about the creation of a parallel track program. Next, Delaney and Eigo emphasized the burning need for such a program and urged that AIDS community members be afforded a central role in its design and implementation. They both contended that PWAs with no treatment alternatives had a "right" to take an informed risk on an experimental drug, and they both rejected the notion that currently infected individuals should make a "sacrifice" for the future greater good. Still, a subtle difference existed between the two men's views, representing a growing East Coast/West Coast divide among AIDS treatment activists. Eigo stressed the importance of obtaining "real world" safety and efficacy information from the parallel track. Delaney, by contrast, favored limiting mandatory data collection in the parallel track. He worried that significant paperwork requirements would "choke the system" and discourage participation by community doctors. Delaney insisted that "the objective of parallel track is not to conduct research. It is to provide treatment."[55]

The right to choose was a recurring refrain in the eloquent and passionate testimony that followed. For example, Michelle Roland of ACT UP San Francisco endorsed Fauci's parallel track proposal only ambivalently because of its restrictions on participation in the parallel track. She warned that her organization would continue to agitate until *all* AIDS patients had "the right to choose to use an experimental therapy once it has been shown to be reasonably safe and there is some indication of efficacy." Larry Kramer, predictably, provided a fiery coda: "If we do not get these drugs you will see an uprising, the likes of which

you have never seen before since the Vietnam War in this country. We will sabo-
tage all of your Phase II studies. We will continue to get our drugs on the underground. Our chemists will duplicate your formulas."[56]

By the end of this August 1989 advisory committee meeting, the parallel track
idea had unstoppable momentum. Indeed, the agency was already on the verge
of allowing post–Phase 1 treatment access to dideoxyinosine (ddI), an antiretroviral product without AZT's severe toxicity. In September, the secretary of HHS
announced a treatment IND for ddI with a protocol—designed by manufacturer
Bristol Myers Squibb with the assistance of ACT UP—that bore all the marks of a
parallel track program.[57]

The Policy

In May 1990, the FDA set forth the parallel track mechanism in a proposed policy
statement. The policy applied only to individuals with AIDS or HIV-related
diseases, although the agency expressed a willingness to consider expanding the
program to other life-threatening diseases later. The proposal limited patient
choice and prioritized the pursuit of data more than Delaney would have preferred. It did not allow patients to join the parallel track if they were eligible for a
controlled study in which they could realistically participate. Moreover, the FDA
emphasized the importance of including "sufficient safeguards and oversight to
ensure that [the parallel track] neither delays nor compromises the controlled
clinical trials." Finally, the proposal emphatically required physicians participating in the parallel track procedure to collect and report safety data, and sometimes efficacy data.[58]

Despite these conditions, the creation of parallel track was an indisputable triumph for the AIDS activists. It allowed many PWAs to try an unapproved drug
after Phase 1, when evidence of efficacy was little more than suggestive. The
activists also prevailed in their demand that the AIDS community play a role
in administering parallel track; under the policy, the FDA would presumptively
refer all parallel track proposals to the AIDS Research Advisory Committee
(ARAC), a body chartered by NIAID that included PWAs as well as scientists and
physicians.[59]

If there was any doubt that the FDA would ultimately finalize the policy, it
disappeared a few months later, when the "Lasagna Committee" convened by
Reagan's Task Force for Regulatory Relief to examine the procedures for approving new cancer and AIDS drugs endorsed a parallel track for treatments
of these diseases. The report observed, "Although [earlier access] will clearly
present greater risks to patients, because some of the drugs may eventually
be found either to be ineffective or to present an unacceptable benefit/risk

ratio, patients with life-threatening diseases who have no alternative therapy are entitled to make this choice." In April 1992, the FDA published its final parallel track policy statement, which remained essentially unchanged from the proposal. Once again, the interests of AIDS activists and Republican deregulators had aligned.[60]

Schism: The Treatment Activists Break Away

Despite the AIDS activist community's success with parallel track, ACT UP was coming apart at the seams. Around 1990, the organization started dividing into two indistinct and overlapping but nonetheless identifiable camps. On one side were the "treatment activists," primarily middle-class, white, HIV-positive gay males who emphasized the goal of getting "drugs into bodies." They increasingly clashed with the "social activists," a group composed largely of women (especially lesbian, HIV-negative women) and people of color (many of them gay and HIV-positive). The social activists focused their energy on issues other than the development and approval of AIDS drugs. They advocated social services for PWAs and equal access to health care, and they demanded that the government pay special attention to the particular challenges confronted by HIV-infected women, African Americans, and Latinos.[61] Although the two groups generally supported each other's agendas, their priorities diverged.

The conflict was particularly bitter within ACT UP/NY, the organization's founding chapter, where members of the Treatment and Data Committee feuded with the Women's Caucus. The most contentious issue was a 1991 proposal by Tracy Morgan, a Caucus leader, that ACT UP impose a six-month moratorium on meetings with government officials. Moratorium proponents believed that T&D members were being corrupted by their increasingly cooperative relationships with the federal AIDS bureaucracy. T&D activists, pleased by their hard-won access to government decision makers, responded to the proposal with horror. David Barr, an HIV-positive treatment activist, scolded Morgan: "You know, what you're saying would kill me."[62] The ACT UP membership voted down the moratorium, but the controversy added to T&D's sense of exasperation and alienation. In January 1992, the T&D leadership split off from ACT UP and formed the Treatment Action Group (TAG), an independent nonprofit organization with invitation-only membership devoted exclusively to speeding the development and availability of AIDS therapies.

Within a couple of years, an equally significant breach opened up within the treatment community itself. The fault line was the inherent tension between freedom of choice and the pursuit of medical truth. The issue that triggered the rupture was a new mechanism called accelerated approval.

The Internecine Battle over Accelerated Approval

Birth of the Procedure

Whereas the parallel track program made drugs available *prior* to FDA approval, accelerated approval—promulgated by the agency as a final rule in 1992— hastened the actual approval of drugs for life-threatening diseases. It authorized approval of an NDA before the acquisition of any concrete evidence that the drug actually lengthened survival. Instead, accelerated approval was based on studies (frequently Phase 2 studies) demonstrating the product's effect on an unvalidated "surrogate endpoint"—a laboratory measurement reasonably likely, but not certain, to correlate with clinical benefit.[63]

Accelerated approval was another product of the unusual alliance between AIDS activists and Republican deregulators. In 1990, to the frustration of many, AZT remained the only FDA-approved drug intended to suppress the HIV virus itself. The August 1990 final report of the Lasagna Committee urged the agency to "exercise its statutory and administrative flexibility to approve AIDS and cancer drugs for marketing at the earliest possible point in their development" and, in particular, to make progress "in approving drugs on the basis of surrogate endpoints." Several months later, a coalition of San Francisco–based AIDS activists petitioned the FDA to approve the NDAs for ddI and another drug, ddC, based on surrogate endpoints rather than improved survival.[64]

On October 9, 1991, before the completion of Phase 2 clinical trials, the FDA approved ddI for patients not helped by AZT. The parallel-track-like program implemented by the drug's manufacturer, Bristol-Meyers, in 1989 had made ddI available to about 23,000 patients and generated important safety data. No evidence yet existed, however, that the drug actually extended the lives of PWAs. Nonetheless, the FDA approved it "conditionally" based on preliminary results showing an increase in patients' T-4 cells (signaling a strengthening of the immune system). The agency said it would revisit the approval when the clinical trial was finished.[65]

The accelerated approval of ddI changed the rules of the drug's distribution in critical ways, compared to parallel track. For example, it would now be available to all PWAs, not just those who satisfied the parallel track's protocol. Moreover, Bristol-Meyers, which had been providing ddI free to patients in the parallel track, would now be permitted to sell it at a profit—for a retail price of about $2,000 per year. Accelerated approval thus gave the company a financial incentive to maximize the drug's distribution. But who would pay for the medication? Insurance drug plans rarely covered experimental treatments outside the cancer area, but they virtually always covered FDA-approved products. The day of ddI's approval, David Kessler, the new FDA commissioner, clarified that accelerated approval was no different from traditional drug approval in this respect. He "expected government and private insurers to pay for ddI like any other F.D.A.-approved drug."[66] The drug's accelerated approval was thus news that industry could cheer along with patient advocates.

On April 15, 1992, the FDA published a proposed rule establishing accelerated approval for drugs intended to treat serious or life-threatening illnesses. The rule stated: "FDA may grant marketing approval for a new drug product on the basis of adequate and well-controlled clinical trials establishing that the drug product has an effect on a surrogate endpoint that is reasonably likely . . . to predict clinical benefit." It also provided, "Such approval will be subject to the requirement that the applicant study the drug further . . . to verify and describe its clinical benefit." The proposal established expedited withdrawal procedures if the mandatory follow-up studies were not performed or failed to verify clinical benefit. In June 1992, even though the rule was not yet finalized, the FDA used the procedure to approve ddC, manufactured by Hoffman–La Roche. In December 1992, the FDA issued a final accelerated approval rule without significant revisions.[67]

TAG's Misgivings

Despite widespread satisfaction among the AIDS movement, some treatment-focused activists were uneasy about accelerated approval. As a member of the advisory committee considering ddC in 1992, Mark Harrington doubted that it had any clinical benefit. He voted in favor of accelerated approval of the drug anyway, because he felt bound to follow the majority sentiment of his community. Later, as Hoffmann–La Roche failed to complete the confirmatory studies it had promised, Harrington and some of his TAG colleagues increasingly regretted his "yes" vote. These East Coast activists began to feel that "the AIDS community, in its understandable desperation, was being manipulated by industry to demand the expeditious approval of inadequately tested drugs." TAG was becoming exasperated by "the access-obsession of other community activists, who no longer seemed to think drugs were worth studying once they were on the market, and yet who clamored endlessly for access to drugs in the early stages of testing."[68]

Two years later, when the advisory committee considered accelerated approval of a drug called d4T, Harrington's seat had been inherited by his TAG colleague Gregg Gonsalves, a thirty-year-old, HIV-positive Tufts dropout. Gonsalves voted "no" on d4T, although the committee as a whole recommended approval and the FDA followed the majority's advice. Enraged by Gonsalves's vote, other AIDS activists launched vicious attacks on him and TAG. A pamphlet circulated at an ACT UP/NY meeting sarcastically urged: "JOIN TAG TODAY. Speak as a 'community representative' while destroying everything AIDS activists have fought and died for! Be a conservative nihilist and . . . be . . . self-hating and GENOCIDAL."[69]

The rancor would soon intensify. In 1994, PWAs were vesting great hope in a new class of antiviral drugs called protease inhibitors. In May, Hoffmann–La Roche announced the results of a small, short-term Phase 2 trial of one of these drugs, saquinavir. The study showed that a triple combination of AZT, ddC, and saquinavir had a modestly positive effect on infection-fighting CD4 cell counts. On June 16, four TAG members (including Harrington and Gonsalves), along with representatives of three other AIDS organizations, sent FDA Commissioner Kessler a letter pleading that the FDA *not* grant accelerated approval to saquinavir. The letter's authors explained: "[W]e believe that people with AIDS are entitled to information about new therapies that is sufficient to make necessary risk/benefit analyses regarding their treatment." Accelerated approval of saquinavir, they argued, "would penalize people with AIDS/HIV by setting an inappropriately low standard of evidential requirements that would govern the regulation of this entire class of therapies."[70]

The TAG letter further contended that accelerated approval of saquinavir would ensure that nobody would ever perform the studies necessary to determine whether the drug had any clinical benefit. "We have learned through difficult experience that [after approval] we cannot depend on the goodwill of pharmaceutical industry sponsors to produce the information that is necessary to make life or death treatment decisions." As an alternative to accelerated approval, the authors urged the commencement of a pre-approval three-arm "large simple trial" (LST) comparing two doses of saquinavir to placebo in a total of 18,000 patients. (An LST is a study with an unusually large sample size, broad eligibility criteria, multiple sites, and a simplified method of data collection.) This approach, they argued, would provide information on actual clinical outcomes.[71]

When ACT UP's membership learned about the TAG letter, it reacted with fury. In a tempestuous weekly meeting, one ACT UP member observed that accelerated approval "is something we've been fighting hard and long for. We've been *arrested* to get accelerated approval through." A female activist roared: "I am not interested in mud-wrestling with the boys. I am absolutely enraged that there are people who have appointed themselves elitist representatives and represent themselves as the single voice of this epidemic. . . . You goddamn well better fight them!"[72]

Advisory Committee Meeting

In September 1994, the FDA Antiviral Drugs Advisory Committee tackled the question of accelerated approval. As Harrington recalled, the meeting was a "circus." Scores of activists hooted, hollered, applauded, and harangued the participants. Strikingly, they directed their vitriol not at government bureaucrats or pharmaceutical industry officials, but at other AIDS activists—TAG members. Gonsalves exploded at Martin Delaney for launching "cheap personal crap" at him and his allies.[73]

The proposed use of a placebo arm in the LST was particularly infuriating to many of TAG's foes. The community had long passionately resisted the use of placebos in clinical trials for AIDS drugs. Indeed, Harrington himself had once described the use of placebo controls as "a shameful legacy . . . [which] stretches [back to] the Tuskegee syphilis experiment of the 1930s." Now, TAG representatives assured their opponents that none of the participants in their proposed saquinavir LST would (like the African American subjects in the notorious Tuskegee study) go *untreated*. Instead, all participants would be permitted concurrently to take any medications they wanted other than protease inhibitors. This did not mollify the anti-TAG forces, however. Martin Delaney explained: "We just don't believe you can put people on a placebo ethically in this disease at this point, even if it's a placebo of the new agent while continuing . . . standard regimens."[74]

In support of accelerated approval, TAG's foes repeatedly invoked the ideal of "personal choice," often elevating it into a quasi-constitutional principle. Brenda Freiburg declared: "I firmly believe that individuals have a basic inalienable right to choose their own treatments." Greg Haas insisted that people with life-threatening illnesses have a "fundamental right" to choose their therapies. Fred Schaich proclaimed: "Our country is based on freedoms. Every PWA should be permitted the freedom to enter a clinic, request a list of AIDS treatment options to combat the HIV virus and make an individual choice."[75]

TAG and its supporters minimized the value of therapeutic choice in the absence of scientific evidence of efficacy. TAG member Spencer Cox testified: "With no reliable information about treatment effects, one sometimes has to make a treatment guess. But this is not an act of reason. This is an act of desperation." TAG demanded only a "right to make *rational* treatment decisions." Its opponents, by contrast, insisted that desperately ill patients had a right to make therapeutic guesses. ACT UP's Bill Bahlman challenged TAG's Cox: "Haven't you realized from your own experience that people respond very differently from [sic] individual drugs and . . . that personal choices and people making decisions for themselves is paramount[?]"[76]

Finally, TAG and its adversaries clashed over accelerated approval's impact on research. In TAG's view, premature approval would undermine the possibility of ever obtaining the evidence necessary for patients to make informed choices about saquinavir. The TAG camp doubted that Hoffman–La Roche would perform the required post-approval studies on clinical benefit and questioned whether the FDA would force the company to do so. TAG thus believed that granting accelerated approval to saquinavir would inappropriately sacrifice the public benefits of scientific knowledge on the altar of personal choice. Cox expounded: "It's easy to construct a rationale allowing patients who are presently ill to make these terrible choices. It's less easy to construct a rationale for committing patients who will be ill in five years to the same kind of ignorance."[77] Dennis Davidson, an allied witness, similarly opined:

> The notion that every citizen with HIV has a right to access new and reasonably safe therapies that show some promise of efficacy, however meager or ambiguous, is certainly appealing, given the cult of individuality which the American culture has so efficiently enshrined. It almost seems patriotic.
>
> However, new and perhaps more informative clinical trials, should they be held hostage to this demand[?] . . .
>
> Perhaps the time has come to defer hypothetical benefit often couched in terms of rights of access to a . . . long-term benefit for all of us. . . .
>
> It may be harsh to frame this debate in terms of selfish individualism versus altruism, but demanding access for individuals without ensuring a process to benefit the group, becomes just that.[78]

By contrast, TAG's opponents suggested that if there was indeed an irresolvable conflict between access and knowledge, the former should prevail. Brenda Freiburg testified: "The acquisition of more meaningful data is very important, but saving lives should always be our number one priority."[79]

In the end, the two sides fought to something of a draw. TAG's intervention doubtless had some impact. Even before the hearing had commenced, Hoffmann–La Roche had agreed to postpone its request for accelerated approval of saquinavir until the company performed an interim analysis of surrogate endpoint data from an ongoing Phase 3 trial. TAG would take credit for this delay, as well as for the company's expansion of the Phase 3 trial and the establishment of a parallel track program to accompany the trial. Nevertheless, the FDA did not embrace all of TAG's proposal. It granted saquinavir accelerated approval on December 7, 1995, without demanding the commencement of the LST proposed by TAG, let alone the presentation of data demonstrating the drug's clinical efficacy. Spencer Cox of TAG ascribed the FDA's action to "Corporate Cynicism, Savvy Schmoozing, and Relentless PR." But it almost certainly also had something to do with Americans' general reluctance to make desperately ill people forgo a potentially useful therapy in the more abstract cause of medical knowledge.[80]

Legacy

By the turn of the millennium, the AIDS movement had lost much of its vitality and visibility in the United States. Although internal divisions probably contributed to this decline, the primary reason was a much happier one: in 1996 and 1997, the FDA granted accelerated approval to three additional protease inhibitors, all superior to saquinavir. These drugs became essential components of the cocktail therapies that made AIDS what it is for many patients today—a manageable chronic disease.[81]

The AIDS movement's influence extended far beyond the development and regulation of AIDS drugs in particular, however. It was remarkably successful at instilling its shared goals and assumptions into America's "drug constitution" in various ways.

Patient Involvement

The AIDS community forged a widely used model for direct patient involvement in FDA decision-making. Today, groups representing people with all sorts of diseases regularly seek to sway FDA drug approval decisions. Some of these organizations receive funding from the pharmaceutical industry, but many do not. Advisory committee meetings are frequently crowded with patients, many offering impassioned testimony. Moreover, thanks to the AIDS movement's efforts, patient representatives are now entrenched in the advisory committees themselves. In 1991, in response to demands of AIDS advocates, the FDA created a position for a patient representative on the Antiviral Drugs Advisory Committee for HIV. The agency's use of patient representatives subsequently expanded, and today they are voting members of a broad array of advisory committees considering drugs for many diseases.[82]

In a 2012 statute, Congress added a new section to the FD&C Act titled "Patient Participation in Medical Product Discussions." This provision obligates the FDA to "develop and implement strategies to solicit the views of patients during the medical product development process and consider the perspectives of patients during regulatory discussions." In a mandatory "goals letter" the agency issued in connection with Prescription Drug User Fee Act (PDUFA) reauthorization in 2011, it committed to holding meetings with patient advocates regarding various disease areas. The FDA has now hosted thirty such meetings, in disease areas ranging from breast cancer to fibromyalgia to narcolepsy to Parkinson's disease. In its 2016 "goals letter," the FDA committed to "enhancing the incorporation of the patient's voice in drug development and decision-making" in various additional ways.[83]

These goals are all part of a broader agency initiative called "Patient-Focused Drug Development" (PFDD), which is organized around the premise that "as experts in what it is like to live with their condition, patients are uniquely positioned to inform the understanding of the therapeutic context for drug development and evaluation." PFDD's debt to the AIDS movement is particularly evident in its efforts to incorporate the patient's voice into the FDA's risk-benefit analyses. As the agency explained when it commenced this initiative, "Patients who live with a disease have a direct stake in the outcome of the review process and are in a unique position to contribute to weighing benefit-risk considerations that can occur throughout the medical product development process."[84]

Even while patients' presence inside the drug review process grows, patient groups continue to pressure the agency from the outside. The FDA now must deal with "freedom of choice" rhetoric whenever it is reviewing the NDA for a product intended to treat an otherwise incurable condition. And in a few prominent instances, the patient choice argument has prevailed. For example, in response to protests by sufferers of irritable bowel syndrome, the FDA in 2002 permitted the return to the market of Lotronex®, a drug earlier withdrawn because of occasional severe side effects. In September 2016, under fierce pressure from patient advocates, FDA granted accelerated approval to a treatment for Duchenne muscular dystrophy, despite the vociferous objections of agency staffers and a negative advisory committee vote.[85]

Faster Drug Approval

Due largely to the AIDS movement's efforts, the FDA's view of its very mission has evolved. It now embraces the task not only of *protecting* the public health by preventing the sale of dangerous and ineffective products, but also of *promoting* the public health by ensuring access to useful remedies in a timely manner. In 1997, Congress added an agency mission statement to the FD&C Act itself, and this statement lists promotion of the public health *before* protection of the public health.[86]

The first major practical addition to the FD&C Act that reflected the efforts of the AIDS movement (as well as other stakeholders) to speed the approval of drugs was the Prescription Drug User Fee Act of 1992 (PDUFA). This statute—which Congress has reauthorized every five years since its initial enactment—has dramatically increased the pace with which the agency reviews drug applications. PDUFA established a system under which drug applicants pay mandatory user fees to the FDA to support the IND/NDA process, while the agency commits to improved performance goals in the operation of this process. Congress enacted this law because of FDA complaints about budget pressures and industry frustration with NDA backlogs, but also, as Representative Henry Waxman emphasized, because "the public will benefit by getting access to life-saving drugs sooner." During hearings on PDUFA reauthorization in 1997, Jeff Bloom of the AIDS group Project Inform, appearing on behalf of a coalition of over a hundred organizations for patients with serious and life-threatening diseases, declared: "The single most important step Congress can take to help patients is to move quickly and revise and extend [PDUFA]."[87]

The implementation of user fees helped slash the median number of months the FDA takes to review and approve NDAs for new molecular entity drugs from 23.0 months in 1993 to 9.8 months by 2012. When implementing the first version of PDUFA, the FDA adopted a "Priority Review Program" that aims to reduce the review time even further for designated drugs that would, if approved, offer a significant improvement over marketed products.[88] In 2012, the median FDA review time for priority products was only 6.0 months.

Beginning in the late 1990s, Congress added various provisions to the FD&C Act focused on speeding the approval of drugs for severe diseases. Section 506, enacted in 1997, expedites the approval of new drugs for serious and life-threatening conditions in the absence of comparable alternatives. This section partly codifies the FDA's 1988 Subpart E regulations (under the name "fast track"). It also includes a liberalized version of the agency's 1992 accelerated approval rule.[89] In 2012, Congress revised Section 506 to further expedite drug review. These amendments expanded the eligibility for and advantages of fast track, granted the FDA greater flexibility and discretion to use accelerated approval, and created a new expedited approval mechanism called "breakthrough therapy," which provides all the benefits of fast track plus more intensive guidance for the applicant and greater involvement by FDA senior managers.[90]

The FDA's various expedited review programs—supported with equal enthusiasm by patient groups and the pharmaceutical industry—have led to faster approval of many drugs for severely ill individuals. For example, in the quarter century since the inception of accelerated approval, the FDA has approved more than two hundred drug and biologics applications based on surrogate endpoints. (Perhaps the most controversial use of the accelerated approval mechanism occurred in June 2021, when—against the almost unanimous advice of an advisory committee—the FDA approved Aduhelm®, a biologic drug for Alzheimer's, based on data demonstrating reduction of plaque in the brain rather than a slowing of cognitive decline.) The FDA also liberally uses the fast track and

breakthrough therapy designations. The use of the various expedited development and review programs has steadily increased over time and has surged in the
past few years. In 2018, more than 70 percent of approved drugs benefitted from
at least one of them.[91]

Notably, the FDA has been increasingly willing to forgo its traditional "Gold
Standard" requirement of two well-controlled human studies prior to drug approval. In 1997, Congress amended the FD&C Act to affirm that "data from one
adequate and well-controlled clinical investigation and confirmatory evidence"
may suffice. A study fifteen years later showed that the agency was approving
36.8 percent of applications on the basis of only a single controlled pivotal trial.
By 2018, that proportion had climbed to nearly one-half. And due in part to the
FDA's increasing use of the Orphan Drug Act designation for drugs to treat rare
diseases, pursuant to which the agency routinely exercises regulatory flexibility
regarding the types of studies required, many of these pivotal trials are small, and
they are frequently nonrandomized, unblinded, or both.[92]

In December 2016, with the overwhelming support of both industry and patient advocacy groups, Congress passed and President Obama signed the 21st
Century Cures Act ("Cures Act"), a law intended to "accelerate the discovery, development, and delivery of" medical products. This statute extensively amended
the FD&C Act in a way that reflects the spirit of AIDS activism in the late 1980s
and early 1990s. For example, the Cures Act requires the agency to issue guidance
regarding the use of "patient experience data" in regulatory decision-making, including ("if appropriate") their use as part of the risk-benefit assessment in drug
approval. It directs the agency to programmatically evaluate and issue guidance concerning the potential use of "real-world evidence" (that is, data "from
sources other than randomized clinical trials") to support the approval of new
indications for existing drugs.[93]

It is not so simple, however, to declare this statute a legacy of the AIDS movement. As we have seen, the AIDS movement itself ultimately divided on how
to balance the provision of early access against the development of complete
data. During the clash over accelerated approval of saquinavir, the Treatment
Action Group (TAG) prioritized the latter much more than many fellow
activists, and they have emphasized the need for data ever since. Today, when
TAG's founders consider the inexorable easing of the FDA's gatekeeping role,
they intimate that by storming the FDA in 1988, they—like Dr. Frankenstein—
created a monster they cannot control. In 2015, TAG's Gregg Gonsalves and
Mark Harrington, along with former FDA Commissioner David Kessler, wrote
an op-ed piece for the New York Times blasting the proposed 21st Century
Cures legislation. They explained that their late-1980s campaign for faster drug
approval risked spawning a "devil's bargain," namely, "quicker access to experimental drugs, but without first determining whether these drugs were safe and

would improve health and extend life." Though celebrating the creation of the fast track and breakthrough therapy designations, the column warned that the Cures Act threatened to "lower the standards for approval of many medical products" and thus undermine "the essential responsibility that drug companies have to patients and the American public: . . . to show that new drugs [are] safe and effective under the usual criteria required by the agency."[94] Their protests went largely unheeded, however; the following year, Congress passed the Cures Act by overwhelming margins.

Access to Unapproved Drugs

The AIDS movement also had a permanent impact on the availability of *unapproved* drugs for people with grave illnesses. In 1997, Congress added a new Section 561 to the FD&C Act, which codified the FDA's 1987 treatment IND rule as well the agency's longtime practice of granting compassionate access to individual patients. In 2009, the FDA revised the treatment IND regulation itself to state that the evidence necessary to support widespread treatment use of an investigational therapy for an immediately life-threatening disease will "ordinarily consist of clinical data from phase 3 or phase 2 trials, *but could be based on more preliminary clinical evidence.*" The FDA thus effectively incorporated parallel track and its lower evidentiary standard into the treatment IND regime. In the 2016 Cures Act, Congress required each manufacturer to publicize its expanded access policies and procedures for investigational drugs.[95]

Americans make quite frequent use of expanded access programs, and the FDA rarely stands in their way. In 2019 (a typical year), the FDA cleared more than 99.5 percent of the expanded access requests it received, for a total of 1,755. Although most of these requests were for single patients, the agency also allowed twenty-five full-sized and thirty-seven intermediate-sized treatment protocols to proceed. Compared to a decade ago, the number of multi-patient treatment protocols has increased dramatically. Between 2015 and 2019, the FDA cleared more than 93 percent of applications for full- or intermediate-sized treatment protocols.[96] It is also important to remember that physicians are virtually always free to prescribe an already-approved drug for any unapproved *use* they deem appropriate, without relying on these expanded use programs.

None of this is to say that desperate, severely ill patients are now able to acquire any unapproved drug they want. The primary remaining obstacle is drug companies' disinclination to pursue treatment INDs. There are various reasons for this aversion, including drug supply challenges, a hesitation to jeopardize the controlled pivotal trials needed for ultimate approval, and potential liability risks. Perhaps the most important reason, however, is the FDA's severe restrictions on charging for investigational drugs. Because Abigail Alliance's constitutional challenge to these limitations (discussed in the Introduction) failed in 2007, the FDA continues to mandate that sponsors obtain agency approval before charging for investigational drugs and to limit permitted charges to the amount required for the recovery of direct costs. The relevant rule also requires a sponsor who wishes to charge for expanded access under a treatment IND to provide the FDA with "evidence of sufficient enrollment in any ongoing clinical trial(s)" and "evidence of adequate progress in the development of the drug for marketing approval." As a practical matter, therefore, the agency's demand for data and its commitment to preserving its gatekeeping role still sometimes constrain therapeutic choice.[97]

Since 2014, forty-one states have sought to evade these remaining FDA restrictions by passing their own "right-to-try" laws based on a model bill disseminated by the libertarian Goldwater Institute. These statutes essentially codify the remedy Abigail Alliance unsuccessfully sought in court; that is, they allow physicians caring for terminal patients with no treatment alternatives to prescribe, and companies to charge for, unapproved drugs that have cleared Phase 1 trials. The Goldwater Institute has ties to the American Legislative Exchange Council (ALEC), a pro-business organization that exploits the "low policy capacity" of busy, part-time state lawmakers by providing them with model bills and supportive materials. Nonetheless, the passage of right-to-try legislation in dozens of states of every political stripe, from Mississippi to California, suggests that a broad swath of Americans remains powerfully devoted to the idea of therapeutic choice for desperately ill individuals. In Arizona, where the law was put to a statewide referendum in 2014, no less than 78.4 percent of voters supported it.[98]

Many people likely do not understand the full implications of a right-to-try regime for pharmaceutical research and FDA's review authority. TAG cofounder Gregg Gonsalves (now a Yale professor and MacArthur "Genius Grant" recipient) does understand, and he is a leading foe of these statutes. In a 2014 letter to the *Washington Post*, Gonsalves explained:

> Two decades ago, [AIDS activists] worked closely with the Food and Drug Administration to streamline access to new medications, but we learned quickly that, as patients, we needed more than access; we needed answers about what these new drugs were doing in our bodies. Unfortunately, conservative think tanks took advantage of desperate patients to push their own agenda— deregulation of the FDA, weakening the agency's ability to vet new agents and give us the very answers we required.
>
> History is repeating itself with right to try laws.[99]

The state right-to-try statutes are mostly symbolic, for they are almost certainly preempted by federal law. Apparently, only a single doctor (a Texas radiologist) has ever invoked one of these state measures to justify treating patients with an unapproved product.[100] The next step in the effort to nationalize the right to try was thus federal legislation.

On May 30, 2018, President Trump signed the Trickett Wendler Right to Try Act into law. The legislation, introduced by Republican senator Ron Johnson of Wisconsin and cosponsored by most of his Republican colleagues, was passed by unanimous consent in the Senate and by an almost strictly party-line vote in the House. It creates an additional pathway for patients with life-threatening illnesses to obtain unapproved drugs once they have exhausted any FDA-approved treatment options. Under new Section 561B of the FD&C Act, these patients and their doctors may ask manufacturers directly for access to an investigational drug that has completed a Phase 1 trial and for which the company is actively pursuing FDA approval. In stark contrast to the established expanded access programs, the FDA has no approval or oversight authority over this right-to-try (RTT) pathway. To encourage manufacturers to participate, the statute shields them from tort liability in the absence of gross negligence or recklessness and presumptively forbids the FDA from considering adverse outcomes when reviewing drug approval applications.[101]

At the signing ceremony, President Trump proclaimed: "For many years, patients, advocates, and lawmakers have fought for this fundamental freedom. . . . We will be saving—I don't even want to say thousands, because I think it's going to be much more, thousands and thousands, hundreds of thousands. We're going to be saving tremendous numbers of lives."[102]

Despite this prediction, two years later, only about ten patients had acquired unapproved drugs through the RTT program. The statute explicitly releases manufacturers from any obligation to use the new pathway, and despite the incentives to participate included in the law, few are interested in doing so. Even if a company is willing to distribute an investigational drug for treatment use, the FDA's long-standing expanded access program remains available as an alternative method. The agency itself far prefers this older process, which generates useful data and offers more safeguards for patients. In addition, due to last minute amendments demanded by Senate Democrats, Trickett Wendler subjects RTT drugs to the same charging limits and promotional bans applicable to other investigational drugs.[103] Why, then, would a company seeking NDA approval risk annoying the FDA by using RTT instead of traditional expanded access?

So with respect to preapproval access, America's Drug Constitution has been liberalized but not utterly transformed. But every time a new crisis arises, the limits are tested.

The COVID-19 Pandemic

As the COVID-19 coronavirus ravaged the country in early 2020, Peter Staley—the "Karate Kid" from the 1988 Parklawn protest—reported that he and other AIDS survivors were suffering from "some version of PTSD."[104] Once again, Americans were protesting the federal government's failure adequately to address a pandemic. Once again, a disease was disproportionately killing socially marginalized populations—this time, people of color and the poor. Once again, right-wing politicians were resisting expert medical opinion. Once again, Dr. Anthony Fauci was appearing regularly in the media as the face of the federal government's science-based response. And once again, people were desperately turning to drugs that had not yet been shown to be effective. This time, however, the nation's leading promoter of an unproven remedy was the president of the United States.

In March and April 2020, Donald Trump repeatedly encouraged the use of the antimalarial drug hydroxychloroquine against COVID-19, calling it a potential "game changer" based on anecdotal reports of success and mixed results in preliminary clinical trials. Echoing the attitude of some early AIDS activists, Trump stated, "I want them to try it [hydroxychloroquine]. And it may work, and it may not work. But if it doesn't work, it's nothing lost by doing it. Nothing." Meanwhile, the conservative outlets Fox News and Fox Business mentioned the drug as a treatment for COVID-19 over a thousand times. In a national poll conducted in mid-April, 46 percent of voters (71 percent of Republicans and 29 percent of Democrats) supported the use of hydroxychloroquine as a treatment for COVID-19 before the completion of full testing.[105]

In late March, the FDA, under pressure from the White House, authorized distribution of hydroxychloroquine (and chloroquine, a related antimalarial drug) by the National Strategic Stockpile for use against COVID-19. The agency did so pursuant to yet another preapproval access program—emergency use authorization (EUA). Congress created this program in the wake of the September 11, 2001, terrorist attacks and subsequent military conflicts. It permits the FDA, during a declared emergency, to authorize the sale of an unapproved medical countermeasure for a biological, chemical, radiological, or nuclear agent if "based on the totality of scientific evidence available . . . the product may be effective." Prior to COVID-19, the FDA had issued EUAs to permit the distribution of unapproved drugs and devices to combat H1N1 influenza, Zika, and Ebola, among other ailments. During COVID-19, the agency would ultimately use this procedure to authorize the sale of numerous unapproved medical products, including the vaccines that helped contain the pandemic in the United States by the summer of 2021.[106]

Because hydroxychloroquine was already on the market as an approved treatment for malaria, lupus, and rheumatoid arthritis, the Stockpile was not the only source of the drug. Physicians could simply prescribe it to their patients off-label for COVID-19. By early April 2020, runs on pharmacies and widespread hoarding had led to shortages of the medicine, risking the health of lupus and arthritis patients. Peter Staley, who had later come to regret his initial demand for access to AIDS drugs based on minimal clinical data, viewed these developments with horror.[107]

The hydroxychloroquine craze started to die down in late April. An NIH expert panel warned against use of the drug in combination with the antibiotic azithromycin (a cocktail repeatedly touted by Trump) because of safety concerns. A Department of Veterans Affairs study showed worse outcomes for COVID-19 victims who used hydroxychloroquine than for those who did not. The FDA warned doctors against the use of the drug outside hospitals and clinical trials because of the risk of heart rhythm problems. By the end of the month, Trump and his Fox News allies were hardly mentioning the hydroxychloroquine at all. A new poll conducted from April 24 to April 26, just two weeks after the previous one, showed that support for using hydroxychloroquine to treat coronavirus had plummeted among voters of all political persuasions. Finally, on June 15, the FDA revoked the emergency use authorization for hydroxychloroquine and chloroquine, explaining that the drugs "are unlikely to be effective in treating COVID-19" and that, in light of serious side effects, the "known and potential benefits of [the drugs] no longer outweigh the known and potential risks." Even after this FDA action, Trump continued to promote the use of hydroxychloroquine against COVID.[108]

Before the FDA revoked the hydroxychloroquine EUA, Gregg Gonsalves observed: "I've seen these boom-and-bust cycles before . . . during the age of HIV/AIDS, when, for over a decade we grasped in desperation for the latest cure." He warned: "Acting without evidence has consequences." Invoking Trump's own words, Gonsalves continued: "If you have Covid-19, what do you have to lose? Without evidence of clinical benefit from well-designed randomized clinical trials, the life you lose could be your own."[109]

But survivors of a pandemic, like Gonsalves, may have a different perspective from people confronting one for the first time.

8

Modern Resistance to Orthodox Medical Domination

In 1993, a group of researchers headed by Dr. David M. Eisenberg published a study in the prestigious *New England Journal of Medicine* titled "Unconventional Medicine in the United States." The article's findings stunned the orthodox medical establishment. It concluded that the "frequency of use of unconventional therapy in the United States is far higher than previously reported." In a national poll conducted by the authors, one-third of respondents reported having used at least one unorthodox therapy in the previous year. According to the authors' calculations, Americans spent $13.7 billion on alternative medicine in 1990 and made more visits to providers of unconventional therapy (425 million) than to primary care physicians (388 million). It is no wonder that American physicians were shocked by these statistics; the study also revealed that 72 percent of patients who used alternative medicine did not inform their doctors.[1]

The media leapt at the story. CNN, ABC News, NPR, the *Washington Post*, the *New York Times*, and the *Boston Globe* immediately ran pieces on it. The *Times* paraphrased the director of the new National Institutes of Health (NIH) Office of Alternative Medicine as stating that "the popularity of alternative medicine demonstrated a hunger among Americans for a more humane and less invasive type of treatment than that ordinarily practiced by standard doctors." According to the *Globe*'s front-page article, the survey's results "suggest that many consumers doubt whether doctors can do the job."[2]

Eisenberg hit the headlines again six years later, when his follow-up study appeared in *JAMA: Journal of the American Medical Association*, the flagship publication of the guardians of orthodox medicine. Eisenberg's team found that alternative medicine use had surged substantially between 1990 and 1997. The proportion of respondents who reported using at least one alternative therapy jumped from 33.8 percent to 42.1 percent. The number of annual visits to alternative medicine practitioners increased by almost 50 percent. The authors estimated that Americans' out-of-pocket expenditures for alternative medicine were now about the same as those for all conventional physician services combined. In a front-page *Washington Post* story about the new findings, a forty-six-year-old user of acupuncture and homeopathy explained that he and his friends were "all

Choose Your Medicine. Lewis A. Grossman, Oxford University Press. © Lewis A. Grossman 2021.
DOI: 10.1093/oso/9780190612757.003.0009

of the age, and we know enough about medicine, that we're willing to consider that perhaps Western medicine doesn't have the only answer."[3]

Surveys backed up the notion that people's trust in orthodox medicine was falling while their use of alternatives rose. Between 1973 and 1996, Americans' faith in the leaders of the country's medical institutions had dropped to the point where a majority expressed "only some" or "hardly any" confidence in them. During this same period, Americans also soured on the methods and bedside manner of the practicing physicians they visited.[4]

In the mid-1990s, scholars began discussing a "new social movement" around alternative medicine—a movement in which "practitioners, patients, and activists coexist in a community where the gap in prestige and knowledge between expert and client is rather narrow." This movement contested the everyday meanings of "medicine" and "health" and entered the political arena to challenge legislative restrictions on unorthodox medicine. The alternative medicine movement was diffuse, comprising many different networks, groups, and individuals with diverse ideological commitments, from cultural progressives to conservative Christians.[5]

The turn to alternative medicine use identified by Eisenberg in the 1990s has proved to be an enduring cultural shift. The data, though sparse, indicate that Americans' use of alternative therapies has remained robust ever since. The widespread embrace of the terms "complementary and alternative medicine" (CAM) and "integrative medicine" since the turn of the century reflect the fact that modern Americans—in contrast to many of their forebears—tend to use unconventional therapies in conjunction with, rather than instead of, orthodox medicine. The increased acceptance of alternative modalities has even affected the medical establishment itself, as reflected in the proliferation of CAM courses in American medical schools; the growing integration of such therapies into orthodox medical practice; and the 1991 establishment of the NIH Office of Alternative Medicine (now called the National Center for Complementary and Alternative Medicine).[6]

The rise of CAM during the past half century raises an underexplored legal puzzle—namely, how did this occur in the context of a legal regime dominated by orthodox physicians? As we saw in Chapter 5, the system of medical regulation established during the mid-twentieth century was starkly inhospitable to alternative therapies. At the federal level, Congress and the FDA embraced the adequate and well-controlled clinical trial as the standard for establishing medical products' efficacy, and thus legality. Few CAM remedies could meet this standard. At the state level, organized medicine controlled and administered licensing regimes that prevented many CAM practitioners from legally ministering to patients.

So why has the explosion in CAM use since the 1970s not been accompanied by a corresponding surge in prosecutions and disciplinary actions? The answer, in short, is that American society's embrace of CAM is reflected in the law itself. To an underappreciated degree, CAM advocates have persuaded legislators to make American law more hospitable to unorthodox treatments. And even where medical regulation remains wedded to conventional standards, government officials often do not enforce it rigorously. Consequently, lawmakers have effectively created a "right to try" many alternative therapies, even as courts have declined to do so. Slowly but surely, the orthodox establishment's stranglehold on medical regulation has loosened.

The law's gradual accommodation of CAM is far from complete. National Health Freedom Action (NHFA), a leading CAM advocacy organization, insists: "There is a tremendous variety of healing arts practitioners, treatments, and therapies, that remain unavailable, and even unknown to many health seekers, because restrictive health practice laws prohibit many practitioners and therapies." This statement, while hyperbolic, reflects a basic truth: American law continues to privilege orthodox medicine's practices, principles, and organizational structures. Nonetheless, it is also true that in recent decades, American law has acquiesced to the growth of CAM in both obvious and subtle ways. As one scholar has observed: "Rather than reflecting biomedical orthodoxy or hostility to competing therapies, the legal system is beginning to reflect a paradigm of integral health care, in which biomedical professionals function cooperatively with complementary and alternative professionals, as well as patients, in a partnership of law and healing."[7]

Federal Regulation of CAM Products

The FD&C Act gives the FDA jurisdiction over all articles intended to cure, treat, or prevent disease or to affect the structure or any function of the body. Thus, virtually every product sold as a CAM therapy is a drug, device, or dietary supplement subject to the agency's authority. Because the FDA regulates medical products, not medical practice (which is governed primarily by the states), CAM modalities such as manual manipulation, touch therapy, meditation, visualization, and faith healing are outside the agency's reach.[8] But the many CAM approaches that depend on products (for example, homeopathy, herbal medicine, and much "energy medicine") are firmly within the FDA's bailiwick. Although the applicable regulatory requirements are complex and variable, as a general matter, these products may legally be sold only if they are both safe and effective. Therefore, even if a CAM drug or contraption is entirely harmless, it usually violates the FD&C Act as a formal matter unless the claims made for it are backed by clinical evidence.

As we have seen, evidence for the efficacy of a medical product must ordinarily derive from randomized and controlled clinical trials (RCTs). In recent years, the FDA—under pressure from Congress—has been considering more and more "real-world evidence," some of which is not generated by clinical trials, but instead gathered from sources like electronic health records, insurance claims data, and billing records. Nonetheless, the randomized, double-blind, placebo-controlled clinical trial remains the "gold standard" for establishing effectiveness. Almost all drug and device approvals require the completion of successful trials with designs that approach this ideal as nearly as possible, in light of practical and ethical limitations. And the FDA has emphasized that it holds CAM to the same regulatory and scientific standards as conventional treatments. A *JAMA* editorial, assuming the same posture, declared: "There is no alternative medicine. There is only scientifically proven, evidence-based medicine supported by solid data or unproven medicine, for which scientific evidence is lacking."[9]

Only a few CAM treatments, such as acupuncture for pain, have been demonstrated to be effective in RCTs. CAM proponents generally base their claims of effectiveness on patient and practitioner testimonials and other anecdotal evidence—data that orthodox medical researchers and regulators deem invalid. When accused of embracing "unscientific" medicine, CAM supporters point to the many conventional therapies (especially surgical procedures and off-label drug uses) that have similarly not been proven effective by controlled investigations. They ascribe the dearth of CAM trials largely to financial factors; government and nonprofit institutions are hesitant to finance such research, and the unavailability of patent protection for many alternative therapies, particularly natural products, deters businesses and investors from doing so. A typical refrain heard at CAM conferences is "the gold standard is well named because it takes a lot of gold to set the standard."[10]

CAM proponents also contend that the RCT is an inapt methodology for assessing many alternative remedies. They argue that blinding and randomization themselves undermine the efficacy of unconventional treatments that work only in the context of fully formed, interpersonal practitioner-patient relationships. They also maintain that clinical trials of products in isolation cannot determine the effectiveness of holistic CAM approaches that employ multiple interventions, including behavioral and spiritual ones. Moreover, CAM advocates argue that their approaches cannot be evaluated without taking into account non-measurable intangible forces and unconventional theories of illness. In sum, they believe that the different epistemological premises of alternative medicine make the "evidence-based" RCT methodology used to assess orthodox medicine inappropriate for CAM. In their worldview, observations of individual patients are an equally valid source of medical knowledge.[11]

The FDA categorically rejects such reasoning. Consequently, the National Health Federation (NHF), the sixty-five-year-old CAM advocacy group we encountered in Chapter 5, continues to demonize the agency as an insatiable, destructive "monster."[12] In fact, however, the FDA has not obstructed the modern flourishing of CAM nearly as much as NHF's rhetoric suggests. Without changing its official stance, the agency has exercised a surprisingly light hand with respect to CAM products in recent decades, sometimes because of congressional dictates and other times because of informal exercises of enforcement discretion.

DSHEA and the Relaxation of Dietary Supplement Regulation

In Chapter 6, we saw how Congress intervened in the 1970s to loosen the FDA's grip on vitamin and mineral supplements. A similar event occurred two decades later, when Congress passed the Dietary Supplement Health and Education Act (DSHEA) of 1994. This statute cabined the FDA's authority over all types of dietary supplements, including not only vitamins and minerals, but also herbs and botanicals, amino acids, and other "dietary substance[s] for use by man to supplement the diet by increasing the total dietary intake."[13]

Prior to DSHEA, the FDA never took a systematic approach to herbs, botanicals, fish oils, and other "natural" supplements. In the absence of medical claims or serious hazards, the agency generally left these products alone, treating them as "generally recognized as safe" food. But in the late 1980s, with the natural supplement market expanding rapidly, the FDA commenced an aggressive enforcement campaign focused on both the content and the labeling of these products.

In 1991, the FDA issued a proposed rule regarding "health claims" (disease prevention claims) for both conventional foods and dietary supplements. In this document, Commissioner David Kessler outraged the supplement industry by declining Congress's invitation to establish a more permissive health claims regime for supplements than for conventional foods. The industry responded with advertisements advocating "freedom of choice regarding natural health alternatives." Then, in May 1992, the FDA conducted a widely publicized raid of an alternative medicine clinic in Kent, Washington. The *New York Times* falsely reported that the FDA agents carried weapons (only the local sheriffs did) and that the proposed rule would lead to a ban on high-potency vitamins. A front-page correction the next week was too late to cool the widespread outrage. Hollywood celebrities had already held a news conference in Beverly Hills urging the public to "start screaming at Congress and the White House not to let the F.D.A. take our vitamins away." In response to a deluge of irate letters and telephone calls from constituents, Congress forbade the FDA from establishing health claims requirements for dietary supplements for one year.[14]

In June 1993, following the end of this moratorium, the agency published effectively the same proposal. Now the fury of supplement manufacturers and users reached a fever pitch. Industry fomented opposition, ominously and inaccurately warning supplement users: "Write to Congress today or kiss your supplements goodbye." They found a receptive audience. An ardent social movement demanding unfettered access to "nontoxic" CAM therapies, including herbal supplements, was by now well established. Although this consumer movement cooperated with industry, it existed independently of it. In the summer and fall of 1993, citizens opposed to the FDA's proposed rule signed petitions, attended demonstrations, and sent an "avalanche" of letters (numbering more than two million) to their senators and representatives. Congress received more mail about dietary supplements that session than about any other topic.[15]

Meanwhile, in April 1993, New Mexico Democratic representative Bill Richardson and Utah Republican senator Orrin Hatch had simultaneously introduced DSHEA in their respective chambers. The law was designed to limit the FDA's power over supplements by categorizing them as food, rather than drugs, for most purposes. The House bill eventually attracted 260 cosponsors drawn almost evenly from both parties, including future Republican Speaker of the House John Boehner and future Democratic Speaker of the House Nancy Pelosi.[16]

At a House committee hearing on the bill in July, some of the pro-DSHEA witnesses represented the supplement industry, but others were not so clearly financially motivated. For example, Fred Bingham, the executive director of a nonprofit AIDS buyers club, testified in favor of the legislation on behalf of an alliance including four ACT UP chapters, the California delegation of the National Organization for Women (NOW), and patient advocacy groups for people with cancer, Alzheimer's disease, and sickle cell anemia. Bingham testified: "We are united in our commitment to informed freedom of choice, and have mobilized to fight the latest round of FDA attacks on this basic human right, to defend our constitutional right to life, to liberty, and the pursuit of happiness." Kachinas Kutenai, an Apache medicine woman representing the Center for Natural and Traditional Medicines, charged that the FDA "has removed the freedom of choice, not just for ethnic minorities who depend on such substances as part of their cultural heritage, but for all free Americans."[17]

Similar Senate hearings followed, as did a nationally aired television commercial in which a fictional SWAT team burst into Mel Gibson's home and arrested the bathrobe-clad actor for vitamin pill possession. Despite the opposition of powerful committee chairs Senator Ted Kennedy and Representative Henry

Waxman, both chambers passed DSHEA easily by voice vote, and President Clinton signed it into law in October 1994.[18]

Ironically, DSHEA did not relax the health claims requirements that triggered the furor in the first place. Nonetheless, it significantly reduced the FDA's authority over dietary supplements in other ways. Most important for our purposes, DSHEA (which is still in effect) exempts supplements that claim to "maintain . . . structure or function" from the rigorous regulatory requirements applicable to drugs so long as the manufacturer satisfies several basic requirements, including the provision of a now familiar disclaimer: "This statement has not been evaluated by the Food and Drug Administration. This product is not intended to diagnose, treat, cure, or prevent any disease." Following the enactment of DSHEA, the dietary supplement industry learned to use structure-function claims extremely creatively. St. John's Wort, consumed overseas as a remedy for depression, might be labeled "Promotes Positive Mood & Healthy Emotional Balance." Saw Palmetto, a well-known European treatment for enlarged prostate, could claim "Supports Healthy Prostate Function." The FDA endorsed just such an approach in its DSHEA regulations. Grocery and drugstore shelves are now filled with supplements that make structure-function claims with a wink at consumers interested in using them to fight disease.[19]

The Access to Medical Treatment Act

In 1994, the year DSHEA passed, Democratic Senate Minority Leader Tom Daschle introduced a bill that would have legalized virtually all alternative medicine that did not present an obvious threat to the health of its users. This measure, called the "Access to Medical Treatment Act" (AMTA), would have allowed licensed medical doctors, osteopaths, chiropractors, and naturopaths working within their legal scope of practice to provide "any method of medical treatment" to a patient so long as the treatment did not represent a "danger" to the patient. The practitioner was required only to provide the patient with certain disclosures. The "methods" allowed by the legislation explicitly included drugs and devices not approved by the FDA—although the labeling and advertising of such products could not make effectiveness claims. Daschle's bill initially attracted eight cosponsors, including three Republicans.[20]

In July 1994, Iowa Democratic senator Tom Harkin, who had become a passionate CAM supporter when bee-pollen capsules seemingly cured his allergies, presided over a committee hearing on the bill. Harkin opened the proceedings by declaring that Americans "want more choices and . . . more control over their health and health care." Daschle lauded his measure as one that "endeavors to enhance consumer freedom of choice in the realm of medical treatment."

Dr. Joan Priestly of Citizens for Health, a "natural health" advocacy organization, declared: "Sovereignty begins with our own bodies." Former Democratic congressman Berkley Bedell proclaimed it "ridiculous to spend all this money for some Government to decide whether something is effective or not. The market does that very clearly." He continued, "The people of America are not going to sit here and continue to give monopoly to the pharmaceutical industry." The only witnesses against the legislation were FDA officials, one of whom warned that it would "provide a green light for charlatans and opportunists to prey on sick and uninformed and frightened customers."[21]

AMTA did not make it out of committee in 1994, but it gathered momentum. The following year, a slightly revised version attracted quite large bipartisan groups of sponsors in both chambers (eighteen in the Senate and fifty-two in the House). The supporters included bizarre bedfellows such as Vermont socialist Bernie Sanders and Texas conservative Republican Tom DeLay.[22] The legislation again failed to advance out of committee, however. AMTA was reintroduced in every Congress through 2011, but the number of sponsors it attracted diminished over time.

Although AMTA did not pass, it is remarkable that it received such serious consideration. In addition to dramatically unraveling the FDA's power, it also represented an unprecedented intrusion into state regulation of medical practice. The original bill expressly provided that state licensing boards could not discipline health care practitioners for using any treatment in compliance with the statute.[23] Even legislators sympathetic to AMTA's goals may ultimately have concluded that the law simply went too far—and recognized that even without such legislation, many CAM products were already widely available.

Homeopathic Drugs and Other Low-Risk CAM Products

Although the FDA's official position is that CAM products are fully subject to the FD&C Act, the agency in modern times has usually declined to impose the Act's stringent drug and device requirements on these products in the absence of a direct threat to the public health. Instead, the FDA has quietly tolerated their presence in the marketplace by exercising enforcement discretion.[24]

Take, for example, homeopathic drugs. The FDA's long relationship with homeopathy is fascinating and complex. Senator Royal Copeland, the sponsor of the 1938 FD&C Act, was himself a homeopathic physician. Apparently at Copeland's behest, the statute identified the Homeopathic Pharmacopoeia of the United States as an official drug compendium (and still does today).[25] As a formal matter, homeopathic drugs are subject to the same safety, efficacy, and premarket approval requirements as allopathic drugs. Nevertheless, the FDA has always systematically withheld its hand with respect to homeopathic medicines, subjecting them to lesser regulation, and often to no regulation whatsoever.

During homeopathy's pinnacle in the nineteenth century, patients obtained homeopathic medicines almost exclusively from the physicians who administered them. By contrast, when Americans' interest in homeopathy resurged in the 1970s, many homeopathic remedies were sold directly to consumers over-the-counter (OTC), as most are today. In 1972, the FDA undertook a major initiative called the OTC Drug Review, a still-unfinished effort to apply the 1962 Drug Amendments' effectiveness requirement to the extant market in OTC products. Shortly after launching the Review, the agency announced that homeopathic medicines would be excluded from its purview because of their "uniqueness." Although the FDA declared it would later address these products separately, the agency's leadership privately doubted that a homeopathic drug review would ever actually occur. To date, it has not.[26]

After 1972, the FDA only rarely brought enforcement actions against homeopathic drugs. For instance, in 1976, the federal government detained an imported shipment of inadequately labeled OTC homeopathic medicines. A federal court, reviewing this detention, affirmed the agency's statutory and constitutional authority to regulate homeopathic remedies as drugs, regardless of how highly diluted (and thus harmless) they were. Nonetheless, the FDA took few additional actions against homeopathic remedies, even as the demand for them expanded dramatically in the late 1970s and 1980s.[27]

In 1988, the agency finally set out an official position regarding homeopathic drugs in a document called a Compliance Policy Guide (CPG). While affirming the applicability of some FD&C Act requirements, the FDA announced a policy of discretionary nonenforcement of others—including the core provisions intended to ensure drug effectiveness. The agency stated that it would challenge homeopathic products' effectiveness only if they were "being offered for use (or promoted) significantly beyond recognized or customary practice of homeopathy." The CPG permitted homeopathic drugs to be marketed directly to consumers, without a prescription, so long as they were "intended solely for self-limiting disease conditions amenable to self-diagnosis . . . and treatment." By spelling out exactly how to steer clear of FDA objections, this document helped the homeopathic drug industry to flourish even more.[28]

In subsequent decades, the FDA continued to maintain a largely hands-off approach to homeopathic drugs, so long as they satisfied the elementary labeling and manufacturing requirements laid out in the 1988 CPG. The agency intervened only in extraordinary situations. For example, in 2009, it issued a warning letter and public advisories regarding Zicam® homeopathic zinc-based nasal gels and swabs. These products, which were labeled for use against the common cold, were much less diluted than traditional homeopathic remedies and apparently caused anosmia (a loss of smell) in some people. The warning letter reaffirmed, however, that the FDA did not ordinarily require manufacturers of homeopathic medicines to submit NDAs demonstrating safety and efficacy.[29]

In 2015, the FDA declared its intention to reexamine its regulatory framework for homeopathic drugs, in light of the industry's enormous growth and the presence of potentially harmful levels of some ingredients. In 2017, the agency issued a draft guidance setting forth a new "risk-based approach" to homeopathic drug regulation. This development sent shudders through the homeopathic community. In a petition to the agency, the nonprofit Americans for Homeopathy Choice contended that the new approach threatened access to homeopathic treatments; it urged the FDA to codify the 1988 CPG instead. In 2019, the agency denied this petition and simultaneously withdrew the CPG. The Alliance for Natural Health condemned these actions as an "attack on homeopathy" fueled by the FDA's "desire to protect [allopathic] drug industry profits."[30]

The 2017 draft guidance states that the agency will prioritize its enforcement and regulatory efforts on specific categories of homeopathic drugs that pose heightened risks to the public health. The document further asserts, however, that *any* unapproved homeopathic drug "is subject to FDA enforcement action at any time." Despite the draft guidance's rigorous tone, it will likely leave most of the homeopathic drug market unscathed. The priority categories consist largely of homeopathic products that the FDA has always maintained authority to act against. And the perpetually cash-strapped agency is unlikely to devote its scarce resources to policing homeopathic drugs outside these categories. Moreover, the FDA would be highly reluctant to trigger the outcry that would inevitably ensue if it removed a highly diluted homeopathic drug for a nonserious condition from the market because of insufficient evidence of efficacy. If history is any guide, Americans will likely retain virtually unfettered access to such remedies.

Homeopathic drugs are not the only CAM products that the FDA tolerates despite their clear violations of the FD&C Act. For instance, the agency has long given a free pass to traditional Chinese medicines sold in Chinese pharmacies. As another example, the FDA has declined to require manufacturers of acupuncture needles to demonstrate the efficacy of acupuncture itself (although it does impose special controls on the needles to ensure their safety). While a growing body of evidence suggests that acupuncture is in fact effective for some conditions, the same cannot be said for many other types of "energy medicine" devices. Nevertheless, a multitude of these products is readily available. Today, one can log on to Amazon.com and purchase an "Elite Orgone Pyramid Energy Generator" as a remedy for "insomnia and chronic nightmares," a "Quantum Value Nano Scalar Energy Zero Point Energy Wand" to "strengthen immunity," or a "Magnetic Migraine Neck Relief Support Headband Wrap." Unless an energy medicine device is marketed as a cure for a fatal illness or emits an actual energy field that may harm consumers, the FDA is extremely unlikely to act against it.[31]

State Regulation of CAM Practice: Medical Licensing Revisited

The history of American alternative medicine is defined by unorthodox practitioners at least as much as by unorthodox products. Many of the leading alternative sects—chiropractic, early osteopathy, and Christian Science, for example—have largely or entirely forsworn the use of drugs and depended entirely on manual manipulations or spiritual guidance by specially trained practitioners. Even product-focused CAM movements, such as homeopathy and naturopathy, have emphasized the critical role of their practitioners. Consequently, as we have seen, American alternative medicine sects have always deemed allopathy-dominated state medical licensing regimes to be a potent—even existential—threat.

Today, licensing reform remains a central component of the CAM community's legislative agenda. We therefore must revisit a topic that dominated the first portion of this book: state medical practice acts. Modern CAM activists, unlike their forerunners in the early nineteenth century, have not succeeded in dismantling the state medical licensing regimes, and they probably never will. Nevertheless, they have campaigned successfully for various reforms that now allow many irregular practitioners to treat patients legally.

CAM in the Courts

As interest in alternative medicine surged in the 1970s, a few litigants brought successful constitutional challenges to orthodoxy-favoring licensing and disciplinary regimes. For example, in 1974, the California Supreme Court ruled that the state board had violated the equal protection rights of osteopathic school graduates by categorically barring them from licensure as physicians. Six years later, the Florida Supreme Court struck down that state board's "arbitrary and unreasonable" punishment of a medical doctor for administering unorthodox chelation therapy for arteriosclerosis. These decisions were idiosyncratic, however. After all, *Dent v. West Virginia* was still good law. A more typical decision was the 1978 rejection by the US Court of Appeals for the Fourth Circuit of a claim that states were constitutionally required to authorize practice by naturopaths. Citing *Dent* and other cases, the court concluded that "the naturopaths' basic claim has been firmly, repeatedly, and authoritatively rejected."[32]

By 1990, it was clear that lawsuits brought by alternative practitioners challenging the constitutionality of state licensing regimes were doomed to fail. That year, in *In re Guess*, the North Carolina Supreme Court upheld the revocation of Dr. George Guess's medical license for practicing homeopathy. The court summarily rebuffed the doctor's assertion that the state board had violated his and his patients' constitutional privacy rights. The court held that the board was required only to show that homeopathy "departs from and does not conform to the standards of acceptable and prevailing medical practice in this state." Similar suits failed in other courts around the country until, by the late 1990s, they had largely disappeared.[33]

The CAM community's most significant litigation triumph in the modern era was a very different sort of case. In 1976, Chester A. Wilk, a cantankerous chiropractor from the Chicago suburbs, filed a Sherman Antitrust Act claim along with four colleagues against the AMA, the American Hospital Association (AHA), and various other parties. Wilk alleged that the defendants had conspired to eliminate the chiropractic profession by prohibiting patient referrals between medical doctors and chiropractors and by blocking chiropractors from gaining hospital admitting privileges. In 1987, after the AHA had settled the claims against it, a US district judge ruled against the AMA and issued a permanent injunction. The US Court of Appeals affirmed this holding, and the Supreme Court let it stand.[34]

The chiropractors' victory in *Wilk v. AMA* suggested that antitrust law could be a powerful weapon in the hands of alternative medicine advocates battling the orthodox establishment. Wilk's attorneys celebrated the district court's ruling "as a landmark event in decades-old legal battles by certain medical groups to break down the hallowed and exclusive barriers of the AMA and other prestigious medical organizations." But within a few years of the decision, it became apparent that various technical requirements of antitrust law severely limited its utility for this purpose.[35] As has so often been the case in American history, CAM advocates would have to conduct their medical freedom campaign primarily in the political rather than the judicial arena.

Separate Licensing of CAM Practitioners

As we have seen, in the late nineteenth century, the homeopathic and eclectic sects sought either nondiscriminatory licensing requirements and representation on state medical boards or, alternatively, entirely distinct licensing regimes. About a quarter of states embraced the latter approach with respect to homeopaths, and some also did so for eclectics. In the early twentieth century, other sects similarly pursued the separate licensing strategy. Approximately twenty-five states passed laws providing for the licensing of naturopaths. In addition, between 1913 and 1939, thirty-nine states enacted chiropractic licensing measures. Whereas the homeopathic, eclectic, and early naturopathic practice statutes were later revoked, the chiropractic practice acts survived. Indeed, since 1974, every state in the union has legally recognized chiropractic and licensed its practitioners—although the scope of practice for chiropractors varies widely between jurisdictions.[36]

Separate licensing regimes for other types of alternative practitioners have proliferated more recently. The thaw in the US-China relationship in the early 1970s triggered a surge of interest in acupuncture among Americans and a corresponding wave of acupuncturist licensing and certification statutes. Today, all but three states have acupuncture practice acts. Naturopathic licensing started rebounding in the 1970s, and today twenty-two states and the District of Columbia have laws licensing or otherwise regulating naturopathic doctors. In the early 1980s, Arizona and Nevada even created new homeopathic boards and began licensing homeopaths—joining Connecticut, which had never revoked its 1902 homeopathy practice act.[37]

Not all CAM practitioners support separate licensing regimes, and many health freedom activists vigorously oppose them. Instead, with growing success, they promote laws that wholly *exempt* CAM providers from licensing—a strategy similar to that pursued by the late nineteenth-century drugless sects. But before we consider the creation of statutory "safe harbors" for unlicensed CAM practitioners, we must first consider a parallel, less radical legislative development: the passage since the early 1990s of numerous "medical freedom acts" protecting licensed medical doctors who use CAM therapies.

Medical Freedom Acts

The growing number of MDs who integrated CAM into their practices in the 1970s and 1980s risked discipline by their state medical boards. In 1990, Alaska became the first state to address this issue, when it amended its medical practice act to declare that "the board may not base a finding of professional incompetence solely on the basis that a licensee's practice is unconventional or experimental in the absence of demonstrably physical harm to a patient." In 1993, the North Carolina legislature amended its code similarly in response to the *Guess* decision. Since then, about fifteen additional states have passed such "medical freedom acts" to shield physicians from disciplinary action for practicing CAM.[38]

These statutes are not all equally protective. The New York version, for example, requires unconventional care, like conventional care, to "effectively" treat the patient, thus leaving the board with enormous discretion to discipline physicians who use unproven CAM remedies. Other states—including some very large ones—have adopted much stronger measures, however. For example, California's law provides that so long as a physician obtains informed consent and does not cause "death or serious bodily injury," he or she may not be disciplined "solely on the basis that the treatment or advice he or she rendered to a patient is alternative or complementary medicine." Florida's statute, enacted with the explicit intent of ensuring that "citizens be able to choose from all health care options," is similarly protective.[39]

Safe Harbor Legislation

In modern times, the first state to legalize the *unlicensed* practice of alternative medicine was Idaho, which in 1977 amended its medical practice act to exempt practitioners who used treatments other than prescription drugs or surgery. Next came Oklahoma, which in 1994 revised its act to provide that nothing "shall prohibit services rendered by any person not licensed by the Board and practicing any nonallopathic healing practice."[40] But the current national movement to promote the passage of such "safe harbor" laws has its real roots in Minnesota.

In 1993, Minnesota criminally charged Herbert Saunders, a dairy farmer and holistic healer, with the unauthorized practice of medicine. For decades, Saunders had offered Minnesotans an unusual treatment for cancer and other serious diseases. He would sell a patient a pregnant cow, inject that person's blood into the cow's udder, and instruct him or her to drink the colostrum (first milk). This procedure supposedly imbued the colostrum with powerful patient-specific antibodies. Two trials of Saunders, in 1995 and 1996, ended in hung juries. The second jury sent the judge a note during its deliberations stating, "We can reach a decision BUT some of us would have to go against our beliefs. Is that what you want?" The state dropped the charges after the second mistrial. Saunders was by this time a heroic figure in the Minnesota alternative medicine community.[41]

The Minnesota Board of Medicine soon riled this community again. The board filed a civil suit to enjoin Helen Healy, a beloved St. Paul naturopath, from practicing medicine without a license. Healy's supporters, dubbing themselves the "Freedom Fund for Naturopathic Medicine," bombarded state legislators and officials with letters and phone calls. In August 1996, they held a rally in downtown St. Paul, carrying signs demanding "Stop the Medical Monopoly" and "Give Health a Chance." A state senator participating in the demonstration proclaimed, "I'm proud to be here in support of people's right to choose." The authorities soon reached a settlement with Healy that permitted her to continue practicing subject to certain limitations, mandatory disclosures, and orthodox medical oversight.[42]

The Minnesota holistic medicine community, outraged by the Saunders and Healy episodes, now mobilized for legislative reform to preclude similar prosecutions in the future. Diane Miller, one of Saunders' attorneys, led this effort as the principal lobbyist for the newly formed Minnesota Natural Health Legal Reform Project. Miller first proposed that the legislature totally exempt alternative providers from the state's medical practice act, but the Minnesota Medical Association blocked this approach. She thus rewrote the measure with enough restrictions and requirements to persuade the MMA to withdraw its opposition.

The Minnesota Complementary and Alternative Health Care Freedom of Access Act became law in May 2000. This statute, still in effect, legalized a new category of "unlicensed complementary and alternative health care practitioners." This category included providers of "the broad domain of complementary and alternative healing methods and treatments," of which the law listed twenty-two examples, including colostrum therapy, herbalism, homeopathy, "mind-body healing practices," naturopathy, and "traditional Oriental practices, such as Qi Gong energy healing." Providers of these treatments could not be charged with the unlicensed practice of medicine if they followed the law's requirements. The statute banned them from providing specified services reserved for licensed professionals, such as surgery, chiropractic adjustments, and prescribing prescription drugs. It also mandated disclosure of their unlicensed status to patients and established disciplinary procedures. It did not, however, establish any sort of registration scheme or impose educational or training requirements.[43]

In the wake of this triumph in her home state, Miller in 2000 co-founded a lobbying organization, National Health Freedom Action (NHFA), and a sister educational group, the National Health Freedom Coalition (NHFC). Since its inception, the NHFA's signature cause has been the passage of "safe harbor practitioner exemption laws" that, like Minnesota's, shield CAM providers from being charged with the unlicensed practice of medicine. The campaign for these statutes has seen slow but steady success over the past twenty years, drawing support from both liberals and conservatives. Since 2000, eight additional states (California, Rhode Island, Louisiana, Arizona, New Mexico, Colorado, Nevada, and Maine) have enacted safe harbor laws, bringing the total to eleven.[44] For unclear reasons, the enactment of these laws has occurred largely under the radar, celebrated on health freedom websites but barely mentioned in the mainstream press.

These safe harbor statutes offer yet another example of the ways in which American law is bending to make room for CAM. This is not to say that CAM providers and their patients no longer confront significant legal obstacles in the United States. After all, even with NHFA's victories, almost four-fifths of Americans still live in states without safe harbor laws. Still, the trend seems clear, as one state or another constantly seems on the verge of joining the ranks of safe harbor jurisdictions.[45]

Health Freedom Rhetoric in the CAM Community

Since its founding in 2000, NHFA/NHFC has become one of the nation's leading advocacy groups for the protection of CAM medicine. NHFA lobbies in coordination with state-level health freedom organizations, not only for safe harbor laws, but also for other bills "promoting freedom of choice in health care," such as legislation protecting philosophical exemptions to vaccine mandates, ensuring access to raw unpasteurized foods, and protecting parental rights to choose CAM. The NHFC disseminates health freedom literature, makes presentations at conferences, and holds workshops. In most years, it hosts a "US Health Freedom Congress" at which dozens of "health freedom leaders and activists" from across the country gather. The Congress's voting members include numerous health freedom advocacy organizations, ranging from groups with an obvious financial stake in the deregulation of alternative medicine to others with little or no obvious connection to industry.[46]

NHFA/NHFC embraces a libertarian approach to health rooted in popular constitutional norms invoked since the country's birth. In 2004, the NHFC issued a "Declaration of Health Freedom" modeled on the Declaration of Independence. After reaffirming the "inalienable rights" of "Life, Liberty, and the pursuit of happiness" asserted by Jefferson in 1776, the NHFC document's own preamble affirmed "that every person has a fundamental right of privacy and self-determination and that the right to make personal choices in pursuit of healing, health, and well-being is encompassed in that right." The Declaration of Health Freedom concluded: "All public policy and laws affecting resources, substances or practitioners used for health care purposes must be drafted only under the highest form of strict scrutiny in order to forever protect the sovereign nature and inherent dignity of the individual."[47]

The US Health Freedom Congress has more recently endorsed various resolutions similarly suffused with quasi-constitutional language. Among the eight "Principles of Health Freedom" set forth in the 2014 resolution is the following: "In order for freedom of choice to be implemented or meaningful, individuals and members of the human family hold the fundamental right and freedom to access their choices, whomever and whatever one deems necessary or prefers for one's health and survival."[48] The following year, the Congress adopted a resolution that explicitly endorsed Benjamin Rush's apocryphal call for incorporating medical freedom directly into the US Constitution. Its proposed amendment: "The People of the United States of America and anyone lawfully residing or sojourning therein shall have freedom of choice and practice of any health or medical care modalities as they deem in their own personal best interest and judgment."[49]

Importantly, from its inception, NHFA/NHFC has opposed *all* licensing of health care providers. As explained by one observer, "Health freedom advocates believe, at root, that the state should not be involved in the healing relationship at all." Therefore, perhaps counterintuitively, the NHFA has consistently battled *against* state legislation establishing licensing regimes for specific categories of CAM practitioners, such as naturopathic and homeopathic doctors, massage therapists, and reflexologists. For example, in 2014 the organization opposed a bill in Hawaii establishing the licensing of herbal therapists. In a lengthy letter to the state legislature, the NHFA contended that the proposed law "would negatively impact consumer choice and jeopardize access to many wonderful unlicensed herbalists, wellness consultants, health coaches, and homeopaths that utilize herbs." The letter continued: "The use of herbs is a non-invasive, natural health care option for thousands of consumers and should not be . . . restricted to a select group of persons with a particular education." The NHFA is so firmly committed to deregulation of the medical sphere that it even opposes laws merely mandating that unlicensed healers *register* with the state.[50]

A major schism thus exists within the broader CAM advocacy movement regarding the best approach for overcoming allopathic doctors' domination of American medicine. Some CAM practitioners (for instance, formally trained naturopathic doctors) actively promote professionalization and licensing in their fields. They strive to become mainstream, with hopes of qualifying for insurance reimbursement and even hospital admitting privileges. By contrast, the NHFA and its health freedom allies oppose virtually every CAM licensing bill. Diane Miller, now the NHFA/NHFC's Legal and Public Policy Director, explains: "Some vocations move forward to seek licensure just so they can get government endorsement and insurance coverage. Constitutionally we do not think that is a valid reason why states can mandate licensing and make other people criminals. Instead of depending on their own academic and good reputation, some professions want the government to do the rubber stamp, but that's not what government is for."[51]

Paradoxically, by resisting licensing, the health freedom movement is helping preserve one of the largest remaining practical obstacles to choosing CAM: the widespread lack of insurance coverage. With the exception of chiropractic (which is now covered by many public and private plans for treatment of neuromusculoskeletal conditions), Americans pay for more than 72 percent of their visits to CAM practitioners entirely out-of-pocket. Medicare and Medicaid do not cover any non-chiropractic CAM services, unless nurse midwifery is counted. Private insurers are similarly parsimonious. Although some offer non-chiropractic CAM coverage pursuant to voluntary riders, few provide it as a standard benefit, unless required to do so by state law. Only a few states have such mandates, and only Washington has gone so far as to require health plans to cover all categories of licensed CAM providers. (In Washington, this list includes chiropractors, naturopaths, acupuncturists, licensed midwives, and massage therapists.) But the main point here is that where CAM coverage exists, it virtually always applies only to *licensed* practitioners, and it is hard to imagine any public or private insurance system ever broadly covering visits to self-declared but unlicensed CAM experts. Thus, in effect, health libertarians like those in NHFA/NHFC prioritize the goal of ending all state regulation of medicine over the goal of providing people with limited resources the practical means to obtain CAM care.[52]

Freedom from Orthodox Medical Compulsion

This book is primarily about the history of resistance to government restrictions on access to medical treatments that people *want*. It has not focused on the intertwined history of resistance to government efforts to *compel* people to undergo treatments or protective measures they *do not want*. Nonetheless, because of the ideological and organizational links between these two issues, the latter has appeared sporadically throughout this book. This chapter will thus conclude with a brief consideration of recent movements that have battled mandatory public health measures favored by the medical establishment.

The Modern Antivaccination Movement

The most prominent example of modern resistance to orthodox compulsion is opposition to vaccination requirements. Although other authors have ably explored the rise of the modern antivaccination movement as a distinct phenomenon, it is important also to understand it as a component of the broader impulse for medical freedom.[53]

Progressive Era medical freedom activists fought mandatory vaccination along with other aspects of orthodox-dominated "state medicine." During America's mid-century romance with scientific medicine, anti-immunization efforts shriveled, although they never disappeared entirely. But in the late 1970s and early 1980s, the same growing distrust of orthodox medical institutions that gave rise to the holistic medicine movement also fueled a resurgence of opposition to immunization, especially compulsory immunization. In 1982, a group of parents who thought the diphtheria-pertussis-tetanus (DPT) vaccine had sickened their children founded Dissatisfied Parents Together. Later renamed the National Vaccine Information Center (NVIC), this organization today remains a leading voice of skepticism regarding vaccine safety and a leading opponent of vaccine compulsion.[54]

At the very end of the twentieth century, public concern about vaccine safety soared. By 1999, Americans were increasingly alarmed about a purported link between the measles-mumps-rubella (MMR) vaccine and autism. In May of that year, Republican Indiana congressman Dan Burton (the grandfather of a child with autism) held the first of a series of widely publicized hearings on vaccine safety. In July, the US Public Health Service and the American Academy of Pediatrics jointly called for the removal of the mercury-based preservative thimerosal from childhood vaccines because of the risk of neurological impairment. Just one week later, the CDC reported that a rotavirus vaccine was associated with intestinal blockage in children.[55]

As the new millennium commenced, this constellation of events triggered a dramatic surge of discussions about vaccine safety and expressions of antivaccination sentiment in the media. The antivaccination movement expanded robustly during this century's first fifteen years, due in large part to the rise of the internet, which became a popular forum for people to express opposition to conventional opinions, medical and otherwise. More parents claimed religious, philosophical, or personal belief exemptions from childhood vaccinations during this period, and several states enacted new exemption laws. A counter-reaction occurred during the latter part of the 2010s, in response to a series of measles outbreaks among uninoculated Americans. Some states tightened the availability of exemptions, including medical exemptions, and a few eliminated one or more types of nonmedical exemptions altogether.[56]

Like so many of the medical freedom causes we have examined, antivaccinationism transcends conventional political divides, drawing from a mishmash of anticorporatists, holistic medicine proponents, chemophobes, evangelical Christians, and small-government libertarians. One leading source of anti-vax rhetoric is Children's Health Defense, an organization founded and chaired by environmental activist Robert F. Kennedy Jr., a scion of the legendary Democratic family. Another is the right-wing conspiracy website Natural News.[57]

The ideological overlaps between CAM legalization activism and antivaccinationism are obvious. They share a fierce commitment to medical freedom of choice. They demand that government officials look beyond population-level statistics and take "anecdotal" evidence seriously. They both allege an insidious conspiracy between the government and pharmaceutical companies, and they use similar tropes of bodily freedom, freedom of conscience, and the superiority of "natural" products and healing methods. The links between the CAM and anti-vax movements are more than philosophical, however. The NVIC counts many CAM enthusiasts among its members, is a voting member of the National Health Freedom Congress, and has received major funding from an osteopath who earned a fortune selling dietary supplements. Natural News publishes articles promoting alternative cures—including supplement products sold by a company in which the site's owner has a financial interest. The Selz Foundation, one of the nation's leading funders of antivaccination advocacy, has also directed its philanthropy toward "homeopathic causes."[58]

The biggest contrast between CAM legalization advocacy and anti-vaccinationism is in their levels of success. Whereas CAM use is extremely widespread in the United States, the number of people who refuse vaccinations is relatively small. And while CAM legalization campaigns have seen substantial victories, compulsory vaccination remains in place nationwide. Court challenges have been futile; *Jacobson v. Massachusetts* (discussed in Chapter 4) remains good law. Moreover, polls consistently show overwhelming support for compulsory vaccination.[59] Recently, mandatory vaccination has become even more pervasive, as some states—in view of the resurgence of measles and other long-dormant diseases—have narrowed or eliminated nonmedical exemptions, despite the fierce resistance of antivaccination activists.

Why has the antivaccine struggle been so much less fruitful than efforts to legalize CAM? The answer is simple; when the health risk in question is a communicable disease, individuals' choices affect the well-being of other individuals and of the community as a whole. As the Supreme Court declared in *Jacobson*, "Real liberty for all could not exist under the operation of a principle which recognizes the right of each individual person to use his own . . . regardless of the injury that may be done to others."[60] Or as stated in an aphorism of uncertain origin: "Your liberty to swing your fist ends where my nose begins."

Nevertheless, even when the United States confronts a new contagious threat, a substantial minority of Americans is always prepared to resist choice-limiting public health measures in the name of personal freedom. During the COVID-19 crisis of 2020–2021, this minority was vociferous and determined.

COVID-19 and the Twenty-First-Century
Battle against State Medicine

On March 19, 2020, as COVID-19 swept through his state, California governor Gavin Newsom issued an executive order directing all Californians to stay at home, with narrow exceptions.[61] One month later, a caravan of enraged protesters departed Orange County and drove north toward Sacramento through a landscape of shuttered businesses, schools, and churches. The motorcade gathered adherents along the way. When the drivers reached Sacramento, they joined hundreds of other demonstrators in an "open up" demonstration, one of many around the United States during spring 2020.

Some protestors circled the State Capitol complex in a convoy of honking cars, while many others lined the surrounding streets. Few wore protective face masks. The crowd waved American flags and carried signs (Fig. 8.1).[62] Some signs made basic pleas. ("Let Us Work"; "Give My Daughter Her Senior Year Back.") Others took a more partisan tack: ("Trump 2020"). Many invoked the country's libertarian tradition ("Don't Tread on Me"; "Life, Liberty, and the Pursuit of Happiness") and condemned autocratic government ("Stop the Tyranny"). A few signs echoed conspiracy theories prominent in right-wing circles. ("The Media is the Real Virus"; "Freedom Trumps the Commie Virus.")

Curiously, one sign declared: "We Do Not Consent to Tyranny or Forced Vaccines." To some observers, the issue of compulsory vaccination may have seemed peripheral to the controversy at hand, especially in view of the fact that no COVID-19 vaccine had yet been developed. But in fact, an antivaccination organization called Freedom Angels had organized the Sacramento demonstration. A trio of conservative Christian "Patriot Mothers" had founded the group in 2019 to wage an ultimately unsuccessful battle against California legislation

Figure 8.1 Demonstration at the California State Capitol in Sacramento protesting a state stay-at-home order during the COVID-19 pandemic, May 23, 2020. *Photo by Stanton Sharpe / SOPA Images/Sipa USA via AP Images.*

strengthening the state's vaccination mandate.[63] Now they had returned to the state capital to continue their struggle against medical despotism.

A week later, a very different type of antivaccine activist allied himself with the national anti-shutdown movement: Robert F. Kennedy Jr. In remarks he delivered at an online conference called the "Health Freedom Summit," Kennedy rued the plight of surfer friends who had been ticketed in Malibu for violating Governor Newsom's beach closure order. In the following weeks, Kennedy and others at Children's Health Defense posted coronavirus-themed diatribes on the organization's website opposing quarantines, contact tracing, and mask wearing.[64]

At first glance, the antivaccination and anti-shutdown agendas may seem entirely distinct, and perhaps even in tension with each other. Wouldn't vaccination skeptics support nonpharmaceutical measures to prevent COVID-19 from spreading? And wouldn't opponents of stay-at-home orders hail the development of a coronavirus vaccine that allowed society to safely reopen? In fact, the ideology of these groups overlapped considerably. They shared a conviction that an unholy alliance of avaricious private interests and power-hungry public officials was conspiring to strip Americans of their fundamental rights.

Consider the most prominent common enemies of the antivaccination and anti-shutdown protestors: Bill Gates and Anthony Fauci. The billionaire co-founder of Microsoft and his wife, Melinda, run the philanthropic Gates Foundation. In April 2020, the foundation pledged up to $250 million to the global fight against COVID-19, including the development of vaccines. Fauci, whom we first met when he was leading the federal response to AIDS in the late 1980s, remains the government's top infectious disease expert. He served on Donald Trump's White House Coronavirus Task Force, where he struggled to navigate the president's unscientific opinions and pronouncements. In January 2021, Fauci transitioned to the role of President Joseph Biden's chief medical advisor.[65]

Throughout the pandemic, COVID-19 skeptics accused Gates and Fauci of exaggerating the severity of the disease (or even inventing the virus) to seize control of the country. One conspiracy theory posited that Gates was plotting with Fauci to enrich himself through sales of a COVID-19 vaccine that would implant a microchip in every American. Cheryl Chumley, the online opinion editor for the *Washington Times*, wrote a column titled "Gates and Fauci: Unelected Destroyers of Freedom." Chumley raged on behalf of "all the freedom-loving Americans watching with dismay as their free America is destroyed by the likes of unelected wonks—unelected, unaccountable to the people, and apparently, unconcerned at all with the God-given rights of constitutionally protected individuals." Robert F. Kennedy Jr. similarly demonized Gates and Fauci, along with all the "despots and billionaires" who would leverage the COVID-19 crisis to convert America into "a tyrannical near-police state operating at the direction of Big Data/Big Telecom, the Medical Cartel, and the Military/Industrial/Intelligence Complex."[66]

Gates and Fauci also played villainous roles in *Plandemic*, a film that proliferated wildly across internet in mid-2020. This documentary, featuring an ex–government researcher named Judy Mikovits, advanced various conspiracy theories about the origins of COVID-19 and the government response to it, while blaming masks and vaccines for exacerbating the pandemic. The film also promoted the use of hydroxychloroquine as a COVID treatment. Indeed, support for unproven COVID therapies abounded among medical freedom activists in 2020 and 2021, including not only hydroxychloroquine, but also, for example, colloidal silver and oleandrin supplements. The internet was replete with allegations that Big Pharma—plotting to profit from expensive COVID vaccines and drugs—was suppressing information about these cheaper treatments' effectiveness.[67]

These types of sentiments and suspicions are deeply rooted in the American political tradition. As we saw in Chapter 4, Progressive Era opponents of "state medicine" similarly battled what they perceived to be a sinister conspiracy of public and private interests scheming to assume dictatorial control over large sectors of American society. Like their modern counterparts, these earlier activists, driven by a profound distrust of experts and elites, struggled against compulsory vaccination and all other coercive instruments of a voracious "medical octopus."[68] Moreover, the Progressive Era medical freedom movement similarly charged a shadowy coalition of the medical establishment and the government with not only despotically imposing compulsory health measures on the people, but also with plotting to deprive them of access to the unorthodox remedies they desired.

Unlike the early twentieth-century medical freedom movement, however, the 2020–2021 version was associated primarily (though not exclusively) with the right wing of the political spectrum. Moreover, with the backing of President Trump and his acolytes in public office, these modern activists had a greater impact on public health policy than the National League for Medical Freedom ever did. Although polls showed that a solid majority of Americans supported government efforts to control COVID-19, the views of the dissenting minority checked the aggressiveness of the federal government's response and shaped much state and local coronavirus policy, especially in the South and West.[69]

The widespread rejection of compulsory (and even voluntary) mask wearing demonstrated that for many Americans, resistance to public health mandates and recommendations was a political act—a marker of one's Trumpian rejection of scientific expertise, the "deep state," and the "fake news." At a July 2020 protest against a Utah requirement that children wear masks at school, demonstrators derided mask wearing as "an act of submission." "We have the right to make our own choices," trumpeted one protestor. "I don't like government mandates," declared another. "COVID is a hoax" added a third.[70]

On January 6, 2021, when a mob invaded the US Capitol in an attempt to overturn the 2020 presidential election, Dr. Simone Gold was part of the crowd. Gold, of Beverly Hills, had risen to prominence in right-wing circles early in 2020 by opposing face masks, lockdowns, and social distancing and advocating the use of hydroxychloroquine. She founded America's Frontline Doctors, a conservative physicians' group dedicated to challenging mainstream narratives about COVID-19. A video of her and fellow members voicing their unorthodox medical theories at a July 2020 event went "viral" on the internet (with an assist from Donald Trump and Donald Trump Jr.) until Facebook, Twitter, and YouTube removed it. On the day of the insurrection, Gold attended a "Rally for Health Freedom" before entering the Capitol with the mob. Inside the rotunda, she denounced the coronavirus vaccine and the "massive medical establishment" to the crowd through a bullhorn. Federal officials arrested Gold later in January, the same week that Joe Biden was inaugurated as president.[71]

In spring 2021, as the rollout of effective vaccines helped subdue COVID-19 and state and local governments began easing lockdowns and mask mandates, the attention of medical freedom advocates turned to another perceived threat: the issuance of "vaccine passports" for domestic and international use. In late March, as President Biden contemplated implementing a system of federal vaccine credentials, reactionary Georgia congresswoman Marjorie Taylor Greene blasted any proof-of-vaccination scheme as "Biden's mark of the beast" and "corporate communism." On April 2, conservative Florida governor Ron DeSantis issued an executive order prohibiting any government in the state from issuing vaccine passports. "People have certain freedoms and individual liberties to make decisions for themselves," DeSantis proclaimed. Notably, this executive order also forbade private businesses from requiring customers to provide documentation of vaccination. DeSantis grumbled, "Give all this information to some big corporation? You want the fox to guard the hen house? I mean, give me a break." After Texas governor Greg Abbott took a similar step a few days later, the Biden administration explicitly disclaimed any intention to establish a federal vaccination database or impose a vaccine credentialing system.[72]

In May 2021, cumulative COVID-19 deaths in the United States climbed past 600,000—more than a sixth of the world's total. Americans nevertheless continued to test the consequences of medical libertarianism during a lethal pandemic.[73]

9

Life, Liberty, [and the Pursuit of Happiness]

The Long Struggle for Legalization of Medical Marijuana

It was 7:45 p.m. on November 5, 1996—Election Day. The thousands of people assembled in and around the Cannabis Buyers Club (CBC) on San Francisco's Market Street were eager for the polls to close in fifteen minutes so they could start smoking weed.[1,2]

The crowd had gathered for a victory party celebrating the expected passage of California Proposition 215, the "California Compassionate Use Act of 1996." If enacted, this initiative would be the first state law in the United States to legalize the use of marijuana for medical purposes. Dennis Peron—the founder and director of the CBC—would later remember: "Our freedom itself was on the ballot. . . . The entire planet was watching."[3]

Many of the partygoers had been ready to light up triumphal joints for hours, but Peron pleaded that they keep their pot in their pockets until 8 p.m. Although polls showed broad support for *medical* marijuana, Californians overwhelmingly opposed recreational use of the drug. Peron later explained, "We just didn't want . . . live television pictures of folks 'getting high' being the last thing people saw before going out to vote."[4]

In each of the two previous years, the California legislature had passed a bill legalizing medical use of marijuana, only to see Governor Pete Wilson veto it. Peron had thus decided to take the issue directly to the people. He had co-drafted Proposition 215, an initiative immune from gubernatorial veto, and started the successful drive to obtain enough signatures to get it in on the ballot. The measure explicitly recognized that Californians had "a right to obtain and use marijuana for medical purposes" when a physician recommended they do so for treatment of "cancer, anorexia, AIDS, chronic pain, glaucoma, arthritis, migraine, or any other illness for which marijuana provides relief." Proposition 215 declared that state prohibitions on the possession and cultivation of marijuana would not apply to such patients or their primary caregivers and that no physician would be sanctioned in any way for making such a recommendation.[5]

Until very recently, the sprawling building where the celebrants gathered had housed the largest non-clandestine marijuana distributor in the country. Peron

Choose Your Medicine. Lewis A. Grossman, Oxford University Press. © Lewis A. Grossman 2021.
DOI: 10.1093/oso/9780190612757.003.0010

had founded the CBC in 1993 to serve the growing population of San Franciscans seeking pot for medical uses. From its inception, many of the CBC's customers were fighting AIDS, an epidemic savaging the largely gay Castro district where the dispensary was initially located. At its current site just northeast of the Castro, the CBC had become an important social center. People with AIDS and other diseases filled the high-ceilinged interior with marijuana smoke while providing each other with medical information and emotional support. Since mid-1996, the building had also served as the de facto headquarters of Californians for Compassionate Use, Peron's pro-Proposition 215 organization.

Then, on August 4, 1996, three months before the election, one hundred armed California narcotics agents raided the CBC on orders from Dan Lungren, the state's conservative and politically ambitious attorney general. They seized more than 150 pounds of pot and interrogated the few staffers and patients who happened to be there on a Sunday, when the club was closed. On Monday, state authorities obtained a court injunction closing the facility.

The following evening, more than five hundred furious protesters marched through the city with signs bearing slogans such as "Marijuana is Medicine" and "Defend Your Right to Smoke Weed." A week later, patient activists conducted a mock public trial of Lungren and then marched to the attorney general's office, where the jury delivered its "guilty" verdict.[6]

Meanwhile, Peron continued to run his Proposition 215 campaign from a second-floor office within the shuttered CBC. One day in October, state authorities arrested and indicted him for the possession and sale of marijuana. He and his comrades implemented a successful media strategy portraying Lungren as a heartless politico. Even cartoonist Garry Trudeau joined the conversation, with a series of sympathetic *Doonesbury* comic strips. In one, the perpetual pothead Zonker bemoans the buyers' club bust, and his friend responds, "Well, if Proposition 215 is approved, it'll never happen again."[7]

By Election Day, political prognosticators were predicting not only victory for Proposition 215, but also the re-election of Democratic president Bill Clinton. As a candidate in 1992, the slick Arkansan had claimed that he tried smoking marijuana once but "didn't inhale." During his first four years in office, President Clinton had been no defender of medical marijuana. His drug czar, Barry McCaffrey, had even flown to California to campaign against Proposition 215, warning that the measure was a "stalking horse for [full] legalization" and had condemned the use of "Cheech and Chong logic to guide our thinking about medicine."[8]

At 8 P.M., Peron announced that the polls were officially closed and immediately, in his own words, "lit up a big fat joint." He puffed away for the news cameras with a broad smile (Fig. 9.1). The crowd followed his example, and soon smoke was pouring out of the CBC's open windows, along with drumbeats and

Figure 9.1 Dennis Peron lights up a joint to celebrate the passage of California Proposition 215, legalizing medical marijuana, on November 6, 1996. © *Andy Kuno/ AP Images.*

triumphant whoops. This festive use of marijuana was unusual for the many celebrants who ordinarily smoked it to relieve the symptoms of serious diseases, such as AIDS and cancer. But the throng also included at least some people like Phil Harris, who told a journalist, "I get high because—gosh—life kind of sucks."[9]

By 11 P.M., it was clear that Proposition 215 would pass. The revelry continued into the early hours of Wednesday morning. The final tally would show that 55.6 percent of California voters voted "yes." The initiative's passage (along with that of a similar measure in Arizona the same day) triggered a wave of state medical marijuana legalization laws that, by 2021, would encompass thirty-six states and the District of Columbia.[10]

Following the election, newspapers around the country published photographs of Peron gleefully toking at the victory party. These images outraged Proposition 215's opponents. A letter to the editor published in the *San Bernardino County Sun* raged: "The joy on [Peron's] face . . . and the absence of any mention of disease . . . send a harmful message to youth about this dangerous drug. What was passed on the premise of aiding people who painfully suffer from a chronic disease . . . now appears to be a license allowing people to smoke marijuana for pleasure."[11]

Then, on November 19, the *New York Times* quoted Peron opining: "I believe all marijuana use is medical—except for kids."[12] His logic: because stress relief is a medical purpose, any adult who uses cannabis does so for medical reasons. Peron became so identified with this statement that it could have been his epi-taph when he died in January 2018.

Peron's proclamation infuriated many. To Proposition 215's enraged opponents, it confirmed that the initiative's true purpose was to enable recrea-tional use. Peron's statement also incensed people who had supported the propo-sition believing it to be a genuine medical measure intended to help people with serious illnesses. Californians for Medical Rights (CMR), a well-funded advo-cacy organization that had run a polished pro-Proposition 215 campaign along-side Peron's grass-roots effort, voiced this view. It quickly issued a press release challenging Peron: "The truth is, the new law applies to relatively few people, under very specific circumstances." Bill Zimmerman, CMR's chief, was blunter. He told the *Washington Post* that the real danger to the new law was not federal officials, but "crazies from our own side," like Peron, who viewed the initiative "as a wedge to legalizing recreational use of marijuana."[13]

Intriguingly, many proponents of legal recreational use were also irritated by Peron's "all marijuana use is medical" declaration. The leadership of the National Organization for the Reform of Marijuana Laws (NORML), the most prominent full-legalization advocacy group, was aghast. Although medical-marijuana-only measures fell far short of NORML's ultimate goal, it had diligently backed them since 1972 and had actively supported Proposition 215.[14] In NORML's view, Peron's post-victory language not only muddied the arguments for full legaliza-tion, but also seemed to disregard the use of marijuana for pure pleasure. Peron thus widened an already-existing rift within the marijuana advocacy commu-nity. As we will see, this fissure between supporters of medical marijuana and proponents of full legalization endures today.

In some ways, the medical marijuana movement examined in this chapter is similar to other movements for freedom of therapeutic choice that we have con-sidered. But the fact that marijuana has an alternative, commonly condemned non-medical use—provision of a recreational high—has engendered some pro-found differences. Pot's widespread recreational use has shaped the tactics and language of medical cannabis proponents and generated fierce intra-movement disputes. Dennis Peron, a hippie stoner genuinely dedicated to helping ill people find relief, embodied all the ambiguities inherent in marijuana itself.

The Medical Alcohol Precedent

Marijuana is not, of course, the only mind-altering substance with both thera-peutic and recreational uses. American law wrestled with the appropriate regula-tion of another dual-use product—alcohol—from the 1830s through the end of national prohibition in 1933. Almost every one of the legal and policy arguments that would later arise in the context of medical marijuana were foreshadowed in this long-standing debate.

In the nineteenth century, American physicians frequently prescribed alcoholic beverages as a treatment for many conditions, ranging from snakebites to rheumatism to pneumonia. The 1863 (4th) edition of the U.S. *Pharmacopoeia* listed brandy, whisky, sherry wine, and port wine. Doctors also recommended the consumption of gin and malt liquors. Nonetheless, many states, at various times, banned the medical use of such products along with other uses. They either prohibited the prescription of intoxicating liquor altogether or allowed it only if the liquor was rendered unfit as a beverage.[15]

Some early state judicial decisions upheld stringent restrictions on the distribution of alcohol for medical purposes. For example, in 1849, Massachusetts' highest court held that even in a dire situation, an unlicensed retailer could not sell "spirituous liquors" pursuant to a physician's prescription, "however strong a necessity there might be for the buyer's using it as medicine, or for the preservation of health." Around mid-century, however, state courts almost uniformly began to strike down complete bans on the sale of alcoholic beverages for medical use. For instance, in 1854, the Missouri Supreme Court reversed the conviction of a physician who sold a glass of brandy to a patient, holding that the jury should have been instructed to acquit the defendant if "he really administered the liquor to a diseased person, as a medicine, upon his professional judgment of its necessity." Through the 1870s, courts read exceptions for medical use into prohibition laws based on the long-standing canon that statutes must be interpreted to avoid absurdity and injustice. In 1885, a Kentucky court suggested that a medical exception was *constitutionally* required. "While the legislature has the power to regulate the sale of liquors to be used as beverage, or to prohibit its sale for that purpose altogether, it cannot exercise that power so arbitrarily as to prohibit the use or sale of it as medicine."[16]

Despite the Kentucky decision, most courts considering the issue after 1880 actually *rejected* the need to read a medical exception into state and local prohibition laws. They concluded that the legislatures in question had intentionally omitted such exceptions and, moreover, that these omissions, far from being absurd, were justifiable. For example, in 1881, the Alabama Supreme Court affirmed the conviction of a physician who had prescribed and sold alcoholic "bitters" to a patient for treatment purposes. "There is no exception made in the statute in favor of physicians, . . . and this court cannot engraft one in their favor without the exercise of legislative power, which it does not possess."[17]

In the early twentieth century, orthodox doctors increasingly expressed doubt about alcohol's value as medicine. The 1916 (9th) edition of the U.S. *Pharmacopoeia* omitted alcoholic beverages altogether. In 1917, the American

Medical Association passed a resolution stating that because alcohol's "use in therapeutics ... has no scientific value," its "use ... as a therapeutic agent should be further discouraged." Not coincidentally, establishment physicians also tended to support temperance; the same resolution condemned the use of alcohol as a beverage because it was "detrimental to the human economy."[18]

Nevertheless, in 1919, when the Eighteenth Amendment to the US Constitution (banning the sale, manufacture, and distribution of alcoholic beverages) was ratified, many doctors still prescribed alcohol. According to a 1921 survey by the *Journal of the American Medical Association*, a slight majority of American physicians thought whiskey was a necessary therapeutic agent, while a smaller but significant percentage held the same opinion about wine and beer. Largely in response to this poll, the AMA reversed course in 1922, resolving that restrictions on medicinal liquor were "a serious interference with the practice of medicine." Whiskey and brandy reappeared in the 1925 (10th) edition of the *U.S. Pharmacopoeia*.[19]

The Volstead Act, enacted by Congress in 1919 to implement the Eighteenth Amendment, recognized the use of alcoholic beverages as medicine. It allowed physicians to prescribe, and pharmacists to dispense, liquor for medicinal purposes, albeit pursuant to a stringent permit scheme. The Act permitted states and localities to regulate alcohol more strictly than the federal government, however, and many did; indeed, about half of states declined to issue any medical permits at all. Moreover, in 1921, Congress passed the Willis-Campbell Act, which prohibited physicians nationwide from prescribing beer and set stricter limits than the Volstead Act on the quantity of spirits and wine they could prescribe.[20]

During the Prohibition Era, medical professionals occasionally fought such restrictions in court, though with almost complete futility. In 1923, a Los Angeles pharmacist convicted of filling a liquor prescription in violation of that city's ordinance alleged that the measure was invalid because, in combination with federal restrictions, it effectively limited sales to therapeutically valueless minute amounts. A California appeals court unequivocally rejected this argument, observing that "the evils which flow from [wine, whiskey, and brandy's] use as a beverage so greatly menace the health, peace, morals, and safety of society that the lawmaking branch of the government may with reason regard those evils as overwhelmingly outweighing the good services which such liquors may perform as medicines." The court remarked that "it is a matter of common notoriety" that "the sale of such liquors for medicinal purposes does greatly facilitate the evasion of the whole scheme of prohibitory legislation."[21]

During the same period, a group of more than one hundred prominent New York physicians formed the Association for the Protection of Constitutional Rights (APCR) to challenge the Willis-Campbell Act's quantity limits on prescriptions. In 1922, the APCR's president, former Columbia Medical School dean Samuel W. Lambert, filed a federal lawsuit alleging that these provisions were unconstitutional. He advanced three main legal theories: (1) the Act exceeded Congress's power under the Eighteenth Amendment to regulate the beverage use of alcohol; (2) it constituted federal regulation of medical practice, an area reserved exclusively to the states; and (3) it violated physicians' "fundamental" right to practice medicine however they deemed necessary to heal the sick. In 1926, the US Supreme Court rejected these arguments in *Lambert v. Yellowley*.[22]

While Lambert litigated his dispute, John Patrick Davin, another respected New York City physician, fought the Willis-Campbell Act outside of court. His main grievance was the law's prohibition on medical use of beer. Davin co-founded a political party called the Medical Rights League in 1922 and launched an unsuccessful campaign for Congress under its aegis.[23]

In 1933, the Twenty-first Amendment was ratified, repealing the Eighteenth. National prohibition disappeared, and only a few states maintained the policy. By 1940, disputes regarding medical alcohol had largely vanished, both because liquor was widely available for any use and because physicians, practicing in the context of emerging "wonder drugs," had largely stopped prescribing it. Whiskey and brandy disappeared from the *U.S. Pharmacopoeia* for good with the 1947 (13th) edition.

As a legal matter, the long struggle over the medical use of alcoholic beverages produced mostly harmful precedents for the later medical marijuana movement. The judicial decisions generally confirmed the power of the state and federal governments to highly restrict or even wholly prohibit the medical use of an intoxicating and addictive product due to its social and moral risks.[24] Moreover, the only notable public campaign in favor of medical use of alcoholic beverages—Davin's short-lived Medical Rights League—was a flop. Davin's campaign represented elite physicians, however; it was not a popular social movement. The country had not yet seen what might happen when a broad coalition of highly motivated patients demanded access to a culturally disfavored medicine.

The Rise and Fall of Marijuana as Medicine
(2700 BCE to 1972 CE)

Cultures around the world have used marijuana therapeutically for millennia. They have taken it orally, smoked it, and applied it topically. In Central Asia, cannabis's native region, people apparently used the plant for medicinal and other purposes for many thousands of years before the dawn of recorded history. The first written mention of the medical use of marijuana appears in Chinese sources from about 2700 BCE. Marijuana was used in ancient Indian Ayurvedic medicine, in African shamanistic healing, and as a peasant folk remedy in Europe. These traditional medical systems employed cannabis to treat a wide variety of conditions, such as rheumatism, fever, malaria, insomnia, digestive problems, and anxiety.[25]

Planters in the American colonies and the early republic—including George Washington and Thomas Jefferson—grew large volumes of cannabis for commercial use. The fiber from the plant's stem (hemp) was used to manufacture rope, paper, and fabric, and the seeds provided hempseed oil. Scholars disagree about how frequently the psychoactive flowers and leaves were used for medical or recreational purposes during the country's early years, although the minimalists seem to have the better of the argument.[26]

In the middle of the nineteenth century, just as hemp fiber was losing much of its commercial value, cannabis entered orthodox western medicine, thanks to the work of an Irish physician-scientist named William B. O'Shaughnessy. While posted in Calcutta as an employee of the British East India Company in the 1830s, O'Shaughnessy researched medical uses of the plant and published his results. In the early 1840s, he brought this knowledge (and a supply of marijuana) back with him to England. There, he oversaw the production of Squire's Extract, the first of many cannabis preparations sold as remedies in Britain and the United States. In 1851, marijuana made its first appearance in the U.S. Pharmacopeia, listed as "Extractum Cannabis. Extract of Hemp."[27]

Medical marijuana use in the United States crested in the late nineteenth century. In 1885, the Dispensatory of the United States (an unofficial companion to the U.S. Pharmacopoeia) noted that extract of hemp was known "to cause sleep, to allay spasm, to compose nervous disquietude, and to relieve pain," and was also prescribed for "neuralgia, gout, rheumatism, tetanus, hydrophobia, epidemic cholera, convulsions, chorea, hysteria, mental depression, delirium tremens, insanity, and uterine hemorrhage." By 1900, medical journals had published more than one hundred articles regarding the drug's efficacy. Although marijuana was never a mainstay of American medicine, more than one in a thousand prescriptions in the early 1900s were for cannabis extracts or tinctures, many of which were manufactured by leading pharmaceutical manufacturers such as Eli Lilly and Squibb. Numerous other companies sold over-the-counter patent drugs containing cannabis, often without listing it as an ingredient. One French business even sold cannabis-based "Indian Cigarettes" in the United States as a treatment for asthma.[28]

The medical use of marijuana plummeted during the first few decades of the twentieth century; by 1933, prescriptions of cannabis preparations had plunged by about 97 percent from their peak. In 1937 congressional hearings, witnesses described medical use of cannabis as "rare" and "disappearing." Probably the most important factor in marijuana's vanishing role in American medicine was the development of superior alternatives to it for many conditions. New synthetic drugs were equally or more effective, highly standardized (thus providing more consistent results), and injectable (thus quicker acting).[29]

Lawmakers also played a role in pushing medical cannabis into oblivion, however, due mainly to their loathing of the drug's recreational use. This attitude was rooted largely in racism; in the early 1900s, most Americans who used marijuana as an intoxicant were either Mexican Americans clustered in the Southwest or African Americans in the urban jazz scene. Congress took an initial baby step into marijuana regulation in 1906, with the passage of the Pure Food and Drug Act. That statute sensibly mandated that labels declare the amount of cannabis present in any drug containing the substance (along with the amount of alcohol, morphine, opium, cocaine, and heroin). The federal Harrison Narcotics Tax Act of 1914, enacted to reduce abuse of opiates and coca-derived drugs, did not mention cannabis, due partly to pressure from drug companies. But shortly after its passage, states began to include prohibitions on the sale of marijuana in their own anti-narcotics statutes. Although these bans were initially concentrated in Western states (where legislators were motivated largely by anti-Mexican prejudice), twenty-two states around the country had passed such laws by 1931.[30]

In 1934, the National Conference of Commissioners on Uniform State Laws promulgated a Uniform Narcotic Drug Act for voluntary adoption by the states. This statute prohibited the sale, distribution, and possession of narcotics, subject to narrow exceptions. The Uniform Act included the option of regulating cannabis like other narcotics. Harry Anslinger, the first commissioner of the Federal Bureau of Narcotics in the Treasury Department, conducted an aggressive campaign to persuade states to embrace the law and include cannabis. His explicitly racist crusade—bolstered by the Hearst newspaper chain—demonized marijuana as a promoter of violence, crime, sexual depravity, and insanity, particularly in minority communities. By 1937, thirty-five states had enacted the Uniform Act with its optional marijuana provisions, and every other state had passed alternative anti-cannabis legislation. This early wave of anti-marijuana laws culminated with the 1937 passage of the federal Marihuana Tax Act. This statute, modeled on the Harrison Act, was another product of Anslinger's anti-drug zealotry. It sought to tax and regulate marijuana out of existence.[31]

None of the anti-marijuana statutes discussed in this section—the early state laws, the Uniform Narcotic Drug Act, and the Marihuana Tax Act—prohibited the medical use of cannabis. Nonetheless, these laws effectively discouraged doctors from prescribing the drug. Not only did they have a stigmatizing effect on cannabis, but they also imposed administrative burdens and taxes on all the actors along marijuana's chain of distribution. The AMA's Legislative Counsel testified against the Marihuana Tax Act, decrying the taxes and additional paperwork it imposed on physicians. He also warned that taxes on growers might eliminate marijuana production—an unacceptable result, because "future investigation may show that there are substantial medical uses for cannabis." Another witness, representing a pharmacists' association, declared that should the law pass, he would destroy all the cannabis drugs he had in stock "so I will not have to register and will not have to pay that extra tax." When the Marihuana Tax Act took effect, many pharmacists presumably did exactly this.[32]

In short, due to both pharmaceutical advances and legal developments, by the start of World War II, American physicians almost never prescribed or recommended marijuana to patients. In 1942, the *U.S. Pharmacopoeia* omitted cannabis after almost a century of listing the drug.[33]

Even as marijuana became increasingly popular as an intoxicant in the 1950s and 1960s (with the beatniks and hippies leading the way), its use as medicine remained rare. President Richard Nixon, first elected in 1968, identified the recreational use of pot with crime and the leftist counterculture. He waged a fierce multipronged "War on Drugs." One of the first shots in that war was the 1970 passage of the federal Controlled Substances Act (CSA). This statute—still in effect today—created a tiered system in which drugs of abuse were put into one of five differently regulated "schedules," depending on various factors. The CSA placed cannabis into Schedule I, the most stringently regulated category, reserved for drugs with a "high potential for abuse," "a lack of accepted safety for use under medical supervision," and "no currently accepted medical use."[34] Schedule I drugs were available only for research purposes, and even scientific investigators had to jump through numerous bureaucratic hoops to obtain them. Heroin and LSD were among other drugs in this category. Cocaine was in Schedule II.

Congress's classification of marijuana as a Schedule I drug in 1970 provoked a reaction that gave birth to the modern medical marijuana movement. The first phase of this movement would take place primarily in courtrooms and federal administrative agencies and would forge an alliance between medical marijuana proponents and advocates of comprehensive legalization.

Reform within the Federal System (1972–1995)

The Reemergence of Medical Marijuana

Just as the CSA went into effect, modern scientific research emerged supporting cannabis's therapeutic potential. Studies published in 1971 suggested that the drug was an appetite stimulant and anticonvulsant and that it might be effective in the treatment of glaucoma, the leading cause of blindness. The next year, the CSA-mandated National Commission on Marihuana and Drug Abuse, known as the "Shafer Commission," issued a report titled *Marijuana: A Signal of Misunderstanding*. This report garnered headlines because of its proposal to decriminalize the personal possession and use of pot. Less noticed was an addendum recommending that the federal government support studies examining the efficacy of marijuana in the treatment of various diseases, including glaucoma, migraine, alcoholism, and cancer.[35]

Two months after the release of this report, NORML and two other organizations commenced a formal challenge to marijuana's Schedule I status. R. Keith Stroup, a young lawyer, had founded NORML in 1970 with the mission of fighting for decriminalization and eventual full legalization. In May 1972, it petitioned the agency known today as the Drug Enforcement Agency (DEA) either to remove marijuana from the ambit of the CSA altogether or to reschedule it into a less regulated category. This petition, which challenged Congress's conclusion that cannabis had "no currently accepted medical use," marked the start of a tortuous journey back and forth between the agency and the courts—an odyssey that did not finally end until the US Court of Appeals for the DC Circuit upheld the DEA's denial of the petition more than twenty years later.[36]

The Trial of Robert Randall

In late 1973, a friend gave Robert Randall a joint. Randall was a twenty-five-year-old aspiring political speechwriter living in the Virginia suburbs of Washington, DC. He suffered from a severe case of glaucoma, a disease that destroys vision by increasing pressure within the eyeball. Randall had already lost much of his sight. But that evening after smoking, the haloes he normally saw around streetlights were absent. Stoned and delighted, Randall immediately hypothesized a link between marijuana use and lowered intraocular eye pressure.

Randall began successfully medicating himself with weed. He obtained the drug on the black market for a couple of years, but the street became an unreliable source with the intensification of Nixon's War on Drugs. Randall thus decided to grow his own pot on the deck of his new home on Capitol Hill. In the summer of 1975, DC police officers spotted and seized Randall's modest cannabis crop and arrested him and his partner, Alice O'Leary.

The couple were charged with criminal possession. Randall, impelled by righteous anger, decided to fight the charge on the theory that illegal drug laws should not apply to people using marijuana for medical reasons. He turned to NORML for help in preparing his case. Keith Stroup gave him a folder of information that the organization had gathered in connection with its rescheduling petition. Stroup also provided Randall with funds for his defense from an arm of NORML called (tellingly) the Center for the Study of *Non*-Medical Drug Use.[37]

Randall's bid for acquittal depended on his successful deployment of the "necessity defense," an oft-discussed, rarely invoked, and almost never applied doctrine in criminal law. Stated broadly, it provides that a crime may be excused if the defendant committed the criminal act in an emergency situation to prevent a greater harm from occurring. Generations of law students have learned this doctrine through the celebrated English case *Regina v. Dudley and Stephens*, in which castaways from a yacht, facing starvation in a lifeboat, killed and ate the cabin boy. As some students forget, this case held that necessity was *not* a defense to murder. It rarely worked in other contexts, either. Defendants typically had trouble satisfying all of the necessity defense's multiple requirements. Particularly problematic for Randall were those cases in which courts had rejected the defense in the context of medical alcohol. These decisions found either that the harms alcoholic beverages caused to society outweighed their benefits to patients or that less offensive alternatives were available.[38]

Randall's trial for marijuana possession took place in July 1976 before DC Superior Court Judge James Washington, formerly the dean of Howard University Law School. While awaiting the verdict, Randall sought to persuade the relevant federal agencies to authorize his marijuana use and provide him with a stable and legal supply of the drug. These agencies included the FDA, which cleared investigational uses of unapproved drugs; the DEA, which controlled access to Schedule I drugs used for research; and the National Institute for Drug Abuse (NIDA), which contracted with the University of Mississippi to grow research-grade marijuana. With NORML's assistance, Randall broke the bureaucratic logjam with a canny media campaign. In November 1976, ophthalmologist John Merritt of Howard University Hospital provided him with forty-five NIDA-supplied marijuana cigarettes pursuant to an FDA-approved Investigational New Drug (IND) application.[39]

In December, Judge Washington issued a daring decision acquitting Randall on the basis of "medical necessity." He found that Randall had no acceptable alternative to smoking marijuana, explaining that "treatment with other drugs has become ineffective, and surgery offers only a slim possibility of favorable results coupled with a significant risk of immediate blindness." The judge also confidently ruled that the harm (blindness) avoided by Randall's personal growth and use of marijuana outweighed the "slight, speculative, and undemonstrable harm" caused by it.

Intriguingly, Washington put a thumb on Randall's side of the scale by citing *Roe v. Wade*, then three years old. He invoked *Roe*'s emphasis on "the fundamental nature of the right of an individual to preserve and control her body." Although he did not go so far as to hold that *Roe* gave Randall a constitutional right to use marijuana, the judge explained that the case was relevant to the application of the necessity defense because of its "revelation of how far-reaching is the right of an individual to preserve his health and bodily integrity."[40]

After this decision, Randall became, in his own words, "America's only legal pot smoker." When Dr. Merritt moved away from Washington in early 1978, Randall filed a lawsuit to compel the federal government to continue supplying marijuana to him under the auspices of a new IND with a different physician-investigator. The government not only settled the case in Randall's favor, but also established a new "Compassionate IND" process that other patients seeking medical marijuana could also use.[41]

ACT's Reform Efforts

In 1980, Randall and O'Leary formed the Alliance for Cannabis Therapeutics (ACT), a nonprofit corporation whose mission was "to promote the public interest in and work to ensure the adequacy of cannabis supplies for legitimate medical, therapeutic, scientific, and research purposes." One of ACT's primary activities was helping other patients negotiate the new Compassionate IND procedure. In 1980, with ACT's assistance, Anne Guttentag (who smoked cannabis to combat nausea caused by chemotherapy for ovarian cancer) became the second American to obtain marijuana from the government through this process. The small community of legal pot smokers grew slowly throughout the decade, as the FDA issued Compassionate INDs for individuals with various conditions. After the FDA approved seven Compassionate INDs in a single day in December 1990, about fifteen people were in the program. In February 1991, Randall launched the Marijuana/AIDS Research Service (MARS), which bundled and partly completed the Compassionate IND forms for people with AIDS to ease their administrative burden.[42]

Randall and O'Leary also fought to get marijuana rescheduled under the Controlled Substances Act. In the early 1980s, Randall co-drafted and lobbied for federal legislation that would reclassify marijuana as Schedule II and create a reliable supply system for patients with "life-threatening and sense-threatening" diseases. Four Republicans introduced this bill—including a young arch-conservative representative from Georgia (and future Speaker of the House) named Newt Gingrich. The bill eventually acquired more than seventy cosponsors from both parties, ranging from ultra-liberal Barney Frank of Massachusetts to religious right-winger William Dannemeyer of California. The odd politics of pot ultimately sank the legislation, however. In early 1983, with the Reagan administration ramping up its anti-drug rhetoric, Gingrich withdrew his sponsorship. He explained to Randall, "The factual case [for medical marijuana] is sustainable, but the cultural case is not." Then California's Henry Waxman—the Democratic consumer protection advocate who chaired the relevant House subcommittee—killed the legislation by refusing to schedule hearings, despite Randall's entreaties. Although the measure was introduced twice more in Congress, it never came to a vote.[43]

Meanwhile, NORML's 1972 rescheduling petition continued its odyssey through the federal bureaucracy. Under the CSA, the DEA administrator is required, before commencing rulemaking procedures to reschedule or de-schedule a controlled substance, to obtain a scientific and medical evaluation and recommendation from the secretary of HHS. In practice, the FDA (a subagency of HHS) carries out this evaluation, and its recommendations are binding on the DEA with respect to scientific and medical matters. In 1983, in accordance with this procedure, the FDA recommended that the DEA retain marijuana's Schedule I classification, concluding that it had no "currently accepted medical use."[44]

The scientific record supporting efficacy was indeed thin, in large part because the DEA, FDA, and NIDA all placed significant regulatory hurdles in front of scientists interested in studying the medical effects of cannabis. Moreover, it was difficult to attract funding for marijuana research because the naturally occurring plant was ineligible for patent protection. Nonetheless, by the early 1980s, a few tenacious scientists had managed to conduct studies on marijuana's potential therapeutic effects. A 1982 Institute of Medicine (IOM) report examined the completed research and concluded that marijuana "might be useful" in the treatment of some conditions, but that "much more work [was] needed." The report further opined that in light of whole marijuana's psychotropic and cardiovascular side-effects, "the greatest therapeutic potential probably lies in . . . synthetic analogues of marijuana derivatives."[45]

In 1987 and 1988, an Administrative Law Judge (ALJ), Francis L. Young, finally conducted hearings regarding NORML's 1972 rescheduling petition. Randall and O'Leary's ACT—despite some reluctance about working alongside NORML—now joined the effort and, indeed, prepared the bulk of the case. In September 1988, Young garnered national headlines by recommending that the DEA reschedule marijuana. He found it "clear beyond any question" that "many" medical professionals, researchers, and patients accepted the use of pot to treat nausea and vomiting accompanying chemotherapy. He also determined that a "significant minority" of physicians embraced marijuana for treatment of spasticity resulting from multiple sclerosis (MS) and other causes. (Interestingly, Young declined to make a similar finding with respect to glaucoma.) The ALJ also opined that "marijuana, in its natural form, is one of the safest therapeutically active substances known to man" and that many physicians recognized its safety. Based on these findings, the ALJ concluded that the terms of the CSA "permit and require the transfer of marijuana from Schedule I to Schedule II."[46]

ACT also advocated for recognition of the medical necessity defense in court. In 1988, Randall helped prepare the successful necessity defense of Elvy Musikka, a glaucoma patient, already blind in one eye, whom Florida prosecuted for growing four marijuana plants in her home. Randall also worked closely with Kenneth and Barbara Jenks, a married Florida couple who contracted AIDS following Kenneth's infection by a contaminated blood transfusion. Florida prosecuted them for growing two marijuana plants for medical use behind their trailer, and they were convicted. In 1991, however, an appeals court, citing both the *Randall* and *Musikka* decisions, overturned the Jenkses' convictions based on the medical necessity defense.[47]

ACT's Accomplishments Unravel

These heady (pun intended) triumphs were only temporary, however. By the mid-1990s, ACT's multipronged medical marijuana strategy was in tatters.

The first devastating blow came at the end of 1989, when the DEA administrator rejected ALJ Young's recommendation and instead denied the NORML/ACT rescheduling petition.[48] The US Court of Appeals for the DC Circuit briefly revived marijuana proponents' hopes in 1991, when it questioned the administrator's precise reasoning and remanded the matter to the agency. But in 1992, the administrator issued a new order that almost contemptuously rejected the petitioners' evidence and kept marijuana in Schedule I. In 1994, the DC Circuit upheld this order and finally laid the twenty-two-year-old rescheduling petition to rest.[49]

For medical marijuana advocates, the most damaging aspect of the DC Circuit's decision was its approval of the DEA's new test for determining whether a drug has "currently accepted medical use." One criterion was that "there must be adequate and well-controlled studies proving efficacy." The DEA explained that the evidence required to satisfy this requirement was generally identical to that needed to obtain FDA approval—that is, two positive adequate and well-controlled Phase 3 clinical trials.[50] By this standard, the scientific record was nowhere close to supporting the rescheduling of marijuana. And because of the administrative burdens on cannabis research and the lack of financial incentives to conduct it, the needed studies might *never* be performed.

Another severe setback occurred in 1991, when the federal government announced that it would phase out the Compassionate IND program, which had been flooded with requests from AIDS patients since Randall established MARS. James Mason, the chief of the Public Health Service (PHS), explained to a journalist that the program sent a "bad signal" that undercut the Bush administration's battle against drug abuse. He urged patients to instead try

THC (marijuana's principal psychoactive cannabinoid) in capsule form. The FDA had approved a synthetic version of THC under the brand name Marinol® in 1985 for treatment of nausea and vomiting associated with cancer chemotherapy. But many patients did not find synthetic THC capsules to be as effective as smoked marijuana, which contained more than sixty additional cannabinoids. Moreover, smoked pot took effect more quickly, its dose could be calibrated more precisely, and it was the only choice for people suffering from severe vomiting.[51]

In 1992, despite ACT's resistance, the PHS officially closed the Compassionate IND program to new patients. Randall could take limited solace from the fact that he and other existing participants were grandfathered in and would continue receiving their marijuana, but nobody else in America would have a legal source for the drug. Over the next quarter of a century, the group of fourteen individuals receiving Mississippi weed from NIDA dwindled as Randall and others died.[52]

The emerging promise of the medical necessity defense also evaporated during this period. *Commonwealth v. Hutchins*, a 1991 decision by Massachusetts' highest court, was particularly influential. Joseph Hutchins, a Navy veteran, smoked marijuana to relieve the debilitating and life-threatening symptoms of scleroderma, a chronic autoimmune disease acquired during his term of service. The court refused to let him plead medical necessity, explaining that "the alleviation of the defendant's medical symptoms . . . would not clearly and significantly outweigh the potential harm to the public were we to declare that [his] cultivation of marihuana and its use for his medicinal purposes may not be punishable." Subsequently, most courts around the country refused to allow defendants charged with marijuana crimes to plead the necessity defense.[53] It became increasingly clear that the defense would be available to cannabis sellers and users only if their states established it explicitly by legislation.

Clinton's 1992 election initially gave Randall and O'Leary hope that they would be able to restore, and perhaps greatly expand, access to medical marijuana. They prepared a booklet of recommendations for Clinton in which they urged him to restore the Compassionate IND program and reschedule marijuana into Schedule II. Clinton, however, quickly revealed himself to be no less opposed to medical marijuana than his predecessor.[54]

By the mid-1990s, Robert Randall's stint as the face of America's medical marijuana movement was ending, as Dennis Peron assumed the role. Randall's buttoned-down, work-within-the-system approach was eclipsed by Peron's more provocative and disruptive tactics. Randall's dedication to federal reform gave way to Peron's almost exclusive focus on state-level activism. Randall's strict interpretation of what constituted valid medical use of marijuana (treatment of serious diseases) was replaced, among some activists, by Peron's view, which blurred the line between medical and recreational use. Under the influence of people with AIDS, medical marijuana advocacy now became a genuine social movement characterized by uninhibited, aggressive, street-level direct action. And the center of activity moved from Washington, DC, to California.

Meanwhile, the relationship between ACT and the broader marijuana legalization movement had frayed irreparably. Randall had concluded that NORML and other drug reform organizations were "exploiting" patients to advance their own broader legalization agendas. NORML, for its part, thought Randall was "putting a stiff arm on NORML at the height of [cultural] anti-druggism, to advocate for medical-only reforms." A breaking point occurred in November 1994, when Randall refused to participate in "National Medical Marijuana Day," a multi-site protest planned by NORML and its allies. Randall demurred not only because he thought the event was poorly planned and futile, but also because he did not want sick people to be used as props.[55]

Going forward, NORML would have to work with the medical marijuana movement's new standard-bearer, Dennis Peron. He would be no less complicated an ally.

Dennis Peron and Proposition 215

California's Proposition 215 was not the first state-level medical marijuana measure. By the mid-1990s, about thirty-five states had enacted a variety of pro-medical pot statutes, often by overwhelming majorities. But these state laws had almost no practical impact. They ranged from utterly useless legislative "recognitions" of marijuana's medical value to actual research programs that failed to survive the 1980s. Proposition 215 was a different sort of law—one that would immunize patients and their caregivers from state criminal prosecution for marijuana possession or cultivation.[56]

Peron's Background

Dennis Peron, a self-proclaimed "hippie faggot," got hooked on marijuana and came out of the closet while serving in Vietnam as an Air Force volunteer. After his 1969 discharge, the native New Yorker settled in San Francisco, where he founded the "Big Top," a commune-cum-marijuana supermarket, in the Castro neighborhood. During the 1970s, he advocated for marijuana legalization and participated in gay rights activism. He served a six-month sentence in the San Francisco County Jail following a drug bust during which a policeman shot him in the leg.

Peron's devotion to marijuana legalization and gay rights merged with the rise of the AIDS epidemic in the 1980s. He learned that people with AIDS smoked marijuana to combat the anorexia, nausea, wasting syndrome, and pain that accompanied the disease and its pharmaceutical treatments. Peron's first concrete action in support of medical marijuana was a special-ops-like mission that smuggled pot into a hospital AIDS ward for a dying man named Richard. This operation, Peron remembered, "started a lot of us thinking about marijuana in a different setting, far from the protest drug that you get from a hippy in a schoolyard."[57]

When Peron's longtime lover, Jonathan West, fell ill with AIDS, he used cannabis for relief. In January 1990, when West was in the very late stages of the disease, police raided Peron's house and found four ounces of marijuana. Donning rubber gloves, they forced Peron's frail partner to the floor, made cruel jokes ("AIDS means 'Asshole in Deep Shit' "), and arrested Peron for drug possession with intent to sell. Peron evaded conviction because West—weak, ashen, and 85 pounds—dragged himself to the trial and testified that the pot was his, not Peron's. The judge dismissed the charges. West's death the following week led Peron, a longtime advocate for full marijuana legalization, to start focusing his activism on medical cannabis.[58]

In 1991, Peron coauthored a San Francisco initiative endorsing the prescription use of medical marijuana and led a successful grass-roots campaign to gather enough signatures to get the measure on the ballot. The initiative, known as Proposition P, passed with 80 percent of the vote. Though legally toothless, Proposition P attracted national media attention. The city's Board of Supervisors issued a resolution urging the mayor, police commissioner, and district attorney to assign "lowest priority" to the arrest and prosecution of individuals possessing or cultivating medical marijuana for personal use. With Peron's support, other municipalities up and down the state issued their own pro-medical-marijuana statements.[59]

In 1993, Peron lobbied for California Senate Joint Resolution 8 (SJR8). This measure, co-drafted by Robert Randall, urged President Clinton and Congress to "enact appropriate legislation to permit cannabis/marijuana to be prescribed by licensed physicians and to ensure a safe and affordable supply of cannabis/marijuana for medical use."[60] SJR8 passed overwhelmingly, but the politicians in Washington took no action. Although the California legislature passed medical marijuana legalization bills the subsequent two years, Governor Pete Wilson vetoed both.

During this period, Peron worked closely with Mary Jane Rathbun, known widely as "Brownie Mary." The ex-IHOP waitress had begun selling her cannabis-laced comestibles in the 1970s on the streets of the Castro and out of Peron's "Big Top." In the 1980s, she started distributing free joints and brownies to friends and customers stricken by AIDS. The national media covered her multiple arrests on drug charges and her cantankerous yet compassionate advocacy for medical marijuana. In the early 1990s, Rathbun helped Peron promote Proposition P and SJR8, while he helped her deliver marijuana edibles and smokable "green bud" to people with AIDS in San Francisco. When the city's Board of Supervisors declared August 25, 1992, "Brownie Mary Day," more than 5,000 people rallied in her honor on the steps of City Hall.[61]

In 1993, to reach more patients, Peron opened the San Francisco Cannabis Buyers Club. He modeled the enterprise on the AIDS Drugs Buyers Club, a San Francisco organization that dispensed unapproved remedies but was not bold enough to traffic in marijuana. The CBC's audacious flouting of state and federal narcotics laws troubled some of Peron's allies, and a fissure opened up in the medical marijuana community. ACT refused to endorse the CBC and similar clubs, not only because Randall and O'Leary were "unwilling to openly encourage illegality," but also because the clubs were "too loosely structured, allowing many with questionable 'ailments' to obtain marijuana." In Randall's view, Peron was cynically exploiting sick people to disguise his true goal of running "a retail pot shop." He worried that this deceitful conduct would harm the medical marijuana movement.[62]

Within two years of its founding, the CBC—the nation's first public marijuana dispensary—had between 8,000 and 10,000 members. It rapidly outgrew its first two locations and settled into an edifice on Market Street affectionately known as the "Brownie Mary Building." At least in theory, the club required every customer to present both a photo ID and a doctor's note stating that he or she had a medical condition (not necessarily a grave one) that marijuana might alleviate. The building was also a social gathering place and the de facto headquarters for California medical marijuana advocacy. In Peron's office on the second floor, he and other activists conceived of a plan to circumvent Governor Wilson; they would present the issue of medical cannabis directly to the voters in a veto-proof ballot initiative.[63]

Selling Proposition 215

Thus was born Proposition 215, the Compassionate Use Act of 1996. A large group of activists and attorneys drafted the measure through a painstaking, eight-month process. The authors strove to make the initiative simultaneously appealing to voters, protective of patients, and immune as possible from legal challenges. The final product was in some ways a modest proposal. It required a physician's recommendation, explicitly declined to condone "the diversion of marijuana for nonmedical purposes," and elided the complicated question of who could legally cultivate and distribute medical cannabis. But at Peron's insistence, Proposition 215 also included one daringly broad provision; it legalized the use of cannabis not only for eight specified ailments, but also for "any other illness for which marijuana provides relief."[64]

Peron formed "Californians for Compassionate Use" to collect the 433,000 valid signatures necessary to get the initiative onto the November 1996 ballot. In an attempt to appeal to citizens outside the progressive Bay Area, Peron cut his shoulder-length hair and traded his tie-dyed tee shirts and beads for Oxford dress shirts and ties. The signature drive nevertheless stalled, and seemed doomed, until billionaire George Soros contributed $350,000 to the effort.[65] Rather than direct the money to CCU, however, Soros hired Bill Zimmerman, a public relations strategist, who created a separate organization called Californians for Medical Rights (CMR). CMR received large donations from several other corporate leaders, including Men's Warehouse CEO George Zimmer (known for his tagline "You'll like the way you look. I guarantee it."). The signature-gathering company retained by Zimmerman far exceeded its target. State officials certified the initiative in June 1996, and Proposition 215 was on the ballot.

In the ensuing months, Zimmerman ran a polished pro-Proposition 215 campaign. It relied largely on television advertisements featuring medical professionals and older women. Zimmerman's Madison Avenue approach departed dramatically from Peron's grass-roots ideal, and the two men often clashed behind the scenes. Peron bristled at his counterpart's philosophy of total message control, his reliance on focus groups, and his strategy of framing medical marijuana as a white, middle-class movement by excluding countercultural figures and people of color from campaign materials.[66]

Peron and Zimmerman also tussled over how to formulate the "Argument in Favor of Proposition 215" that would be included in the official "Ballot Pamphlet" mailed to all voters. They submitted competing versions to the Republican secretary of state, who unsurprisingly selected the PR man's more conservative language. Peron was particularly upset about a passage explaining that under Proposition 215, police officers would still be allowed to arrest people for marijuana possession, because the measure merely provided an affirmative defense to use in court.[67]

The "Argument in Favor" reflected the fact that scientific evidence for the medical effectiveness of smoked cannabis remained preliminary, at best. Although a growing body of research suggested that, in isolation, the cannabinoids THC and CBD (cannabidiol) might be useful in a treating a range of conditions, the number of human efficacy studies on smoked whole marijuana remained tiny. Moreover, none of the completed studies came anywhere near the size, rigor, and design of the Phase 3 trials that the FDA ordinarily requires for drug approval. The "Argument in Favor" thus relied largely on the testimonials and endorsements of medical professionals who had "witnessed firsthand the medical benefits of marijuana" and on the argument that "doctors and patients should decide what medicines are best."[68]

For uncertain reasons, the rhetoric used by Peron's forces diverged strikingly from that used by Zimmerman's team. This difference is reflected in the names of their respective organizations: Californians for Compassionate Use (CCU) versus Californians for Medical Rights (CMR). Peron and his associates generally emphasized tropes of "compassion" and "common sense." For example, in an op-ed, Peron called Proposition 215 a "mission of mercy" that would "herald a turn toward a more loving and compassionate society." A CCU pamphlet explained that the organization's "sole purpose is to relieve suffering." By contrast, the CMR's principal stated mission was to "protect the rights of patients and doctors." In one brochure, a state legislator proclaimed: "It's your life, it's your freedom." Conservative libertarians who supported Proposition 215 were comfortable with such language. For example, David Boaz of the libertarian Cato Institute praised Proposition 215's "less government, more freedom" message.[69]

Despite their differences, CCU and CMR agreed that to win the election, they must clearly dissociate Proposition 215 from the cause of comprehensive legalization. Although every poll showed Californians overwhelmingly in favor of medical marijuana, fewer than one quarter wanted to legalize recreational use. In recognition of this fact, the law enforcement officials leading the opposition to the initiative characterized it as a "cruel hoax" that "exploit[ed] public compassion for the sick in order to legalize and legitimize the widespread use of marijuana in California." In turn, the CMR-drafted "Argument in Favor" of the initiative emphasized, "MARIJUANA WILL STILL BE ILLEGAL FOR NON-MEDICAL USE." Peron was similarly striving to resist any linkage between Proposition 215 and recreational use when on Election Day, he frantically urged revelers to refrain from toking until the polls closed.[70]

The tactical imperative to separate medical legalization from recreational legalization created an awkward situation for organizations like NORML that advocated both. They were authentically committed to providing succor to sick individuals, but they were also worried, in Keith Stroup's words, that "the emerging medical use debate might make it more difficult for us to focus public attention on the issue we preferred they consider; i.e., whether to decriminalize or legalize marijuana for everyone, recreational users as well as medical users." Nonetheless, throughout the Proposition 215 campaign, supporters of full legalization were disciplined and devoted warriors for medical-only cannabis. Shortly before the November 1996 election, Kevin Zeese of Common Sense for Drug Policy warned fellow members of the full legalization movement that they should respond with "extreme restraint" to the initiative's likely victory, so as not to jeopardize progress on medical marijuana in other states. He cautioned them

that even if they saw Proposition 215 as a step toward comprehensive legalization, "it is a mistake to say so publicly."[71]

This posture explains why the comprehensive legalization community was
so exasperated with Peron's antics after Proposition 215 won. For months, they
had shelved their primary ambition to focus on the medical marijuana cause.
Now, Peron—with his celebratory joint and his "all marijuana use is medical"
assertion—was insinuating that he shared their goal of full legalization, though
he cloaked this objective in the language of medical policy. As Allen St. Pierre of
NORML later recalled:

Dennis and his minions became obsessed with two propagandistic notions.
Only refer to marijuana as "medicine" [and] *Declare ALL cannabis use medicinal.* The above two strategies were found to be so vexing at places like NORML,
that clear divisions opened up[:] intellectually honest vs. dishonest . . . trans-
parent vs. non-transparent.[72]

Implementing Proposition 215

Although Proposition 215 "encouraged" state officials to "implement a plan to
provide for the safe and affordable distribution of marijuana" to patients, it left
the details to local lawmakers. The result was a hodgepodge of policies. Some
counties—with Attorney General Lungren's backing—proceeded as though the
new law did not exist. In these jurisdictions, law enforcement continued to ap-
prehend medical cannabis users, who highly regretted Zimmerman's concession
that the initiative provided only an affirmative defense at trial, rather than a complete shield from arrest. Meanwhile, authorities in other areas (particularly liberal bastions like the San Francisco Bay Area) left medical marijuana users alone.

More permissive counties also allowed medical marijuana dispensaries
to emerge and flourish, based on the legal fiction that these entities were their
customers' "primary caregivers" and thus protected by Proposition 215. One
group of dispensaries cooperated with local law enforcement, banned on-site
smoking, rigorously verified prescriptions, sold only to patients suffering from
an enumerated list of serious illnesses, and generally conducted themselves
like medical clinics. The most prominent dispensary of this type was the Los
Angeles Cannabis Resource Center (LACRC), founded in West Hollywood by
a gay Methodist minister named Scott Imler. Peron's newly named "Cannabis
Cultivators' Club" (CCC), which opened on San Francisco's Market Street
in January 1997, was extremely different. The CCC, like its predecessor, was a
thriving social hub with abundant on-site toking. In a state lawsuit, Lungren accused it of "an indiscriminate and uncontrolled pattern of sale" to people without

doctors' recommendations, including undercover officers. Peron adamantly denied this charge. But he openly acknowledged implementing his "all marijuana use is medical" philosophy by selling to *everyone* with a physician's recommendation (including older minors), regardless of the severity of their illness.[73]

Imler and Peron—once close allies on the Proposition 215 campaign—became symbols of bitterly competing camps in the blossoming medical marijuana industry. The taxpaying, rule-following medical entrepreneurs on one side fought to distance themselves from the antigovernment, anticorporatist, countercultural ethos embraced by the other. Imler accused Peron of running a "clown show." Peron called his rival "Benedict" Imler. One observer described the Imler-Peron split as "legendary" within the medical marijuana community. After a California appeals court upheld a state injunction shutting down the CCC's operations, Imler ungenerously observed that Peron had served himself up to Lungren "on a silver platter." Peron's club—under legal attack from federal as well as state authorities—closed permanently on May 25, 1998.[74]

When Peron lost a whimsical challenge to Lungren for the Republican gubernatorial nomination in 1998, his reign as leader of the medical marijuana movement ended. Lungren also departed the scene around this time, after losing the general election in a landslide to Democrat Gray Davis. For the next decade, California basically continued Lungren's approach of allowing each county to forge its own path with respect to medical cannabis. Some counties issued medical marijuana identification cards and countenanced sales by retail outlets, while others aggressively arrested patients and caregivers. Although a state law enacted in 2003 was intended to create a more uniform statewide policy, local sovereignty continued to create a variegated jigsaw puzzle of regulations and enforcement priorities. Depending on the county, dispensaries ranged from shabby beachfront retailers to high-caliber professionalized providers. Medical cannabis became such an indelible feature of California's commerce and culture that whether you were a seriously ill person patronizing Imler's dispensary in West Hollywood or a stoner with an easily obtained Patient ID Card scoring weed on Venice Beach, it was easy to forget that every seller and purchaser of pot was still violating federal law.[75]

State-Federal Divergence (1996–Present)

Other States Follow California

California's enactment of Proposition 215 in 1996 (along with Arizona's passage the same day of an even broader measure later declared void due to a technicality) was a seminal moment in the evolution of American medical marijuana regulation. The day after the election, Bill Zimmerman changed the name of his organization to "*Americans* for Medical Rights" and vowed to press the issue throughout the nation.[76] Two years later, the people of Alaska, Nevada, Oregon, Washington, and Arizona (again) legalized medical marijuana, although the schemes they created were generally more restrictive than California's.

When urging further expansion of legalization, medical marijuana advocates made liberal use of quasi-constitutional rhetoric. Terminal patient Terry Stephenson, from Illinois, demanded his "constitutional and God given right to use cannabis for medical purposes." Larry Nickerson of Texas invoked the "inalienable rights" of "Life, Liberty, and the Pursuit of Happiness" enumerated in the Declaration of Independence and asserted that the government's prohibition of medical marijuana constituted denial of "that most basic right: life itself."[77]

Since the passage of Proposition of 215, thirty-six states and the District of Columbia have passed medical marijuana legalization laws, some by initiative, some by legislation, and one (Florida) by constitutional amendment. Almost every measure that has come to a vote has passed. This national wave of legalization has occurred simultaneously with a surge in public support for the policy. When California passed Proposition 215, between 60 percent and 70 percent of the country already supported giving physicians the right to prescribe marijuana. According to a recent poll, 91 percent of Americans now believe marijuana should be legal for medical use.[78]

Despite the spread of state-level medical marijuana legalization, medical cannabis users have never felt completely safe from prosecution anywhere in the United States. Pot remains illegal under the CSA, regardless of the reason for its use. Even the most protective state laws provide no protection from a knock on the door by federal DEA agents.

Clinton and Bush: Federal Recalcitrance

The Clinton administration did not modify its fierce anti-medical marijuana stance following the 1996 passage of Proposition 215. Clinton's drug czar, Barry McCaffrey, swiftly issued a formal response to the enactment in which he emphasized that the United States would continue to treat cannabis as both an illegal Schedule I controlled substance and an unapproved drug prohibited by the FD&C Act. In 1998, the federal government obtained preliminary injunctions shuttering six northern California cannabis clubs, including Peron's, for violations of the CSA. Although Peron abandoned the dispensary business, the other defendants, led by the Oakland Cannabis Buyers' Cooperative, would fight the injunctions all the way to the Supreme Court.[79]

Upon taking office in 2001, George W. Bush made marijuana a major law enforcement priority. His administration continued its zealous pursuit of medical
cannabis-related cases even after the devastating attacks of September 11, 2001.
For example, in October 2001, the DEA raided Scott Imler's West Hollywood
dispensary, despite his assiduous efforts to comply with every jot and tittle of
Proposition 215. The following year, the federal government arrested and prosecuted Ed Rosenthal, a California medical pot activist, horticulturist, and *High
Times* magazine columnist who grew cannabis for distribution to medical
marijuana dispensaries pursuant to an agreement with the City of Oakland.
Rosenthal's January 2003 conviction infuriated patients and activists—and five
of the jurors themselves, who learned only after the trial about the defendant's
arrangement with Oakland.[80]

As has almost always been the case with respect to American movements for
freedom of therapeutic choice, the courts provided little help to medical marijuana legalization advocates during this period. The California cannabis clubs
closed by the Clinton administration sought to persuade the federal courts that
an implied defense of medical necessity should be read into the CSA's prohibition on manufacturing and distributing marijuana. The Supreme Court rejected
this argument in 2001, in *United States v. Oakland Cannabis Buyers' Cooperative*.
The following year, Angel McClary Raich and Diane Monson, both of whom
used medical cannabis in compliance with California's Proposition 215, filed a
federal constitutional claim seeking to enjoin Bush's DEA from enforcing the
CSA against them. Monson cultivated her own pot within the state, while Raich
used state-grown pot her caregivers provided to her at no cost. The plaintiffs
contended that the CSA could not apply to such noncommercial, intrastate activity without exceeding Congress's power to regulate interstate commerce pursuant to the US Constitution's commerce clause. In 2005, the US Supreme Court
ruled against them, too. *Gonzales v. Raich* held that Congress had a rational basis
for concluding that the plaintiffs' local activities affected interstate commerce
sufficiently to fall within the commerce power.[81]

Raich and Monson also contended that the CSA violated their rights under
the due process clause of the Fifth Amendment. The Ninth Circuit addressed this
issue on remand in 2007. Angel Raich (now proceeding without Monson) alleged
that she had a fundamental, substantive due process right to "mak[e] life-shaping
medical decisions that are necessary to preserve the integrity of her body, avoid
intolerable physical pain, and preserve her life." But the moment in the late 1970s
when it seemed that courts might expand the *Roe v. Wade* holding into a full-
blown right to medical choice had long passed. Because of the test established
by *Glucksberg* (the 2005 assisted suicide decision discussed in the Introduction),
Raich was forced to contend that medical marijuana use was "deeply rooted in
[the country's] history and tradition." The Ninth Circuit predictably rejected

this assertion. But Raich also advanced a more promising substantive due process argument based on *Lawrence v. Texas*, the Supreme Court's 2003 decision declaring anti-sodomy laws unconstitutional. *Lawrence* had ignored *Glucksberg* and instead applied a test asking whether there was an "emerging awareness" that the right in question was fundamental. To demonstrate that such an awareness was, indeed, "emerging" for medical marijuana, Raich pointed to the eleven states that had passed laws legalizing it by 2007. The Ninth Circuit acknowledged that the legalization of medical cannabis was "gaining traction," but it concluded that it had "not yet reached the point where . . . the right to use medical marijuana is 'fundamental.'" The court's reasoning raised the tantalizing possibility that as more and more states legalized medical cannabis, a cognizable fundamental right might emerge. To date, however, nobody has tested this possibility.[82]

Obama and Trump: Mixed Signals

In 2008, medical marijuana proponents had cause for optimism when Democrat Barack Obama, an admitted inhaler, was elected president. Medical marijuana advocates were further buoyed on October 19, 2009, when Deputy Attorney General David Ogden circulated a memorandum to US Attorneys serving in states that had authorized medical cannabis use. The "Ogden Memo" instructed these prosecutors to prioritize the pursuit of significant marijuana traffickers rather than "individuals whose actions are in clear and unambiguous compliance with existing state laws providing for the medical use of marijuana." But one week later, Deputy Attorney General James M. Cole issued a clarifying memorandum emphasizing that the enforcement discretion set forth in the Ogden Memo applied only to patients and caregivers, not to businesses. Federal agents subsequently raided two dispensaries in central California and a medical cannabis farm in eastern Washington.[83]

During Obama's second term, the federal government once again sent out inconsistent messages regarding medical marijuana. In August 2013, Cole released yet another memo, reasserting the Department of Justice's intention generally to defer to state laws legalizing the possession and sale of marijuana for medical use—or even recreational use—except when certain federal law enforcement priorities (such as preventing distribution to minors) were threatened. Then, after years of rejecting similar measures, Congress in 2014 passed the Rohrabacher-Farr Amendment. This provision, which has been renewed repeatedly since, prohibits the DOJ from using funds to prevent states from implementing their medical marijuana regimes. Obama's DOJ interpreted Rohrabacher-Farr narrowly, however. Until the courts intervened, it continued to prosecute defendants on marijuana charges even though they were likely in compliance with state law.[84]

Obama's successor, Donald Trump, took medical marijuana proponents on a roller coaster ride. He claimed as a candidate to be "100 percent" in favor of medical marijuana, and his administration did not conduct raids against medical marijuana patients or providers in states where it is legal. In January 2018, however, Trump's first attorney general, Jeff Sessions, threw the medical marijuana industry into a temporary panic when he issued a memorandum rescinding the Ogden and Cole memos. This move had little practical effect because of Congress's regular reauthorization the Rohrabacher-Farr (now the Rohrabacher-Blumenauer) Amendment. Nonetheless, Trump twice signaled in signing statements that he reserved the right to ignore this provision. Sessions's successor, William Barr, pledged to honor the Cole Memorandum—but not to formally reissue it. In December 2018, Trump signed a farm bill that entirely descheduled "hemp," defined as cannabis or any of its derivatives containing less than 0.3 percent THC (the main psychoactive cannabinoid in marijuana). But cannabis containing greater amounts of THC—as does almost all the crop used as medical marijuana—remains an illegal Schedule I drug.[85]

Notably, in defining "hemp," the 2018 farm bill did not limit the amount of cannabidiol (CBD)—a less psychoactive cannabinoid thought by many to be helpful for a wide range of health conditions. Soon, American store shelves were replete with CBD tinctures, edibles, vape pens, and creams. Most of these remain illegal under the FD&C Act. (Perhaps the only indisputably legal CBD product is Epidiolex®, a prescription drug the FDA approved in 2018 for treatment of certain seizure disorders.) Nonetheless, the FDA—under enormous public pressure—has exercised its enforcement discretion to permit countless CBD products to remain on the market.[86]

CBD products lack not only THC, but also more than a hundred other cannabinoids naturally present in whole leaf marijuana. It is thus difficult to see the rise of CBD as a triumph for the medical marijuana movement. After all, Richard Randall and Dennis Peron were struggling for the legalization of smokable and edible "green bud," not isolated constituents extracted in a laboratory.

The Failure to Reschedule

Marijuana's continued classification as an illegal Schedule I drug is not due to a lack of effort by medical marijuana advocates. Since the DEA rejected the NORML/ACT rescheduling petition in 1989, the government has denied at least four other petitions submitted by various groups and individuals.[87]

What explains the federal government's failure to budge on the rescheduling of marijuana, under both Democratic and Republican presidents, even as states have moved in the other direction? Rightly or wrongly, the federal bureaucracy has approached the issue as a purely scientific one and has followed the cogent recommendations of a scientific agency—the FDA. The CSA requires any drug of abuse with "no currently accepted medical use" to be placed in Schedule I. The DEA and FDA interpret this phrase as embracing the same standards that the FDA uses to assess safety and efficacy in its drug approval decisions. The FDA has not ignored the available research but rather has accurately concluded that the completed studies are not of the size and quality that would support NDA approval. In 2015, in connection with the most recently denied rescheduling petitions, the FDA performed a rigorous review of all clinical research on inhaled marijuana for therapeutic purposes. The agency identified eleven completed Phase 2 controlled investigations for various indications. While acknowledging that such research had "progressed" since the agency's previous literature review in 2006, and that the new studies showed "positive signals," the FDA reasonably concluded that they provided only preliminary evidence of effectiveness because of their small size and the inconsistency of doses delivered, among other issues.[88]

The government's strict interpretation of "currently accepted medical use" is open to criticism. After all, many unapproved uses of drugs are widely "accepted" by the medical community even though they have never been systematically investigated. Indeed, the DEA generally does not sanction physicians for prescribing legal controlled substances off-label for "legitimate medical purposes."[89] Perhaps in determining whether a substance is Schedule I, the DEA should construe the phrase "currently accepted medical use" to include any indication for which the drug is commonly prescribed or recommended, regardless of the state of the science.

Federal regulators should also keep in mind a core strand of medical freedom ideology throughout American history—freedom of inquiry. Medical cannabis advocates have long decried the Catch-22 they are trapped in; the government refuses to reschedule marijuana without further research while simultaneously making such research onerous or impossible. A 2015 Brookings report, *Ending the U.S. Government's War on Medical Marijuana Research*, confirmed this "circular policy trap," ascribed it to "statutory, regulatory, bureaucratic, and cultural barriers," and blamed it for the absence of "research freedom" in this area. The report recommended rescheduling cannabis under the CSA, ending the NIDA monopoly on legal production of marijuana for research, and reopening the FDA's long-dormant compassionate use IND program.[90]

However, if it is valid to ask whether federal law and policy are too tough on medical marijuana, it is also valid to ask whether some states are too *lenient*. Since 1996, state after state has legalized medical cannabis with far less proof of safety and efficacy than Americans generally demand for medical products. Why should pot be subject to lower scientific standards than other drugs? Those who embrace this position seem to rely largely on the argument that the government should not interfere with cannabis use because it is a "natural" product. As medical marijuana user Terry Stephenson declared, "Cannabis has a lot of therapeutic effects and is less harmful to the body than manufactured drugs by a pharmaceutical company. It is bound to be; it is organic and put on earth by God and Nature."[91] But of course the mere fact that a drug is "natural" does not mean that it is free of risks, nor that its benefits outweigh these risks.

Medical Marijuana and the Rise of Legal Recreational Pot

In November 2010, California nearly became the first state to legalize marijuana for nonmedical uses. By a margin of only seven percentage points, voters rejected Proposition 19, an initiative that would have allowed local governments to authorize the retail sale of marijuana for recreational use and to regulate and tax these transactions. A surprising group joined law enforcement and anti-drug organizations in opposing the initiative: some (though hardly all) medical cannabis patients, sellers, growers, and advocates. They dominated a web-based advocacy group, "Stoners against Proposition 19," which contended that the measure would harm patients. One vociferous member of this informal organization was none other than Dennis Peron. He asserted that legalization of "recreational" marijuana simply made no sense because all cannabis use is medical.[92]

Proposition 19 advocates were apoplectic over this opposition from within the marijuana movement. NORML's blog charged medical dispensary owners who opposed the initiative with having an "I gots mine" attitude. The website "Loopy Lettuce" accused Peron of trying to suppress new competition for his "pot friendly" bed and breakfast in San Francisco. These intra-movement tensions exploded at the International Cannabis and Hemp Expo held in San Francisco in September 2010. The previous Expo had been a mellow celebration of public toking. This one devolved into near chaos. After the election, legalization proponents blamed the initiative's defeat on a "greedy, reactionary . . . fifth column within the medical cannabis community."[93]

Two years later, on November 6, 2012, the citizens of both Colorado and Washington State, by comfortable margins, voted in favor of measures that legalized the possession and use of small amounts of marijuana for recreational purposes purchased from state-licensed dispensaries while also taxing such sales and imposing various restrictions. Many medical marijuana advocates fervently and noisily resisted these initiatives. In Washington, they denounced that state's I-502 as a pathetic, less-than-halfway legalization measure that would expose patients to DWI charges and prohibit personal cultivation. As the Washington legislature debated how to structure the state's new non-medical cannabis distribution system, Americans for Safe Access (ASA), the nation's leading medical marijuana advocacy organization, coordinated a campaign called "Health before Happy Hour." The campaign's goal was to inform politicians that "the needs of patients are much different from those of recreational marijuana users, and they will not be easily brushed aside."[94]

Since 2012, fifteen more states and the District of Columbia have legalized recreational marijuana—in each case despite resistance from some in the medical marijuana community. One of these states is California, which in 2016 easily passed Proposition 64 (the "Adult Use of Marijuana Act"), despite opposition from medical cannabis proponents, including Dennis Peron, by then a cannabis farmer in rural Humboldt County.[95]

As we have seen, tensions have existed between proponents of medical legalization and recreational legalization (I will call them Medicals and Recreationals) for at least a quarter of a century. But the recent comprehensive legalization measures have elevated the acrimony to new levels. Some Medicals actively oppose full legalization and many others take a posture of calculated passivity. ASA's official policy, for example, is not to take a position on the legalization of recreational use, while warning policymakers "against letting the debate surrounding legalization of cannabis for recreational use obscure the science and policy regarding the medical use of cannabis." This lack of support infuriates Recreationals. In the opinion of NORML's ex–executive director Allen St. Pierre, ASA's stance is based not on principle, but on the goal of protecting the material interests of its dispensary-owner members, whose business model is threatened by the rise of recreational pot retailers.[96]

To Recreationals, the Medicals' position is not only selfish and ungrateful, but also positively harmful. Many embrace the "Box Canyon" theory, which, as explained by cannabis blogger and podcaster Russ Belville, "means that if you fight only for medical marijuana, your marijuana will become only medical." Inevitably, Belville explains, "tighter and stricter forms of medical marijuana laws are passed to appease the powers that wish marijuana prohibition to continue." Recreationals thus fear that "medical only" advocacy will inadvertently bring about a highly regulated "medical only" future that even most medical marijuana advocates (at least those outside pharmaceutical companies) would despise: FDA regulation, production controls, inventory caps, distribution limits, prohibition of home cultivation, elimination of high-THC products, and, potentially, the total abolition of smoked whole leaf pot.[97]

The rancor runs in both directions. Despite the Recreationals' longtime support of medical marijuana, the Medicals have long been skeptical about their true motives. Many Medicals believe the Recreationals support medical marijuana legalization only as a stepping stone to full legalization and do not actually care about patients. To bolster this point, Medicals frequently invoke NORML founder Keith Stroup's ill-phrased assertion in 1979 that his organization would use cannabis treatment of cancer as a "red herring to give marijuana a good name." Their suspicions were stirred up again in 2012, when Allen St. Pierre was quoted on the Celebstoner.com website calling the medical cannabis industry a "political and legal farce" and "sham." Though St. Pierre explicitly stated that he was not demeaning medical marijuana itself, this subtlety was lost on many enraged Medicals.[98]

Medicals who have resisted comprehensive legalization have not done so merely out of pique, however. They believe that legalization of recreational use will have concrete negative consequences for medical marijuana growers, sellers, and users. Most fundamentally, medical marijuana dispensaries fear economic ruination from competition with recreational sellers owned by big business.[99] Indeed, a recent analysis shows that states that have embraced full legalization have seen precipitous drops in both medical marijuana cardholders and dispensaries; in Oregon, almost two-thirds of patients abandoned their cards and the number of medical-only retailers plummeted from four hundred to two.

In the eyes of many Medicals, the disappearance of dedicated medical marijuana shops through absorption into recreational stores harms patients as well as merchants. First, they argue, recreational retailers are unlikely to stock the specialized strains and products needed by small classes of patients. Second, the prices of these dedicated medical cannabis products are soaring as the supply shrinks. Third, the employees of recreational marijuana outlets are generally less qualified to advise patients about medical cannabis use. Finally, many Medicals believe that the interiors, exteriors, and neighborhoods of recreational stores have a "head-shoppy" (and even dangerous) aura rather than the serious, controlled, medical atmosphere preferred by many patients.[100]

Time is likely on the side of comprehensive legalization. Support for this policy has climbed dramatically since the turn of the millennium, and about 60 percent of Americans now say marijuana should be legal for all uses. This trend is due in part to the fact that marijuana policy preferences are increasingly shaped by the ineradicable racial discrimination that characterizes the enforcement of drug laws. Until quite recently, much of the African American community supported marijuana prohibitions. For example, in the mid-1970s, Washington, DC, rejected a bill to decriminalize cannabis possession, because most African American government officials and pastors, and the bulk of the city's black population, concluded that marijuana use harmed the community in ways that outweighed other concerns. Although attitudes started to shift in the 1990s, even as late as 2010 the California NAACP faced fierce opposition from black religious and community leaders when it supported Proposition 19.[101]

Michelle Alexander's bestseller *The New Jim Crow*, published the same year, helped turn the tide by detailing the drug war's devastating effect on African Americans. In November 2014, the residents of Washington, DC, by a 70 to 30 margin, passed an initiative fully legalizing the use and cultivation of small amounts of pot. Although white Washingtonians supported the initiative at a higher rate than their black counterparts, a comfortable majority of African American voters (about 58 percent) also favored it. And in 2016, when Californians overwhelmingly passed Proposition 64, legalizing recreational marijuana, African Americans backed the measure at a rate higher than any other group. As minority communities add their support for comprehensive legalization to the already robust support among whites, more "medical only" states will likely legalize recreational marijuana use.[102]

Perhaps no phenomenon presents a greater challenge to medical marijuana sellers and activists than the burgeoning legalization of recreational marijuana. NORML founder Keith Stroup predicts that "we are approaching a time when medical use laws will become irrelevant to the marijuana legalization movement. Once marijuana is legalized for all adults, there is no need for a medical use law." Allen St. Pierre similarly opines: "I don't think the distinction between medical and recreational marijuana will hold up." When Robert Randall commenced his fight in the mid-1970s, who could have predicted that forty-five years later, the primary threat to a thriving medical cannabis industry would not be prohibition, but rather full legalization?[103]

10

The Right to Be Covered

Therapeutic Choice and Health Insurance

The many breast cancer survivors in the room had good reason to feel anxious when the presiding officer called the FDA public hearing to order on the morning of June 28, 2011. After all, from these women's perspective, the topic for debate was whether they could continue taking the drug that was keeping them alive.

The hearing, held in the FDA's conference center in Silver Spring, Maryland, was convened to consider a proposal by the agency to withdraw approval of Avastin® (bevacizumab) for the treatment of breast cancer. Avastin is a biologic product (large-molecule drug) sold by Genentech. It is a "tumor-starving" drug that works differently from traditional chemotherapy.[1] In 2004, the agency approved Avastin for use against colorectal cancer in combination with conventional chemotherapy. Approval for combination use against lung cancer followed in 2006. Then, in 2008, the FDA granted Avastin accelerated approval for use in combination with conventional chemotherapy against metastatic breast cancer. The agency based this decision on a clinical study showing that patients taking Avastin had a 5.5-month improvement in median progression-free survival (PFS)—that is, the amount of time they lived without their tumors growing.

Like all accelerated approvals, this one was contingent on the results of confirmatory studies. Genentech completed these studies, and they, too, showed improvements (though smaller ones) in PFS. Nevertheless, in 2010, the FDA's Oncological Drugs Advisory Committee voted 12–1 to recommend that the agency withdraw approval of Avastin for breast cancer, and the FDA's Office of Oncology Drug Products (OODP) embraced that recommendation. In explaining the proposed withdrawal of approval, the office's director pointed to the smaller PFS benefit in the confirmatory trials and the failure of any of the trials to show a statistically significant improvement in overall survival time—an endpoint the studies were not designed to measure. He also emphasized the frequency of serious adverse events in patients taking Avastin. In summary, the OODP director explained: "The modest benefit observed with Avastin together with the substantial adverse reactions observed in breast cancer trials to date fail to provide a favorable risk-benefit profile."[2]

Genentech demanded the June 2011 hearing to challenge the proposed withdrawal. The advisory committee attended the hearing and would, at

Choose Your Medicine. Lewis A. Grossman, Oxford University Press. © Lewis A. Grossman 2021.
DOI: 10.1093/oso/9780190612757.003.0011

its conclusion, make a recommendation to FDA Commissioner Margaret Hamburg, who would have the final say. The agency initially was not going to permit patients to speak at the event, but it had bowed to intense pressure and allocated the first two hours of the proceedings to "nonparty" testimony. Each patient would have only three minutes to persuade the expert panel that her life depended on its decision.[3]

One of the first witnesses to take the microphone was Patricia Howard, a sixty-six-year-old grandmother and metastatic breast cancer patient who "owe[d] her life to Avastin." Howard acknowledged that the overall data in favor of Avastin were less than overwhelmingly positive, but she identified herself as a "super-responder" for whom the drug's effect was "nothing short of miraculous." Just the previous morning, her doctors had declared her cancer-free. Pleading for the choice to continue using Avastin, Howard declared, "I'm not just a piece of anecdotal evidence. . . . I'm not just a statistic."[4]

A while later, Terrence Kalley took the floor on behalf of his sixty-four-year-old wife, Arlene. He was familiar to some of the other patients as the founder of Freedom of Access to Medicines, an organization that the previous day had a staged a protest outside the FDA building opposing the agency's proposed action on Avastin. Arlene, first diagnosed with breast cancer in the 1980s, had begun taking Avastin when her disease metastasized in 2008. In an op-ed published in anticipation of the hearing, Arlene stated that due to this "miracle drug," she had lived longer than her "medical team ever imagined." She insisted that she, her doctor, and her family should have the right to decide whether Avastin's possible benefits outweighed its potential risks.[5]

At the hearing, Terrence Kalley accused the FDA of treating breast cancer patients as "expendable, innocent statistics in the face of a regulatory machine on autopilot." He blasted the agency for contemptuously dismissing super-responders like Arlene as "anecdotal evidence" and ignoring "the details behind the medians." Terrence pointed out that both the European Medicines Agency and the National Comprehensive Cancer Network (a consortium of US oncology centers) had recently reaffirmed their endorsements of Avastin for use against breast cancer. Turning to the FDA representatives, he forcefully insisted: "It should not be for you, but for my wife and her oncologist, to make this life-and-death decision."[6]

Soon afterward, Christi Turnage—a forty-nine-year-old practicing nurse and mother of four—approached the microphone (Fig. 10.1). Her Stage IV metastatic breast cancer had disappeared when she started on Avastin three years earlier, and she remained cancer-free. Turnage defended the use of progression-free survival, as opposed to overall survival, as an indicator of benefit, remarking, "I believe that the definition of a clinical benefit is a personal question that each patient needs to answer with their doctor." After observing that only 4 percent

Figure 10.1 Christi Turnage testifies in favor of preserving the approval of Avastin for breast cancer at an FDA advisory committee hearing in Silver Spring, Maryland, June 28, 2011. © *Joshua Roberts/Bloomberg via Getty Images.*

of people suffered serious side effects from Avastin, Turnage conceded, "And no, I wouldn't want one of those side effects, but if I don't have this drug, I know that I will have death." At the conclusion of her remarks, she presented the chairwoman with an online petition to preserve Avastin's approval signed by 11,000 people. The petition proclaimed: "We . . . cherish individual freedom and the right of a patient to choose her medical options with her physician. By acting on this, you will confirm our belief that Life, Liberty and the Pursuit of Happiness is an inalienable right for all, including the seriously ill."[7]

During the two hours devoted to nonparty testimony, twenty-eight witnesses—patients, relatives, physicians, and members of advocacy groups—spoke in favor of preserving Avastin's approval. For the patients, choice was the dominant theme. One pled for "freedom to choose the best option," another insisted that breast cancer victims "deserve the choice," and still another demanded that the FDA "not deny me this choice." Representatives of various disease groups warned that a negative decision on Avastin would inhibit medical research and innovation.[8] The audience hailed the comments of each pro-Avastin witness with enthusiastic applause.

Only four speakers—representatives of breast cancer and women's health advocacy organizations—testified in favor of withdrawing approval. They observed that Avastin had actually *shortened* some women's lives, due to its side effects. They contended that progression-free survival was not an appropriate endpoint, unless it correlated with longer overall survival or improved quality of life. They asserted that the FDA should not approve a drug that helped only some patients unless the company first identified biomarkers distinguishing women who might benefit from those who would not. After one of these witnesses demanded that the FDA base its decision on "science" rather than "anecdotes," the next speaker, a pro-Avastin breast cancer survivor, growled, "I am completely disgusted to have to follow somebody like that."[9]

The remainder of the two-day hearing was devoted to presentations by Genentech and the FDA and questions from the advisory committee to each of them. At the conclusion of the meeting, the committee voted unanimously (6–0) to recommend that the FDA revoke Avastin's accelerated approval for metastatic breast cancer.

The Avastin breast cancer controversy in many ways paralleled the furor surrounding the FDA's review of AIDS drugs twenty years earlier. There was one critical difference, however. In contrast to the entirely new antiretroviral medications sought by AIDS patients in the late 1980s and early 1990s, Avastin would be legally available to breast cancer patients regardless of whether the FDA approved it for that particular use. The drug was also approved for colorectal and lung cancer and would thus remain on the market even if the FDA withdrew the breast cancer approval. And even though such an action by the agency would require Genentech to remove the breast cancer indication from Avastin's labeling, physicians would retain full authority to prescribe the drug for that purpose "off-label."

What, then, was all the fuss at the FDA hearing about? The answer is money or, more precisely, health insurance coverage. Avastin cost nearly $90,000 per year, an amount most patients could not afford. An FDA withdrawal of the approval for breast cancer *might* lead some third-party payers to stop covering Avastin for this use. As we will explore later, the risk of this occurring was not as high as the witnesses and many commentators seemed to believe, because the breast cancer indication for Avastin was included in an official "compendium" that listed not only FDA-approved uses for pharmaceuticals, but also many widely accepted off-label uses. Medicaid would thus continue to cover Avastin for breast cancer, as would Medicare (at least for the time being). Furthermore, many—likely most—private insurers would continue to cover it regardless of the FDA's decision. Nevertheless, as the witnesses correctly observed, at least some plans might respond to a negative FDA verdict by eliminating coverage for Avastin's use against breast cancer. As a practical matter, this would make the drug inaccessible for all but their wealthiest beneficiaries battling this disease.[10]

In short, when witnesses at the hearing demanded that the FDA preserve women's "freedom of choice," they were not seeking *freedom from* government interference, but rather continued access to the resources that gave them *freedom to* obtain an extremely costly product. As the great political philosopher Isaiah Berlin observed: "It is argued, very plausibly, that if a man is too poor to afford something on which there is no legal ban—a loaf of bread, a journey round the world, recourse to the law courts—he is as little free to have it as he would be if it were forbidden him by law." Breast cancer survivor Crystal Hannah manifested exactly this viewpoint at the hearing: "If the FDA removes breast cancer indication from the label, my insurance likely won't pay, and I can't afford the drug otherwise. If you were me ... wouldn't you want ... the freedom to choose the best options?"[11]

On November 18, 2011, five months after the hearing, FDA Commissioner Hamburg followed the advisory committee's recommendation to withdraw Avastin's breast cancer approval. In a seventy-page decision, she explained that there was a lack of "credible, objective evidence that the drug is safe and effective." Breast cancer patients who were taking the drug and believed they were responding well to it were predictably distressed. Patricia Howard, who testified at the June 2011 hearing, was "devastated" by the decision. Terry Kalley (Arlene's husband) protested, "It is impossible to see how the health care of Americans is improved by limiting their choices. . . . The wealthy will find ways to obtain Avastin, while the rest will be rationed according to their health insurance coverage." Lorraine Pace, the co-president of Breast Cancer Help in Bay Shore (NY), opined: "It ticks me off. . . . If there's a medication that's out there, people should have access to it."[12]

Hamburg's decision also provoked a negative, sometimes vicious, reaction from the political right. US Representative Alan Nunnelee of Mississippi grumbled: "The American people do not like to be told that the government will limit their access to treatments." Republican Louisiana senator David Vitter blasted the FDA for "tak[ing] that option away" from patients and "rationing access." On the Fox News website, "19marion66" asserted: "This is nothing but more ObamaCrapCare death panel rationing."[13] Many additional posters on this site echoed the sentiment that Hamburg's decision was a tyrannical action by a despotic government agency.

But how can an agency decision that might indirectly lead health insurers to stop paying for a drug be tyrannical? Indeed, how could even the noncoverage decision itself be characterized this way? Virtually any health insurance system, public or private, must limit various types of patient choice—the choice not only of drugs, but also of physicians, hospitals, procedures, and insurance plans. Consequently, if any refusal to cover all the services and products a patient wants constitutes a denial of her rights, all health insurance is rights-stripping.

Despite this country's continuing failure to provide universal health care, most Americans now have some form of health insurance. Consequently, the assumption that third parties will pay for medical treatments is engraved so deeply into the American consciousness that people often do not distinguish between a denial of coverage and a direct interference with their therapeutic choice—especially when they are confronting a personal medical crisis. But when one considers the overall cost of a health care system that enables rather than restricts patient choice, the distinction between "freedom to choose" and "freedom to be covered" becomes inescapable.

A Constitutional Right to Be Compensated?

Because only a state actor can violate one's constitutional rights, no colorable argument exists that denial of coverage by a purely private insurance policy might be unconstitutional. Government insurance programs like Medicare and Medicaid, by contrast, can—in theory—be administered in a way that violates their enrollees' constitutional rights. On rare occasions, beneficiaries have actually filed federal civil rights lawsuits challenging a denial of coverage under Medicare or Medicaid as unconstitutional. Today, such suits are doomed to fail, however, because the US Supreme Court has made clear that nobody has a constitutional "right" to *reimbursement* for a particular product or procedure—even if that procedure is abortion, which receives special constitutional protection against government *interference* under *Roe v. Wade*.

Soon after the US Supreme Court decided *Roe* in 1973, disputes arose regarding whether Medicaid must cover abortion.[14] At the time, many states' Medicaid programs covered medically necessary abortions, but not elective abortions. A number of lower federal courts held in the years immediately following *Roe* that a state's refusal to provide Medicaid coverage for nontherapeutic abortions violated the equal protection clause of the Fourteenth Amendment by treating pregnant women seeking abortions differently from women seeking other types of pregnancy-related care. In 1977, the Supreme Court rejected this reasoning in *Maher v. Roe*.[15]

The Court soon delivered an even harsher blow to the notion that women were ever constitutionally entitled to reimbursement for abortion. Starting in 1976, Congress annually enacted the "Hyde Amendment," which barred any use of federal funds to pay for the cost of an abortion, including a *medically necessary* abortion, except in narrowly defined situations. In a 1980 decision titled *Harris v. McRae*, the Supreme Court rejected a claim by indigent pregnant women that the Hyde Amendment violated their liberty interests as articulated in *Roe v. Wade*. The Court reasoned that a state's decision not to "subsidize" abortion did not raise the same concerns as "direct state interference" with the procedure, even if the lack of financial support made it impossible for some women to obtain abortions. "Although government may not place obstacles in the path of a woman's exercise of her freedom of choice, it need not remove those not of its own creation. Indigency falls in the latter category."[16]

Harris v. McCrae thus drew a dispositive distinction between the freedom to choose an abortion without direct government interference, on the one hand, and the asserted right to receive public assistance for an abortion, on the other. In the language of legal scholars, the former is a constitutionally protected "negative" right, whereas the latter is a "positive" right outside constitutional protection. *Harris's* reasoning ensured that almost all future judicial determinations of a right to Medicaid or Medicare coverage for any service or product would be based on statutory, rather than constitutional, grounds. After all, if destitute women do not have a constitutional right to financial assistance for a medically necessary abortion, why would a person have such a right with respect to a medical procedure that, unlike abortion, is not granted special constitutional status?[17]

Ever since *Harris*, "freedom of choice" debates in the insurance context have thus occurred entirely outside court-based constitutional jurisprudence. As we have seen with respect to other American disputes about freedom of therapeutic choice, however, the fact that a dispute concerns the interpretation of statute, or occurs wholly outside of court, does not mean that it is not a *constitutional* debate in the "popular constitutional" arena, where the public struggles over the meaning of the country's fundamental commitment to liberty.

Health Insurance and the Freedom to Choose a Doctor

A patient's choice of a doctor is the gateway to many other choices regarding her health care. She cannot obtain a prescription drug unless she has a physician willing to write her a script. She cannot undergo surgery or other procedure unless she has a doctor willing to perform it. She cannot be treated at a particular hospital unless her doctor has admitting privileges there. As it turns out, the very first disputes about health insurance's implications for "freedom of choice" occurred with respect to patients' choice of a physician.

In the early 1930s, very few Americans had any form of health insurance—with the notable but limited exception of the workers' compensation schemes enacted by most of the states. The United States was a laggard in this respect; many European nations had established government-run or government-supported health insurance systems (in some instances compulsory ones) during the late nineteenth and early twentieth centuries. Progressive reformers' efforts to introduce compulsory insurance in the United States during the 1910s had been a resounding failure, and the issue was largely dormant in the 1920s. But following the start of the Great Depression in 1929, Americans increasingly recognized the need for health insurance, and the country belatedly and haphazardly began embracing various forms of it on a wide scale. On the private side, prepaid hospital plans began to proliferate under the name "Blue Cross." On the public side, although the 1935 Social Security Act omitted any form of health insurance, the federal Resettlement Administration began that year to establish cooperative medical prepayment plans among the nation's small farmers.[18]

The American Medical Association (AMA) viewed these developments with trepidation. They threatened to undermine physicians' independence by giving third-party payers control over doctors' practice decisions and incomes. Dr. R. G. Leland, director of the AMA's Bureau of Medical Economics, thus assumed an ominous tone when he delivered an address titled "The Insurance Principle in the Practice of Medicine" at a September 1933 meeting of industrial accident commissioners. Leland condemned the forty prepaid hospital care schemes that had been proposed around the country during the previous year. He predicted that "without check or guidance," this phenomenon would inexorably spread to non-hospital-based medical services. This, he warned, would cause "the degredation [sic] of the medical profession to the position of employees of commercially minded lay organizations, with hurried mass diagnosis and treatment of patients." But the most insidious consequence of "the insurance principle" in medicine was the restriction of patient choice:

> An essential feature of good medical care, which is often denied to the patient under the health-insurance systems, is the freedom of choice of a physician. For centuries the medical profession has held that any enforced choice of physicians by lay interests destroys the very foundation of those relations between patient and practitioner which are essential to the best treatment. . . . Any change in the organization of medical service which destroys the right of the patient to choose his own physician . . . destroys social values which it has taken ages to establish.[19]

The following year, the AMA published ten principles that should apply to all private health plans. Rule 3 stated: "Patients must have absolute freedom to choose a duly qualified doctor of medicine . . . from among all those qualified to practice and who are willing to give service."[20]

Although the AMA portrayed the free choice of physician as an ideal status quo threatened by the insurance beast, Americans' choice of doctors had never actually been completely unfettered. As we have seen, ever since the country's founding, state medical licensing regimes—when not successfully suppressed

by unorthodox sects—had prevented uncounted numbers of patients from re-
taining their preferred alternative practitioners. It is nonetheless true that
Americans had always had the right, under the principle of liberty of contract,
to retain any duly licensed *orthodox* physician willing to serve them. Of course,
even this "free choice of doctor" was not so unconstrained in reality. Physicians
routinely rejected patients who could not afford their fees. Many rural communities had only one doctor—or none. Moreover, sick patients (then, as now) were
often dependent on their treating physicians' emotional support and knowledge
about their case and thus did not feel as "free" to switch doctors as to change
tailors or plumbers.[21] Nonetheless, the free market for orthodox physicians celebrated by establishment medicine in the 1930s existed as a formal legal matter.

As the organized profession slowly accommodated itself to the inexorable rise
of health insurance in subsequent decades,[22] it continued to promote—and often
demand—the freedom of patients to select their doctors. Almost without com-
ment, however, the meaning of this "freedom" evolved into a positive right to
receive *insurance coverage* for a visit to the physician of one's choice. The medical establishment largely succeeded in establishing this notion of "free choice of
doctor" as a societal ideal that policymakers violated at their peril. Commitment
to this principle contributed to the continuing dominance of "fee for service"
medical care, as opposed to, for example, closed-network managed care plans
that limited such choice.

The various US presidents who offered comprehensive federal health insurance proposals in the decades following World War II proceeded on the assumption that Americans shared an unwavering devotion to "free choice." Thus, when
President Harry S. Truman urged Congress to enact his national health program
in 1946, he stressed: "People should remain free to choose their own physicians
and hospitals. . . . Under the plan I suggest, our people would continue to get
medical and hospital services just as they do now—on the basis of their own voluntary decisions and choices." The medical establishment's successful campaign
against Truman's proposal, by contrast, stressed the plan's alleged denial of free
choice. The president of the State Medical Association of Texas asserted in a congressional hearing: "The people of Texas . . . wish to retain their full liberty to
select and patronize the physicians of their choice without being handicapped in
even the smallest way by any Federal law or directive."[23]

Unsurprisingly, the two most significant federal health care programs established during the twentieth century—Medicare and Medicaid—both contained
"free choice of provider" guarantees. The Medicare statute, enacted along with
Medicaid in 1965, has always stated: "Any individual entitled to insurance
benefits under this title may obtain health services from any institution, agency,
or person qualified to participate under this title if such institution, agency,
or person undertakes to provide him such services." Congress added similar

language to the Medicaid statute in 1968. In multiple subsequent legal disputes (many involving challenges by Planned Parenthood against state laws barring Medicaid enrollees from obtaining family planning services from abortion providers), courts have uniformly interpreted the Medicaid "free choice" provision as creating a private right for patients, enforceable through a federal civil rights lawsuit.[24]

In 1994, President Bill Clinton promoted his own plan for universal health coverage by declaring: "Our goal is . . . most of all, the freedom to choose a plan and the right to choose your own doctor." Oregon senator Ron Wyden, a supporter of Clinton's effort, warned his colleagues: "If Congress enacts a plan that doesn't give people real freedom of choice among providers, you're darn near going to have a revolt in the streets." Nonetheless, the plan's foes, led by the AMA, defeated it largely by successfully portraying it as restricting choice. One commentator ascribed Clinton's failure to pass health reform to the opposition's tactic of "hitting on people's fears that reform would mean less choice of doctors."[25]

When he took office in 2009, President Barack Obama's main priority was the passage of the Patient Protection and Affordable Care Act (ACA), which sought to increase the percentage of Americans covered by health insurance in several ways: by mandating that most Americans carry a minimum level of insurance, by establishing "insurance exchanges," and by expanding Medicaid to a broader population. In promoting the legislation, Obama predictably catered to Americans' devotion to the free choice of doctor. He repeatedly claimed: "If you like your doctor, you can keep your doctor." Although the Pulitzer Prize–winning website PolitiFact characterized this unqualified assertion as a "Pants on Fire" lie, a majority of Americans apparently bought it—at least for a while.[26] Congress passed "Obamacare" by nail-bitingly close margins in 2010.

Polls appear to validate politicians' continuing impulse to accommodate Americans' desire for doctor choice. Two years after the ACA's passage, 60 percent of respondents in a CBS News/New York Times poll were at least somewhat concerned they would have to change doctors under the new health law, and about two-thirds of these were "very concerned."[27] In a survey the following year, no less than 82 percent of registered voters said that it was "very important" to be able to "choose your doctor when you need care."[28]

In light of all this political rhetoric and survey data, one might assume that most insured Americans actually have a free choice of physicians. In fact, however, a striking contrast exists between the country's professed ideal and the degree of choice patients actually have as a practical matter. First of all, about 30 percent of doctors refuse to accept any new patients insured by Medicaid, approximately 15 percent reject new patients covered by Medicare (which has higher payment rates), and 10 percent turn away new patients covered by private plans.[29]

Furthermore, in 2016, more than ninety million Americans—more than 30 percent of those with health insurance—were enrolled in HMO plans that restricted patients to a list of specified doctors. Indeed, even in Medicare and Medicaid, with their "free choice of provider" provisions, tens of millions of beneficiaries are enrolled in managed care plans with restricted networks of physicians. State Medicaid programs can seek HHS approval for plan amendments or waivers that allow them to provide coverage through managed care organizations with limited doctor choice, and the government routinely grants such permission. Indeed, more than 80 percent of Medicaid beneficiaries are now enrolled in managed care, largely on a mandatory basis. Medicare, by contrast, can never require its beneficiaries to enroll in managed care. Nevertheless, it offers a managed care option: Medicare Part C, or "Medicare Advantage" (MA). Such plans offer enrollees a more restricted choice of providers than does traditional Medicare, but they also offer countervailing benefits, such as low-cost expanded coverage. About one-third of Medicare enrollees have opted for MA plans, demonstrating that however highly Americans value unrestricted physician choice, a significant number are willing to trade it for other benefits.[30]

Are politicians thus routinely underestimating the public's willingness to exchange some of their doctor choice for other concrete advantages? Perhaps. The polling data on this question are inconsistent, and largely outdated, but some surveys conducted over the past thirty years have shown that a majority of respondents would be willing to limit physician choice in exchange for other values, such as universal coverage or cost control.[31] But it is easier to reach such a conclusion in the abstract than when confronted with an actual involuntary switch of doctors. And in a 2016 survey, nearly half of people who were forced to change their doctors because of insurance coverage described it as a "big problem," and an overwhelming majority characterized it as a "problem."[32]

As we will see, a similar tension exists within Americans' attitudes toward prescription drug coverage.

Health Insurance and the Freedom to Choose a Drug

The Rise of the Formulary System

Outpatient prescription drugs—that is, medications used by patients without a concurrent hospital stay—were late to receive widespread insurance coverage. The first major expansion of such coverage was the 1957 enactment of MediCal, California's health insurance system for the indigent. Medicaid, enacted in 1965, extended such coverage to impoverished people nationwide; although the Medicaid statute does not require states to pay for outpatient drugs, every state has chosen to do so. Medicare Part B, created in 1965 to serve primarily the elderly, pays only for outpatient prescription drugs administered to beneficiaries in settings such as doctors' offices. Medicare did not begin paying for most prescription drugs sold at retail outlets until the passage of Part D in 2003.

Private insurance plans were also slow to begin covering drugs. In 1970, despite the passage of Medicaid five years earlier, only 16.5 percent of retail prescription drug expenditures in the United States were paid for by *any* sort of insurance, government or private. Since then, the percentage of these purchases covered by insurance has risen dramatically, to 81.3 percent in 2012. The enactment of Medicare Part D explains only part of this increase; an even bigger factor is the dramatic expansion of prescription drug coverage by private insurers in the 1980s and 1990s.[33]

The advent of prescription drug coverage in the second half of the twentieth century fueled the proliferation of a new phenomenon: the restrictive (or "closed") outpatient formulary. *Formularies* in their broadest sense—that is, listings of formulas for medicines—have existed for millennia; the earliest known example is a Sumerian tablet dating from about 3000 BCE. In the late eighteenth and early nineteenth centuries, modern iterations of such compilations, often titled "Pharmacopoeia," emerged in Europe and the United States. By the end of the 1800s, these volumes, issued by hospitals, municipalities, medical societies, and other entities, became lengthier and more detailed with the addition of purity and potency standards.[34]

The concept of a *restrictive* formulary first appeared in the middle of the twentieth century, in the hospital inpatient setting. Hospitals began to control physicians' prescription drug selection by adopting formularies obligatory on all doctors with admitting privileges. In the mid-1960s, Medicare and the Joint Commission on Accreditation of Hospitals (JCAH) started requiring hospitals to obtain guidance about drug selection from "pharmacy and therapeutics committees." As these P&T committees proliferated, they established formularies in more and more hospitals. By 1975, 60 percent of large hospitals and 82 percent of community hospitals were using restrictive formularies. Although pharmaceutical manufacturers and others occasionally protested the use of this mechanism, it was relatively uncontroversial overall.[35]

Formularies became more contentious in the late 1960s and early 1970s, as private insurers used them in their new plans covering outpatient drugs.[36] Formularies also made their way into Medicaid around this time. Despite the statute's silence on the matter, many state Medicaid programs were using outpatient formularies, including closed formularies, by the early 1970s.[37]

Generic substitution was a particularly important function of early outpatient formularies. During the 1970s, insurers increasingly required the substitution of brand-name medicines with cheaper, generic copies containing the same active ingredients. Physicians and drug manufacturers condemned mandatory substitution as an infringement of doctors' traditional right to prescribe drugs according to the dictates of their professional judgment, as a prioritization of cost over quality of care, and even as a form of "dictatorship." Patients were much less troubled by generic substitution requirements, though their attitude was more ambivalent than supportive.[38]

By the end of the twentieth century, formularies had evolved into complex formulary *systems*. Although these systems sometimes excluded particular drugs or drug classes from coverage entirely, they also employed a variety of less extreme cost-saving methods. These techniques included not only mandatory generic substitution, but also compulsory therapeutic interchange (replacement of a non-formulary drug with a formulary drug in the same drug class), step protocols (requiring the use of cheaper drugs first), and the establishment of higher copayment amounts and prior approval requirements for non-formulary medications.[39]

Meanwhile, the use of formularies in public insurance programs expanded. In 1993, Congress amended the Medicaid statute to reflect long-standing actual practice by expressly allowing states to establish formularies. The revised statute permits states to exclude from these formularies drugs with no "significant, clinically meaningful therapeutic advantage" over listed drugs, although they must permit coverage of excluded drugs pursuant to a prior authorization program. The Veterans Health Administration adopted a partially closed formulary in 1997. And in 2003, when Congress enacted Medicare Part D, it permitted the companies providing the plans to adopt closed formularies containing only two drugs for each therapeutic class, although it later created an exception for six "protected" categories of drugs.[40]

Patient Resistance to the Formulary System

Doctors have long understood that individual patients' responses to drugs vary and, therefore, that two patients with the same disease should not necessarily receive the same medication.[41] Until the late twentieth century, however, the general public was only dimly aware of this phenomenon. Phrases like "people respond to drugs differently," now commonplace in the popular media, were virtually absent before about 1990. Most patients did not care which drug within a therapeutic class their physician prescribed—or which one their insurer's formulary included. After all, the FDA had deemed all of them to be safe and effective.

One of the first areas of medicine in which millions of patients asked their physicians for a particular type of drug, or even a particular brand, was psychiatry. A signal moment occurred in 1987, when the FDA approved Eli Lilly's

Prozac® (fluoxetine) for treatment of depression. It was the first selective sero-tonin reuptake inhibitor (SSRI), a targeted type of antidepressant with fewer side effects than older options. The public was primed to take an interest in Prozac's introduction by a wave of articles in high-end popular media about psycho-pharmacology in general and about the imminent availability of the SSRIs in particular.[42] Prozac quickly became a blockbuster product, especially among women. One author has observed, "It would be hard to overstate the degree to which Prozac became famous as a commercial product—a medicine but also a widely available consumer good that just happened to be available only through physicians." Whereas earlier psychiatric drugs, such as Valium, had been the target of a feminist backlash alleging they were a tool of male oppression, the media portrayed the use of Prozac as an empowering choice made by women themselves.[43]

The FDA approved three other SSRI's in fairly quick succession: Zoloft® (1991), Paxil® (1992), and Celexa® (1998). During the same period, the FDA also approved two serotonin-norepinephrine reuptake inhibitors (SNRIs), a related class of medications. Thus, by the turn of the century, psychiatrists treating de-pressed patients had a choice of six new-generation antidepressants. But who was making the choice—physicians or patients? It became increasingly clear that patients were often driving the decision.

In 1996, companies began advertising antidepressants directly to consumers in popular magazines. The following year, the FDA began allowing television advertisements for prescription drugs, and a significant number of the new commercials were for antidepressants. The very existence of TV spots for com-peting antidepressants implicitly conveyed the message that there were signifi-cant differences among them—and that patients should be personally involved in selecting one. In 2005, a thirty-two-year-old patient told a reporter, "If a person is having a problem in life . . . someone my age will be like, 'Do I need to switch from Paxil to Prozac?'" Omnipresent TV ads for the arthritis drugs Celebrex and Vioxx and the allergy medicines Claritin, Zyrtec, and Allegra instilled the same attitude in patients with other conditions. Not coincidentally, by the early 2000s, articles in the popular press frequently contained statements like "antidepressants affect different patients differently" and "each patient's al-lergy is different, so people may have to try a variety of options to find the ones that work best for them."[44]

In the late 1990s and early 2000s, another development further height-ened consumers' interest in having a variety of drugs available for each disease: the well-publicized efforts of the Human Genome Project, an inter-national consortium dedicated to mapping all the genes of human beings. Even prior to the publication of the project's results in 2001 and 2004, more and more articles in the popular press began discussing the emerging field of pharmacogenetics—the study of the effect of genetics on individual responses to drugs. Around the time of the project's completion, media mentions of the concept of pharmacogenetics soared. In 2006, for example, *Newsweek* declared: "Scientists are uncovering genetic differences in the way people respond to . . . widely used medications, like antidepressants." Between 2006 and 2009, Americans became significantly less sympathetic to proposals that insurance companies refuse to cover new drugs until they were proven to be more effective than older, cheaper treatments.[45]

In light of these trends, it is not surprising that the late 1990s and early 2000s was also the period in which patients began organizing against private insurers' formulary systems. In 1995, a coalition of over fifty patient, consumer, and health provider groups formed Citizens for the Right to Know in California. This organization initially focused on transparency; it lobbied (successfully) for the California legislature to require health care plans to disclose certain information prior to enrollment, including the existence and content of any formularies. Within a few years, however, Citizens for the Right to Know was part of a broader movement combatting the use of overly restrictive formularies by insurers and HMOs. In 1999, the group joined a larger coalition that, in the name of "patients' rights," successfully pressured California regulators to order a number of payers to maintain drugs in their formularies that they were planning to cut.[46]

Patient advocates also turned to federal lawmakers for protections against perceived formulary abuse. In 1999, US Representative Luis Gutierrez of Illinois introduced the Patients' Formulary Rights Act, which would have required health plans not only to make various disclosures regarding their formularies, but also to provide continuity of coverage to patients following the removal of drugs from these lists. Various other bills were introduced in Congress during this period that would have provided formulary-related rights to patients, including the right to obtain medically indicated non-formulary drugs. Although none of these became law, numerous states passed similar measures.[47]

In recent years, as knowledge of variable patient responses to drugs has increased, more and more patient advocacy organizations have battled the use of restricted formularies. For instance, the National Alliance on Mental Illness (NAMI) fights for "open access" to all approved psychiatric drugs in both public and private insurance plans. Its director of legislative advocacy explains: "People living with disorders such as major depression, bipolar disorder, or schizophrenia don't always respond to the first or second rounds of treatment and often require multiple attempts with multiple combinations of medications before finding a treatment that works." In 2012, Gary Puckrein of the National Minority Quality Forum, a nonprofit healthcare advocacy organization, launched an "open formulary movement" that fought for the elimination of all prescription drug formularies in the name of "consumer choice." Puckrein condemned formularies for ignoring "medical need, ability to pay, genetic variability, culture, and gender."[48]

In their resistance to restricted formularies, patient groups have found enthusiastic allies—and patrons—in the pharmaceutical industry. Indeed, according to a 2009 congressional investigation, NAMI received the majority of its donations from drug manufacturers.[49] Drug companies participate in this struggle because they want insurers to pay for their newest, most expensive products, which tend to be excluded from restricted formularies. Moreover, when third-party payers use restricted formularies, drug companies often must offer price concessions in exchange for formulary placement. The combined advocacy of patient groups and industry can be a potent force against the adoption of restricted formularies.

The efficacy of such organized resistance is illustrated by recent proposals regarding Medicare Part D. As noted earlier, Part D, enacted in 2003, covers primarily self-administered drugs purchased at retail outlets. The program generally requires plans' formularies to include only two products per therapeutic class. In 2005, however, the Centers for Medicare and Medicaid Services (CMS) issued a regulatory guidance identifying six "protected" classes of treatments for which the Part D formularies had to include "all or substantially all" drugs. The protected classes were antidepressants, antipsychotics, anticonvulsants, antiretrovirals (HIV/AIDS treatments), antineoplastics (cancer treatments), and immunosuppressants (transplant drugs). Congress subsequently amended the statute to explicitly authorize this policy, although the law permits CMS to amend the list of protected classes by regulation.[50]

In a 2014 rulemaking, President Obama's CMS proposed to revoke the protected status of antidepressants, antipsychotics, and immunosuppressants. The administration's primary goal was cost savings; analyses suggested that Medicare Part D plan sponsors would pay less for these drugs if the formularies were closed and sponsors were thus able to negotiate price concessions in exchange for formulary placement. CMS proposed that a drug class should be required to have an open formulary only if (1) variability in disease manifestations and drug responses demanded the full range of treatment options; and (2) a delay in getting access to non-formulary drugs through special procedures would put patients at severe risk. According the CMS proposal, the three designated classes failed one or both of these criteria, and Medicare Part D sponsors could thus start limiting the formularies for these classes to two drugs each.[51]

The response was fierce. Leaders of patient advocacy groups met with White House officials to express their consternation. Bipartisan groups of Senate and House members wrote letters to the HHS secretary and the CMS administrator urging preservation of the "six protected classes" policy. A new nonprofit entity sprouted up: Partnership for Part D Access, a self-described "coalition of leading national patient groups, pharmaceutical industry participants and other advocates committed to maintaining open access to all available medications under Medicare Part D." Charles Ingoglia, the executive director of the Partnership, insisted in newspapers throughout the country: "Restricting patient choice does not provide effective care, nor does it control costs." Two months after publishing the proposal, CMS withdrew it, citing "the complexities of these issues and stakeholder input."[52]

In November 2018, the Trump administration—as part of a broader effort to reduce drug prices—advanced its own plan to weaken the "protected classes" policy. This proposed CMS rule, applicable to all six classes, would (among other reforms) have allowed Part D sponsors to exclude a drug from the formulary in the event of a price increase greater than inflation. The Partnership for Part D Access launched another aggressive resistance campaign with the slogan "When you limit drug choices, you threaten lives." In protest of the proposal, the Partnership sent CMS Administrator Seema Verma a letter signed by 140 patient advocacy organizations. The letter contended: "Patients with complex conditions often use multiple medications, and they must work closely with their doctors to find the best treatment regimen. . . . Patients facing medical issues that the protected classes were meant to help treat must be able to access the full range of treatment options." In May 2019, the Trump administration, like its predecessor, bowed to the demands of activists and industry. In the final rule, it abandoned the price-based exception to the protected-class policy in light of the many comments it received contending that this change would "greatly compromise[] access to needed therapy . . . for patients taking protected class Part D drugs, which would lead to adverse health outcomes, and, in the case of HIV, endanger public health."[53]

Voters today consistently rank high prescription drug costs as one of their main concerns with respect to health care.[54] But this attitude is stated in the abstract. The impassioned negative response that inevitably arises among patient groups in response to actual efforts to reduce health care costs by restricting insurance formularies suggests that many Americans prioritize selection over savings with respect to the particular diseases they care about. As with the choice of doctors, this country remains conflicted about whether and when it is acceptable to limit the choice of drugs to lower health care costs.

The Impact of Personalized Medicine on Formulary Policy

Although trial and error remains the main method for determining which drug within a class works best for a patient, this may be changing. Scientists are identifying more and more biomarkers that show whether a particular drug will be safe and effective for a particular person. In response, companies are producing "companion" diagnostic products to identify these biomarkers. In the future, doctors—and insurers—may frequently know in advance which drug, if any, will work best for a patient. This emerging treatment approach is known as "personalized medicine" or "precision medicine."

It is difficult to forecast personalized medicine's impact on formulary policies. Certainly, personalized medicine in its idealized form would diminish the role of "choice" in drug selection. In a hypothetical world in which the detection of biomarkers perfectly determined the best drug for each patient, there would be no "choice" for doctor and patient to make—except for the choice of whether to pursue pharmaceutical treatment in the first place. The notion that every patient should have access to the full menu of drugs for every condition would disappear. But this development would not necessarily lead to smaller formularies. To the contrary, if every drug in a class served some identifiable segment of the patient population best, third-party payers would be under great pressure to cover all of them—despite the upward pressure on prices that might result from the fragmentation of the patient market and the reduced competition among pharmaceutical companies for restricted formulary placement.

Personalized medicine also promises to alter, or even eliminate, the role of "choice" with respect to drugs that work for some people but not others. Imagine how different the Avastin story would have been if before the hearing, scientists had discovered a biomarker that, with absolute certainty, identified a subset of breast cancer patients who were "super-responders" to the drug. The FDA would have maintained its approval of Avastin for such patients, all insurers would likely have covered it, and nobody—including the breast cancer survivors themselves—would have characterized the use of the product primarily as a matter of "choice."

Today's demand for pharmaceutical "choice" is largely a product of medical science's uncertainty. And no situation breeds more impassioned demands for therapeutic choice than those in which there is a scientific reason to believe a product *might* treat a deadly disease in at least some people, but the evidence is insufficient to support FDA approval. We saw this dynamic when examining the battle over FDA regulation of AIDS drugs in the late 1980s and early 1990s. The FDA's withdrawal of approval of Avastin for breast cancer created a similar situation, but with the added twist that the drug was still approved for other indications and thus remained available to be prescribed for breast cancer.

Patients resisting the FDA's decision were thus fighting to protect their insurance coverage for Avastin rather than their legal access to it.

Avastin Revisited

Health Insurance Coverage of Drugs for Unapproved Uses

The dire predictions that FDA's action on Avastin would lead to widespread cessation of insurance coverage did not in fact come true.[55] The reason—seemingly not grasped by some of the agency's critics—is that both public and private insurers frequently cover unapproved uses, particularly in the cancer area.

The American health insurance system once covered virtually all off-label prescriptions of FDA-approved drugs, effectively rubber-stamping physicians' determinations that these products were "medically necessary" for their patients. When payers began to reassess this practice in the 1980s, in the face of a growing number of off-label prescriptions for extremely expensive AIDS and cancer medications, patients fought back.[56]

Unsurprisingly, some of the earliest organized patient protests against insurers' denials of off-label drug coverage occurred in the AIDS community. One prominent controversy concerned the drug pentamidine, a preventative treatment for a fungal pneumonia found in many people with AIDS. Although the FDA had approved pentamidine only in injectable form, many physicians started using an unapproved aerosolized version in their AIDS patients. The John Hancock Insurance Company, among others, refused to pay for aerosolized pentamidine. In October 1988, AIDS activists blocked the entrance to Boston's Hancock Tower to protest this policy. The company reversed course several months later.[57]

AIDS patients also successfully battled limitations on Medicaid coverage of the drug AZT. Even after the FDA approved AZT in March 1987, the Missouri Medicaid Program refused to cover the drug, one of the most expensive ever at that point in history. AIDS patients—many of whom were eligible for Medicaid due to their desperate financial straits—filed a class action, contending that this denial of coverage violated their statutory right to benefits. The lawsuit was organized by an advocacy organization called St. Louis Effort for AIDS and litigated by civil rights and legal services lawyers.[58] In response to the suit, the Missouri Department of Social Services issued a rule providing for coverage of AZT, but only for AIDS patients with specific symptoms listed in the FDA-approved labeling. Patients without these symptoms continued the lawsuit.

Prior to 1990, the Medicaid Act did not contain specific requirements for coverage of prescription drugs. The resolution of this case, *Weaver v. Reagen*, thus turned on the statute's general mandate that state plans be "reasonable" and "consistent with the objectives of [the Act]," along with the implicit requirement that the program pay for all "necessary treatment." Missouri contended that the Act and its implementing regulations permitted the state, as a reasonable act of discretion, to cover AZT only for its FDA-approved indications. The US Court of Appeals for the Eighth Circuit disagreed, however, holding in 1989 that the "Medicaid statute and regulatory scheme create a presumption in favor of the attending physician in determining the medical necessity of treatment." The court concluded that the mere fact of FDA non-approval could not overcome this presumption with respect to off-label use of AZT, particularly in light of "the widespread recognition by the medical community and scientific literature that AZT is the only known antiviral treatment for individuals with AIDS."[59]

In 1990, the *Final Report of the National Committee to Review Current Procedures for Approval of New Drugs for Cancer and AIDS* (the "Lasagna Committee") urged third-party payers to look beyond FDA approval in determining reimbursement eligibility. Citing *Weaver*, the report recommended: "The cost of investigational drugs, and marketed drugs prescribed for unlabeled indications . . . should be covered by Medicare, Medicaid, and private insurance, if the use has been approved by expert government agencies, in authoritative medical compendia, or by a committee established by the Secretary of [HHS]."[60]

Just days after the publication of this report, Congress revised the Medicaid statute by adding complex drug coverage provisions that, in slightly amended form, are still in effect today. The law now requires states offering drug benefits under the program (as every state does) to cover drugs for almost all "medically accepted indications." It treats FDA approval as an automatic indicator of "medical acceptability" and thus requires coverage of drugs for all FDA-approved uses. But the Medicaid statute also defines "medically accepted indication" to include any other use for an FDA-approved drug supported by a citation in at least one of a designated group of privately compiled compendia. A state Medicaid program may deny coverage for a medically accepted indication only if the drug in question has no clinically meaningful advantage over covered drugs. Even then, the plan must ultimately permit coverage pursuant to an often-burdensome "prior authorization program."[61]

In 1993, Congress amended Medicare Part B (the part covering physician-administered injectable outpatient drugs like Avastin) to establish similar coverage requirements for off-label use of anticancer medications. Part B now categorizes as "medically accepted," and thus as presumptively covered, not only any FDA-approved anticancer use of a drug, but also any unapproved anticancer use if it is either recognized in one of the compendia or supported by clinical evidence in peer reviewed literature.[62]

Soon before the FDA's 2011 Avastin hearing, the National Comprehensive Cancer Networks voted unanimously to keep Avastin's breast cancer indication in the NCCN Compendium. Consequently, both Medicaid and Medicare were required to continue coverage for the time being, regardless of what the FDA decided. Indeed, the day following the hearing, CMS announced that Medicare would continue to pay for Avastin for breast cancer. Some risk existed, however, that Medicare might eventually withdraw coverage. Even if an anticancer use for a drug is listed in one of the compendia, CMS may, pursuant to a specified procedure, deem it to be "not medically appropriate" and issue a "National Coverage Determination" (NCD) excluding it from Medicare coverage. Because CMS's announcement did not rule out eventually employing the NCD procedure for Avastin, Medicare beneficiaries with breast cancer faced at least a theoretical possibility that the program would one day stop paying for their use of the drug. It was also possible that one of the Medicare contractors that determined coverage for particular regions of the country would issue a Local Coverage Determination (LCD) dropping coverage for Avastin for breast cancer.[63]

The breast cancer patients with the most reason to worry about the FDA's Avastin decision were those covered by private insurance plans—a category apparently comprising most, if not all, of the survivors who testified at the hearing. So long as Avastin was FDA-approved for breast cancer, almost all private policies would pay for that use; indeed, forty-six states have laws *requiring* private payers to cover drugs for all FDA-approved anticancer indications. This safe harbor was lost when the FDA withdrew approval. Although thirty states, representing almost two hundred million people, have laws requiring private payers to cover anticancer drugs for off-label indications listed in the compendia, all but seven of these states make "medical necessity" an additional criterion for mandatory coverage. Consequently, the breast cancer community faced a real possibility that at least some private insurers in forty-three states would stop covering Avastin after the FDA withdrew approval. Indeed, in October 2011, the huge Blue Shield of California announced that it would do just that.[64]

Moreover, an enormous group of Americans enrolled in employer-provided health insurance plans falls entirely outside the protection of state law. Under a federal statute called ERISA, companies that provide "self-funded" group health plans for employees and their families are exempt from most state insurance regulation—including formulary mandates. In 2011, 58.5 percent of Americans with insurance provided by their employers were in such plans. The sponsors of these plans were free to end coverage of Avastin for breast cancer and justify this action to their workers by citing the FDA's withdrawal of approval.[65]

In short, patients had cogent reasons for worrying that some private insurers would stop covering Avastin for breast cancer in response to the agency's unfavorable decision. The worst-case scenario would be if CMS were eventually to issue a NCD rejecting Medicare coverage. In that event, much of the private

278 CHOOSE YOUR MEDICINE

market would likely follow along, for Medicare coverage determinations are hugely influential on private insurers' coverage decisions.[66]

The FDA's action on Avastin did not in fact cause widespread cessation of insurance coverage. This may have been due partly to the fact that by the time Hamburg issued her decision, Avastin for breast cancer represented a diminishing financial burden on payers, as oncologists rapidly abandoned the drug for this use. This trend, which continued after the FDA's final action, did not result from any change in coverage policies, but rather from physicians' reassessment of the drug's safety and effectiveness for breast cancer in light of the unfavorable evidence presented to the FDA.[67]

The Paradoxical Conservative War on the FDA's Avastin Decision

Nonetheless, critics of the FDA's Avastin decision earnestly believed that insurance coverage was at risk. The episode thus offers a rich opportunity to examine "freedom of choice" ideology in the context of reimbursement. We have already extensively discussed the views and fears of one group: breast cancer survivors taking Avastin and seemingly thriving on it. Before we leave the topic, we should also consider the more opaque and sometimes surprising arguments made by another outraged group: conservative politicians and commentators.

The conservative defense of Avastin first kicked into high gear in December 2010, when the agency initially announced its intention to withdraw approval. On *American Spectator Online*, Jeffrey Lord condemned the inappropriate insertion of "the judgment of political bureaucrats for medical science—and the freedom of patients to order the drug." In a *Wall Street Journal* op-ed, David Rivkin and Elizabeth Foley contended: "Government-imposed cost-benefit rationing raises serious constitutional concerns. . . . If government can limit Americans' choice of effective medical treatments, there's no limit to its control over our bodies, and the right to bodily autonomy is an illusion." Columnist Peter Ferrara offered the most extreme reaction: "When a third party, not a patient with his doctor's advice, weighs your health and life in the balance like this, I call it Fascism. It is a perfect analogue to Nazi practices."[68] The phrase "Death Panel" appeared in the title of every one of these pieces.

Conservative critics of the FDA—or at least the better-informed ones—understood that even if the agency withdrew Avastin's approval for breast cancer, the drug would still be available for purchase and doctors would be permitted to prescribe it off-label for this use. They realized that withdrawal of FDA approval would thus decrease "access" to Avastin only indirectly. As Sally Pipes recognized, "Public insurance programs could use the decision as justification to stop covering Avastin for breast cancer. Private insurers are likely to follow suit." In short, sophisticated conservatives grasped what was actually at stake—although even some of them greatly overstated the certainty that insurers would widely stop covering Avastin for breast cancer in response to the FDA's move.[69]

What precise problem, then, did small-government conservatives have with the FDA's action? Why did Sally Pipes (the president of the Pacific Research Institute, a think tank devoted to "free-market policy solutions" and "personal responsibility") characterize the agency's move as a "disgrace"?[70] People with such views do not typically condemn unequal access to goods based on unequal wealth distribution. They ordinarily do not oppose reductions in spending by massive government programs. They usually laud the freedom of private enterprises—such as insurance companies—to take rational, profit-maximizing actions.

Certainly, some conservative condemnation of the FDA's Avastin decision was merely unprincipled political opportunism at a time when the political right was quick to denounce any action taken by the Obama administration. After all, "He is killing breast cancer patients" is a potent line to use against a political opponent. Nevertheless, if we consider the conservative critique carefully, we will find that there is a certain logic to it, despite its intrinsic inconsistencies.

The key to understanding conservatives' response to the FDA's 2010 statement of intention regarding Avastin is revealed by their constant references to "death panels." Earlier that year, Congress passed and Obama signed the ACA, the health care law that induced (and still induces) a sputtering fury among conservatives. An August 2009 Facebook post by former Alaska governor and vice-presidential candidate Sarah Palin helped shape many Americans' negative views of "Obamacare":

> And who will suffer the most when they ration care? The sick, the elderly, and the disabled, of course. The America I know and love is not one in which my parents or my baby with Down Syndrome will have to stand in front of Obama's "death panel" so his bureaucrats can decide, based on a subjective judgment of their "level of productivity in society," whether they are worthy of health care. Such a system is downright evil.[71]

Palin apparently posted this statement in response to a provision in an Obamacare bill then under consideration by the House that would have required Medicare to cover voluntary end-of-life counseling. Her post triggered an outcry that spooked Congress into excluding any such language from the law that ultimately passed in March 2010. Then, in December 2010, a week after the FDA proposed to withdraw Avastin's breast cancer indication, news broke that the CMS had slipped a similar end-of-life counseling provision into a rule implementing the ACA. The contemporaneity of these two incidents created a false linkage between them in many observers' minds, solidifying an already-extant notion that breast cancer patients seeking Avastin would be the victims of the federal government's grand plan to "ration" health care in the name of financial savings.[72]

Dishonest and manipulative though it was, Palin's statement touched a nerve in a huge swath of citizens for a variety of reasons. First of all, many Americans share a visceral unease about the idea of rationing health care based on cost concerns. Second, many are bitterly opposed to having bureaucrats and experts make personal decisions for them. As one scholar has observed, the "death panels" dust-up of 2010 reveals a great deal about "the public's deep discomfort with the notion of rationing essential medical care and, especially, the government's involvement in that process." Third, the public and private facets of our health care system have become so inextricably intertwined that it is possible to see the government's hand in almost any reimbursement decision, whether by a public or private entity. Though this blurring of the public-private distinction commenced long before passage of the ACA, that statute significantly advanced the phenomenon.[73]

The Avastin question got caught up in these developments. Hence the frequent charge by conservatives (and some patients) that the FDA was conducting cost-based "rationing." For example, in their op-ed, Rivkin and Foley declared: "The FDA made a crude cost calculation; as everyone in Washington knows, it wouldn't have banned Avastin if the drug cost only $1,000 a year, instead of $90,000." In his *Washington Times* column, Milton Wolf proclaimed just as confidently, "For the first time in our history, the government has banned the use of a cancer drug based not on its safety or even efficacy, but on its financial cost."[74]

The assertion that the FDA's action constituted a "ban" on Avastin's use for breast cancer was, of course, blatantly untrue. Moreover, the accusation that the FDA made its decision for economic reasons was almost certainly unjustified. In fact, the FDA is prohibited from taking economic factors into consideration when deciding whether or not to approve a drug. Accordingly, the Office of New Drugs' 2010 withdrawal proposal and Commissioner Hamburg's final order a year later both focused exclusively on the scientific evidence.[75] If the FDA's Avastin decision constituted economic "rationing," it was a silent conspiracy.

It was also an ineffective one. The FDA itself was perfectly aware that some physicians would continue to prescribe Avastin for breast cancer and that many insurers would continue to cover it for this indication. Indeed, CMS announced that Medicare would continue to cover Avastin for breast cancer five months *before* Hamburg issued her final decision. Moreover, if the FDA was willing to cold-bloodedly trade lives for savings, it was hardly consistent about it; not long after the Avastin ruling, it approved the cystic fibrosis treatment Kalydeco, which cost more than $300,000 per year, and the hepatitis C drug Sovaldi, which entered the market at $84,000 for a twelve-week course of treatment.[76]

One aspect of the anti–death panel rhetoric swirling around Avastin was at least rooted in fact—namely, the charge that FDA drug approval decisions prioritized the judgment of "government-anointed medical patriarchs" over the decisions of individual physicians and patients. Peter Ferrara condemned the "bureaucratic dictat" by which the FDA substituted "its own judgment about clinical meaningfulness for those of practicing oncologists and terminally ill cancer patients." Peter Roff maintained: "People should be free to choose the medicines they want, especially if there is no viable alternative available. . . . When death is the alternative, the FDA and its . . . bureaucratic instincts should not be able to stand in the way." This anti-bureaucratic strain of the attack on the FDA was accompanied by resistance to the modern clinical scientific method itself. The *Wall Street Journal* editorial page characterized Hamburg's demand for "credible, objective evidence" as "merely another way of imposing a blanket government abstraction over the individual choices of a patient and her physicians."[77]

These criticisms were cogent within the libertarian worldview. After all, an FDA decision on whether to approve a drug *does* elevate the conclusions of an expert bureaucracy over those of patients and their doctors. And the FDA *does* look at the averages of clinical study populations rather than at individual patient responses—as it must, since the Food, Drug, and Cosmetic Act defines the requisite "substantial evidence" of efficacy to mean data from adequate and well-controlled clinical trials. Ultimately, however, these are critiques of the FDA's drug review function, not of reimbursement policies, which the FDA does not determine. And because Avastin—still approved for other cancers—remained on the market following the FDA's decision and could be prescribed off-label for breast cancer, reimbursement (not FDA approval) was the truly pertinent issue in this instance.

If the agency's conservative detractors really believed that insurers should be required to disregard FDA's risk-benefit assessments when deciding whether to cover an anticancer drug, it is difficult to square this position with their free-market, small-government philosophy. Critics of the FDA's Avastin decision bewailed the prospect that it would lead Medicare to stop covering the drug for breast cancer. But if Congress removed FDA approval as a factor in Medicare reimbursement policy, and instead required the program to pay for any drug chosen by a patient in consultation with her physician, an already extremely expensive government program would become even more costly. Conservative commentators also decried the fact that *private* insurers might stop covering Avastin for breast cancer as a result of the FDA's decision. But private payers would be free to continue paying for this use regardless of what the FDA (or CMS) said. If they stopped doing so, this behavior would be a rational response to new information by profit-motivated private entities—something conservatives normally celebrate.

Only a few conservative commentators explicitly articulated that their problem with the Avastin decision was that "all but the wealthiest and most politically connected will have to go without." Nevertheless, this objection lay at the root of every protest against the FDA's decision, or at least every protest by someone who truly understood the decision's implications.[78] Therefore, the conservative critique was, at its essence, a plea for a *positive* right to health for people of limited means—not normally a theme of American conservatism. Opponents of the FDA's Avastin ruling were never able to articulate a coherent political vision that simultaneously embraced individuals' right to make their own therapeutic choices *and* guaranteed third-party payment for these choices *and* controlled public and private health care expenditures. Perhaps nobody ever could.

11

The End

Freedom to Choose and the Right to Die

On Tuesday, November 6, 2012, Massachusetts citizens had some important choices to make when they entered the polls. Should they support President Barack Obama for a second term or pull the lever for his opponent, their former governor Mitt Romney? In the US Senate election, should they vote for the Democratic candidate, Harvard law professor Elizabeth Warren, or the incumbent Republican, Scott Brown? And finally, did they support freedom of therapeutic choice?

Of course, this third issue was not stated so broadly. Rather, voters opined on two separate ballot questions concerning specific exercises of medical freedom. One of them ("Question 2") asked whether a doctor should be permitted, at a terminally ill patient's request, to prescribe medication that would end that patient's life. The other ("Question 3") asked whether the commonwealth should eliminate legal penalties for marijuana possession and use by patients diagnosed with debilitating medical conditions.

From Pittsfield to Provincetown, more than three million Bay Staters flooded polling places. In terms of raw numbers, the turnout was the highest in the commonwealth's history. And most of the results were what one might expect in the famously liberal state. Obama beat Romney 61 percent to 38 percent. Warren—weighed down by a controversy regarding her unsubstantiated claims of Native American heritage—prevailed over Brown by a narrower 54 percent to 46 percent. Question 3, the medical marijuana measure, outperformed even Obama, garnering the support of 63 percent of voters.[1]

One might assume that this electorate also approved Question 2, the physician-assisted suicide (PAS) initiative. After all, like Question 3, it sought to ensure patient autonomy by guaranteeing access to particular drugs. Indeed, during the preceding summer, the same coalitions had coalesced around both questions: choice-embracing liberals and small-government conservatives (in favor) versus religious conservatives and the medical establishment (opposed). As late as September 2012, polls showed at least 60 percent support for Question 2.[2] But on Election Day, the PAS measure narrowly failed, 51 percent to 49 percent.[3]

Choose Your Medicine. Lewis A. Grossman, Oxford University Press. © Lewis A. Grossman 2021.
DOI: 10.1093/oso/9780190612757.003.0012

What happened? We will consider the Massachusetts battle more closely later. For now, we should simply acknowledge the obvious fact that although treating disease and hastening death can both provide relief from pain and misery, they are strikingly different methods for achieving this goal. Death is sui generis. It is irreversible. It is unfathomable and terrifying. While most of us spend our lives *seeking* good health (at least in theory), we strive even more assiduously to *avoid* death—until the moment we don't. Helping someone to attain health is almost invariably a noble act; intentionally precipitating another's death is, in most circumstances, the epitome of evil.

For many Americans, access to PAS thus stands apart from other forms of medical freedom. Millions of religious people who would allow others to try almost any drug in pursuit of health and longevity also believe that it is sinful to ever take a life, including one's own. Moreover, significant numbers of disabled, elderly, black, and impoverished Americans who might ordinarily embrace therapeutic freedom of choice fiercely oppose PAS. They question whether PAS is ever truly a "free choice" in a society that routinely devalues the lives of certain citizens. They fear that such people will confront insidious pressure to end their lives prematurely—pressure applied by a health care system striving to reduce costs and by relatives seeking to alleviate caretaking burdens and to accelerate inheritances. They worry that society will nudge "expendable" people toward suicide through undertreatment—or, even worse, that society will slide down the slippery slope to involuntary physician-administered euthanasia.[4] Although Americans' deep-seated suspicion of conspiracies and clandestine motives has bolstered movements for therapeutic choice in other contexts, it has had the opposite effect with respect to PAS.

State-level ballot measures to legalize PAS emerged slightly before California approved the nation's first medical marijuana initiative in 1996. Yet the PAS legalization movement has had meager success compared with medical cannabis. Today, thirty jurisdictions have legalized medical marijuana, but only ten have legalized PAS. Every medical cannabis measure put directly to American voters has passed, whereas PAS initiatives have failed as often as they have succeeded. Clearly, a different medical freedom dynamic is at work when the "therapy" is death.

The Right to Refuse Life-Sustaining Medical Treatment

In the United States, the first widespread discussions regarding a "right to die" concerned the right to *refuse* life-sustaining medical treatment, rather than the right to *obtain* pharmaceutical or professional assistance in hastening death. In other words, the modern right-to-die movement coalesced around concepts of "negative liberty" rather than "positive liberty."

American law generally supports the right to decline medical care. Judge Benjamin Cardozo offered one of the most famous statements of this principle in a 1914 New York Court of Appeals case concerning a woman operated on without her consent: "Every human being of adult years and sound mind has a right to determine what shall be done with his own body."[5] This tenet has long been riddled with exceptions, however. Indeed, nine years before Cardozo wrote these words, the US Supreme Court declared in *Jacobson v. Massachusetts* that a state government could constitutionally compel a person to undergo medical treatment when necessary to advance the public interest. *Jacobson* upheld a mandatory smallpox vaccination law over an objector's assertion that every American has an "inherent right to care for his own body and health in such way as to him seems best." Although the Court did not deny the existence of such a liberty interest, it emphasized that this right was not absolute and sometimes had to give way to the "common good."[6]

In 1927, this reasoning took a darker turn in the US Supreme Court's notorious *Buck v. Bell* decision. The Court upheld a Virginia statute authorizing the mandatory sterilization of Carrie Buck, an institutionalized woman purportedly "afflicted with an hereditary form of . . . imbecility." Justice Oliver Wendell Holmes Jr. rejected Buck's contention that the law unconstitutionally violated her bodily integrity. Instead, he insisted that the statute properly advanced the general welfare by preventing society from being "swamped with incompetence." Citing *Jacobson*, Holmes declared: "The principle that sustains compulsory vaccination is broad enough to cover cutting the Fallopian tubes. Three generations of imbeciles are enough."[7]

As the twentieth century progressed, *Jacobson* and *Buck* remained the law of the land. Following the triumphant conclusion of the Salk polio vaccine trial in 1955, compulsory immunization statutes proliferated throughout the country. By the end of the 1970s, nearly every state had such laws.[8] After World War II, states began repealing their eugenic sterilization laws in light of the revelation of the Nazi horrors, but these programs disappeared only gradually. And when the fluoridation of public water supplies to prevent dental cavities arose as a controversial issue in the postwar years, courts remained deferential to government officials' efforts to advance the public health. Though fluoridation opponents contended that the practice "invade[d] the private rights of persons to choose for themselves what medication they will take," judges—often citing *Jacobson*—uniformly rejected such arguments.[9]

But what if a compelled treatment did not so clearly implicate the public health? Even then, American law before 1970 did not unambiguously protect the right to refuse medical care. A 1965 piece in the *California Law Review* observed that courts were divided on whether an adult of sound mind could be required to undergo a life-saving medical intervention involuntarily. The article, which focused on patients who objected to emergency treatment on religious grounds, concluded that courts should allow hospitals to compel care in such situations due to "the sanctity of human life and the interest society has in the life of the individual."[10]

When this article appeared, the epitome of a patient refusing medical care was a Jehovah's Witness rejecting a blood transfusion following an accident. By 1970, however, a new personification of the right-to-refuse debate was emerging in the public's mind: a terminally ill or profoundly disabled patient kept alive by machines. The postwar years saw the introduction of technologies—most importantly mechanical respirators and total parenteral (intravenously administered) nutrition—that could extend life significantly, even indefinitely. Other advancements, such as antibiotics, chemotherapy, and heart transplants, could also ward off death in terminally ill patients, but often for only a limited time and with great discomfort. In a phenomenon known as the "hospitalization of death," physicians employed these technologies liberally in end-of-life care, with relatively little concern about their drawbacks. As one scholar has noted: "In American hospitals between the 1950s and 1970, life's prolongation had taken precedence over the lives, the biographies, the experiences, wishes, and relationships of persons who possessed life."[11]

Even as these technologies emerged, a few critics rejected the notion that the extension of life should trump all other goals, including the cessation of agony. Then, in the 1970s, resistance to the medicalization of death went mainstream, along with a broader cultural interest in the notion of a "good death." By the mid-1970s, American culture was awash with books, magazine articles, and television programs on dying well. In his unlikely 1976 bestseller, *Medical Nemesis*, the Croatian-Austrian philosopher Ivan Illich blasted the modern approach to caring for critically ill patients: "Society, acting through the medical system, decides when and after what indignities and mutilations [a man] shall die. . . . Western man has lost the right to preside at his act of dying." Perhaps the most popular and influential contribution to this genre was *On Death and Dying* by the psychiatrist Elisabeth Kübler-Ross. This 1969 book opens with a portrait of a failing patient who "may cry for rest, peace, and dignity, but . . . will get infusions, transfusions, a heart machine, or tracheostomy if necessary."[12]

The right-to-die movement was a natural outgrowth of this general anxiety about doctors' aggressive use of medical technology at the end of life. In its resistance to the medical establishment's use of excruciating and ultimately futile measures, the movement echoed the rhetoric of the opponents of orthodox "heroic" medicine in the country's early years.

Americans' embrace of the right to refuse treatment was just one component of the broader "rights revolution" that occurred in the 1970s. Right-to-die activism was bolstered by the patients' rights movement, with its emphasis on informed consent, and by the women's health movement, with its resistance to the male-dominated, hyper-technologized medical system. In 1973, the first Patient's Bill of Rights promulgated by the American Hospital Association included "the right to refuse treatment to the extent permitted by law." That same year, 62 percent of Americans opined that a terminal patient "ought to be able to tell his doctor to let him die"—a number that increased to 71 percent in 1977.[13]

Nothing during this period galvanized discussions about the right to die more than the tragic circumstances of a twenty-one-year-old New Jersey woman named Karen Ann Quinlan. In April 1975, Karen stopped breathing following a friend's birthday party, apparently due to her consumption of alcohol and drugs. By the time she reached the hospital and was placed on a respirator, she was comatose. As spring turned to summer, Karen remained unconscious, withering away while receiving oxygen, water, nutrition, and antibiotics through tubes. By the end of July, both of Karen's parents reluctantly accepted that she almost certainly would never emerge from her "chronic persistent vegetative state." The Quinlans consulted with a priest about the morality of removing their daughter's respirator. In accordance with a 1957 address by Pope Pius XII to anesthesiologists, the priest told them it was permitted. On July 31, the Quinlans directed Karen's physician to "discontinue all extraordinary measures, including the use of a respirator." When the doctor refused to do so, Joseph Quinlan filed a lawsuit seeking the authority to discontinue his daughter's life support.[14]

The Quinlan litigation was an epic news story that thrust end-of-life issues into the nation's everyday discourse. In 1976, the New Jersey Supreme Court ruled in Joseph's favor. It held that Karen's physicians should remove her respirator pursuant to Joseph's instructions if the hospital ethics committee determined there was no reasonable possibility she would ever emerge from her coma. Two months later, following such a conclusion by the committee, Karen's doctors withdrew her ventilator. She unexpectedly continued breathing on her own, however, and lived until 1985, when she finally succumbed to pneumonia, never having regained consciousness.[15]

Much of the public controversy surrounding the Quinlan case revolved around the fact that Karen herself could not express a choice regarding her medical care. At trial, her father introduced evidence of statements by Karen suggesting she would not want to prolong her life in such a situation. The New Jersey Supreme Court ruled that this evidence was "without sufficient probative weight," but it nevertheless allowed Joseph, acting as Karen's guardian, to make the decision for her "under the peculiar circumstances here present." In this respect, the Quinlan saga was merely the first of a series of prominent contentious legal battles concerning when a state must accept the "substituted judgments" of an incompetent patient's close family members regarding the withdrawal of life support. In subsequent decades, the country would be convulsed by similar cases regarding two other women in persistent vegetative states: Nancy Cruzan and Terri Schiavo.[16]

This chapter will not dwell on the "substituted judgment" problem. For our purposes, the important aspect of the *Quinlan* decision is the New Jersey Supreme Court's unambiguous declaration that if Karen were "miraculously lucid for an interval," she would have had a constitutional right to choose to discontinue her life support. To support this assertion, the court cited most of the leading US Supreme Court decisions affirming the existence of a constitutional right to privacy, including *Roe v. Wade*. The court concluded: "Presumably this right [of privacy] is broad enough to encompass a patient's decision to decline medical treatment under certain circumstances, in much the same way as it is broad enough to encompass a woman's decision to terminate pregnancy under certain conditions." Subsequent decisions by other courts confirmed this principle, and even expanded it. For example, the California Court of Appeal ruled in 1986 that Elizabeth Bouvia, a mentally competent quadriplegic woman with cerebral palsy who was *not* terminally ill, had a constitutional right "to refuse any medical treatment or medical service," including the forced feedings through a nasogastric tube that were keeping her alive. In 1990, while deciding Nancy Cruzan's fate, the US Supreme Court stated in dictum that "a competent person has a constitutionally protected liberty interest in refusing unwanted medical treatment."[17]

Such holdings were in accord with the public's views. During the Quinlan controversy, polls suggested that Americans overwhelmingly supported the right to die for both Karen in particular and terminal patients in general. The Quinlan situation contributed to an upsurge of interest in living wills, in which adults specified what medical treatments they would want if rendered incompetent. Although these instruments had been around since 1969, they were rarely used, legally nonbinding, and routinely ignored by doctors and hospitals. However, in 1976, just months after the *Quinlan* decision, California governor Jerry Brown signed that state's Natural Death Act, which gave adults the right to execute enforceable directives instructing their physicians to withhold or withdraw life-sustaining procedures if they became terminally ill. By 1986, thirty-eight additional states had passed similar living-will statutes. And in 1990, Congress passed the Patient Self Determination Act, which requires hospitals and other facilities to inform patients of their right to execute advanced directives under state law.[18]

In the 1970s, many Americans who embraced dying people's right to refuse treatment perceived a connection between this right and the more general rights to privacy and bodily integrity articulated in *Roe v. Wade*. For example, a 1976 *Los Angeles Times* editorial in favor of the Natural Death Act, titled "The

Ultimate Right of Choice," urged Governor Brown to sign the bill "in the interest of humane recognition of individual rights: of the right to privacy, of informed freedom of choice, of avoidance of suffering, of dignity in dying."[19] But whereas the *Quinlan* case and living wills concerned the freedom not to be *compelled* to undergo treatment, the abortion rights movement and many of the other therapeutic choice movements we have examined in this book were about *access* to medical treatment. Did the "right to die" extend this far? Did people have a right to end their own lives using drugs or medical devices? Did they have a right to receive a physician's assistance in doing so? Americans were far more divided on these issues than they were on the question of voluntary withdrawal of life support.

America's Rejection of Physician-Administered Euthanasia

Physician aid-in-dying encompasses two practices, physician-assisted suicide (PAS) and voluntary physician-administered euthanasia (PAE). PAS normally entails a doctor providing a patient with a lethal dose of a drug in oral form for self-administration. PAE, by contrast, usually involves a doctor delivering a lethal dose by needle or intravenous catheter to a patient who requests it. Many people around the world view the two as ethically equivalent, and most countries outside the United States that have legalized PAS (the Netherlands, Belgium, Luxembourg, Canada) have also legalized PAE. The exception is Switzerland, in which only PAS is permitted.[20]

The United States appears to be following the Swiss path. PAS is now legal in ten states, whereas PAE remains prohibited nationwide. Before examining the PAS-legalization movement, however, it is worth separately considering PAE and its rejection by American voters and lawmakers.

American doctors have always possessed drugs that could—in addition to treating pain and other conditions—hasten a patient's death. During the country's first century, the most commonly used drug of this type was laudanum, a liquid opium preparation. In the mid-1800s, two other possible euthanasia agents entered the American armamentarium: ether and chloroform, both used primarily by surgeons as anesthesia. Until the late nineteenth century, however, doctor-administered euthanasia was so utterly contrary to both medical ethics and the profession's paramount goal of "reviving expiring life" that few if any physicians advocated for it, let alone publicly acknowledged performing it. After all, the ancient Hippocratic Oath includes a pledge not to "give a lethal drug to anyone if I am asked."[21]

The first open debates within the American medical profession about the propriety of euthanasia were triggered by the 1873 appearance in *Popular Science*

Monthly of a summary of an essay on the topic by Samuel D. Williams, an English schoolteacher. This essay defended the proposition that "in all cases of hopeless and painful illness it should be the recognized duty of the medical attendant, whenever so desired by the patient, to administer chloroform . . . so as to destroy consciousness at once, and put the sufferer at once to a quick and painless death." Although Williams's proposal provoked earnest discussions about euthanasia in American medical societies and journals, the profession overwhelmingly continued to condemn the practice. In 1885, a *JAMA* editorial condemned the "ghastly" specter of letting "the physician don the robes of an executioner, and apply what [Williams] is pleased to term *a remedy*." This editorial invoked the likelihood that physicians would sometimes make incorrect terminal diagnoses and even the possibility that disreputable doctors would accept payment to provide people "a certain and easy method of being rid of an objectionable relative."[22]

During the next three decades, some lawyers and social reformers spoke in favor of voluntary euthanasia, but most doctors remained unalterably opposed. In 1906, the Ohio legislature considered a bill legalizing PAE, but the measure lost overwhelmingly. Although public interest in euthanasia waned in the United States following this defeat, it resurged thirty years later following the formation of the British Voluntary Euthanasia Society in 1935 and the Euthanasia Society of America (ESA) in 1938. Polls in the late 1930s showed that 46 percent of Americans favored the legalization of voluntary physician-administered euthanasia for patients with incurable diseases.[23]

Some of the ESA's members and supporters—including its founder, Charles Francis Potter—were thoroughgoing eugenicists who also supported the *involuntary* euthanization of "unfit" (that is, mentally and physically disabled) people, including infants. Nazi Germany implemented this horrific program. Hitler—inspired in part by American eugenicists—ordered the widespread "mercy killing" of the disabled in a program run by German doctors. The revelation of this ghastly effort after World War II made Americans uneasy about a possible slippery slope from voluntary PAE to involuntary eugenic culling. Support for physician-administered euthanasia dropped to 37 percent in 1947.[24]

For the next two decades, Americans rarely spoke openly about the possible benefits of voluntary euthanasia. Hospital personnel sometimes ended the lives of incurably ill and suffering patients, but they did so secretively. (In a 1948 speech to the staff of the Massachusetts General Hospital, the dean of Harvard Divinity School referred to the "many examples" of PAE known to his audience.) In a widely followed—and passionately debated—1950 incident, Hermann Sander, a New Hampshire doctor, was tried for murder after he injected air into the vein of an unconscious patient with terminal cancer. On the stand, Sander implausibly claimed that he thought the man was already dead. Although leading religious figures urged the doctor's conviction, the jury acquitted him in barely over an hour. Nonetheless, Sander's lawyer felt compelled after the verdict to emphasize that "euthanasia is not the defense."[25]

American interest in the topic of PAE soared in the 1970s, and approval of the practice began to climb until it reached a high of 70 percent in 1991. The same forces that drove growing support for voluntary withdrawal of life support were also at play here: ambivalence about the modern medicalization of death and a "rights revolution" emphasizing the freedom to control one's own body and health.[26] Euthanasia proponents increasingly shifted their rhetorical emphasis from physicians' compassion to patients' autonomy. Hemlock Society founder Derek Humphry, who supported PAE as well as physician-assisted suicide (PAS), framed the issue as follows:

> Individual freedom requires that all persons be allowed to control their own destiny, especially at life's end. Existing law does not permit this basic right. Therefore, the law must be reformed to permit a terminally ill patient the right to request and receive the assistance of a physician in dying. . . . This is the ultimate civil liberty. . . . If we cannot die by our choice, then we are not a free people.[27]

But even as public support for PAE rose, religious leaders, particularly representatives of the Catholic Church, continued to condemn it. So did the organizational leaders of the medical profession and a plurality of its members. In 1988, *JAMA* published an essay, "It's Over Debbie," in which an anonymous gynecology resident acknowledged giving a lethal morphine injection to a dying cancer patient after she uttered, "Let's get this over with." Most doctors who voiced an opinion on the piece were outraged. Although some of these objections were based on the fact that the resident barely knew "Debbie," many physicians attacked the very notion of PAE under any circumstances.[28]

American voters have opined directly on the legalization of physician-administered euthanasia on two occasions, and they rejected it both times. Washington State's Initiative 119 and California's Proposition 161—both of which would have legalized PAE along with PAS—were voted down in 1991 and 1992, respectively, both by 54–46 margins. In each instance, a substantial early lead in the polls disintegrated by Election Day. Although a number of factors contributed to this crumbling of support, the most important may have been the ardent, organized, and well-funded opposition of two influential institutions: the Catholic Church and the state medical associations.

The Catholic Church fiercely fought these measures because of its doctrines regarding the sanctity of life. In a letter read at all masses in the nation's largest archdiocese, Cardinal Roger M. Mahony of Los Angeles called on Catholics to pray and do penance for the defeat of Proposition 161, which he characterized as "a profound and disturbing assault on the dignity and integrity of human life."[29]

Organized medicine opposed the Washington and California initiatives for a variety of reasons. Representatives of the state medical associations asserted that the measures, as worded, did not contain sufficient safeguards against mistakes and abuse. A spokesman for the Washington body, for example, warned, "This initiative has the chance for adversely affecting some of the most vulnerable in our society, the frail elderly, the disabled and the poor." More broadly, many doctors insisted that both PAE and PAS were fundamentally inconsistent with their profession's healing function. A flyer distributed by "Washington Physicians Against 119" proclaimed, "We want to care for our patients and not kill them." In essence, doctors opposed to the Washington and California measures contended that their profession should enable only *therapeutic* choices—as opposed to the one choice that obviates all other choices.[30]

Since the defeat of California Proposition 161 in 1992, Americans have never again been asked to vote on the legalization of PAE, either in isolation or in combination with PAS. Today, the practice remains unlawful throughout the country.

Caveat: Pain Relief and the "Double Effect" Principle

This is not to say, however, that physicians never in fact hasten terminally ill patients' deaths by delivering high doses of sedatives or opioids. In a 1996 anonymous survey of physicians working in the ten specialties most likely to receive requests for aid-in-dying, almost 5 percent of respondents responded "yes" to the question "Have you ever given a patient a lethal injection?"[31]

The number of positive responses would have been significantly higher if the question had been: "Have you ever administered medication to ease a dying patient's pain that might also have hastened his or her death?" From a moral perspective, many physicians (and medical ethicists) distinguish between interventions intended to kill a patient and interventions intended to assuage a patient's suffering that incidentally also accelerate the dying process. According to the widely embraced doctrine of "double effect," an action with a foreseeable bad effect on another (for example, earlier death) is permissible if the actor *intends* a good effect (for example, relief from unbearable pain) and the good effect is proportional to the bad.[32]

Although the double-effect principle is often linked to the thought of St. Thomas Aquinas, one does not have to be a theologian or moral philosopher to grasp and embrace it. American doctors—the vast majority of whom would reject a patient's explicit request for a lethal injection, even if it were legal— frequently provide palliative care they expect to shorten their patients' lives.

Indeed, they do so with such regularity that one internist has called the practice "the dirty little secret of medicine." In a 1999 survey of Connecticut internists, 96 percent agreed that it was ethically appropriate to use analgesics to relieve pain in terminal illness even at the risk of hastening death. While the AMA's ethical principles declare that "euthanasia is fundamentally incompatible with the physician's role as healer," they also state the following: "Physicians have an obligation to relieve pain and suffering and to promote the dignity and autonomy of dying patients in their care. This includes providing effective palliative treatment even though it may foreseeably hasten death."[33]

Lay people also broadly embrace the double-effect principle, though few identify the concept by this name. According to polls, about 80 percent of Americans believe it should be permissible for a doctor, on request, to administer pain-reducing drugs that might also shorten the patient's life. This level of support is 15 to 20 percent higher than that for physician-administered euthanasia on request.[34]

Some experts dispute whether an appropriate dose of pain medication ever actually shortens a dying patient's life.[35] The important point, however, is that most people, including many practicing physicians, assume that this does occur and nevertheless defend such palliative measures. The double-effect principle allows doctors and the general public to frame access to death-hastening pain relief as a traditional right to *therapeutic* choice, while circumventing the common concern that precipitating death is intrinsically contrary to the physician's role. And as with most questions of therapeutic choice, Americans tend toward a position of government noninterference when it comes to end-of-life pain relief.

In 1998, two conservative Republican members of Congress, Representative Henry Hyde and Senator Don Nickles, introduced the Lethal Drug Abuse Prevention Act. This law (a response to Oregon's legalization of PAS, discussed later) would have punished doctors who dispensed or distributed "a controlled substance with a purpose of causing, or assisting in causing, the suicide or euthanasia of any individual."[36] Although the bill apparently permitted double-effect administration, an important theme of the successful campaign against it was the risk that the statute would have a chilling effect on doctors' provision of palliative care and thus would violate dying patients' "right" to pain relief. A coalition of more than fifty patient, professional, and industry groups (including the AMA) warned that the law would "be a disaster for those who suffer from chronic, intractable pain."[37]

In the next Congress, Hyde and Nickles tried again by introducing the substantively similar but cleverly titled Pain Relief Promotion Act of 1999. They sought, successfully, to mollify the AMA by tweaking the statute's language and by establishing a federal program for palliative care research and training. The measure nonetheless faced ardent opposition from state medical associations, pain treatment advocates, and others concerned that it would "discourage physicians nationwide from adequately treating the suffering of their dying patients." Not coincidentally, in 2000, the Joint Commission on the Accreditation of Healthcare Organizations adopted a standard stating: "All patients . . . have the right to have their pain assessed and managed appropriately."[38]

This second bill failed, as well.In sum, during the final years of the twentieth century—before the rise of the tragic opioid addiction crisis we confront today— patient groups and many within the medical profession emphatically promoted access to end-of-life pain treatment, invoking rights as well as compassion. By embracing the double-effect principle, pain treatment advocates presented the choice to use potentially life-shortening palliative medication as a variety of therapeutic freedom instead of as a "right to die." They thus garnered far more support than proponents of purposeful euthanasia have ever achieved.

America's Hesitant Embrace of Physician-Assisted Suicide

Although American law still universally prohibits doctors from directly administering lethal drugs for the primary purpose of hastening death, the country has started—haltingly—to take a different stance with respect to physicians who provide terminally ill patients with the means to end their own lives.

PAS's Emergence from the Shadows

For most of American history, most jurisdictions have prohibited aiding another's suicide for any reason. Nevertheless, physician-assisted suicide has likely always existed in the secret corners of medical practice. Mentions of PAS began appearing in scholarly literature in the second half of the twentieth century. In the mid-1960s, two scholars researching end-of-life care in hospitals identified a surreptitious practice known as "auto-euthanasia," in which suffering patients were left alone with pills in "dying rooms." In the 1970s, a few ethicists began publicly defending PAS.[39]

The person most responsible for making PAS a topic of public debate in the United States was Derek Humphry, a British-born reporter. In a 1978 book titled *Jean's Way*, he described how he had recently helped his cancer-ridden, pain-racked wife end her own life with a lethal dose of medication prescribed by an unnamed London doctor. Although American sales of the book were modest, its publication garnered Humphry many prominent media appearances in the United States. He and his second wife, Anne Wickett, soon moved to California where, in 1980, they cofounded the Hemlock Society to advocate for the social acceptance and legalization of PAS by terminally ill people.[40]

In 1981, Hemlock published Humphry's *Let Me Die before I Wake*, essentially a "how-to" guide for those seeking to end their own lives. Interest in PAS began to build. In 1986, Humphry co-drafted a model initiative, the Humane and Dignified Death Act. This audacious measure raced well ahead of evolving public opinion by legalizing PAE as well as PAS and by making both options available to people who were irreversibly ill but not near death. In 1988, the Hemlock Society's political arm attempted to get a watered-down version of the initiative (applicable only to the terminally ill) onto the California ballot, but it gathered only one-third of the requisite signatures. This failed effort nonetheless attracted national attention to the aid-in-dying movement.

In 1991, the Hemlock Society published Humphry's *Final Exit*, an explicit and detailed suicide manual. It became a surprise blockbuster—the fourth-highest-selling nonfiction book of the year. Hemlock used its earnings from this controversial volume to support state ballot initiatives, including the unsuccessful Washington and California measures of 1991 and 1992. Increasingly, however, Americans viewed Humphry, who retired as president of the Hemlock Society in 1992, as a "ghoulish" extremist. Indeed, the organizers of these early state initiatives publicly distanced themselves from him even while courting his financial support.[41]

By 1994, Humphry's role as the leading advocate for PAS had been assumed by an even more divisive figure, a highly eccentric, unemployed pathologist from Michigan named Jack Kevorkian. Dr. Kevorkian's professional interests had always tended toward the macabre. As a medical resident in the 1950s, he observed the appearance of people's eyes at the precise moment of their demise and published his results in a journal article titled "The Fundus Oculi and the Determination of Death." Kevorkian subsequently also wrote papers about consensual medical experimentation on death-row inmates and about transfusing blood from cadavers to living patients. In the 1980s, he turned his scholarly attention to euthanasia and suicide, producing a body of work that culminated in a 1988 article titled "The Last Fearsome Taboo: Medical Aspects of Planned Death."[42]

Around this time, Kevorkian began advertising his services in and around Detroit as a "Physician-Consultant" for terminally ill people wishing to "die with dignity." His career as a "Special Death Counselor" got off to a slow start; he received only two requests for assistance and declined both as inappropriate. In 1988, Kevorkian approached the Hemlock Society with a proposal to open a "suicide clinic" in California, but Humphry rejected the idea, choosing instead to maintain the organization's focus on state-level legal reform efforts. The two men never spoke again.

In 1989, back in Michigan, Kevorkian used $30 worth of bric-a-brac he acquired in garage sales and hardware stores to build a "Thanatron" (Greek for "death machine"). The device enabled a patient to self-administer a lethal drug cocktail intravenously by pressing a button. In June 1990, Kevorkian observed as Janet Adkins—a fifty-four-year-old Oregonian with early-stage Alzheimer's disease—became the first person to end her life using his invention. The procedure took place in Kevorkian's rusted Volkswagen bus, parked at a secluded campsite an hour outside Detroit. Widespread media coverage of this event— including a front-page story in the *New York Times*—launched Kevorkian into the national spotlight. Then, in October 1991, Kevorkian attended the joint suicide of Marjorie Wantz, suffering from severe chronic pelvic pain, and Sherry Miller, a woman with multiple sclerosis. Wantz used the Thanatron, but Miller, whose veins were too weak, inhaled carbon monoxide through a mask. During the next three years, Kevorkian oversaw the suicides of about twenty additional people. Many were not terminally ill, and none of them were patients of his prior to the procedure.

The cadaverous, grey-haired Kevorkian, who apparently had not treated a living person since medical school, was not an ideal spokesperson for physician-assisted suicide. With his Rube Goldberg suicide machine, he struck some as a sinister mad scientist. Journalists nicknamed him "Dr. Death"—a moniker he proudly embraced.[43] A late 1993 story in *Newsweek* titled "The Real Jack Kevorkian" highlighted his longtime "obsession with death" and his enthusiasm for human experimentation. The article even quoted Kevorkian opining that Nazi doctors' experiments on concentration camp inmates were "not *absolutely* negative." Thereafter, most advocates for aid-in-dying legislation viewed "Dr. Death" as politically radioactive and assiduously avoided any association with him.[44]

For its part, organized medicine vociferously denounced Kevorkian from the moment he commenced his PAS campaign. AMA representatives reaffirmed the organization's condemnation of the practice. Michigan and California revoked Kevorkian's medical licenses. Prominent physicians and medical ethicists quoted in newspapers almost unanimously decried Kevorkian's conduct. (Kevorkian, in turn, compared the rest of the profession to "those immoral Nazi doctors.") Interestingly, however, polls of practicing physicians showed that nearly half of them approved of Kevorkian's activities.[45]

During the early 1990s, Kevorkian's creepy "Dr. Death" caricature was counterbalanced by the emergence of Dr. Timothy Quill, an utterly respectable internist and palliative care specialist in Rochester, New York. In the March 1991 issue of the *New England Journal of Medicine* (*NEJM*), Quill described how he had knowingly provided a leukemia patient, "Diane," with the barbiturates she used to commit suicide. Diane took her own life rather than pursuing a grueling course of chemotherapy that would have given her a 25 percent chance of long-term survival. Quill explained, "I have been a longtime advocate of active, informed patient choice of treatment or nontreatment, and of a patient's right to die with as much control and dignity and possible." After discovering Diane's identity, the Rochester district attorney brought Quill's case before a grand jury, but it declined to indict him.[46]

Quill's approach to PAS was very different from Kevorkian's. Whereas "Dr. Death" assisted patients he had just met, Diane had been under Quill's care for eight years. Diane, unlike many of Kevorkian's patients, was near death when she took the pills. Moreover, Quill was not present when she did so. In light of these distinctions, doctors seemed more likely to support Quill than Kevorkian. Indeed, a poll of Washington State doctors taken soon after the "Diane" episode showed that far more than half thought PAS was sometimes ethically justified. More important, many commentators from the medical establishment defended Quill, including George Annas (one of the nation's leading medical ethicists) and Arnold Relman, the editor of *NEJM*.[47] The New York disciplinary board cleared Quill of any medical misconduct.[48] The professional response to Quill's article suggested that even organized medicine might support PAS in some situations.

Outside medical circles, Quill was never nearly as prominent as Kevorkian, who remained the face of PAS for most Americans. But even as troubling information about "Dr. Death" emerged and the medical establishment railed against him, the general public supported his conduct. In national polls conducted near the end of 1993, many more Americans approved of Kevorkian's actions than disapproved.[49] Thanks to sympathetic juries, Kevorkian avoided legal consequences for a surprisingly long time. In spring 1994 (after Michigan lawmakers amended the state's criminal code to explicitly ban assisted suicide), Kevorkian stood trial for his role in the carbon monoxide death of Thomas Hyde, a man with amyotrophic lateral sclerosis (ALS), also known as Lou Gehrig's disease. The prosecutor portrayed Kevorkian as a "lonely medical outlaw" with a "lifelong, morbid fascination with death." In response, Kevorkian advanced a "double-effect" defense, asserting that because he was motivated primarily by a compassionate desire to ease Hyde's suffering, he fell within an exception to the statute.[50] On May 2, 1994, the jury acquitted the doctor. Two other juries subsequently acquitted Kevorkian of homicide charges regarding other assisted suicides.

Kevorkian's lawyer, Geoffrey Fieger, repeatedly succeeded in painting Kevorkian as a caring physician providing a legitimate *treatment* option for his patients. In the words of medical historian Keith Wailoo: "In these ... acquittals, juries saw the case for PAS in terms of pain relief and the freedom to choose. In privileging pain relief in their decisions, juries voiced a popular sentiment. They accepted that Kevorkian was driven by compassion and concern for pain; he acted as a doctor."[51]

As the 1990s progressed, Kevorkian attended more and more suicides, including about thirty in 1997 alone. His legal escape act ended in 1999, when a jury finally convicted him of murder. Kevorkian, increasingly bold, had boxed himself into a corner by injecting an ALS patient with lethal drugs himself, sending a videotape of the procedure to CBS's *60 Minutes*, and representing himself in the ensuing trial. Dr. Death remained in prison until 2007, when he was paroled for good behavior. He died four years later of natural causes.[52]

Triumph in Oregon

In 1994, following their failures in Washington and California, PAS advocates turned their attention to Oregon. They gathered enough signatures to put the Oregon Death with Dignity Act (ODDA) on the ballot. If approved by the state's voters, this initiative, also known as Measure 16, would permit doctors to prescribe life-ending medications to terminally ill patients who requested them. The proposed law mandated that the patient make a written request witnessed by two individuals and that the attending physician and an additional consulting physician certify that the patient had less than six months to live. In these respects, Oregon's Measure 16 was identical to the recently defeated Washington and California initiatives.

To improve the ODDA's prospects, however, its framers made several critical modifications. Most important, Measure 16 legalized PAS but *not* PAE. This change was largely intended to neutralize organized medicine's opposition. Unlike the Catholic Church, which condemns PAE and PAS equally, physicians do not necessarily view the two practices as morally equivalent. Indeed, polls show that doctors are more inclined to support PAS than PAE, probably because of their visceral discomfort with the notion of administering a fatal medication themselves. Measure 16's exclusive focus on PAS probably explains why the Oregon Medical Association took no position on the initiative, in contrast to its Pacific Coast counterparts earlier in the decade.[53]

By limiting the ODDA to PAS, the law's drafters also helped assure lay voters that physician-assisted death in Oregon would always be truly voluntary and would not extend to incompetent patients.[54] Measure 16 contained additional new safeguards to ensure voluntariness. It required a patient to make two oral requests in addition to the written request, and it imposed waiting periods prior to the writing of the prescription. It obligated the attending and consulting doctors to certify that the patient was "capable" and "acting voluntarily," and it allowed either physician to refer the patient to a psychiatrist or psychologist for counseling and a mental health evaluation.

Finally, the ODDA—in contrast to the defeated Washington and California measures—made PAS available only to state residents. This feature of Measure 16 assuaged the concerns of voters who were worried that Oregon would become a national suicide destination.[55]

Oregon Right to Die, the political action committee that drafted and promoted Measure 16, assembled a broad coalition of professional and community leaders similar to those that had supported the Washington and California initiatives. But notably for our purposes, the aid-in-dying movement now also received support from two groups struggling for freedom of therapeutic choice in other contexts: AIDS activists and abortion advocates. The former, while fighting for access to emerging treatments that might temporarily delay the ravages of AIDS, also demanded freedom to determine the timing and circumstances of their deaths. One leading Measure 16 proponent was Tim Shuck, a Portland AIDS activist (and abortion counselor), who declared his intention to take his own life when his brain turned to "mush." Meanwhile, the National Organization for Women and the American Civil Liberties Union framed the "right to die" as a logical extension of the bodily liberty they demanded with respect to abortion. A month before the vote, an ACLU lawyer proclaimed: "Just as we recognize a woman's free choice, we're going to recognize a terminally ill person's choice to go on living or the choice to hasten inevitable death."[56]

Rights talk and the theme of free choice suffused the pro–Measure 16 campaign. For example, the "Arguments in Favor" of the initiative in the official Voters' Pamphlet mailed to all Oregon voters emphasized "the fundamental right of dying patients to choose a humane and dignified death." A pro–Measure 16 television commercial featured a series of people declaring: "This is my body. I don't need you. I don't need government. I don't need any church playing politics with my choices, with my life."[57]

The last assertion was directed mainly at the Catholic Church, which was (with the Oregon Medical Association on the sidelines) far and away the most prominent and energetic foe of Measure 16. While priests preached religious objections to their congregants, a church-funded opposition effort disseminated secular concerns to the broader public. This anti-ODDA campaign contended, for instance, that PAS undermined doctors' professional role as healers; that diagnoses of imminent death were sometimes mistaken; that legalization of PAS would create a slippery slope to legalization of physician-administered euthanasia; and that poor, elderly, and disabled people would face pressure to opt for PAS. Opponents of Measure 16 also criticized specific features of the proposed law, including its lack of mandatory psychiatric counseling and family notification. Overall, however, the carefully drafted Oregon initiative was less vulnerable to charges of insufficient safeguards than its Washington and California antecedents.[58]

Once again, PAS supporters saw a robust lead in the polls shrivel by Election Day. Nevertheless, on November 4, 1994, Measure 16 narrowly passed with 51 percent of the vote. The battle was not over, however. Opponents challenged the constitutionality of the ODDA in court. In August 1995, a US district judge counterintuitively held that the law violated terminally ill patients' equal protection rights by providing them with less protection than other people from suicidal impulses. The US Court of Appeals for the Ninth Circuit reversed this decision in February 1997 on jurisdictional grounds. A few months later, however, the Oregon legislature—in an unprecedented move—referred the ODDA, with no amendments, back to the voters for reconsideration and possible repeal. Oregonians were widely outraged that lawmakers were second-guessing their judgment. In November 1997, they resoundingly rejected the repeal initiative, by a 20 percent margin. The night following the election, the state attorney general confirmed that America's first-ever PAS legalization law was in effect.[59]

The ODDA's enactment apparently convinced aid-in-dying proponents that their surest path to victory in other states was legalization of PAS alone, without PAE. Although polls have not clearly demonstrated that the public favors the former practice over the latter, every subsequent measure put before American voters (successful or not) has been PAS-only.

The *Glucksberg* Case

Earlier in 1997, the death with dignity movement was denied a much more comprehensive victory that would have made PAS available nationwide. In June, the US Supreme Court held, in *Washington v. Glucksberg* and *Vacco v. Quill*, that states violated neither the due process clause nor the equal protection clause of the US Constitution by prosecuting physicians for helping mentally competent, terminally ill patients take their own lives.[60] In these companion decisions, as in many other cases we have considered, the Court thus deferred a question of therapeutic freedom to the political sphere.

The *Glucksberg* litigation commenced when four physicians, three gravely ill patients, and the nonprofit organization Compassion in Dying filed a suit in US district court seeking a declaration that Washington State's ban on assisted suicide violated the patients' due process rights to "self-sovereignty" and "personal autonomy." The plaintiffs eventually earned a favorable decision from the full US Court of Appeals for the Ninth Circuit, which held that they had demonstrated "that the Constitution encompasses a due process liberty interest in controlling the time and manner of one's death—that there is, in short, a constitutionally-recognized 'right to die.'" *Vacco v. Quill* originated with a similar suit in New York

State brought by, among others, Dr. Timothy Quill. The US Court of Appeals for the Second Circuit ruled that New York violated the equal protection clause by applying its ban on assisted suicide to physicians prescribing death-hastening drugs but not to doctors removing life-support systems.[61] Both states appealed the decisions against them to the US Supreme Court.

A broad array of parties filed *amicus* briefs with the Supreme Court in support of a constitutional right to PAS. They included, among others, the ACLU, the Center for Reproductive Law and Policy, the National Women's Health Network, the Gay Men's Health Crisis, the American Medical Student Association, the Washington State Psychological Association, and representatives of various mainstream Protestant denominations. The list of *amici* urging reversal was even longer, however. It included the US government, numerous state attorneys general, the US Catholic Conference, the Evangelical Lutheran Church in America, the Union of Orthodox Jewish Congregations, the American Medical Association, the National Hospice Organization, the National Right to Life Committee, and—notably—organizations representing the elderly and people with disabilities and spinal cord injuries.[62]

On June 26, 1997, the Supreme Court ruled unanimously in both cases against the existence of a constitutional right to physician-assisted suicide. In *Glucksberg* (a decision we first encountered in the Introduction), the majority held that substantive due process extends only to "carefully described" rights that are both "deeply rooted in the Nation's history and tradition" and "implicit in the concept of ordered liberty." In applying the "history and tradition" test, Chief Justice William Rehnquist emphasized that "for over 700 years, the Anglo-American common-law tradition has punished or otherwise disapproved of both suicide and assisting suicide." Rehnquist reviewed centuries of legal sources and concluded, "We are confronted with a consistent and almost universal tradition that has long rejected the asserted right, and continues explicitly to reject it today, even for terminally ill, mentally competent adults."

After explaining why access to physician-assisted suicide was not a fundamental right, Rehnquist observed that a state ban on it would nonetheless violate due process unless it was "rationally related to a legitimate government interest." The Chief Justice then catalogued multiple reasons why a state might legitimately prohibit PAS. Here, the Chief Justice echoed the standard arguments against PAS commonly advanced in both the legal and political arenas. Washington State had an "unqualified interest in the preservation of human life." It also had an interest in "protecting the integrity and ethics of the medical profession." Furthermore, "the State may fear that permitting assisted suicide will start it down the path to voluntary and perhaps even involuntary euthanasia."[63]

The Chief Justice devoted a full page of his opinion to a fourth "legitimate government interest" that was becoming an increasingly prominent component of anti-PAS rhetoric by 1997. He affirmed that "the State has an interest in protecting vulnerable groups—including the poor, the elderly, and disabled persons—from abuse, neglect, and mistakes." After warning about the "real risk of subtle coercion and undue influence in end-of-life situations," the famously conservative Rehnquist quoted language (from a New York State task force report on assisted suicide and euthanasia) that even the most ardent liberal could embrace: "The risk of harm is greatest for the many individuals in our society whose autonomy and well-being are already compromised by poverty, lack of access to good medical care, advanced age, or membership in a stigmatized social group."[64] This line of reasoning largely explains why anti-PAS advocacy was becoming increasingly bipartisan at the moment the *Glucksberg* decision flung the issue back to the political sphere for resolution.

The Chief Justice differentiated the Court's suggestion in *Cruzan* seven years earlier that the due process clause protects competent patients' right to refuse life-saving hydration and nutrition. He asserted that requesting the withdrawal of life support was "widely and reasonably regarded as quite distinct" from committing suicide with the assistance of another in light of the "long legal tradition protecting the decision to refuse unwanted medical treatment." Rehnquist examined this distinction in greater depth in *Quill*, the companion case, which held that New York did not violate the equal protection clause by banning PAS while permitting withdrawal of life-sustaining treatment.[65]

Although *Glucksberg* and *Quill* rejected the contention that terminally ill patients have a constitutional right to PAS, the opinions strongly suggested that there might be a constitutional right to pain relief, including death-hastening pain relief. In *Quill*, Rehnquist implicitly embraced the double-effect principle. In a concurrence addressed to both cases, Justice Sandra Day O'Connor intimated that "patients have a constitutionally cognizable interest in obtaining relief from the suffering that they may experience in the last days of their lives." She found it unnecessary to address the issue, however, because under both Washington and New York law, dying patients could already indisputably "obtain palliative care, even when doing so would hasten their deaths." One prominent legal scholar interpreted *Glucksberg* and *Quill* as "effectively require[ing] all states to ensure that their laws do not obstruct the provision of adequate palliative care, especially for the alleviation of pain and other physical symptoms of people facing death."[66]

In sum, following the decisions in *Cruzan*, *Glucksberg*, and *Quill*, terminally ill Americans had a constitutional right to request the withdrawal of life-sustaining treatment and, perhaps, to demand pain relief even if it accelerated their deaths. But the question of physician-assisted suicide would—like most questions of therapeutic choice in American history—be decided at the ballot box.

Failure in Other States

In other situations we have considered—Laetrile, medical marijuana, "right to try"—the enactment of the first state law protecting therapeutic choice has opened the floodgates to many more across the country. The aftermath of the passage of the Oregon Death with Dignity Act was very different. Although many comparable PAS legalization bills were proposed in state legislatures between the ODDA's enactment in 1994 and the turn of the millennium, not a single one passed. Ballot measures put directly to voters also failed. In 1998, Michigan (where Kevorkian was increasingly unpopular) overwhelmingly rejected Proposal B, a PAS-legalization initiative, by more than a 2–1 margin. In 2000, Maine voters narrowly rejected a similar referendum. During this period, a few states actually passed laws explicitly *prohibiting* assisted suicide—joining the overwhelming majority that had already done so.[67]

Meanwhile, a new interest group surged to the forefront of the anti-PAS movement: disabled Americans. The Catholic Church and other PAS opponents had long warned that if the practice were legalized, vulnerable and devalued people such as minorities, the elderly, and the disabled would face intense pressure to use it. Some critics went further and warned that PAS legalization would create a "slippery slope" to involuntary euthanasia for these populations. But until the mid-1990s, organizations representing these groups remained largely out of the fray while other PAS foes advanced such arguments on their behalf.

In 1996, disabled citizens began to organize against PAS legalization themselves. Disability-rights advocate Diane Coleman founded a new group, Not Dead Yet (NDY), to resist the aid-in-dying agenda. NDY's first major public action occurred on the sidewalk in front of the Supreme Court on January 8, 1997, the day of the *Glucksberg* arguments. About two hundred shivering disabled protestors, far outnumbering counter-demonstrators from the Hemlock Society, chanted, "We want to live." One activist, Evan Kemp (a former chairman of the Equal Employment Opportunity Commission who used a wheelchair due to ALS) told a reporter observing the protest: "I do think disabled people are going to be the target for the same reason as Nazi Germany—cost savings." Kathi Wolfe, another demonstrator, explained in a post-event op-ed: "We fear cost-conscious HMOs and government programs. Because health-care dollars are scarce and our society devalues the disabled, I believe the so-called right to die could become a duty rather than a choice for people like me."[68]

In its early years, NDY focused much of its attention on Michigan, where many of Jack Kevorkian's clients were chronically disabled but not terminally ill. In 1998, the organization joined Citizens for Compassionate Care, an anti–Proposal B coalition that also included, among many other groups, the Michigan Catholic Conference, the Michigan State Medical Association, and Right to Life of Michigan. Although the Catholic Church provided the bulk of the coalition's funds, many news stories leading up to the Election Day defeat of the ballot measure prominently featured the voices of disability advocates. In 2000, NDY turned its focus to Maine, where it helped defeat that state's referendum on doctor-assisted suicide. As the twenty-first century commenced, the anti-PAS alliance had become a powerful conglomeration of conservative religious groups, professional medical organizations, and left-leaning disability activists.[69]

Federal Resistance

Meanwhile, the federal government took its own steps to inhibit PAS. In 1997, Congress passed the Assisted Suicide Funding Restriction Act, a law still in effect that prohibits the use of federal funds "to pay for items and services ... the purpose of which is to cause (or assist in causing) the suicide, euthanasia, or mercy killing of any individual." That same year, President Clinton's DEA administrator, Thomas Constantine, declared that prescribing controlled substances to help people commit suicide was not a "legitimate medical purpose" for such drugs and thus violated the federal Controlled Substances Act (CSA). This action, which effectively squelched implementation of the ODDA, initiated a long struggle regarding federal versus state power over physician-assisted suicide—a counterpart to the roughly simultaneous federal-state tug of war over medical marijuana.[70]

In June 1998, Attorney General Janet Reno overruled Constantine, assuring physicians that they would suffer no federal consequences if they prescribed controlled substances to patients in compliance with a state's PAS legalization law. She explained, "There is no evidence that Congress, in the CSA, intended to displace the states as the primary regulators of the medical profession, or to override a state's determination as to what constitutes legitimate medical purpose."[71] In reaction to Reno's decision, Senator Don Nickles and Representative Henry Hyde introduced the aforementioned Lethal Drug Use Abuse Prevention Act of 1998, which would have amended the CSA to expressly outlaw prescription of a controlled substance for use in a suicide. As we saw, both this bill and a less severe 1999 version failed.

In November 2001, President George W. Bush's attorney general, John Ashcroft, issued a memorandum reversing Reno. Ashcroft's memo declared that suicide assistance was not a "legitimate medical purpose" under the CSA regardless of state law, and that a physician prescribing a controlled substance for this use thus risked suspension or revocation of his DEA registration. So long as this federal policy was in place, state-level legalization of PAS (a stalled effort in any event) was largely irrelevant. In 2006, however, the US Supreme

Figure 11.1 Activists demonstrate in favor of the Oregon Death with Dignity Act as the US Supreme Court hears arguments in *Gonzalez v. Oregon*, October 5, 2005. © *Charles Dharapak/AP Images.*

Court, in *Gonzales v. Oregon*, revived the possibility of meaningful state action by ruling that the CSA did not authorize the attorney general to prohibit doctors from prescribing controlled substances for PAS use in compliance with state law (Fig. 11.1).[72]

Sputtering Success

In 2008—two years after *Gonzales* and fourteen years after the initial triumph in Oregon—a second state finally legalized physician-assisted suicide. Washington State voters approved a virtual copy of the ODDA by a comfortable 58–42 percent margin. The next year, Montana effectively legalized PAS by judicial decision.[73] Had the country reached a tipping point?

The narrow loss of Massachusetts Question 2 in 2012 suggested that it had not. The defeat of PAS legalization in liberal Massachusetts revealed the issue's curious political dynamics. Although Catholic organizations provided most of the funding for the anti–Question 2 campaign, disability advocates played a greater role than ever in advancing the ground game and shaping the campaign's mostly secular themes. In the months leading up to the election, the media spotlighted the impassioned opposition efforts of "Second Thoughts," a Massachusetts group representing anti-PAS disabled people. John Kelly, Second Thoughts' director, ascribed Question 2's ultimate defeat to the organization's success in preventing the vote from being framed as a purely partisan struggle. "We were able to get enough of a disabled rights perspective so that the archetypal culture war—religious conservatives versus secular Democrats—was not set up." Notably, Second Thoughts endorsed Question 3, the victorious medical marijuana legalization measure that appeared on the very same ballot. The group believed its commitment to "patients' rights" dictated both its antagonism toward Question 2 and its support for Question 3.[74]

Since 2012, seven additional states (Vermont, California, Colorado, Hawaii, New Jersey, Maine, and New Mexico) and the District of Columbia have joined Oregon, Washington, and Montana in legalizing physician-assisted suicide. In contrast to medical marijuana legalization, the states' primary method for taking this step has been legislation, not the ballot initiative.[75] Does this recent spate of PAS-legalization statutes foreshadow a coming wave? Perhaps. In Gallup polling, national support for legalization of PAS (if requested by a terminally ill patient in severe pain) has risen from 51 percent in 2013 to 65 percent in 2018. But an even higher level of support for PAS in 2001 did not translate into widespread legal reform.[76] And PSA-legalization laws continue to fail much more often than they succeed in state legislatures. Indeed, several states have recently enacted or strengthened *bans* on assisted suicide.

Explanations

Overall, since the ODDA went into effect in 1997, states have passed more laws prohibiting physician-assisted suicide than laws allowing it.[77] During essentially the same period, thirty-six states have legalized medical marijuana. Why have Americans, who generally support freedom of therapeutic choice, hesitated to endorse PAS? As I stated at the start of this chapter, the answer certainly lies in the ineluctable difference between health and death. This assertion deserves some unpacking.

Some of the very same distinctive aspects of American culture that have nourished other movements for freedom of therapeutic choice have had the opposite effect with respect to PAS. Take, for example, the country's high level of religiosity. In this book, we have encountered various examples of religious devotion fueling medical liberty movements. By contrast, American religiosity generally generates a powerful impulse *against* freedom of choice with respect to PAS (as well as abortion).

Most modern religions embrace some version of the principle that life is a divine gift that human beings should not destroy. A recent Pew Research Center survey of sixteen major American religious groups regarding end-of-life issues (ten Protestant denominations, Catholicism, Latter-day Saints, Judaism, Islam, Buddhism, and Hinduism) concluded that eleven of these creeds explicitly oppose physician-assisted suicide and three impliedly do so. Only the United Church of Christ and the Unitarian Universalist Association embrace a right to PAS.[78] Of course, many people adhere to a religion while rejecting some of its tenets. But organized religion remains a powerful force in American society, and that force generally resists the legalization of physician-assisted suicide.

The profit motive is another pillar that has bolstered many American medical freedom movements. The United States, more than any other nation, treats health care as a bundle of *commercial* goods and services. Consequently, commercial interests have supported many of the medical freedom movements we have examined. But—to put it bluntly—there is little money to be made from PAS. Its methods are cheap, and once a person is dead, nobody can profit off him or her. Therefore, no health care provider has a monetary motive to lobby for PAS legalization. Indeed, the one commercial entity with an obvious financial stake in the issue—the hospice care industry—reliably campaigns *against* PAS. This is not to suggest that individual hospice professionals are primarily profit-driven—only that financial incentives tend to work against the legalization of PAS, not for it.[79]

Another aspect of American culture that has fueled therapeutic choice activism throughout the country's history, but not in the PAS context, is the country's deep-seated distrust of elites, experts, and establishment institutions. Since the founding of the nation, American advocates of freedom of therapeutic choice have claimed to be battling a shadowy combination of tyrannical government, scientific bureaucracies, and powerful financial interests. This very same conspiratorial mindset has led many Americans to *oppose* the legalization of physician-assisted suicide. PAS foes ominously warn that once this door is opened, the United States—under the control of such forces—will be on the path to embracing *involuntary* euthanasia.

The conservative right-to-life movement advances this argument, but so do constituencies on the political left, including disability activists and African Americans. Fear of a eugenic turn is one of the chief reasons (along with religiosity) that African Americans are dramatically less likely than whites to support PAS legalization. In light of the infamous "Tuskegee Study of Untreated Syphilis in the Negro Male" from the 1930s to the 1970s and of the systematic undertreatment of black patients today, many African Americans understandably fear that PAS will be employed in a discriminatory manner. The Reverend James Perkins, a black minister in Detroit, explained: "There is a sort of paranoia in the back of our minds that, if assisted suicide becomes legal, then lawmakers will somehow find a way to manipulate the law . . . to where African Americans are . . . receiving less medical care and are more often eliminated." His colleague in Boston, the Reverend Eugene Rivers III, has characterized PAS legalization as "back end eugenics" aimed at eliminating poor African Americans.[80]

American health care is extremely expensive and funded by budget-constrained governments and profit-seeking insurance companies. African Americans worry that these entities will promote the use of PAS as a cost-saving measure and will pressure blacks to resort to it more than whites. For their part, many disabled people fear that society will embrace PAS as a cheaper alternative to providing them with the health care and accommodations they require. Elderly and poor Americans disproportionately oppose PAS legalization for similar reasons. In short, many Americans view physician-assisted suicide not as a valuable therapeutic choice, but as a surreptitious method for denying people—especially people in certain categories—medical treatment, palliative care, disability accommodations, and social services. The lack of evidence that these populations use assisted suicide disproportionately in Oregon or Holland has not quieted this argument.[81]

At root, PAS opponents reject the very notion that legalization of this practice enhances medical autonomy. In their view, resort to this measure is rarely a true exercise of "free choice." The Disability Rights Education and Defense Fund (DREDF) website declares: "Legalizing assisted suicide would not increase choice and self-determination, despite the assertions of its proponents. It would actually augment real dangers that negate genuine choice and control." The website goes on to explain how individuals who decide to pursue PAS do so in a web of societal and emotional coercion. In a country without universal health care, universal hospice care, or universal long-term care, suicide may seem like the only practical alternative for some people of limited means. Even those who can afford care might not want to impose a financial or caretaking burden on their families—and self-interested relatives may pressure them not to do so. The DREDF site further argues that because elderly and disabled people internalize society's devaluation of them, they may elect suicide to avoid a supposed "loss of dignity." Moreover, some requests for PAS are made by clinically depressed patients, and doctors may honor these requests instead of treating the underlying mental disorder.[82]

Such considerations explain why PAS opponents believe they are the true defenders of patients' rights. Indeed, one of the leading organizations fighting PAS legalization is called the "Patients Rights Council." The patients' rights movement is mainly about autonomy, and PAS foes essentially reject the notion that people would ever *freely* choose death over life, even in life's waning moments. PAS proponents, with no less passion, assert that their battle for end-of-life choice makes *them* the true champions of the rights of dying patients. Compassion & Choices, the leading advocacy organization for medical aid-in-dying, declares in its mission statement: "We envision a patient-driven system. . . . We are working toward an America that respects everyone's right to make their own end-of-life care decisions, in consultation with doctors and loved ones." Compassion & Choices thus emphasizes the agency, rather than the vulnerability, of dying people, and it vows to protect "our hard-earned rights to autonomy and liberty at life's end." When framed in this way, the PAS legalization campaign is another expression of the values that have defined medical freedom movements throughout American history.[83]

Notes

Introduction

1. Julie Hofler, "Battling for Life," *Cavalier Daily*, April 27, 2001; Steven Ginsberg, "One Life Galvanizes Thousands," *Washington Post*, May 7, 2001; Steven Ginsberg, "'We've Gone from Hopeless to Hope,'" *Washington Post*, June 6, 2001; Steven Ginsberg, "Student Dies after Fight with Drug Firms," *Washington Post*, June 12, 2001; "Cancer-Stricken U.Va. Student Dies," *Richmond Times Dispatch*, June 13, 2001.
2. 21 C.F.R. § 312.21(a).
3. Robert Langreth and Michael Waldholz, "Drug Progress on Hard-to-Treat Cancers Is Cited," *Wall Street Journal*, November 17, 1999; Richard Saltus, "2 New Cancer Fighters Hold Promise in Trials," *Boston Globe*, May 22, 2000; Daniel Q. Haney, "Drug Targets Growth Gene in Cancers; IMC-C225 Shows Potential in Victims of Colon Cancer and Head and Neck Cancer," *Portland Press Herald*, May 22, 2000; F. Robert et al., "Phase I Study of Anti-Epidermal Growth Factor Receptor Antibody Cetuximab in Combination with Radiation Therapy in Patients with Advanced Head and Neck Cancer," *Journal of Clinical Oncology* 19, no. 13 (July 1, 2001): 3234–43, https://doi.org/10.1200/JCO.2001.19.13.3234.
4. Ginsberg, "One Life Galvanizes Thousands."
5. "Letter from Patricia Keegan, CDER-FDA, to Cheryl Anderson, ImClone," March 1, 2006.
6. *Abigail Alliance v. Eschenbach*, 495 F.3d 695 (D.C. Cir. 2007).
7. *Abigail Alliance for Better Access to Developmental Drugs v. von Eschenbach*, 445 F.3d 470, 480, 483 (D.C. Cir. 2006).
8. *Abigail Alliance v. Eschenbach*, 495 F.3d 695 (D.C. Cir. 2007).
9. Larry D. Kramer, *The People Themselves: Popular Constitutionalism and Judicial Review* (New York: Oxford University Press, 2005).
10. Mark Tushnet, *Taking the Constitution Away from the Courts* (Princeton, NJ: Princeton University Press, 1999). Other examples of the literature on popular constitutionalism include William N. Eskridge Jr., "Some Effects of Identity-Based Social Movements on Constitutional Law in the Twentieth Century," *Michigan Law Review* 100 (2002): 2062; Reva B. Siegel, "Constitutional Culture, Social Movement Conflict and Constitutional Change: The Case of the de Facto ERA—2005–06 Brennan Center Symposium Lecture," *California Law Review* 94 (2006): 1323. See also Daniel W. Hamilton, ed., "A Symposium on the People Themselves: Popular Constitutionalism and Judicial Review," *Chicago-Kent Law Review* 81, no. 3 (2006): 809–1182.
11. Judy Foreman, "Unproven Drugs Tempt the Seriously Ill," *Star Tribune*, September 28, 2003.

Chapter 1

1. This chapter is drawn largely from Lewis A. Grossman, "The Origins of American Health Libertarianism," *Yale Journal of Health Policy, Law, and Ethics* 13 (2013): 76–134.

2. See generally Alyn Brodsky, *Benjamin Rush: Patriot and Physician* (New York: Truman Talley Books, 2004); Stephen Fried, *Rush: Revolution, Madness, and Benjamin Rush, the Visionary Doctor Who Became a Founding Father* (New York: Crown, 2018).

3. Fried, *Rush*, 8.

4. Benjamin Rush, "Lecture 6. On the Causes Which Have Retarded the Progress of Medicine, and on the Means of Promoting Its Certainty, and Greater Usefulness," in *Sixteen Introductory Lectures, to the Courses of Lectures upon the Institutes and Practice of Medicine* [. . .] (Philadelphia: Bradford and Inskeep, 1811).

5. Fried, *Rush*, 336, 413.

6. John Harley Warner, *The Therapeutic Perspective* (Princeton, NJ: Princeton University Press, 1997), 85.

7. James C. Whorton, *Nature Cures: The History of Alternative Medicine in America* (New York: Oxford University Press, 2004), 18.

8. Warner, *Therapeutic Perspective*, 91.

9. Warner, *Therapeutic Perspective*, 11.

10. Ron Chernow, *Washington: A Life* (New York: Penguin Press, 2010), 807–9; Jared Sparks, *The Life of George Washington* (Boston: Ferdinand Andrews, 1839), 531–35; Fried, *Rush*, 401.

11. Benjamin Rush, *The Autobiography of Benjamin Rush: His "Travels through Life" Together with His Commonplace Book for 1789–1813*, ed. George W. Corner, new ed. of 1948 ed. (Westport, CT: Greenwood Press, 1970), 361–66 App. 1 ("Rush Medical Theories"); Warner, *Therapeutic Perspective*, 29–31, 36, 98; Edmund D. Pellegrino, "The Sociocultural Impact of Twentieth-Century Therapeutics," in *Therapeutic Revolution: Essays in the Social History of American Medicine*, eds. Charles E. Rosenberg and Morris J. Vogel (Philadelphia: University of Pennsylvania Press, 1979), 247; Charles E. Rosenberg, "The Therapeutic Revolution: Medicine, Meaning, and Social Change in Nineteenth-Century America," in *Therapeutic Revolution: Essays in the Social History of American Medicine*, eds. Charles E. Rosenberg and Morris J. Vogel (Philadelphia: University of Pennsylvania Press, 1979), 19–21.

12. William G. Rothstein, *American Physicians in the Nineteenth Century: From Sects to Science* (Baltimore: Johns Hopkins University Press, 1992), 63–72, 87–100; Paul Starr, *The Social Transformation of American Medicine: The Rise of a Sovereign Profession and the Making of a Vast Industry*, repr. ed. (New York: Basic Books, 1984), 46.

13. See generally Victoria Johnson, *American Eden: David Hosack, Botany, and Medicine in the Garden of the Early Republic* (New York: Liveright, 2018). On Rush, see Johnson, 197; The Benjamin Rush Medicinal Plant Garden, https://collegeofphysicians.org/garden.

14. Starr, *Social Transformation*, 32–37, 47–51; Rothstein, *American Physicians*, 32–34.

15. "The Correspondent, No. XIV," *Connecticut Journal*, March 19, 1773; "Untitled," *New-London Gazette*, October 8, 1773.

16. Richard Harrison Shryock, *Medical Licensing in America, 1650–1965* (Baltimore: Johns Hopkins University Press, 1967), 15. On colonial licensing laws and resistance to them, see Shryock, *Medical Licensing*, 13–19; Starr, *Social Transformation*, 44; James H. Cassedy, *Medicine in America: A Short History* (Baltimore: Johns Hopkins University Press, 1991), 18–19; Rothstein, *American Physicians*, 37–38.

17. Shryock, *Medical Licensing*, 17; Starr, *Social Transformation*, 44; Cassedy, *Medicine in America*, 19.

18. "Untitled Letter," *Essex Gazette*, March 15, 1774.

19. "Untitled," *New-London Gazette*, April 15, 1774.

20. Rothstein, *American Physicians*, 74, 332–39 App. II; Shryock, *Medical Licensing*, 23–27.

21. Shryock, *Medical Licensing*, 76.

22. Rothstein, *American Physicians*, 76; Starr, *Social Transformation*, 44–45.

23. Rothstein, *American Physicians*, 75–77.

24. Rothstein, 327–31 App. I; John S. Haller, *The People's Doctors: Samuel Thomson and the American Botanical Movement, 1790–1860* (Carbondale: Southern Illinois University Press, 2000), 35–36.

25. "Untitled," *Connecticut Courant*, July 31, 1769, 5.

26. "State of Connecticut, In the House of Representatives, May 22," *Connecticut Journal*, June 6, 1787, 3. On the defeat of this measure, see Rothstein, *American Physicians*, 68.

27. Steven G. Calabresi and Larissa C. Leibowitz, "Monopolies and the Constitution: A History of Crony Capitalism," *Harvard Journal of Law & Public Policy* 36, no. 3 (2013): 1003–8.

28. Gordon S. Wood, *The Idea of America: Reflections on the Birth of the United States* (New York: Penguin Books, 2011), 88, 104.

29. Wood, *The Idea of America*, 81–126. On anti-aristocratic sentiments in the Revolutionary generation, see Gordon S. Wood, *The Radicalism of the American Revolution*, repr. ed. (New York: Vintage, 1993), 240–43.

30. "State of Connecticut, In the House of Representatives, May 22." The Society of the Cincinnati was a hereditary fraternal order of army officers, of whom George Washington was the first president. The society was widely scorned as a secretive, elitist, aristocratic institution, and in 1787, George Washington tried, with mixed success, to force reforms on it, including abandonment of its hereditary character. Chernow, *Washington*, 497–500.

31. "Untitled," *Independent Gazetteer*, December 16, 1788, 3.

32. Lance Banning, *The Jeffersonian Persuasion: Evolution of a Party Ideology* (Ithaca, NY: Cornell University Press, 1978), 120–21; Stanley Elkins and Eric McKitrick, *The Age of Federalism: The Early American Republic, 1788–1800* (New York: Oxford University Press, 1995), 459; Rush, *Autobiography*, 58; Fried, *Rush*, 312, 341.

33. Elkins and McKitrick, *Age of Federalism*, 459; Rush, *Autobiography*, 78–79, 88–89.

34. Rush, *Autobiography*, 106; Benjamin Rush, *Duties of a Physician, and the Methods of Improving Medicine Accommodated to the Present State of Society and the Manners of the United States.* [. . .] *Conclusion of a Course of Lectures* [. . .] (Philadelphia: Prichard & Hall, 1789), 10; Rush, *Autobiography*, 88–89 ("science so simple"); Rush, "Lecture VI.," 156 ("mystery or imposture"), 157 ("meanest capacities").

35. Brodsky, *Benjamin Rush*, 91–92; Rush, *Autobiography*, 70, 88, 96, 361–66 App. 1 ("Rush's Medical Theories"); Shryock, *Medical Licensing*, 67–72.

36. Rush, *Autobiography*, 97–98; Elkins and McKitrick, *Age of Federalism*, 823 n. 182; Brodsky, *Benjamin Rush*, 326, 329–32.

37. Brodsky, *Benjamin Rush*, 345.

38. Rush, "Lecture VI.," 151–52.

39. Brodsky, *Benjamin Rush*, 79; Rush, *Autobiography*, 339–40. On the Jeffersonian Republican commitment to the separation of church and state, see Gordon S. Wood, *Empire of Liberty: A History of the Early Republic, 1789–1815*, repr. (New York: Oxford University Press, 2011).

40. Thomas Jefferson, *Thomas Jefferson: Writings: Autobiography/Notes on the State of Virginia/Public and Private Papers/Addresses/Letters* (New York: Library of America, 1984), 285.

41. Shryock, *Medical Licensing*, 16–17; Rothstein, *American Physicians*, 339; Samuel Lee Baker, "Physician Licensure Laws in the United States, 1865–1915," *Journal of the History of Medicine and Allied Sciences* 39, no. 2 (April 1984): 196.

42. Wood, *Empire of Liberty*, 461.

43. Rush, "Lecture VI.," 151.

44. Rush, *Duties of a Physician*, 10.

45. Wood, *Empire of Liberty*, 725–28.

46. Samuel Thomson, *A Narrative of the Life and Medical Discoveries of Samuel Thomson*, 8th ed. (Columbus, OH: Pike, Platt, 1832), 123–24.

47. Thomson, *Narrative of the Life*, 124–25.

48. Samuel Thomson, *New Guide to Health; or Botanic Family Physician* (Boston: J. Q. Adams, 1835).

49. Thomson, *Narrative*, 125–26.

50. Thomas Hersey, "A Lecture on the Comparative Merits of the Patent Steam Practice of Dr. Samuel K. Jennings and Dr. Samuel Thomson," *Thomsonian Recorder* 2, no. 13 (March 29, 1834): 197.

51. R. H. Brumby, "Medical Botanist," *Thomsonian Recorder* 2, no. 23 (August 16, 1834): 368.

52. James Harvey Young, *Toadstool Millionaires: A Social History of Patent Medicines in America before Federal Regulation*, Illustrated (Princeton, NJ: Princeton University Press, 1972), 37.

53. "Proceedings of the Mecklenburg Branch Society: Lecture by M. W. McCraw," *Thomsonian Recorder* 2, no. 26 (September 27, 1834): 406.

54. Samuel Robinson, *A Course of Fifteen Lectures, on Medical Botany* (Columbus, OH: Horton Howard, 1829), 10.

55. An Association of Homeopathic Physicians, ed., *Miscellanies on Homoeopathy* (Philadelphia: W. L. J. Kiderlen, 1839), 159.

56. "Directory of Members (Attachment)," *Journal of the American Osteopathic Association* 6, no. 6 (February 1, 1907): 29.

57. One scholar, while correctly dismissing the Rush quotation about the need for a constitutional amendment as "bogus," mistakenly asserts that Rush was not in

fact a proponent of medical freedom. Thomas Szasz, "A Bogus Benjamin Rush Quote: Contribution to the History of Pharmacy," *History of Psychiatry* 16, no. 1 (March 2005): 89–98.

Chapter 2

1. This chapter is drawn largely from Lewis A. Grossman, "The Origins of American Health Libertarianism," *Yale Journal of Health Policy, Law, and Ethics* 13, no. 1 (2013): 76–134.
2. William G. Rothstein, *American Physicians in the Nineteenth Century: From Sects to Science* (Baltimore: Johns Hopkins University Press, 1992), 75–76, 145–46; John S. Haller Jr., *The People's Doctors: Samuel Thomson and the American Botanical Movement 1790–1860* (Carbondale: Southern Illinois University Press, 2001), 98, 132; "Political," editorial, *Botanico-Medical Recorder* 6, no. 24 (August 25, 1838): 376.
3. Alex Berman, "Neo-Thomsonianism in the United States," *Journal of the History of Medicine and Allied Sciences* 11, no. 2 (April 1, 1956): 133–55.
4. "Political," 376.
5. Haller, *People's Doctors*, 99.
6. Rothstein, *American Physicians*, 332–39; James H. Cassedy, *Medicine in America: A Short History* (Baltimore: Johns Hopkins University Press, 1991), 26; Haller, *People's Doctors*, 200; James C. Whorton, *Nature Cures: The History of Alternative Medicine in America* (New York: Oxford University Press, 2004), 36; Richard Harrison Shryock, *Medical Licensing in America, 1650–1965* (Baltimore: Johns Hopkins Press, 1967), 27.
7. Rothstein, *American Physicians*, 77–78, 332–39.
8. Charles Coventry, "History of Medical Legislation in the State of New York," *New York Journal of Medicine and Collateral Sciences*, March 1845, 160.
9. Lemuel Shattuck, *Report of a General Plan for the Promotion of Public and Personal Health* (Boston: Dutton & Westworth, 1850), 58; John S. Haller Jr., *American Medicine in Transition, 1840–1910* (Urbana: University of Illinois Press, 1981), 201.
10. Samuel Thomson, *New Guide to Health; or Botanic Family Physician* (Boston: J. Q. Adams, 1835), 24–26; Haller, *People's Doctors*, 10–13.
11. Haller, *People's Doctors*, 14–19, 32–43, 143–47.
12. Whorton, *Nature Cures*, 39.
13. Haller, *People's Doctors*, 17–30, 39–40.
14. Whorton, *Nature Cures*, 10–12; Haller, *People's Doctors*, 51.
15. Haller, *People's Doctors*, 67–73, 94–99, 139, 147–59, 170–73, 215; Berman, "Neo-Thomsonianism in the United States."
16. Charles E. Rosenberg, *The Cholera Years: The United States in 1832, 1849, and 1866* (Chicago: University of Chicago Press, 1987), 72. See also Haller, *People's Doctors*, 143; Rothstein, *American Physicians*, 141. On the links between Thomsonianism and Jacksonian Democracy, see Paul Starr, *The Social Transformation of American Medicine: The Rise of a Sovereign Profession and the Making of a Vast Industry*, 2nd

ed. (New York: Basic Books, 2017), 56–57; Haller, *The People's Doctors*, 63; Whorton, *Nature Cures*, 33–35; Shryock, *Medical Licensing*, 31. One author questions the strength of this connection, at least with respect to Connecticut. Toby A. Appel, "The Thomsonian Movement, the Regular Profession, and the State in Antebellum Connecticut: A Case Study of the Repeal of Early Medical Licensing Laws," *Journal of the History of Medicine and Allied Sciences* 65, no. 2 (2010): 153–86.

17. Daniel Walker Howe, *What Hath God Wrought: The Transformation of America, 1815–1848* (New York: Oxford University Press, 2007), 505; William J. Novak, *The People's Welfare: Law and Regulation in Nineteenth-Century America* (Chapel Hill: University of North Carolina Press, 1996), 43. For a discussion of the "republican theory and practice" that bridged the Jeffersonian and Jacksonian political cultures, see Harry L. Watson, *Liberty and Power: The Politics of Jacksonian America*, rev. ed. (New York: Hill & Wang, 2006), 42–72. Marvin Meyers, *The Jacksonian Persuasion: Politics and Belief* (New York: Vintage Books, 1960), 12; Watson, *Liberty and Power*, 42–72, 167; Meyers, *Jacksonian Persuasion*, 12, 194–95.

18. Arthur Meier Schlesinger Jr., *The Age of Jackson* (Boston: Little, Brown, 1953), 137–40, 352–56; Watson, *Liberty and Power*, 242, 245; Howe, *What Hath God Wrought*, 583. On Catholic support, see Howe, *What Hath God Wrought*.

19. Howe, *What Hath God Wrought*, 583; John L. O'Sullivan, "The Great Nation of Futurity," *The United States Democratic Review*, November 1839, 430.

20. Caleb Nelson, "Re-Evaluation of Scholarly Explanations for the Rise of the Elective Judiciary in Antebellum America," *American Journal of Legal History* 37, no. 2 (April 1993): 191; Jed Handelsman Shugerman, "Economic Crisis and the Rise of Judicial Elections and Judicial Review," *Harvard Law Review* 123, no. 5 (March 2010): 1061–1150; Mark A. Graber, "Resolving Political Questions into Judicial Questions: Tocqueville's Thesis Revisited," *Constitutional Commentary* 21, no. 2 (Summer 2004): 529–30.

21. Larry D. Kramer, *The People Themselves: Popular Constitutionalism and Judicial Review* (New York: Oxford University Press, 2004), 25, 167–68; Keith E. Whittington, "Give the People What They Want," *Chicago-Kent Law Review* 81, no. 3 (2006): 918.

22. Andrew Shulze, "To the Assembly Vetoing 'An Act to Regulate the Practice of Physics and Surgery within This Commonwealth' (Dec. 8, 1824)," in *Pennsylvania Archives, Vol. 5: Papers of the Governors, 1817–1832*, ed. George Edward Reed (London: Forgotten Books, 2019), 542.

23. John W. Comfort, *The Practice of Medicine on Thomsonian Principles* [. . .] *Containing a Biographical Sketch of Dr. Thomson* [. . .] *with Practical Directions for Administering the Thomsonian Medicines* (Philadelphia: A. Comfort, 1850), xxxv–xxxvi; Samuel Waterhouse, "Copy of a Letter from Dr. Benjamin Waterhouse, Formerly Lecturer on the Theory and Practice of Physic, in Cambridge University, to the Late Samuel L. Mitchell, of New-York," *Thomsonian Recorder* 1, no. 5 (December 1, 1832): 104.

24. Honestus [pseud.]. "An Essay in Relation to the Unconstitutionality, Injustice, and Injurious Effects, Resulting from Our Present Aristocratical Medical Law in the State of Ohio," *Thomsonian Recorder*, no. 6 (December 15, 1832): 124, 130–31.

25. The petition to be presented at the Ohio legislature is reproduced in *Thomsonian Recorder* 1, no. 1 (September 15, 1832): 24.

26. The preamble and resolutions of the Society, adopted on April 7, 1834, are reproduced in "Meeting," *Botanic Watchman* 1, no. 4 (April 1, 1834): 57.

27. "Declaration of Independence," *Thomsonian Recorder* 5, no. 21 (July 15, 1837): 326.

28. "Declaration of Independence," 329.

29. Honestus, "Essay," 130; "Declaration of Independence," 329; Rothstein, *American Physicians*, 145.

30. "Meeting," 243; "Petition to the Hon. The Legislature of the State of New Jersey," *Reformed Medical Journal* 1, no. 2 (February 15, 1832): 1.

31. Michael Les Benedict, "Laissez-Faire and Liberty: A Re-Evaluation of the Meaning and Origins of Laissez-Faire Constitutionalism," *Law and History Review* 3, no. 2 (October 1, 1985): 314–26; Haller, *American Medicine*, 138; Honestus, "Essay," 124.

32. "The Die Is Cast," *Thomsonian Recorder* 2, no. 16 (May 10, 1834): 241.

33. Meyers, *The Jacksonian Persuasion*, 10.

34. "Speech of Mr. Smart," *Botanico-Medical Recorder* 8, no. 17 (May 16, 1840): 271.

35. "The Cause in New York," *Botanico-Medical Recorder* 9, no. 16 (May 1, 1841): 248–49.

36. Benedict, "Laissez-Faire and Liberty," 321–23; *Calder v. Bull*, 3 U.S. 386, 388 (1798) (Chase, J.).

37. Honestus, "Essay," 131; "Declaration of Independence," 327; "Memorial," *Botanic Watchman* 1, no. 6 (June 1, 1831): 82.

38. "The Medical Pension Bill," *Botanic Watchman* 1, no. 4 (April 1, 1834): 57.

39. Coventry, "History of Medical Legislation," 160.

40. Honestus, "Essay," 123.

41. Honestus, "Essay," 123.

42. Whorton, *Nature Cures*, 40; "Legislature of Georgia. Equal Rights," *Thomsonian Recorder* 5, no. 9 (January 28, 1837): 137.

43. "Maryland Legislature," *Thomsonian Recorder* 2, no. 12 (March 15, 1834): 188.

44. Thomson, *New Guide to Health*, 8–10. Although the preface is written "By a Friend," Haller ascribes it to Thomson himself. Haller, *People's Doctors*, 50.

45. Haller, *People's Doctors*, 163–67, 180 ("mongrelism"), 201–2, 252; "Medical Organizations," *Thomsonian Recorder* 5, no. 15 (April 22, 1837): 236.

46. Honestus, "Essay," 130–31.

47. Michael W. McConnell, "The Origins and Historical Understanding of Free Exercise of Religion," *Harvard Law Review* 103, no. 7 (May 1990): 1493.

48. B. W. S., "A Second Voice from New York," *Thomsonian Recorder* 2, no. 16 (May 10, 1834): 252; Honestus, "Essay," 123.

49. Honestus, "Essay," 123; Editorial Department, *Thomsonian Recorder* 2, no. 16 (May 10, 1834): 246; Thomson, *New Guide to Health*, 5.

50. Robert C. Fuller, *Alternative Medicine and American Religious Life* (New York: Oxford University Press, 1989), 36; "To Our Patrons," *Thomsonian Recorder* 1, no. 1 (September 15, 1832): 1.

51. "Petition to the Hon. The Legislature of the State of New Jersey," 1.

52. *Cantwell v. Connecticut*, 310 U.S. 296 (1940); "The Governor's Veto," *Arkansas Gazette*, November 9, 1831, 1.

53. *Laws of the State of New York, Passed at the Second Meeting of the 50th Session of the Legislature* (Albany: E. Croswell, 1827), chap. 185; Haller, *The People's Doctors*, 134–35; Rothstein, *American Physicians*, 338; *Laws of the State of New York, Passed at the 53rd Session of the Legislature* (Albany: Wm. Gould and Co., 1830), chap. 126, § 2; *Laws of the State of New York, Passed at the 57th Session of the Legislature* (Albany: E. Croswell, 1834), chap. 68, § 2.

54. "The Botanic State Convention," *Botanic Watchman* 1, no. 10 (October 1, 1834): 145.

55. "Proceedings of the Botanic State Convention," *Thomsonian Recorder* 3, no. 2 (October 25, 1834): 18.

56. "Proceedings of the Botanic State Convention," 20; Editorial Department, *Thomsonian Recorder* 3, no. 10 (February 14, 1835): 160; Editorial Department, *Thomsonian Recorder* 3, no. 16 (May 9, 1835): 253; Haller, *The People's Doctors*, 137–38; Whorton, *Nature Cures*, 36; James Harvey Young, *Toadstool Millionaires: A Social History of Patent Medicines in America before Federal Regulation*, Illustrated (Princeton, NJ: Princeton University Press, 1972), 55; *Laws of the State of New York, Passed at the Second Meeting of the 67th Session of the Legislature*, chap. 275, § 3.

57. "Proceedings of the Botanic State Convention," 18–19.

58. "Proceedings of the Botanic State Convention," 18.

59. "Proceedings of the Botanic State Convention," 19–20.

60. "Proceedings of the Botanic State Convention," 19–20.

61. "Proceedings of the Botanic State Convention," 19. Legislative committee quoted in Rothstein, *American Physicians*, 241, 243–44, 265, 268.

62. "Proceedings of the Botanic State Convention," 19–20.

63. Berman, "Neo-Thomsonianism in the United States," 135. See also Berman, 139–42; Haller, *The People's Doctors*, 180, 184–46.

64. See William G. Rothstein, "The Botanical Movements and Orthodox Medicine," in *Other Healers: Unorthodox Medicine in America*, ed. Norman Gevitz (Baltimore: Johns Hopkins University Press, 1988), 29, 47–50; James C. Whorton, "From Cultism to CAM: Alternative Medicine in the Twentieth Century," in *The Politics of Healing: Histories of Alternative Medicine in Twentieth-Century North America*, ed. Robert D. Johnston (New York: Routledge, 2004), 287–88; William G. Rothstein, "Botanical Movements," 47–50; Whorton, "From Cultism to CAM," 288.

Chapter 3

1. William James, "The Medical Registration Act," letter to the editor, *Boston Evening Transcript*, March 24, 1894.

2. James introduced the name "pragmatism" to the world in an August 1898 talk, but in that address, he attributed its coinage to Charles S. Peirce in the early 1870s. Louis Menand, *The Metaphysical Club: A Story of Ideas in America* (New York: Farrar,

Straus & Giroux, 2002), 350. On James's audience, see George Cotkin, *William James, Public Philosopher* (Urbana: University of Illinois Press, 1994), 11–13. For a complete list of James's Harvard courses, see http://www.uky.edu/~eushe2/Pajares/JamesTeachingSchedule.html.

3. *Acts and Resolves Passed by the General Court of Massachusetts* (Boston: Wright & Potter Printing, 1894), chap. 458, §11. For a discussion of James's role in the 1894 debate, see John T. Matteson, "'Their Facts Are Patent and Startling': WJ and Mental Healing (Part One)," *Streams of William James* 4, no. 1 (2002): 5–6. *The Medical Question. The Great Contest of 1898: Addresses before the Committee on Public Health* (Boston: Banner of Light Printing, 1898).

4. *Addresses before the Committee on Public Health*, 31.

5. James H. Cassedy, *Medicine in America: A Short History* (Baltimore: Johns Hopkins University Press, 1991), 24; John Harley Warner, *The Therapeutic Perspective* (Princeton, NJ: Princeton University Press, 1997), 24, 185–96; John S. Haller Jr., *American Medicine in Transition, 1840–1910* (Urbana: University of Illinois Press, 1981), 79–80.

6. On therapeutic skepticism and its effects on actual practice, see Warner, *The Therapeutic Perspective*, 83–161; Charles E. Rosenberg, "The Therapeutic Revolution: Medicine, Meaning, and Social Change in Nineteenth-Century America," in *Therapeutic Revolution: Essays in the Social History of American Medicine* (Philadelphia: University of Pennsylvania Press, 1979), 17–19; Edmund D. Pellegrino, "The Sociocultural Impact of Twentieth-Century Therapeutics," in *Therapeutic Revolution: Essays in the Social History of American Medicine*, ed. Morris J. Vogel and Charles E. Rosenberg (Philadelphia: University of Pennsylvania Press, 1979), 247.

7. On the germ theory in America, see Russell C. Maulitz, "Physician versus Bacteriologist: The Ideology of Science in Clinical Medicine," in *Therapeutic Revolution: Essays in the Social History of American Medicine* (Philadelphia: University of Pennsylvania Press, 1979), 91–98; Cassedy, *Medicine in America*, 77–78, 84; Haller, *American Medicine in Transition, 1840–1910*, 216–17; William G. Rothstein, *American Physicians in the Nineteenth Century: From Sects to Science* (Baltimore: Johns Hopkins University Press, 1992), 253–59. On professional authority, see Warner, *The Therapeutic Perspective*.

8. Sherman M. Mellinkoff, "Chemical Intervention." *Scientific American*, September 1973, 103.

9. A 1900 national medical directory listed 104,094 regular physicians, 10,944 homeopaths, and 4,752 eclectics and others. William G. Rothstein, "The Botanical Movements and Orthodox Medicine," in *Other Healers*, ed. Norman Gevitz (Baltimore: Johns Hopkins University Press, 1988), 50. On the social status of homeopathy followers, see Martin Kaufman, *Homeopathy in America: The Rise and Fall of a Medical Heresy* (Baltimore: Johns Hopkins Press, 1971), 145; Paul Starr, *The Social Transformation of American Medicine: The Rise of a Sovereign Profession and the Making of a Vast Industry* (New York: Basic Books, 2017), 99.

10. Kaufman, *Homeopathy in America*, 99–107; James C. Whorton, *Nature Cures: The History of Alternative Medicine in America* (New York: Oxford University Press, 2004), 49–75.

11. Rothstein, "Botanical Movements," 47–51; John S. Haller Jr., *The People's Doctors: Samuel Thomson and the American Botanical Movement, 1790–1860* (Carbondale: Southern Illinois University Press, 2000), 241–48.

12. Rothstein, "Botanical Movements," 50; Kaufman, *Homeopathy in America*, 141–55.

13. Whorton, *Nature Cures*, 108–12.

14. Whorton, 103–15; Robert C. Fuller, *Alternative Medicine and American Religious Life* (New York: Oxford University Press, 1989), 40–53. On Quimby, see Robert C. Fuller, *Alternative Medicine and American Religious Life* (New York: Oxford University Press, 1989), 40–53; Whorton, *Nature Cures*, 115–19. On Eddy and Christian Science, see Rennie B. Schoepflin, *Christian Science on Trial: Religious Healing in America* (Baltimore: Johns Hopkins University Press, 2002), 55–72. On New Thought, see Fuller, *Alternative Medicine and American Religious Life*, 61–63.

15. Benjamin Orange Flower, "Restrictive Medical Legislation and the Public Weal," *Arena* 19, no. 103 (June 1898): 789–90. For the testimony of Reverend Benjamin Fay Mills, see *Addresses before the Committee on Public Health*, 13.

16. Derived from data in Samuel Lee Baker, "Physician Licensure Laws in the United States, 1865–1915," *Journal of the History of Medicine and Allied Sciences* 39, no. 2 (April 1984): 174–76; Samuel Lee Baker, "Medical Licensing in America: An Early Liberal Reform" (PhD diss., Harvard University, 1977), 54; Starr, *Social Transformation*, 104.

17. Baker, "Physician Licensure Laws," 178; Starr, *Social Transformation*, 104; Haller, *People's Doctors*, 223; "Medical Practice Laws," *American Medical Association Bulletin* 3, no. 2 (November 15, 1907): 34–106.

18. "A Conversation with Alexander Wilder, M.D., F.A.S. on Medical Freedom," *Arena* 26, no. 6 (December 1901): 641. On the AMA's influence, see James C. Mohr, *Licensed to Practice: The Supreme Court Defines the American Medical Profession* (Baltimore: Johns Hopkins University Press, 2013); Rothstein, *American Physicians*, 114–21, 200–201; Starr, *Social Transformation*, 90–91, 109; Whorton, *Nature Cures*, 135; Richard Harrison Shryock, *Medical Licensing in America, 1650–1965* (Baltimore: Johns Hopkins University Press, 1967), 44; Baker, "Medical Licensing in America," S4–5; Mohr, *Licensed to Practice*, 157–58.

19. Mohr, 25–79; Baker, "Medical Licensing in America," 78; Dorothy Ross, *The Origins of American Social Science* (New York: Cambridge University Press, 1992), 62; Thomas L. Haskell, *The Emergence of Professional Social Science: The American Social Science Association and the Nineteenth-Century Crisis of Authority* (Baltimore: Johns Hopkins University Press, 2000), xx, 5–6, 12; Baker, "Medical Licensing in America," 78, 118.

20. Reginald H. Fitz, "The Legislative Control of Medical Practice," *Boston Medical and Surgical Journal* 130, no. 24 (June 14, 1894): 581–85.

21. "Shall the Practice of Medicine Be Regulated?," editorial, *New England Medical Gazette* 15, no. 3 (March 1880): 65–70; Baker, "Medical Licensing in America," 101–3, 158–60, 203–4.

22. *The Code of Virginia: With the Declaration of Independence and the Constitution of the United States; and the Constitution of Virginia* (Richmond: James E. Goode, 1887), chap. 77, § 1747; *General Laws of the State of Rhode Island and Providence*

Plantations to Which Are Prefixed the Constitutions of the United States and of the State, (Providence: E. L. Freeman & Son, 1896), chap. 165, § 6; Tex. Const. of 1876, Art. XVI, § 31.

23. "Medical Practice Laws," 44–46.

24. "Conversation with Alexander Wilder," 640; Starr, *Social Transformation*, 102, 107; *Code of Ethics of the American Medical Association, Adopted May* 1847 (Philadelphia: T. K. & P. G. Collins, 1848), chap. II, art. IV, § 1.

25. "Medical Practice Laws," 74.

26. *Laws of the State of New York Passed at the Ninety-Seventh Session of the Legislature* (Albany: Hugh J. Hastings, 1874), chap. 436, § 1.

27. "The State and Quackery," editorial, *New York Times*, February 13, 1885; William Archer Purrington, *A Review of Recent Legal Decisions Affecting Physicians, Dentists, Druggists, and the Public Health* (New York: E. B. Treat, 1899), 16. On these developments, see *Transactions of the Medical Society of the State of New York* (Philadelphia: Dornan, 1889), 15–16, 23–24.

28. *Transactions of the Medical Society* (1890), 27–28; "Medical Examinations," editorial, *New York Times*, March 21, 1890.

29. *Transactions of the Medical Society*, 27; *The General Statutes of the State of New York for the Year 1890* (Albany, NY: Weed, Parsons, 1890), chap. 507, §§ 1–5.

30. Starr, *Social Transformation*, 107.

31. Clifford P. Smith, *Christian Science: Its Legal Status: A Defense of Human Rights* (Boston: Christian Science Publishing Society, 1914), 30.

32. The circular is reproduced in "Mr. Gross' Closing Argument in Favor of the Bill," in *Proceedings of the Connecticut Medical Society 1893* (Bridgeport: Connecticut Medical Society, 1893), 289. On the NCCL, see Benjamin Orange Flower, *Progressive Men, Women, and Movements of the Past Twenty-Five Years* (Boston: New Arena, 1914), 314; "Doctors and 'Doctors,'" *Hartford Courant*, March 9, 1893, 2.

33. "Doctors and 'Doctors,'" 2; NCLL advertisement is reproduced in "Mr. Gross' Closing Argument," 288.

34. "The Medical Practice Bill," *New York Times*, April 1, 1893, 10.

35. *Special Acts and Resolutions of the General Assembly of the State of Connecticut at the January Session, 1893* (Hartford: Press of the Case, Lockwood & Brainard, 1893), chap. 158, § 1.

36. *Acts and Resolves Passed by the General Court of Massachusetts* (Boston: Wright & Potter Printing, 1894), chap. 459, §§ 10–11; Matteson, "Their Facts Are Patent and Startling," 5–6; *Laws of the State of New Hampshire, Passed January Session, 1897* (Manchester: Arthur E. Clarke, 1897), chap. 63, § 11; *Acts and Resolves of the Seventieth Legislature of the State of Maine 1901* (Augusta: Kennebec Journal Print, 1901), chap. 275, § 8.

37. "Medical Practice Laws," 102; Smith, *Christian Science: Its Legal Status*, 59–64; Clifford P. Smith, "Christian Science and Legislation," *Christian Science Journal* 23, no. 7 (October 1905): 407–12; Schoepflin, *Christian Science on Trial*, 72–75, 164, 212–18.

38. Baker, "Physician Licensure Laws," 183. For the 1899 treatise, see Purrington, *Legal Decisions Affecting Physicians*, 86.

39. Schoepflin, *Christian Science on Trial*, 146, App.

40. *General Laws of the State of Texas Passed at the Session of the Fifteenth Legislature* (Austin: Shaw & Blaylock, 1876), chap. 231, § 5.

41. Richard L. Abel, *American Lawyers* (New York: Oxford University Press, 1989), 40–43, 63; Lawrence M. Friedman, *A History of American Law*, rev. ed. (New York: Touchstone, 1986), 606–7, 649, 654; *Dent v. West Virginia*, 129 U.S. 114 (1889).

42. The background of this case is related in detail in Mohr, *Licensed to Practice*.

43. Argument in Behalf of Plaintiff in Error at 4, *Dent v. West Virginia*, 129 U.S. 114 (1889) (No. 390).

44. *Yick Wo v. Hopkins*, 118 U.S. 356, 370 (1886); *Slaughterhouse Cases*, 83 U.S. 36, 105, 110 (1873) (Field, J., dissenting). In *Slaughterhouse*, Field rooted this right in the privileges and immunities clause of the Fourteenth Amendment. In his majority opinions in the "Test Oath Cases": *Cummings v. Missouri*, 71 U.S. 277 (1866) and *Ex parte Garland*, 71 U.S. 333 (1866), Field identified such a right when applying the ex post facto clause of Art. 1, § 10.

45. Charles W. McCurdy, "Justice Field and the Jurisprudence of Government-Business Relations: Some Parameters of Laissez-Faire Constitutionalism, 1863–1897," in *American Law and the Constitutional Order: Historical Perspectives*, ed. Lawrence M. Friedman and Harry N. Scheiber (Cambridge, MA: Harvard University Press, 1978), 248–51.

46. *Dent*, 129 U.S. at 121–22.

47. *Dent*, 129 U.S. at 122–23.

48. See cases cited in Purrington, *Legal Decisions Affecting Physicians*, 75–76; *People v. Phippin*, 37 N.W. 888, 898–903 (Mich. 1888).

49. Mohr, *Licensed to Practice*, 59, 67, 73, 87; *Dent*, 129 U.S. at 115 (emphasis mine).

50. Mohr, 101–2. A list of former Cincinnati Medical Schools and Colleges is available on the website of the University of Cincinnati Libraries, Archival and Rare Books Library: https://libraries.uc.edu/libraries/arb/collections/university-archives/former. Rothstein, *American Physicians*, 225–26.

51. Carl Brent Swisher, *Stephen J. Field: Craftsman of the Law* (1930; repr. ed. Hamden, CT: Archon Books, 1963), 21; *Biographical Notice of Stephen J. Field* (printed for private use, 1892), 8–9.

52. *Ohio v. Marble*, 73 N.E. 1063, 1067 (Ohio 1905); *Parks v. State*, 64 N.E. 862 (Ind. 1902); *State v. Heath*, 101 N.W. 429 (Iowa 1904).

53. "Medical Practice Laws," 109.

54. *State v. Buswell*, 58 N.W. 728, 732 (Neb. 1894).

55. *State v. Mylod*, 40 A. 753, 755–56 (R.I. 1898); Schoepflin, *Christian Science on Trial*, 54; *People v. Cole* 113 N.E. 790 (N.Y. 1916).

56. *Bennett v. Ware*, 61 S.E. 546, 549 (Ga. Ct. App. 1908); *State v. Biggs*, 46 S.E. 401, 403 (N.C. 1903).

57. "Speech of Dr. G. L. Porter," in *Proceedings of the Connecticut Medical Society, 1893* (Bridgeport: Connecticut Medical Society, 1893), 274; Flower, "Restrictive Medical Legislation," 808.

58. Mark Tushnet, *Taking the Constitution Away from the Courts* (Princeton, NJ: Princeton University Press, 1999), 9–14.

59. Henry Wood, "Medical Slavery through Legislation," *Arena* 8, no. 48 (November 1893): 680–81; A. A. Chevaillier, "Constitutional Liberty," *Arena* 1, no. 4 (March 1890), 432.

60. *Boston Transcript*, quoted in Septimus J. Hannah, "Editor's Table," *Christian Science Journal* 16, no. 1 (April 1898): 70; J. W. Lockhart, "Socialistic Medical Legislation," *Medical Brief: A Monthly Journal of Scientific Medicine and Surgery* 28, no. 7 (July 1900): 1012.

61. R. C. Bayly, *The Legal Status of Doctors Everywhere under the Flag and State Recognition of the Supremacy of National Law and Legal Courtesy to Physicians of Other States— Fraudulent Practice Acts* (Decatur, IL: Lesson Leaf Publishing, 1900), xiii, 50–52, 54, 62, 97, 112, 120–22, 125, 129–30, 132. This book is largely a compilation of articles that Bayly published in Volume 28 (1900) of *Medical Brief: A Monthly Journal of Scientific Medicine and Surgery*.

62. F. E. R., "The Medical Bill. A Woman Who Objects—She Suggests a Sensible Addition," letter to the editor, *Hartford Courant*, April 5, 1893; "Conversation with Alexander Wilder," 634.

63. "Conversation with Alexander Wilder," 632; Packard, "Christian Science and the Constitution," 348; James, "Medical Registration Act."

64. Packard, "Christian Science and the Constitution," 348; *Addresses before the Committee on Public Health*, 9; James B. Stewart, "How Broccoli Landed on Supreme Court Menu," *New York Times*, June 13, 2012.

65. James, "Medical Registration Act," 233 (emphasis added); Brief for New Women Lawyers et at., as Amici Curiae, *Roe v. Wade*, 410 U.S. 113 (1973) (No. 70-18 & 70-40). While finding a right to obtain an abortion, the Court explicitly rejected the assertion that "one has an *unlimited* right to do with one's body as one pleases." 410 U.S. at 152–53 (emphasis added).

66. Howard Gillman, *The Constitution Besieged: The Rise & Demise of Lochner Era Police Powers Jurisprudence* (Durham, NC: Duke University Press, 1992); Michael Les Benedict, "Laissez-Faire and Liberty: A Re-Evaluation of the Meaning and Origins of Laissez-Faire Constitutionalism," *Law and History Review* 3, no. 2 (October 1, 1985): 293–331; Lewis A. Grossman, "James Coolidge Carter and Mugwump Jurisprudence," *Law and History Review* 20, no. 3 (October 1, 2002): 577–629.

67. "Conversation with Alexander Wilder," 632, 636.

68. Bayly, *Legal Status of Doctors*, v, 65.

69. McCurdy, "Justice Field," 259–61; *Addresses before the Committee on Public Health*, 16; Lockhart, "Socialistic Medical Legislation," 1012–13.

70. *Lochner vs. New York*, 198 U.S. 45, 64 (1905). The opinion did not specify what "other motives" were at play in this case. Scholars disagree on what the justices thought these motives were. Compare David E. Bernstein, *Rehabilitating Lochner: Defending Individual Rights against Progressive Reform* (Chicago: University of Chicago Press, 2011), 23–39 to Paul Kens, review of *Rehabilitating Lochner: Defending Individual*

Rights against Progressive Reform, by David E. Bernstein H-Law, H-Net Reviews, June, 2013.

71. Packard, "Christian Science and the Constitution," 350; "Conversation with Alexander Wilder," 636; Bayly, *Legal Status of Doctors*, 72; Smith, *Christian Science: Its Legal Status*, 42; Packard, "Christian Science and the Constitution," 350.

72. Benedict, "Laissez-Faire and Liberty"; Bayly, *Legal Status of Doctors*, 77; Alexander Wilder, "Medical Liberty," *Mind*, July 1898, 197.

73. Grossman, "James Coolidge Carter and Mugwump Jurisprudence."

74. Fuller, *Alternative Medicine*, 53; Sydney E. Ahlstrom, *A Religious History of the American People*, 2nd ed. (New Haven, CT: Yale University Press, 2004), 1019; Kaufman, *Homeopathy in America*, 25–26; Fuller, *Alternative Medicine*, 55; Whorton, *Nature Cures*.

75. *Addresses before the Committee on Public Health*, 25.

76. *Addresses before the Committee on Public Health*, 41–42.

77. Packard, "Christian Science and the Constitution," 347.

78. Bayly, *Legal Status of Doctors*, 64–65; Flower, "Restrictive Medical Legislation," 808; Lockhart, "Socialistic Medical Legislation;" "Doctors and 'Doctors,'" 2.

79. Ahlstrom, *Religious History*, 483–90, 1019–22, 1038–42; Fuller, *Alternative Medicine*, 38–65.

80. Schoepflin, *Christian Science on Trial*, 148–49.

81. Packard, "Christian Science and the Constitution," 342, 348–49; Smith, "Christian Science and Legislation," 406, 410. See also Schoepflin, *Christian Science on Trial*, 156.

82. Schoepflin, *Christian Science on Trial*, 156; John Mickey is quoted in Smith, *Christian Science: Its Legal Status*, 59; Margery Fox, "Conflict to Coexistence: Christian Science and Medicine," *Medical Anthropology* 8, no. 4 (1984): 296.

83. *Addresses before the Committee on Public Health*, 17–25. James's testimony is also reproduced at 48 Cong. Rec. S5532–33 (1912).

84. William James, *The Varieties of Religious Experience* (New York: Touchstone, 2004), 57–91.

85. *Addresses before the Committee on Public Health*; "Christian Science Protests," *New York Times*, March 5, 1898; Matteson, "Their Facts Are Patent and Startling," 5–6.

86. Flower, "Restrictive Medical Legislation," 808; "Conversation with Alexander Wilder," 637.

87. Benjamin Orange Flower, "Governor Thomas's Notable Veto of the Medical Trust Bill," editorial, *The Coming Age: A Magazine of Constructive Thought* 2, no. 2 (August 1899).

88. Smith, "Christian Science and Legislation," 411; James, "Medical Registration Act."

89. Herbert Spencer, *Social Statics: or, The Conditions Essential to Human Happiness Specified, and the First of Them Developed* (London: John Chapman, 1851), 103, 372–95. In 1894, Fitz stated: "Herbert Spencer is usually quoted as the leading exponent of [the anti-licensing] view." Fitz, "The Legislative Control of Medical Practice," 280. *Addresses before the Committee on Public Health*, 37. Horton and Garrison also paraphrased Spencer's first principle in this hearing. Fitz, *Legislative Control*, 5, 15.

90. Spencer, *Social Statics*, 378; "Conversation with Alexander Wilder," 636; Wood, "Medical Slavery through Legislation," 681. For other examples of statements linking

medical freedom to the general freedom of choice necessary in a democratic system, see Bayly, *Legal Status of Doctors*, 65–66, 68; Packard, "Christian Science and the Constitution," 343.

91. Michael Willrich, *Pox: An American History* (New York: Penguin, 2011), 252–53. David Rabban labels this tradition "libertarian radicalism." David M. Rabban, *Free Speech in Its Forgotten Years, 1870–1920* (New York: Cambridge University Press, 1999), 23–76. Mark Elliott calls a similar cluster of ideas "radical individualism." Mark Elliott, *Color Blind Justice: Albion Tourgée and the Quest for Racial Equality from the Civil War to "Plessy v. Ferguson"* (New York: Oxford University Press, 2008), 7–9, 314–16; Rabban, *Free Speech*, 23–24.

92. Allen J. Matusow, "The Mind of B. O. Flower," *New England Quarterly* 34, no. 4 (December 1961): 492–94.

93. Flower, *Progressive Men, Women, and Movements*, 290.

94. Roy P. Fairfield, "Benjamin Orange Flower: Father of the Muckrakers," *American Literature* 22, no. 3 (November 1950): 276–77.

95. Matusow, "The Mind of B. O. Flower," 495.

96. Harriet Hyman Alonso, *Growing Up Abolitionist: The Story of the Garrison Children* (Amherst: University of Massachusetts Press, 2002), 283, 286–92; Marion Hohenstein, "William Lloyd Garrison II, the Universal Reformer in the Gilded Age" (master's thesis, Smith College, 1954), 37–51, 71–72, 92–94. Garrison's wife, Ellen Wright, came from a family similarly committed to social reform. Ellen was the niece of Lucretia Mott, the celebrated advocate for abolition and women's rights. William Lloyd Garrison II (speech, New England Free Trade League, 1895), quoted in Hohenstein, "Universal Reformer," 88.

97. Matusow, "The Mind of B. O. Flower," 500–7; Fairfield, "Benjamin Orange Flower," 275, 278; Alonso, *Growing Up Abolitionist*, 286–87; Hohenstein, "Universal Reformer," 86–90, 95; Stephen J. Leonard, "Swimming against the Current: A Biography of Charles S. Thomas, Senator and Governor," *Colorado Heritage*, (Autumn 1994): 31; Darcy Richardson, *Others: Fighting Bob La Follette and the Progressive Movement: Third-Party Politics in the 1920s* (Lincoln, NE: iUniverse, 2008), 133–38.

Chapter 4

1. Amended Bill of Complaint at 7, *American School of Medical Healing v. McAnnulty*, 187 U.S. 94 (1902) (No. 146).

2. Harold Walter Eickhoff, "The Organization and Regulation of Medicine in Missouri, 1883–1901" (PhD diss., University of Missouri, 1965), 225–26.

3. Amended Bill of Complaint, 10.

4. "Fighting Fraud Order: 'Magnetic Healers' Appear before Post-Office Authorities," *Washington Post*, May 13, 1900, 3.

5. Amended Bill of Complaint, 11; Pub. L. No. 51-908, §§ 2–3, 26 Stat. 466 (1890); Pub. L. No. 53-191, § 4, 28 Stat. 964 (1895).

6. The details of Weltmer's biography are derived from Ferriss Clay Bailey, "'Preachers without Pulpits': New Thought and the Rise of Therapeutic Self-Help in Progressive America" (PhD diss., Vanderbilt University, 1999), chap. 4; Eickhoff, "Medicine in Missouri," chap. 10; Patrick Brophy, "Weltmer, Stanhope, and the Rest: Magnetic Healing in Nevada, Missouri," *Missouri Historical Review* 91, no. 3 (April 1997): 275–94; *History of Cole, Moniteau, Morgan, Benton, Miller, Maries and Osage Counties, Missouri* (Chicago: Goodspeed Publishing, 1889).

7. Eickhoff, "Medicine in Missouri," 226–27; Brophy, "Weltmer, Stanhope, and the Rest," 287, 292.

8. Sidney A. Weltmer, *The Mystery Revealed or the Hand-Book of Weltmerism* (Kansas City, MO: Hudson-Kimberly Publishing, 1901), 58.

9. *Longan v. Weltmer*, 79 S.W. 655 (Mo. 1904); Eickhoff, "Medicine in Missouri," 241–51; Weltmer, *Mystery Revealed*, chap. 14.

10. *Weltmer v. Bishop*, 71 S.W. 167 (Mo. 1902); Eickhoff, "Medicine in Missouri," 219, 229ff.

11. *American School of Magnetic Healing v. McAnnulty*, 187 U.S. 94 (1902); "Weltmerism Again," *Journal of the American Medical Association* 39, no. 22 (November 29, 1902): 1396.

12. *Magnetic Healing*, 187 U.S. at 104 (emphasis added).

13. *Magnetic Healing*, 187 U.S. at 37–38.

14. *Lochner v. New York*, 198 U.S. 45 (1905); James W. Ely Jr., "Rufus W. Peckham and Economic Liberty," *Vanderbilt Law Review* 62, no. 2 (2009): 591–638.

15. William James, *The Varieties of Religious Experience* (New York: Touchstone, 2004); Fletcher Battershall, *Henry Arnold Peckham and Rufus Wheeler Peckham, Jr.: A Memoir* (Albany, NY: J. B. Lyon, 1909); Sheila M. Rothman, *Living in the Shadow of Death: Tuberculosis and the Social Experience of Illness in American History* (Baltimore: Johns Hopkins University Press, 1995), 211–26; *Magnetic Healing*, 187 U.S. at 105.

16. Samuel G. Dixon, *Law, the Foundation of State Medicine, Oration on State Medicine, Delivered at the 58th Annual Session of the American Medical Association, Atlantic City, June, 1907* (Chicago: Press of the American Medical Association, 1907), 5; H. B. Anderson, *State Medicine: A Menace to Democracy* (New York: Citizens Medical Reference Bureau, 1920); *Jacobsen v. Massachusetts*, 197 U.S. 11 (1905).

17. James G. Burrow, *Organized Medicine in the Progressive Era: The Move toward Monopoly* (Baltimore: Johns Hopkins University Press, 1977); Robert H. Wiebe, *The Search for Order, 1877–1920* (New York: Hill & Wang, 1966), 111–23; Paul Starr, *The Social Transformation of American Medicine: The Rise of a Sovereign Profession and the Making of a Vast Industry*, repr. ed. (New York: Basic Books, 1984), 110.

18. Harry M. Marks, *The Progress of Experiment: Science and Therapeutic Reform in the United States, 1900–1990* (New York: Cambridge University Press, 1997), 17–42; Starr, *Social Transformation*, 118, 131–32; Daniel Carpenter, *Reputation and Power: Organizational Image and Pharmaceutical Regulation at the FDA* (Princeton, NJ: Princeton University Press, 2010), 76; Abraham Flexner, *Medical Education in the United States and Canada: A Report to the Carnegie Foundation for the Advancement of Teaching, Bulletin Number Four* (Boston: Merrymount Press, 1910), 48.

19. Starr, *Social Transformation*, 118, 120–21; Flexner, *Medical Education*, 156–66; Martin Kaufman, "Homeopathy in America: The Rise and Fall and Persistence of a Medical Heresy," in *Other Healers: Unorthodox Medicine in America*, ed. Norman Gevitz (Baltimore: Johns Hopkins University Press, 1988), 112; William G. Rothstein, "The Botanical Movements and Orthodox Medicine," in *Other Healers: Unorthodox Medicine in America*, ed. Norman Gevitz (Baltimore: Johns Hopkins University Press, 1988), 29–51.

20. Anne Taylor Kirschmann, "Making Friends for 'Pure' Homeopathy," in *The Politics of Healing*, ed. Robert D. Johnston (New York: Routledge, 2004), 30; Kaufman, "Homeopathy in America," 106–7; Rothstein, "Botanical Movements," 50–51; Burrow, *Organized Medicine*, 71–87.

21. Burrow, 73, 83–84; Starr, *Social Transformation*, 107; Kaufman, "Homeopathy in America," 109–10; "One Board Is Enough," editorial, *New York Times*, February 26, 1907, 10; *Laws of the State of New York Passed at the One Hundred and Thirtieth Session of the Legislature* (Albany, NY: J. B. Lyon, 1907), chap. 344, § 3.

22. Stephen Petrina, "Medical Liberty: Drugless Healers Confront Allopathic Doctors, 1910–1931," *Journal of Medical Humanities* 29, no. 4 (December 2008): 222; James C. Whorton, *Nature Cures: The History of Alternative Medicine in America* (New York: Oxford University Press, 2004), 192–214, 223; Starr, *Social Transformation*, 99, 127. In his testimony to the Committee on Interstate and Foreign Commerce, NLMF vice president Miller said eighteen million Americans were partial to the practitioners of irregular schools. *Hearings on Bills Relating to Health Activities of the General Government before the H. Comm. on Interstate & Foreign Com.*, 61st Cong. 267 (1910) (testimony of Mr. Miller). In his testimony to the Committee on Interstate and Foreign Commerce, Mr. Sheridan from the Illinois Voters and Taxpayers' Association counted 110,000 regular practitioners, 9,000 osteopaths, 18,000 homeopaths, and 4,000 eclectic practitioners. *Hearings on Bills Relating to Health Activities of the General Government before the H. Comm. on Interstate & Foreign Com.*, 61st Cong. 374–75 (1910) (testimony of Mr. Sheridan).

23. Margery Fox, "Conflict to Coexistence: Christian Science and Medicine," *Medical Anthropology* 8, no. 4 (Fall 1984): 295; Whorton, *Nature Cures*, 192–214, 223.

24. Norman Gevitz, "Osteopathic Medicine: From Deviance to Difference," in *Other Healers*, ed. Norman Gevitz (Baltimore: Johns Hopkins University Press, 1988), 125–28; Robert C. Fuller, *Alternative Medicine and American Religious Life* (New York: Oxford University Press, 1989), 68–69, 71–72, 81–84; Frank J. Helminski, "The Legal Creation of Osteopathic Medicine" (master's thesis, Wayne State University, 1981); J. Stuart Moore, *Chiropractic in America* (Baltimore: Johns Hopkins University Press, 1993).

25. See data presented by Miller of NLMF in *Bills Relating to Health Activities*, 267 (testimony of Mr. Miller); Fox, "Conflict to Coexistence," 295–96; Rennie B. Schoepflin, *Christian Science on Trial: Religious Healing in America* (Baltimore: Johns Hopkins University Press, 2002), 146.

26. *Eastman v. People*, 71 Ill. App. 236 (1896); *Eastman v. Ohio*, 4 Ohio N.P. 163 (Ct. Com. Pl. 1897); Gevitz, "Osteopathic Medicine," 132; Whorton, *Nature Cures*, 2004, 153.

27. Whorton, *Nature Cures*, 154–55; Gevitz, "Osteopathic Medicine," 132–33.

28. Walter I. Wardwell, "Chiropractors: Evolution to Acceptance," in *Other Healers: Unorthodox Medicine in America*, ed. Norman Gevitz (Baltimore: Johns Hopkins University Press, 1988), 165–66; Moore, *Chiropractic in America*, 76; Whorton, *Nature Cures*, 2004, 176–82.

29. Paul Starr, *The Social Transformation of American Medicine: The Rise of a Sovereign Profession and the Making of a Vast Industry*, repr. ed. (New York: Basic Books, 1984), 156–57, 180–97; James H. Cassedy, *Medicine in America: A Short History* (Baltimore: Johns Hopkins University Press, 1991), 107–18; John Duffy, *From Humors to Medical Science: A History of American Medicine*, 2d ed. (Urbana: University of Illinois Press, 1993), 188–95.

30. Edmund D. Pellegrino, "The Sociocultural Impact of Twentieth-Century Therapeutics," in *Therapeutic Revolution: Essays in the Social History of American Medicine*, ed. Morris J. Vogel and Charles E. Rosenberg (Philadelphia: University of Pennsylvania Press, 1979), 246–53; "Leading Causes of Death, 1900–1998," Centers for Disease Control and Prevention, last modified November 6, 2015, https://www.cdc.gov/nchs/data/dvs/lead1900_98.pdf.

31. Act to Encourage Vaccination, ch. 37, 2 Stat. 806 (1813), *repealed by* ch. 50, 3 Stat. 677 (1822); Manfred Waserman, "The Quest for a National Health Department in the Progressive Era," *Bulletin of the History of Medicine* 49, no. 3 (Fall 1975): 355; Cassedy, *Medicine in America*, 113–17.

32. The Postmaster General first used these statutes to attack health fraud sometime around the turn of the century; it is unclearly exactly when. James Harvey Young, *The Medical Messiahs: A Social History of Medical Quackery in 20th Century America*, repr. ed. (Princeton, NJ: Princeton University Press, 1975), 67; Pub. L. No. 57-244, 32 Stat. 728 (1902); Pub. L. No. 59-384, 34 Stat. 768 (1906); Burrow, *Organized Medicine*, 97.

33. Samuel Hopkins Adams, *The Great American Fraud: Articles on the Nostrum Evil and Quacks, Reprinted from Collier's Weekly*, 4th ed. (Chicago: Press of the American Medical Association, 1907); Carpenter, *Reputation and Power*, 77.

34. Pub. L. No. 59-384, 34 Stat. 768, § 8 (1906); see list of these cases in Brief for the United States at 54–60, *United States v. Johnson*, 221 U.S. 488 (1910) (No. 786).

35. *U.S. v. Johnson*, 177 F. 313, 317 (W.D. Mo. 1910).

36. All of the facts below are drawn from the U.S. Supreme Court Transcript of Record, Transcript of Record, *United States v. Johnson*, 221 U.S. 488 (1910) (No. 786); Brief ("Statement") for Johnson at 4.

37. Flexner, *Medical Education*, 210–11; "Bennet Medical College," http://www.lostcolleges.com/bennett-medical-college; Walter Barlow Stevens, *Centennial History of Missouri (The Center State): One Hundred Years in the Union, 1820–1921*, Vol. 5 (St. Louis: S. J. Clarke Publishing, 1921), 679–80; Additional Brief on Behalf of O. A. Johnson, Defendant in Error at 38–40, Additional app.

38. Additional Brief on Behalf of O. A. Johnson, Defendant in Error, 7–37.

39. Brief ("Statement") for Johnson, 39; Additional Brief on Behalf of O. A. Johnson, 43, 69; Reply Argument on Behalf of the Government, 18.

40. Brief ("Statement") for Johnson, 21, 38–39.

41. Additional Brief on Behalf of O.A. Johnson, 54–55.
42. Reply Argument on Behalf of the Government, 54–55; Marks, *The Progress of Experiment*, 37. Physician quoted in Burrow, *Organized Medicine*, 77.
43. *Johnson*, 221 U.S. at 488.
44. 62 H.R. 11877, 62nd Cong., 1st Sess. (1911); 47 Cong. Rec. 2434 (1911).
45. *The Pure-Food Law: Hearing on H.R. 11877 before the H. Comm. on Interstate & Foreign Com.*, 62 Cong. 20–21 (1912) (statement of Rep. Sherley).
46. *The Pure-Food Law*, 4.
47. Appendix to the Cong. Rec. at 675 (Aug. 19, 1912) (also Report. No. 1138).
48. Pub. L. No. 62-301, 37 Stat. 416 (1912). For example, from June to October 1915, the government brought forty-four civil and criminal enforcement actions under the amendment and prevailed every time—in all but one instance by a default or guilty plea. In that one case, the defendant was convicted. Brief for the United States at 36, *Seven Cases . . . Eckman's Alterative v. United States*, 239 U.S. 510 (1916) (No. 51).
49. *Seven Cases*, 239 U.S. at 514.
50. The Supreme Court had decided *Magnetic Healing* solely on the basis of statutory interpretation, thus leaving open the question of whether Congress could constitutionally prohibit fraudulent therapeutic claims even if it wanted to do so.
51. Brief for Plaintiff in Error at 30–32, *Seven Cases*, 239 U.S. 510 (No. 51). Eckman also contended that the Sherley Amendment exceeded Congress's power under the commerce clause. Brief for Plaintiff in Error at 23–29. Eckman further argued, unconvincingly, that Congress's restriction on its right to advertise and "puff" its drug violated the company's property rights under the Fifth Amendment. Brief for Plaintiff in Error at 30–31.
52. *Seven Cases*, 239 U.S. at 517–18.
53. *Kar-Ru Chemical Co. v. U.S.*, 264 F. 921, 927 (9th Cir. 1920).
54. U.S. Dept. of Agric., 8021, Notices of Judgment under the Food & Drugs Act (1918); *Kar-Ru Chemical Co*, 264 F. at 921. On homeopathic practice during the Progressive Era, see Suzanne White Junod, "An Alternative Perspective: Homeopathic Drugs, Royal Copeland, and Federal Drug Regulation," *Food and Drug Law Journal* 55, no. 1 (2000): 4–9.
55. Quotation from 1921 catalogue, in Robert A. Buerki and Louis D. Vottero, *Ethical Responsibility in Pharmacy Practice*, 2nd ed. (Madison, WI: American Institute of the History of Pharmacy, 2002), 26.
56. *U.S. v. Tuberclecide Co.*, 252 F. 938, 941 (S.D. Cal. 1916).
57. Waserman, "National Health Department," 356–66.
58. 45 Cong. Rec. 3677 (1910).
59. *Proposed Department of Public Health: Hearing on S. 6049 to Establish a Dept. of Health and for Other Purposes before the S. Comm. on Public Health & National Quarantine*, 61st Cong. 14 (1910) (testimony of L. K. Frankel, Rep., Metro. Life Ins. Co.), 24 (testimony of Dr. William Welch, President, American Med. Ass'n of Baltimore), 6 (testimony of Joseph Y. Porter, President, Conf. of State Bds. of Health).
60. "Do You Want the 'Doctors' Trust' to Be Able to Force Its Opinions on You?," advertisement, *Washington Post*, n.d. The advertisement appeared in numerous other papers, including the *New York Times*, the *Chicago Tribune*, and the *Los Angeles Times*.

61. For background information on the NLMF, see Petrina, "Medical Liberty," 206–20.

62. For information on the life and thought of B. O. Flower, see Roy P. Fairfield, "Benjamin Orange Flower: Father of the Muckrakers," *American Literature* 22, no. 3 (November 1950): 272–82; Allen J. Matusow, "The Mind of B. O. Flower," *New England Quarterly* 34, no. 4 (December 1961): 492–509; David H. Dickason, "Benjamin Orange Flower, Patron of the Realists," *American Literature* 14, no. 2 (May 1942): 148–56; Jean-Louis Marin-Lamellet, "'What Is the Cocoon but a Dark Cabinet?': Benjamin O. Flower, Print Culture and the Legitimisation of Fringe Science in the 1890s," *Mémoires du livre* 6, no. 1 (Fall 2014); Jean-Louis Marin-Lamellet, "What's the Matter with Benjamin O. Flower?," *European Journal of American Studies* 8, no. 1 (Spring 2013); Edd Applegate, "Benjamin Orange Flower (1858–1918)," in *Muckrakers: A Biographical Dictionary of Writers and Editors* (Lanham, MD: Scarecrow Press, 2008): 58–60.

63. Herbert Spencer, *Social Statics* (London: John Chapman: 1851), quoted in Benjamin Orange Flower, *Progressive Men, Women, and Movements of the Past Twenty-Five Years* (Boston: New Arena, 1914), 311.

64. Dickason, "Patron of the Realists," 149.

65. Flower, *Progressive Men, Women, and Movements*; Fairfield, "Benjamin Orange Flower," 282.

66. "Constitution of the American Psychical Society," *Psychical Review* 1, no. 1 (August 1992): 33; Benjamin Orange Flower, "The Relation of the New Thought to Social and Economic Progress," in *Proceedings of the 2d Annual Convention of the International Metaphysical League, Held at New York, N.Y., October 23–26, 1900* (Boston: International Metaphysical League, 1901), 203–11; Benjamin Orange Flower, *Christian Science as a Religious Belief and a Therapeutic Agent* (Boston: Twentieth Century Company, 1910).

67. Benjamin Orange Flower, "Restrictive Medical Legislation and the Public Weal," *Arena* 19, no. 103 (June 1898): 809.

68. *Bills Relating to Health Activities*, 200, 202.

69. On telegrams, see *Bills Relating to Health Activities*, 92, 99. For a list of the NLMF's officers and advisors, see *First Report of The National League for Medical Freedom* (New York: NLMF, 1910), 4–5.

70. 47 Cong. Rec. 2673 (1911) (statement of Sen. Owen).

71. "A Bad Bunch," *Collier's*, May 6, 1911; "Liberty," *Collier's*, June 3, 1911; 47 Cong. Rec. 2473–79 (1911) (statement of Sen. Owen).

72. 47 Cong. Rec. 2661, 2675 (1911) (statement of Sen. Works).

73. "Untitled," *Medical Freedom*, November 1911, 4; "Medical Freedom Championed, Federal Interference Decried in Enthusiastic Mass Meeting," *Medical Freedom*, November 1911, 5; "First General League Conference," *Medical Freedom*, December 1911; "Protest the Owen Bill: Meeting in San Francisco under Auspices of National League for Medical Freedom," *Medical Freedom*, December 1911, 13.

74. 48 Cong. Rec. 5532 (1912) (statement of Sen. Works); Lydia Avery Coonley-Ward, "A Distinguished Woman Protests," *Medical Freedom*, July 1912, 10; An Act to Change the Name of the Public Health and Marine Hospital Service . . ., Pub. L. No. 62–265, 37 Stat. 309 (1912); Waserman, "National Health Department," 376, 378–79.

75. Richard Hofstadter, "The Paranoid Style in American Politics," *Harper's Magazine*, November 1964. One scholar has examined the "paranoid" style of Flower's world-view. Marin-Lamellet, "What's the Matter with Benjamin O. Flower?"

76. *Bills Relating to Health Activities*, 311 (testimony of Fred Bangs, Rep. of the NLMF).

77. *Bills Relating to Health Activities*, 258 (testimony of Mr. Miller); "The League—Its Work and Its Mission," *Medical Freedom*, September 1911, 2; "Medical Freedom Championed, Federal Interference Decried in Enthusiastic Mass Meeting."

78. *Bills Relating to Health Activities*, 103 (Prof. Irving Fisher, Chairman of the Comm. of One Hundred on Pub. Health of the Am. Ass'n for the Advancement of Sci., and Prof. of Pol. Econ. at Yale Univ.), 258 (testimony of Mr. Miller); Waserman, "National Health Department," 366; Burrow, *Organized Medicine*, 100; *Proposed Department of Public Health*, 23–27 (testimony of Dr. Welch).

79. Jeffrey Lionel Berlant, *Profession and Monopoly: A Study of Medicine in the United States and Great Britain* (Berkeley: University of California Press, 1975).

80. Howard Markel, *The Kelloggs: The Battling Brothers of Battle Creek* (New York: Pantheon, 2017), 214–15; *Bills Relating to Health Activities*, 153 (testimony of Dr. Kellogg).

81. "A New Combination against the American Medical Association," *Journal of the American Medical Association* 54, no. 22 (May 28, 1910): 1792.

82. *Bills Relating to Health Activities*, 199–235 (testimony of Mr. Bates, Rep. NLMF); 47 Cong. Rec. 2673 (1911) (testimony of Sen. Works).

83. *Bills Relating to Health Activities*, 310 (testimony of Mr. Bangs).

84. *Proposed Department of Public Health*, 23 (testimony of Dr. Welch).

85. *Medical Freedom*, August 1912, cover, April 1914, cover; "The Spirit of '76," *Medical Freedom*, n.d., 2; "Untitled," *Connecticut Courant*, July 31, 1769; "Dr. Benjamin Rush," *Medical Freedom*, May 1914, cover.

86. Benjamin Orange Flower, "Privilege of the People," *Medical Freedom*, November 1911, 4.

87. Daniel T. Rodgers, "In Search of Progressivism," *Reviews in American History* 10, no. 4 (December 1982): 123–24.

88. "Have You Protested against the Medical Trust?," *Atlanta Constitution*, May 31, 1911, 7; *Bills Relating to Health Activities*, 261–63 (testimony of Hon. Miller), 288–93, 296 (testimony of Mr. Bangs).

89. *Bills Relating to Health Activities*, 377 (statement of Sen. Bartlett).

90. *Bills Relating to Health Activities*, 238 (testimony of Dr. Laws, President, Arkansas Eclectic Bd. of Med. Exam'rs).

91. Benjamin Orange Flower, "The Menace of a National Health Bureau," *Twentieth Century Magazine*, June 1910, 237.

92. Douglas Laycock, "The Benefits of the Establishment Clause," *DePaul Law Review* 42 (Fall 1992): 373–82; *Bills Relating to Health Activities*, 308 (testimony of Mr. Bangs).

93. *Bills Relating to Health Activities*, 277 (testimony of Mr. Miller), 330 (testimony of Dr. Crutcher, Fac., Hahnemann Homeopathic Med. C.), 360–66 (testimony of Mr. Sheridan).

94. Cong. Rec. at 5539 (statement of Sen. Works); *Bills Relating to Health Activities*, 247 (testimony of Rev. Dr. Williams).

95. "What Standardizing of Medical Practice Laws Means," *Medical Freedom*, May 1913, 4.

96. "Making Law-Abiding Citizens Law Breakers," *Medical Freedom*, December 1912, 3.

97. *Bills Relating to Health Activities*, 232–33 (testimony of Mr. Bates), 237 (testimony of Dr. Laws).

98. *Bills Relating to Health Activities*, 315 (testimony of Diana Belais, President, Anti Vaccination and Vivisection Soc'y). On the anti-vaccinationists' emphasis on the notion of bodily autonomy and integrity, see Michael Willrich, *Pox: An American History* (New York: Penguin Press, 2011), 252, 270–72.

99. Willrich, *Pox*, 271–74; See generally Rodgers, "In Search of Progressivism"; Marin-Lamellet, "What's the Matter with Benjamin O. Flower?," 2.

100. Clifford P. Smith, *Christian Science: Its Legal Status: A Defense of Human Rights* (Boston: Christian Science Publishing Society, 1914), 26; Flower, *Progressive Men, Women, and Movements*.

101. *Bills Relating to Health Activities*, 237 (testimony of Dr. Laws).

102. Cassedy, *Medicine in America*, 120–21; Basil Achilladelis, "Innovation in the Pharmaceutical Industry," in *Pharmaceutical Innovation: Revolutionizing Human Health*, ed. Ralph Landau, Basil Achilladelis, and Alexander Scriabine (Philadelphia: Chemical Heritage Foundation, 1999), 51–55; John C. Burnham, "American Medicine's Golden Age: What Happened to It?," *Science* 215, no. 4539 (March 1982): 1474–75.

Chapter 5

1. "Dr. Winrod's Letter," *National Health Federation Bulletin*, February 1957, 14; "Gerald B. Winrod Is Dead, Pro-Nazi 'Fundamentalist,'" *New York Herald Tribune*, November 13, 1957, 22; "Gerald B. Winrod, Wichita Minister," *New York Times*, November 13, 1957, 35.

2. Geo. P. Larrick, "Public Warning against Hoxsey Cancer Treatment," *Canadian Medical Association Journal* 74, no. 9 (May 1, 1956): 740; "Dr. Winrod's Letter," 18.

3. Background information on Hoxsey is derived from James Harvey Young, *The Medical Messiahs: A Social History of Medical Quackery in 20th Century America* (Princeton, NJ: Princeton University Press, 1967), 360–89; James T. Patterson, *The Dread Disease: Cancer and Modern American Culture* (Cambridge, MA: Harvard University Press, 1987), 106–7; Harry M. Hoxsey, *You Don't Have to Die!* (New York: Milestone Books, 1956); "Public Warning by FDA . . . Against Hoxsey Cancer Treatment, Extension of Remarks," 84 Cong. Rec. app. at A3071–72 (April 17, 1956) (statement of Rep. Heselton).

4. *Hoxsey v. State*, 159 S.W.2d 886 (Tex. Crim. App. 1942); "Hoxsey—Cancer Charlatan," *Journal of the American Medical Association* 133, no. 11 (March 15, 1947): 774–75; *Hoxsey v. Fishbein*, 83 F. Supp. 282 (N.D. Tex. 1949).

5. Young, *Medical Messiahs*, 371–74; Hoxsey, *You Don't Have to Die!*, 204–5.

6. David J. Hess, "CAM Cancer Therapies in Twentieth-Century North America: The Emergence and Growth of a Social Movement," in *The Politics of Healing: Histories of Alternative Medicine in Twentieth-Century North America*, ed. Robert D. Johnston (New York: Routledge, 2004), 236.

7. Young, *Medical Messiahs*, 378; *United States v. Hoxsey Cancer Clinic*, 94 F. Supp. 464 (N.D. Tex. 1950); *United States v. Hoxsey Cancer Clinic et al.*, 198 F.2d 273 (5th Cir. 1952).

8. *Hoxsey Cancer Clinic*, 198 F.2d at 277–81.

9. *Hoxsey Cancer Clinic v. United States*, 344 U.S. 928 (1953); 346 U.S. 897 (1953); Young, *Medical Messiahs*; Food, Drug, & Cosmetic Act § 705(b), 21 U.S.C. § 375(b) (1952); Larrick, "Public Warning against Hoxsey Cancer Treatment," 740.

10. Larrick, 740; The poster is reproduced in David Cantor, "Cancer, Quackery and the Vernacular Meanings of Hope in 1950s America," *Journal of the History of Medicine and Allied Sciences* 61, no. 3 (July 2006): 328.

11. "Court Upholds Hoxsey Cancer Pills Warning," *National Health Federation Bulletin*, December 1957, 20; "Texan Assailed on Cancer Clinic," *New York Times*, April 5, 1956, 60; "National Health Federation Hold Mass Meetings," *National Health Federation Bulletin*, July 1957, 5–6.

12. Cantor, "Cancer, Quackery and the Vernacular Meanings," 336; Young, *Medical Messiahs*, 384; 85 Cong. Rec. app. at A1857–58 (March 7, 1957) (statement of Rep. Dingell).

13. *United States v. 10 Cartons . . . Drug Labeled in Part "Hoxsey,"* 152 F. Supp. 360 (W.D. Penn. 1957); Young, *Medical Messiahs*, 387–88; Hess, "CAM Cancer Therapies," 236.

14. Hess, 236; Gretchen Ann Reilly, "'Not a So-Called Democracy': Anti-Flouridationists and the Fight over Drinking Water," in *The Politics of Healing: Histories of Alternative Medicine in Twentieth Century North America*, ed. Robert D. Johnston (New York: Routledge, 2004), 139–40.

15. Daniel Carpenter, *Reputation and Power: Organizational Image and Pharmaceutical Regulation at the FDA* (Princeton, NJ: Princeton University Press, 2010), 197–204; Young, *Medical Messiahs*, 390–407.

16. Hess, "CAM Cancer Therapies," 234–35.

17. Stephen Petrina, "Medical Liberty: Drugless Healers Confront Allopathic Doctors, 1910–1931," *Journal of Medical Humanities* 29 (December 2008): 220–23; S. L. Kotar and J. E. Gessler, *Smallpox: A History* (Jefferson, NC: McFarland, 2013), 284.

18. James Colgrove, "'Science in a Democracy': The Contested Status of Vaccination in the Progressive Era and the 1920s," *Isis* 96, no. 2 (June 2005): 174–77; H. B. Anderson, *State Medicine: A Menace to Democracy* (New York: Citizens Medical Reference Bureau, 1920).

19. James C. Whorton, *Nature Cures: The History of Alternative Medicine in America* (New York: Oxford University Press, 2004), 178–80; Walter I. Wardwell, "Chiropractors: Evolution to Acceptance," in *Other Healers: Unorthodox Medicine in America*, ed. Norman Gevitz (Baltimore: Johns Hopkins University Press, 1988), 165–66; J. Stuart Moore, *Chiropractic in America: The History of a Medical Alternative* (Baltimore: Johns Hopkins University Press, 1993), 89–90, 151–52.

20. Petrina, "Medical Liberty," 223.

21. John C. Burnham, "American Medicine's Golden Age: What Happened to It?," *Science* 215, no. 4539 (March 19, 1982): 1474–79; Eliot Freidson, "Professionalism and Institutional Ethics: Salvaging the Future of American Medicine," *Revue française d'études américaines*, no. 77 (June 1998): 21–37; Charles Rosenberg, "A Therapeutic Revolution Revisited," in *Therapeutic Revolutions: Pharmaceuticals and Social Change in the Twentieth Century*, ed. Jeremy A. Greene, Flurin Condrau, and Elizabeth Siegel Watkins (Chicago: University of Chicago Press, 2016), 302–10.

22. James C. Whorton, "'Antibiotic Abandon': The Resurgence of Therapeutic Rationalism," in *The History of Antibiotics: A Symposium*, ed. John Parascandola (Madison, WI: American Institute of the History of Pharmacy, 1980), 125–36; Scott H. Podolsky and Anne Kviem Lie, "Futures and Their Uses: Antibiotics and Therapeutic Revolutions," in *Therapeutic Revolutions: Pharmaceuticals and Social Change in the Twentieth Century*, ed. Jeremy A. Greene, Flurin Condrau, and Elizabeth Siegel Watkins (Chicago: University of Chicago Press, 2016), 20–24; "Leading Causes of Death, 1900–1998," Centers for Disease Control and Prevention, last modified November 6, 2015, https://www.cdc.gov/nchs/data/dvs/lead1900_98.pdf.

23. Laura E. Bothwell et al., "Assessing the Gold Standard—Lessons from the History of RCTs," *New England Journal of Medicine* 374, no. 22 (June 2, 2016): 2175–81; Laura E. Bothwell and Scott H. Podolsky, "The Emergence of the Randomized, Controlled Trial," *New England Journal of Medicine* 375, no. 6 (August 11, 2016): 501–4; Anton J. M. de Craen et al., "Placebos and Placebo Effects in Medicine: Historical Overview," *Journal of the Royal Society of Medicine* 92, no. 10 (October 1999): 511–15; Harry M. Marks, *The Progress of Experiment: Science and Therapeutic Reform in the United States, 1900–1990* (New York: Cambridge University Press, 1997); "Streptomycin Treatment of Pulmonary Tuberculosis: A Medical Research Council Investigation," *British Medical Journal* 2, no. 4582 (October 30, 1948): 769–82,

24. Sinclair Lewis, *Arrowsmith* (New York: Signet, 2008), 348.

25. Lewis, *Arrowsmith*, 350, 382, 392.

26. "'Polio' Vaccines," editorial, *New England Journal of Medicine* 213, no. 14 (October 3, 1935): 687–88.

27. David M. Oshinsky, *Polio: An American Story* (New York: Oxford University Press, 2005), 215; Liza Dawson, "The Salk Polio Vaccine Trial of 1954: Risks, Randomization and Public Involvement in Research," *Clinical Trials* 1, no. 1 (February 2004): 122–30. A search of Salk, Mantle, and Dean on Google Books N-gram Viewer suggests that they followed remarkably similar, contemporaneous paths to prominence in the 1950s.

28. Burnham, "American Medicine's Golden Age"; Allan Mazur, "Opinion Poll Measurement of American Confidence in Science," *Science, Technology, & Human Values* 6, no. 36 (Summer 1981): 17; Evelyn Barkins, *Are These Our Doctors?* (Hollywood, FL: Frederick Fell, 1952), 171–72.

29. The President Presents Plan No. 1 to Carry Out the Provisions of the Reorganization Act, 8 Pub. Papers 261–65 (April 25, 1939); Reorganization Plan No. IV, 5 U.S.C. § 12 (1940); Harlan Miller, "Food and Drug Agency Shift Is under Study," *Washington Post*, March 19, 1940, 2.

30. Herbert McClosky, "Consensus and Ideology in American Politics," *American Political Science Review* 58, no. 2 (June 1964): 370; "Trust in Government: 1958–2015," Pew Research Center, November 23, 2015, http://www.people-press.org/2015/11/23/1-trust-in-government-1958-2015/; David Goldfield, *The Gifted Generation: When Government Was Good* (New York: Bloomsbury, 2017), 225–26.

31. Norman Gevitz, "'A Coarse Sieve': Basic Science Boards and Medical Licensure in the United States," *Journal of the History of Medicine and Allied Sciences* 43, no. 1 (January 1988): 36–63; Whorton, *Nature Cures*, 230–32.

32. Cal. Health & Safety Code, ch. 789 (1959) (repealed 1995); Cal. Health & Safety Code § 1700–21 (1959) (repealed 1995). Robert Blanchard, "Assembly Passes Cancer Quack Bill," *Los Angeles Times*, May 22, 1959, 1; Cal. Dept. of Pub. Health, *The Cancer Law: 1959–1964* (1964).

33. *A Bill to Prevent the Manufacture, Shipment, and Sale of Adulterated or Misbranded Food, Drugs, and Cosmetics . . . To Prevent the False Advertisement of Food, Drugs, and Cosmetics, and for Other Purposes: Hearing on S. 1944 before a S. Subcomm. of the Comm. on Com.*, 73rd Cong. 44 (1933) (statement of Walter G. Campbell, Chief, FDA).

34. FD&C Act § 502(a)(1), 21 U.S.C. § 352(a)(1) (1938); Wheeler-Lea Act §§ 3–4, 1 Pub. L. No. 75-447, 52 Stat. 111, 111, 115–16 (1938).

35. *Research Labs v. United States*, 167 F.2d 410 (9th Cir. 1948), *cert. denied*, 335 U.S. 843 (1948). See, e.g., Harvey Wickes Felter, *The Eclectic Materia Medica, Pharmacology and Therapeutics* (Cincinnati: John K. Scudder, 1922).

36. Brief for the United States in Opposition at 12, *Research Labs*, 335 U.S. 843 (No. 134).

37. *Research Labs*, 167 F.2d at 413–17.

38. N-gram "medical quackery."

39. Google Books Ngram Viewer "medical quackery"; Carpenter, *Reputation and Power*, 197–99.

40. Bess Furman, "U.S. Food Aide Asks Drive on 'Quacks,'" *New York Times*, December 10, 1952, 46; "U.S. Aide Scores Medical Quacks," *New York Times*, December 9, 1954, 28; Jonathan Spivak, "Crusade on Quacks: Federal, State, Private Agencies Step Up Fight against False 'Cures,'" *Wall Street Journal*, June 22, 1960, 1; "All-Out War on Quacks Is Urged," *Washington Post*, October 7, 1961, B17,; Marjorie Hunter, "U.S. and A.M.A. Pledge Drive to End Billion-a-Year Quackery," *New York Times*, October 7, 1961, 1; "Parley in Capital Fights Quackery," *New York Times*, October 26, 1963, 30; H. C. Long, "Health Freedom Battle Is On," *National Health Federation Bulletin*, December 1963, 5–6.

41. Robert K. Plumb, "Deformed Babies Traced to a Drug," *New York Times*, April 12, 1962, 37; Morton Mintz, "'Heroine' of FDA Keeps Bad Drug off of Market," *Washington Post*, July 15, 1962, A1; Carpenter, *Reputation and Power*, 251; Accounts of the thalidomide crisis appear in Carpenter, 256–60; Morton Mintz, *By Prescription Only*, rev. ed. (Boston: Beacon Press, 1967), 248–64.

42. FD&C Act § 505(i), 21 U.S.C. § 355(i) (1963); 28 Fed. Reg. 179 (Jan. 8, 1963) (codified as amended at 21 C.F.R. pt. 312).

43. FD&C Act § 505(a), (d); 21 U.S.C. § 355(a), (d) (1972).

44. FD&C Act § 505(d), 21 U.S.C. § 355(d) (1962); Carpenter, *Reputation and Power*, 136, 159 n. 62; 35 Fed. Reg. 7250 (May 8, 1970) (codified as amended at 21 C.F.R. § 314.126).

45. Carpenter, *Reputation and Power*, 118–227.

46. Whorton, *Nature Cures*, 246–47; Selwyn D. Collins, "Frequency and Volume of Doctors' Calls among Males and Females in 9,000 Families, Based on Nation-Wide Periodic Canvasses, 1928–31," *Public Health Reports (1896–1970)* 55, no. 44 (November 1, 1940): 1977–2020; Norman Gevitz, "Three Perspectives on Unorthodox Medicine," in *Other Healers: Unorthodox Medicine in America*, ed. Norman Gevitz (Baltimore: Johns Hopkins University Press, 1988), 22–23; White House Commission on Complementary & Alternative Medicine Policy, Final Report (2002).

47. Young, *Medical Messiahs*, 206.

48. Martin Kaufman, *Homeopathy in America: The Rise and Fall of a Medical Heresy* (Baltimore: Johns Hopkins University Press, 1971), 117; Gevitz, "Coarse Sieve," 48.

49. James H. Cassedy, *Medicine in America: A Short History* (Baltimore: Johns Hopkins University Press, 1991), 138–39; Erika Janik, *Marketplace of the Marvelous: The Strange Origins of Modern Medicine* (Boston: Beacon Press, 2014), 251; Charles E. Rosenberg, *Our Present Complaint: American Medicine, Then and Now* (Baltimore: Johns Hopkins University Press, 2007), 122–25; "Principles of Medical Ethics—1957," *Journal of the American Medical Association* 164, no. 13 (June 27, 1957).

50. Paul Starr, *The Social Transformation of American Medicine: The Rise of a Sovereign Profession and the Making of a Vast Industry*, repr. ed. (New York: Basic Books, 1984), 107–8; Anne Taylor Kirschmann, "Making Friends for 'Pure' Homeopathy," in *The Politics of Healing*, ed. Robert D. Johnston (New York: Routledge, 2004), 273–74; Kaufman, *Homeopathy in America*, 174–83; Peter Barton Hutt, Richard A. Merrill, and Lewis A. Grossman, *Food and Drug Law: Cases and Materials*, 3rd ed. (Washington, DC: Foundation Press: 2007), 800.

51. Whorton, *Nature Cures*, 234–35, 288–89; Rodney Stark, "The Rise and Fall of Christian Science," *Journal of Contemporary Religion* 13, no. 2 (May 1, 1998): 189–214.

52. Gevitz, "Coarse Sieve," 57–58; Norman Gevitz, "Osteopathic Medicine: From Deviance to Difference," in *Other Healers*, ed. Norman Gevitz (Baltimore: Johns Hopkins University Press, 1988), 144; Whorton, *Nature Cures*, 236–37.

53. Gevitz, "Ostopathic Medicine," 147–50, 153; Whorton, *Nature Cures*, 237–40.

54. Moore, *Chiropractic in America*, 113ff., 151–52; Wardwell, "Chiropractors: Evolution to Acceptance," 168; Whorton, *Nature Cures*, 233; Gevitz, "Coarse Sieve," 51–53, 58.

55. Whorton, *Nature Cures*, 287; Wardwell, "Chiropractors: Evolution to Acceptance," 169–70, 185; Moore, *Chiropractic in America*, 124.

56. *A. Schlessing v. United States*, 239 F.2d 885 (9th Cir. 1956); *United States v. Article . . . Lindquist Chronosonic Ultrasound Model 401B*, 255 F. Supp. 374 (W.D. Ark. 1966). *Contra United States v. 22 Devices . . . Halox Therapeutic Generator*, 98 F. Supp. 914 (S.D. Cal. 1951).

57. Michael Ackerman, "Science and the Shadow of Ideology in the American Health Foods Movement, 1930s–1960s," in *The Politics of Healing*, ed. Robert D. Johnston (New York: Routledge, 2004), 55–67; Young, *Medical Messiahs*, 1975, 333–59.

58. Ackerman, "Science and the Shadow of Ideology," 56; *Health Frauds and Quackery, Hearing before the S. Subcomm. on Frauds & Misrepresentations Affecting the Elderly of the Spec. Comm. on Aging,* 88th Cong. 129–30 (1964) (Memorandum from U.S. Food and Drug Administration).

59. *V. E. Irons, Inc. v. United States,* 244 F.2d 34 (1st Cir. 1957), *cert. denied* 354 U.S. 923 (1957); Young, *Medical Messiahs,* 333–59.

60. The details of the FDA's dispute with the Church of Scientology, described later in this chapter, are drawn from Jeanne Cavanaugh, *Scientology and the FDA: A Look Back, A Modern Analysis, and a New Approach* (Harvard Law School Third-Year Paper, 2004) (available at https://dash.harvard.edu/handle/1/8965552). *Founding Church of Scientology of Washington, D.C. v. United States,* 409 F.2d 1146 (D.C. Cir. 1969); *United States v. Article or Device . . . "Hubbard Electrometer,"* 333 F. Supp. 357 (D.D.C. 1971).

61. *Founding Church,* 409 F. 2d at 1162.

62. *"Hubbard Electrometer,"* 333 F. Supp. at 361, 364; *United States v. An Article or Device,* 1969–1974 FDLI Jud. Rec. 131 (D.C. Cir. 1973) (per curiam).

63. On mid-twentieth-century device quackery and its leading figures, see Young, *Medical Messiahs,* 137–42, 239–59, 383; "What the Health Hucksters Are Up To," *Changing Times,* September 1964, 27; "NHF Founder Fred J. Hart Dies after 2-Year Illness," *National Health Federation Bulletin,* June 1975, 1–2; Kenneth L. Milstead, "Quackery in the Medical Device Field," *American Physical Therapy Association,* October 1963, 654–62.

64. *Drown v. United States,* 198 F.2d 999 (9th Cir. 1952); *United States v. Ellis Research Labs,* 300 F.2d 550 (7th Cir. 1962); *United States v. Electronic Products Ass'n,* Food Drug Cosm. L. Rep. ¶ 40,126Z (N.D. Cal. 1962); "Decree Filed to Ban Electron 'Quackery,'" *New York Times,* March 18, 1954, 55; Young, *Medical Messiahs,* 383; "What the Health Hucksters Are Up To," 24.

65. James Harvey Young and Richard E. McFadyen, "The Koch Cancer Treatment," *Journal of the History of Medicine and Allied Sciences* 53, no. 3 (July 1, 1998): 254–84.

66. Patterson, *Dread Disease,* 162–167, 191–97, 238–40.

67. Richard Hofstadter, "The Paranoid Style in American Politics," *Harper's Magazine,* November 1964, 77.

68. Young and McFadyen, "The Koch Cancer Treatment," 273–77; Young, *Medical Messiahs,* 381–82.

69. Don C. Matchan, "Fred J. Hart—Farmer, Scholar, Gentleman," *National Health Federation Bulletin,* April 1960, 9–12; "NHF Founder Fred J. Hart Dies after 2-Year Illness," *National Health Federation Bulletin,* June 1975; "What Outland Thinks of the Farmer's Judgment," advertisement, *Press-Courier,* October 20, 1944, 5; Daniel K. Williams, *God's Own Party: The Making of the Christian Right,* repr. ed. (New York: Oxford University Press, 2012).

70. Fred J. Hart, "It's Time for Co-Ordinated Action," *National Health Federation Bulletin,* February 1957, 9; "America Wake Up," *National Health Federation Bulletin,* August 1957, 7; "The National Health Council," *National Health Federation Bulletin,* August 1957, 9–11.

71. The original elected Board of Governors is listed on p. 8 of the Sept.–Oct. 1956 issue of *The National Health Federation Bulletin*.

72. "National Health Federation Resolution," *National Health Federation Bulletin*, September–October 1956, 8; Young and McFadyen, "Koch Cancer Treatment," 276–81; Roy Gibbons, "Cancer 'Cure' Assailed by U.S., Peddled Again," *Chicago Daily Tribune*, September 11, 1949.

73. "Program of the National Health Federation," *National Health Federation Bulletin*, July 1955, 2.

74. David M. Kasson, "A Cancer Victim Speaks," *National Health Federation Bulletin*, August 1957, 20.

75. "What Is the NHF?," editorial, *National Health Federation Bulletin*, November 1956, 3.

76. "Untitled," *National Health Federation Bulletin*, May 1955, 3; Ray H. Overaker, "Health Freedom by Constitutional Amendment," *National Health Federation Bulletin*, December 1959, 5.

77. Kasson, "A Cancer Victim Speaks," 19; [Fred. J. Hart], "A Dangerous Ideology," *National Health Federation Bulletin*, August 1955, 2; "National Health Federation Hold Mass Meetings," *National Health Federation Bulletin*, August 1957, 5; "Suggested Program for the N.H.F. for 1958," *National Health Federation Bulletin*, December 1957, 5.

78. Fred J. Hart, "National Health Federation a Force to Be Reckoned With," *National Health Federation Bulletin*, January 1957, 4; "Congress Always Responds to the Will of the People," *National Health Federation Bulletin*, June 1957, 3.

79. Robert Blanchard, "Assembly Bill Is Blow at Cancer Cure Quacks," *Los Angeles Times*, January 22, 1957, 17; "Cancer Bill Draws Raft of Letters," *Wilmington Daily Press Journal*, March 6, 1957, 2; Robert Blanchard, "Bill Aimed at Cancer Quacks Wins Approval," *Los Angeles Times*, March 20, 1957, 12; "Committee Sidetracks Anticancer Quack Bill," *Los Angeles Times*, April 19, 1957, 7.

80. Harold Edwards, "Position of the National Health Federation," *National Health Federation Bulletin*, March 1960, 9–10; Fred J. Hart, "Cancer Control Act S.B. 194 Report," *National Health Federation Bulletin*, June 1959, 3–4; Fred J. Hart, "Final Report on the Cancer Control Act," *National Health Federation Bulletin*, August 1959, 11–12; "The Cancer Law, 1959–1964," 5.

81. Fred J. Hart, "National Health Federation a Force to Be Reckoned With," *National Health Federation Bulletin*, January 1957, 4; Fred J. Hart, "President's Annual Report," *National Health Federation Bulletin*, February 1958, 9; "Washington Office Opens Feb. 1," *National Health Federation Bulletin*, February 1958, 2–3; Helen Frost, "Cancer 'Quacks' Add to Victims' Misfortune," *The Republic*, May 11, 1960, 11 (NHF reports 10,000 members).

82. Robert C. Toth, "U.S. Investigation of Krebiozen Due," *New York Times*, January 16, 1963, 9; Elinor Langer, "Krebiozen: FDA, NIH Still on Trail of Anticancer Drug, and Congress on Trail of Agencies," *Science* 141, no. 3585 (September 1963): 1021–23; Nate Haseltine, "Rally at Capitol Hails Medicine Facing Ban," *Washington Post*, May 15, 1963, A12; "Cancer Drug Ban Opposed," *The Sun*, May 15, 1963, 23; Martin J. Weil, "FDA Aides Refuse Krebiozen Demand," *Washington Post*, March 29, 1966, B2; "Drug Protest," photograph, *The Austin Statesman*, March 30, 1966.

83. Weil, "FDA Aides Refuse Krebiozen Demand," B2.

84. James F. Holland, "The Krebiozen Story: Is Cancer Quackery Dead?," *Journal of the American Medical Association* 200, no. 3 (April 1967): 213–18; "Tests Indicate New Drug Benefits Cancer Cases," *New York Times*, March 27, 1951, 31.

85. Young, *Medical Messiahs*, 401; Keith Wailoo, *How Cancer Crossed the Color Line* (New York: Oxford University Press, 2011), 123–29; Holland, "The Krebiozen Story"; Patterson, *Dread Disease*, 1989, 163–66.

86. James E. Hague, "A Cancer 'Cure' and Its Backer Found Wanting," *Washington Post*, November 18, 1951, B3.

87. Fitzgerald Report, 83 Cong. Rec. A5350 (1953) (statement of Sen. Langer).

88. Fitzgerald Report, 83 Cong. Rec. A5350 (1953) (statement of Sen. Langer); Herbert Bailey, *Krebiozen—Key to Cancer?* (New York: Hermitage House, 1955; Andrew Conway Ivy, *Observations on Krebiozen in the Management of Cancer* (Chicago: H. Regnery, 1956); Robert K. Plumb, "Cancer Drug Test Balked at Parley," *New York Times*, October 25, 1958, 18; Percy Wood, "Cancer Group Hits Ivy Rules on Drug Test," *Chicago Daily Tribune*, March 9, 1959, B12; "Cancer Group to Evaluate Krebiozen Value," *Fort Lauderdale News*, October 1, 1961, 38; "Krebiozen Backer Disputes U.S. Aide," *New York Times*, August 26, 1962, 57; James F. Holland, "Krebiozen Story."

89. FD&C Act § 505(a), (i); 28 Fed. Reg. 179 (Jan. 8, 1963) (codified at 21 C.F.R. pt. 312).

90. Toth, "U.S. Investigation of Krebiozen Due," 9; "Cancer Drug Ban Opposed," 23; Haseltine, "Rally at Capitol," A12; "Demonstrator Arrested at White House," photograph, *Washington Post*, June 5, 1963, B6; "An Open Letter," advertisement, *Washington Post*, June 6, 1963, A14; Langer, "Krebiozen: FDA Deadline Brings New, but Not the Final, Episode in Controversy over Cancer Drug," *Science* 141, no. 3575 (July 5, 1963): 31–33.

91. Robert C. Toth, "Showdown Near over Krebiozen," *New York Times*, June 6, 1963, 22; Robert C. Toth, "U.S. Is Receiving Krebiozen Data," *New York Times*, June 8, 1963, 52; Robert C. Toth, "Krebiozen Maker Criticized by U.S.," *New York Times*, July 4, 1963, 19; "Krebiozen Maker Ends Tests Plea," *New York Times*, July 13, 1963, 15; W. Joynes McFarlan, "U.S. Calls Krebiozen Inexpensive Acid, Ineffective in Treatment of Cancer," *Washington Post*, September 8, 1963, A3; John Kelly, "A Cure-All for Cancer?: Early Federal Chemist Proved Them Wrong," *Washington Post*, August 27, 2017, C03; Langer, "Krebiozen: FDA, NIH Still on Trail," 1021–23; Nate Haseltine, "U.S. Finds Krebiozen Has No Value," *Washington Post*, September 27, 1963, B10; Nate Haseltine, "Krebiozen Ruled Completely Useless as a Cancer Cure by U.S. Officials," *Washington Post*, October 16, 1963, A1.

92. "Cancer Group Asks Probe of Krebiozen Ban," *Hartford Courant*, February 3, 1964; "Krebiozen Ban Hit at Rally; Ask Probe," *Newsday*, February 3, 1964;; "Krebiozen Backers Demand Study," *Pocono Record*, February 10, 1964; "National Group Formed to Fight for Krebiozen," *Lebanon Daily News*, February 12, 1964; "Picket Cancer Society Office over Krebiozen," *Lebanon Daily News*, February 12, 1964; "Cancer 'Cure' Picket Arrested," *Washington Post*, June 23, 1964, C1; "Krebiozen Sit-Ins Ask for LBJ's Intervention," *Austin Statesman*, October 30, 1964; "Krebiozen Protest Held at White House," *New York Times*, November 1, 1964, 42; "Krebiozen Protest to LBJ?," *Boston Globe*, November 1, 1964.

93. Donald Janson, "Maker of Krebiozen Freed on All Counts," *New York Times*, February 1, 1966, 1.

94. Laine Friedman Robins, Obituary, June 17, 2003, on file with author; "Senators Ask Relaxing of Drug Shipping Ban," *Los Angeles Times*, July 31, 1964, 22; 109 Cong. Rec. 14412 (1963).

95. Keith Wailoo, *How Cancer Crossed the Color Line*; Mazur, "Opinion Poll Measurement of American Confidence in Science," 17.

96. "Delaney Bill Deemed Most Effective of Four: NHF Members Urged to Write Harris," *National Health Federation Bulletin*, April 1958, 3; *Food Additives: Hearing before a H. Subcomm. of the Comm. on Interstate & Foreign Com.*, 85th Cong. 488–96 (1958) (statement of Willard Gleeson, Vice President, NHF); *Drug Industry Act of 1962: Hearings on H.R. 11581 and H.R. 11582 Before the H. Comm. on Interstate & Foreign Commerce*, 87 Cong. 513–18 (1962) (statement of Clinton R. Miller, Assistant to the President, NHF); "House Group Toughens Bill on Drug Control," *Philadelphia Inquirer*, September 20, 1962; Clinton R. Miller, "Statement on the FTC's Proposed Rule-Making Pertaining to Advertising and Labeling of Cigarettes," *National Health Federation Bulletin*, May 1964; George H. Fisher, "The Fight against Smog," *National Health Federation Bulletin*, January 1961, 19–20; " 'Silent Spring' and 'Stay Young Longer,' " *National Health Federation Bulletin*, January 1963, 13.

Chapter 6

1. The headlines are from the first page of the *San Francisco Examiner* on November 8, 18, and 27, 1973. Philip Elwood, "The Who's First Show on the Road Falls Apart," *San Francisco Examiner*, November 21, 1973, 22.

2. "Rally Protests Vitamin Curbs," *San Francisco Examiner*, November 12, 1973, 26; 38 Fed. Reg. 20,708, 20,723, 20,725, 20,730 (Aug. 2, 1973).

3. Harvey A. Levenstein, *Paradox of Plenty: A Social History of Eating in Modern America* (New York: Oxford University Press, 1994), 162–66; Laura J. Miller, *Building Nature's Market: The Business and Politics of Natural Foods* (Chicago: University of Chicago Press, 2017), 175–77; James Harvey Young, *American Health Quackery: Collected Essays of James Harvey Young* (Princeton, NJ: Princeton University Press, 2014), 72.

4. "Come to the Health Freedom Rally," advertisement, *San Francisco Examiner*, November 8, 1973, 33; Jim Wood, "1st S.F. Work Day: BART Packs 'em In," *San Francisco Examiner*, November 5, 1973, 1; Jeffrey Haydu, "Cultural Modeling in Two Eras of U.S. Food Protest: Grahamites (1830s) and Organic Advocates (1960s–70s)," *Social Problems* 58, no. 3 (August 2011): 461–87; Levenstein, *Paradox of Plenty*, 178–88; Miller, *Building Nature's Market*, 145–55.

5. "Go to Health, FDA!," advertisement, *Daily Independent Journal*, November 8, 1973, 19; "Rally Protests Vitamin Curbs," 26; "Vitamin Restrictions Opposed," *Times-Advocate*, November 12, 1973, 4; "New Curbs on Vitamins Ires Health Enthusiasts," *Fresno Bee*, November 13, 1973, 28; Elaine Woo, "Gypsy Boots, 89: Colorful Promoter of Healthy Food and Lifestyles," *Los Angeles Times*, August 10, 2004.

6. "Editorial Comments," *National Health Federation Bulletin*, January 1973, 1; Charles Creculius, "The President's Message," *National Health Federation Bulletin*, January 1973, 3; Richard D. Lyons, "Disputed Health Lobby Is Pressing for a Bill to Overturn Any Limits on Sales of Vitamins," *New York Times*, May 14, 1973, 17; Ralph Lee Smith, "Amazing Facts about a 'Crusade' That Can Hurt Your Health," *Today's Health*, October 1966.

7. H.R. 643, 93rd Cong. (1973); Clinton R. Miller, "What You Should Know about the Hosmer Bill," *National Health Federation Bulletin*, April 1973, 10; "Of Vitamins, Minerals: Fighting the FDA," *Washington Post*, January 20, 1974, L5.

8. Clinton R. Miller, "Annual Report of Activities by NHF's Legislative Advocate," *National Health Federation Bulletin*, January 1974, 8; H.R. 7474, 93rd Cong. (1973); James J. Kilpatrick, "Food for Thought," op-ed, *Baltimore Sun*, February 4, 1973, K6; James J. Kilpatrick, "What Gives FDA Right to Play Papa to Us All," op-ed, *Baltimore Sun*, August 16, 1973, A15; Nicholas von Hoffman, "A and D as Mother's Little Helpers," Commentary, *Washington Post*, June 6, 1973, B1; Dan Hurley, *Natural Causes: Death, Lies and Politics in America's Vitamin and Herbal Supplement Industry* (New York: Broadway Books, 2006), 48.

9. "Pro-Vitamin Group Pickets FDA Office," *Napa Valley Register*, October 24, 1973, 32; Nancy L. Ross, "Defending the Right to Vitamins and Minerals: Battling the FDA," *Washington Post*, October 30, 1973, E1; "Vitamin, Mineral, and Diet Supplements," § Subcommittee on Public Health and Environment of Committee on Interstate and Foreign Commerce (1973), 738 (Broomfield testimony); *Hearings on H.R. 643, H.R. 10093, H.R. 10206, H.R. 10994, H.R. 11085, H.R. 11203 before a H. Subcomm. on Pub. Health & Env't of the Comm. on Interstate & Foreign Com.*, 93rd Cong. 733 (1973) (statement of Rep. Sisk).

10. *Food Supplement Legislation, 1974: Hearing on S. 2801 & S. 3867 before a S. Subcomm. on Health of the Comm. on Labor & Pub. Welfare*, 93rd Cong. 850–52 (1974) (statement of Mr. King).

11. *Nat'l Nutritional Foods Ass'n v. FDA*, 504 F.2d 761 (2d Cir. 1974); Pub. L. No. 94-278, 90 Stat. 410, Title V (1976); "Congress Blocks Efforts by F.D.A. to Curb Vitamins," *New York Times*, April 14, 1976, 16.

12. Edward D. Berkowitz, *Something Happened: A Political and Cultural Overview of the Seventies* (New York: Columbia University Press, 2005), 6; Peter N. Carroll, *It Seemed Like Nothing Happened: America in the 1970s*, repr. ed. (New Brunswick, NJ: Rutgers University Press, 1990), 235; see also Bruce J. Schulman, *The Seventies: The Great Shift in American Culture, Society, and Politics*, repr. ed. (Cambridge, MA: Da Capo Press, 2002), 140; "The ANES Guide to Public Opinion and Electoral Behavior," Resources, ANES, website. Even more dramatically, the subset of respondents saying they "just about always" trusted the federal government plummeted from 17 percent in 1966 to only 2 percent in 1980.

13. *Confidence in Leaders of Institutions: Medicine (1966–1980)*, distributed by The Harris Poll; *General Social Survey: Confidence in Scientific Community (1973–2018)*, distributed by University of Chicago, National Opinion Research Center; Roger D. Launius, "Public Opinion Polls and Perceptions of US Human Spaceflight," *Space Policy* 19, no.

3 (August 2003): 163–75; Richard D. Lyons, "2 Moon Landings Dropped by NASA in Economy Move," *New York Times*, September 3, 1970, 1; John Noble Wilford, "Apollo 17 Splashes Down Accurately in Successful Finale to Moon Project," *New York Times*, December 20, 1972, 1.

14. "Kohoutek Fades Out as Star Attraction: Too Clean to Shine: NASA Revises Estimate of Comet's Brilliance, Says It Doesn't Have Enough Dust," *Wall Street Journal*, December 28, 1973, 6; Victor K. McElheny, "Viewers of Kohoutek in Dark, but Expert Sees Ray of Hope," *New York Times*, January 11, 1974, 13; Carroll, *It Seemed Like Nothing Happened*, 218–19; Berkowitz, *Something Happened*, 128–30. On the decline in the faith in science generally in the 1970s, see "Science, Technology, and Political Conflict," in *Controversy: Politics of Technical Decisions*, 3rd ed., ed. Dorothy Nelkin (Thousand Oaks, CA: Sage Publications, 1992), x–xiii.

15. Arthur Allen, *Vaccine: The Controversial Story of Medicine's Greatest Lifesaver* (New York: W. W. Norton, 2008), 259–61; Thomas O'Toole, "Why the Swine Flu Program Failed," *Washington Post*, January 30, 1977, 35; Carroll, *It Seemed Like Nothing Happened*, 306–7; Nicholas von Hoffman, "Placing the Blame for the Swine Flu Fiasco on the Doctors," *Washington Post*, January 22, 1977, E2; Elena Conis, *Vaccine Nation: America's Changing Relationship with Immunization* (Chicago: University of Chicago Press, 2016), 94–95.

16. Allen, *Vaccine*, 261; Conis, *Vaccine Nation*, 94–95, 140–49.

17. Ivan Illich, *Medical Nemesis: The Expropriation of Health* (New York: Pantheon, 1982), 3–4; James C. Whorton, *Nature Cures: The History of Alternative Medicine in America* (New York: Oxford University Press, 2004), 245–49; Paul Starr, *The Social Transformation of American Medicine: The Rise of a Sovereign Profession and the Making of a Vast Industry*, repr. ed. (New York: Basic Books, 1984), 408–11; John C. Burnham, *Health Care in America: A History* (Baltimore: Johns Hopkins University Press, 2015), 424–27; Morton Mintz, *The Therapeutic Nightmare*, 4th ed. (Boston: Houghton Mifflin, 1965); Rick J. Carlson, *The End of Medicine* (New York: Wiley, 1975); John H. Knowles, ed., *Doing Better and Feeling Worse: Health in the United States* (New York: W. W. Norton, 1977); Robin Cook, *Coma* (New York: Signet, 2002).

18. Whorton, *Nature Cures*, 221, 245–79; *Cambridge Reports National Omnibus Survey* (January 1979), distributed by Cambridge Reports and Research International.

19. Robert C. Fuller, *Alternative Medicine and American Religious Life* (New York: Oxford University Press, 1989), chap. 5.

20. Fuller, *Alternative Medicine and American Religious Life*, 114–17; Schulman, *The Seventies*, 96–100.

21. Berkowitz, *Something Happened*, 133–57; Dominic Sandbrook, *Mad as Hell: The Crisis of the 1970s and the Rise of the Populist Right*, repr. ed. (New York: Anchor, 2012), 249–50; James T. Patterson, *Restless Giant: The United States from Watergate to Bush v. Gore*, repr. ed. (New York: Oxford University Press, 2007), 10.

22. Ruth R. Faden and Tom L. Beauchamp, *A History and Theory of Informed Consent* (New York: Oxford University Press, 1986), 93; David J. Rothman, *Strangers at the Bedside: A History of How Law and Bioethics Transformed Medical Decision Making* (New York: Basic Books, 1991), 145.

23. Faden and Beauchamp, *Informed Consent*, 59, 86–87, 89, 90–91, 94.

24. B. D. Colen, "Dispute over Laetrile Focuses Attention on Rights of Patients," *Washington Post*, May 29, 1977, 18. See generally Lewis A. Grossman, "FDA and the Rise of the Empowered Consumer," *Administrative Law Review* 66, no. 3 (Summer 2014): 627–77.

25. Sandra Morgen, *Into Our Own Hands: The Women's Health Movement in the United States, 1969–1990* (Piscataway, NJ: Rutgers University Press, 2002); Carol S. Weisman, *Women's Health Care: Activist Traditions and Institutional Change* (Baltimore: Johns Hopkins University Press, 1998); *Roe v. Wade*, 410 U.S. 113, 164 (1973). Mary Ziegler, *After Roe: The Lost History of the Abortion Debate* (Cambridge, MA: Harvard University Press, 2015), 160–69.

26. On the rhetorical transformation of *Roe v. Wade* from a medical rights decision to a women's rights decision, see Ziegler, *After Roe*, 157–85; Mary Ziegler, *Beyond Abortion: Roe v. Wade and the Battle for Privacy* (Cambridge, MA: Harvard University Press, 2018), 158–60. On the use of *Roe* in medical freedom campaigns in the 1970s, see Ziegler, *Beyond Abortion*, 140–57. On the abortion movement's increasing focus on the "choice" theme in the late 1970s, see Ziegler, *After Roe*, 138–41.

27. Amy Sue Bix, "Engendering Alternatives: Women's Health Care Choices and Feminist Medical Rebellions," in *The Politics of Healing: Histories of Alternative Medicine in Twentieth-Century North America*, ed. Robert D. Johnson (New York: Routledge, 2004), 156–62; Elizabeth Siegel Watkins, *On the Pill: A Social History of Oral Contraceptives, 1950–1970*, repr. ed. (Baltimore: Johns Hopkins University Press, 2001), 103–28; Grossman, "FDA and the Rise of the Empowered Consumer," 652–53; 35 Fed. Reg. 5962 (Apr. 10, 1970) (proposed rule); 35 Fed. Reg. 9001 (June 11, 1970) (final rule).

28. Barbara Seaman, "Health Activism, American Feminist," *Jewish Women's Archive* (blog), March 20, 2009; Morgen, *Into Our Own Hands*, 29–30; Requirement for Labeling Directed to the Patient, 42 Fed. Reg. 37,636 (July 22, 1977) (to be codified at 21 C.F.R. pt. 310); Grossman, "FDA and the Rise of the Empowered Consumer," 653–54; *Pharm. Mfrs. Ass'n v. FDA*, 484 F. Supp. 1179 (D. Del. 1980), *aff'd per curiam*, 634 F.2d 106 (3d Cir. 1980) (emphasis added).

29. On the feminist women's health clinic movement, see Morgen, *Into Our Own Hands*, 22–24; Judith A. Houck, "The Best Prescription for Women's Health: Feminist Approaches to Well-Woman Care," in *Prescribed: Writing, Filling, Using, and Abusing the Prescription in Modern America*, ed. Jeremy A. Greene and Elizabeth Siegel Watkins (Baltimore: Johns Hopkins University Press, 2012), 134–56; "Rally Aids Feminist Court Fight," *Independent*, November 16, 1972, 39.

30. Raymond G. DeVries, *Making Midwives Legal: Childbirth, Medicine, and the Law*, 2nd ed. (Columbus: Ohio State University Press, 1996); Katherine Beckett and Bruce Hoffman, "Challenging Medicine: Law, Resistance, and the Cultural Politics of Childbirth," *Law & Society Review* 39, no. 1 (March 2005): 125–70; "CPMs Legal Status by State," *The Big Push for Midwives* (blog).

31. Boston Women's Health Collective, *Women and Their Bodies: A Course* (Boston: The Collective, 1970), 101; Bix, "Engendering Alternatives," 157–58, 163; "Our Bodies, Ourselves: The Nine U.S. Editions," *Publications* (blog), *Our Bodies, Ourselves*.

32. Bix, "Engendering Alternatives," 154–56; Arianne Shahvisi, "Medicine Is Patriarchal, but Alternative Medicine Is Not the Answer," *Journal of Bioethical Inquiry* 16, no. 1 (December 2018): 99; D. M. Eisenberg et al., "Trends in Alternative Medicine Use in the United States, 1990–1997: Results of a Follow-Up National Survey," *JAMA* 280, no. 18 (November 11, 1998): 1569–75; Peter M. Wolsko et al., "Insurance Coverage, Medical Conditions, and Visits to Alternative Medicine Providers: Results of a National Survey," *Archives of Internal Medicine* 162, no. 3 (February 11, 2002): 281–87.

33. Margaret Wooddell and David J. Hess, *Women Confront Cancer* (New York: New York University Press, 1998), 1, 197–208.

34. Laetrile: Commissioner's Decision, 42 Fed. Reg. 39768, 39772 (Aug. 5, 1977) (hereinafter "Commissioner's Decision").

35. Two excellent sources for this history are Young, *American Health Quackery*, 205–55, and Commissioner's Decision, 42 Fed. Reg. at 39768.

36. Young, *American Health Quackery*, 208–17, 239; "The Cancer Law, 1959–1964: Cal. Dept. of Pub. Health, The Cancer Law: 1959–1964, 4, 32–40 (1964); Ron Einstoss, "Doctor Indicted on Cancer Drug Charges," *Los Angeles Times*, September 14, 1968, B1; "Doctor Jailed for Useless Cancer 'Cure,'" *Los Angeles Times*, July 18, 1969, B10; William Drummond, "Cancer Victims Cross Border to Be Treated at Tijuana Clinics," *Los Angeles Times*, December 11, 1967, 3; for a detailed profile of McNaughton, see Marci McDonald, "Cashing In on Cancer," *Maclean's*, January 1, 1976, 22–28.

37. James C. Petersen and Gerald E. Markle, "Politics and Science in the Laetrile Controversy," *Social Studies of Science* 9, no. 2 (May 1979): 149.

38. Petersen and Markle, "Politics and Science in the Laetrile Controversy"; Drummond, "Cancer Victims Cross Border to Be Treated at Tijuana Clinics," 3; Lloyd Shearer, "The Cancer Clinics of Tijuana," *Parade*, March 10, 1968, 132.

39. Daniel Carpenter, *Reputation and Power: Organizational Image and Pharmaceutical Regulation at the FDA* (Princeton, NJ: Princeton University Press, 2010), 413; Young, *American Health Quackery*, 214; Ernst T. Krebs, "The Nitrilosides (Vitamin B-17)—Their Nature, Occurrence, and Metabolic Significance (Antineoplastic Vitamin B-17)," *Journal of Applied Nutrition* 22, no. 3 (1970): 76–78; Nicholas von Hoffman, "And If It Works . . .," commentary, *Washington Post*, June 4, 1971, B1.

40. Krebs, "Nitrilosides," 76–78; Young, *American Health Quackery*, 219.

41. Leroy F. Aarons and Stuart Auerbach, "Cancer Relief or Quackery?: Cancer Treatment or Quack Drug?," *Washington Post*, May 26, 1974, C1; Wooddell and Hess, *Women Confront Cancer*, 199–203.

42. Young, *American Health Quackery*; Benjamin Wilson, "The Rise and Fall of Laetrile," *Quackwatch* (blog); Aarons and Auerbach, "Cancer Relief or Quackery?"

43. Young, *American Health Quackery*, 218–19; Morton O. Wagenfeld et al., "Notes from the Cancer Underground: Health Attitudes and Practices of Participants in the Laetrile Movement," *Social Science & Medicine. Part A: Medical Psychology & Medical Sociology* 13, no. 4 (June 1979): 483–85; David J. Hess, "Technology- and Product-Oriented Movements: Approximating Social Movement Studies and Science and Technology Studies," *Science, Technology, & Human Values* 30, no. 4 (October 1, 2005): 522; David Hess, *Evaluating Alternative Cancer Therapies: A Guide*

to the Science and Politics of an Emerging Medical Field (New Brunswick, NJ: Rutgers University Press, 1998), 103.

44. Hess, *Evaluating Alternative Cancer Therapies*, 16–17; Lynn Lilliston, "Doctor Hurls FDA Challenge on Cancer Drug," *Los Angeles Times*, July 16, 1973, C1; Frank Cousineau, "History of the Cancer Control Society," *Our History* (blog), *Cancer Control Society*; Wagenfeld et al., "Notes from the Cancer Underground"; Ziegler, *Beyond Abortion*, 142; Petersen and Markle, "Politics and Science in the Laetrile Controversy," 151; David J. Hess, "CAM Cancer Therapies in Twentieth-Century North America," in *The Politics of Healing: Histories of Alternative Medicine in Twentieth-Century North America*, ed. Robert D. Johnston (New York: Routledge, 2004), 238.

45. Matthew Schneirov and Jonathan David Geczik, "Beyond the Culture Wars: The Politics of Alternative Health," in *The Politics of Healing*, 245–56.

46. "Transcript of Questions and Answers in President Carter's Call-In," *New York Times*, March 6, 1977, 30–33; "Carter Answers the Last Question," *New York Times*, March 9, 1977, 14.

47. "The Cancer Drug Dilemma," editorial, *New York Times*, February 11, 1977, A26; "Clutching at Apricot Pits," editorial, *Los Angeles Times*, May 30, 1977, D4; James J. Kilpatrick, "Laetrile: Good News and Bad," op-ed, *Los Angeles Times*, April 26, 1977, C5; Nicholas von Hoffman, "A Cure for High Medical and Hospital Costs: Doctors in Competition," op-ed, *Washington Post*, May 13, 1977, D8.

48. *Roper Reports Poll: Consumerism/Government/Retirement* (July 9, 1977), distributed by The Roper Organization; "Why Not a Laetrile Bill?," editorial, *Washington Post*, May 22, 1977; F. J. Ingelfinger, "Laetrilomania," *New England Journal of Medicine* 296, no. 20 (May 19, 1977): 1167–68.

49. "Laetrile Again Termed Worthless by the FDA," *Washington Post*, April 15, 1977, A9; "Federal Agents Raid Laetrile Manufacturers," *Chicago Tribune*, July 15, 1977, 8; Everett R. Holles, "19 Indicted by U.S. in Cancer Drug Plot," *New York Times*, 1976, 81; Carpenter, *Reputation and Power*, 416–17; Ziegler, *Beyond Abortion*, 147–52. The figure of thirteen states in 1977 was compiled by the author from various sources. The figure of twenty-seven states by 1987 is from Young, *American Health Quackery*, 91–92; Hess, *Evaluating Alternative Cancer Therapies*, 191.

50. H.R. 12573, 94th Cong. (1976); H.R. 54, 95th Cong. (1977); "Legalize Laetrile as a Cancer Drug?: Interview with Representative Steven D. Symms," *U.S. News & World Report*, June 13, 1977; H.R. 54 had nineteen co-sponsors but other versions of the bill garnered support as well. See H.R. 4051 95th Cong. (1977) (24 co-sponsors); H.R. 4648, 95th Cong. (1977) (24 co-sponsors); H.R. 6611, 95th Cong. (1977) (23 co-sponsors); H.R. 8544, 95th Cong. (1977) (14 co-sponsors); H.R. 10397, 95th Cong. (1977) (1 co-sponsor); and H.R. 11261, 95th Cong. (1978) (1 co-sponsor).

51. *Banning of the Drug Laetrile from Interstate Commerce by FDA: Hearing before the S. Subcomm. on Health & Sci. Res. of the Comm. on Human Res.*, 95th Cong. 250, 252–53 (1977); Carpenter, *Reputation and Power*, 418.

52. *Rutherford v. United States*, 399 F. Supp. 1208 (W.D. Okla. 1975).

53. *Rutherford v. United States*, 542 F.2d 1137, 1140, 1144 (10th Cir. 1976); *Rutherford v. United States*, 424 F. Supp. 105, 107 (W.D. Okla. 1977). The "generally recognized

as safe and effective" exception and one grandfather clause are contained in section 201(p) of the FD&C Act, 21 U.S.C. § 321(p). The other grandfather clause, which is not codified in the FD&C Act, appears in section 107(c) of the Drug Amendments of 1962, Pub. L. 87-781, 76 Stat. 780, 788–89 (1962).

54. Phillip S. Brimble, "Laetrile Ineffective, FDA Hearing Told," *Washington Post*, May 3, 1977, A4; U.S. Food & Drug Admin., Docket No. 77N-0048, Laetrile Administrative Rule Making Hearing Oral Argument, 38, 50, 191, 308 (1977).

55. Laetrile Oral Argument, 291 (testimony of Philip B. Lipsin, Educ. Dir., Truth about Cancer), 100 (testimony of Carol M. Dunn, Sec. of the Bd. of Pol. of Liberty Lobby), 81–82 (testimony of Betty Lee Morales, Sec. of the Nat'l Health Found).

56. Laetrile Oral Argument, 70 (testimony of James Gordon Roberts), 259 (testimony of Walter Ermer, D.D.), 311 (testimony of Glenn L. Rutherford), 226–27 (testimony of Norma Manke).

57. Laetrile Oral Argument, 226–27 (testimony of Ms. Manke), 455 (testimony of Kenneth Coe).

58. Laetrile Oral Argument, 293 (testimony of John Litle, Dir., Citizens Truth about Cancer), 345, 349, 352, 354, 357 (testimony of Robert W. Bradford, President, Comm. for Freedom of Choice in Cancer Therapy).

59. Laetrile Oral Argument, 17–27 (testimony of Ed Griffin, President, Am. Media), 48–51 (testimony of Michael Culbert, Comm. for Freedom of Choice in Cancer Therapy), 251 (testimony of Mr. Ermer), 348–54 (testimony of Mr. Bradford), 410–12 (testimony of Dean Burk, President, Dean Burk Foundation, Inc.), 452–53 (testimony of Mr. Coe).

60. Peter Barton Hutt, Richard A. Merrill, and Lewis A. Grossman, *Food and Drug Law: Cases and Materials*, 4th ed. (St. Paul, MN: Foundation Press, 2014), 660–67.

61. Commissioner's Decision, 42 Fed. Reg. at 39803.

62. *Rutherford v. United States*, 438 F. Supp. 1287, 1299, 1300–1 (W.D. Okla. 1977).

63. Mary Knudson, "Laetrile Ruling Delights Seller, Shocks FDA," *The Sun*, December 7, 1977, C1; *Rogers v. St. Bd. of Med. Exam'rs*, 371 So.2d 1037 (Fla. Dist. Ct. App. 1979); *Andrews v. Ballard*, 498 F. Supp. 1038, 1057 (S.D. Tex. 1980).

64. Jace Weaver, *Then to the Rock Let Me Fly: Luther Bohanon and Judicial Activism* (Norman: University of Oklahoma Press, 1993), xii, 71–116, 157; *Dowell v. Board of Education*, 338 F. Supp. 1256, 1273 (W.D. Okla. 1972); Ziegler, *Beyond Abortion*, 147–52.

65. *Rutherford v. United States*, 582 F.2d 1234 (10th Cir. 1978); Commissioner's Decision, 42 Fed. Reg. at 39,786–87, 39, 802–3.

66. *United States v. Rutherford*, 442 U.S. 544, 556 (1979).

67. *California v. Privitera*, 591 P.2d 919 (Cal. 1979), *cert. denied*, 444 U.S. 949 (1979); *Privitera*, 591 P.2d at 932–36 (Bird, J., dissenting).

68. *Rutherford v. United States*, 616 F.2d 455, 457 (10th Cir. 1980), *cert. denied*, 449 U.S. 937 (1980); *Carnohan v. United States*, 616 F.2d 1120, 1122 (9th Cir. 1980).

69. Laura Kalman, *The Strange Career of Legal Liberalism* (New Haven, CT: Yale University Press, 1998), 6–7, 58–59; Ziegler, *Beyond Abortion*, 202–38.

70. "McQueen Death Renews Cancer Treatment Debate," *New York Times*, November 9, 1980, 21; Young, *American Health Quackery*, 232–34.

Chapter 7

1. This chapter is drawn primarily from Lewis A. Grossman, "AIDS Activists, FDA Regulation, and the Amendment of America's Drug Constitution," *American Journal of Law & Medicine* 42, no. 4 (November 1, 2016): 687–742.

2. Centers for Disease Control and Prevention, "CDC Fact Sheet: Today's HIV/AIDS Epidemic," August 2016; *ACT UP & ACT NOW Seize Control of the FDA* (SuchIsLifeVideos, 2014), video, https://www.youtube.com/watch?v=s70aCOflRgY.

3. Daniel Carpenter, *Reputation and Power: Organizational Image and Pharmaceutical Regulation at the FDA* (Princeton, NJ: Princeton University Press, 2010), 436–38; Investigational New Drug, Antibiotic, and Biological Drug Product Regulations; Treatment Use and Sale, 52 Fed. Reg. 19,466 (May 22, 1987).

4. Philip M. Boffey, "New Initiative to Speed AIDS Drugs Is Assailed," *New York Times*, July 5, 1988, C1; William C. Buhles, "Compassionate Use: A Story of Ethics and Science in the Development of a New Drug," *Perspectives in Biology and Medicine* 54, no. 3 (Summer 2011): 310–11.

5. Michael Nesline, interview by Sarah Schulman, *ACTUP Oral History Project*, March 24, 2003, 43. Transcripts of *ACTUP Oral History Project* interviews are available online at http://www.actuporalhistory.org/interviews/. The details of the demonstration related in this chapter are drawn from various sources, including *ACT UP & ACT NOW Seize Control of the FDA*; David France, *How to Survive a Plague* (Public Square Films, 2012); *ACTUP Oral History Project* (various interviews); Paul Duggan, "1,000 Swarm FDA's Rockville Office to Demand Approval of AIDS Drugs," *Washington Post*, October 12, 1988, B1; "176 Arrested at FDA AIDS Drug Protest, Many Employees Don't Go to Work," *Health Daily*, October 12, 1988, 2–4; "FDA Resumes Business after AIDS Demonstration," *Health Daily*, October 17, 1988, 7.

6. On "superstatutes," see William N. Eskridge Jr. and John A. Ferejohn, *A Republic of Statutes: The New American Constitution* (New Haven: Yale University Press, 2010); William N. Eskridge Jr. and John A. Ferejohn, "Super-Statutes," *Duke Law Journal* 50, no. 5 (March 2001). "Federal Food, Drug, and Cosmetic Act," Pub. L. No. 75–717, 52 Stat. 1040 (1938); "Drug Amendments of 1962," Pub. L. No. 87–781, 76 Stat. 80 (1962); "Medical Device Amendments of 1976," Pub. L. No. 94–295, 90 Stat. 539 (1976). Eskridge and Ferejohn identify the 1938 FD&C Act as a "superstatute" in "Super-Statutes,"1257–58. On FDA's positive reputation, see Carpenter, *Reputation and Power*.

7. Marc Stein, *Rethinking the Gay and Lesbian Movement* (New York: Routledge, 2012), 157–63; Sean Strub, "Condomizing Jesse Helms' House," *Huff Post*, May 25, 2011.

8. Steven Epstein, *Impure Science: AIDS, Activism, and the Politics of Knowledge* (Berkeley: University of California Press, 1996), 13.

9. Drug Amendments of 1962, Pub. L. No. 87-781 § 103, 76 Stat. 780, 782–84 (1962) (codified as amended at 21 U.S.C. § 355(i)); New Drugs; Procedural and Interpretative Regulations; Investigational Use, 28 Fed. Reg. 179 (Jan. 8, 1963). These regulations, as amended, are now at 21 C.F.R. Part 312 (2016).

10. § 102, 76 Stat. at 781 (codified at 21 U.S.C. § 355(d)) at 781 (codified at 21 U.S.C. § 355(d)). FDA reviewers had in fact been taking efficacy considerations into account when considering NDAs since the late 1940s. Carpenter, *Reputation and Power*, 118–227.

11. *Drug Safety (Part 1): Hearings before a Subcomm. of the H. Comm. on Gov't Operations*, 88th Cong. 150, 153–54 (1964) (statement of FDA Commissioner George P. Larrick).

12. § 102, 76 Stat. 780, 781 (codified as amended at 21 U.S.C. § 355(d)); FDA, *Guidance for Industry: Providing Clinical Evidence of Effectiveness of Human Drugs and Biological Products* (1998), 3.

13. Carpenter, *Reputation and Power*, 374–80; Peter Barton Hutt, Richard A. Merrill, and Lewis A. Grossman, *Food and Drug Law: Cases and Materials*, 3rd ed. (St. Paul, MN: Foundation Press, 2007, 744–51; Joseph A. DiMasi, "New Drug Development in the United States 1963 to 1999," *Clinical Pharmacology and Therapeutics* 69, no. 5 (May 2001): 291; Jim Eigo et al., *FDA Action Handbook* (n.p.: ACT UP, 1988).

14. Carpenter, *Reputation and Power*, 433–42; *AIDS Drug Development and Related Issues: Hearing before a Subcomm. of the H. Comm. on Gov't Operations*, 99th Cong. 103 (1986) (statement of Harry Meyer, Dir., Ctr. for Drugs & Biologics).

15. Peter Barton Hutt, Richard A. Merrill, and Lewis A. Grossman, *Food and Drug Law: Cases and Materials*, 4th ed. (St. Paul, MN: Foundation Press, 2014), 768–70; Richard A. Merrill, "The Architecture of Government Regulation of Medical Products," *Virginia Law Review* 82, no. 8 (1996): 1843.

16. Thomas O. McGarity, "Regulatory Reform in the Reagan Era," *Maryland Law Review* 45, no. 2 (1986): 253, 261; New Drug and Antibiotic Regulations, 47 Fed. Reg. 46,622, 46,622 (proposed Oct. 19, 1982) (to be codified at 21 C.F.R. pts. 310, 312, 314, 450, 431, and 433); Proposed New Drug, Antibiotic, and Biologic Drug Product Regulations, 48 Fed. Reg. 26,720, 26,742 (proposed June 9, 1983) (codified at 21 C.F.R. pt. 312).

17. Buhles, "Compassionate Use"; Caroline Rand Herron and Katherine Roberts, "A Ray of Hope for AIDS Patients," *New York Times*, September 21, 1986, A4; Carpenter, Reputation and Power, 436–37; Dale Gieringer, "Twice Wrong on AIDS," *New York Times*, January 12, 1987, A21.

18. 52 Fed. Reg. 8850, 8554, 8855–57 (proposed Mar. 19, 1987) (to be codified at 21 C.F.R. pt. 312).

19. *FDA Proposals to Ease Restrictions on the Use and Sale of Experimental Drugs: Hearing before a Subcomm. of the H. Comm. on Gov't Operations*, 100th. Cong., 2 (opening statement of Chairman Weiss), 38 (statement of Dr. Charles Moertel, Prof. of Oncology, Mayo Clinic & Mayo Med. Sch.), 100 (comments from Chairman Weiss); Gina Kolata, "Odd Alliance Would Speed New Drugs," *New York Times*, November 26, 1988, 9; Jonathan Kwitny, *Acceptable Risks* (New York: Simon & Schuster, 1992), 141, 148–49; "Drug-Lag Defenders," editorial, *Wall Street Journal*, May 15, 1987, 14.

20. 52 Fed. Reg. at 19,466, 19,476 (codified at 21 C.F.R. § 312.7(d)(2), (3)).

21. Philip M. Boffey, "Bush Favors Requiring AIDS Tests for Marriage License Application," *New York Times*, April 9, 1987, B8; Michael Hirsley, "Talk of AIDS Quarantine Spreads Like a Disease," *Chicago Tribune*, November 12, 1985, 1; Richard Restak, "Worry about Survival of Society First; Then AIDS Victims' Rights,"

Washington Post, September 8, 1985, C1; William F. Buckley Jr., "Identify All the Carriers," op-ed, *New York Times*, March 18, 1986, A27; Fran Smith, "Anxiety over AIDS Prompts Attacks Against Gays," *Philadelphia Inquirer*, January 27, 1985, C3.

22. Gregg Bordowitz, interview by Sarah Schulman, *ACTUP Oral History Project*, December 17, 2002, 31–32.

23. Deborah Gould, "Rock the Boat, Don't Rock the Boat, Baby: Ambivalence and the Emergence of Militant AIDS Activism," in *Passionate Politics: Emotions and Social Movements*, ed. Jeff Goodwin, James M. Jasper, and Francesca Polletta (Chicago: University of Chicago Press, 2001), 152–55; Deborah B. Gould, *Moving Politics: Emotion and ACT UP's Fight against AIDS* (Chicago: University of Chicago Press, 2009). The insight regarding the impact of the increase in HIV testing was provided by David Barr in a private communication with the author on February 2, 2020.

24. Kwitny, *Acceptable Risks*.

25. Elaine Woo, "Martin Delaney, Dies at 63; Crusader for Patients with AIDS," *Los Angeles Times*, January 27, 2009, B5; Kwitny, *Acceptable Risks*, 149.

26. Hutt, Merrill, and Grossman, *Food and Drug Law*, 2014, 772; Kwitny, *Acceptable Risks*, 141, 154, 195–97, 203–7; Marilyn Chase, "For Some AIDS Patients, Bootleg Drugs Are One Way to Preserve Some Hope," *Wall Street Journal*, October 5, 1987, 20; Robert Reinhold, "Infected but Not Ill, Many Try Unproved Drug to Block Aids," *New York Times*, May 20, 1987, B12; Philip M. Boffey, "F.D.A. Will Allow AIDS Patients to Import Unapproved Medicines," *New York Times*, July 24, 1988, 1; William Booth, "An Underground Drug for AIDS," *Science* 241, no. 4871 (September 9, 1988): 1279; Donald C. McLearn, *FDA Responds to ACT UP Demands* (Rockville, MD: FDA, 1988).

27. "This Is about People Dying: The Tactics of Early ACT UP and Lesbian Avengers in New York City," *ACT UP* (blog), n.d.; *FDA Proposals to Ease Restrictions on the Use and Sale of Experimental Drugs: Hearing before a Subcomm. of the H. Comm. on Gov't Operations*, 100th. Cong., 132 (1987) (testimony of Mr. Robinson).

28. Kwitny, *Acceptable Risks*, 150; Randy Shilts, a*nd the Band Played On: Politics, People, and the AIDS Epidemic* (New York: Macmillan, 2000), 135, 166–67, 209–10, 275, 309–11. See the following interviews by Sarah Schulman for the *ACTUP Oral History Project*: Larry Kramer, November 15, 2002, 7–8; Nesline, 8–9; Ron Goldberg, October 25, 2003, 59–60; and interview by Jim Hubbard: Maxine Wolfe, February 19, 2004, 40–42.

29. Larry Kramer, "The F.D.A.'s Callous Response to AIDS," *New York Times*, March 23, 1987, A19.

30. Linda Hirshman, *Victory: The Triumphant Gay Revolution*, repr. ed. (New York: Harper Perennial, 2013), 197.

31. 5 U.S.C. § 553(c), (e) (2018); "FDA Resumes Business after AIDS Demonstration."

32. See the following interviews by Sarah Schulman for the *ACTUP Oral History Project*: Bordowitz, 23 (paraphrasing Barr and Wheatley); David Barr, May 15, 2007, 36.

33. Bordowitz, interview, *ACTUP Oral History Project*, 23. Tarrow examines the "outsiders inside" phenomenon extensively in Sidney Tarrow, *Strangers at the Gates: Movements and States in Contentious Politics* (New York: Cambridge University Press, 2012).

34. See the following interviews by Sarah Schulman for the *ACTUP Oral History Project*: Mark Harrington, March 8, 2003, 45; David Kirschenbaum, October 19, 2003, 45.

35. *Crossfire*, aired October 12, 1988, on CNN, excerpted in France, *How to Survive a Plague*; Patrick J. Buchanan, *Right from the Beginning* (Washington, DC: Regnery Gateway, 1988), 339–40.

36. Kolata, "Odd Alliance Would Speed New Drugs," 9.

37. "An AIDS Crisis Proposal," editorial, *Wall Street Journal*, June 15, 1988, 1; Kolata, "Odd Alliance Would Speed New Drugs," 9; Eigo, et al, "FDA Action Handbook."

38. Larry Kramer, "A 'Manhattan Project' for AIDS," *New York Times*, July 16, 1990, A15; Ronald Reagan, "Inaugural Address," January 20, 1981; Bernard Weinraub, "Reagan Orders AIDS Report, Giving High Priority to Work for Cure," *New York Times*, February 6, 1986, B7; Erik Eckholm, "AIDS: Scientists Voice Concern over Research," *New York Times*, November 4, 1986, C1.

39. "The Denver Principles," (1983); American Hospital Association, Patients' Bill of Rights (1973), reprinted in Ruth R. Faden and Tom L. Beauchamp, *A History and Theory of Informed Consent* (New York: Oxford University Press, 1986), 94; Kevin Michael DeLuca, "Unruly Arguments: The Body Rhetoric of Earth First!, ACT UP, and Queer Nation," *Argumentation and Advocacy* 36, no. 1 (Summer 1999): 9–21.

40. See the following interviews by Sarah Schulman for the *ACTUP Oral History Project*: Jean Carlomusto, December 19, 2002, 12; Marion Banzhof, April 18, 2007, 15–21; Risa Denenberg, July 11, 2008, 9–19, 33; Robert Vazquez-Pacheco, December 14, 2002, 63. On the "teach-in," see Barbara Seaman, "Health Activism, American Feminist," *Jewish Women: A Comprehensive Historical Encyclopedia* (blog), *Jewish Women's Archive*, March 20, 2009.

41. See the following interviews by Sarah Schulman for the *ACTUP Oral History Project*: Brian Zabcik, September 8, 2008, 40; Steve Quester, January 17, 2004, 16. Jim Serafini, "ACT UP's Challenge to the Establishment," *San Francisco Chronicle*, June 20, 1990, A19.

42. Sam Kazman, "Protected to Death: The FDA's Misbegotten AIDS Rules Are Killing with Kindness," *Washington Post*, July 16, 1989, B5; FDA, Early Availability of Drugs for Serious or Life-Threatening Diseases: FDA Antiviral Drugs Advisory Committee, 177–78 (1994) (statement of Mr. Milano).

43. Procedures for Drugs Intended to Treat Life-Threatening and Severely Debilitating Illnesses, 53 Fed. Reg. 41,516, 41,516 (Oct. 21, 1988).

44. Michael Specter, "FDA Amends Rules to Speed AIDS Drugs," *Washington Post*, October 20, 1988, A1.

45. 21 U.S.C. § 356(b), (d) (2018); 21 C.F.R. § 312.82 (2019); 53 Fed. Reg. at 41,518, 41,520.

46. Specter, "FDA Amends Rules to Speed AIDS Drugs"; Warren Leary, "Panel Seeks to Streamline F.D.A. for Cancer and AIDS Drugs," *New York Times*, January 5, 1989, B12.

47. Martin Delaney, "The Case for Patient Access to Experimental Therapy," *Journal of Infectious Diseases* 159, no. 3 (March 1989): 416–19.

48. Delaney, "Case for Patient Access," 416–19.

49. ACT UP/New York, "A National AIDS Treatment Research Agenda" (V International Conference on AIDS Montreal, June 1989), 6–7.

50. Gina Kolata, "AIDS Researcher Seeks Wide Access to Drugs in Tests," *New York Times*, June 26, 1989, A1; Victor F. Zonana and Marlene Cimons, "Ease AIDS Drug Rules, Health Chief Urges," *Los Angeles Times*, June 24, 1989, 23; Jeffrey Levi, "Unproven AIDS Therapies: The Food and Drug Administration and DdI," in *Biomedical Politics*, ed. Kathi E. Hanna (Washington, DC: National Academy Press, 1991), 9–37; "ACTUP Capsule History 1989," *Capsule History* (blog), *ACTUP*.

51. Kolata, "AIDS Researcher Seeks Wide Access to Drugs in Tests," A1; Levi, "Unproven AIDS Therapies."

52. *AIDS Issues (Part 2): Hearings before the Subcomm. on Health & the Env't of the H. Comm. on Energy & Com.*, 101st. Cong., 1 (statement of Chairman Waxman), 5–26 (statements of James O. Mason, Assistant. Sec., Dep't of HHS, Frank E. Young, Comm'r, FDA, Anthony S. Fauci, Nat'l Inst. of Allergy & Infectious Diseases, NIH, and Samuel Broder, Dir., Nat'l Cancer Inst.) (1989).

53. *AIDS Issues (Part 2)*, 30 (statement of Martin Delaney, Project Inform).

54. FDA, Transcript of Proceedings: FDA Anti-Infective Drugs Advisory Committee (1989).

55. "Transcript of Proceedings," 80, 83–85 (statement of Mr. Eigo), 90–91, 99 (statement of Mr. Delaney).

56. "Transcript of Proceedings," 171 (statement of Ms. Roland), 194 (statement of Mr. Kramer).

57. Levi, "Unproven AIDS Therapies," 26–28. ACT UP's participation was confirmed by David Barr in a private communication with the author on February 2, 2020.

58. Expanded Availability of Investigational New Drugs Through a Parallel Track Mechanism for People with AIDS and HIV-Related Disease, 55 Fed. Reg. 20,856, 20,857, 20,859 (May 21, 1990).

59. 55 Fed. Reg. at 20,858.

60. Nat'l Cancer Inst., Final Report of the National Committee to Review Current Procedures for Approval of New Drugs for Cancer and AIDS (Aug. 15, 1990); Expanded Availability of Investigational New Drugs Through a Parallel Track Mechanism for People with AIDS and Other HIV-related Disease, 57 Fed. Reg. 13,250 (April 15, 1992).

61. Gould, *Moving Politics*, 328–94.

62. Tracy Morgan, interview by Sarah Schulman, *ACTUP Oral History Project*, October 12, 2012, 52.

63. New Drug, Antibiotic, and Biological Drug Product Regulations: Accelerated Approval, 57 Fed. Reg. 58,942, 58,958 (Dec. 11, 1992) (codified at 21 C.F.R. § 314.510).

64. "Final Report of the National Committee," iii–iv; Gina Kolata, "Petition Seeks to Speed Approval of AIDS Drugs," *New York Times*, December 21, 1990, A31.

65. Malcolm Gladwell, "Second AIDS Drug Given Conditional Approval," *Washington Post*, October 10, 1991, A4; Milt Freudenheim, "F.D.A. Approves a Second Drug, Still Being Tested, to Treat AIDS," *New York Times*, October 10, 1991, B2.

66. Freudenheim, "F.D.A. Approves a Second Drug."

67. 57 Fed. Reg. 13,234, 13,240 (proposed April 15, 1992) (to be codified at 21 C.F.R. § 314.510); Marlene Cimons, "FDA Approves AIDS Drug for Use with AZT," *Los Angeles Times*, June 23, 1992, A1; New Drug, Antibiotic, and Biological Drug Product Regulations: Accelerated Approval, 57 Fed. Reg. at 58,942.

68. Mark Harrington, introduction to *Ten Texts on Saquinavir: Its Rapid Rise and Fall*, ed. Mark Harrington (Treatment Action Group, 2001), 3; Mark Harrington, "Access Versus Answers," in *Ten Texts on Saquinavir*, 7.

69. Harrington, 8; Laurie Garrett, "Battle on AIDS Drugs," *Newsday*, September 6, 1994, 4.

70. Roland Bassett, David Schoenfeld, and Ann Collier, "ACTG 229: AZT/DdC/Saquinavir vs. AZT/Saquinavir v. AZT/DdC (May 1994)," in *Ten Texts on Saquinavir*, 12–13; David Barr, et al., "Letter to David Kessler (June 16, 1994)," in *Ten Texts on Saquinavir*, 14–15.

71. Barr, 14–15.

72. France, *How to Survive a Plague*, 1:32:00–34:00.

73. "Early Availability of Drugs," 388–89; Harrington, "Access versus Answers," 6, 10.

74. [Martin Delaney], "Placebos: Time to Say No," *PI Perspective*, October 1988; "Transcript of Proceedings," 178 (statement of Mr. Harrington); "Early Availability of Drugs," I-385 (statement of Mr. Delaney).

75. "Early Availability of Drugs," I-78 (Freiburg testimony), II-70 (Haas testimony), II-104 (Schaich testimony).

76. "Early Availability of Drugs," II-36, 43 (Cox testimony), II-45 (Bahlman testimony).

77. "Early Availability of Drugs," II-36 (Cox testimony).

78. "Early Availability of Drugs," II-36 (Cox testimony), I-123-24 (Davidson testimony).

79. "Early Availability of Drugs," I-75 (Freiburg testimony).

80. "Early Availability of Drugs," I-154 (Soo testimony); Harrington, "Access versus Answers," 10, 25; *FDA Approves First Protease Inhibitor Drug for Treatment of HIV*, U.S. Department of Health and Human Services. (Dec. 7, 1995), https://perma.cc/3NR9-8Y3J; Spencer Cox, "Giving Away the Farm: How Corporate Cynicism Savvy Schmoozing & Relentless PR Paved the Way to Unqualified Approval for Two New Antiretrovirals," in *Ten Texts on Saquinavir*, 29.

81. These drugs were Norvir (ritonavir) (1996), Crixivan (indinavir) (1996), and Viracept (nelfinavir) (1997).

82. Between 30 percent and 70 percent of patient advocacy organizations receive funding from the pharmaceutical industry. Susannah L. Rose, "Patient Advocacy Organizations: Institutional Conflicts of Interest, Trust, and Trustworthiness," *Journal of Law, Medicine & Ethics* 41, no. 3 (2013): 681; *Patient Representative Program*, US Food & Drug Admin., https://perma.cc/3NR9-8Y3J.

83. Food and Drug Administration Safety and Innovation Act, Pub. L. No. 112-144, § 1137, 126 Stat. 993, 1124 (2012) (codified in FD&C Act 569C, 21 U.S.C. § 360bbb-8c); "FDA-led Patient-Focused Drug Development (PFDD) Public Meetings," FDA, website; FDA, "PDUFA Reauthorization Performance Goals and Procedures Fiscal Years 2013 through 2017," (2011), 25; FDA, "PDUFA Reauthorization Performance Goals and Procedures Fiscal Years 2018 Through 2022," (2016), 27–30.

84. "CDER Patient-Focused Drug Development," FDA, website; Prescription Drug User Fee Act Patient-Focused Drug Development; Public Meeting, 77 Fed. Reg. 58,849, 58,850 (Sept. 24, 2012).

85. Denise Grady, "U.S. Lets Drug Tied to Deaths Back on Market," *New York Times*, June 8, 2002, A1; Sabrina Tavernise, "F.D.A. Clears Debated Drug That Patients Lobbied For," *New York Times*, 2016, B1.

86. Peter Arno and Karen L. Feiden, *Against the Odds: The Story of AIDS Drug Development, Politics and Profits* (New York: HarperPerennial, 1992), 109; Pub. L. No. 105-115, § 406, 111 Stat. 2296, 2369 (1997) (codified at FD&C Act 1003[b], 21 U.S.C. § 393[b]).

87. Prescription Drug User Fee Act of 1992, Pub. L. No. 102-571, 106 Stat. 4491–4505 (1992) (codified at 21 U.S.C. §§ 735–736B)); reauthorized by Pub. L. No. 105-115, 111 Stat. 2296 (1997); Pub. L. No. 107-188, 116 Stat. 594, 687–694 (2002); Pub. L. No. 110-85, 121 Stat. 823, 825–42 (2007); Pub. L. No. 112-144; 126 Stat. 993, 996–1008 (2012); Pub. L. No. 112-144, 126 Stat. 993, 996–1002 (2017); 138 Cong. Rec. H9098 (daily ed. Sept. 22, 1992) (Waxman statement); *Reauthorization of the Prescription Drug User Fee Act and FDA Reform: Hearing before the Subcomm. on Health & Env't of the H. Comm. on Com.*, 105th Cong. 107 (1997) (statement of Mr. Bloom, Volunteer, Project Inform).

88. Hutt, Merrill, and Grossman, *Food and Drug Law*, 2014, 749–50; CDER Manual of Policies and Procedures 6020.3 Rev. 2 (2013).

89. Food and Drug Administration Modernization Act of 1997, Pub. L. No. 105-115, § 112, 111 Stat. 2296, 2309-10 (1997) (codified at 21 U.S.C. § 356).

90. Food and Drug Administration Safety and Innovation Act, Pub. L. No. 112-144, § 901, 902, 126 Stat. 993, 1082-88 (2012) (codified at 21 U.S.C. § 356).

91. FDA, "Drug and Biologic Approvals Based on a Single Endpoint, as of June 30, 2020," (July 2020); Pam Belluck and Rebecca Robbins, "F.D.A. Approves New Medication for Alzheimer's," *New York Times*, June 8, 2021, A1; "Fast Track Approvals," FDA, website; "Number of Breakthrough Therapy Designation Approvals," About FDA, FDA, website; IQVIA, "The Changing Landscape of Research and Development", April 2019, 5; Jonathan J. Darrow, Jerry Avorn, and Aaron S. Kesselheim, "FDA Approval and Regulation of Pharmaceuticals, 1983–2018," *JAMA* 323, no. 2 (January 14, 2020): 169

92. Food and Drug Administration Modernization Act of 1997, Pub. L. No. 105-115, § 115, 111 Stat. at 2313 (codified at 21 U.S.C. § 355(d)); Nicholas S. Downing et al., "Clinical Trial Evidence Supporting FDA Approval of Novel Therapeutic Agents, 2005–2012," *JAMA* 311, no. 4 (January 22, 2014): 368–77; "The Changing Landscape of Research and Development," 7; Darrow, Avorn, and Kesselheim, "FDA Approval and Regulation of Pharmaceuticals, 1983–2018"; Aaron S. Kesselheim, Jessica A. Myers, and Jerry Avorn, "Characteristics of Clinical Trials to Support Approval of Orphan vs. Nonorphan Drugs for Cancer," *JAMA* 305, no. 22 (June 8, 2011): 169.

93. 21st Century Cures Act, Pub. L. No. 114-255, 130 Stat. 1033 (2016), § 3022 (codified at 21 U.S.C. § 355g, FD&C Act § 505F).

94. Gregg Gonsalves, Mark Harrington, and David A. Kessler, "Don't Weaken the F.D.A.'s Drug Approval Process," *New York Times*, June 11, 2015.

95. Pub. L. No. 105-115, § 402, 111 Stat. at 2365–67 (1997) (codified at 21 U.S.C. § 360bbb, FD&C Act § 561); Expanded Access to Investigational Drugs for Treatment Use, 74 Fed. Reg. 40,900, 40,910–11, 40,945 (August 13, 2009) (codified at 21 C.F.R. 312.320(a)(3)(ii) (emphasis added); Pub. L. No. 114-255, § 3032, 130 Stat. at 1100–1 (2016) (codified at 21 U.S.C. § 360bbb-0, FD&C Act § 561A).

96. "CDER, CBER and CDRH Expanded Access INDs and Protocols (2015-2019)," Expanded Access (Compassionate Use) Submission Data, FDA, website.

97. Jerome Groopman, "The Right to a Trial: Should Dying Patients Have Access to Experimental Drugs?," *New Yorker*, December 18, 2006; *Abigail Alliance v. Eschenbach*, 495 F.3d 695 (D.C. Cir. 2007); 21 C.F.R. § 312.8(c), (d) (2020).

98. Goldwater Institute, "Right to Try Model Legislation," Goldwater Institute, (2016); "Right to Try in Your State," Right to Try; Alexander Hertel-Fernandez, "Who Passes Business's 'Model Bills'?: Policy Capacity and Corporate Influence in U.S. State Politics," *Perspectives on Politics* 12, no. 3 (September 2014): 582–602; "A Reporter's Guide to the Goldwater Institute: What Citizens, Policymakers, and Reporters Should Know," Arizona Working Families & Center for Media and Democracy, March 14, 2013; "State of Arizona Official Canvass: 2014 General Election (Nov. 4, 2014)," Historical Election Results & Information, State of Arizona, website.

99. Gregg Gonsalves, "Going Around FDA Will Not Serve Patients' Interests," letter to the editor, *Washington Post*, May 21, 2014, A14; Matthew Perrone, "Former FDA Foe Now Is in Its Corner," *Boston Globe*, August 12, 2014, B7.

100. Laurie McGinley, "Fight over FDA and 'Right-to-Try' Moves from States to Congress," *Washington Post*, March 27, 2017, A01.

101. Pub. L. No. 115-176, 132 Stat. 1372 (2018) (codified in part at 21 U.S.C. § 360bbb-0a, FD&C Act §561B).

102. Remarks by President Trump at S.204, "Right to Try" Bill Signing, White House Documents and Publications (May 30, 2018).

103. Christopher Rowland, Carolyn Y. Johnson, and Laurie McGinley, "Trump Calls Drug a 'Game Changer,' but FDA Says It Needs Further Study," *Washington Post*, March 20, 2020, A20, "Johnson Agrees to Drop Hold on FDARA in Exchange for Vote on Revised Right-to-Try Bill," *Inside Health Policy* (blog), August 2, 2017; 21 U.S.C. § 360bbb-0a(b).

104. Jacob Bernstein, "For H.I.V. Survivors, a Feeling of Déjà Vu," *New York Times*, April 9, 2020, D1.

105. Philip Bump, "The Rise and Fall of Trump's Obsession with Hydroxychloroquine; Forty Days of Promotion, Hype—and Eventual Retreat," *Washington Post*, April 24, 2020; "National Tracking Poll #200436" (Morning Consult & Politico, April 10, 2020), 253.

106. Christopher Rowland, "FDA Approves Use of Unproven Treatments, Saying the Risks Are Worthwhile," *Washington Post*, March 31, 2020, A5; Pub. L. No. 108-136, Div. A, Title XVI, § 1603(a), 117 Stat. 1392, 1684 (2003), *amended by* Project Bioshield Act of 2004, Pub. L. No. 108-276, § 4(a), 118 Stat. 835, 853 (2004) (codified as further amended at 21 U.S.C. § 360bbb-3 (2020).

107. Bernstein, "For H.I.V. Survivors, a Feeling of Déjà Vu"; Denise Grady, "Malaria Drug Helps Virus Patients Improve, in Small Study," *New York Times*, April 1, 2020.

108. Denise Grady, "New U.S. Treatment Guidelines for Covid-19 Don't See Much Progress," *New York Times*, April 22, 2020; Christopher Rowland, "VA Study Links Anti-Malarial Drug Trump Touted to Higher Death Rates," *Washington Post*, April 22, 2020, A23; "FDA Drug Safety Communication: FDA Cautions against Use of Hydroxychloroquine or Chloroquine for COVID-19" (FDA, April 24, 2020); Bump, "The Rise and Fall of Trump's Obsession with Hydroxychloroquine"; "National Tracking Poll #200482" (Morning Consult & Politico, April 24–26, 2020); FDA, "Coronavirus (COVID-19) Update: FDA Revokes Emergency Use Authorization for Chloroquine and Hydroxychloroquine," June 15, 2020; Sheera Frankel and Davey Alba, "Despite Safeguards, a Misleading Video Goes Viral, with Help from the Trumps," *New York Times*, July 29, 2020, A5.

109. Gregg Gonsalves, "Beating Covid-19 Will Take Coordination, Experimentation, and Leadership," *The Nation*, April 23, 2020.

Chapter 8

1. David M. Eisenberg et al., "Unconventional Medicine in the United States— Prevalence, Costs, and Patterns of Use," *New England Journal of Medicine* 328, no. 4 (January 28, 1993): 246–52.

2. Natalie Angier, "Patients Rushing to Alternatives," *New York Times*, January 28, 1993, A12; Larry Tye, "Unconventional Cures; Many Turn to Alternative Treatment," *Boston Globe*, January 28, 1993, 1.

3. D. M. Eisenberg et al., "Trends in Alternative Medicine Use in the United States, 1990–1997: Results of a Follow-Up National Survey," *JAMA* 280, no. 18 (November 11, 1998): 1569–75; Susan Okie, "Widening the Medical Mainstream; More Americans Using 'Alternative' Therapies," *Washington Post*, November 11, 1998, A1.

4. "Confidence in Medicine," General Social Survey, National Opinion Research Center (February 1973 and February 1996); Bernice A. Pescosolido, Steven A. Tuch, and Jack K. Martin, "The Profession of Medicine and the Public: Examining Americans' Changing Confidence in Physician Authority from the Beginning of the 'Health Care Crisis' to the Era of Health Care Reform," *Journal of Health and Social Behavior* 42, no. 1 (March 2001): 1–16.

5. Matthew Schneirov and Jonathan David Geczik, "A Diagnosis for Our Times: Alternative Health's Submerged Networks and the Transformation of Identities," *Sociological Quarterly* 37, no. 4 (Autumn 1996): 630–31; Melinda Goldner, "The Dynamic Interplay between Western Medicine and the Complementary and Alternative Medicine Movement: How Activists Perceive a Range of Responses from Physicians and Hospitals," *Sociology of Health & Illness* 26, no. 6 (September 20, 2004): 710–36.

6. Patricia M. Barnes, Barbara Bloom, and Richard L. Nahin, "Complementary and Alternative Medicine Use among Adults and Children: United States, 2007," *National*

Health Statistics Reports 10, no. 12 (December 10, 2008): 1–23; Lindsey I. Black et al., "Use of Yoga, Meditation, and Chiropractors among U.S. Children Aged 4–17 Years," NCHS Data Brief (U.S. Department of Health and Human Services, November 2018); James C. Whorton, *Nature Cures: The History of Alternative Medicine in America* (New York: Oxford University Press, 2004), 292–95, 297–300; Goldner, "Dynamic Interplay."

7. "About NHFA," National Health Freedom Action, website; Michael H. Cohen, *Complementary and Alternative Medicine: Legal Boundaries and Regulatory Perspectives* (Baltimore: Johns Hopkins University Press, 1998), 118.

8. FD&C Act § 201(g)(1), (h) (21 U.S.C. § 321(g)(1), (h)) (2018); FDA, "Guidance for Industry on Complementary and Alternative Medicine Products and Their Regulation by the Food and Drug Administration: Draft Guidance" (2006), 5–6.

9. "Real World Evidence," FDA, website; FD&C Act § 505F (21 U.S.C. § 355g); CAM Guidance; Phil B. Fontanarosa and George D. Lundberg, "Alternative Medicine Meets Science," *JAMA* 280, no. 18 (November 11, 1998): 1618–19.

10. Barbara L. Atwell, "Mainstreaming Complementary and Alternative Medicine in the Face of Uncertainty," *UMKC Law Review* 72, no. 3 (Spring 2004): 609–10; David J. Hufford, "Evaluating Complementary and Alternative Medicine: The Limits of Science and of Scientists," *Journal of Law, Medicine & Ethics* 31, no. 2 (June 1, 2003): 203, 208; 21 C.F.R. §§ 314.126(e), 860.7(c)(2) (2019); E. Haavi Morreim, "A Dose of Our Own Medicine: Alternative Medicine, Conventional Medicine, and the Standards of Science," *Journal of Law, Medicine & Ethics* 31, no. 2 (Summer 2003): 222–35; quotation on "gold standard" is from David Hess, "Technology, Medicine, and Modernity: The Problem of Alternatives," in *Modernity and Technology*, ed. Thomas J. Misa, Philip Brey, and Andrew Feenberg (Cambridge, MA: MIT Press, 2004), 289.

11. Michael Ruggio and Lauren DeSantis-Then, "Complementary and Alternative Medicine: Longstanding Legal Obstacles to Cutting Edge Treatment," *Journal of Health & Life Sciences Law* 2, no. 4 (July 2009): 137–70; Mark R. Tonelli and Timothy C. Callahan, "Why Alternative Medicine Cannot Be Evidence-Based," *Academic Medicine* 76, no. 12 (December 2001): 1218; Robert Tillman, "Paying for Alternative Medicine: The Role of Health Insurers," *The Annals of the American Academy of Political and Social Science* 583, no. 1 (September 2002): 70; Atwell, "Mainstreaming Complementary and Alternative Medicine," 609.

12. Scott Tips, "The FDA Bubble," *National Health Federation* (blog), 2011, website.

13. Dietary Supplement Health and Education Act, Pub. L. No. 103–417 (1994); Lewis A. Grossman, "Food, Drugs, and Droods: A Historical Consideration of Definitions and Categories in American Food and Drug Law," *Cornell Law Review* 93, no. 5 (July 2008): 1091–1148; Lewis A. Grossman, "FDA and the Rise of the Empowered Consumer," *Administrative Law Review* 66, no. 3 (Summer 2014): 648–49; FD&C Act § 201(ff), 21 U.S.C. § 321(ff) (1994).

14. Labeling; General Requirements for Health Claims for Food, 56 Fed. Reg. 60,537, 60,539 (proposed Nov. 27, 1991); Dan Hurley, *Natural Causes: Death, Lies and Politics in America's Vitamin and Herbal Supplement Industry* (New York: Broadway, 2006), 83–87; Lena Williams, "F.D.A. Steps Up Effort to Control Vitamin Claims," *New York*

Times, August 9, 1992, 1; "Correction: F.D.A. on Vitamin Policy," *New York Times*, August 16, 1992, A1; Prescription Drug User Fee Act, Pub. L. No. 102-571, 106 Stat. 4491, 4500 (1992).

15. Food Labeling; General Requirements for Health Claims for Dietary Supplements, 58 Fed. Reg. 33,700 (proposed June 18, 1993) ; Michael Weisskopf, "In the Vitamin Wars, Industry Marshals an Army of Citizen Protesters," *Washington Post*, September 14, 1993, A7; David Hess, "Technology, Medicine, and Modernity," 283; David J. Hess, "Technology- and Product-Oriented Movements: Approximating Social Movement Studies and Science and Technology Studies," *Science, Technology, & Human Values* 30, no. 4 (October 1, 2005): 516, 523; John Schwartz, "Next Week, FDA Will Take Vitamins," *Washington Post*, December 7, 1993, A23.

16. Dietary Supplement Health and Education Act of 1993, H.R. 1709 (1993), S. 784 (1993).

17. *Regulation of Dietary Supplements: Hearing on Bills H.R. 509, H.R. 1709, and S. 784 before the Subcomm. on Health & Env't of the H. Comm. on Energy & Com.*, 103rd Cong., 126 (statement of Fred Bingham), 138 (statement of Kachinas Kutenai) (1993); Bob Lederer, "The FDA's Dirty Little War," *POZ* (blog), August 1, 1994, website.

18. Hurley, *Natural Causes*, 94–103; Dietary Supplement Health and Education Act, Pub. L. No. 103-417, 108 Stat. 4325 (1994) (codified in scattered sections of 21 U.S.C. §§ 321, 331, 341, 342, 343).

19. Grossman, "Food, Drugs, and Droods," 1141–43; FD&C Act §§ 201(g), 403(r)(6); 21 U.S.C. §§ 321(g), 343(r)(6); 65 Fed. Reg. 1000 (Jan. 6, 2000) (codified at 21 C.F.R. § 101.93).

20. Access to Medical Treatment Act, S. 2140, 103rd Cong. (1994).

21. Guy Gugliotta, "Unlikely Allies Aid Industry; Harkin, Hatch Are Supplement Users," *Washington Post*, December 25, 2000, A4; Kenneth Silber, "Alternative-Medicine Agency Can't Bridge Gap," *Washington Times*, December 8, 1994, A10; Access to Medical Treatment Act, 2 (statement of Sen. Harkin), 3 (statement of Sen. Daschle), 8 (statement of Mary Pendergast, Deputy Comm'r & Senior Advisor to the Comm'r, FDA), 43 (testimony of Dr. Priestley), 48–49 (statement of Sen. Bedell).

22. Access to Medical Treatment Act, S. 1035, 104th Cong. (1995); Access to Medical Treatment Act, H.R. 2019, 104th Cong. (1995).

23. S. 2140, § 6.

24. "CAM Guidance," 2.

25. Suzanne White Junod, "An Alternative Perspective: Homeopathic Drugs, Royal Copeland, and Federal Drug Regulation," *Food and Drug Law Journal* 55, no. 1 (2000): 161–83; 21 U.S.C. § 201(g)(1)(A).

26. Junod, 162, 178; Procedures for Classification of OTC Drugs, 37 Fed. Reg. 9464, 9466 (May 11, 1972).

27. *Meserey v. United States*, 447 F. Supp. 548 (D. Nev. 1977); Junod, "Alternative Perspective," 179; James C. Whorton, "From Cultism to CAM: Alternative Medicine in the Twentieth Century," in *The Politics of Healing: Histories of Alternative Medicine in Twentieth-Century North America*, ed. Robert D. Johnston (New York: Routledge, 2004), 303.

28. FDA, CPG Sec. 400.400, Conditions under Which Homeopathic Drugs May Be Marketed (1988).

29. Letter to William J. Hemelt, Matrixx Initiatives, Inc. from Deborah M. Autor, FDA (June 15, 2009).

30. Homeopathic Product Regulation: Evaluating the FDA's Regulatory Framework after a Quarter Century; Public Hearing, 80 Fed. Reg. 16, 327 (Mar. 27, 2015); Americans for Homeopathy Choice, Citizen Petition to FDA (July 25, 2018); Janet Woodcock, FDA, to Americans for Homeopathy Choice (Oct. 24, 2019); 84 Fed. Reg. 57,439 (Oct. 25, 2019); FDA, Draft Guidance, Drug Products Labeled as Homeopathic (Oct. 2019); FDA Renews Attack on Homeopathy, Alliance for Natural Health, November 21, 2019, website.

31. Peter Barton Hutt, Richard A. Merrill, and Lewis A. Grossman, *Food and Drug Law: Cases and Materials*, 4th ed. (St. Paul, MN: Foundation Press, 2014), 800–1; 21 C.F.R. § 880.5580 (2019); Rick Weiss, "FDA Removes Bar to Coverage for Acupuncture by Insurance," *Washington Post*, March 30, 1996, A3; Christine Willmsen and Michael J. Berens, "Public Never Warned about Dangerous Device," *Seattle Times*, updated March 19, 2016; Michael J. Berens and Christine Willmsen, "Fraudulent Medical Devices Targeted," *Seattle Times*, January 30, 2008; "FDA Safety Communication: FDA Warns Against Use of Energy-Based Devices to Perform Vaginal 'Rejuvenation' or Vaginal Cosmetic Procedures," FDA, July 30, 2018.

32. *D'Amico v. Bd. of Med. Exam'rs*, 520 P. 2d 10, 27 (Cal. 1974) (in bank); State Bd. of Med. Exam'rs v. Rogers, 387 So. 2d 937 (Fla. 1980); Idaho Ass'n of Naturopathic Physicians v. FDA, 582 F.2d 849, 851 (4th Cir. 1978), *cert. denied* 440 U.S. 976 (1979). See also *Maguire v. Thompson*, 957 F.2d 374 (7th Cir. 1992), *cert. denied* 506 U.S. 822 (1992) (naprapathy).

33. *In re Guess*, 393 S.E.2d 833, 835 (N.C. 1990). See, e.g., Mitchell v. Clayton, 995 F.2d 772 (7th Cir. 1993) (rejecting challenge by acupuncturists and patients); see also, e.g., *Sammon v. N.J. Bd. of Med. Exam'r*, 66 F.3d 639 (3d Cir. 1995) (rejecting suit brought by aspiring midwives and prospective parents); *Ohio Coll. of Ltd. Med. Practice v. Ohio St. Med. Bd.*, 670 N.E. 2d 490 (Ohio Ct. App. 1995) (ruling against mechanotherapists and patient).

34. *Wilk v. Am. Med. Ass'n.*, 895 F.2d 352 (7th Cir. 1990), *cert. denied* 496 U.S. 927 (1990).

35. William B. Crawford and Jon Van, "Judge Cites AMA for Chiropractic Plot," *Chicago Tribune*, August 29, 1987, 1; Lori B. Andrews, "The Shadow Health Care System: Regulation of Alternative Health Care Providers," *Houston Law Review* 32, no. 5 (1996): 1293–95.

36. Walter I. Wardwell, "Chiropractors: Evolution to Acceptance," in *Other Healers: Unorthodox Medicine in America*, ed. Norman Gevitz (Baltimore: Johns Hopkins University Press, 1988), 165–66; Mabel Chang, "The Chiropractic Scope of Practice in the United States: A Cross-Sectional Survey," *Journal of Manipulative and Physiological Therapeutics* 37, no. 6 (July 2014): 363–76.

37. "State Licensure Requirements Interactive Map," NCCAOM, website; Whorton, *Nature Cures*, 214, 289, 291; "Naturopathic Doctor Licensure," AANMC, website; Stefano Maddalena, *Alternative Medicines: On the Way towards Integration?: A*

Comparative Legal Analysis in Western Countries (Bern: Peter Lang, 2005), 232–33; Martin Kaufman, "Homeopathy in America: The Rise and Fall and Persistence of a Medical Heresy," in *Other Healers: Unorthodox Medicine in America,* ed. Norman Gevitz (Baltimore: Johns Hopkins University Press, 1988), 121–22.

38. Cohen, *Complementary and Alternative Medicine,* 92–93; 1990 Alaska Sess. Laws 126, *codified at* Alaska Stat. § 08.64.326(a)(8)(A); 1993 N.C. Sess. Laws 241, *codified at* N.C. Gen. Stat. § 90-14(a)(6); one scholar counted seventeen states in 2006. John Lunstroth, "Voluntary Self-Regulation of Complementary and Alternative Medicine Practitioners," *Albany Law Review* 70, no. 1 (2006): 222 n. 86.

39. Michael H. Cohen, "Medical Freedom Legislation: Illusory Progress?," *Alternative & Complementary Therapies,* April 12, 2006, 100; Joseph A. Barrette, "The Alternative Medical Practice Act: Does It Adequately Protect the Right of Physicians to Use Complementary and Alternative Medicine?," *St. John's Law Review* 77, no. 1 (Winter 2003): 86; 2004 Cal. Stat. 742 (2004), *codified at* Cal. Bus. & Prof. Code § 2234.1 (2019); 2001 Fla. Laws 116, *codified at* Fla. Stat. § 456.41(1), (3)(c) (2019). The statute defines "complementary or alternative health care treatment" to include any treatment "*designed to* provide patients with an effective option" to conventional treatment methods. § 456.41(2)(a) (emphasis added).

40. Idaho Code Ann. § 54-1804(l) (2019); 1994 Okla. Sess. Laws 323, *codified at* Okla. Stat. tit. 59, § 492(F).

41. Robert Franklin, "A Snag in the Milk/Cancer Cure-Case," *Star Tribune,* March 11, 1995, 2; *Minnesota v. Saunders,* 542 N.W.2d 67 (Minn. Ct. App. 1996); James Walsh, "Farmer-Healer Is an Elusive Target for Prosecutors," *Star Tribune,* May 22, 1996, 19; David Chanen, "Odin Dairy Farmer Won't Be Tried Again," *Star Tribune,* May 30, 1996.

42. Maura Lerner, "St. Paul Holistic Healer Finds Herself under the State's Microscope," *Star Tribune,* August 19, 1996, 1; Maura Lerner, "Supporters Rally for Holistic Healer," *Star Tribune,* August 22, 1996, 31; Maura Lerner, "Case against Healer Settled out of Court," *Star Tribune,* September 19, 1996, 27.

43. Maura Lerner, "Alternative-Care Law Is Proposed," *Star Tribune,* March 30, 2000, 1; Minn. Stat. § 146A.01 (2019). Because chiropractors and acupuncturists were already subject to separate licensing regimes, these methods were not included in the list.

44. Alan Dumoff, "The Ins and Outs, Pros and Cons of Nonlicensed Practice," *Alternative & Complementary Therapies,* June 2006, 140. Six of the laws are excerpted in Dumoff, 137–39.

45. "Safe Harbor Practitioner Exemption Laws," NHFA, website; "State Organizations," NHFA, website; Cal. Bus. & Prof. Code § 2053.5-6 (2019); Me. Rev. Stat. Ann. tit. 32, § 1, chap. 113-B, subchap. 5 (2019). See "Action Alerts," NHFA, website.

46. NHFA, *NHFA: State Action Update: For Safe Harbor Exemption Laws for Independent Health Care Practitioners* (NHFA, 2010), website; NHFA, *NHFA: State Action Update: For Safe Harbor Exemption Laws for Independent Health Care Practitioners* (NHFA, 2011), website; NHFA, *NHFA: State Action Update* (NHFA, 2012); "History of the U.S. Health Freedom Congress," US Health Freedom Congress, website; *Schedule* (Northfield, MN: National Health Freedom Coalition, 2016) (on file with author).

47. "2004—NHFC Declaration of Health Freedom," National Health Freedom Coalition, website.

48. "Principles of Health Freedom," NHFC, September 27, 2014, website.

49. "Principles of Health Freedom," NHFC, September 27, 2014, website; "Resolution to Support the Adoption of a National Health Freedom Constitutional Amendment," Texas Health Freedom Coalition, October 20, 2015, website.

50. Dumoff, "Ins and Outs," 141; NHFA, *NHFA State Action Update: Occupational and Other Laws Impacting Health Freedom* (2016), website; NHFA to Hawaii Office of the Auditor, Hawaii, November 6, 2014, 1, 10, website; "Opposition of Registration of Unlicensed Health Care Practitioners" (National Health Freedom Action, 2004), website.

51. Dumoff, "Ins and Outs," 141–42; Diane Miller, "Protecting Your Access to Health Care Freedom," interview by Carol Bedrosian, NHFC, March 14, 2019, 4, website.

52. Research shows that the extent of insurance coverage correlates strongly with frequent of use of CAM providers, and there are reasons to believe that insurance coverage drives frequent visits rather than vice-versa. Peter M. Wolsko et al., "Insurance Coverage, Medical Conditions, and Visits to Alternative Medicine Providers: Results of a National Survey," *Archives of Internal Medicine* 162, no. 3 (February 11, 2002): 281, 285. On CAM coverage generally, see Atwell, "Mainstreaming CAM," 612. On chiropractic generally, see 42 U.S.C. § 1395x(r); 42 C.F.R. § 410.2; HHS, *Chiropractic Care: Controls Used by Medicare, Medicaid, and Other Payers* (Atlanta: HHS Department of the Inspector General, 1998); "Medicaid Benefits: Chiropractor Services," KFF, website; Richard L. Nahin, Patricia M. Barnes, and Barbara Stussman, *Insurance Coverage for Complementary Healthy Approaches among Adult Users: United States, 2002 and 2012* (Hyattsville, MD: National Center for Health Statistics, January 2016), 4. On insurance statistics, see Ronald Sturm and Jürgen Unützer, "State Legislation and the Use of Complementary and Alternative Medicine," *Inquiry* 37, no. 4 (Winter 2000): 423–29; Tillman, "Paying for Alternative Medicine," 68; Eisenberg et al., "Trends in Alternative Medicine." On midwivery, see Elizabeth Kukura, "Giving Birth under the ACA: Analyzing the Use of Law as a Tool to Improve Health Care," *Nebraska Law Review* 94, no. 2 (2016): 834, 854; H. G. Hall, L. G. McKenna, and D. L. Griffiths, "Midwives' Support for Complementary and Alternative Medicine: A Literature Review," *Women Birth* 25, no. 1 (March 2012): 4–12; Marie Hastings-Tolsma and Masako Terada, "Complementary Medicine Use by Nurse Midwives in the U.S.," *Complementary Therapies in Clinical Practice* 15, no. 4 (November 2009): 212–19. On private insurers, see Tillman, 66; Tammy Worth, "It's a Prickly Subject: Many Patients Turn to Alternative Medicine. But Such Treatment May Not Be Covered," *Los Angeles Times*, September 27, 2010, E3. On Washington, see Wash. Rev. Code § 48.43.045(1).

53. Robert D. Johnston, "Contemporary Anti-Vaccination Movements in Historical Perspective," in *The Politics of Healing*, 259–86; for comprehensive examinations of vaccines in American history, including the modern era, see Arthur Allen, *Vaccine: The Controversial Story of Medicine's Greatest Lifesaver* (New York: W. W. Norton, 2008); James Keith Colgrove, *State of Immunity: The Politics of Vaccination*

in Twentieth-Century America, California/Milbank Books on Health and the Public 16 (Berkeley: University of California Press, 2006); Elena Conis, *Vaccine Nation: America's Changing Relationship with Immunization* (Chicago: University of Chicago Press, 2016).

54. Johnston, 262, 278–81; Colgrove, 237.

55. Allen, *Vaccine*; Colgrove, *State of Immunity*; Conis, *Vaccine Nation*.

56. Eileen Wang et al., "Nonmedical Exemptions from School Immunization Requirements: A Systematic Review," *American Journal of Public Health* 104, no. 11 (November 2014): e62; Liz Szabo, "Measles Outbreak Could Reverse Anti-Vaccination Trend," *USA Today*, January 30, 2015. See, e.g., Kevin McDermott, "Populist Politics Is the Perfect Breeding Ground for Anti-Vaccination Nonsense," editorial, *St. Louis Post-Dispatch*, April 21, 2019; Jan Hoffman, "How Anti-Vaccine Sentiment Took Hold in the United States," *New York Times*, September 23, 2019; "States with Religious and Philosophical Exemptions from School Immunization Requirements," National Conference of State Legislatures, website.

57. Johnston, "Anti-Vaccination Movements," 277–78; Colgrove, *State of Immunity*, 219, 238–39; Lena H. Sun, "Majority of Anti-Vaccine Ads on Facebook Were Funded by Two Groups," *Washington Post*, November 15, 2019; Kathleen Kennedy Townsend, Joseph P. Kennedy II, and Maeve Kennedy Mckean, "RFK Jr. Is Our Brother and Uncle. He's Tragically Wrong about Vaccines.," *Politico Magazine*, May 8, 2019, website; Kelly Weill, "The New Infowars Is a Vitamin Site Predicting the Apocalypse," *The Daily Beast*, June 8, 2019, website.

58. Johnston, 271, 273; Colgrove, 237–38; Conis, *Vaccine Nation*, 131–57; Neena Satija and Lena H. Sun, "A Major Funder of the Anti-Vaccine Movement Has Made Millions Selling Natural Health Products," *Washington Post*, December 20, 2019; Lena H. Sun and Amy Brittain, "Anti-Vaccine Movement Receives Millions from One N.Y. Couple," *Washington Post*, June 20, 2019.

59. See, e.g., *Phillips v. City of New York*, 775 F.3d 538 (2d Cir. 2015), *cert. denied* 136 S. Ct. 104 (2015). Hoffman, "How Anti-Vaccine Sentiment Took Hold in the United States"; Nina Shapiro, "A Win for Vaccines, but Worries Remain," op-ed, *Wall Street Journal*, July 23, 2015; Amanda Paulson, "Beyond Us and Them: The Role of Trust in Vaccine Controversy," *Christian Science Monitor*, May 7, 2019; Melody Gutierrez, "Californians Strongly Back Vaccine Law in New Statewide Poll," *Los Angeles Times*, September 30, 2019;; Emily Baumgaertner, "How Civic Discord Can Lead to Lower Vaccination Rates," *Los Angeles Times*, May 13, 2019. In a 2019 Pew Research Center Poll, 16 percent of respondents supported the proposition that "parents should be able to decide not to vaccinate their children, even if that may create health risks for other children and adults," while 82 percent favored requiring children to be vaccinated to attend school. Pew Research Center's American Trends Panel Poll (Oct. 2019).

60. *Jacobson v. Massachusetts*, 197 U.S. 11, 26 (1905).

61. Cal. Exec. Order N-33-20 (March 19, 2020).

62. Laurel Rosenhall and Emily Hoeven, "Calif. Lawmakers Want Info; Protesters Want to End Lockdown," *Cal Matters*, April 20, 2020.

63. Alexei Koseff, "Protesters Call for State to End Virus Shutdown," *San Francisco Chronicle*, April 21, 2020; Freedom Angels Foundation, website.

64. Peter Jamison, "Anti-Vaccination Leaders Seize on Coronavirus to Push Resistance to Inoculation," *Washington Post*, May 5, 2020; Robert F. Kennedy Jr., "As the Quarantine Guts the Economy, America's Five Wealthiest People Have Gotten 75 Billion Dollars Richer," May 29, 2020, website; "Tell Congress That H.R. 6666 'COVID19 Testing, Reaching, and Contacting Everyone (TRACE) Act' Is Unconstitutional and Threatens the Liberty of All Americans," Children's Health Defense, May 14, 2020, website; Alan Palmer, "The Risks vs. Benefits of Face Masks—Is There an Agenda?," May 26, 2020, website.

65. "Gates Foundation Expands Commitment to COVID-19 Response, Calls for International Collaboration," Bill & Melinda Gates Foundation, April 15, 2020, website; Tina Nguyen, "MAGA World Finds Its Coronavirus Scapegoats," *Politico*, updated April 21, 2020, website; Michael D. Shear, "Fauci Says He Can Again 'Let the Science Speak' Unfettered," *New York Times*, Jan. 22, 2021, A6.

66. Cheryl K. Chumley, "Gates and Fauci: Unelected Destroyers of Freedom," *Washington Times*, April 11, 2020, website; Kennedy Jr., "Quarantine Guts the Economy"; "Fauci: Steering the Pandemic Narrative toward Vaccine 'Solutions' Is Nothing New," Children's Health Defense, June 11, 2020, website; "Coronavirus Provides Dictators and Oligarchs with a Dream Come True," Children's Health Defense, April 9, 2020.

67. Sheera Frankel and Davey Alba, "Despite Safeguards, a Misleading Video Goes Viral with Help from the Trumps," *New York Times*, July 29, 2020, A5; Davey Alba, "Virus Conspiracists Elevate a Discredited Scientist as a New Champion," *New York Times*, May 11, 2020, B4; "In the News: Coronavirus and 'Alternative' Treatments," National Center for Complementary and Integrative Health, September 15, 2020, website.

68. Stephen Petrina, "Medical Liberty: Drugless Healers Confront Allopathic Doctors, 1910–1931," *Journal of Medical Humanities* 29, no. 4 (December 2008): 205–30.

69. Kenneth P. Vogel, Jim Rutenberg, and Lisa Lerer, "They Amplify the Fight against Lockdowns, Quietly," *New York Times*, April 22, 2020, A3; Koseff, "Protesters Call for State to End Virus Shutdown"; Brian Yermal Jr., "As COVID-19 Restrictions Ease, at Least 70% of Voters Would Support Same Moves to Mitigate Second Wave," *Morning Consult* (blog), May 18, 2020, website; Ricardo Alonso-Zaldivar and Zeke Miller, "Biden Vows Pandemic Help 'Is on the Way': President Ramps Up Federal Response with Orders on Masks, Vaccine Plan," *Houston Chronicle*, Jan. 22, 2021, A1.

70. Courtney Tanner, "In Separate Rallies, Utahns Protest Mask Mandate and Demand in-Person Classes," *Salt Lake Tribune*, updated July 16, 2020.

71. Neena Satija, "'I Do Regret Being There': Simone Gold, Noted Hydroxychloroquine Advocate, Was Inside the Capitol during the Riot," *Washington Post*, Jan. 12, 2021; Peter Stone, "'Wilful Ignorance': Doctor Who Joined Capitol Attack Condemned for Covid Falsehoods," *The Guardian* (London), Jan. 22, 2021; Daniel Funke, "Who Are the Doctors in the Viral Hydroxychloroquine Video?" *Politifact*, July 29, 2020 (website).

72. Alexandra Hutzler, "Marjorie Taylor Green Rebukes Vaccine Passports as 'Biden's Mark of the Beast,'" *Newsweek.com*, March 30, 2021, online; Steven Lemongello and Gray Rohrer, "DeSantis Vows to Ban 'Vaccination Passports,'" *Orlando Sentinel*, March 30, 2021, A1; Christine Sexton, "DeSantis Order Blocks COVID-19 Passports,"

Florida Times-Union, April 3, 2021, A1; Sheryl Gay Stolberg and Adam Liptak, "Fight Brewing on 'Passports' for Vaccinated," *New York Times*, April 7, 2021.

73. Ed Young, "How the Pandemic Defeated America," *Atlantic*, September 2020, https://www.theatlantic.com/magazine/archive/2020/09/coronavirus-american-failure/614191/. Data drawn from Worldometer, Coronavirus Updates (website).

Chapter 9

1. This chapter is an edited version of Lewis A. Grossman, "Life, Liberty, [and the Pursuit of Happiness]: Medical Marijuana Regulation in Historical Context," *Food and Drug Law Journal* 74, no. 2 (2019): 280–321.

2. Dennis Peron and John Entwistle Jr., *Memoirs of Dennis Peron: How a Gay Hippy Outlaw Legalized Marijuana in Response to the AIDS Crisis* (San Francisco: Medical Use Publishing House, 2012), loc. 3708 of 10370.

3. Peron and Entwistle, loc. 3706–8 of 10370.

4. Peron and Entwistle, loc. 3730 of 10370.

5. Cal. Health & Safety Code § 11362.5 (West 2008), added by initiative, Proposition 215, as approved by voters, General Election (Nov. 5, 1996).

6. "500 S.F. Protestors Protest Closure of Cannabis Club," *Los Angeles Times*, August 7, 1996, A22; Dan Reed and Alan Gathright, "Pot Supporters Take to the Streets over Raid. Demonstrators Call State Move 'Political,'" *San Jose Mercury News*, August 6, 1996, 10A; Californians for Medical Rights, "Jury of Medical Marijuana Patients Delivers 'Guilty' Verdicts, Personal Pleas to Attorney General Lungren," press release, October 15, 1996, on file with author.

7. Gary Trudeau, "Doonesbury," comic strip, *Washington Post*, October 2, 1996, B3.

8. John Hudak, *Marijuana: A Short History* (Washington, DC: Brookings Institution Press, 2016), 83–84; Office of the Assistant Secretary, *Talking Points on Medicinal Marijuana Policy* (Washington, DC: HHS, 1994); Carey Goldberg, "Medical Marijuana Use Winning Backing," *New York Times*, October 30, 1996, A12.

9. "Happy Smoker," photo, *The Desert Sun*, November 6, 1996, 13; "Prop. 215 Faces Many Questions," *The Desert Sun*, November 7, 1996, 6; "Voters Say Marijuana Should Be Legal Medicine," *Ukiah Daily Journal*, November 6, 1996, 10; Peron and Entwistle, *Memoirs of Dennis Peron*, loc. 3729–33 of 10370.

10. "California Proposition 215, the Medical Marijuana Initiative (1996)," Ballotpedia, website; "Map of Marijuana Legality by State," DISA Global Solutions, updated July 2020, website.

11. Carl Irby, "Marijuana Use," letter to the editor, *San Bernardino County Sun*, November 19, 1996, 11.

12. Christopher S. Wren, "Votes on Marijuana Are Stirring Debate," *New York Times*, November 17, 1996, 16.

13. Californians for Medical Rights, "Responsible Guidelines for Marijuana Patients Issued," press release, November 19, 1996, on file with author; William Claiborne

and Roberto Suro, "Medicinal Marijuana Brings Legal Headache," *Washington Post*, December 5, 1996, A1.

14. "It's Official! California Voters Will Decide on Medical Marijuana Issue This Fall," *Freedom @ NORML* 2 (September 1996).

15. *The Pharmacopoeia of the United States of America*, 4th ed. (Philadelphia, 1863), 51, 52, 55. At the time of the ratification of the Eighteenth Amendment, more than half of the states banned the prescription of alcoholic beverages. *Lambert v. Yellowley*, 272 U.S. 581, 590 n. 2 (1926).

16. *Commonwealth v. Sloan*, 58 Mass. 52, 54 (1849); *State v. Larrimore*, 19 Mo. 391, 392 (1854); *Donnell v. State*, 2 Ind. 658, 659 (1851); *State v. Wray*, 72 N.C. 253, 255 (1875); *Ball v. State*, 50 Ind. 595, 597 (1875); *Sarris v. Commonwealth*, 83 Ky. 327, 331 (1885) (dictum).

17. *Carson v. State*, 69 Ala. 235, 240 (1881). *See also State v. McBryer*, 2 S.E. 755 (N.C. 1887); *Carl v. State*, 8 So. 156 (Ala. 1890); *State v. Durein*, 78 P. 152, 156 (Kan. 1904).

18. Bartlett C. Jones, "A Prohibition Problem: Liquor as Medicine 1920–1933," *Journal of the History of Medicine and Allied Sciences* 18, no. 4 (October 1963): 353–54; "American Medical Association and Prohibition," *Boston Medical and Surgical Journal* 176, no. 25 (June 21, 1917): 884–85; Jacob M. Appel, "'Physicians Are Not Bootleggers': The Short, Peculiar Life of the Medicinal Alcohol Movement," *Bulletin of the History of Medicine* 82, no. 2 (2008): 355–86.

19. "The Referendum on the Use of Alcohol in the Practice of Medicine," *Journal of the American Medical Association* 78, no. 3 (1922): 210–31; Jones, "Prohibition Problem," 358; *Pharmacopoeia of the United States of America*, 10th ed. (Philadelphia: J. B. Lippincott, 1925).

20. National Prohibition Act of 1919, Pub L. No. 66-66, §§ 6–8, 41 Stat. 305, 310–11; Ernest H. Cherrington, *Anti-Saloon League Year Book* (Westerville, OH: Anti-Saloon League of America, 1921), 15; Willis-Campbell Act, Pub. L. No. 67-96, 42 Stat. 222 (1921).

21. Ex Parte Application of Hixson, 214 P. 677, 679 (Cal. App. 1923).

22. Appel, "Physicians Are Not Bootleggers," 376–83; Brief for Appellant at 6, 21, 23, *Lambert*, 272 U.S. 581 (No. 47) (1926); *Lambert*, 272 U.S. at 581.

23. Appel, "Physicians Are Not Bootleggers," 367–76.

24. See, however, *Linder v. United States*, 268 U.S. 5, 18, 22 (1925), in which the Court questioned federal power to regulate medical practice while overturning the conviction of a physician under the 1914 Harrison Narcotics Tax Act.

25. Martin A. Lee, *Smoke Signals: A Social History of Marijuana—Medical, Recreational and Scientific* (New York: Scribner, 2012), 3–5, 13–14, 20–21; Martin Booth, *Cannabis: A History* (New York: Picador, 2003), 22–23, 70–72; Robert Deitch, *Hemp—American History Revisited: The Plant with a Divided History* (New York: Algora Publishing, 2003), 9–10.

26. Compare Lee, *Smoke Signals* (use was limited to seeds and fiber) to Deitch, *Hemp*, 25–27 (colonial Americans commonly smoked cannabis for medicinal and recreational purposes).

27. W. B. O'Shaughnessy, "On the Preparations of the Indian Hemp, or Gunjah," *Transactions of the Medical and Physical Society of Bengal* 8 (1839): 421–61; W. B. O'Shaughnessy, "Case of Tetanus, Cured by a Preparation of Hemp (the Cannabis Indica)," *Transactions of the Medical and Physical Society of Bengal* 8 (1843): 462–69; Lee, *Smoke Signals*, 24–25; Martin Booth, *Cannabis: A History*, 109–14; John Geluardi, *Cannabiz: The Explosive Rise of the Medical Marijuana Industry* (Sausalito, CA: PoliPointPress, 2010), 19–21; *Pharmacopoeia of the United States of America*, 3rd ed. (Philadelphia, 1853), 50.

28. H. C. Wood, Joseph P. Remington, and Samuel P. Sadtler, *The Dispensatory of the United States of America*, 15th ed. (Philadelphia, 1885), 341; Lee, *Smoke Signals*, 25–26; *Taxation on Marihuana: Hearing on H.R. 6385 before the H. Comm. on Ways & Means*, 75th Cong. 114 (1937); John Geluardi, *Explosive Rise*, 22.

29. *Taxation of Marihuana*, 17 (statement of Mr. Hester, Ass't Att'y Gen., Dep't of the Treasury), 49 (statement of Dr. Munch, Pharmacologist, Temp.), 114 (statement of Dr. Woodward, Leg. Counsel, AMA); Lee, *Smoke Signals*, 54; Booth, *Cannabis: A History*, 116–19; Geluardi, *Explosive Rise*, 22–23.

30. Richard J. Bonnie and Charles H. Whitebread II, "The Forbidden Fruit and the Tree of Knowledge: An Inquiry into the Legal History of American Marijuana Prohibition," *Virginia Law Review* 56, no. 6 (October 1970): 1010–16, 1035–36; Lee, *Smoke Signals*, 42; Booth, *Cannabis: A History*, 162–63; Federal Food and Drugs Act of 1906, Pub. L. No. 59-384, § 8, 34 Stat. 768, 770; Harrison Narcotics Tax Act of 1914, Pub. L. No. 63-233, 38 Stat. 785.

31. Adoption of the Uniform Narcotic Drug Act for the District of Columbia, see Pub. L. No. 75-682, 52 Stat. 785 (1938); Lee, *Smoke Signals*, 48–54; Booth, *Cannabis: A History*, 174–94; Hudak, *Marijuana*, 25–26, 35–40; John Geluardi, *Explosive Rise*, 26–31; Bonnie and Whitebread, "Forbidden Fruit," 1034, 1037–53.

32. Bonnie and Whitebread, "Forbidden Fruit," 1027; *Taxation of Marihuana*, 91, 96–97, 106–7 (statements of Woodward), 122 (statement of Hilton, Rep., AMA).

33. *Pharmacopoeia of the United States of America*, 12th ed. (Philadelphia: Mack Printing, 1942).

34. Comprehensive Drug Abuse Prevention and Control Act of 1970, § 202(b)(1) (emphasis added).

35. Institute of Medicine, *Marijuana and Health* (Washington, DC: National Academy Press, 1982); *Marihuana: A Signal of Misunderstanding, The Official Report of the National Commission on Marihuana and Drug Abuse* (New York: Signet, 1972), 176; Fred P. Graham, "National Commission to Propose Legal Private Use of Marijuana," *New York Times*, February 13, 1972, 1.

36. *All. for Cannabis Therapeutics v. DEA*, 15 F.3d 1131 (D.C. Cir. 1994).

37. Robert C. Randall and Alice M. O'Leary, *Marijuana Rx: The Patients' Fight for Medicinal Pot* (New York: Thunder's Mouth Press, 1998), 9–18, 66–67.

38. *Regina v. Dudley & Stephens*, 14 Q.B.D 273 (1884); *Commonwealth v. Sloan*, 58 Mass. 52 (1849); *Bice v. State*, 34 S.E. 202 (Ga. 1899).

39. Randall and O'Leary, *Marijuana Rx*, 85–123.

40. *United States v. Randall*, 104 Dly. Wash. L. Rptr. 2249 (1976).

41. Randall and O'Leary, *Marijuana Rx*, 134, 160–63, 191–92, 197–99; "Glaucoma Victim Gets Marijuana Use Rights," *Washington Post*, May 19, 1978, B3.

42. Randall and O'Leary, *Marijuana Rx*, 229–31, 254, 304, 353, 358–61.

43. H.R. 4498, 97th Cong., 1st Sess. (Sept. 16, 1981); H.R. 4498, 97th Cong., 1st Sess. (March 3, 1982) (new cosponsors); Randall and O'Leary, *Marijuana Rx*, 263–67, 271–77; Lee, *Smoke Signals*, 166–67; Gingrich quotation at Randall and O'Leary, *Marijuana Rx*, 275.

44. 21 U.S.C. § 811(b) (2018); Notice of Petition Denial, 66 Fed. Reg. 20,038 (Apr. 18, 2001); Schedules of Controlled Substances: Marijuana Petition Hearing, 51 Fed. Reg. 22,946 (June 24, 1986).

45. John Hudak and Grace Wallack, *Ending the U.S. Government's War on Medical Marijuana Research* (Washington, DC: Brookings Institution, 2015); Jonathan P. Caulkins, Beau Kilmer, and Mark A. R. Kleiman, *Marijuana Legalization: What Everyone Needs to Know* (New York: Oxford University Press, 2012), 98–100; Institute of Medicine, *Marijuana and Health*, 4.

46. Hearing on Petition to Reschedule Marijuana, 51 Fed. Reg. 22,946 (June 24, 1986); Randall and O'Leary, *Marijuana Rx*, 285; Robert C. Randall, *Marijuana, Medicine & the Law: Volume II* (Washington, DC: Galen Press, 1989); Francis L. Young, ALJ, U.S. Dep't of Justice, DEA, In the Matter of Marijuana Rescheduling Petition, Docket No. 86-22, 5–6, 26, 38, 54, 58–59, 66–67 (Sept. 6, 1988).

47. Kevin B. Zeese, "Legal Issues Related to the Medical Use of Marijuana," in *Cannabis in Medical Practice: A Legal, Historical and Pharmacological Overview of the Therapeutic Use of Marijuana*, ed. Mary Lynn Mathre (Jefferson, NC: McFarland, 1997), 24–26; Randall and O'Leary, *Marijuana Rx*, 302–5; *Jenks v. State*, 582 So.2d 676 (Fla. Dist. Ct. App. 1991).

48. Marijuana Scheduling Petition; Denial of Petition, 54 Fed. Reg. 53,767 (Dec. 29, 1989).

49. 57 Fed. Reg. 10,499 (Mar. 26, 1992); *All. Cannabis Therapeutics v. DEA*, 930 F.2d 936 (1991); *All. Cannabis Therapeutics v. DEA*, 15 F.3d 1131 (1994).

50. *All. Cannabis Therapeutics*, 15 F.3d at 1135; 57 Fed. Reg. at 10,503–6.

51. Michael Isikoff, "HHS to Phase Out Marijuana Program," *Washington Post*, June 22, 1991, A14; Young Opinion, 10–13; Robert C. Randall and Alice M. O'Leary, *Marijuana as Medicine, Initial Steps: Recommendations for the Clinton Administration* (Washington, DC: Galen Press, 1993), 28–34.

52. Randall and O'Leary, *Marijuana Rx*, 372–77, 389–90, 396–97, 400–1; Isikoff, "HHS to Phase Out Marijuana Program." The history of the development and cancellation of the Compassionate IND program is related in *Kuromiya v. United States*, 78 F. Supp. 367 (E.D. Pa. 1999).

53. *Commonwealth v. Hutchins*, 575 N.E.2d 741, 745 (Mass. 1991); Jay M. Zittler, Annotation, *Construction and Application of Medical Marijuana Laws and Medical Necessity Defense to Marijuana Laws*, 50 A.L.R.6th 353, §§ 43–54 (2018).

54. Randall and O'Leary, *Marijuana Rx*, 418; Randall and O'Leary, *Marijuana as Medicine*.

55. Allen St. Pierre, Deputy National Director, NORML, email message to author, February 28, 2018; Randall and O'Leary, *Marijuana Rx*, 446–47. On planning

shortfalls, see letter from Eric E. Sterling, Criminal Justice Policy Foundation, to Allen St. Pierre, Deputy National Director, NORML (Dec. 5, 1994) (on file with author).

56. Marijuana Scheduling Petition; Denial of Petition, 54 Fed. Reg. 53,767, 53,771, 53,774 (Dec. 29, 1989); Lee, *Smoke Signals,* 166; Randall & O'Leary, *Marijuana Rx,* 267, 302, 359; Randall and O'Leary, *Marijuana as Medicine,* 11, 33–63 (1993); *State Legislation or Resolutions Recognizing Marijuana's Medical Value,* NORML (1995) (on file with author).

57. Peron and Entwistle, *Memoirs of Dennis Peron,* loc. 662 of 10370.

58. Peron and Entwistle, *Memoirs of Dennis Peron*; Paul DeRienzo, "Dennis Peron: The Marijuana Mouse Who Roared," *High Times,* August 1998, 44–50; Mark Evans, "Hero or Villain: Passion Drives Pot-Measure Supporter," *San Bernardino County Sun,* November 24, 1996, B4; Richard Sandomir, "Dennis Peron, an Early Advocate for Medical Marijuana, Dies at 71," *New York Times,* January 31, 2018, B12; Zack Ruskin, "Dennis Peron, the Patron Saint of Legal Cannabis, Has Died," *SF Weekly,* January 29, 2018, online.

59. San Francisco Board of Supervisors, Resolution 741–92 (Aug. 31, 1992).

60. S.J. Res. 8 (Cal. Mar. 3, 1993); Randall and O'Leary, *Marijuana Rx,* 428–29.

61. Emily Dufton, *Grass Roots: The Rise and Fall and Rise of Marijuana in America* (New York: Basic Books, 2017), 212–21; Lee, *Smoke Signals,* 228–29; Peron and Entwistle, *Memoirs of Dennis Peron.*

62. Peron and Entwistle, *Memoirs of Dennis Peron,* loc. 1151–63 of 10370; Randall and O'Leary, *Marijuana Rx,* 417–18, 432.

63. On the CBC, see Lee, *Smoke Signals,* 232, 235–38; Peron and Entwistle, *Memoirs of Dennis Peron*; Carey Goldberg, "Marijuana Club Helps Those in Pain," *New York Times,* February 25, 1996, 16.

64. Lee, *Smoke Signals,* 239–40; Peron and Entwistle, *Memoirs of Dennis Peron,* loc. 1593–1615 of 10370.

65. Jeordan Legon, "Marijuana Maverick Continues Campaign: Compassion Is Key to Prop. 215, Says Measure's Author," *San Jose Mercury News,* October 28, 1996, 1A; Carey Goldberg, "Wealthy Ally for Dissidents in the Drug War," *New York Times,* September 10, 1996, A12.

66. Lee, *Smoke Signals,* 243; Peron and Entwistle, *Memoirs of Dennis Peron,* loc. 2369–2413, 2839–77 of 10370; Dufton, *Grass Roots,* 218–19.

67. "California Ballot Pamphlet: 215 Medical Use of Marijuana. Initiative Statute" (1996); Lee, *Smoke Signals,* 243.

68. Institute of Medicine, *Marijuana and Health*; "California Ballot Pamphlet: 215 Medical Use of Marijuana. Initiative Statute"; Dana Wilkie, "Marijuana as Medicine: Is Measure a Remedy, or Ruse?," *San Diego Union-Tribune,* October 21, 1996, E1.

69. Medical Marijuana Campaign Goes National," press release (Californians for Medical Rights, November 6, 1996); CMR Brochures (1996); Dennis Peron, "Yes on Prop. 215: A Mission of Mercy," *San Francisco Examiner,* October 20, 1996, C15; CCU Brochure (1996).

70. Lee, *Smoke Signals,* 243; "California Ballot Pamphlet: 215 Medical Use of Marijuana. Initiative Statute."

71. Kevin Zeese, email to "aro-list," October 28, 1996.

72. Allen St. Pierre, email to author, October 12, 2018.

73. Lee, *Smoke Signals*, 254–60.

74. Matt Krasnowski, "L.A.'s Prescription Pot Rebel: He Gets Along with Cops," *Copley News Service*, March 27, 1998; Peron and Entwistle, *Memoirs of Dennis Peron*, loc. 3518, 5054–65, 5264–73 of 10370; Mary Curtius, "Activist's Tactics Anger Many in Medical Marijuana Movement," *Los Angeles Times*, December 28, 1997, A3; Lee, *Smoke Signals*, 260–64; *People ex rel. Lungren v. Peron*, 70 Cal. Rptr. 2d 20 (Cal. Ct. App. 1997).

75. Lee, *Smoke Signals*, 334–35, 350–51, 353–54.

76. "Medical Marijuana Campaign Goes National."

77. Terry Stephenson, "Dear Sir" Letter (1997); Steve Kubby, "Bill of Rights Is the Cure for Government Disease," op-ed, *WorldNetDaily*, October 18, 2000, online; Norah Vincent, "A New 'Worst' Drug Stirs up the Snoops," op-ed, *Los Angeles Times*, July 19, 2001, 15; Larry Nickerson, "Life and Marijuana," letter to the editor, *Ft. Worth Star-Telegram*, June 25, 2002, online.

78. "State Medical Marijuana Laws," Health, Research, NCSL, website; Texas A&M, Sam Houston State University Survey, June 6–June 26, 1995; Henry J. Kaiser Foundation, Harvard School of Public Health Survey, Dec. 13–17, 1996; ABC News Poll, May 27, 1997; Andrew Daniller, "Two-Thirds of Americans Support Marijuana Legalization," Pew Research Center, November 14, 2019.

79. Barry R. McCaffrey, "The Administration's Response to the Passage of California Proposition 215 and Arizona Proposition 200" (Dec. 30, 1996); *United States v. Cannabis Cultivators Club*, 5 F. Supp. 2d 1086 (N.D. Cal. 1998).

80. Lee, *Smoke Signals*, 295, 299–300, 303–6, 309; Bob Pool, "Medical Marijuana Center in Mourning," *Los Angeles Times*, October 30, 2001, 3; *United States v. Rosenthal*, No. CR 02-00053 CRB, 2007 WL 2012734, at *1 (N.D. Cal. 2007)

81. *United States v. Oakland Cannabis Buyers Coop.*, 532 U.S. 483 (2001); *Gonzalez v. Raich*, 545 U.S. 1 (2005).

82. *Raich v. Gonzales*, 500 F.3d 850, 864–66 (9th Cir. 2007); *Lawrence v. Texas*, 539 U.S. 558 (2003); *Washington v. Glucksberg*, 521 U.S. 702, 721–23 (1997).

83. Memorandum from David W. Ogden, Deputy Att'y Gen., Memorandum for Selected United States Attorneys (Oct. 19, 2009); Memorandum from James M. Cole, Deputy Att'y Gen., Guidance Regarding the Ogden Memo in Jurisdictions Seeking to Authorize Marijuana for Medical Use (June 29, 2011); Mark K. Osbeck and Howard Bromberg, *Marijuana Law in a Nutshell* (St. Paul, MN: West Academic Publishing, 2017), 113–14.

84. Memorandum from James M. Cole, Deputy Att'y Gen., Guidance Regarding Marijuana Enforcement (Aug. 29, 2013); Pub. L. No. 113-235, § 538, 128 Stat. 2130 (2014); *United States v. Marin All. for Med. Marijuana*, 139 F. Supp. 3d 1039 (N.D. Cal. 2015); *United States. v. McIntosh*, 833 F.3d 1163 (9th Cir. 2016).

85. Fox News Network, The O'Reilly Factor, Feb. 10, 2016; Memorandum from Jefferson B. Sessions, Att'y Gen., Marijuana Enforcement (Jan. 4, 2018); Evan Halper, "Trump Inclined to Back Ending Pot Ban," *Los Angeles Times*, June 9, 2018,

A1; Sean Williams, "Trump Continues to Flip-Flop on Medical Marijuana," The Motley Fool (blog), April 18, 2019; Tom Angell, "Trump Issues Signing Statement on Medical Marijuana Provision of Funding Bill," Marijuana Moment (blog), February 15, 2019; Tom Angell, "Trump Attorney General Pick Puts Marijuana Enforcement Pledge in Writing," Marijuana Moment (blog), January 28, 2019; Agriculture Improvement Act of 2018, Pub. L. No. 115-334, §§ 10113, 12619, 132 Stat. 4908–9, 5018.

86. "FDA Advances Work Related to Cannabidiol Products with Focus on Protecting Public Health, Providing Market Clarity," FDA, March 24, 2020; "FDA Approves First Drug Comprised of an Active Ingredient Derived from Marijuana to Treat Rare, Severe Forms of Epilepsy," FDA, March 27, 2020.

87. Hudak, Marijuana, 134–36; 81 Fed. Reg. 53,688, 53,767 (Aug. 12, 2016).

88. 81 Fed. Reg. at 53,713–15.

89. 21 C.F.R. 1306.04(a) (2019); David A. Kessler, "Regulating the Prescribing of Human Drugs for Nonapproved Uses under the Food, Drug, and Cosmetic Act," *Harvard Journal on Legislation* 15, no. 4 (June 1978): 695–97.

90. Hudak and Wallack, "Ending the U.S. Government's War on Medical Marijuana Research," 1–2, 8.

91. Stephenson, "Dear Sir" letter.

92. Marcus Wohlsen, "Proposition 19 Shows State's Conflicted Link to Pot," *Monterey County Herald*, October 12, 2010.

93. Russ Belville, "'I Gots Mine': Dispensary Owners against Marijuana Legalization," NORML, July 14, 2010; Steve Elliot, "'Stoners against 19' Hand Victory to the Cops: BOYCOTT THEM," *Cannabis Culture*, November 4, 2010; Angela Bacca, "Chaos Erupts over Prop 19 at California Cannabis Expo," *Cannabis Culture*, September 27, 2010.

94. Use and Regulation of Marijuana, Colorado Amendment 64 (2012); Washington Marijuana Legalization and Regulation, Washington Initiative 502 (2012); Kirk Johnson, "Marijuana Referendum Divides Both Sides," *New York Times*, October 14, 2012, 18; *Evergreen: The Road to Legalization in Washington*, directed by Riley Morton (New York: First Run Features, 2013); Kris Hermes, "Medical Marijuana Patient Advocates Launch 'Health before Happy Hour' Campaign," press release, Americans for Safe Access, August 13, 2013.

95. "Map of Marijuana Legality by State"; Natalya Estrada, "Prop. 215 Author Fights Prop. 64," *Eureka Times-Standard*, October 12, 2016.

96. "Legalization of Cannabis for Recreational Use," Americans for Safe Access; Allen St. Pierre email to author, October 12, 2018.

97. Russ Belville, "New York Governor Steering Medical Marijuana Into the Box Canyon," *Huffpost*, June 17, 2014; Allen St. Pierre, email message to author, March 7, 2014; Keith Stroup, email message to author, March 23, 2015; Allen St. Pierre, email message to Rick Cusick, March 4, 2015.

98. "NORML Chairman Keith Stroup Talks on Pot Issues," *The Emory Wheel*, February 6, 1979; Michael Roberts, "Medical Marijuana v. Recreational Use: NORML Controversy, Colorado Connection," Westword (blog), January 25, 2012.

99. Patrick Whittle, "Pot Ballot Drives Put Medical, Recreational Users at Odds," *Associated Press Financial Wire*, October 29, 2016; Patrick McGreevy, "Pot Community Deeply Divided over Prop. 64: Some Fear Measure Will Disrupt Medical Cannabis Market," *Los Angeles Times*, October 6, 2016, A13; Hilary Bricken, "The 'Why' behind California's Battle to Legalize Marijuana," Canna Law Blog (blog), November 21, 2014.

100. Gillian Flaccus and Angeliki Kastanis, "AP Analysis: Medical Pot Takes Hit When Weed Legal for All," *AP News*, June 11, 2019; Don Duncan, "ASA Broadcast: What Legalization Means for Medical Cannabis," November 20, 2014, Americans for Safe Access, broadcast recording, https://www.youtube.com/watch?v=Tk8nCOm4UQs; Dan Adams, "Advent of Legal Pot Use Challenges Medicinal Shops," *Boston Globe*, May 10, 2017, B11.

101. Danmiller, "Two-Thirds of Americans Support Marijuana Legalization"; Jeffrey M. Jones, "U.S. Support for Legal Marijuana Steady in Past Year," *Gallup*, October 23, 2019; James Forman, *Locking Up Our Own: Crime and Punishment in Black America* (New York: Farrar, Straus & Giroux, 2018), 17–46; Patrick McGreevy, "NAACP Leader's Ouster Is Sought," *Los Angeles Times*, July 8, 2010, AA4.

102. Forman, *Locking Up Our Own*, 204–5; Michelle Alexander, *The New Jim Crow: Mass Incarceration in the Age of Colorblindness* (New York: The New Press, 2010); Aaron C. Davis and Peyton M. Craighill, "Poll: D.C. Voters Poised to Legalize Pot, Elevating National Debate Over Marijuana," *Washington Post*, September 19, 2014; "IGS Poll Finds Support for Gun Control, Marijuana Legalization" (Institute of Governmental Studies, August 17, 2016).

103. Keith Stroup, email message to author, March 23, 2015; Maggie Clark, "For Medical Pot, a New Legal Haze: Colorado's OK of Recreational Use Worries Dispensaries," *Sun-Sentinel*, January 31, 2013, A10.

Chapter 10

1. For clarity, this chapter will refer to Avastin as a "drug" rather than as a "biologic."

2. Memorandum to the File: BLA 125085 Avastin (Bevacizumab), Richard Pazdur, Dir., FDA-OODP, to Janet Woodcock, Dir., FDA-CDER (Dec. 15, 2010).

3. Alicia Mundy, "Resistance to FDA on Avastin Limits," *Wall Street Journal*, April 8, 2011, B1; Terrence D. Kalley, "FDA to Breast Cancer Patients: Shut Up and Die," *Washington Times*, May 12, 2011, online.

4. Caleb Hellerman, "Patients, Scientists at Odds over Breast Cancer Drug," *CNN*, June 28, 2011, online; "Proposal to Withdraw Approval for the Breast Cancer Indication for Bevacizumab (Avastin): FDA Public Hearing," June 28, 2011, 27–30.

5. Arlene Kalley, "Eliminating Avastin Will Be a Death Sentence for Some Cancer Victims," *San Jose Mercury News*, June 27, 2011, online.

6. "FDA Public Hearing," June 28, 2011, 87–90 (testimony of Terrence Kalley); Kalley, "Eliminating Avastin;" Kalley, "FDA to Breast Cancer Patients;" Sandra J. Horning, Michael S. Labson, Paul W. Schmidt, "Docket No. FDA-2010-N-0621: Pre-Hearing

Summary of Evidence and Arguments of Genentech, Inc," May 13, 2011. "FDA Public Hearing."

7. "FDA Public Hearing," 99–102 (testimony of Christi Turnage); "Petition to Protect the Avastin Women," Freedom of Access to Medicines, accessed June 27, 2011, website, on file with author.

8. "FDA Public Hearing," 35 (testimony of Crystal Hanna), 66 (testimony of Beth Baugham Dupree), 111 (testimony of Carolyn Law), 76 (testimony of Erin Ehrlich), 81–82 (testimony of Helen Schiff), 86 (testimony of Ivy Ahmed), 119 (testimony of Theresa Morrow).

9. "FDA Public Hearing," 80–83 (testimony of Helen Schiff), 91–93 (testimony of Christine Brunswick), 94 (testimony of Kimberley Jewett), 97–99 (testimony of Vernal Branch), 123–25 (testimony of Diana Zuckerman).

10. Mundy, "Resistance to FDA on Avastin Limits," B1.

11. Isaiah Berlin, "Two Concepts of Liberty," in *Liberty: Incorporating Four Essays on Liberty*, ed. Henry Hardy, 2nd ed. (Oxford: Oxford University Press, 2002), 169; "FDA Public Hearing," 35 (testimony of Crystal Hannah).

12. Margaret A. Hamburg, Comm'r, FDA, "Decision of the Commissioner on the Proposal to Withdraw Approval for the Breast Cancer Indication for AVASTIN (Bevacizumab), Docket No. FDA-2010-N-0621" (Nov. 18, 2011); Freedom of Access to Medicines, "Breast Cancer Advocates Decry FDA Vote to Remove Life-Saving Drug from Market," November 18, 2011; Delthia Ricks, "LI Reacts: Dismay, Support for Order," *Newsday*, November 19, 2011, A5.

13. "Mississippi Lawmakers Knock FDA Decision Federal Agency Withdraws Best-Selling Cancer Drug," *Federal Information & News Dispatch*, November 21, 2011; Sen. David Vitter, "Vitter Comments on FDA Withdrawal of Approval for Avastin Use for Breast Cancer Treatment," *Federal Information & News Dispatch*, November 18, 2011; screen shots of Nov. 18, 2011, posts on Fox News website on file with author.

14. Because Medicare originally covered only people of age sixty-five and older, abortion never arose in that context; it occasionally does now, because Medicare was expanded in 1972 to cover younger Americans with long-term disabilities and end-stage renal disease.

15. See, e.g., *Doe v. Wohlgemuth*, 376 F. Supp. 173, 186–92 (W.D. Pa. 1974); *Doe v. Westby*, 383 F. Supp. 1143 (D.S.D. 1974); *Doe v. Ceci*, 384 F. Supp. 7 (E.D. Wis. 1974); *Roe v. Norton*, 408 F. Supp. 726 (D. Conn. 1975); *Maher v. Roe*, 432 U.S. 464 (1977).

16. *Harris v. McCrae*, 448 U.S. 297, 316 (1980); *Maher*, 432 U.S. at 474–76.

17. On "negative" versus "positive" rights to health, see Abigail R. Moncrieff, "The Freedom of Health," *University of Pennsylvania Law Review* 159 (June 2011): 2209–52; Jessie B. Hill, "What Is the Meaning of Health?: Constitutional Implications of Defining 'Medical Necessity' and 'Essential Health Benefits,'" *American Journal of Law and Medicine* 38, no. 2 (June 2012): 460–69. Constitutional issues may still arise if, for example, government medical benefits are distributed differently to different groups of people, implicating the equal protection clause, or if a government medical insurance program denies coverage to a beneficiary without affording him sufficient notice and opportunity for a hearing, implicating the due process clause.

18. Workers' compensation covered medical treatment for work-related injuries and, in a few cases, occupational disease. Paul Starr, *The Social Transformation of American Medicine: The Rise of a Sovereign Profession and the Making of a Vast Industry* (New York: Basic Books, 2017), 237–57, 270–75, 294–98.

19. R. G. Leland, "The Insurance Principle in the Practice of Medicine," in *Discussions of Industrial Accidents and Diseases at the 1933 Meeting of the International Association of Industrial Accident Boards and Commissions, Chicago, Ill.* (Washington, DC: U.S. Bureau of Labor Statistics, 1934), 60–61.

20. "Proceedings of the Cleveland Session Minutes of the Eighty-Fifth Annual Session of the American Medical Association, Held at Cleveland, June 11–15, 1934," *Journal of the American Medical Association* 102, no. 26 (June 30, 1934): 2200.

21. Jay W. Friedman, "The Value of Free Choice in Health Care," *Medical Care* 3, no. 2 (June 1965): 121–27; Starr, *Social Transformation*, 23–24.

22. Starr, 306–10.

23. Harry S. Truman, Message from the President of the United States Transmitting His Request for Legislation for Adoption of a National Health Program, H.R. Doc. 380, at 9 (1945); *National Health Program: Hearings on S. 1606, Part 2 before the S. Comm. on Educ. & Labor*, 79th Cong. 605 (1946) (letter from H. F. Connally, President, St. Med. Ass'n of Tex., to Sen. James E. Murray, Chairman, Comm. on Educ. & Labor, Apr. 15, 1946). For other discussions of the subject, see, e.g., *National Health Program: Hearings on S.1606*, 620–21, 643, 756–57, 1150–54; *National Health Program: Hearings on S. 1606, Part 3 before the S. Comm. on Educ. & Labor*, 79th Cong., 1321–28, 1346–49, 1531–33 (1946).

24. Social Security Amendments of 1965, Pub. L. No. 89-97, § 1802, 79 Stat. 286, 291 (codified at 42 U.S.C. § 1395a(a)). "Any individual eligible for medical assistance (including drugs) may obtain such assistance from any institution, agency, community pharmacy, or person, qualified to perform the service or services required." Pub. L. No. 90-248, § 227, 81 Stat. 821, 903 (1968) (codified as amended at 42 U.S.C. §1396a(a)(23)). *Planned Parenthood of Gulf Coast, Inc. v. Gee*, 862 F.3d 445 (5th Cir. 2016); *Planned Parenthood of Ariz., Inc. v. Betlach*, 727 F.3d 960 (9th Cir. 2013); *Planned Parenthood of Ind., Inc. v. Comm'r of Ind. St. Dep't of Health*, 699 F.3d 962 (7th Cir. 2012). *See also Harris v. Olszewski*, 442 F.3d 456 (6th Cir. 2006) (free choice of supplier of incontinence products).

25. Bill Clinton, President of the United States, State of the Union Address (Jan. 25, 1994); Sandy Rovner, "Can I Keep My Doctor?: Freedom of Choice Is a 'Hot-Button' Issue," *Washington Post*, November 2, 1993, 6; Robert Pear, "Clinton's Health Plan: A.M.A. Rebels over Health Plan in Major Challenge to President," *New York Times*, September 30, 1993, A1; Abigail Trafford, "What Went Wrong: How Wonks and Pols—and You—Fumbled Universal Care," *Washington Post*, August 21, 1994, C1.

26. Louis Jacobson, "Barack Obama says [. . .].," *PolitiFact*, November 4, 2013, website; Greenberg, Quinlan, Rosner, Research, "Democracy Corps Questionnaire," Democracy Corps Poll, June 25, 2009. By 2013, 61 percent of respondents opined that "the Obama administration knew before the new system was launched that under the exchanges not everyone would be able to keep their current doctor unless they paid

more to do so." Dana Blanton, "Fox News Poll: 67 Percent Say Delay Obamacare, 53 Percent Would Vote to Repeal It," *Fox News*, December 21, 2015.

27. "New York Times/CBS News Poll: March 21–25, 2012," March 26, 2012.

28. Blanton, "Fox News Poll."

29. Kayla Holgash and Martha Heberlein, Physician Acceptance of New Medicaid Patients, Medicaid and CHIP Payment Access Commission (Presentation, January 24, 2019), online.

30. Calculated from 2016 "Health Insurance Coverage of the Total Population" and "Total HMO Enrollment," State Health Facts, Kaiser Family Foundation, website; *Medicaid Managed Care Enrollment and Program Characteristics* (Washington, DC: CMS, Spring 2018); Amy B. Monahan, "The Interactions Between Public and Private Health Insurance," in *Oxford Handbook of US Health Law*, ed. I. Glenn Cohen, Allison K. Hoffman, and William M. Sage (New York: Oxford University Press, 2017), 799–800; Integrated Care Resource Center, "'At-a-Glance' Guide to Federal Medicaid Authorities Useful in Restructuring Medicaid Health Care Delivery or Payment," April 2012; Gretchen Jacobson, Anthony Damico, Tricia Neuman, and Marsha Gold, "Medicare Advantage 2017 Spotlight: Enrollment Market Update," *KFF*, June 6, 2017, website; Monahan, "Interactions Between Public and Private Health Insurance," 798–99.

31. In an April 28, 1989, NBC News/Wall Street Journal poll, support for "a comprehensive national health plan that would cover all Americans, and be paid for by federal tax revenues" dropped from 67 percent to 53 percent—still a majority—"if you were not able to choose your own doctor." "NBC News Poll: April 1989," Roper, April 25, 1989, website. In a January 1992 telephone poll by Aetna, "being able to choose a doctor" was only the fourth most important characteristic of a health care system, behind holding down costs, high quality, and universal access. Only 12 percent identified it as the most important. In a 1993 poll, a majority of people said they would be willing to choose a doctor from a limited list rather than going to see their current doctor if it would reduce their health care costs. Robin Toner, "Clinton's Health Plan," *New York Times*, September 22, 1993, A1. In a July 2007 Democracy Corps poll, 58 percent of respondents said "knowing I will always have health coverage" was a more important personal health priority than "maintaining choices and seeing my own doctor." By contrast, in a different 1993 poll, 71 percent of respondents said that it would be "completely unacceptable" and 15 percent said that it would be "somewhat unacceptable" for a health reform plan to cause them to "lose the ability to choose your own doctor." Voter/Consumer Research (April 1993). A 1998 survey showed that 56 percent were willing to pay more in exchange for "greater freedom of choice of doctor, hospitals, medications, etc." "Wirthlin Worldwide Poll: April 1998," Wirthlin Worldwide, April 6, 1998, website.

32. "Kaiser Health Tracking Poll: January 2016," *KFF*, January 28, 2016.

33. Lewis A. Grossman, "Drugs, Biologics, and Devices: FDA Regulation, Intellectual Property, and Medical Products in the American Healthcare System," in *Oxford Handbook of US Health Law*, ed. I. Glenn Cohen, Allison K. Hoffman, and William M. Sage (New York: Oxford University Press, 2017), 656.

34. *Description and Analysis of the VA National Formulary* (Washington, DC: National Academies Press, 2000), 15–16.

35. *Description and Analysis*, 17; Jeremy A. Greene, *Generic: The Unbranding of Modern Medicine* (Baltimore: Johns Hopkins University Press, 2014), 144–45.

36. Greene, *Generic*, 145; *Description and Analysis*, 17.

37. *Description and Analysis*, 17; Bryan L. Walser, Dennis Ross-Degnan, and Stephen B. Soumerai, "Do Open Formularies Increase Access to Clinically Useful Drugs?," *Health Affairs* 15, no. 3 (Fall 1996): 95–109.

38. Greene, *Generic*, 143–47, 197–208.

39. *Description and Analysis*, 184.

40. 42 U.S.C.§ 1396r-8(d)(4); *Description and Analysis*, 2; Medicare Prescription Drug, Improvement, and Modernization Act of 2003, Pub. L. 108-173, § 101, 117 Stat. 2066, 2084 (codified at 42 U.S.C. § 1395w-104(b)(3)).

41. David Jones, "The Prospects of Personalized Medicine," in *Genetic Explanation: Sense and Nonsense*, ed. Sheldon Krimsky and Jeremy Gruber (Cambridge, MA: Harvard University Press, 2013), 147–48.

42. See, e.g., "Eli Lilly Drug Passes a Test," *New York Times*, September 12, 1987, 40; Judith Valente, "Eli Lilly's New Antidepressant Drug Clears FDA Hurdle, Stock Jumps $10," *Wall Street Journal*, September 14, 1987, 28; Deborah Licklider, "New Drug Fights Depression: Reduced Side Effects Make Prozac a Better Choice for Some," *Philadelphia Daily News*, September 14, 1988, 31; Erin Marcus, "Prozac: Is It Really the 'Wonder Drug' for Depression?," *Washington Post*, August 28, 1990, 12.

43. David Herzberg, *Happy Pills in America: From Miltown to Prozac* (Baltimore: Johns Hopkins University Press, 2010), 177–79.

44. Milt Freudenheim, "Psychiatric Drugs Are Now Promoted Directly to Patients," *New York Times*, February 17, 1998, A1; Wendy L. Bonifazi, "Hard Sell: Drug Makers Are Spending Billions on 'Direct to Consumer Ads,'" *Wall Street Journal*, March 25, 2002, R8; Amy Harmon, "Young, Assured and Playing Pharmacist to Friends," *New York Times*, November 16, 2005, A1; Francesca Lunzer Kritz, "Ask Your Doctor about . . . Which of the Many Advertised Allergy Drugs Are Right for You?," *Washington Post*, June 6, 2000, 9.

45. International Human Genome Sequencing Consortium, "Initial Sequencing and Analysis of the Human Genome," *Nature* 409, no. 6822 (February 15, 2001): 860–921; International Human Genome Sequencing Consortium, "Finishing the Euchromatic Sequence of the Human Genome," *Nature* 431, no. 7011 (October 21, 2004): 931–45; Gina Kolata, "Using Gene Tests to Customize Medical Treatment," *New York Times*, December 20, 1999, A1; Claudia Kalb, "Peering into the Future; Genetic Testing Is Transforming Medicine—and the Way Families Think about Their Health.," *Newsweek*, December 11, 2006, 52. In a 2006 poll, 62 percent of respondents responded positively to the statement, "If a doctor recommends an expensive new drug or medical treatment, do you think insurance companies should pay for it only if it's been proven to be more effective than other, less expensive treatments." "Health Care in America 2006 Survey," *ABC News/Kaiser Family Foundation/USA Today*, October 2006. An almost identical question in 2009 found that only 38 percent of

people believed insurance companies should not have to pay in this situation. "The Public and the Health Care Delivery System," *Kaiser/Harvard/NPR*, March 2009, 15.

46. "Consumer Group Vows to Shine Light on Managed Care," press release, *PR Newswire*, March 29, 1995; Barbara Marsh, "HMO Drug Lists New Focus of Backlash," *Los Angeles Times*, January 18, 1998, 1; Bill Ainsworth, "HMO Law Gives Women Direct Access to Specialist," *San Diego Union-Tribune*, April 17, 1998, A-1; Amy Pyle, "State Denies HMOs' Bid to Drop Coverage of Some Drugs," *Los Angeles Times*, April 18, 1999, 8.

47. Patients' Formulary Rights Act of 1999, H.R. 3274, 106th Cong., 1st Sess. (Nov. 9, 1999). See, e.g., Health Insurance Bill of Rights Act of 1997, S. 353, § 2776, 105th Cong., 1st Sess. (Feb. 25, 1997); Patients' Bill of Rights Act of 1998, § 107, S. 1890, 105th Cong., 2nd Sess. (Mar. 31, 1998); "Managed Care Again Tops State Law Lists," *Reuters Health Medical News*, February 16, 2000.

48. Andrew Sperling, "Health Reform and Access to Prescription Drugs," *Care for Your Mind* (blog), website; Gary Puckrein, "The Democratization of Health Care: The Open Formulary Movement," *Huffpost*, October 12, 2012, website.

49. Gardiner Harris, "Drug Makers Are Advocacy Group's Biggest Donors," *New York Times*, October 22, 2009, A23.

50. Access to Covered Part D Drugs, 42 C.F.R. § 423.120(b)(2)(i) (2019); The Medicare Improvements for Patients and Providers Act, Pub. L. 110-275, § 176, 122 Stat. 2494, 2581 (2008), was amended by the Patient Protection and Affordable Care Act, Pub. L. 111-148, § 3307, 124 Stat. 119, 471–72 (2010) (codified at 42 U.S.C. § 1395w-104(b) (3)(G)). The history is described at 79 Fed. Reg. 1918, 1937 (Jan. 10, 2014).

51. 79 Fed. Reg. at 1937–38, 1941–47. Anticonvulsants, antiretrovirals, and antineoplastics (anticancer drugs) would remain protected classes.

52. Chuck Grassley and Sherrod Brown, Letter to Andy Slavitt (June 30, 2016); Office of Congressman Leonard Lance, "Bipartisan Lawmakers Defend Medicare," news release, March 7, 2014, website; Charles S. Ingoglia, "CMS Proposal to Strip Patient Safeguards Stopped," op-ed, *The Highlander*, June 24, 2014, 6A; Katie Thomas and Robert Pear, "Plan to Limit Some Drugs in Medicare Is Criticized," *New York Times*, February 22, 2014, B1; Robert Pear, "White House Withdraws Plan Allowing Limits to Medicare Coverage for Some Drugs," *New York Times*, March 11, 2014, A13.

53. Modernizing Part D and Medicare Advantage, 83 Fed. Reg. 62152 (Nov. 30, 2018); "Tell CMS: Preserve Medicare's Six Protected Classes," *Care for Your Mind* (blog), January 15, 2019, website; Letter from Patient Groups to Seema Verma, January, 25, 2019; Modernizing Part D and Medicare Advantage, 84 Fed. Reg. 23,832, 23,843 (May 23, 2019).

54. See, e.g., Ashley Kirzinger, Bryan Wu, and Mollyann Brodie, "Kaiser Health Tracking Poll—March 2018: Views on Prescription Dug Pricing and Medicare-for-All Proposals," *KFF*, March 23, 2018, website.

55. Kati Sadiwnyk, "Mixed Response to Avastin's Indication Removal," *Zitter Health Insights*, May 21, 2012, website.

56. Drusilla S. Raiford, Sheila R. Shulman, and Louis Lasagna, "Determining Appropriate Reimbursement for Prescription Drugs: Off Label Uses and Investigational Therapies," *Food and Drug Law Journal* 49, no. 1 (1994): 37–76.

57. Richard A. Knox, "AIDS Drug Protest Targets Hancock," *Boston Globe*, October 25, 1988, 60; Steven Morris, "AIDS-Related Drug Wins Limited OK," *Chicago Tribune*, February 7, 1989, 1.

58. Peter Arno and Karen L. Feiden, *Against the Odds: The Story of AIDS Drug Development, Politics and Profits* (New York: HarperPerennial, 1992), 54–57; Roger Signor, "Missouri Medicaid to Cover Drug to Treat AIDS Patients," *St. Louis Post-Dispatch*, July 11, 1987, 5; Tim Bryant and Robert Manor, "AIDS Patients Win Medicaid Victory," *St. Louis Post-Dispatch*, September 26, 1989, 1.

59. *Weaver v. Reagen*, 886 F.2d 194, 197–98, 200 (8th Cir. 1989) (citing 42 U.S.C. § 1396a(a)(17) and *Beal v. Doe*, 432 U.S. 438 (1977)); *Weaver v. Reagen*, 701 F. Supp. 717, 723 (W.D. Mo. 1988). There was an apparent flaw in the court of appeals' reasoning. It relied in part on a Medicaid regulation providing that the "Medicaid agency may not arbitrarily deny or reduce the amount, duration, or scope of a required service . . . to an otherwise eligible beneficiary solely because of the diagnosis, type of illness, or condition." *Weaver*, 886 F.2d at 197 (citing 42 C.F.R. § 440.230). Prescription drugs are an *optional* service under Medicaid. This fact has led some courts to reject *Weaver v. Reagen* and hold that the medical necessity standard does not apply to optional services. See, e.g., *Ohlson v. Weil*, 953 P.2d 939, 943 (Colo. App. 1997).

60. National Cancer Institute, *Final Report of the National Committee to Review Current Procedures for Approval of New Drugs for Cancer and AIDS*, August 15, 1990, vii, 13.

61. Omnibus Budget Reconciliation Act of 1990, Pub. L. No. 101-508, § 4401, 104 Stat. 1388-143 (codified at 42 U.S.C. § 1396r-8; 42 U.S.C. § 1396r-8(k)(6). The 1990 amendments defined "medically accepted indications" to include uses "appear[ing] in peer reviewed medical literature" and uses supported by any of the compendia, but in 1993 Congress removed the reference to "peer reviewed medical literature." Omnibus Budget Reconciliation Act of 1993, Pub. L. No. 103-66, § 13602; 42 U.S.C. § 1396r-8(d)(1), (4); (g)(1)(B); (k)(6). Although prescription coverage is an "optional service category" under Medicaid, every state has chosen to provide it. For states that opt in, Medicaid, with some exceptions not relevant here, requires coverage of all FDA-approved prescription drugs and biological products. 42 U.S.C. § 1396r-8(k)(2)(A)(i), (B). See also § 1396r-8(d)(1)(B)(i), (k)(6). States are, however, allowed to use formulary management tools to promote the use of cheaper products.

62. 42 U.S.C. 1395x(t)(2); Peter B. Bach, "Limits on Medicare's Ability to Control Rising Spending on Cancer Drugs," *New England Journal of Medicine* 360, no. 6 (February 5, 2009): 626–33; Lindsey Gabrielson, "Bias at the Gate?: The Pharmaceutical Industry's Influence on the Federally Approved Drug," *American Journal of Law and Medicine* 40, no. 1 (2014): 141; David Armstrong, "By the Book: How Drug Directory Helps Raise Tab for Medicaid and Insurers," *Wall Street Journal*, October 23, 2003, A1; on the high frequency of off-label use in the oncology field, see Rena M. Conti et al., "Prevalence of Off-Label Use and Spending in 2010 Among Patent-Protected Chemotherapies in a Population-Based Cohort of Medical Oncologists," *Journal of Clinical Oncology* 31, no. 9 (March 20, 2013): 1134–39; Omnibus Budget Reconciliation Act of 1993, § 13553(b), 107 Stat. 312 (codified at 42 USC § 1395x(t)). Medicare Part B requires coverage of drugs and biological products used in anticancer chemotherapeutic regimens

for any "medically accepted indication," which is defined to include all uses approved by the FDA. 42 U.S.C. 1395x(t)(2). Although Medicare Part B also provides that, notwithstanding this provision, "no payment should be made" for items or services "not reasonable and necessary," this exclusion has rarely if ever been invoked with respect to an FDA-approved cancer indication. 42 U.S.C. § 1395y(a). Medicare Part D, for self-administered drugs, uses the same standard for "medically accepted" anticancer indications. 42 U.S.C. § 1395w-102(e)(4).

63. Andrew Pollack, "Medicare Will Pay for Avastin in Treating Breast Cancer," *New York Times*, June 30, 2011, website; 42 U.S.C. § 1395x(t)(2)(B)(ii). Indeed, based on the FDA's initial negative decision in December 2010, one regional contractor (Palmetto GBA) threatened to do just this, but quickly reversed course in response to protests. Andrew Pollack, "Medicare to Pay for Cancer Drug," *New York Times*, January 8, 2011, B2.

64. Raiford, Shulman, and Lasagna, "Determining Appropriate Reimbursement for Prescription Drugs: Off Label Uses and Investigational Therapies," 39; Andrew Pollack, "Blue Shield of California Won't Cover Breast Cancer Drug," *New York Times*, October 2, 2011, B3.

65. Paul Fronstin, "Self-Insured Health Plans: State Variation and Recent Trends by Firm Size," *Employee Benefit Research Institute* 33, no. 11 (June 2015): 2; *Report to Congress: Annual Report on Self-Insured Group Health Plans* (Washington, DC: Department of Labor, 2017).

66. Rebecca S. Eisenberg and W. Nicholson Price, "Promoting Healthcare Innovation on the Demand Side," *Journal of Law and the Biosciences* 4, no. 1 (April 2017): 31; William Atkinson, "The Impact of CED on Private Payers," *Biotechnology Healthcare* 4, no. 2 (April 2007): 24–30; Ryan Abbott and Ian Ayres, "Evidence and Extrapolation: Mechanisms for Regulating Off-Label Uses of Drugs and Devices," *Duke Law Journal* 64, no. 3 (December 2014): 406; Monahan, "Interactions between Public and Private Health Insurance," 796–97.

67. Kati Sadiwnyk, "Mixed Response"; Rob Stein, "Breast Cancer Option Gone: Drug Harms More than It Helps, FDA Rules," *Augusta Chronicle*, November 19, 2011, A1; Kristen Leigh Painter, "Local Opinions Differ on Avastin," *Denver Post*, November 19, 2011, A12; Deborah Kotz, "FDA Revokes Approval of Drug for Breast Cancer," *Boston Globe*, November 19, 2011, A1; Stacie B. Dusetzina et al., "How Do Payers Respond to Regulatory Actions?: The Case of Bevacizumab," *Journal of Oncology Practice* 11, no. 4 (July 2015): 315.

68. Jeffrey Lord, "Berwick Sets Up Death Panels by Fiat," *The American Spectator Online*, December 28, 2010; David B. Rivkin Jr. and Elizabeth Price Foley, "'Death Panels' Come Back to Life," op-ed, *Wall Street Journal*, December 30, 2010, A15; Peter Ferrara, "The Death Panel's First Murder," *The American Spectator Online*, December 22, 2010.

69. Sally C. Pipes, "Avastin Decision Is a Nightmare for Many Breast Cancer Patients," *The Examiner*, December 27, 2010, 21. The *Wall Street Journal* editorial page, for example, inaccurately warned that Medicare "never" reimburses for oncology therapies that are not FDA-approved. "Breast Cancer and the FDA," editorial, *Wall Street Journal*, December 17, 2010, A18.

70. Pipes, "Avastin Decision Is a Nightmare for Many Breast Cancer Patients."
71. Sarah Palin, "Statement on the Current Health Care Debate," Facebook, August, 7, 2009.
72. Elizabeth Weeks Leonard, "Death Panels and the Rhetoric of Rationing," *Nevada Law Journal* 13, no. 3 (Spring 2013): 873. For an earlier linkage of the Avastin decision to cost-conscious rationing by "central planners," see "The Avastin Mugging," editorial, *Wall Street Journal*, August 18, 2010, A16.
73. Leonard, "Death Panels and the Rhetoric of Rationing," 873; Monahan, "Interactions Between Public and Private Health Insurance."
74. Rivkin and Foley, "'Death Panels' Come Back to Life"; Milton R. Wolf, "The FDA's One-Man Death Panel," *Washington Times*, June 21, 2011.
75. "Memorandum to the File"; Hamburg, "Decision of the Commissioner."
76. Liz Szabo, "A Timeline of Eye-Popping Drug Prices," *USA Today*, August 26, 2016, B2.
77. "Avastin Mugging," A16; Ferrara, "Death Panel's First Murder"; Peter Roff, "FDA Musn't [sic] Restrict Freedom to Use Avastin to Fight Breast Cancer," *U.S. News*, June 25, 2011, website; "The Avastin Denial," editorial, *Wall Street Journal*, November 19, 2011, A14.
78. Rivkin and Foley, "'Death Panels' Come Back to Life"; Ferrara, "The Death Panel's First Murder"; Pipes, "Avastin Decision Is a Nightmare."

Chapter 11

1. "State Results: Massachusetts," Election 2012, *New York Times*, website.
2. Paula Span, *How the "Death with Dignity" Initiative Failed in Massachusetts*, New York Times Blogs, December 6, 2012.
3. "State Results: Massachusetts."
4. Neil M. Gorsuch, *The Future of Assisted Suicide and Euthanasia* (Princeton, NJ: Princeton University Press, 2009), 126.
5. *Schloendorff v. Soc'y of N.Y. Hospital*, 105 N.E. 92, 93 (1914).
6. *Jacobson v. Massachusetts*, 197 U.S. 11, 26–27 (1905).
7. *Buck v. Bell*, 274 U.S. 200, 207 (1927).
8. Arthur Allen, *Vaccine: The Controversial Story of Medicine's Greatest Lifesaver* (New York: W. W. Norton, 2008), 244; Michael Willrich, *Pox: An American History* (New York: Penguin, 2011), 339.
9. Harry Bruinius, *Better for All the World: The Secret History of Forced Sterilization and America's Quest for Racial Purity* (New York: Vintage Books, 2007), 317–21; *Rogowski v. City of Detroit*, 132 N.W.2d 16, 18, 20–24 (Mich. 1965). See also *Kaul v. Chehalis*, 277 P.2d 352 (Wash. 1954); *Minnesota State Bd. of Health by Lawson v. City of Brainerd*, 241 N.W.2d 624 (Minn. 1976).
10. Kenney F. Hegland, "Unauthorized Rendition of Lifesaving Medical Treatment," *California Law Review* 53 (1965): 860, 877.
11. Harold Y. Vanderpool, "Doctors and the Dying of Patients in American History," in *Physician-Assisted Suicide*, ed. Robert F. Weir (Bloomington: Indiana University

Press,1997) 33–66, 43–47; Lisa Yount, *Physician-Assisted Suicide and Euthanasia* (New York: Facts on File, 2000), 11; Stanley J. Dudrick, "History of Parenteral Nutrition," *Journal of the American College of Nutrition* 28, no. 3 (June 2009): 243–51; Peter G. Filene, *In the Arms of Others: A Cultural History of the Right-to-Die in America* (Chicago: Ivan R. Dee, 1998), 53–55; Vanderpool, "Doctors and the Dying of Patients," 46.

12. Vanderpool, 46–49; Yount, *Physician-Assisted Suicide and Euthanasia*, 12; Filene, *In the Arms of Others*, 63–67; Ivan Illich, *Medical Nemesis: The Expropriation of Health* (New York: Pantheon, 1982), 207; Elisabeth Kübler-Ross, *On Death and Dying* (New York: Macmillan, 1971), 8.

13. Yount, *Physician-Assisted Suicide and Euthanasia*, 12; Filene, *In the Arms of Others*, 67–73; James T. Patterson, *Restless Giant: The United States from Watergate to Bush v. Gore* (New York: Oxford University Press, 2007), 67; "Patient's Bill of Rights: American Hospital Association," Healthcare for the Aging, website; Louis Harris, "Terminally Ill Should Have Right to Die," The Harris Survey, for release May 14, 1981.

14. Filene, *In the Arms of Others*, 17–19; Pope Pius XII, "The Prolongation of Life: An Address to an International Congress of Anesthesiologists, November 24, 1957," *Pope Speaks* 4, no. 4 (Spring 1958): 393–98.

15. *In re Quinlan*, 348 A.2d 801 (N.J. Super. Ct. Ch. Div. 1975); 355 A.2d 647 (N.J. 1976). Quinlan's story is related in detail in Filene, *In the Arms of Others*.

16. *In re Quinlan*, 355 A.2d at 664; *Cruzan v. Missouri Dep't of Health*, 497 U.S. 261 (1990); Arthur L. Caplan, James J. McCartney, and Dominic A. Sisti, eds., *The Case of Terri Schiavo: Ethics at the End of Life* (Amherst, NY: Prometheus Books, 2006).

17. *In re Quinlan*, 355 A.2d at 603, 663; *Bouvia v. Superior Court*, 225 Cal. Rptr. 297 (Cal. Ct. App. 1986); *Cruzan*, 497 U.S. at 278.

18. Filene, *In the Arms of Others*, 25, 41–42, 106; Yount, *Physician-Assisted Suicide and Euthanasia*, 15–16; Tom Goff, "Right-to-Die Bill Frees Terminally Ill," *Los Angeles Times*, October 2, 1976, B1; Patient Self-Determination Act of 1990, H.R. 5067, 101st Cong. (incorporated into Omnibus Budget Reconciliation Act, H.R. 5835, § 4206).

19. "The Ultimate Right of Choice," editorial, *Los Angeles Times*, September 8, 1976, C6.

20. Yale Kamisar, "Physician-Assisted Suicide: The Last Bridge to Active Voluntary Euthanasia," in *Euthanasia Examined*, ed. Daniel Callahan (Cambridge, UK: Cambridge University Press, 1995), 230–33; L. W. Sumner, *Physician-Assisted Death: What Everyone Needs to Know* (New York: Oxford University Press, 2017), 44–45, 67–85.

21. Vanderpool, "Doctors and the Dying of Patients," 33–37; William G. Rothstein, *American Physicians in the Nineteenth Century: From Sects to Science* (Baltimore: Johns Hopkins University Press, 1992), 251–53; Ezekiel J. Emmanuel, "The History of Euthanasia Debates in the United States and Britain," *Annals of Internal Medicine* 121, no. 10 (November 15, 1994): 794; Hippocrates, *Hippocratic Oath*, trans. Michael North (National Library of Medicine, 2002).

22. "Euthanasia," *Popular Science Monthly*, May 1873, 90–91; "The Moral Side of Euthanasia," editorial, *Journal of the American Medical Association* 5 (1885): 382–83.

23. Ezekiel J. Emmanuel, "The History of Euthanasia Debates in the United States and Britain," 796–97; Yount, *Physician-Assisted Suicide and Euthanasia*, 8–9, 11.

24. Gorsuch, *The Future of Assisted Suicide and Euthanasia*, 35–36; Robert J. Blendon et al., *American Public Opinion and Health Care* (Washington, DC: SAGE, 2011), 339, Table 13-6.

25. Vanderpool, "Doctors and the Dying of Patients," 45; Willard L. Sperry, "Moral Problems in the Practice of Medicine," *New England Journal of Medicine* 239, no. 26 (December 23, 1948): 988; Filene, *In the Arms of Others*, 7–8; Russell Porter, "Sander Acquitted in an Hour; Crowd outside Court Cheers," *New York Times*, March 10, 1950, 1.

26. Blendon et al., *American Public Opinion and Health Care*, 339, Table 13-6; Yount, *Physician-Assisted Suicide and Euthanasia*, 11–12.

27. Derek Humphry, *Lawful Exit: The Limits of Freedom for Help in Dying* (Junction City, OR: Norris Lane Press, 1993), 19.

28. Jerald G. Bachman et al., "Attitudes of Michigan Physicians and the Public toward Legalizing Physician-Assisted Suicide and Voluntary Euthanasia," *New England Journal of Medicine* 334, no. 5 (1996): 303–9; Jonathan S. Cohen et al., "Attitudes toward Assisted Suicide and Euthanasia among Physicians in Washington State," *New England Journal of Medicine* 331, no. 2 (1994): 89–94; "It's Over, Debbie," *Journal of the American Medical Association* 259, no. 2 (1988); "Account of Assisted Suicide in Journal Advances Debate," *Medical Ethics Advisor* 7, no. 4 (1991): 44–47; Vanderpool, "Doctors and the Dying of Patients," 54.

29. Daniel Hillyard and John Dombrink, *Dying Right: The Death with Dignity Movement* (New York: Routledge, 2001), 46–48, 56, 60; United Press International (UPI), *Cardinal Mahony Urges Defeat of Euthanasia Proposition*, October 30, 1992.

30. Tom Paulson, "Initiative 119 from the Inside," *Seattle Post-Intelligencer*, September 20, 1991, A1; Cohen et al., "Attitudes toward Assisted Suicide and Euthanasia," 89–94; E. D. Pellegrino, "Doctors Must Not Kill," *Journal of Clinical Ethics* 3, no. 2 (Summer 1992): 95–102; Hillyard and Dombrink, *Dying Right*, 32, 45–53, 58–67; Robert Jones, *Liberalism's Troubled Search for Equality: Religion and Cultural Bias in the Oregon Physician-Assisted Suicide Debates* (Notre Dame, IN: University of Notre Dame Press, 2007), 74–76.

31. Diane E. Meier et al., "A National Survey of Physician-Assisted Suicide and Euthanasia in the United States," *New England Journal of Medicine* 338, no. 17 (April 23, 1998): 1199.

32. Gorsuch, *Future of Assisted Suicide and Euthanasia*, 53–57.

33. Gina Kolata, "'Passive Euthanasia' in Hospitals Is the Norm, Doctors Say," *New York Times*, June 28, 1997, 10; Meier et al., "National Survey," 1199; Yount, *Physician-Assisted Suicide and Euthanasia*, 5; L. C. Kaldjian et al., "Internists' Attitudes towards Terminal Sedation in End of Life Care," *Journal of Medical Ethics* 30, no. 5 (October 1, 2004): 499–503; American Medical Association, Council on Ethical and Judicial Affairs, *Code of Medical Ethics of the American Medical Association: Current Opinions with Annotations*, 2015, Opinions 5.8, 2.20.

34. Blendon et al., *American Public Opinion and Health Care*, 335–36 (comparing Tables 13-5 and 13-6).

35. Sumner, *Physician-Assisted Death*, 31–33.

36. Lethal Drug Abuse Prevention Act of 1998, H.R. 4006, 105th Cong. (2d Sess. 1998).
37. "Coalition Opposes Hyde-Nickles Lethal Drug Abuse Prevention Act," *U.S. Newswire*, September 23, 1998.
38. Pain Relief Promotion Act, H.R. 2260, 106th Cong. (2d Sess. 1999); David Orentlicher and Arthur Caplan, "The Pain Relief Promotion Act of 1999," *JAMA* 283, no. 2 (January 12, 2000): 255–58; Sue Ellen Christian, "Medical Treatment of Pain Enters New Regulatory Era," *Chicago Tribune*, May 23, 2000, D1.
39. Gorsuch, *Future of Assisted Suicide and Euthanasia*, 32–33; Vanderpool, "Doctors and the Dying of Patients," 43, 55–56; Yount, *Physician-Assisted Suicide and Euthanasia*, 7–8; Barney G. Glaser and Anselm L. Strauss, *Awareness of Dying* (New Brunswick, NJ: Aldine Transaction, 2005), 223–25.
40. Derek Humphry and Mary Clement, *Freedom to Die: People, Politics, and the Right-to-Die Movement* (New York: St. Martin's Griffin, 2000), 100–9.
41. Humphry and Clement, *Freedom to Die,* 109–16, 215–17; Yount, *Physician-Assisted Suicide and Euthanasia,* 28–30; Hillyard and Dombrink, *Dying Right,* 53–58, 82–83, 243.
42. Information on Kevorkian's career and activities through the early 1990s is drawn from Michael Betzold, *Appointment with Doctor Death*, 2nd ed. (Troy, MI: Momentum Books, 1993), 22–36, 41–46; Humphry and Clement, *Freedom to Die*, 125–31; Michael DeCesare, *Death on Demand: Jack Kevorkian and the Right-to-Die Movement* (Lanham, MD: Rowman & Littlefield, 2015), 7–100; Lisa Belkin, "Doctor Tells of First Death Using His Suicide Device," *New York Times*, June 6, 1990, 1; Jack Kevorkian, "The Last Fearsome Taboo: Medical Aspects of Planned Death," *Medicine and Law* 7, no. 1 (January 1988): 1–14.
43. "'Dr. Death' Undisturbed by Nickname," *St. Louis Post-Dispatch*, June 7, 1990, 19.
44. "'Dr. Death' Undisturbed by Nickname," 19; Mark Hosenball, "The Real Jack Kevorkian," *Newsweek*, December 6, 1993, 28; Hillyard and Dombrink, *Dying Right,* 76, 243–45.
45. Rogers Worthington, "Kevorkian Fires Up Ethics Debate," *Chicago Tribune*, October 23, 1993, N1; "Kevorkian Criticizes Medical Ethics," *Washington Post*, November 2, 1991, A12; DeCesare, *Death on Demand*, 61–62.
46. Timothy E. Quill, "Death and Dignity," *New England Journal of Medicine* 324, no. 10 (March 7, 1991): 691–94; Yount, *Physician-Assisted Suicide and Euthanasia*, 27.
47. Cohen et al., "Attitudes toward Assisted Suicide and Euthanasia"; Shari Roan, "Doctor Describes Aiding Cancer Patient's Suicide: Many Authorities Support Physician," *Los Angeles Times*, March 8, 1991, A1; Vanderpool, "Doctors and the Dying of Patients," 57.
48. Nicholas Goldberg and John Riley, "NY Panel Clears Suicide Doctor," *Newsday*, August 17, 1991, 2.
49. A Harris poll published in December 1993 showed 58 percent approval versus 38 percent disapproval Humphrey Taylor, "Majority Support for Euthanasia and Dr. Kevorkian Increases," *The Harris Poll*, for release December 6, 1993. A CBS poll showed 52 percent versus 41 percent, and a *New York Times* poll showed 46 percent versus 39 percent. An outlier in December 1993 was a Gallup poll that showed 43 percent approval and 47 percent disapproval.

50. DeCesare, *Death on Demand*, 101–5.

51. Keith Wailoo, *Pain: A Political History*, repr. ed. (Baltimore: Johns Hopkins University Press, 2015), 146.

52. DeCesare, *Death on Demand*, 152, 166–86.

53. For the public, see Blendon et al., *American Public Opinion and Health Care*, 339–40, Tables 13-6, 13-7, 13-8; Bachman et al., "Attitudes of Michigan Physicians," 306; Hillyard and Dombrink, *Dying Right*, 31. For physicians, see Cohen et al., "Attitudes toward Assisted Suicide and Euthanasia," 81; Ezekiel J. Emanuel, "Attitudes and Practices of U.S. Oncologists regarding Euthanasia and Physician-Assisted Suicide," *Annals of Internal Medicine* 133, no. 7 (2000): 527; Bachman et al., "Attitudes of Michigan Physicians," 306; Hillyard and Dombrink, *Dying Right*, 83–84.

54. Hillyard and Dombrink, *Dying Right*, 74, 81–84.

55. Oregon Death with Dignity Act, Or. Rev. Stat. (1994); Hillyard and Dombrink, *Dying Right*, 80–81.

56. "After Others Fail, Oregon Offers Death with Dignity," *USA Today*, October 25, 1994, A12; Hillyard and Dombrink, *Dying Right*, 42–43, 144; Yount, *Physician-Assisted Suicide and Euthanasia*, 18; Filene, *In the Arms of Others*, 187–88; Mary Ziegler, *Beyond Abortion: Roe v. Wade and the Battle for Privacy* (Cambridge, MA: Harvard University Press, 2018), 163–201; Carol J. Castaneda and Stuart Wasserman, "Oregon to Take Measure of Right-to-Die Issue," *USA Today*, October 26, 1994, A10; William McCall, "Oregon Will Decide Whether to Allow Doctors to Prescribe Suicide Pill," *Associated Press*, October 12, 1994.

57. Hillyard and Dombrink, *Dying Right*, 89; *Voters' Pamphlet*, State of Oregon General Election November 8, 1994, 127–29.

58. Hillyard and Dombrink, *Dying Right*, 90–93, 95–96. See also the "Arguments in Opposition" in *Voters' Pamphlet*, State of Oregon General Election, November 8, 1994, 129–34.

59. Hillyard and Dombrink, *Dying Right*, 92–93, 99–118; *Lee v. Oregon*, 891 F. Supp. 1429 (1995); *Lee v. Oregon*, 107 F.3d 1382 (1997); William Claiborne and Thomas B. Edsall, "Affirmation of Oregon Suicide Law May Spur Movement," *Washington Post*, November 6, 1997, A19.

60. *Washington v. Glucksberg*, 521 U.S. 702 (1997); *Vacco v. Quill*, 521 U.S. 793 (1997).

61. *Compassion in Dying v. Washington*, 79 F.3d 790, 816 (1996) (en banc); *Quill v. Vacco*, 870 F.3d 716 (2d Cir. 1996).

62. *Glucksberg*, 521 U.S. at 704–6.

63. *Glucksberg*, 521 U.S. at 728–35.

64. *Glucksberg*, 521 U.S. at 731–32.

65. *Glucksberg*, 521 U.S. at 720–25; *Quill*, 521 U.S. at 800–3.

66. *Quill*, 521 U.S. at 802; *Glucksberg*, 521 U.S. at 736–37 (O'Connor, J., concurring); Robert A. Burt, "The Supreme Court Speaks—Not Assisted Suicide but a Constitutional Right to Palliative Care," *New England Journal of Medicine* 337, no. 17 (October 23, 1997): 1234.

67. Jennifer Dixon, "State OKs Ban on Aided Suicides; Kevorkian Will Defy Measure, Lawyer Says," *Detroit Free Press*, July 4, 1998, 1A; DeCesare, *Death on Demand*, 167; Hillyard and Dombrink, *Dying Right*, 212–18; *Glucksberg*, 521 U.S. at 717–18.

68. Ziegler, *Beyond Abortion*, 193; Jones, *Liberalism's Troubled Search for Equality*, 177; Sandy Banisky, "Protesters Fear Ruling Could Be Death Sentence; Disabled Urge Upholding Ban on Assisted Suicide," *Baltimore Sun*, January 9, 1997, 13A; Lori Montgomery, "Outside Court, Disabled Urge: 'Keep Me Alive,'" *Detroit Free Press*, January 9, 1997, 6A;; Kathi Wolfe, "Give Us the Right to Health Care," *San Jose Mercury News*, January 16, 1997, 9B.

69. Thomas Maier, "This Group's Alive—and Kicking/Disabled Fight, Fear Legalized Suicide," *Newsday*, June 9, 1997, A8; "Assisted Suicide Advocates, Disabled Clash at Conference," *Los Angeles Times*, June 7, 1998, 22; David Broder, "Choice on Physician-Assisted Suicide Comes Home," *Washington Post*, October 8, 1998, A20; Dee-Ann Durbin, "Catholic Church the Major Backer in Fight against Proposal B," *Associated Press*, October 28, 1998; Glenn Adams, "Mainers Weigh Doctor-Assisted Suicide," *Associated Press*, October 15, 2000; Wailoo, *Pain*.

70. Pub. L. No. 105-12, § 3, 111 Stat. 23 (codified at 42 U.S.C. § 14402); Yount, *Physician-Assisted Suicide and Euthanasia*, 36; "Physician-Assisted Suicide and the Controlled Substances Act," CRS Report for Congress (Congressional Research Service, February 7, 2006), 3.

71. Yount, *Physician-Assisted Suicide and Euthanasia*, 36; "Statement of Attorney General Janet Reno on Oregon's Death with Dignity Act," June 5, 1998.

72. 66 Fed. Reg. 56,608 (Nov. 9, 2001); *Gonzales v. Oregon*, 546 U.S. 243 (2006).

73. Sumner, *Physician-Assisted Death*, 88–89; *Baxter v. State*, 224 P.3d 1211 (Mont. 2009).

74. Diane Coleman and Stephen Drake, "'Second Thoughts' Grow on Assisted Suicide," *Wall Street Journal*, April 6, 2012, A13; Maurice T. Cunningham, "Defeating 'Death with Dignity': Morality and Message in a Massachusetts Referendum," *American Catholic Studies* 125, no. 2 (Summer 2014): 23–43; Valerie Richardson, "Inclusion Key in Anti-Suicide Drive; Diverse Coalition, Focus on Details Defeated Initiative," *Washington Times*, November 15, 2012, A8.

75. Besides Oregon and Washington, only Colorado has used the latter procedure.

76. Lydia Saad, "U.S. Support for Euthanasia Hinges on How It's Described," *Gallup*, May 29, 2013, online; Megan Brenan, "Americans' Strong Support for Euthanasia Persists," *Gallup*, May 31, 2018, online; Blendon et al., *American Public Opinion and Health Care*, 339 (Table 13-7).

77. "Map: Assisted Suicide in the States," End of Life, Charles Lozier Institute, updated June 13, 2019, website.

78. "Religious Groups' Views on End-of-Life Issues," *Pew Research Center, Religion and Public Life*, November 21, 2013. By contrast, every one of these sixteen faiths allows the cessation of extraordinary medical measures and artificial life support in some circumstances. In other words, they all draw a distinction between a doctor causing a patient's death and a doctor allowing it to occur.

79. National Hospice and Palliative Care Organization, "Statement on Legally Accelerated Death," November 4, 2018.

80. Jones, *Liberalism's Troubled Search for Equality*, 43; Lori Montgomery, "Blacks Fearful of White Doctors Pulling the Plug," *Detroit Free Press*, February 26, 1997, 1A. Stephen Vicchio, "Doctor Death's Logic," *Baltimore Sun*, April 4, 1999, 1C; Fenit Nirappil,

"D.C. Council Set to Approve Aid-in-Dying Measure," *Washington Post*, October 18, 2016, A1.

81. Jones, *Liberalism's Troubled Search for Equality*, 43; Stephen Vicchio, "Doctor Death's Logic," 1C; L. W. Sumner, *Physician-Assisted Death*, 137–42.

82. "Why Assisted Suicide Must Not Be Legalized," *Disability Rights Education & Defense Fund* (blog), website.

83. Richardson, "Inclusion Key in Anti-Suicide Drive," A8; "Our Mission, Our Work," Compassion & Choices, website; Wailoo, *Pain*, 146.

Index